S0-AHI-352

Fundamental Statistics for Psychology

ROBERT B. McCALL

The Fels Research Institute and Antioch College

Fundamental Statistics for Psychology

HARCOURT, BRACE & WORLD, INC.

New York Chicago San Francisco Atlanta

Library of Congress Catalog Card Number: 77-115865
ISBN: 0-15-529410-5

Cover painting by Thomas Upshur

Printed in the United States of America

preface

This book is designed for undergraduates in the behavioral sciences who are taking a first course in applied statistics. Although most of the examples are from psychology and education, the topics are taken from basic descriptive and inferential statistics and are therefore appropriate to a variety of disciplines. In order to give the students a thorough understanding of the basic concepts rather than a limited familiarity with a variety of techniques, I have emphasized concepts and have presented relatively few specific techniques.

In order to impress on the student the rationale and logic of each concept and its application to data, I have refrained from presenting any fundamental concept solely by giving its formula. Instead, I have tried to discuss the logic of each formula, with frequent recourse to graphic illustrations, examples of the use of the concept, and explanations of the rationale involved. Sometimes I have presented contrasting sets of data to enable the student to observe the "behavior" of the statistics under different circumstances. Some sections are devoted to the factors that govern the interpretation of a statistical result, and the problems and questions at the end of each chapter are designed not only to test the student's command of the correct use and computation of the statistic but, more important, his conceptual understanding of its logic and purpose.

I feel that the mathematically uninitiated student is better served by a presentation that follows the principles of the psychology of learning than by a strictly mathematical presentation. Further, students want to understand what they are studying, at least at a level that is satisfying to them, and when they do grasp the rationale and logic of statistics it becomes for them the intriguing system of thought and techniques that it is.

Consequently, throughout the book I have introduced various features in an effort to facilitate learning: (1) Important definitions are set off in distinctive type. (2) Mathematical proofs are put in tables so that the reader will not lose the train of thought. (3) No steps are omitted in the algebraic proofs or derivations, and the reason for each step is given. (4) The use of statistical tables is explained at each table as well as in the text. (5) Symbols are accompanied by their verbal name several times so that the reader has more than one opportunity to associate the meaning with the symbol. (6) Concepts and formulas are briefly reviewed as needed.

The book has been organized in such a way that the instructor may emphasize either descriptive and correlational methods or inferential statistics, as he chooses. Chapters 1 through 6 cover basic descriptive and correlational techniques. Chapter 7 presents a limited introduction to probability and a more detailed discussion of the general logic of hypothesis testing. Chapters 8 through 11 outline some techniques of hypothesis testing, including simple and two-factor analysis of variance and some nonparametric statistics. Chapter 12 presents a more extensive treatment of elementary topics in probability. Thus, the instructor who wants to emphasize descriptive and correlational methods might concentrate on Chapters 1 through 8 and portions of Chapter 11, while the instructor who wishes to give more weight to inferential statistics might concentrate on Chapters 1 through 4 and Chapters 7 through 12.

A knowledge of high-school algebra and plane geometry is assumed, and, with the exception of summation signs, no new methematical operations or techniques are introduced. For more advanced students some calculus is presented, but it may be omitted without loss of continuity.

Many people shared their time and knowledge with me as I prepared successive drafts of the manuscript. Mark Appelbaum's incisive comments were invaluable to me as I tried to blend my personal approach to teaching the subject matter with the demands of formal theory. Jerome Kagan has helped enormously throughout the project. Numerous people read selected chapters. The comments of Henri Barrik, Mary Chronister, Nancy Cole, Fred Grote, Michael Lester, Karen Reinfurt, Pamela Savoy, Mariam Young, and the suggestions of untold numbers of students are greatly appreciated.

The book could not have been completed had it not been for the help (and patience) of my own teachers—Curtis Thompsen, Ray Frankmann, Lloyd Humphreys, William Kappauf, Ledyard Tucker, and Donald Burkholder.

I am indebted to the Literary Executor of the late Sir Ronald A. Fisher, F.R.S., to Dr. Frank Yates, F.R.S., and to Oliver & Boyd Ltd., Edinburgh, for permission to reprint Tables III, IV, VII, and XXXIII from their book *Statistical Tables for Biological, Agricultural and Medical Research.*

Numerous people from several institutions helped to type what must have been a frustrating manuscript. My appreciation goes to the Social Science Research Council and the Department of Psychology of the University of North Carolina and to the Fels Research Institute, which supported much of the clerical work. In particular, I am grateful to Nancy Boynton, Patricia Brewer, Ileen Brown, Lynne Christensen, Deeanne Treadway, Doris Simpson, Joanne Peterson, Katherine Pryor, and Mary Warnock.

Lastly, thanks of a special kind go to my wife, Rozanne, for her encouragement and for the absence of complaints while she was temporarily widowed for this cause.

ROBERT B. MCCALL

contents

1 **1** The study of statistics

measurement and the statistical method *1*

the study of statistics *3*

7 **2** Frequency distributions

measurement *7*

summation sign *14*

frequency distributions *19*

38 **3** Characteristics of distributions

measures of central tendency *38*

estimation *47*

measures of variability *51*

61 **4** Measures of relative standing

percentiles *61*

changing the properties of scales *66*

standard scores and the normal distribution *73*

86 **5** Regression

linear relationships *86*

regression constants *94*

factors in the use of the regression line *103*

113 **6** Correlation

derivation of the correlation coefficient *114*

properties of the correlation coefficient *118*

factors influencing the size of the correlation coefficient *127*

138 **7** Introduction to hypothesis testing

overview of probability *138*

sampling and sampling distributions *145*

hypothesis testing *153*

differences between population and sample means with $\sigma_{\bar{x}}$ estimated by $s_{\bar{x}}$ *165*

176 **8** Elementary techniques of hypothesis testing

the difference between means *177*
homogeneity of variance *190*
inferences about correlation coefficients *195*
the interpretation of significance *200*
a comparison of the difference between means and correlation *205*
proportion of variance accounted for *207*

214 **9** Simple analysis of variance

the logic of the analysis of variance *216*
computational procedures *233*
the relation between the analysis of variance and other statistics *241*

246 **10** Two-factor analysis of variance

derivation of formulas *253*
computation *268*

282 **11** Nonparametric techniques

parametric versus nonparametric tests *282*
tests on independent samples *284*
correlated samples *304*
rank-order correlation *308*
when to use nonparametric tests *315*

323 **12** Further topics in probability

set theory *323*
simple classical probability *327*
probability of complex events *334*
methods of counting *340*
advanced probability problems *345*

350 Appendix I Review of Basic Mathematics
361 Appendix II Tables
393 Answers to the Exercises
409 Glossary
413 Index

Fundamental Statistics for Psychology

1

the study of statistics

measurement and the statistical method

One can find measurement everywhere in our society. It exists from the measurement of flight times between major cities to the intricate calibration of manned rockets. **Measurement** is the systematic assignment of numbers to objects or events. But, although measurement is common in society, it forms the very basis of science. If an event or attribute cannot be measured, it does not find its way into the domain of science.

The result of scientific observation is usually a collection of measurements. These measurements are called **data.** Most of what is discussed in this text concerns techniques for organizing and summarizing data and for making generalizations and inferences from data.

Statistics is the study of methods of handling quantitative information. These methods can be grouped into two broad classes. First, the term **descriptive statistics** refers to procedures for organizing, summarizing, and describing quantitative information or data. Most people are partially familiar with this aspect of statistics. The baseball fan is accustomed to checking over his favorite player's batting average, the sales manager relies on charts showing the sales distribution and cost-efficiency of his enterprise, the housewife may consult articles describing the average domestic expenditures of families of comparable size and income, and the actuary possesses charts outlining the life expectancy of people in various professions. These are relatively simple statistical tools which facilitate the description of data, but additional techniques also are available to describe such things as the extent to which values deviate from one another and the relationship between performance of one kind and that of another. For example, what is the degree of relationship between scores on a college entrance examination and later performance in college?

The second major aspect of statistics, known as **inferential statistics,** concerns the methods by which inferences are made to a large group on the basis of observations made on a smaller subgroup. For example, suppose a social psychologist wished to compare two approaches to changing people's attitudes about a given political issue. Specifically, are attitudes changed more easily if the persuader adopts a position just slightly different from the original attitude of the people being converted or if the persuader presents quite a discrepant stand? To study this question, two groups of people might be given an attitude questionnaire. Then each group is exposed to a persuader who attempts to change their attitude about a given political issue. For one group, the persuader presents a statement that is slightly more positive than the original opinion of the people, whereas for the other group his statement is considerably more positive than their initial feelings. Later, a similar attitude questionnaire is again given to the people to determine whether one group shifted their attitude about the issue more than the other.

Suppose this experiment is performed and the first group averages an 8-point change in attitude while the second group averages a 5-point change. These data show that for the subjects studied, a small discrepancy between original attitude and the tenor of the persuasion produces more attitude change than a large discrepancy, but a more interesting question is whether this would be true for every set of two groups tested. That is, is this observation of an average difference of 8 versus 5 only characteristic of the particular subjects tested or might this also be true of larger groups of subjects—indeed, of all people?

One feels a moderate uncertainty about answering this question. It is possible that the observed difference could be due to the fact that more members of the group showing greater attitude change were people who could be influenced very easily, so that the degree of discrepancy in opinion had nothing to do with the result. On the other hand, these subjects, indeed, may be faithful representatives of "people in general," and the slightly discrepant position does, in fact, win more converts. What is needed is some way to quantify the uncertainty that one feels about this decision so that it would be possible to say that in n of every 100 such experiments one should expect a difference of this magnitude or greater between the groups purely by "chance" factors associated with the particular subjects selected to be in the observations. If the probability is high that the observed difference is just "lucky" or due to chance, then one might conclude that the two persuasion strategies probably do not differentially affect the degree of attitude change. Conversely, if the probability is quite small that the observed difference is due to chance, then perhaps the two strategies do, in fact, determine the differing amounts of attitude change. This quantification of uncertainty is done with *probability*, and the task of statistical inference is to attach a probability value to the validity of certain statements, often for the purpose of making inferential decisions.

One common kind of decision that scientists are often required to make occurs when a theory is tested. A scientific theory attempts to explain certain phenomena. Deductions are made from the theory which predict what will happen in a special experimental situation. The experiment is executed and the data are evaluated to decide whether or not they are in accord with the theory. Statistical procedures are often used to make this decision.

Thus, statistics is the study of methods of handling data. Descriptive statistics organizes, summarizes, and describes data, while making inferences from small to larger groups of subjects or events is the province of inferential statistics.

the study of statistics

WHY IS STATISTICS NECESSARY?

There are several reasons why a knowledge of statistics is necessary in handling data. Of major importance is the fact that very often the only measurement available is not very accurate. For example, if you were to get on a reasonably sensitive scale and test your weight ten times within a two-hour period, it is likely that the scale would read the same number on each of the ten occasions. But if it were possible to take a personality test ten times in succession, it is likely that you would not receive precisely the same score each time.

There may be several reasons why the personality test does not always give the same score. First, the measurement may be crude. Imagine that your shoe is approximately a foot long and you want to set up a baseball field with first base 90 feet from homeplate. If you pace it off using your foot as a measure, the distance might not be the same each time you did it because of the crudity of the measuring process. The analogue in personality testing may be that sometimes the cluster of everyday experiences may predispose a person to respond to a given item one way one time but quite differently the next time.

But measurement may be crude for another reason; namely, the concept being measured may not be faithfully reflected in behavioral events that can be measured easily and accurately. For example, suppose one desires to measure how favorably the electorate views its president. The simple question, "Do you like President Smith?" may be interpreted to mean, "Do you like his personality?" or "Do you think he is performing his job competently?" or many other possibilities.

Even if people respond with the same interpretation of the question, uniform responses by a single individual are not necessarily guaranteed. Suppose all people interpreted the question to be concerned with the competency of the president. A person might respond positively because he thinks foreign affairs are running smoothly and the domestic machinery is doing well. The next day, however, interest rates may be raised, making mortgage money harder to obtain and the same person might suddenly reverse his opinion because of unfavorable performance in a single area which affects him (even though foreign affairs are still going well). Thus, measurement may be crude because the concept being measured (e.g., opinion of the president) is not clearly and unequivocally reflected in behavior or events that can be accurately measured.

One of the primary concepts of psychology suffers from a very similar problem. The concept of learning cannot easily be observed in the behavior of organisms without the simultaneous influence of motivation. If a mother asks her young son to play the piano for her visitors and he does not do it, it is not clear whether the child has not **learned** to perform this action or if he merely does not **want** to do it at this time.

The result of what has been called crude measurement is that the link between the concept of interest and the available measurement of that concept may be very tenuous. Most people have a reasonably good idea of what intelligence is, although they may have trouble verbalizing precisely what they mean. After reviewing the items on an intelligence test, however, many people remark, "Does that test intelligence?" This apparent skepticism that an intelligence test measures their intuitive concept of what intelligence really is, illustrates one of the greatest problems for research, the discrepancy between the definition of a concept and its measurement.

The lack of precision in measurement means that less faith can be placed in a single score. Obviously, if the scale yields the same weight time after time within a short time interval, one comes to accept its initial reading and does not return for additional measurements. However, if the measurement is not so precise, it may be necessary to measure a single subject several times in order to gain enough confidence in the ascribed values, or many subjects or events must be sampled in order to have confidence that the data faithfully reflect the characteristics supposedly being measured.

The fact that measurement is crude, that a variety of factors other than those being studied frequently govern the behavior of interest, and that one subject is not the same as the next, all conspire to make conclusive decisions about the results of controlled observations difficult to draw. It is the task of inferential statistics to quantify the uncertainty and to provide a set of techniques that permit orderly decisions to be made in spite of such imprecision.

WHY STUDY STATISTICS?

There are good reasons for studying statistics. First, if a person ever expects to intelligently read and evaluate social science research literature, a knowledge of statistics is almost essential. Obviously, if one is going to design and carry out his own experiments, he will have to describe the results and make inferences from his data, which will require a knowledge of statistical techniques. It is for this reason that statistics is usually required of undergraduate and graduate students in a variety of subjects.

However, even if one will never be a researcher himself, he will want to maintain his acquaintance with certain topics, perhaps because his profession requires him to apply research literature (e.g., a clinical psychologist, a special education teacher, etc.). He will be expected to comprehend and evaluate detailed research literature, much of which is couched in statistical terms. For example, it is of considerable interest to a psychologist, an educator, a teacher, a mother, etc. to know the relative contributions of heredity and environment to intelligence. Although the question is not really an either-or problem, it is often conceived in that manner. For example, a correlation (degree of relationship) of .35 was found between the intelligence of adopted children and the intelligence of their biological mothers but child IQ correlated only .09 with the intelligence of the mothers that reared those children.[1] Yet, the average IQ of the children was approximately equal to the average IQ of their rearing mothers and much higher than that of their biological mothers. The correlations seem to support heredity while the averages appear to favor environment as the more powerful determinant of intelligence. How is this possible? What does it mean to have a correlation or a difference between means? How shall this collection of information be interpreted? A knowledge of statistics—even the basic introduction that this book will hopefully provide—would answer these questions (e.g., see Chapter 8).

Therefore, it should be clear that if the individual is going to produce research himself or evaluate the reports of others, some knowledge of statistical principles is necessary. Consequently, if the student expects to attend graduate school in any of a variety of disciplines, this course will but foreshadow a far deeper and broader encounter with such quantitative procedures.

But what about the student who does not expect to attend graduate school and who will probably not read professional scientific literature? Of what benefit is an acquaintance with statistics to him? First, rudimentary statistics finds its way into the communications media. For example, the **average** family income in the United States is higher than the **median** income, yet both are used as measures of typical incomes? Why are they different, and which is most appropriate as an expression of typical income?

Consider another set of facts once reported in newspapers and magazines[2] across the country and not atypical of presentations that may prompt unreasoned conclusions. Ordinarily, at conception each person is given 23 pairs of chromosomes, and these determine much of the individual's development.

[1] M. Skodak and H. M. Skeels, "A final follow-up study of one-hundred adopted children," *Journal of Genetic Psychology*, 1949, LXXV, 85–125.

[2] *Time*, May 3, 1968, 41.

One such pair of chromosomes determines the sex of the individual. If this pair is XX a female results, whereas if the pair is XY a male results. Occasionally, in the course of the generation of sex cells, an extra chromosome is contributed to a cell such that the result is XYY. This person is a male, tends to be approximately six inches taller than the average, and has other distinguishing characteristics. Interestingly, among male prisoners the incidence of an XYY condition is estimated to be 60 times more common than in the general population. What does such a statistic imply? Does this argue for giving each male individual a chromosomal analysis and keeping track of the XYY people or even restricting their freedom? Does this observation mean that the XYY grouping causes hyperaggressiveness or criminal behavior? Again a knowledge of statistics might help in interpreting these data.

Lastly, a course in statistics, like a course in logic, generally breeds a healthy skepticism in its participants for the way they approach issues and problems, statistical or otherwise. Consider the above information on genetic combinations and criminals. Suppose that an XYY combination occurs in every 2000 male births. For convenience, assume there are 100,000,000 males in the United States and 120,000 men in prisons. Therefore, in the general population there are approximately 50,000 men in the country with an XYY combination, only 3600 of which (7.2%) are in prison. Is one then to set up a program, even if the genetic anomaly were the cause of criminal tendencies, to observe or even restrict the liberty of 50,000 men when 46,400 of them are not likely to cause any trouble? The point here is not that a knowledge of statistics was required to refine the interpretation of the data as illustrated, but rather statistical experience is more likely to have fostered a critical attitude that would prompt a person to make this analysis.

Consequently, if one attends graduate school in any one of a variety of fields, he will be expected to arrive with some statistical experience and take more courses in it in the progress of his training in order to perform or evaluate scientific research. If the student does not continue on for an advanced degree, he is likely to come away with a healthy skepticism of glibly presented facts and a few tools to assist him in interpreting some of the statistical information presented in newspapers, magazines, and the electronics media.

2

frequency distributions

measurement

One of the major functions of statistics is to describe efficiently the nature of (1) experimental results, (2) observations on large groups of subjects, and (3) relationships between performance on two different tasks. In each case an attempt is made to describe the nature of a group of measurements that have been made. This chapter presents a basic method of describing such data, the frequency distribution. However, the description depends in part on how the measurements were made, so it is necessary first to discuss some aspects of the measurement process.

SCALES OF MEASUREMENT

properties of scales A major concern about a measurement technique is that it faithfully reflect the attribute being measured. For example, if one wants to measure the heights of people in the class, it is necessary to have a number scale that indeed reflects the "tallness" of the class members. Although this proposition appears trivial at first, it happens that in many sciences the concepts of interest to the scientist can only be measured in relatively rudimentary ways. For example, suppose a researcher wanted a single number that would represent the aggressiveness of people involved in his research on personality. He might have a clinical psychologist interview and then rate the subjects from 1 through 10 on their aggressiveness. The important point for the present discussion is what general attributes of the dimension "aggressiveness" does the measurement scale created by rating subjects 1 through 10 reflect?

What attributes of a concept can measurement scales possibly possess? For this discussion there are three: **magnitude, equal intervals,** and an **absolute zero point.**

> When a scale has **magnitude,** one instance of the attribute can be judged greater than, less than, or equal to another instance of the attribute.

If the clinical psychologist in the preceding example assigns a score of 8 to John and a score of 5 to Harry, this scale of measurement reflects the difference in magnitude of aggressiveness in the two boys—John is more aggressive than Harry.

Another attribute a scale may possess is **equal intervals.**

> **Equal intervals** denotes that the magnitude of the concept represented by a unit of measurement on the scale is equal regardless of where on the scale the unit falls.

Take the measurement of height in inches as an example. One is confident that the difference in height between someone measuring 61 inches versus someone measuring 60 inches is of the same magnitude as the difference in height that exists between someone measuring 75 inches versus someone measuring 74 inches. In short, an inch reflects a certain amount of height regardless of where that inch falls on the scale. However, consider the measurement of intelligence with the customary IQ scale. The amount of difference in intelligence between someone scoring 80 versus someone scoring 100 is not the same as the amount of difference in intelligence between someone scoring 180 and someone scoring 200. In the last instance, since a unit of the measuring scale does not always reflect the same amount of the attribute being measured (e.g., intelligence) depending upon where on the scale the unit lies, that scale does not possess equal intervals.[1]

A third attribute a scale may possess is an **absolute zero point.**

> An **absolute zero point** is a value that indicates that nothing at all of the attribute being measured exists.

Thus, "0 inches" of height is a scale value that implies no height whatsoever—absolute zero. However, in the case of rating aggressiveness, the lowest score

[1] In the middle range of values (e.g., 80–120) IQ is approximately an equal interval scale but the total scale is probably ordinal.

that the psychologist can assign (i.e., "1"), does not indicate "no aggressive tendencies whatsoever." Rather, it denotes less aggressiveness than a score of "2" and that is about all one can say. Even if the value "0" were a part of the scale, it might not actually mean a total absence of aggressive characteristics. Thus, the rating scale for aggressiveness does not possess an absolute zero point.

types of scales It is clear from the previous discussion that if the attribute of height is measured in inches then the scale has magnitude, equal intervals, and an absolute zero. Many of the measurements one makes in everyday life possess all three of these attributes.

> Any scale of measurement possessing magnitude, equal intervals, and an absolute zero point is called a **ratio scale.**

This scale is termed "ratio" because the collection of properties that it possesses allows ratio statements to be made about the attribute being measured. If a father is 70 inches tall and his son is 35 inches, it is correct to infer that the father is twice as tall as his son. Such ratio statements may be made only if the scale possesses all three of these attributes.

Not all scales used in research in psychology, education, sociology, etc. are ratio scales. That is, many variables cannot be measured with scales that reflect all three of these attributes about the concept under consideration.

> An **interval scale** possesses the attributes of magnitude and equal intervals but not an absolute zero point.

The most frequent example of an interval scale is the scale for measurement of temperature in degrees Fahrenheit. Although from the standpoint of physics or chemistry the absolute zero point is reached when all molecular movement ceases, for all practical purposes there is no point at which one says that there is no temperature whatsoever.[2] Note that neither 0° Fahrenheit nor 0° centigrade denotes the point at which there is no temperature at all, i.e., absolute zero. Further, if the temperature today is 30° and yesterday it was 15° one does not proclaim that it is "twice as hot" today as yesterday. Ratio statements cannot be made without an absolute zero point. However, the temperature scale does possess the properties of magnitude and equal intervals. For example, 25° is a greater temperature than 19°, and the difference between 50° and 40° represents the same difference in temperature as between 90° and 100°. Hence, the temperature scale has the attributes of magnitude and equal intervals, but not absolute zero, and is therefore an interval scale.

[2] The Kelvin scale of temperature does have an absolute zero and is therefore a type of ratio scale.

Some scales do not have all of the properties of an interval scale.

> An **ordinal scale** reflects only magnitude and does not possess the attributes of equal intervals or an absolute zero point.

For example, take the people in the class and line them up according to height, and then rather than measuring them with a tape measure merely rank them according to their height, the tallest receiving a rank of "1," the next tallest "2," etc. The result is an ordinal scale of height.

Clearly the scale has the attribute of magnitude but does it possess equal intervals? In order to assess this, one must be aware of the distinction between the scale and the aspect of nature which the scale is supposed to measure. The rank order constitutes the scale, but the scale is being used to assess the height of people in the class. Therefore, although the scale says that there is one unit difference between ranks 1 and 2 and between ranks 2 and 3, the height of these people (in terms of inches) may be the following:

		Difference in	
Rank	**Height (Inches)**	**Rank**	**Inches**
1	78		
		1	6
2	72		
		1	1
3	71		

The ranking assigns a difference of one unit between ranks 1 and 2 and between ranks 2 and 3; yet in terms of height, these units are not at all equal. Indeed, one represents a difference in height of 6 inches and the other of 1 inch. Thus, in terms of the concept being measured, namely height, the rank ordering scale does not have equal intervals.

Neither has it a zero point, because there is no ranking (not even if we started with rank "0") that always expresses "no height at all." Hence, the ranking of height produces an ordinal scale because it possesses the attribute of magnitude but not equal intervals or an absolute zero.

Rank ordering is not the only kind of ordinal scale. Consider the IQ scale. It does not have equal intervals—the difference (of 20) between IQs of 80 and 100 does not indicate the same amount of "intelligence" as the difference (of 20) between 180 and 200—nor does the IQ scale have a useful zero point of "no intelligence at all." Hence, the IQ scale is merely an ordinal scale, and it should not be used as if it were an interval or ratio scale (e.g., an IQ of 140 does not represent twice as much intelligence as an IQ of 70).

It is possible to have a "scale" which has none of the three attributes discussed in the preceding material, but one would hardly think of it as a "scale," a term usually reserved for measurements which imply differences in magnitude.

A **nominal scale** refers to the classification of items into discrete groups which do not bear any magnitude relationships to one another.

For example, if a person were to stand on a busy street corner and name cars, he could classify a car as a Ford, a Chevrolet, a Plymouth, etc. The dimension of classification is "make of car." However, one would not say that Ford is more or less of a "make of car" than is Chevrolet. It may be more or less expensive or eye appealing, but not more or less a make of car. Hence, grouping cars according to make represents a nominal scale, which does not possess the properties of magnitude, equal intervals, or an absolute zero point.

VARIABLES

variables versus constants Most data consist of values of a variable. A **variable** is a type of quantity that may take on several values. If the quantity is the height in inches of members of a class, then height is a variable because the heights of members of the class will differ from one to another. Thus, since height assumes several values in this context, it is a variable.

In contrast, a **constant** is a numerical value which does not change within a given context. The mathematical symbol, π, is a constant because it always equals approximately 3.1416. Its value does not change. Thus, if one obtains the heights of people in a class in terms of inches and wishes to report these measurements in terms of feet, height would be considered a variable but the 12:1 conversion factor of inches to feet is a constant.

discrete versus continuous variables Variables may be either **discrete** or **continuous.**

A **discrete** variable is one in which there are a finite number of potential values that the variable can assume between any two points on the scale.

For example, the number of children in a family is a discrete variable because there can be only one child between the values of 1 and 3. One does not conceive of a family having $1\frac{1}{2}$ children.

A **continuous** variable is one which theoretically can assume an infinite number of values between any two points on the scale.

Consider, for example, weight. Even between 100 and 101 pounds there is an unlimited number of values possible. Time is another example of a continuous variable.

The discrete-continuous distinction is really only a theoretical one, because in practice most variables are measured in such a way that one obtains only discrete scores. For example, IQ is a continuous variable but only whole numbers are actually obtained—no one speaks of a person having an IQ of $113\frac{1}{4}$. Thus, regardless of how one goes about measuring a variable, it is continuous if theoretically there is an underlying dimension for the trait or behavior which permits an infinite number of values to be obtained if one had an ultimately sensitive instrument for measuring them. Therefore, just because a variable is measured only in whole numbers or because all numbers are rounded to the nearest tenth's digit, it does not make that variable discrete.

Notice that the discrete-continuous distinction is applied to variables not to the type of scale used to measure them. A continuous variable and some discrete variables may be measured with ratio, interval, or ordinal scales. For example, IQ is a continuous variable because given a sufficiently fine instrument, theoretically there could be an infinite number of values between any two points. Yet, the current measurement of IQ is relatively crude and constitutes an ordinal scale.

REAL LIMITS

If a continuous, as opposed to a discrete, variable is one such that an infinite number of values exist between any two points on the scale, then the obtained measurements are necessarily approximate. For example, since the continuous variable of time may be measured in years, months, days, hours, minutes, seconds, milliseconds, etc., if one measured to the nearest second, it is clear that more refined approximations could be made with more sophisticated timers. Consequently, if a young child is asked to solve a given mathematics problem and he does so in "33 seconds," the value 33 probably does not mean "**exactly** 33 seconds" but "**approximately** 33 seconds." More precisely, it means between 32.5 and 33.5 seconds, which values are called the **real limits** of 33 seconds. The **lower real limit** is 32.5 because any number lower than this (e.g., 32.4) would be rounded to a whole number other than 33 seconds (i.e., 32), and the **upper real limit** is 33.5 because any number greater than this also would be rounded to a whole number other than 33 (i.e., 34). Real limits may be defined in two ways.

(a) The **real limits** of a number are those points which define an interval within which all values would be rounded to that number.
(b) The **real limits** of a number are those points falling one-half a unit above and one-half a unit below that number.

To illustrate, if measurement is being made in whole seconds, the unit of measurement is one second and thus the real limits of 33 seconds are 32.5 seconds and 33.5 seconds, one-half unit (.5 second) below and above 33 seconds, respectively. However, note that the definition states that the limits fall one-half **unit** above and below the number. Therefore, the real limits of 33 seconds are different for measurements made in units other than whole seconds. Suppose that a stop watch is available and that the length of time to solve a problem is recorded in terms of tenths of a second. In this case, the unit of measurement is .1 second and one-half unit is .05 second. Consequently, when measuring in tenths of a second the real limits of 33.0 are 32.95 and 33.05. Similarly, if measurement is made in hundredths of a second, the real limits of 33.00 are 32.995 and 33.005. These points are presented graphically in Figure 2–1.

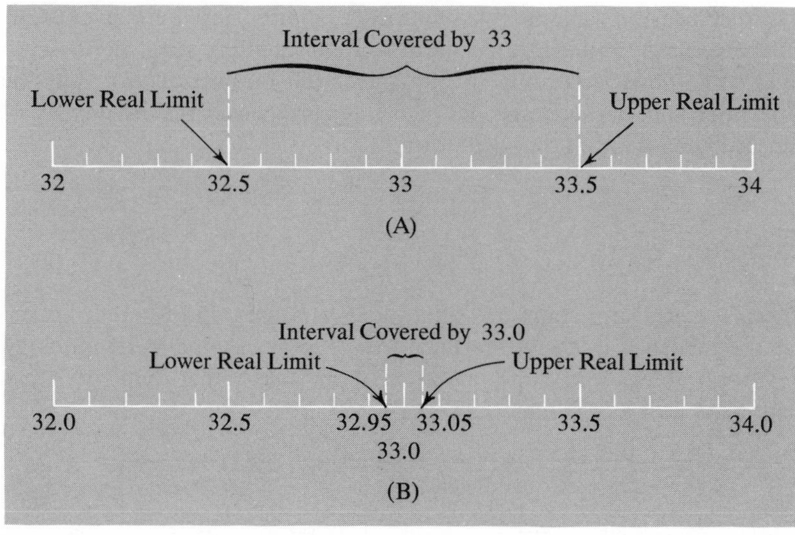

Fig. 2–1. The real limits of 33 when the measurement is in whole units (top) and when it is in tenths of units (bottom).

ROUNDING

If measurements are taken in tenths of a second but are to be reported in terms of whole seconds, they are said to be **rounded** to the nearest whole second. Numbers are rounded according to the following convention:

(a) If the remaining decimal fraction is less than .5 unit, drop the remaining fraction.

(b) If the remaining decimal fraction is greater than .5 unit, increase the preceding digit by one.

(c) If the remaining decimal fraction is exactly .5 unit, add 1 to the preceding digit if that digit is an odd number but drop the remaining decimal fraction if the preceding digit is an even number.

For example, if the unit of measurement is a whole second and the value 33.4 is obtained, round this to 33 seconds in accordance with convention (a) for rounding. If the obtained value is 32.6, round to 33 in accordance with (b). If the obtained value is 34.5, convention (c) dictates to round to 34 because the preceding digit (i.e., 4) is even; but if 33.5 is to be rounded the result is 34 because the preceding digit (e.g., 3) is odd. Note, however, that 34.51 is rounded to 35 because the remaining decimal fraction is more than .5 unit.

The reason that some numbers whose remaining decimal fractions are exactly .5 are rounded up and some are rounded down is so that over many instances of rounding numbers approximately half will be rounded up and half rounded down. In contrast, if a simple rule of always rounding .5 up were invoked, more numbers would be rounded up than down. By rounding some of these cases up and some down according to the convention outlined in (c), this "bias" is eliminated. On the average half the numbers considered in this way are rounded up and half are rounded down.

summation sign

Statistics are measures computed on a group of scores, and when formulas are given for statistics it is convenient to have some symbolic terminology to represent groups of scores and operations on groups rather than single scores. Consider the group of five scores below:

Subject	Score Symbol	Score Value
1	X_1	2
2	X_2	3
3	X_3	8
4	X_4	4
5	X_5	7

Suppose the measure reflected by these scores is called X. Actually, the measure may be inches, seconds, frequency, etc., but since it will be useful to express formulas which can be used for any measure, such a general measure will be called X. There are five scores in the above group and each score represents a specific example of an X. In order to be able to distinguish one specific score from another, each score is given a subscript corresponding to the number of the subject who made that score. Customarily, in a group of five scores, these subscripts would be 1, 2, 3, 4, 5. In general, if there are N scores, the subscripts would run from 1 to N. Frequently, it is useful to be able to refer to a single score, but not necessarily any particular one—just any single score in the distribution of X's. This single score is referred to as the ith score in the distribution and it is written X_i. Thus, in this example the distribution of X_i has five scores and if one refers to X_i where $i = 3$ one refers to X_3 which has a score value of 8.

In later chapters of this book it will be necessary to consider more than one group of scores of the same type of measurement. In this case, in order to specify a particular score it is necessary to indicate both the group and the subject within that group. Two subscripts are used to accomplish this type of score designation. For example, any particular score would be written X_{ij}, where i indicates the subject and j specifies the group. The score for the fourth subject in the third group would be designated as X_{43}. This topic will be considered again in the sections on the analysis of variance in Chapter 9.

One of the most frequent operations performed in statistics is the summation of all or a portion of the scores in a group. For example, in computing the average of a group of measurements, one sums all the scores and divides by the number of scores. However, when writing the formula for the average it is cumbersome to use

$$\text{Average} = \frac{\text{sum of all the scores}}{\text{the number of scores}}$$

Usually, N is used to refer to the number of scores in the distribution, but the operation of summing all the scores also requires a symbolic abbreviation because it occurs in so many formulas.

The Greek capital letter sigma, $\sum$, is employed to indicate the operation of summing. This summation sign is often written in a form comparable to

$$\sum_{i=1}^{N} X_i$$

The small notations under and over the $\sum$ are called the "limits of the summation." The entire symbol is read, "sum of the X_i from $i = 1$ to N." It means to add X_1 plus X_2 plus . . . plus X_N. In symbols,

$$\sum_{i=1}^{N} X_i = X_1 + X_2 + X_3 + \cdots + X_N$$

Thus, $\sum_{i=1}^{5} X_i$ implies the sum of the first five X scores and $\sum_{i=2}^{4} X_i$ means the sum of the second through the fourth scores. In terms of the above data,

$$\sum_{i=1}^{5} X_i = 2 + 3 + 8 + 4 + 7 = 24$$

and

$$\sum_{i=2}^{4} X_i = 3 + 8 + 4 = 15$$

Often, when all the scores in a distribution are to be summed, the limits of the summation are not written and the subscript i is often omitted:

$$\sum X = \sum_{i=1}^{N} X_i$$

There are three short cuts for using the summation sign in algebraic operations which will help the student in working with the summation sign.

1. **The sum of a constant times a variable equals the constant times the sum of the variable.** If c is a constant and X_i a variable,

$$\sum_{i=1}^{N} cX_i = c \sum_{i=1}^{N} X_i$$

First, consider what the expression means:

$$\sum_{i=1}^{N} cX_i = cX_1 + cX_2 + cX_3 + \cdots + cX_N$$

But, this series of terms may be factored in the same manner as $ca + cb = c(a + b)$ with the following results:

$$\sum_{i=1}^{N} cX_i = c\underbrace{(X_1 + X_2 + X_3 + \cdots + X_N)}_{c \sum_{i=1}^{N} X_i}$$

Since the expression within the parentheses is what has been defined to be the $\sum_{i=1}^{N} X_i$, the sum of a constant times a variable is the constant times the sum of the variable:

$$\sum_{i=1}^{N} cX_i = c \sum_{i=1}^{N} X_i$$

2. **The sum of a constant taken N times is N times the constant.** If c is a constant,

$$\sum_{i=1}^{N} c = Nc$$

This fact can be seen easily by writing out the expression being considered.

$$\sum_{i=1}^{N} c = \underbrace{c + c + c + \cdots + c}_{N \text{ terms}}$$

The symbol $\sum_{i=1}^{N} c$ implies adding N c's together. However, the operation of multiplication is precisely this repetitive addition, so that adding N c's is identical to multiplying c by N. Therefore, the sum of a constant c taken N times is Nc.

3. **The summation of a sum of terms is the sum of these individual summations.** If X and Y are variables,

$$\sum_{i=1}^{N} (X_i + Y_i) = \sum_{i=1}^{N} X_i + \sum_{i=1}^{N} Y_i$$

Again, writing out the expression,

$$\sum_{i=1}^{N} (X_i + Y_i) = (X_1 + Y_1) + (X_2 + Y_2) + \cdots + (X_N + Y_N)$$

removing parentheses,

$$= X_1 + Y_1 + X_2 + Y_2 + \cdots + X_N + Y_N$$

and regrouping produces

$$\sum_{i=1}^{N} (X_i + Y_i) = \underbrace{X_1 + X_2 + \cdots + X_N}_{\sum_{i=1}^{N} X_i} + \underbrace{Y_1 + Y_2 + \cdots + Y_N}_{\sum_{i=1}^{N} Y_i}$$

This result may be generalized to any number of terms. For example,

$$\sum(X_i + Y_i + W_i) = \sum X_i + \sum Y_i + \sum W_i$$

Understanding and being facile in the use of the summation sign is imperative in order to follow the rest of this text. The student is advised to practice the exercises until he has mastered the use of the summation sign.

Those students needing a review of basic algebra will find a brief description of the most frequently used techniques in Appendix I.

EXERCISES

1. Indicate the scale of measurement presented for each of the following concepts and justify your choice:
   a. A social psychologist obtains a measure of leadership for 20 people in a group discussion by having an observer assign points (1 through 10) to each member of the group in accordance with the observer's judgment of leadership potential.
   b. An experimental psychologist records the number of bar presses that an animal makes as a measure of the reinforcing potential of a change in illumination. Each bar press results in a change of illumination in the cage.
   c. After making a response to a Rorschach inkblot the person is asked to report the characteristics of the figure that prompted his stated interpretation. A clinical psychologist determines whether the responses focused on the form, color, or shading of the figure.
   d. Discuss the difference in the scales of temperature produced by the centigrade versus the Kelvin methods. (The Kelvin method uses −273°C as its zero point. This is the point at which all molecular movement ceases.)

2. The following table shows a small distribution of scores on an examination. Take these scores and rank order the students assigning a rank of 1 to the highest score. Compare the difference between students numbers 8 and 9 with the difference between students numbers 8 and 7. What is the nature of the information that is lost when an ordinal as opposed to an interval (or ratio) scale is used?

Student	Score
1	4
2	6
3	3
4	1
5	0
6	8
7	9
8	10
9	18
10	7

3. Which of the following variables are discrete and which are continuous?
   a. IQ
   b. number of responses made by a rat in a bar-pressing situation
   c. the rate of bar pressing (responses/time)
   d. biological sex

4. What are the real limits for the following numbers?
   a. 1 d. 1.1 g. 3.84
   b. 18 e. 24.3 h. 12.61
   c. 77 f. 1002.4 i. 129.80

5. Round the following numbers to tenths.
   a. 4.63 d. 6.75
   b. 3.48 e. 8.050
   c. 2.05001

6. Given the following data, determine the numerical value of each of the following expressions.

Subject (*i*)	X_i	Y_i
1	3	2
2	8	3
3	2	7
4	1	5
5	5	4

a. $\sum_{i=1}^{5} X_i$ e. $\sum_{i=1}^{5} (X_i + Y_i)$

b. $\sum_{i=1}^{3} Y_i$ f. $\sum_{i=1}^{5} X_i Y_i$

c. $\sum_{i=3}^{5} X_i$ g. $\sum_{i=1}^{5} X_i^2$

d. $\sum Y$ h. $\left(\sum_{i=1}^{5} X_i\right)^2$

7. Given the data from Exercise 6 for X and Y and that c, a constant, equals 3, determine the numerical value of each of the following expressions.

a. $\sum cX_i$ d. $\sum_{i=1}^{5} c$

b. $\sum cXY$ e. $\sum_{i=1}^{3} (X + c)$

c. $\sum c(X + Y)$

8. Simplify the following expressions (W and Z are variables, k is a constant).

a. $\dfrac{\sum (kW + W)}{\sum W}$

b. $\dfrac{\sum (W + k) + \sum (Z - k)}{\sum (W + Z)}$

c. $\dfrac{\sum (k - W) + \sum (Z + W) + (\sum k)(\sum Z)}{N\left(\sum kZ + \dfrac{\sum k}{N}\right)}$

frequency distributions

Given that a variable and a scale of measurement have been selected and a group of scores has been obtained, how can one efficiently describe this collection of observations? It is often desirable to be able to characterize the entire group of scores rather than to denote any single value. For example, one might want to know the range of score values included in the group, the values about which most of the scores seem to cluster, the dispersion of the scores over the measurement scale, etc. It would be highly cumbersome and inefficient to enumerate each score every time these questions were posed, and furthermore such a listing would not provide a ready picture of the characteristics of the group.

> A **frequency distribution** shows a tallying of the number of times each score value (or interval of score values) occurs in a group of scores.

Suppose a short history quiz was given to a class of 10 students, and the essay was graded on a 10-point scale. The scores are presented in Part A of Table 2–1. The first thing to do in order to obtain a clearer picture of this small group of scores is to list them in descending order as in Part B of Table 2–1. Next, observe that there was one score of 10, two of 9, three of both 8 and 7, and one of 6. If the score value is designated as "X" and a tally is made next to the X for each occurrence of that value, the result is the frequency distribution presented in Part C of Table 2–1 in which f indicates the frequency for any given value of the variable X.

2–1 The Development of a Frequency Distribution.

A. Scores on a History Quiz

8	8
10	7
9	6
7	8
9	7

B. Scores on a History Quiz Presented in Decreasing Order

10	8
9	7
9	7
8	7
8	6

C. Frequency Distribution of Scores on a History Quiz

X	*Tally*	f
10	/	1
9	//	2
8	///	3
7	///	3
6	/	1
		$N = 10$

A second example of a frequency distribution might involve an opinion researcher who gives a questionnaire in which he asks a sample of people to what extent they approve of the way the President of the United States is carrying out his duties. The researcher provides five possible responses and he arbitrarily attaches a number to each level of response:

1. disapprove to a great extent,
2. generally disapprove but do agree with some policies,
3. disapprove of about half of his actions and approve of half,
4. generally approve but disapprove of some policies,
5. approve to a great extent.

Suppose 80 people were questioned and asked to indicate one of these five opinions. The frequency of their responses is presented in Table 2–2. It is clear from this frequency distribution that people seem to be somewhat split on their opinion about the President's actions. A sizable group generally disagrees while another sizable group agrees with his actions. Few people seem either ambivalent ($X = 3$) or adamantly positive or negative. Such descriptive conclusions would be difficult to arrive at if all 80 scores were written down without the assistance of the frequency distribution. Hence, not only does a frequency distribution save time in displaying data, it also organizes data in a way in which the data may be summarized more easily than a mere accounting of each score would allow.

A distribution that indicates the percentage of the total number of cases which were observed at each score value (or interval of values) is called a **relative frequency distribution.**

An example of a relative frequency distribution is given in the last column of Table 2–2. The advantage of a relative frequency distribution is that it expresses the pattern of scores in a manner which is not so dependent on the specific number of cases involved. Thus, an opinion pollster would not say

2–2 Frequency Distribution of Opinions on Presidential Policy.

	X	f	$Rel. f$
Disapprove Greatly	1	6	.08
Disapprove	2	25	.31
Ambivalent	3	10	.12
Approve	4	30	.38
Approve Greatly	5	9	.11
		$N = 80$	1.00

that 9 people emphatically approved of the President's actions, but rather that 11% did. Of course it is always informative to know the total number of people polled.

The two examples illustrating the concept of a frequency distribution have had either a small number of cases or they have involved only a few score values. While arranging data in the form of a frequency distribution in these cases demonstrated two assets of this technique, the frequency distribution is used to its greatest advantage when there are a large number of scores and a wide range of score values.

To illustrate, suppose 112 eighth-grade children were given a mathematics ability test prior to taking an algebra course. The scores for these children are presented in Table 2–3. This display emphasizes the fact that enumerating all the scores does not provide much immediate information about the nature of the group of scores. A frequency distribution is necessary.

2–3 Mathematics Ability Test Scores for 112 Eighth-Grade Students.

79	51	67	50	78	71	77	75
62	89	83	73	80	67	74	63
88	48	60	71	79	79	47	55
89	63	55	93	71	81	72	68
41	81	46	50	61	72	86	66
59	50	90	75	61	82	73	57
75	98	53	79	80	64	67	51
70	37	42	72	74	78	91	69
67	73	79	67	85	74	70	62
91	73	77	36	77	45	39	59
53	67	85	74	77	78	73	61
71	43	42	96	83	83	84	67
70	92	59	86	53	71	49	68
32	67	67	71	71	59	80	66

If a frequency distribution were constructed from these scores in the previous manner, namely stating each possible score value between 0 and 100 and its corresponding frequency, there would be almost no gain in the efficiency of characterizing this data. In order to retain the advantage of concise presentation of data, several score values could be grouped together forming a **class interval.** For example, how many frequencies were there for the score values of 30, 31, 32, 33, and 34 all together?

Table 2–4 was constructed with this ordering and grouping in mind. From this table, one can see that there were only two cases of a score between 95 and 99 inclusive (namely, 98 and 96), five cases within the interval between

2–4 Ordering of Mathematics Ability Test Scores.

—	74, 74, 74, 74	49
98	73, 73, 73, 73, 73	48
—	72, 72, 72	47
96	71, 71, 71, 71, 71	46
—	70, 70, 70	45
—	69	—
93	68, 68	43
92	67, 67, 67, 67, 67, 67, 67, 67, 67	42, 42
91, 91	66, 66	41
90	—	—
89, 89	64	39
88	63, 63	—
—	62, 62	37
86, 86	61, 61, 61	36
85, 85	60	—
84	59, 59, 59, 59	—
83, 83, 83	—	—
82	57	32
81, 81	—	—
80, 80, 80, 80	55, 55	—
79, 79, 79, 79, 79	—	
78, 78, 78	53, 53, 53	
77, 77, 77, 77	—	
76	51, 51	
75, 75, 75	50, 50, 50	

90 and 94 inclusive, seven between 85 and 89 inclusive, etc. A summary of this accounting is presented in the frequency distribution shown in the two left-most columns of Table 2–5. The only difference between this frequency distribution and previous ones is that rather than having frequencies stated for each possible score value, frequencies are listed as falling within certain class intervals, e.g., 30–34, 35–39, 40–44, etc. When scores are presented in this manner, they are sometimes referred to as **grouped data.**

In addition to the frequency distribution of raw scores, the relative frequency distribution provides another method of examining grouped data. An example of it is presented in the third column of Table 2–5. Two other distributions are

2–5 Distributions for 112 Math Ability Scores.

Class Interval	*f*	Rel. *f*	Cum. *f*	Cum. Rel. *f*
95–99	2	.02	112	1.00
90–94	5	.04	110	.98
85–89	7	.06	105	.94
80–84	11	.10	98	.88
75–79	16	.14	87	.78
70–74	20	.18	71	.64
65–69	14	.12	51	.46
60–64	9	.08	37	.34
55–59	7	.06	28	.26
50–54	8	.07	21	.20
45–49	5	.05	13	.13
40–44	4	.04	8	.08
35–39	3	.03	4	.04
30–34	1	.01	1	.01
	$N = 112$	1.00		

also displayed. They are the **cumulative frequency** and **cumulative relative frequency** distributions.

> A **cumulative frequency distribution** is one in which the entry for any class interval is the sum of the frequencies in that interval and all class intervals below. A **cumulative relative frequency distribution** is one in which the entry for any class interval is the relative frequency corresponding to the sum of the frequencies in that interval and all intervals below.

Quite simply, these are respective modifications of the frequency and relative frequency distribution in which the entries are progressively accumulated starting from the lowest class interval. Cumulative distributions provide a means for rapidly ascertaining the number or proportion of scores that fall below the upper limit of a given class interval.

Suppose for this mathematics test, Johnny had a score of 64. The cumulative percentage for scores in the interval 60–64 in Table 2–5 is .34, which says that 34% of the scores were equal to or below the score of 64. Johnny is sometimes said to be at the 34th percentile. Percentiles will be discussed in more detail in Chapter 4.

A distribution, then, is a group of scores classified according to frequency, relative frequency, cumulative frequency, or cumulative relative frequency.

The advantage of such a distribution is that it is an efficient method of organizing and presenting a large group of scores in such a fashion that certain characteristics of the group as a whole become apparent.

CONSTRUCTING FREQUENCY DISTRIBUTIONS FOR GROUPED DATA

number of class intervals It is somewhat easier to read and understand a frequency distribution of the variety just discussed than it is to organize a group of scores into that form because certain decisions must be made about the nature of the class interval to be used. In the above case, an interval such as 30–34 was selected, but would 30–32 or 30–47 have done just as well? Table 2–6 illustrates these two alternatives.

2–6 Two Distributions with Class Intervals of Different Sizes.

Class Interval	*f*	Class Interval	*f*
96–98	2	84–101	15
93–95	1	66–83	60
90–92	4	48–65	26
87–89	3	30–47	11
84–86	5		$N = 112$
81–83	6		
78–80	12		
75–77	8		
72–74	12		
69–71	9		
66–68	13		
63–65	3		
60–62	6		
57–59	5		
54–56	2		
51–53	5		
48–50	5		
45–47	3		
42–44	3		
39–41	2		
36–38	2		
33–35	0		
30–32	1		
	$N = 112$		

Consider these examples from the standpoint of the general goal of frequency distributions which is **summarization** of data into a form which **accurately pictures** the group as a whole. In the first instance (left-hand distribution) with 23 different class intervals the summarization advantage of the frequency distribution is lost. Taking the proliferation of class intervals to a ridiculous extreme, one could enumerate each possible score value just as in Table 2–4. Several scores would have no frequencies (e.g., 33, 34, 35, 38, etc.), and there would be little advantage in making a frequency distribution at all. Further, the frequencies at the left of Table 2–6 do not provide a smooth picture or description of the pattern of frequencies in relation to the scores. This distribution is too spread out or diffuse.

Conversely, the right-hand distribution in Table 2–6 has too few class intervals. It is clear that most of the scores fall between 66–83, but this interval is so big that considerable accuracy and detail have been lost in grouping the data into only four classes. For example, it is not known if the 11 cases between 30–47 fell rather near the value of 47, nearer to 30, or were relatively evenly spaced within the interval. The lowest score in the group could be anywhere between 47 and 30 according to this distribution.

From these examples it should be clear that too many class intervals do not provide adequate summarization or description of the group of scores, whereas too few intervals reduce the accuracy of the description. One must select a number of class intervals that represents a compromise between these extremes.

It is usually suggested that between 10 and 20 class intervals be chosen, but there can be a great difference between the picture one obtains of a distribution if it is displayed with 10 or with 20 intervals. Hence, although this is a good rule of thumb to employ, one has to make an intelligent decision depending upon the nature of the data. In the example illustrated in Table 2–5, 14 intervals were chosen. In general, if the total number of frequencies is small (e.g., 20–50) one would tend to pick fewer intervals than if there were 100 or 200 cases. If the distribution had only 10 scores one would want even fewer intervals than 10, perhaps 4 or 5; but if there were 2000 cases as many as 20 or more intervals might be contemplated. Hence, although the guideline of between 10 and 20 intervals is one which is usually appropriate, it merely reflects the concern for an accurate summarization and display of a group of scores.

the size of the class interval Once a tentative decision on the approximate number of class intervals has been made, the size of the interval must be determined. A good approach is to subtract the smallest score from the largest. This provides a crude measure of the span of values covered by the group of scores which must be broken into intervals. If this result is divided by the approximate number of intervals, an estimate of the size of the intervals is obtained. For example, if approximately 15 intervals would be appropriate for the data in Table 2–4 and the difference between the largest and smallest scores was 98 − 32 = 66, then

$$\begin{array}{r} 4.4 \\ 15\overline{)66.} \\ \underline{60} \\ 60 \\ \underline{60} \end{array}$$

yields an approximate interval size. However, it is inconvenient to use intervals involving fractions like 4.4. Hence, one might use an interval of 5, thus covering a range of 66 with 14 intervals.

To determine the size of a class interval from a distribution already constructed subtract the lower **real limit** from the upper **real limit** of the interval. For the interval 30–34 (30 and 34 are called the **stated limits**), the lower real limit is 29.5 and the upper real limit is 34.5 which yields an interval size of 5:

$$34.5 - 29.5 = 5$$

It may seem a bit puzzling that the size of the interval 30–34 is 5 and not 4 as it might initially appear, but if the various scores which are contained within the range of 30–34 are listed (30, 31, 32, 33, 34) there are clearly 5 not 4 of them. This notion is further illustrated in Figure 2–2 in which the linear scale of measurement is drawn and the real limits for each score in the interval are shown.

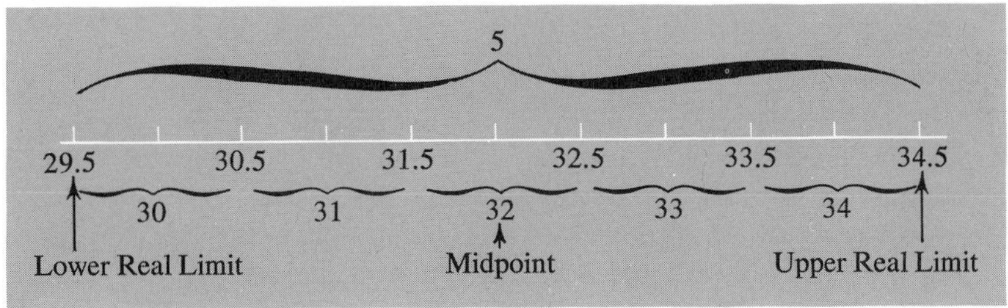

Fig. 2–2. Illustration of the fact that the size of the interval 30–34 is 5.

the lowest interval Now that the number and size of the class intervals have been established, all that remains is to specify the first interval and the scale will be completely determined. There is a custom that the first **stated** limit (not the lower **real** limit) be evenly divisible by the size of the interval. Thus, the size of the lowest interval 30–34 is 5 and the lowest **stated** limit is 30. Since 30 divided by 5 is an even 6, this meets the requirement. If the lowest score in a distribution is 49 and an interval of size 4 is selected, the first interval would be 48–51, because 48, but not 49, is evenly divisible by 4.

midpoint of an interval The **midpoint** of a class interval is the precise center of that interval or half-way between the endpoints. It is determined by adding one-half of the size of the interval to its lower real limit.

For the interval 30–34 whose size is five and whose lower real limit is 29.5, the midpoint is

$$29.5 + 2.5 = 32$$

For the interval 45.6–48.3 whose size is 2.8 and lower real limit is 45.55, the midpoint is

$$45.55 + 1.4 = 46.95$$

The important thing to remember is to take the lower **real** limit (e.g., 45.55) not the **stated** limit (e.g., 45.6).[3]

summary illustration As a final presentation of some of these topics, Table 2–7 provides a summary of the guidelines for constructing a frequency distribution using class intervals and Table 2–8 displays the resulting distribution for the sample data presented in Table 2–5 including the real limits, interval size, and midpoints.

2–7 Summary of Guidelines for Constructing Frequency Distributions with Grouped Data.

1. Estimate the number of class intervals. This usually should be 10 to 20, but it may be less if the total number of cases is small or it may be more if the total is very large.
2. Estimate the size of the class interval by dividing the difference between the largest and smallest score in the distribution by the number of intervals selected in Step 1.
3. Adjust the number of intervals and their size so that
   a. the size is indicated by a whole number (or a convenient fraction if a whole number is not appropriate), and
   b. the number of intervals of this size will cover the entire range of scores.
4. Select the lowest class interval such that its lowest **stated** limit is evenly divisible by the size of the interval.
5. Place the lowest interval at the bottom of the table which contains the class intervals and their respective frequencies.

[3] Since the midpoint of a class interval is the point falling in the center of the interval, it may be computed by taking half the distance between the **stated** limits and adding that result to the lower **stated** limit. Thus, in the case of the interval 30–34, $(34 - 30)/2 + 30 = 32$ yields the same result as above. Since other procedures require use of the real limits and since the size of the interval is usually known (note that the difference between **stated** limits is **not** the size of the interval), the text uses the form involving real limits and interval size.

2–8 Frequency Distribution with Real Limits, Interval Size, and Midpoint.

Class Interval	Real Limits	Interval Size	Midpoint	Frequency
95–99	94.5–99.5	5	97	2
90–94	89.5–94.5	5	92	5
85–89	84.5–89.5	5	87	7
80–84	79.5–84.5	5	82	11
75–79	74.5–79.5	5	77	16
70–74	69.5–74.5	5	72	20
65–69	64.5–69.5	5	67	14
60–64	59.5–64.5	5	62	9
55–59	54.5–59.5	5	57	7
50–54	49.5–54.5	5	52	8
45–49	44.5–49.5	5	47	5
40–44	39.5–44.5	5	42	4
35–39	34.5–39.5	5	37	3
30–34	29.5–34.5	5	32	1
				$N = 112$

GRAPHS OF FREQUENCY DISTRIBUTIONS

frequency histogram The descriptive function of frequency distributions is served by drawing a graph of the distribution. One type of graph is a frequency histogram, and it is presented in Figure 2–3 for the data in the example of the math ability scores of 112 eighth-grade children (Table 2–8).

When constructing this histogram, a horizontal scale was drawn corresponding to the math ability scale of scores. The horizontal dimension of such a plot is called the **abscissa.** Notice that the numbers along the abscissa are the midpoints of the intervals as found in Table 2–8. The vertical dimension is called the **ordinate,** and in the case of frequency distributions it will correspond to "Frequency." The abscissa and ordinate are collectively called **axes.** Note that the axes are clearly marked with the numbers of their respective scales and then labeled.

frequency polygon The **frequency polygon** uses precisely the same abscissa and ordinate as the frequency histogram, and an example is presented in Figure 2–4. The graph is constructed by placing a point above the midpoint of each class interval corresponding to the frequency within that interval. The adjacent points are connected by straight lines. Note also that the line formed by connecting the points intersects the abscissa at both ends. If there were two additional class intervals, each with zero frequencies and one

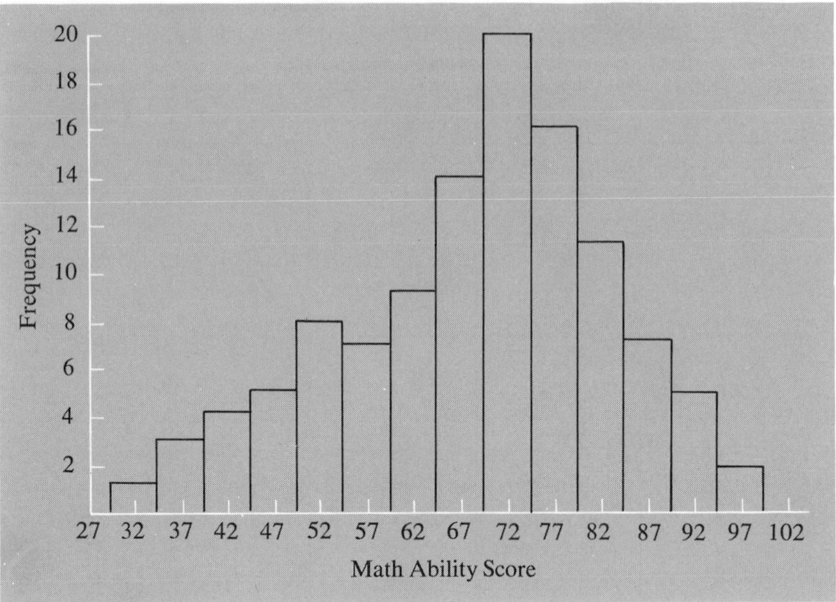

Fig. 2–3. Frequency histogram for the math ability scores of 112 eighth-grade students as presented in Table 2–5.

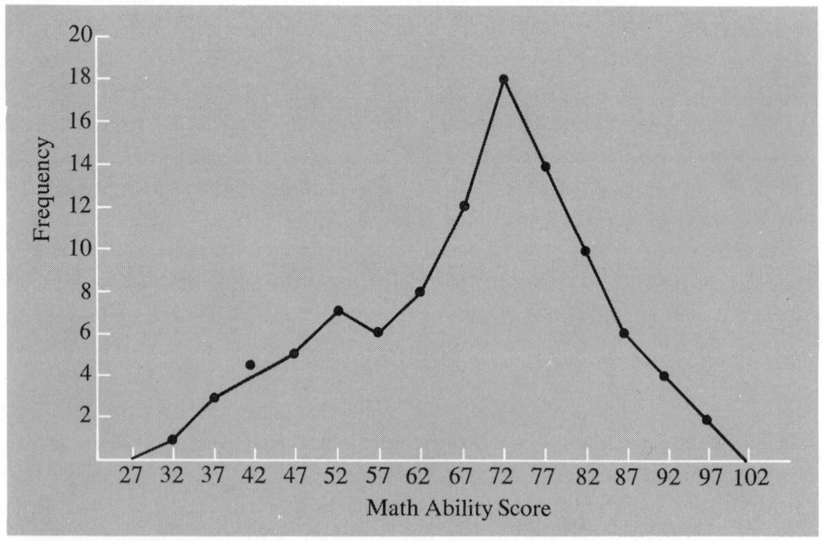

Fig. 2–4. Frequency polygon for the math ability scores of 112 eighth-grade students as presented in Table 2–5.

placed at each end of the distribution, the line of the polygon would intersect the abscissa (indicating "no frequencies") at the midpoints of these extreme intervals. This closing of the line with the abscissa completes the formation of a polygon from which this graph derives its name.

relative frequency histogram and polygon Figure 2–5 presents a relative frequency histogram and polygon for these same data. Note that these plots are graphically similar to the corresponding frequency distribution of scores except that the ordinate is relative frequency and the values are taken from the column labeled "Rel. *f*" in Table 2–5.

cumulative frequency histogram and polygon Just as frequency and relative frequency distributions have been plotted in the form of polygons, the two cumulative distributions in Table 2–5 similarly can be graphed. For example, Figure 2–6 presents a cumulative frequency polygon.

One difference between the graph of a frequency distribution and a cumulative frequency distribution is that the ordinate changes from frequency to cumulative frequency.

The cumulative frequency polygon contains another important difference from the frequency polygon: the point on the graph is now placed over the upper real limit of the interval rather than over its midpoint. This is because this point must indicate that up to the end of that interval, a certain number of cases have occurred. Since the scores that fall within a given interval may be

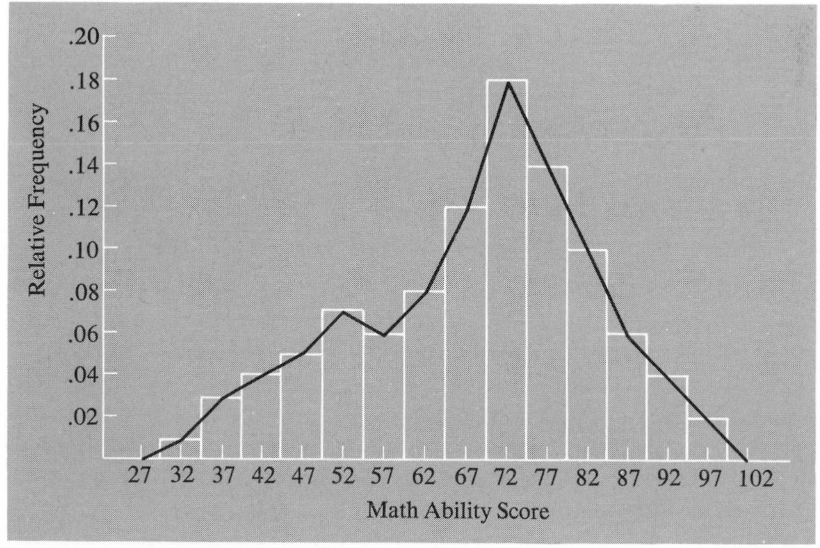

Fig. 2–5. A relative frequency polygon and histogram for the data on mathematics ability presented in Table 2–5.

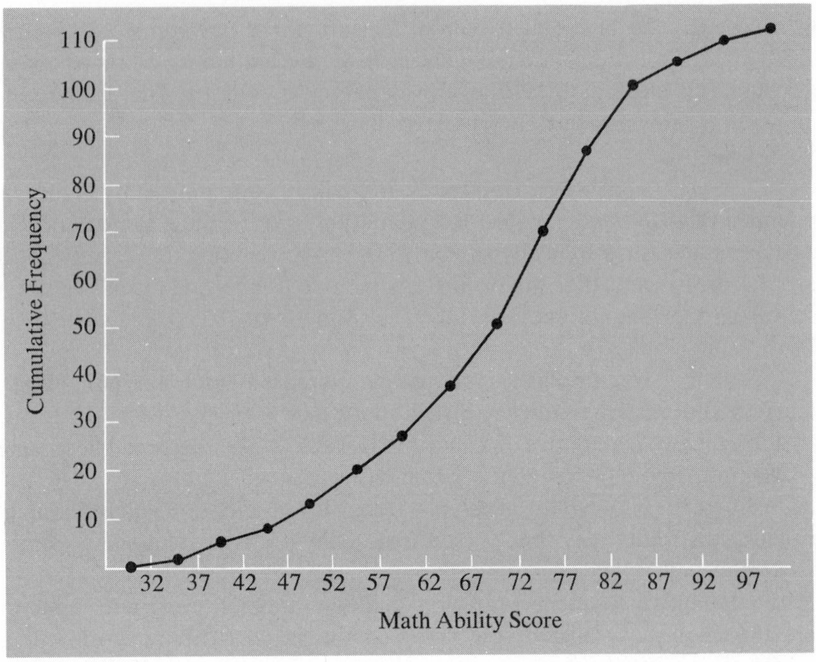

Fig. 2-6. A cumulative frequency polygon.

located anywhere within that interval, the point representing the accumulation of all frequencies within and below this interval is placed at the upper real limit of the interval.

HOW DISTRIBUTIONS DIFFER

Distributions differ one to another with respect to (1) **central tendency,** (2) **variability,** (3) **kurtosis,** and (4) **skewness.** The next chapter will take up measures of some of these characteristics. It will be profitable to preface this material with an overview of the general meaning of these concepts.

> The **central tendency** of a distribution is a typical or representative score.

There are several more specific definitions of central tendency, each with its own set of characteristics and implications. Three of these will be discussed in Chapter 3: the **mean, median,** and **mode.**

To illustrate the concept of central tendency, consider the two curves (smoothed frequency polygons) in Figure 2–7. They differ only with respect to

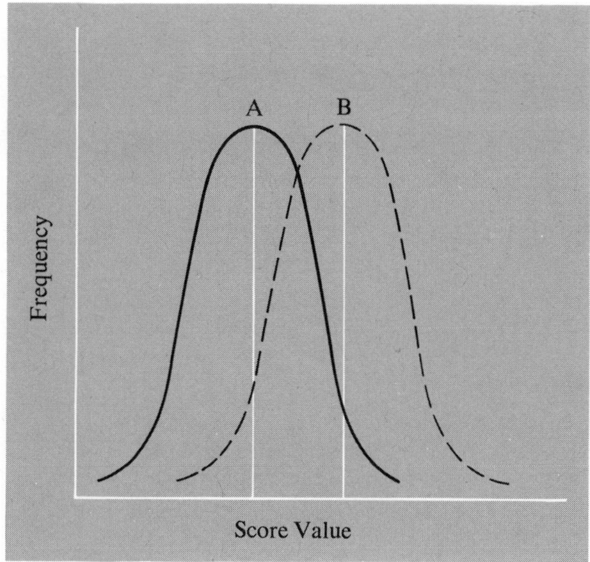

Fig. 2–7. Two distributions which differ only with respect to central tendency.

central tendency. They are the same shape, but occupy different places on the score dimension.

> **Variability** is the degree to which scores deviate from their central tendency.

Figure 2–8 shows two curves with similar central tendencies but different amounts of variability. The cases in Distribution A tend to cluster more closely about the central tendency of the distribution which is indicated by the vertical line. In contrast, there is a disproportionate number of cases in Distribution B that do not fall as closely around that central value as do the cases in the A curve. There is more variability in B than in A. The concept of variability is probably the most central idea in statistics.

> The **kurtosis** of a distribution is the "curvedness" or "peakedness" of the graph.

Figure 2–9 depicts two curves with similar central tendencies but different kurtoses. Curve A is more peaked than B, and the changes in the height of the curve as the score value increases are more marked for A than for B. Kurtosis is frequently used in a relative sense. Distribution A is more **leptokurtic** than B.

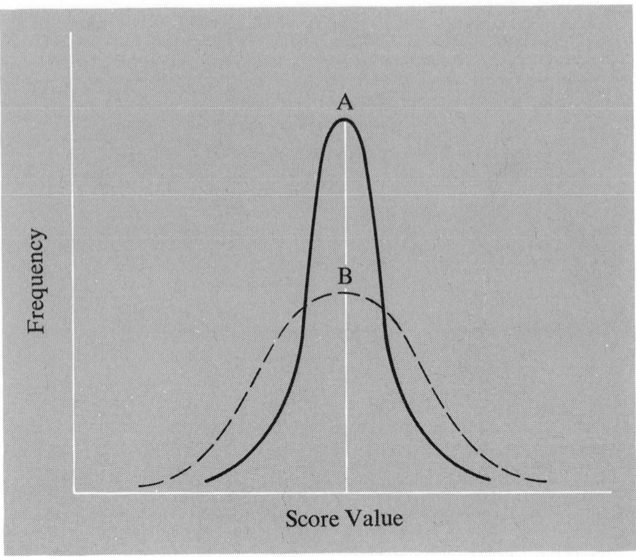

Fig. 2–8. Distributions with similar central tendency but with different variability.

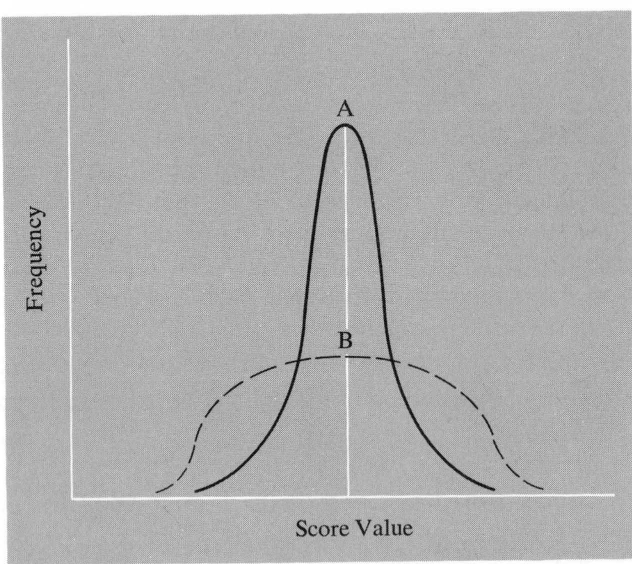

Fig. 2–9. Distributions with similar central tendency but different kurtosis.

The Greek *lepto* means "thin," so leptokurtic means thinly curved which seems appropriate to describe curve A relative to B. On the other hand, B is said to be more **platykurtic** than A. *Platy* means "flat" (e.g., *platy*helminthes—flatworms, *platy*pus—a flat-billed mammal). Hence, B is flatter than A.

> **Skewness** refers to the bunching of scores on one side of the central tendency or to the trailing out of scores in one direction from the central tendency.

These traits are reflected in the lack of symmetry of some distributions. Figure 2–10 presents two skewed distributions. Both lack symmetry, and B is more skewed than is A because the scores tend to bunch more at one end and trail off to the other end.

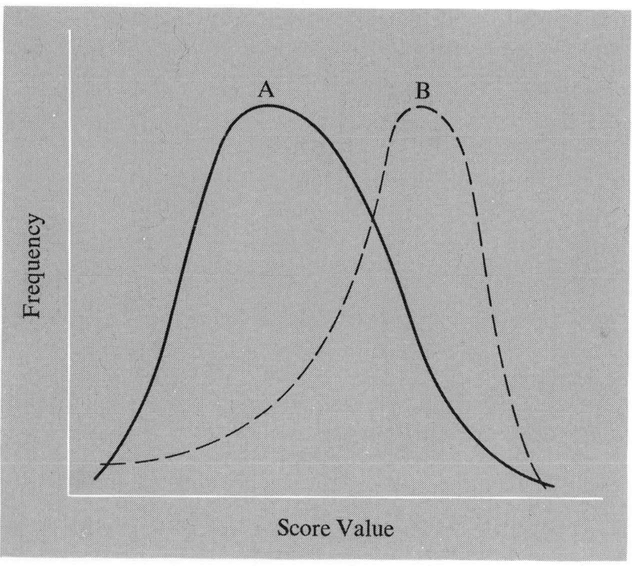

Fig. 2–10. Distributions with different skewness.

Skewness has direction as well as magnitude. In Distribution A the scores tend to trail off to the right or positive end of the scale. It is said to be **positively skewed** or **skewed to the right.** Distribution B, conversely, trails off to the left or to the negative end of the scale (recall that the first integer to the left of 0 is -1, i.e., negative). Distribution B is said to be **negatively skewed** or **skewed to the left.**

These terms may be used to describe the general form of a distribution. Thus, one might say that a distribution is positively skewed and rather platykurtic.

This verbal description gives one some idea of the form the curve of this distribution. However, one might wish to be more precise than merely to use these relative terms. For purposes of comparing distributions it would be helpful if mathematical indices were available that reflect these characteristics. Although measures of skewness and kurtosis are available[4] they are not often used. Therefore, only indices of central tendency and variability will be taken up in the next chapter.

EXERCISES

1. Below is a set of scores on a mathematics exam. Construct a frequency distribution appropriate for these data. Present the distribution in the manner of Table 2–8, with real limits, midpoint, interval size, and frequency indicated. Then compose a relative frequency distribution, cumulative frequency distribution, and cumulative relative frequency distribution for these data.

67	91	21	64	59
92	12	72	65	68
31	41	52	74	51
38	64	68	88	55
62	60	84	33	60
50	78	42	26	80
48	25	47	72	63
75	83	35	57	39
35	42	48	43	50
40	60	93	69	49

2. Construct polygons and histograms for the frequency, relative frequency, and cumulative frequency distributions above.

3. Perform the tasks required in Exercises 1 and 2 with the following data:

40	41	38	43	35	42
41	37	36	34	38	34
34	31	35	41	45	39
30	38	40	36	32	32
46	38	30	29	38	41
36	34	36	44	42	41
32	43	38	35	36	37
50	35	33	38	31	46
37	36	41	39	44	35
42	37	44	39	39	38

[4] See, for example: G. A. Ferguson, *Statistical Analysis in Psychology and Education.* New York: McGraw-Hill, 1966, (76).

4. The procedures for constructing a frequency distribution were described for data composed of whole numbers. Obviously, many of the measurements made by scientists are in decimal form. The guidelines for constructing frequency distributions listed in Table 2–7 also apply to decimal data. Perform the tasks required in Exercises 1 and 2 with the numbers below.

1.8	1.5	2.3	2.7
2.5	1.9	1.3	1.5
2.0	3.1	2.4	1.1
2.1	2.2	1.6	2.0
1.6	2.2	.4	2.0
1.3	1.4	2.2	1.2
2.8	.6	.9	2.3

3

characteristics of distributions

The purpose of this chapter is to introduce indices of some of those characteristics of frequency distributions discussed at the end of Chapter 2. For example, it is often convenient to talk about the central tendency of a distribution, the point on the distribution that represents a typical score. To make the meaning of central tendency more precise, a numerical index of this attribute is needed. One such central point is the mean or average score. Other indices of central tendency are the median and the mode. However, central tendency is not the only characteristic of a distribution that requires numerical description. Another attribute of a group of scores is their variability, the extent to which the scores differ from one another. Variability is reflected in the range, variance, and standard deviation. In conjunction with the presentation of these concepts, a discussion of statistical estimation will show how measures obtained from a limited number of observations may be used to estimate characteristics of much larger groups of subjects.

measures of central tendency

THE MEAN

definition The most common measure of the central tendency of a group of scores is the average or mean.

The **mean,** symbolized by $\overline{X}$ (read "X bar"), is given by the formula

$$\overline{X} = \frac{\sum_{i=1}^{N} X_i}{N}$$

in which X_i is the ith score in the distribution, N is the number of scores, and $\sum_{i=1}^{N}$ instructs one to add all the scores. Usually, the limits of the summation and the subscript on X are not written since it is always understood that the summation is over all N scores. Therefore, the most common expression for the mean is simply

$$\overline{X} = \frac{\sum X}{N}$$

The mean is also called the arithmetic average of the scores.[1]

computational example The mean is calculated in the following manner if the values of X are 8, 3, 4, 10, 7, and 1.

X
8
3
4
10
7
1

$$\sum X = 33$$
$$N = 6$$
$$\overline{X} = \frac{\sum X}{N} = \frac{33}{6} = 5.5$$

deviations about the mean The mean possesses several properties that make it very useful.

The sum of the deviations of the separate scores from the mean in a distribution is zero. Stated symbolically,

$$\sum_{i=1}^{N} (X_i - \overline{X}) = 0$$

[1] Texts differ in the symbols given to different statistical concepts. Although this text will use the notation $\overline{X}$ to denote the sample mean, other books use M.

Consider the following specified numerical example:

	X_i	$\overline{X}$	$(X_i - \overline{X})$
	3	5	$3 - 5 = -2$
	6	5	$6 - 5 = 1$
	5	5	$5 - 5 = 0$
	1	5	$1 - 5 = -4$
	10	5	$10 - 5 = 5$
$\sum X_i =$	25		$\sum_{i=1}^{N} (X_i - \overline{X}) = 0$
$N =$	5		
$\overline{X} =$	5		

This fact can be proven true of all distributions. The proof, presented in Table 3–1, uses two of the summation rules discussed in Chapter 2 plus the fact that the mean ($\overline{X}$) of any distribution is a constant.

It is important to notice that while the sum of the deviations of all the scores about the mean is always zero, the sum of the **squared** deviations about the mean usually is not zero.

That is, while

$$\sum_{i=1}^{N} (X_i - \overline{X}) = 0$$

the expression

$$\sum_{i=1}^{N} (X_i - \overline{X})^2$$

3–1 Proof that the Sum of the Deviations about the Mean Equals Zero.

Operation	Explanation
1. $\sum(X_i - \overline{X}) = \sum X_i - \sum \overline{X}$	1. The sum of the differences between two quantities equals the difference between their sums.
2. $= \sum X_i - N\overline{X}$	2. The sum of a constant added to itself N times (i.e., $\overline{X}$) is N times the constant.
3. $= \sum X_i - N\left(\frac{\sum X_i}{N}\right)$	3. Substitution of $\frac{\sum X_i}{N}$ for $\overline{X}$
4. $\sum(X_i - \overline{X}) = \sum X_i - \sum X_i = 0$	4. Cancellation

is usually not equal to zero. Returning to the numerical example given above, squaring the numbers in the right-hand part of third column and summing one obtains

$$(-2)^2 + (1)^2 + (0)^2 + (-4)^2 + (5)^2 = 46$$

Although this may appear to be a trivial distinction at this point, these two expressions will appear frequently and the student must be alert to which equals zero and which does not.

A second property of the mean concerns the squared deviations.

> The sum of the squared deviations of all the scores about the mean is less than the sum of the squared deviations about any other value.

This is a fundamental principle and will be invoked in the explanation of many subsequent concepts. The proposition states that although the sum of the **squared** deviations about the mean usually does not equal zero, this sum is smaller than if the squared deviations were taken about any other value. For example, in the above illustration the sum of the squared deviations about the mean equaled 46. The mean of that distribution was 5.0. The sum of the squared deviations about the number 6.0 equals 51, about the number 4.0 it equals 51, and about the number 7.0 it equals 66. The sum (46) taken about the mean is less than any other of these examples, and it can be shown (see the following) that it always will be less than about any other value. It is in this sense that the mean is a measure of central tendency: The mean is "closer" (in terms of squared deviations) to the individual scores over the entire group than is any other single value.

The proof that the sum of the squared deviations about the mean is less than about any alternative value is presented in Table 3–2. The logic of the proof is that "any other value" may be expressed in terms of the mean, $\overline{X}$, plus some value. Specifically, the alternative to the mean will differ from the mean by some value, call it c. Thus, the alternative value may be expressed by $(\overline{X} + c)$, where it is understood that the value of c may be positive or negative. The procedure in proving that the sum of the squared deviations about the mean is a minimum involves determining the sum of squared deviations about any other value (i.e., the value $\overline{X} + c$), and then demonstrating that this sum will always be greater than if the deviations were taken about $\overline{X}$.

THE MEDIAN

definition One measure of central tendency is the median.

> The **median,** symbolized by M_d, is the point that divides the distribution into two parts such that an equal number of scores fall above and below the point.

3–2 Proof that the Sum of the Squared Deviations about the Mean Is a Minimum.

Operation	Explanation
1. $(\overline{X} + c)$, $c \neq 0$, is a value other than $\overline{X}$.	1. Assumption
2. The sum of the squared deviations about $\overline{X}$ equals $\sum(X_i - \overline{X})^2$ and about $(\overline{X} + c)$ it equals $\sum[X_i - (\overline{X} + c)]^2$	2. Definition
3. To prove $\sum(X_i - \overline{X})^2 < \sum[X_i - (\overline{X} + c)]^2$	3. To prove
4. $\sum[X_i - (\overline{X} + c)]^2 = \sum[(X_i - \overline{X}) - c]^2$	4. Regrouping
5. $= \sum[(X_i - \overline{X})^2 - 2c(X_i - \overline{X}) + c^2]$	5. Binomial expansion of the form: $(a - b)^2 = a^2 - 2ab + b^2$
6. $= \sum(X_i - \overline{X})^2 - \underbrace{2c \sum(X_i - \overline{X})}_{\downarrow} + \underbrace{\sum c^2}_{\downarrow}$	6. The sum (or difference) of several variables is the sum (or difference) of their sums, and the sum of a constant times a variable is the constant times the sum of the variable.
7. $\sum[X_i - (\overline{X} + c)]^2 = \sum(X_i - \overline{X})^2 - \quad 0 \quad + Nc^2$	7. $\sum(X_i - \overline{X}) = 0$ and the sum of N c^2's equals N times c^2.
8. $\sum(X_i - \overline{X})^2 < \sum(X_i - \overline{X})^2 + Nc^2$	8. Substituting in 3 above. The expression is true because Nc^2 will always be greater than zero.

computational examples The computation of the median varies under different circumstances.

(a) **There is an odd number of scores in the distribution.** When there is an odd number of scores and no duplication of scores near the median (see (c) below), the median is the middle score. Consider the distribution (3, 5, 6, 7, 10). In this case, the point that divides the distribution into two equal parts is 6.

(b) **There is an even number of scores in the distribution.** By convention, when there is an even number of scores in the distribution and no duplication exists near the median (see (c) below), the average of the middle two scores is taken as the median. Suppose the distribution was (3, 5, 6, 7, 10, 14). The point that divides the distribution in half lies between 6 and 7. The average of these points (6.5) is taken as the median. Another example illustrates the convention that is followed when the scores near the median are not adjacent. If the distribution is (3, 4, 8, 14), the median is 6, since $(4 + 8) \div 2 = 6$.

(c) **There is a duplication of scores near the median.** When more than one instance of the score value falling near the median exists, the median is obtained by interpolation. For example, suppose the distribution is (3, 4, 5, 5, 5, 6, 6, 7). This situation is diagrammed in Figure 3–1 which shows the scores occupying the space on the scale of measurement between their real limits. Since four of the eight scores are required to be below the median, the median must fall within the interval 4.5–5.5. Since two scores already fall below that interval, two of the three scores existing between 4.5 and 5.5 are required to be below the median. Therefore, two-thirds or .67 of the one-unit interval is added to its lower limit: $4.5 + .67 = 5.17$. Thus, 5.17 is the median. If Figure 3–1 is examined carefully and if fractions of frequencies are considered, the student can observe that the distribution is divided in half at the point 5.17.

The above example represents a case involving an even number of scores. Suppose there are an odd number of cases in the distribution. The solution proceeds in the same manner. If the distribution contains the 9 scores (3, 4, 5,

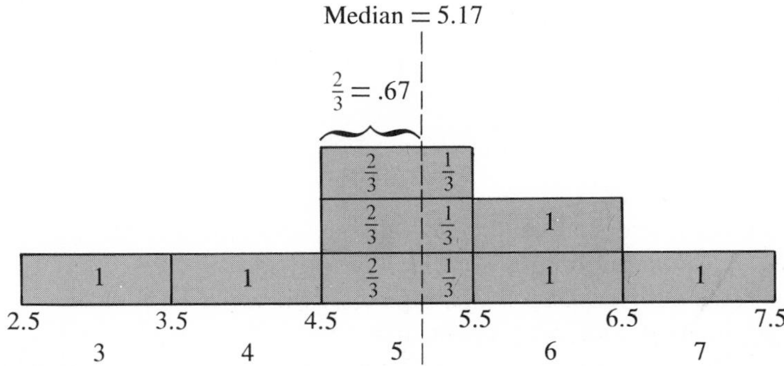

Fig. 3–1. Computing the median when there is duplication of scores.

5, 5, 6, 6, 7, 7), the median again falls within the score interval 4.5–5.5. The problem is diagrammed in Figure 3–2. Since there are 9 scores in the distribution, $4\frac{1}{2}$ of them must lie below the median. Again, two scores exist below 4.5, and therefore $2\frac{1}{2}$ of the 3 scores in the interval 4.5–5.5 must fall below the median. That is,

$$\frac{2\frac{1}{2}}{3} = \frac{\frac{5}{2}}{3} = \frac{5}{6} = .83$$

of the one-unit interval must fall below the median. Therefore,

$$4.5 + .83 = 5.33$$

is the median. Again, by examining Figure 3–2 one can observe that the distribution is divided in half at the point 5.33.

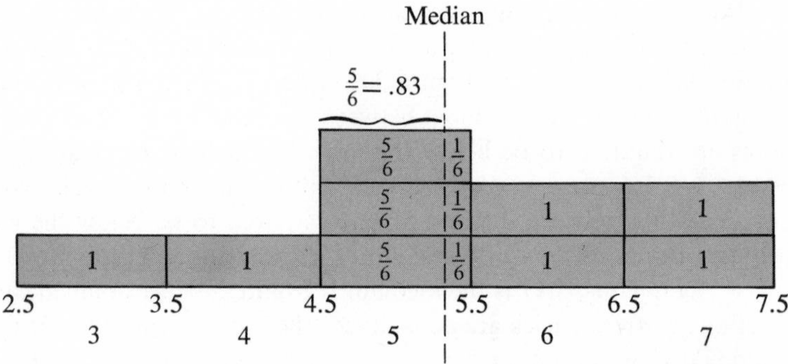

Fig. 3–2. Computing the median when there is duplication of scores.

Although the logic of this process is quite simple, an expression exists which formalizes these steps:

$$M_d = L + \left[\frac{N/2 - n_b}{n_w}\right] i$$

in which

M_d = the median
L = the lower limit of the interval containing the median
N = the number of scores in the total distribution
n_b = the number of scores falling below the lower limit of the interval containing the median
n_w = the number of scores within the interval containing the median
i = the size of the interval.

In terms of the last example,

$$\begin{aligned} L &= 4.5 \\ N &= 9 \\ n_b &= 2 \\ n_w &= 3 \\ i &= 1 \end{aligned}$$

Then

$$\begin{aligned} M_d &= L + \left[\frac{N/2 - n_b}{n_w}\right] i \\ &= 4.5 + \left[\frac{\frac{9}{2} - 2}{3}\right] 1 \\ &= 4.5 + \frac{\frac{5}{2}}{3} \\ &= 4.5 + .83 \\ M_d &= 5.33 \end{aligned}$$

THE MODE

definition A third measure of central tendency is the mode.

The **mode,** symbolized M_o, is the most frequently occurring score.

If the distribution is (3, 4, 4, 5, 5, 5, 6, 8), the mode is 5. Sometimes a distribution will have two modes, such as the distribution (3, 4, 4, 4, 5, 6, 6, 7, 7, 7, 8). In this case, the modes are 4 and 7 and this distribution is called **bimodal.**

COMPARISON OF THE MEAN, MEDIAN, AND MODE

The essential difference between the mean and the median is that the mean reflects the values of each score in the distribution whereas the median is based largely on where the midpoint of the distribution falls without regard for the particular value of many of the scores. For example, consider the following illustration:

Scores	Mean	Median
1, 2, 3, 4, 5	3	3
1, 2, 3, 4, 50	12	3
1, 2, 3, 4, 100	22	3

Only the last number differs from one distribution to the other. The mean reflects these differences but the median does not. This is because the median is the midpoint of the distribution such that an equal **number** of scores fall above and below it. The particular value of the extreme scores does not matter, only the fact that those scores exist and are above the midpoint is considered. In contrast, the mean takes into account the value of every score. This fact can be seen by inspecting the numerator of the formula for $\overline{X}$, $\sum X_i$. Thus, changing a score value will change the value of the mean.

The mode is a simple measure of central tendency and reflects only the most frequently occurring score. It is used very little in the social sciences.

Because the three different measures of central tendency are sensitive to different aspects of the group of scores, frequently they are not the same value in a given distribution. If the distribution is symmetrical and unimodal (one mode), then the mean, median, and mode are identical. This condition is graphed in Part A of Figure 3–3. If the distribution is symmetrical but has two modes, such as in Part B, the mean and median are the same but the modes are different (the distribution is **bimodal**). In Chapter 2, a skewed distribution was defined to be one that was not symmetrical, having scores bunched on one end. Parts C and D of Figure 3–3 illustrate two skewed distributions and the relative positions of the three measures of central tendency. The distribution in Part C is fairly common and illustrates a condition in which most scores have moderate values but a few are very high. In this case, the mean, being sensitive to those extreme values, is somewhat higher than the median which divides the area under the curve into two equal parts. A common illustration of this situation occurs in the reporting of typical family income. In a given year mean family income in the United States is usually higher than the median income. Part D of Figure 3–3 illustrates the relative positions of the measures of central tendency when the skewness of the distribution is in the other direction.

Ordinarily, the mean is selected as the measure of central tendency. There are several reasons for preferring the mean, but one of the major considerations is that the mean is required by so many other statistical procedures. For example, later in this text techniques for asking questions about the central tendency of one group versus another group of scores will be described, and these calculations require that the means of the groups be used. Consequently, in most situations the mean is the preferred measure of central tendency.

However, sometimes the circumstances are such that the median would reflect the central tendency of the distribution more accurately than would the mean. For example, when the distribution is very skewed, the mean may not yield a value that coincides with one's intuitive impression of what the "typical score" should be. For example, the distribution (1, 2, 3, 4, 100) has a mean of 22 and a median of 3. In this case the median seems to characterize the central tendency of the group more faithfully than does the mean of 22 which is not close in value to any score in the distribution. Thus, in the case of a skewed

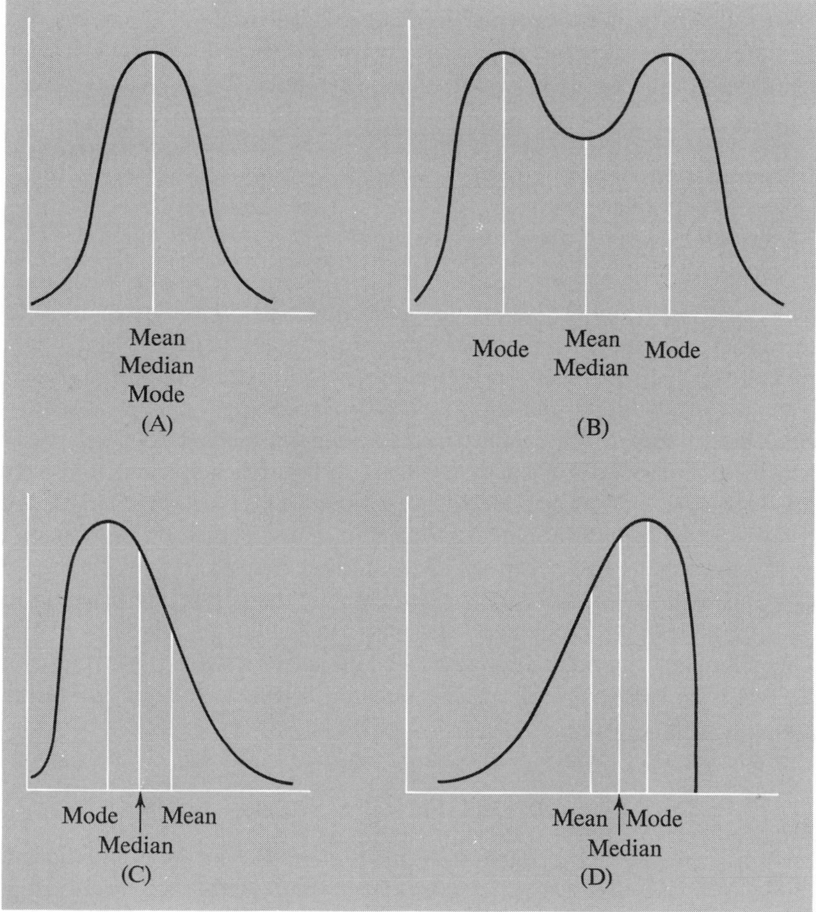

Fig. 3–3. The mean, median, and mode in different distributions.

distribution the median demonstrates a distinct advantage in characterizing the central tendency.

estimation

POPULATION AND SAMPLE

Frequently, a scientist performs an experiment on a relatively small group of subjects. At the conclusion of the research, however, he generalizes his results to a much larger group of subjects of which his sample is a small part. For example, an experiment might be performed using a group of 40 male students at State University, but the results are discussed in terms of "all college men." The small group actually used as subjects in the experiment is known as a **sample** whereas the larger group of subjects to which the researcher wishes to generalize his results is called the **population.** Succinctly stated:

> A **population** is a collection of subjects or events that have some common characteristic.[2]
> A **sample** is a subgroup of a population.

It is important to note that sample and population are relative terms. "All men enrolled at State University" might be the population from which a sample of 50 male students is drawn for a given experiment, but it might also function as a sample of the larger population of "all college men."

One obvious reason why samples rather than populations are used in research is that the populations are usually too large to be studied efficiently. However, it is somewhat trivial for the scientist to consider his results as being appropriate only to the specific subjects he experimented upon. Therefore, he designs the experiment so that he may generalize from his sample to the population. One goal of this process is to **estimate** characteristics in the population by computing various measures on the sample.

Characteristics of a population are called **parameters,** while those of a sample are termed **statistics.** Therefore, the research scientist attempts to estimate parameters with statistics.

CHARACTERISTICS OF A "GOOD" ESTIMATOR

Frequently, a researcher wants to estimate the mean of the population. For example, suppose a research program was being established to investigate procedures for teaching mynah birds to talk. It would be important to know how much vocalization an untrained mynah bird emits in the course of a 12-hour day before special procedures are attempted to mold that natural vocalization into something resembling human speech. Consequently, the mean time spent vocalizing in a 12-hour period for all mynah birds would be desired, but it will be estimated from a small sample of 20 birds. Suppose the mean time in this sample is 88 minutes, the median is 83, the mode is 92, and the longest single time was 112. Which sample statistic should be used to estimate the population mean, and on what grounds should this choice be made?

There are several criteria for a good estimator. The one that will be of major concern in this book is the quality of **unbiasedness.**

[2] Very frequently, although not always, a population is considered to be composed of an infinite number of cases. While such a conception of the population has certain advantages, particularly for theoretical mathematical statistics, the definition presented here will be used for certain pedagogical reasons.

> An **unbiased estimator** of a population parameter is one whose average over all possible random samples equals the value of the parameter.

Suppose that the sample mean is to be used to estimate the population mean time spent vocalizing by mynah birds in a 12-hour period. If the sample mean is an unbiased estimator of the population mean the following would be true: If many, many samples of 20 mynah birds were selected and the mean were computed for each sample, then as the number of such samples becomes very large the average of the sample means would tend to equal the population mean. Theoretically, if all possible random samples were taken, the average of all of those means would equal the population mean. Actually, of course, scientists do not take repeated samples in order to test whether or not a particular statistic is an unbiased estimate of a given population parameter. There exist certain mathematical procedures (called "expectation") that can be used to show that the sample mean averaged over many samples approaches the precise value of the population parameter.[3]

Consider taking the highest score in a sample of 20 birds as an estimate of the population mean. It can be shown that the highest score is not an unbiased estimator of the population mean because over all possible samples of a given size the average of the highest scores would not equal the value of the population mean. Thus, while there are other criteria for determining a "good estimator," unbiasedness is a valuable characteristic for an estimator to possess.

The fact that this course is usually called "statistics" and not "parameters" indicates that the focus is on computing measures on samples and not on populations. Consequently, for some statistics presented in this volume, the relationship between sample value and corresponding parameter will be discussed (e.g., the variance—see following), whereas in other cases only the sample statistic will be considered (e.g., median, mode). To facilitate distinguishing between statistics and parameters, statistics are usually abbreviated with Roman letters while parameters often have Greek designations. This custom will be illustrated in the following discussion on sample and population means.

SAMPLE AND POPULATION MEANS

The sample mean was symbolized by $\overline{X}$ and was computed with the formula

$$\overline{X} = \frac{\sum X}{N}$$

The **population mean** is symbolized by the Greek letter μ. $\overline{X}$ is frequently used as an estimator of the population mean, μ.

[3] For more details on the characteristics of good estimators, see: W. L. Hays, *Statistics for Psychologists* (New York: Holt, Rinehart, & Winston, 1963, 196–201).

EXERCISES

A	B	C	D
1	1	1	1
3	3	2	3
5	4	2	4
6	6	2	5
7	7	3	6
7	8	5	6
8	8	6	6
	9	6	9
	9	6	25
	9	8	
		9	

1. Compute the mean, median, and mode for each of the above distributions.
2. Which measure of central tendency is most appropriate for each distribution and why?
3. Of what importance is the skewness of the distribution in deciding which measure of central tendency to use?
4. Find the median for the following distributions.
   (a) 1, 4, 6, 7, 10
   (b) 1, 3, 4, 7, 8, 11
   (c) 1, 2, 3, 3, 3, 3
   (d) 1, 2, 3, 3, 3, 3, 5
   (e) 5, 10, 11, 11, 15
5. Draw the distributions such that the following are true.
   (a) The mean, median, and mode are identical.
   (b) The mean and median are identical but the mode is different.
   (c) The mean is greater than the median.
   (d) The median is greater than the mean.
6. Show that the sum of the deviations about the mean of Distribution A is zero. Compute the sum of the deviations about the median of Distribution A. Which is less, the sum of the deviations about the mean or about the median?
7. Demonstrate with a numerical example using Distribution A that

$$\sum_{i=1}^{N} (X_i - M_d)^2 > \sum_{i=1}^{N} (X_i - \overline{X})^2$$

   Will this be true for any distribution?
8. In what way are the terms "population" and "sample" relative?
9. Why is this course called "statistics" and not "parameters?"
10. How would you compare the sample mean with the statistic "the next to the last score" in terms of the unbiasedness of their estimation of the population mean?

measures of variability

In order to characterize a distribution more fully, a measure of variability is needed in addition to an index of central tendency.

> **Variability** refers to the extent to which the scores differ from each other.

For example, suppose two groups of scores, A and B, are defined to be

$$A = (5, 7, 9)$$
$$B = (3, 7, 11)$$

Set B has more variability than A even though they both have the same mean of 7. The purpose of this section is to discuss measures that provide a numerical index of the extent of the variability in a distribution.

THE RANGE

One measure of the variability in a distribution is the range. The **range** is the largest score minus the smallest score in the distribution.[4] In the distribution (3, 5, 6, 6, 8, 9), the range is 6.

However, the range is limited in its ability to reflect the variability of a distribution. It is certainly true that as the variability increases in a distribution, the range of scores is also likely to increase. However, the range is not sensitive to the variability of all the scores, only the two most extreme values. Further, the range itself is a statistic with a great deal of variability from sample to sample. Therefore, although the range is easily computed, it is usually employed only as a crude approximation of variability.

THE VARIANCE AND STANDARD DEVIATION

An index that reflects the degree of variability in a group of scores but which does not have the limitations of the range is the **variance,** and its derivative, the **standard deviation.**

> The **variance,** symbolized by s^2, is defined to be
>
> $$s^2 = \frac{\sum_{i=1}^{N} (X_i - \overline{X})^2}{N - 1}$$

[4] Technically, the range should probably be defined as the difference between the upper real limit of the largest score minus the lower real limit of the smallest score. Since the range is an approximate index of variability at best, it does not seem appropriate to insist upon this level of "accuracy."

In words, the variance is the sum of the squared deviations of the scores (X_i) from their mean ($\overline{X}$) divided by the number of scores minus one ($N - 1$). Conceptually, it is very much like the average squared deviation of the scores about their mean except that the squared deviations are divided by $N - 1$ rather than N. The reason for having $N - 1$ as the denominator is that this "correction" makes s^2 an unbiased estimator of the population variance. The **population variance** is symbolized by σ^2 (read "SIG-mah squared"). Since most uses of the variance involve estimating σ^2, the formula for s^2 with $N - 1$ in the denominator will be used throughout this text.

computational example The computation of the variance proceeds as follows:

	X_i	$\overline{X}$	$(X_i - \overline{X})$		$(X_i - \overline{X})^2$
	5	7	-2		4
	7	7	0		0
	9	7	$+2$		4
$\sum_{i=1}^{N} X_i =$	21		0	$\sum_{i=1}^{N} (X_i - \overline{X})^2 =$	8
$N =$	3				
$\overline{X} =$	7				

$$s^2 = \frac{\sum_{i=1}^{N} (X_i - \overline{X})^2}{N - 1}$$

$$s^2 = \tfrac{8}{2}$$

$$s^2 = 4.00$$

Notice that the mean is computed first ($\overline{X} = 7.0$). The mean is subtracted from each score ($X_i - \overline{X}$) and this difference is squared [$(X_i - \overline{X})^2$]. The sum of the squared deviations from the mean is divided by $N - 1$ to obtain the variance.

The variance is difficult to "explain" because it cannot be diagrammed or "pointed at." Rather, the variance is an abstract numerical index that increases with the amount of variability in the group of scores. Despite the fact that the variance escapes being pictured, it does have a certain logic to it. The mean is the central value of the distribution and it seems natural to base a measure of variability upon the extent to which the scores deviate from their central tendency [i.e., $(X_i - \overline{X})^2$]. In addition one may recall from the discussion of the mean that the sum of the squared deviations about the mean is less than the sum about any other value. This fact adds to the logic of selecting squared deviations about the mean as an index of variability.

Consider the implications of squaring the deviations $(X_i - \overline{X})^2$. Initially, all of the deviations make a positive contribution to the total because squaring a negative number results in a positive value. If the deviations were not squared then the negative deviations would cancel out the positive and their sum would be zero because

$$\sum_{i=1}^{N} (X_i - \overline{X}) = 0$$

Second, large deviations, when squared, contribute disproportionately to the total (e.g., a deviation of 4 units becomes 16 when squared, but a deviation of twice that size, 8 units, contributes 64 to the total sum of squared deviations). Thus, the final index is especially sensitive to extreme departures from the mean because of the squaring procedure.

Third, the fact that the squared deviations are divided by $N - 1$, makes the variance a sort of "average squared deviation," and thus the variance of distributions having different numbers of scores may be compared just as means from distributions having different N's may be compared.

A last point to be made about the variance as a measure of variability is this: Recall that the definition of variability is "the extent to which the scores deviate from one another." One way to measure such variability would be to sum the squared deviations between each score and every other score in the distribution and divide this total by the number of such pairs $[N(N - 1)]$. This procedure for obtaining a measure of variability follows the definition of variability quite closely, and it is important to note that the variance is directly proportional to this alternative index. Therefore, the variance is indeed closely associated with the concept of variability which it measures.

the standard deviation, *s* The variance measures variability in squared units. If the researcher recorded how long it took animals to find their way to a goal box at the end of a maze, the mean time would be in seconds but the variance would be in "squared seconds." This results from the fact that the formula for the mean uses the scores as they are (e.g., $\sum X$) but the formula for the variance squares the deviations (e.g., $\sum(X - \overline{X})^2$) thus changing them from seconds to "squared seconds." However, it will be convenient to have a measure of variability in terms of the original units of measurement, not squared units.

The **standard deviation** (symbolized by s) is defined to be the positive square root of the variance:

$$s = \sqrt{s^2}$$

or (without subscripts)

$$s = \sqrt{\frac{\sum(X - \overline{X})^2}{N - 1}}$$

Since the variance was in squared units, by taking its square root, a return is made to the original units of measurement.[5] The population standard deviation is symbolized by σ (read "SIG-mah").

[5] The notation *SD* is used in some other texts to symbolize the standard deviation.

SPECIAL COMPUTATIONAL PROCEDURES FOR s^2 AND s

The formulas given above are called "definitional formulas" because they define and usually provide the most logical explanation of the concept. However, when sufficient amounts of data are collected, the definitional formulas are frequently not very convenient to use in making the calculations. An expression for a statistic that is mathematically equivalent to the definitional formula but more convenient for calculating is called a "computational formula." In the case of the variance and standard deviation, it is tedious to first compute the mean and then subtract it from each score, particularly if the mean is a lengthy decimal. Not only is the decimal subtraction laborious, but the squaring of these decimal remainders is even more cumbersome. Therefore, an expression more appropriate for calculation is desirable.

The computational formula for the variance is (summations of X are from $i = 1, N$)

$$s^2 = \frac{N\sum X^2 - (\sum X)^2}{N(N-1)}$$

It follows that the computational formula for the standard deviation is

$$s = \sqrt{\frac{N\sum X^2 - (\sum X)^2}{N(N-1)}}$$

It is important to realize that these computational formulas yield results which are equivalent (within rounding error) to those calculated by the definitional formulas. Table 3–3 demonstrates the algebraic equivalence of the two formulas.

The computational formula has the advantage of having only one division, not requiring that the mean be calculated first, and facility in computing on a standard hand calculator. Only three quantities are needed: $\sum X^2$, $\sum X$, and N. Consider the variance and standard deviation of the following numbers:

	X		X^2
	3		9
	4		16
	7		49
	8		64
	8		64
	9		81
	10		100
$\sum X =$	49	$\sum X^2 =$	383
$N =$	7		

variance

$$s^2 = \frac{N\sum X^2 - (\sum X)^2}{N(N - 1)}$$

$$s^2 = \frac{7(383) - (49)^2}{7(7 - 1)} = \frac{2681 - 2401}{42}$$

$$s^2 = \frac{280}{42}$$

$$s^2 = 6.67$$

standard deviation

$$s = \sqrt{s^2}$$

$$s = \sqrt{6.67}$$

$$s = 2.58$$

It is very important to distinguish between two quantities used in the formula: $\sum X^2$ and $(\sum X)^2$. The first, $\sum X^2$, means the sum of all the squared scores; square each score and then add them. The second, $(\sum X)^2$, means the square of the sum of the scores; add all the scores and then square this sum. Pointing this out may appear trivial, but the student should be alerted to the difference between these two quantities because they both occur frequently in the remainder of this book and confusion between them is often the source of computational error.

PROPERTIES OF s^2 AND s AS MEASURES OF VARIABILITY

The first property of the variance as a measure of variability is that it is proportional to the average squared deviation of each score from every other score. As previously noted, the intuitive concept of variability embodies the extent to which each of the scores deviates from every other score. Since the variance is proportional to the average squared deviation of each score from every other score, it follows that the variance indeed reflects the variability of the scores.

Second, if the definitional formula for the variance is considered

$$s^2 = \frac{\sum(X_i - \overline{X})^2}{N - 1}$$

since all quantities are squared, the variance will always be positive.

Third, if there is no variability among the scores, that is, all the scores in the distribution are identical to one another, then each quantity $(X_i - \overline{X})^2$ and their sum will be zero because X_i and $\overline{X}$ will always be identical. Therefore, when there is no variability among the scores of a distribution, $s^2 = 0$.

3–3 The Algebraic Equivalence of the Definitional and Computational Formulas for the Variance.

Operation	Explanation
To prove $\dfrac{\sum(X_i - \overline{X})^2}{N-1} = \dfrac{N\sum X_i^2 - (\sum X_i)^2}{N(N-1)}$	
1. $s^2 = \dfrac{\sum(X_i - \overline{X})^2}{(N-1)}$	1. Definition
2. $= \dfrac{\sum(X_i^2 - 2X_i\overline{X} + \overline{X}^2)}{(N-1)}$	2. Expanding $\sum(X_i - \overline{X})^2$ in the manner: $(a-b)^2 = (a^2 - 2ab + b^2)$
3. $= \dfrac{(\sum X_i^2 - \sum 2X_i\overline{X} + \sum \overline{X}^2)}{(N-1)}$ (a) (b)	3. The sum of several terms is the sum of the separate terms: $\sum(X+Y+Z) = \sum X + \sum Y + \sum Z$
4. $= \dfrac{(\sum X_i^2 - 2\overline{X}\sum X_i + N\overline{X}^2)}{(N-1)}$	4. a. The sum of a constant times a variable equals the constant times the sum of the variable ($\overline{X}$ is a constant): $\sum kX = k\sum X$ b. The sum of a constant taken N times is N times the constant: $\sum_{i=1}^{N} k = Nk$

Step	Explanation
5. $= \dfrac{\left[\sum X_i^2 - 2\left(\frac{\sum X_i}{N}\right)\sum X_i + N\left(\frac{\sum X_i}{N}\right)\left(\frac{\sum X_i}{N}\right)\right]}{(N-1)}$	5. Substitution: $\overline{X} = \dfrac{\sum X_i}{N}$
6. $= \dfrac{\left[\sum X_i^2 - 2\left(\frac{\sum X_i}{N}\right)\sum X_i + (\sum X_i)\left(\frac{\sum X_i}{N}\right)\right]}{(N-1)}$	6. Cancellation in the third term.
7. $= \dfrac{\left[\sum X_i^2 - \left(\frac{\sum X_i}{N}\right)\sum X_i\right]}{(N-1)}$	7. Subtraction involving the last two terms of the numerator.
8. $= \dfrac{\left[N\sum X_i^2 - N\left(\frac{\sum X_i}{N}\right)\sum X_i\right]}{N(N-1)}$	8. Multiplying numerator and denominator by N.
9. $s^2 = \dfrac{N\sum X_i^2 - (\sum X_i)^2}{N(N-1)}$	9. Cancellation

Fourth, as the variability of the scores increases, the variance also increases. This can be seen in the few examples listed below:

Scores	s^2
10, 10, 10	0
8, 10, 12	4
6, 10, 12	10
6, 10, 14	16
2, 10, 20	82

As the scores show more and more variability, the value of s^2 increases, faithfully reflecting the extent to which the scores deviate from one another. Similar arguments can be made for the standard deviation.

Fifth, s^2 and s are more sensitive to variability in a group of scores and they are less variable in themselves (different samples tend to yield more similar values) than the range. The range is neither a precise nor a very stable measure of variability, and s^2 and s are much preferred in this regard.

Sixth, the variance frequently is used in other statistical manipulations, and therefore its computation as a measure of variability also finds application in the calculation of other formulas.

Seventh, under certain conditions the variance may be partitioned into various parts which can be attributed to different sources. This capability of being partitioned permits statisticians to ask the following types of questions: A group of scores possesses a certain amount of variability. What portion of that variability can be attributed to cause A as opposed to cause B? This aspect of the variance will be taken up in more detail later in the chapters on the analysis of variance.

FORMULAS

1. Mean

Sample Mean:

$$\overline{X} = \frac{\sum X_i}{N}$$

Population mean symbolized by μ.

Deviations about $\overline{X}$: $\sum(X_i - \overline{X}) = 0$

Squared Deviations about $\overline{X}$:

$$\sum(X_i - \overline{X})^2 \text{ less than } \sum[X_i - (\text{any other value})]^2$$

2. Median

(a) **There is an odd number of scores:**

M_d is the middle score.

(b) **There is an even number of scores:**

M_d is the average of the two middle scores.

(c) **There is duplication of scores near the median:**

$$M_d = L + \left[\frac{N/2 - n_b}{n_w}\right] i$$

where L = lower limit of the interval containing the median
N = number of scores in the distribution
n_b = number of scores falling below the lower limit of the interval containing the median
n_w = number of scores within the interval containing the median
i = the size of the interval.

3. Mode

The mode, M_o, is the most frequent score.

4. Range

The range is the largest minus the smallest score.

5. Variance

$$s^2 = \frac{\sum(X_i - \overline{X})^2}{N - 1} \qquad \text{(definitional)}$$

$$s^2 = \frac{N\sum X_i^2 - (\sum X_i)^2}{N(N - 1)} \qquad \text{(computational)}$$

Population variance symbolized by σ^2

6. Standard Deviation

$$s = \sqrt{s^2} = \sqrt{\frac{\sum(X_i - \overline{X})^2}{N - 1}} \qquad \text{(definitional)}$$

$$s = \sqrt{\frac{N\sum X_i^2 - (\sum X_i)^2}{N(N - 1)}} \qquad \text{(computational)}$$

Population standard deviation symbolized by σ

EXERCISES

1. Define variability and compose three distributions which differ in their amount of variability.

2. Discuss the limitations of the range as a measure of variability and whenever possible present some numerical examples to illustrate your points.

3. Compute with both the definitional and computational formulas the variance and standard deviation for each of the following distributions. Also compare the means of these distributions.

   (a) 6, 7, 7, 8
   (b) 4, 5, 9, 10
   (c) 0, 1, 3, 4, 7, 7, 8, 8, 9, 9, 9, 10, 10, 10, 10

4. Why does the formula for the variance have $N - 1$ in the denominator and not N?

5. Suppose a researcher believes that boys are more variable in IQ than are girls. After testing 20 boys and 30 girls he computes the variance for both sexes. Is it meaningful to compare the two variances when they are based upon different numbers of cases? (This would be similar to comparing s^2 for (a) or (b) with (c) in Exercise 3.) Suppose height was measured in feet in one group and in inches in another group. Can the variance of these two groups be meaningfully compared? Explain.

6. Discuss the properties, characteristics, and advantages of s^2 as a measure of variability. Does s have any potential advantages over s^2?

4

measures of relative standing

Although the measures of characteristics of a distribution discussed in the previous chapter assist in describing that distribution, they do not provide direct assistance in interpreting individual scores. For example, suppose you received a grade of 88 on a statistics examination. Just knowing your numerical score without any knowledge of the nature of the distribution does not offer much information. Further, knowing that the mean was 81 tells you that you were above the mean but very little else. What is needed in order to interpret a score of 88 is some measure of your relative standing within the total distribution. Percentiles and standard scores perform this function.

percentiles

One of the most common measures of relative standing is the percentile.

DEFINITION

The ***n*th percentile** is that scale value below which $n\%$ of the cases in the distribution fall. The scale value of the variable is called a **percentile point,** while its corresponding percentage value is known as its **percentile rank.**

Thus, if a score of 88 was at the 92nd **percentile rank,** 92% of the people in the group scored less than the **percentile point** of 88. The **upper quartile** is determined by the score value separating the top 25% from the remainder of the distribution while the **lower quartile** is determined by the score value separating the bottom 25% of the distribution. The **interquartile range** is determined by the score values that separate the middle 50% of the distribution from the remainder, that is, the percentile points corresponding to $P_{.25}$ and $P_{.75}$ where $P_{.25}$, for example, signifies the 25th percentile.

COMPUTATION OF PERCENTILE POINTS

Computing percentile points is very similar to computing the median, and the procedure is somewhat different under various circumstances. First, consider how to determine the score value corresponding to a given percentile.

(a) no duplication near percentile The distribution of scores on a statistics test for 40 students is presented in Table 4–1. Suppose the score value corresponding to $P_{.30}$ is desired. The 30th percentile is defined to be that point below which 30% of the class lies. Thirty percent of 40 students is 12 students. Therefore, 12 students must be below $P_{.30}$. Looking at the table, one can see that the 12th student scored 59 and the 13th student scored 60. There-

4–1 Distribution of Scores on a Statistics Examination for a Class of 40 Students.

Student	Score	Student	Score	Student	Score
1	46	16	70	31	82
2	48	17	71	32	83
3	49	18	72	33	84
4	49	19	72	34	85
5	51	20	72	35	85
6	55	21	74	36	88
7	55	22	75	37	91
8	55	23	75	38	92
9	55	24	76	39	93
10	56	25	78	40	97
11	58	26	78		
12	59	27	78		
13	60	28	78		
14	61	29	79		
15	65	30	80		

fore, the desired point must fall between those two values. By convention the mean of the 12th and 13th scores is taken as the 30th percentile:

$$P_{.30} = \frac{59 + 60}{2} = 59.5$$

It is important to note that 59.5 is the upper limit of the score value of 59 and the lower limit of the score value of 60. Therefore, the value 59.5 does indeed allow 30% or 12 students' scores to fall below it and 70% or 28 students' scores to fall above it.

Suppose the percentile point corresponding to $P_{.60}$ was required. This would mean that 60% or 24 scores should fall below this point. The 24th student scored 76 while the 25th student scored 78. Therefore, the desired point is located somewhere between the upper limit of the score 76 and the lower limit of the score 78. Again, the mean of these two score values provides the desired point:

$$P_{.60} = \frac{76 + 78}{2} = 77.0$$

(b) duplication near percentile A different procedure is used in the event that the score value corresponding to the desired percentile has more than one frequency. For example, consider the score value corresponding to $P_{.20}$. Twenty percent of 40 students is 8 students, and thus the desired point must be such that 8 students score below that value. However, the 8th and 9th, as well as the 6th and 7th, students all had scores of 55. The lower limit of the score value of 55 is 54.5. Five students scored below 54.5. Thus, 3 of the 4 students scoring 55 should theoretically fall below the 20th percentile, so $\frac{3}{4}$ or .75 of the interval 54.5–55.5 is added to its lower limit:

$$P_{.20} = 54.5 + .75 = 55.25$$

This procedure is quite analogous to that described for computing the median in Chapter 3.

COMPUTATION OF PERCENTILE RANKS

The two illustrations just given show how one computes the score (i.e., percentile point) corresponding to a given percentile. However, the question can be reversed. What is the percentile rank corresponding to a given score?

(a) no duplication near percentile What is the percentile rank of a score of 83? The score of 83 is 32nd in the distribution. This means that 31 people scored less than the lower limit of 83 which is 82.5. Since

$$\tfrac{31}{40} = 77.5\%$$

77.5% of the distribution falls below 82.5, the lower limit of a score of 83. Eight people must have had scores above the upper limit of a score of 83. Therefore,

$$\tfrac{8}{40} = 20.0\%$$

of the distribution lies above the upper limit, 83.5. But the 77.5% of the distribution falling below the lower limit of a score of 83 and the 20.0% of the distribution falling above the upper limit of 83 add up to only 97.5% of the total distribution. Therefore, the score interval 82.5–83.5 must contain

$$100\% - 97.5\% = 2.5\%$$

of the distribution. Indeed, one person falls in this interval and the ratio of 1 to 40 is 2.5%. The space in the distribution which is occupied by the score being considered is divided equally. Half is placed above the score of 83 and half below. Therefore, in addition to the 77.5% of the distribution falling below 82.5, another 1.25% of the distribution falls between 82.5 and 83.0. Consequently,

$$77.5\% + 1.25\% = 78.75\%$$

of the distribution falls below a score of 83. Since percentile ranks are commonly rounded off to the nearest whole percentage, 83 is the score value corresponding to $P_{.79}$. The logic of the approach is shown graphically in Figure 4–1.

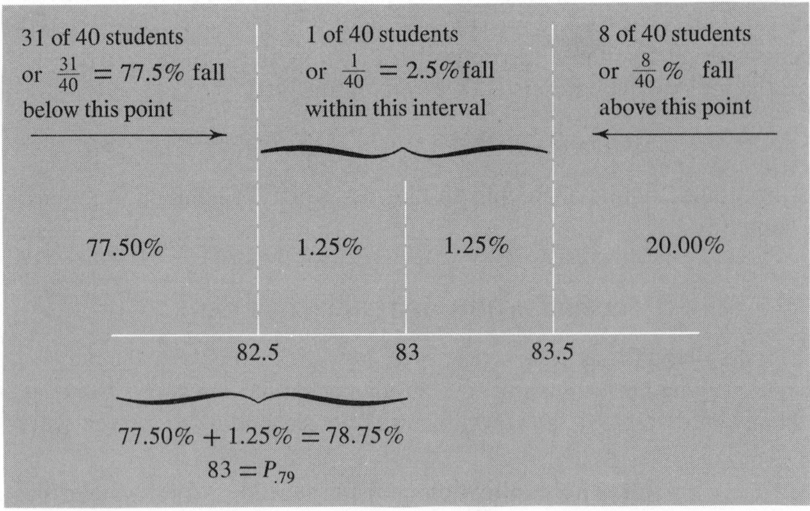

Fig. 4–1. Determining the percentile rank corresponding to the score value of 83.

(b) duplication near percentile The general procedure is still the same if more than one frequency exists at the score value being evaluated. Suppose one wanted to know the percentile rank corresponding to a score of 72. The score 72 has as lower and upper limits, 71.5 and 72.5, respectively. Three scores exist within that interval. Seventeen students' scores or

$$\tfrac{17}{40} = 42.50\%$$

of the distribution falls below its lower limit. Since there are three scores or frequencies within the interval, they cover

$$\tfrac{3}{40} = 7.5\%$$

of the distribution. Half of this percentage or

$$\frac{7.5\%}{2} = 3.75\%$$

is considered to fall below the score of 72, and therefore

$$42.5\% + 3.75\% = 46.25\%$$

of the distribution falls below a score of 72. Thus, $X = 72$ falls at $P_{.46}$ This procedure is diagrammed in Figure 4–2.

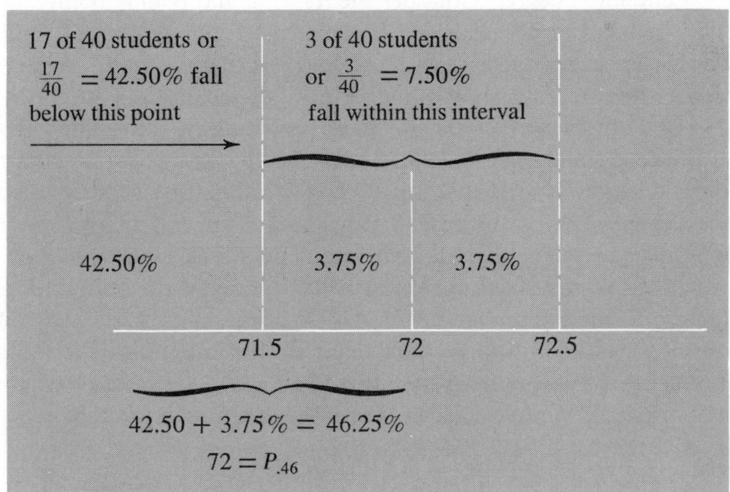

Fig. 4–2. Determining the percentile rank corresponding to a score value of 72.

EXERCISES

1. Using the frequency distribution presented in Table 4–1, determine the score values corresponding to the following percentile ranks.

   (a) $P_{.30}$ (c) $P_{.10}$ (e) $P_{.45}$ (g) $P_{.675}$
   (b) $P_{.65}$ (d) $P_{.85}$ (f) $P_{.475}$ (h) $P_{.50}$

2. Using Table 4–1, determine the percentile ranks corresponding to the following score values.

   (a) 51 (c) 82 (e) 55 (g) 85
   (b) 75 (d) 78 (f) 60 (h) 49

changing the properties of scales

Centigrade and Fahrenheit are two different scales of temperature. They differ in that they have different origins (not to be confused with absolute zero) and units of different sizes. The transformation formula for converting degrees centigrade to degrees Fahrenheit is given by

$$°F = °C(1.8) + 32°$$

The 1.8 is the factor used to convert the size of the centigrade degree to the size of the Fahrenheit degree. Consider the freezing and boiling points of water on the two scales. For the Fahrenheit scale, these points are 32° and 212°, respectively, whereas for the centigrade scale they are 0° and 100°, respectively. Thus, between the freezing and boiling point of water on the Fahrenheit scale there are 180 Fahrenheit degrees. Between the freezing and boiling point of water on the centigrade scale there are only 100 centigrade degrees. Therefore the centigrade degree is larger, and it takes 1.8 Fahrenheit degrees to equal 1 centigrade degree. This is the reason why the 1.8 appears in the conversion formula; it changes the centigrade unit into a Fahrenheit unit.

However, the two scales are not yet equivalent. Even if the centigrade degree is transformed to the Fahrenheit degree, the freezing point is still at 0° and the boiling point is at (1.8)(100) = 180°. That is, the origins of the scales are different. One is 32°F away from the other. To change the origin to match the Fahrenheit origin, 32° must be added. Thus, the conversion formula is

$$°F = °C(1.8) + 32°$$

in which the 1.8 converts the centigrade unit to the Fahrenheit unit and the 32 adjusts the origin of the centigrade scale to match that of the Fahrenheit scale.

One scale can be transformed to another by changing the size of its unit and changing its origin, as was just done. To formalize these rules:

> To change the size of the unit of measurement, multiply or divide the old values by the proper constant (conversion factor). To change the origin of a scale, add or subtract the appropriate number of units.

Most transformations common to everyday life are ones in which only the size of the unit is converted. For example:

$$\text{inches} = (12)\ \text{feet} \quad \longleftarrow \text{conversion factor}$$

$$\text{miles} = \frac{\text{kilometers}}{.6} \quad \longleftarrow \text{conversion factor}$$

However, in research in the social sciences, transformations are frequently made from one scale to another which do involve changing both the unit size and the origin of the scale. Since these transformations are common, it will be instructive to consider what happens to the mean and variance of a distribution as a function of altering the unit size and origin.

EFFECTS OF SCALE CHANGES ON THE MEAN

The origin of a scale is changed by adding or subtracting a constant from every score. If a constant is added to (or subtracted from) every score in the distribution, the mean of the new distribution is the mean of the old plus (or minus) that constant. If $\overline{X}'$ is the new mean, $\overline{X}$ is the old mean, and c is the constant, then

$$\overline{X}' = \overline{X} + c$$

This proposition can be easily proven. The formula for the mean is

$$\overline{X} = \frac{\sum X}{N}$$

and if a new scale of measurement is to be constructed by adding (or subtracting) a constant c, the transformation to a new scale of X' would be

$$X' = X + c$$

The mean of this new distribution of X' in terms of the old mean, $\overline{X}$, is derived in Table 4–2. This shows that adding a constant to every score in the distribution results in adding that constant to the mean. If the constant is negative (that is, subtracting a constant from every score), the mean would be diminished by that constant. If the mean of a distribution is 15 and 3 is added to every score,

4-2 Change in the Mean with a Change in Origin.	
Operation	**Explanation**
1. $\overline{X}' = \frac{\sum(X+c)}{N}$	1. Definition of the mean.
2. $= \frac{\sum X + \sum c}{N}$	2. The sum of several terms is the sum of the separate terms.
3. $= \frac{\sum X + Nc}{N}$	3. The sum (from 1 to N) of a constant is N times that constant.
4. $= \frac{\sum X}{N} + \frac{\cancel{N}c}{\cancel{N}}$	4. Simplification.
5. $\overline{X}' = \overline{X} + c$	5. Substitution: $\frac{\sum X}{N} = \overline{X}$

the new mean would be 18. If 3 were subtracted from every score, the new mean would be 12.

The unit of a scale is changed by multiplying or dividing every score by a constant. If every score in a distribution is multiplied (or divided) by a constant, the mean of the new distribution is the mean of the old distribution multiplied (or divided) by that constant. In symbols,

$$\overline{X}' = c\overline{X}$$

This fact can also be demonstrated by letting the new score (X') equal c times the old score:

$$X' = cX$$

The proof presented in Table 4–3 shows that under this transformation the new mean is $c\overline{X}$. Therefore, if every score is multiplied by 12, the mean will be

4-3 Change in the Mean with a Change in Unit.	
Operation	**Explanation**
1. $\overline{X}' = \frac{\sum cX}{N}$	1. Definition.
2. $= \frac{c\sum X}{N}$	2. The sum of a constant times a variable is the constant times the sum of that variable.
3. $\overline{X}' = c\overline{X}$	3. Substitution: $\frac{\sum X}{N} = \overline{X}$

multiplied by 12. Since dividing each score by c is the same as multiplying each score by $1/c$, if every score is divided by 3, the mean will be divided by 3.

In summary, if the scale of measurement is altered, the mean will also change in the same manner and to the same extent as the scale. This makes sense because the mean can be conceived to be a "typical score," and thus if every score is incremented or multiplied by a constant, it should follow that the mean, as a typical score, should also undergo the same change.

EFFECTS OF SCALE CHANGES ON THE VARIANCE AND STANDARD DEVIATION

Consider now these same transformations of scale as they are reflected in the variance and standard deviation of a distribution.

> If a constant is added to (or subtracted from) every score in the distribution, the variance and standard deviation are not changed. In symbols,
>
> $$s_{x'}^2 = s_x^2$$
>
> $$s_{x'} = s_x$$

This makes intuitive sense if one considers that s^2 and s are really functions of the distance between the various points of the distribution, not the distance those points are from the origin. For example, consider the distance between points in the following distribution before and after a change of origin (5 is added to each score):

	X				$X' = X + 5$		
	3	7	11		8	12	16
$(X - \overline{X})$:	4	4		$(X - \overline{X})$:	4	4	

Since s^2 and s are based upon the distances between the points and the mean $(X - \overline{X})$ and since these distances do not change when the origin is changed, s^2 and s remain the same.

This proposition may also be demonstrated by letting the new score (X') equal the old (X) plus c:

$$X' = X + c$$

The proof that such a change in origin leaves s^2 and s unaffected is presented in Table 4–4.

4-4 No Change in the Variance (and Standard Deviation) with a Change in Origin.

Operation	Explanation
1. $s_{x'}^2 = \dfrac{\sum[(X+c) - (\overline{X}+c)]^2}{N-1}$	1. Definition and if a constant is added to every score, the mean will also be incremented by that constant.
2. $\quad = \dfrac{\sum[X + c - \overline{X} - c]^2}{N-1}$	2. Removing parentheses.
3. $s_{x'}^2 = \dfrac{\sum(X - \overline{X})^2}{N-1} = s_x^2$	3. Subtraction.

If the unit of measurement is changed by multiplying (or dividing) every score in the distribution by a positive constant, the new variance will equal the old variance multiplied (or divided) by the square of that constant and the new standard deviation will equal the old standard deviation multiplied (or divided) by that constant. In symbols,

$$s_{x'}^2 = c^2 s_x^2$$

and

$$s_{x'} = cs_x$$

While changing the origin does not alter the variance, changing the unit does. This is because multiplying or dividing by a constant changes the size of the units of the scale. Consider the deviations and squared deviations which are part of the variance when the scale undergoes a change in unit (every score is multiplied by 2):

	X				$X' = 2X$		
	3	7	11		6	14	22
$(X - \overline{X})$:	4	4		$(X - \overline{X})$:	8	8	
$(X - \overline{X})^2$:	16	16		$(X - \overline{X})^2$:	64	64	

Two important points are to be gained from this example. First, notice that when the unit of measurement is changed by multiplying every score by 2, the distances between points are also multiplied by 2. Second, when these deviations are squared, the differences in the size of the squared deviations between the two scales increases by $2^2 = 4$ (in general, c^2). Since the variance uses these squared deviations in its formula, the size of the variance will be multiplied by

c^2 if each score is multiplied by c. On the other hand, the formula for the standard deviation takes the positive square root of these squared deviations, and thus it will be changed by a factor of c (assuming c is a positive constant).[1]

The proof of this proposition can be found in Table 4–5 with

$$X' = cX$$

4–5 Changes in Variance and Standard Deviation with a Change in Unit.

Operation	Explanation
Variance	
1. $s_{x'}^2 = \frac{\sum(cX - c\overline{X})^2}{N-1}$	1. Definition and if each score is multiplied by a constant the mean is multiplied by that same constant.
2. $= \frac{\sum[c(X - \overline{X})]^2}{N-1}$	2. Factoring in the manner of $ca - cb = c(a - b)$.
3. $= \frac{\sum[c^2(X - \overline{X})^2]}{N-1}$	3. Simplification in the manner of $(ab)^2 = a^2b^2$.
4. $= \frac{c^2\sum(X - \overline{X})^2}{N-1}$	4. The sum of a constant times a variable is that constant times the sum of the variable.
5. $s_{x'}^2 = c^2 s_x^2$	5. Substitution.
Standard Deviation	
1. $s_{x'} = \sqrt{s_{x'}^2}$	1. Definition.
2. $= \sqrt{c^2 s_x^2}$	2. Substitution.
3. $s_{x'} = cs_x$	3. Simplification in the manner of $\sqrt{a^2b^2} = ab$ in which c is a positive constant.

It shows that if every score is multiplied by a positive constant, the variance is multiplied by the square of that constant, and the standard deviation is multiplied by the constant. If every score is divided by a positive constant, the variance is divided by the square of the constant, and the standard deviation is divided by the constant.

A numerical example illustrating all of these principles is given in Table 4–6.

[1] If c is negative, $s_{x'} = |c|s_x$.

4–6 Numerical Example of the Effects of Changing the Origin and Unit of the Scale of Measurement.

X		Y = X + 5		W = 3X	
X	X^2	Y	Y^2	W	W^2
3	9	8	64	9	81
5	25	10	100	15	225
6	36	11	121	18	324
10	100	15	225	30	900
$\sum X = 24$	$\sum X^2 = 170$	$\sum Y = 44$	$Y^2 = 510$	$\sum W = 72$	$\sum W^2 = 1530$

X

$$N = 4$$

$$\overline{X} = \frac{\sum X}{N} = \frac{24}{4} = 6$$

$$s_x{}^2 = \frac{N\sum X^2 - (\sum X)^2}{N(N-1)} = \frac{4(170) - (24)^2}{4(4-1)} = 8.67$$

$$s_x = \sqrt{8.67} = 2.94$$

Y = X + 5

$$N = 4$$

$$\overline{Y} = \frac{\sum Y}{N} = \frac{44}{4} = 11$$

$$s_y{}^2 = \frac{N\sum Y^2 - (\sum Y)^2}{N(N-1)} = \frac{4(510) - (44)^2}{4(4-1)} = 8.67$$

$$s_y = \sqrt{8.67} = 2.94$$

W = 3X

$$N = 4$$

$$\overline{W} = \frac{\sum W}{N} = \frac{72}{4} = 18$$

$$s_w{}^2 = \frac{N\sum W^2 - (\sum W)^2}{N(N-1)} = \frac{4(1530) - (72)^2}{4(4-1)} = 78.00$$

$$s_w = \sqrt{78.0} = 8.82$$

Summary	X	**Change the Zero Point** $Y = X + 5$	**Change the Unit** $W = 3X$
Mean	6	11	18
Variance	8.67	8.67	78.00
Standard Deviation	2.94	2.94	8.82

EXERCISES

1. If the mean of a distribution was 50, and the standard deviation was 8, what would be the mean, variance, and standard deviation if each of the following operations was done?
   (a) 10 was added to each score.
   (b) 12 was subtracted from each score.
   (c) Each score was multiplied by 10.
   (d) Each score was divided by 5.
   (e) Each score was divided by 8 and then 50 was subtracted from it.

2. If an original set of measurements was made in inches and had a mean of 24 and a variance of 36, what would be the mean, variance, and standard deviation if the unit was changed to feet? If 16 inches had to be added to each measurement to correct for an error? If the measures were converted to centimeters (2.5 centimeters = 1 inch) and then 6 inches were subtracted from each score?

standard scores and the normal distribution

STANDARD SCORES

One reason for introducing changes in the origin and unit of measurement was to describe how the transformation from one scale of measurement to another may take place. Within this context it would be of great importance if two very different scales could somehow be made comparable. For example, suppose a teacher gave two exams to his class. A score of 88 on each exam might mean quite different things. It could be an extremely high score on the first test but quite a low score on the second or vice-versa. While percentiles provide some idea of relative standing, they only represent an ordinal expression of position within a distribution. That is, percentiles reveal only the proportion of people scoring below a given score, but they do not indicate how much below that score the remainder of the distribution was. For example, the results of two tests might be

$$A = (78, 81, 87, 88)$$
$$B = (59, 61, 63, 88)$$

The person who scored 88 would have the same percentile value within each distribution, but the 88 on Test *B* represents a considerably greater relative achievement than it did on Test *A* because it stands so far apart from the remaining scores. Therefore, it would be desirable to be able to characterize the position of a score within a distribution in a more refined manner than merely by indicating its ordinal position.

The interpretation of a score within a distribution is based upon both (a) its relative standing with respect to the mean and (b) the variability of the scores within the distribution. Consider the following example:

$$A = (10, 36, 38, 40, 42, 44, 70)$$
$$B = (10, 20, 30, 40, 50, 60, 70)$$

In both distributions, the mean is 40, but the variability is much greater in the B distribution. A score of 70 deviated $+30$ points from the mean in both distributions, but since the variability was greater in the second distribution, somewhat less value is placed on a score of 70 in Group B than in Group A since other scores also were likely to deviate a great deal from the mean. Therefore, the interpretation of a score is relative not only to the mean of the distribution but also to the variability of the scores in the distribution.

If a single scale of measurement were adopted as being "standard", then all distributions being considered, regardless of origin and unit, could be transformed to that single scale for mutual comparison by subtracting and dividing the scores by appropriate constants. This is essentially what is done when measures are converted into standard scores. By this "standardization" process the relative standing of a person in one distribution may be compared with his standing in another distribution.

A **standard score** is defined to be

$$z_i = \frac{X_i - \overline{X}}{s_x}$$

In words, to transform a score into standard score form (z_i) subtract the mean of the distribution from that score and divide the result by the standard deviation of the X_i (symbolized by s_x).

Consider what this formula does in terms of the origin and unit of measurement. First, it subtracts the mean from the score. Since the mean is a constant and this subtraction could be performed for all scores, the mean of the new distribution of all

$$X_i - \overline{X}$$

will be zero because if a constant (the mean) is subtracted from each score in a distribution, the new mean will be the old mean minus that constant:

$$\text{New Mean} = \overline{X} - c$$
$$c = \overline{X}$$
$$\text{New Mean} = \overline{X} - \overline{X}$$
$$\text{New Mean} = 0$$

Therefore, subtracting the mean from every score makes the mean of the new distribution zero.

Further, recall two facts: (1) subtracting a constant does not alter the standard deviation of a distribution, and (2) the variability of a group of scores influences the interpretation of relative standing. Therefore, the distribution of the scores $(X_i - \overline{X})$ has a mean of zero but a standard deviation of s_x. Suppose, however, that every score in this distribution of $(X_i - \overline{X})$ were divided by s_x. If every score in a distribution is divided by a constant (and s_x is a constant), the standard deviation of the new distribution will equal the original standard deviation divided by that constant:

$$\begin{aligned} \text{New Standard Deviation} &= s_x/c \\ c &= s_x \\ \text{New Standard Deviation} &= s_x/s_x \\ \text{New Standard Deviation} &= 1 \end{aligned}$$

Note that dividing by s_x does not change the mean in this case because the mean is zero and $0/s_x = 0$. Therefore, if every score in the distribution of X_i has the mean subtracted from it and this result divided by the standard deviation, the new distribution will have a mean of 0 and a standard deviation of 1.

The task of interpreting the relative position of a score by considering the mean and variability (standard deviation) of the distribution is accomplished by changing the measures into standard scores which possess a mean of 0 and a standard deviation of 1. For example, if you had a score of 88 on an examination, the class mean was 79, and the standard deviation was 6, the standard score, z, corresponding to $X = 88$ is given by

$$z = \frac{X - \overline{X}}{s_x} = \frac{88 - 79}{6} = \frac{9}{6} = 1.50$$

Standard scores are in standard deviation units. For example, in the above case, the standard deviation was 6. The z score represents the number of standard deviations the score X is from the mean, $\overline{X}$. Since $(X - \overline{X})$ was 9, X is $\frac{9}{6} = 1.5$ standard deviations from the mean.

Standard scores become useful when one wishes to compare performance on several measures, each of which has a different mean and standard deviation. Suppose a teacher gave three examinations and wanted to combine their scores into a single score for the purpose of grading at the end of the course. Merely adding the scores on the three tests weights the scores in accordance with the variabilities of the separate distributions. A score of 14 points above the mean carries a different connotation if the variability of the distribution were quite small (e.g., $s = 3$) than if it were rather large (e.g., $s = 20$). With small variability, a score 14 points above the mean would be quite outstanding relative to the group performance, whereas with large variability it would not be nearly so distinguishing. If each set of measurements is converted to standard scores, then the variability of each of these new distributions will be equal ($s = 1$). In this case, a standard score of 1.3, for example, will be comparable in each standardized distribution and will connote the same quality of performance relative to the group in each case.

Table 4–7 compares adding raw scores across tests with adding standard scores for the same data. Notice that the rank order of the students is not the same using standard scores as when raw scores are employed. This is particularly striking when Students 2 and 3 are compared. They had identical raw score totals (245), but Student 3 had a total z score of 1.50 compared to −.29 for Student 2. This difference was primarily a result of Student 3 scoring 90 on the third test. The 90 was an extremely high score in a distribution that otherwise did not have much variability. Therefore, that performance was weighted more in terms of standard deviation units than in terms of raw scores. A comparison of Students 2 and 5 shows the case in which two students scored quite differently in terms of raw score but had the same standard score total. In general, adding

4–7 The Effect of Computing Standard Scores and Adding across Distributions.

	Raw Scores			
Student	*Test 1*	*Test 2*	*Test 3*	*Total*
1	93	80	85	258
2	81	80	84	245
3	70	85	90	245
4	76	81	85	242
5	65	89	82	236
6	65	90	81	236
7	69	86	79	234
	$\overline{X} = 74.14$	$\overline{X} = 84.43$	$\overline{X} = 83.71$	
	$s = 10.14$	$s = 4.20$	$s = 3.55$	

	Standard Scores			
Student	*Test 1*	*Test 2*	*Test 3*	*Total*
1	1.86	−1.05	.36	1.17
2	.68	−1.05	.08	− .29
3	− .41	.14	1.77	1.50
4	.18	− .82	.36	− .28
5	− .90	1.09	− .48	− .29
6	− .90	1.32	− .76	− .34
7	− .51	.37	−1.33	−1.47

scores in standard score form provides a fairer, truer index of performance than does adding raw scores because the variances of the individual distributions are equated.

THE NORMAL DISTRIBUTION

Standard scores take on greater meaning when their relationship to the normal distribution is understood. The **normal distribution** follows a symmetrical bell-shaped curve. An example is pictured in Figure 4–3. The mean, median, and mode are identical and divide the area under the curve in half. The curve is said to be **asymptotic** to the X-axis, which means that the tails of the distribution draw closer and closer to the X-axis but never quite join it. Since this is true, the curve really extends from $-\infty$ to $+\infty$ on the X-axis.

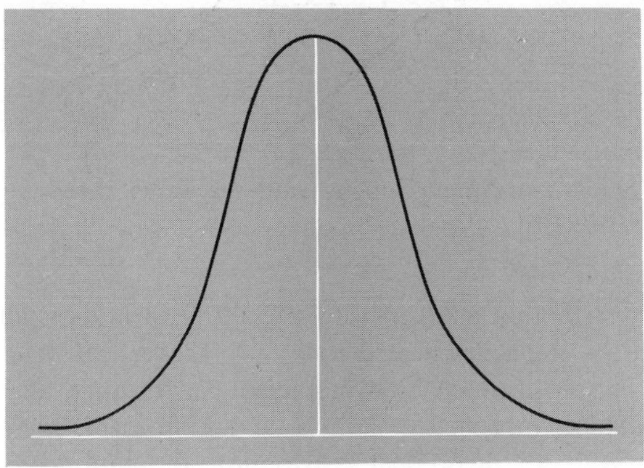

Fig. 4–3. A normal distribution.

Since the normal distribution is plotted on two axes, it has a formula which describes the height of the curve (Y) at any given place along the X-axis (X):

$$Y = \frac{1}{\sqrt{2\pi\sigma^2}} e^{-(X-\mu)^2/2\sigma^2}$$

in which

Y = the height of the curve at point X
X = any point along the X-axis
μ = mean of the distribution
σ^2 = variance of the distribution
π = a constant, 3.1416 . . .
e = the base of Napierian logarithms, 2.7183 . . .

The fact that the mean and variance enter into the formula implies that there is not just one normal distribution but many, one for each of the infinite number of combinations of means and variances that might occur. Three normal curves having the same mean but different variances are shown in Figure 4–4.

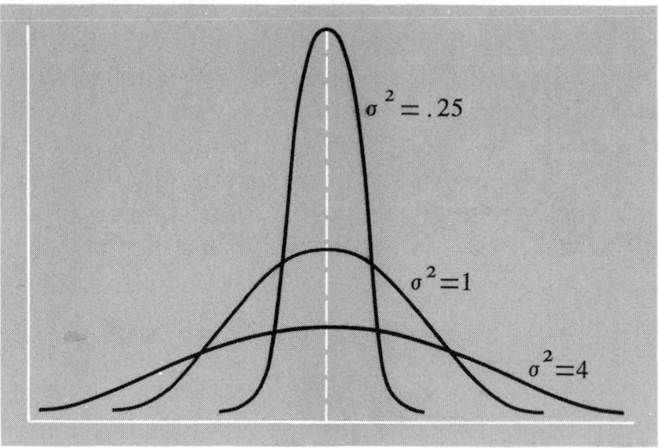

Fig. 4–4. Three normal distributions with the same mean but different variances.

The normal distribution as defined by the above formula is an example of a **theoretical relative frequency distribution.**[2] A theoretical relative frequency distribution is one determined by a mathematical formula, and its values are those that would be approached if more and more cases were continuously sampled. Because it is a theoretical distribution, the parameters μ and σ^2 are used in the formula rather than $\overline{X}$ and s^2. Because it is a relative frequency distribution, the proportion of frequencies that fall between any two points along the X-axis can be determined.

standard normal distribution Just as any distribution may undergo a change of the scale of measurement by converting scores to standard score form, so too may the scale underlying a normal distribution be changed by converting the measures into standard scores. Since one is dealing with a theoretical distribution, the conversion to standard scores uses the parameters μ and σ rather than $\overline{X}$ and s:

$$z_i = \frac{X_i - \mu}{\sigma}$$

[2] This is also called a probability distribution.

> Now, **if the X_i distribution is normal in form** then the distribution of the z_i as given above will also have a normal distribution but with a mean equal to zero and a variance (and standard deviation) equal to 1. This new distribution is known as the **standard normal distribution.** Any single z_i is called a **standard normal deviate** because it signifies the amount any given score deviates from the mean of its distribution in terms of the units of the standard normal distribution.

The advantage of transforming the X_i into standard scores is that the infinite number of normal distributions with different means and variances all can be related to a single theoretical relative frequency distribution by the transformation $z = (X_i - \mu)/\sigma$. Since the distribution of z_i corresponding to the X_i has a mean of zero and a standard deviation of one, all the various normal distributions can be converted into a single distribution and the proportions of frequencies occurring between various points of that single distribution can be applied. Because the normal distribution in terms of z scores is used as a common reference for all normal distributions, it is called the **standard normal distribution.** The standard normal distribution has the parameters $\mu_z = 0$ and $\sigma_z = 1$.

The standard normal distribution is presented in Figure 4–5. Recall that it is a relative frequency distribution which implies that the curve represents the proportion of frequencies which occur at various values of z. Thus, the area under the curve located between two points along that axis represents the proportion of frequencies falling between those two z values. For example, in the standard normal distribution the mean, median, and mode are all located

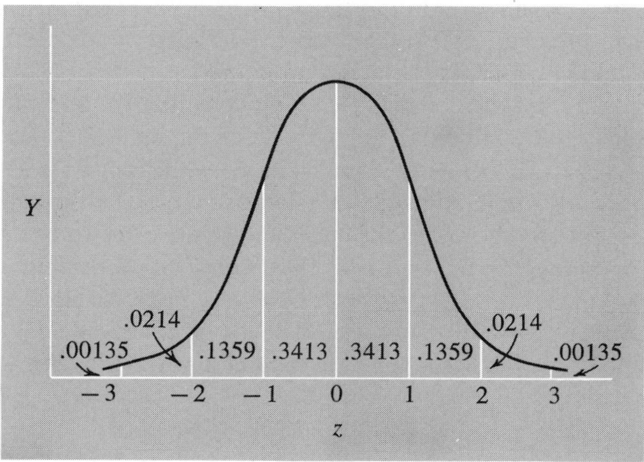

Fig. 4–5. Areas under the curve of the standard normal distribution.

at $z = 0$. The area under the curve between $z = 0$ and $+\infty$ is one-half the total area and thus one would expect that 50% of the cases should fall above $z = 0$. In a relative frequency distribution, area implies relative frequency (or proportion of cases).

With this in mind, certain points can be selected along the z-axis and the portions of the total area under the curve can be illustrated as has been done in Figure 4–5. Here it can be seen that 34.13% of the cases are between $z = 0$ and $+1$ and between $z = 0$ and -1. Further, almost all the cases in a normal distribution (all but .27%) will be included between $z = -3$ and $z = +3$. This means that in any normal distribution, almost all the cases will be within three standard deviations of the mean, because the z scale is in standard deviation units. If the mean of a normal distribution is 55 and the standard deviation is 10, then all the scores are likely to fall between

$$\mu \pm 3(\sigma)$$
$$55 \pm 3(10)$$
$$55 \pm 30$$
$$25 \text{ and } 85$$

The few points along the z-axis which were selected for Figure 4–5 were chosen for convenience. Actually, many points along the z-axis are listed in Table A of Appendix II in the back of this book. The first column is labeled z and corresponds to values along the z-axis which have been transformed from a normal distribution of X_i by

$$z_i = \frac{(X_i - \mu)}{\sigma}$$

The second column gives the proportion of area under the curve (i.e., proportion of frequencies) falling between the mean ($z = 0$) and the z value for that row. The third column provides the area beyond z (i.e., between the z value and $+\infty$) which in every case equals .50 − (area between 0 and z). Thus, for a $z = .35$, the proportion of area falling between the mean ($z = 0$) and $z = .35$ is .1368, and the proportion of area falling between $z = .35$ and $z = +\infty$ is .3632. Notice also that although the standard normal distribution contains negative z values to the left of the mean and positive values to the right of it, the table presents only the positive values. Since the distribution is perfectly symmetrical, the areas relating to each positive z value are equally appropriate for each negative z value. However, it must be remembered that the third column of the table implies area to the right of a positive z value or area to the left of a negative z value.

application of the standard normal distribution Several types of questions can be answered by using the percentiles of the standard normal distribution.

(1) In a normal distribution with mean 45 and standard deviation 10, at what percentile rank does a score of 58 fall?

(a) Determine the z score corresponding to $X = 58$:

$$z = \frac{X - \mu}{\sigma} = \frac{58 - 45}{10} = 1.30$$

(b) Look in the table for the area between the mean ($z = 0$) and a $z = 1.30$. This area constitutes .4032 of the total. Since all of the distribution to the left of the mean also falls below a z of 1.30, .5000 should be added to .4032 to obtain

$$.4032 + .5000 = .9032$$

Thus, an $X = 58$ corresponds to the 90th percentile rank.

(2) In the normal distribution described above, what score is at the 23rd percentile? This is the same type of problem as before only it is solved in the reverse direction.

(a) Draw a picture of the normal distribution such as Figure 4–6. The question asks for the X score corresponding to the 23rd percentile. In the standard normal distribution, the z score corresponding to $P_{.23}$ will have 23% of the cases below it. The third column of the table gives the proportion of cases between z and $+\infty$. However, since the distribution is symmetrical, it also gives the relative frequency between $-z$ and $-\infty$. Therefore, look down the third column until you find .23. The closest figure is .2296, and the z corresponding to that area is .74. Since the left side of the distribution is being worked with, the z value for the 23rd percentile is $-.74$.

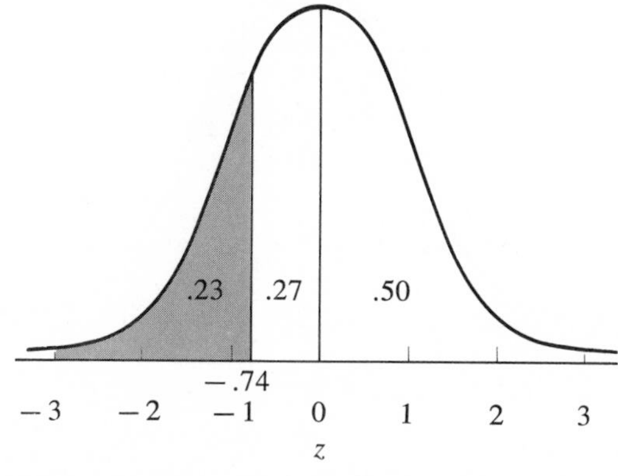

Fig. 4–6. Finding the X score at the 23rd percentile of a normal distribution.

(b) Since 23% of the area falls below $z = -.74$, the problem may be solved by converting $z = -.74$ into its corresponding X value:

$$z = \frac{X - \mu}{\sigma}$$

$$-.74 = \frac{X - 45}{10}$$

$$X = 45 - 7.4$$

$$X = 37.6$$

Therefore, $X = 37.6$ represents the 23rd percentile.

(3) What percent of the cases in a frequency distribution will fall between $z = -1.00$ and $z = 1.00$?

(a) The problem is solved by determining the area between the mean and $z = 1.00$ and between the mean and $z = -1.00$, and then adding these together. The table shows that the area between the mean and $z = 1.00$ is .3413 of the total. Therefore,

$$.3413 + .3413 = .6826$$

gives the right answer.

(4) What proportion of the frequencies fall between $X = 88$ and $X = 95$ if the normal distribution of X_i has a mean of 85 and a standard deviation of 5?

(a) Draw a picture similar to that presented in Figure 4–7 describing the problem. This diagrams the X distribution and indicates that the desired area falls between 88 and 95.

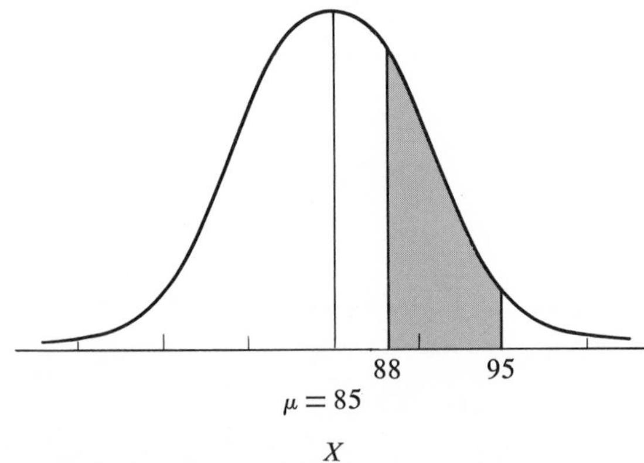

Fig. 4–7. Determining the proportion of cases falling between $X = 88$ and $X = 95$.

(b) Convert 88 and 95 to z values:

$$z = \frac{X - \mu}{\sigma} = \frac{88 - 85}{5} = .60$$

$$z = \frac{X - \mu}{\sigma} = \frac{95 - 85}{5} = 2.00$$

(c) Look in the table under $z = 2.00$ (corresponding to $X = 95$). The area between the mean and this point is .4772. However, the area between the mean and $z = .60$ (corresponding to $X = 88$) is not to be included in the desired answer. Therefore, since this area amounts to .2257, subtract it from the proportion of area between the mean and $z = 2.00$.

$$.4772 - .2257 = .2515$$

to obtain the required proportion.[3]

standard scores and the standard normal distribution

Because the standard normal distribution is a theoretical distribution, conversions between other normal distributions and the standard normal require μ and σ rather than their corresponding sample statistics, $\overline{X}$ and s. However, the standard normal distribution may be used even if only a sample rather than a population is at hand under two conditions:

(1) The population distribution from which the sample is drawn must be normal in form. One way to examine the tenability of this assumption is to plot the sample distribution and casually observe its general form. If the sample distribution does not depart severely from a normal pattern and there is no reason that it should not be normal, then this condition is satisfied.

(2) There must be enough measurements in the sample. A reasonable number of cases is needed in order to determine if the sample is normal in form and in order for $\overline{X}$ and s to be accurate estimators of μ and σ. For samples of approximately 30 or more, $\overline{X}$ and s^2 are sufficiently good estimators of their respective parameters, but it must be remembered that they are still only estimates or approximations to μ and σ.

If these two conditions are met, then with some caution, one can relate the sample distribution to the theoretical standard normal distribution in the same manner as has been illustrated for normal populations by using the formula

$$z_i = \frac{(X_i - \overline{X})}{s_x}$$

[3] The solution presented for this type of problem assumes that the values of 88 and 95 are exactly 88.000 . . . and 95.000 . . . . If not, then their real limits would be 87.5 to 88.5 and 94.5 to 95.5, respectively, in which case the interval of concern would be (87.5–95.5) rather than (88–95).

The logic of this procedure is that $\overline{X}$ and s_x are estimators of μ and σ, and therefore may be used to estimate these parameters when only sample data are available. However, the accuracy of the results of using sample data and this procedure depend upon the normality of the distribution and the sample size which in turn determines the accuracy of $\overline{X}$ and s_x as estimators of their corresponding parameters. Therefore, this practice may be employed only with the knowledge that it will yield approximate results.

OTHER "STANDARDIZED" DISTRIBUTIONS

The standard normal distribution discussed in the preceding section had a mean of zero and a standard deviation of one because the mean was subtracted from each score and the result divided by the standard deviation. However, these parameter values are arbitrarily designated. It could just as easily be made to have a mean of 100 and a standard deviation of 20 by the transformation

$$\text{standard score} = 20\left[\frac{X_i - \overline{X}}{s_x}\right] + 100$$

or a mean of 500 and a standard deviation of 100 by the transformation

$$\text{standard score} = 100\left[\frac{X_i - \overline{X}}{s_x}\right] + 500$$

The Army General Classification Test of World War II used the former standard score and the Graduate Record Exam has employed the latter. Thus, it is obvious that the concept of standard scores is perfectly general, and that the selection of a mean of zero and a standard deviation of one is arbitrary.

EXERCISES

1. What are the limitations of percentiles as measures of relative position and how do standard scores overcome these limitations?

2. Explain and illustrate why it is necessary to consider the variance of a distribution in order to accurately reflect the relative position of a score.

3. Compute the standard score for each of the members of the following distribution. Then calculate the mean and the standard deviation of the z_i. Would you have predicted these last two values? Why?

$$X_i = (5, 7, 7, 8, 9, 12)$$

4. What does the area under a theoretical relative frequency distribution signify?

5. What proportion of the cases of a normal distribution will fall to the left of $z = 0$? To the right of $z = 0$? To the right of $z = 1.00$? To the right of $z = -1.00$?

6. Determine the proportion of cases falling under the normal curve in the following circumstances.
   (a) Between $z = -1$ and $z = +1$.
   (b) Between $z = 1.0$ and $z = 2.0$.
   (c) To the right of $z = 1.5$.
   (d) To the left of $z = -1.96$ plus the cases to the right of $z = 1.96$.
   (e) To the left of $z = -2.575$ and to the right of $z = 2.575$.
7. If the mean of a normal distribution is 38 and the standard deviation is 3, within how many standard deviations of the mean would you expect almost all of the cases to fall? What score values correspond to these points?
8. In a normal distribution with mean of 35 and standard deviation 15, at what percentile is a score of 45 likely to fall? $X_i = 20$? $X_i = 38$?
9. In a normal distribution with mean 50 and standard deviation 8, what score is likely to fall at the 95th percentile? 25th? 1st?
10. What percent of the cases are likely to fall between the values of 38 and 55 in a normal distribution with mean 40 and standard deviation 6? Between 46 and 58? Between 19 and 24?

5

regression

Thus far the discussion has focused upon the several ways to characterize or describe a frequency distribution: the central tendency and variability of the scores. Such statistics can provide an efficient method of describing the distribution.

In addition to characterizing the properties of a distribution one also might want to consider how scores in one distribution relate to those in another. For example, it may be of interest to determine if there is a relationship between scores on college entrance tests, such as the Scholastic Aptitude Test (SAT), and college grades so that this relationship could be used to predict how applicants will fare in college. Further one may wish to describe the magnitude or degree of this relationship. Is there quite a close correspondence between SAT scores and grades or is there only a hint that the two are related? These questions fall under the topic of regression and correlation.

linear relationships

Relationships between two variables can be plotted and the resulting graph often approximates a straight line that relates specific values of one variable to values of the other. Since a very precise description of such graphic displays is needed, it will be beneficial first to consider the geometric and algebraic characteristics of straight lines and then to show how these concepts can be used to describe approximate relationships between variables.

THE EQUATION FOR A STRAIGHT LINE

Suppose a baby sitter charges $1.00 per hour for her services. Consider the relationship between money earned (call it Y) and hours worked (labeled X). If the baby sitter does not work at all ($X = 0$), then she earns no money ($Y = 0$). If she works two hours ($X = 2$) she makes $2.00 ($Y = 2$). If she works four hours she earns $4.00. A table displays these values:

X	Y
0	0
2	2
4	4

The basis of this table is the relationship: an hour worked is a dollar earned. Using the symbols, Y for dollars earned and X for hours worked, this statement reduces to:

$$Y = X$$

This is a simple mathematical equation to describe the relationship between hours worked and money earned, and it will indicate the earnings for any amount of time worked. For example, if the baby sitter worked $3\frac{1}{2}$ hours ($X = 3.5$), then she would be paid $3.50.

$$\begin{aligned} X &= 3.5 \text{ (hours)} \\ Y &= X \\ Y &= 3.5 \text{ (dollars)} = \$3.50 \end{aligned}$$

The same information may be expressed by graphing this equation, letting specific values for X and Y be the coordinates of a point. Figure 5–1 shows the X and Y axes and the three points from the preceding table [(0, 0), (2, 2), (4, 4)]. The line passing through them is described by the equation, $Y = X$. The line really represents an infinite number of points which indicate the amount of money earned for a given amount of time worked; therefore, if the baby sitter worked $3\frac{1}{2}$ hours, a vertical line could be drawn at $X = 3.5$ which would intersect the graphed line of the relationship at $Y = \$3.50$. This fact is indicated in the figure. Hence, the table, the equation ($Y = X$), and the graph of that equation in Figure 5–1 all describe the relationship between money earned and hours worked and provide a method to predict one (Y) from the other (X).

The previous example illustrates a **linear relationship.**

> A **linear relationship** is an association between two variables which may be accurately represented on a graph by a straight line.

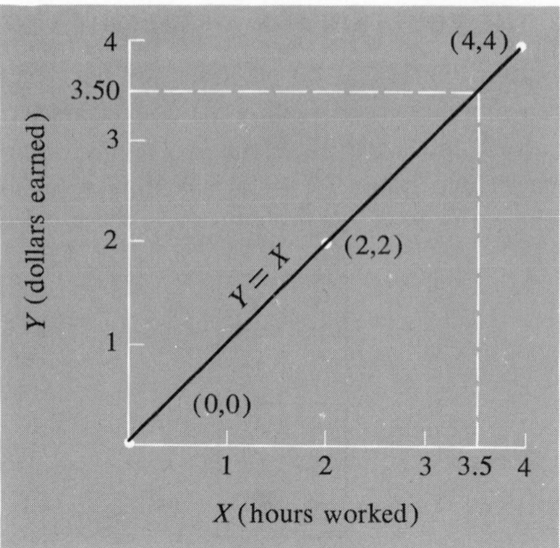

Fig. 5–1. Graph of the line, $Y = X$.

In this case, the association was between money earned and hours worked, and the equation $Y = X$ describes the graph in Figure 5–1 which is indeed a straight line. Relationships are not always linear. If they are not, they are called **non-linear** or **curvilinear relationships.** Their graphs will not be straight lines.

The above example of a linear relationship is one of the simplest kind. Suppose the baby sitter was paid only $.75 an hour. Once again if she worked zero hours ($X = 0$), she would not be paid ($Y = 0$); if she worked 1 hour ($X = 1$), she would earn 75¢ ($Y = .75$); and if she worked 3 hours, she would earn $2.25. Putting these values into a table, one obtains

X	Y
0	0
1	.75
3	2.25

The table uses the relationship: dollars earned equals $.75 times the number of hours worked, which symbolically stated is

$$Y = .75X$$

Figure 5–2 graphically describes this relationship. Note that the two lines, $Y = X$, (Figure 5–1) and $Y = .75X$ (Figure 5–2), are quite similar, differing only in terms of the tilt or **slope** of the line.

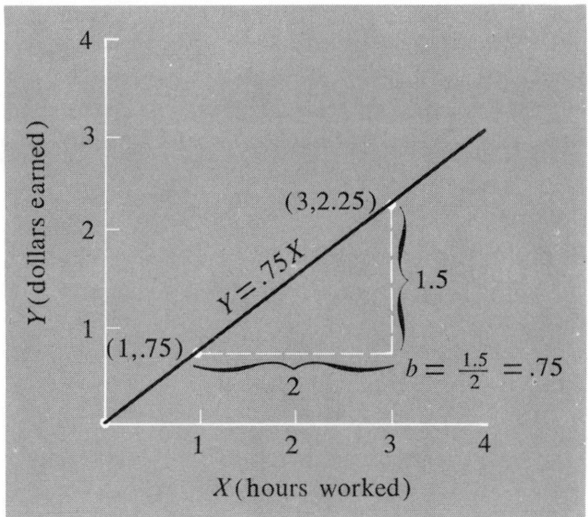

Fig. 5–2. Graph of the line, $Y = .75X$, indicating the slope of the line, b, to equal .75.

The **slope** of a line is defined to be the vertical distance divided by the horizontal distance between any two points on the line. In symbols, given the two points (x_1, y_1) and (x_2, y_2), the slope b of the line is

$$\text{slope} = b = \frac{\text{vertical distance}}{\text{horizontal distance}} = \frac{y_2 - y_1}{x_2 - x_1}$$

For example, two points found for the line above were (1, .75) and (3, 2.25). Putting them in the formula one obtains

$$b = \frac{y_2 - y_1}{x_2 - x_1} = \frac{2.25 - .75}{3 - 1} = \frac{1.5}{2}$$

$$b = .75$$

Graphically, this fact can be seen in Figure 5–2. Recalling that the slope equals the vertical distance between any two points on the line divided by the horizontal distance between the same two points, one can see that this ratio of distances is always equal to .75 for this line. In particular, this fact is illustrated for the points (1, .75) and (3, 2.25).

It is not just coincidence that the slope of this line equals .75 and the equation of the line is $Y = .75X$. The coefficient of X in an equation of this sort is identical to the slope of the line that the equation describes. In the first illustration, $Y = X$, the coefficient of X is 1 [e.g., $Y = (1)X$]. An examination of Figure 5–1 reveals that two points on the graph are (2, 2) and (4, 4), yielding a slope of 1:

$$b = \frac{4 - 2}{4 - 2} = \frac{2}{2} = 1$$

The slope of a line may be negative as well as positive. Consider the line in Figure 5–3. Two points on that line are (2, 3) and (4, 2), which substituted into the formula for the slope, b, yield

$$b = \frac{y_2 - y_1}{x_2 - x_1} = \frac{2 - 3}{4 - 2} = \frac{-1}{2}$$
$$b = -.50$$

In terms of the graph, to get from the point (2, 3) to (4, 2) one must go down a unit, equivalent to going −1 vertical units, and to the right two units (+2), giving a slope of

$$b = \frac{-1}{2} = -.50$$

The slope of the line determines whether the relationship is positive or negative.

> A line with a positive slope indicates a **positive** or **direct** relationship and a line with a negative slope represents a **negative** or **inverse** relationship.

Notice that lines with positive slope tend to run upward from left to right across the graph, indicating that low values on one variable are associated with low values on the other, and high values on one go with high values on the other. In terms of the baby sitting example, few hours worked returned few dollars and many hours worked earned many dollars. Since the slope in such a situation

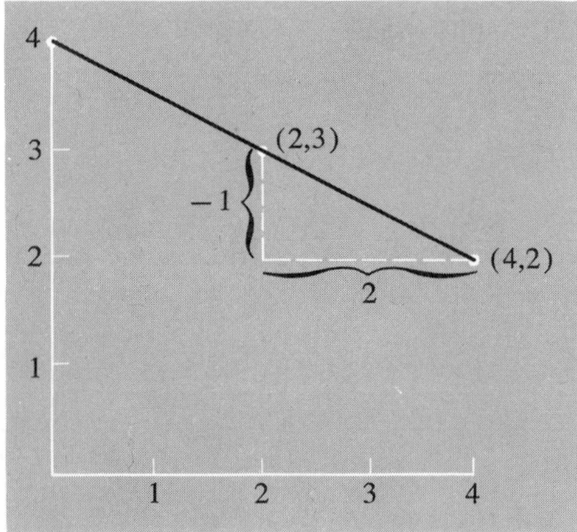

Fig. 5–3. An illustration of a line with negative slope, $b = -\frac{1}{2} = -.5$. Note that low values of X are associated with high values of Y, an inverse or negative relationship.

is positive the relationship is called positive, or it may be referred to as being direct because of the direct correspondence of values on the two dimensions. In contrast, if the slope is negative the line tends to run down from left to right on the graph, indicating that low values on one dimension go with high values on the other. Because the slope is negative in these instances, the relationship is called negative, or it also might be called inverse because high values are associated with low values (rather than high with high and low with low as in direct relationships).

As a final example of a linear relationship, suppose the baby sitter works for an agency. The agency operates in the following manner: Once parents contact and arrange for a baby sitter there is a \$1.00 charge which is made regardless of whether or not the engagement is fulfilled. Baby sitting is paid at the rate of \$.75 an hour in addition to the \$1.00 service charge. Thus, if parents make an appointment and then have to cancel it, in terms of the number of hours worked ($X = 0$), the cost to the parents is \$1.00. If the date is completed and the sitter was occupied for three hours ($X = 3$), the charge is 3 hours at \$.75 an hour plus \$1.00 service charge for a total of \$3.25. A five-hour evening would cost 5 × \$.75 plus \$1.00 or \$4.75. In tabular form:

X	Y
0	1.00
3	3.25
5	4.75

These values were arrived at by multiplying .75 times the number of hours worked and adding 1.00 which can be expressed by the general equation

$$Y = .75X + 1.00$$

The plot of these points together with the previously discussed lines are presented in Figure 5–4. Observe first that the line $Y = X$ has a slope of 1 while the other two lines both have a slope of .75 ($Y = .75X$ and $Y = .75X + 1$). On the graph, the line for ($Y = X$) definitely has a different tilt or slope, while the two lines which have identical slopes are parallel. But these two parallel lines differ in another way. One is always one unit above the other. If the Y-axis is arbitrarily selected as the place to measure this separation, the line $Y = .75X + 1$ goes through the Y-axis at 1 whereas the line $Y = .75X$ goes through the Y-axis at 0.

The point at which lines intersect the Y-axis is called the **y-intercept** and its value is symbolized by a.

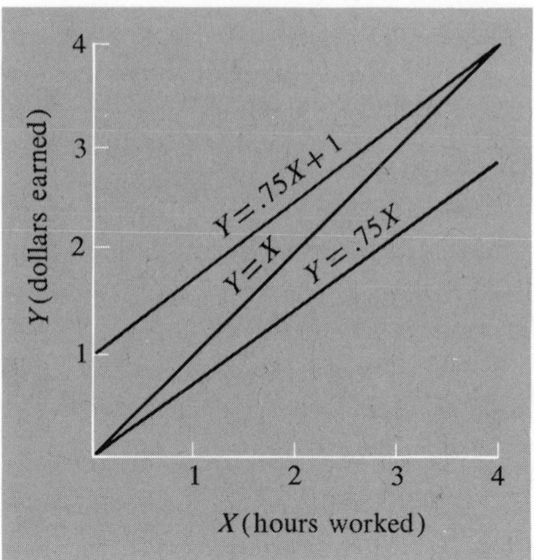

Fig. 5–4. A plot of the three lines discussed in the text having different slopes and intercepts.

Note that the value of the y-intercept, or a, equals the constant which is added to the equation

Equation	Y-intercept
$Y = .75X + 1$	$a = 1$
$Y = .75X \rightarrow Y = .75X + 0$	$a = 0$

The y-intercept can be found from the equation of the line by letting $X = 0$, which is, in fact, the point on the X scale where the Y-axis is located. Thus, to compute the y-intercept:

$$
\begin{aligned}
Y &= .75X + 1 \\
Y &= .75(0) + 1 \\
Y &= +1 = y\text{-intercept}
\end{aligned}
$$

Thus, there are two values to know if one wants the equation of a straight line: The y-intercept (a) and the slope (b). Further, since a provides one point and b tells one how to arrive at some other point on the line, a and b completely specify a particular line.

Therefore, any straight line will have the general equation of

$$Y = bX + a$$

If $a = 1$ and $b = .75$, then the equation

$$Y = .75X + 1$$

describes the line with slope .75 and y-intercept at 1.

The usefulness of the equation of a linear relationship lies in determining a Y value given an X score. Suppose the appropriate equation is $Y = .75X + 1$, and one wishes to know the Y score corresponding to an X of 2, then, substituting $X = 2$,

$$\begin{aligned} Y &= .75X + 1 \\ Y &= .75(2) + 1 \\ Y &= 1.5 + 1 \\ Y &= 2.5 \end{aligned}$$

Thus, in the baby sitting example if the parents are to be gone for 2 hours, they could plan on spending \$2.50 for a baby sitter through the agency.

The baby sitting examples illustrate that graphs of linear relationships have a slope and a y-intercept and that they can provide the basis for predicting a Y value given a certain X value. However, all of these cases have dealt with perfect linear relationships. That is, all of the points have fallen precisely on the line. None has deviated from it. Regrettably, most of the relationships observed in nature are not so precise. A plot of an approximate linear relationship is presented in Figure 5–5. Observe first that the relationship does have a positive linear trend as indicated by the straight line drawn through it, but this line is certainly only an approximation. Yet it still might be useful to have its

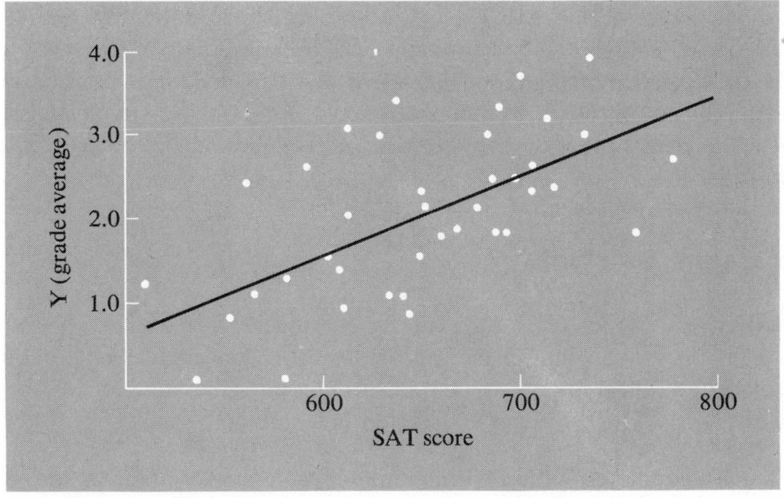

Fig. 5–5. An approximate linear relationship between SAT scores and freshman grades (Table 5–1).

equation in order to make approximate predictions of Y given X. This plot represents the hypothetical relationship between Scholastic Aptitude Test (SAT) scores and freshman college grades in a certain year. If the equation of the line were known, educated guesses of the scholastic performance for next year's applicants could be made on the basis of their SAT scores, assuming the relationship would be much the same from year to year. Previously in this chapter the determination of the equation of the line has been rather obvious, but this task is no longer so intuitive when the relationship is not linearly perfect. In fact, it may not be immediately obvious that the data do indeed follow a linear trend. The first step is to check on the linear trend by constructing a scatterplot.

SCATTERPLOTS

One way to obtain some information on the linearity of a relationship is to construct a graph of it. Suppose that a college admissions officer had 40 freshman students with both SAT score and first year college grades ($A = 4.0$) as presented in Table 5–1. This collection of pairs of scores may be treated in the same manner as the small tables of values described in the previous section, and a point may be placed on a graph corresponding to each pair of values.

A **scatterplot** is a graph of a collection of pairs of scores.

Figure 5–5 is an example of a scatterplot. It was constructed simply by recording a point corresponding to each pair of scores. The variable about which predictions are to be made (predicted variable) is placed on the ordinate. Thus, to plot the first pair of scores in Table 5–1, a point is placed directly over 510 on the SAT scale and precisely to the right of a grade average of 1.3.

Although precise techniques exist which assist in making a decision about linearity, for our purposes now an observation of the total scatterplot is usually sufficient to determine if the trend in the data is approximately linear or if it is curvilinear.

regression constants

Obviously, if the scatterplot tends to be curvilinear, trying to describe it with a straight line would hardly be appropriate. If, however, the relationship is approximately linear, the next task is to determine the equation of the line which best describes the linear association between the two observed variables.

The line describing the relationship between two variables is known as the **regression line** and is expressed in the form, $\tilde{Y} = bX +$ [illegible]. The variable $\tilde{Y}$ is called **predicted Y,** and the values a and b are known as **regression constants.**

5–1 SAT Scores and Grades for a Sample of 40 College Students.

SAT	Freshman Grades	SAT	Freshman Grades
510	1.3	659	2.1
533	0.1	663	1.7
558	0.8	670	1.8
565	2.4	678	2.1
569	1.1	679	2.9
580	0.1	680	2.3
581	1.3	687	1.8
590	2.6	688	3.2
603	1.5	693	1.8
610	1.3	698	2.4
612	0.9	700	3.6
615	2.0	710	2.5
618	3.0	710	2.2
630	2.9	718	3.1
633	1.1	724	2.3
639	3.3	734	2.9
643	1.1	739	3.8
645	0.9	750	3.9
651	1.5	767	1.7
654	2.2	778	2.6

Fitting such lines to observed data is called a problem in **regression.** The term was originated by Francis Galton who found that while the sons of tall men were above average in height, they tended to be a little closer to the mean height of all men than were their fathers. Galton called this **regression toward the mean,** and the term is still used today. However, the word regression also became associated with the process of determining the line which describes the relationship between two variables. In Galton's case the relationship is between the heights of fathers and their sons. As a result, the line has become known as the **regression line.** The constants in the equation, a and b, are called the **regression constants.**

The task, then, is to specify the regression constants for the regression line that best describes the relationship. In order to do this with some degree of precision, a criterion is needed to determine which line of the many possible lines is "best." The criterion selected is called the **least squares criterion.**

The **least squares criterion** states that the line which best characterizes the data is the one which makes the sum of the squared deviations of the points from the line a minimum.

In order to examine the meaning of this concept it is necessary to observe a scatterplot in more detail. For purposes of illustration the following few subjects have been selected from the original sample of 40 students. Their scores are as shown.

X_i	Y_i
510	1.3
533	0.1
603	1.5
670	1.8
750	3.9

A scatterplot of just these five points is presented in Figure 5–6.

For the purpose of explaining the least squares criterion, several definitional points must be reviewed. First, note that when a linear relationship is not perfect, the points do not all fall directly on the line. The vertical distance between the abscissa and any point on the graph is simply its Y_i value. Therefore, the actual vertical locus of any point is symbolized by Y_i. Since every Y_i value is associated with some X value, one could ask what the proposed relationship between X and Y would predict the Y_i value to be. That is, what would the regression line predict the Y_i value to be on the basis of the subject's X score? The predicted value of Y_i would be the vertical height of the line at that particular X value. This point is called $\tilde{Y}$ and read either "Y tilde" or "Y predicted." Any one subject in the distribution will have an actual X and Y score. His actual Y_i value may be predicted from knowledge of his X score and the relationship between X and Y. More specifically, one would predict $\tilde{Y}$. However,

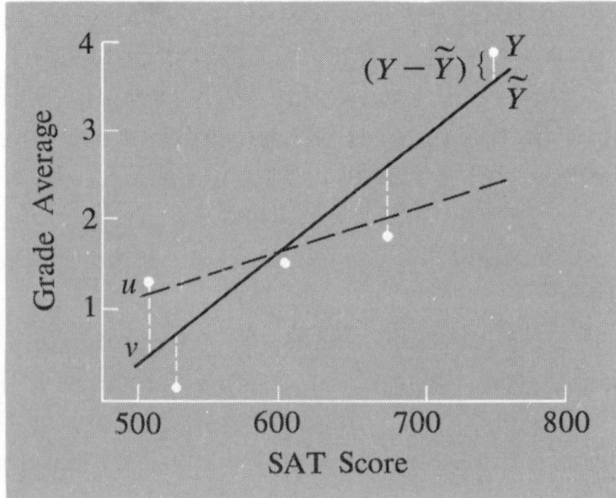

Fig. 5–6. A plot of a selected group of points with two possible regression lines, *u* and *v*.

$\tilde{Y}$ will probably not equal the subject's actual Y_i score. That is, there will be some error in predicting Y_i with $\tilde{Y}$. The quantity $(Y_i - \tilde{Y})$ represents the amount of this error. It is the difference between the predicted and the actual value of the subject's Y_i score.

Consider the two lines in Figure 5–6. Notice that in the upper right-hand corner of the graph the distance between Y_i and $\tilde{Y}$ is shown. Observe that this distance is a vertical rather than a perpendicular distance between the point Y_i and the line $\tilde{Y}$. The error in prediction should be measured in terms of Y units. If the error is measured along the perpendicular from the point Y_i to the line $\tilde{Y}$, the measurement would not be in Y units since such a measurement scale would not be parallel to the Y-axis. Therefore, the error is measured in the vertical dimension in order to state these deviations in Y units.

The distances between the actual points and their respective predicted values represent the error in prediction. It would be advantageous to select regression lines which make such error as small as possible. For example, using the vertical distance between each point and the line as a criterion in Figure 5–6, it is obvious that the points cluster more closely about line v than about line u. These distances between the points and the line might give a convenient measure of how closely the points group about the line and thus be a criterion for which line "best" fits the data. However, notice that if the simple distances $(Y_i - \tilde{Y})$ are used, some of these deviations are positive and some are negative. Thus, points could deviate markedly from the line but if the positive deviations were balanced by equally large negative deviations, the sum $\sum(Y_i - \tilde{Y})$ could be zero for many lines, leaving unresolved the choice of which line is best. This same situation occurred in the case of the variance, s^2, because the sum of the deviations of scores about the mean is always zero. In that instance, the **squared** deviations about the mean were used which resulted in summing only positive values. The same solution is used in the case of regression. Just as $\sum(X_i - \overline{X})^2$ yields a measure of the extent to which points deviate about their mean,

$$\sum(Y_i - \tilde{Y})^2$$

provides an index of how much the points deviate from the regression line. It would be desirable to have this total as small as possible, making the line fit the data points as closely as possible. Therefore, one picks the line so that

$$\sum(Y_i - \tilde{Y})^2$$

is as small as possible. This is the criterion of least squares.

Since the regression line is completely determined if a and b are known, the task reduces to the selection of these regression constants in accordance with the least-squares criterion. The formulas for a and b are derived by the calculus in Table 5–2.[1]

[1] If you have had experience with calculus you will profit from this derivation, while if you are unfamiliar with calculus you may omit this material.

5–2 Deriving Regression Constants by Calculus.

Purpose. To derive formulas for a and b such that the sum of the squared deviations of points about the line $[\sum(Y - \tilde{Y})^2]$ is a minimum.

Since:

$$\tilde{Y} = bX + a$$

Substituting:

$$\sum(Y - \tilde{Y})^2 = \sum[Y - (bX + a)]^2$$
$$\sum(Y - \tilde{Y})^2 = \sum[Y - bX - a]^2$$

Squaring:

$$\sum(Y - \tilde{Y})^2 = \sum(Y^2 - 2aY - 2bXY + b^2X^2 + 2abX + a^2)$$

Distributing the summation operation through the parenthesis gives:

$$\sum Y^2 - 2a\sum Y - 2b\sum XY + b^2\sum X^2 + 2ab\sum X + Na^2$$

Call the above expression S. Then, to minimize S set the partial derivative of S with respect to a equal to zero:

(1) $$\frac{\partial S}{\partial a} = -2\sum Y + 2b\sum X + 2aN = 0$$

Then set the partial derivative of S with respect to b equal to zero:

(2) $$\frac{\partial S}{\partial b} = -2\sum XY + 2b\sum X^2 + 2a\sum X = 0$$

Solving for a in Equation (1):

$$-2\sum Y + 2b\sum X + 2aN = 0$$
$$2aN = 2\sum Y - 2b\sum X$$
$$a = \frac{\cancel{2}\sum Y}{\cancel{2}N} - \frac{\cancel{2}b\sum X}{\cancel{2}N}$$
$$a = \frac{\sum Y}{N} - b\frac{\sum X}{N}$$
$$a = \overline{Y} - b\overline{X}$$

continued

OBTAINING THE REGRESSION LINE

In Table 5–2, it was found that the formulas for a and b are

$$b = \frac{N(\sum XY) - (\sum X)(\sum Y)}{N\sum X^2 - (\sum X)^2}$$
$$a = \overline{Y} - b\overline{X}$$

5-2 continued

Substituting the next to last expression obtained for a in Equation (2):

$$-2\sum XY + 2b\sum X^2 + 2a\sum X = 0$$

$$-2\sum XY + 2b\sum X^2 + 2\sum X\left[\frac{\sum Y}{N} - b\left(\frac{\sum X}{N}\right)\right] = 0$$

Multiplying:

$$-2\sum XY + 2b\sum X^2 + 2(\sum X)\left(\frac{\sum Y}{N}\right) - 2b(\sum X)\left(\frac{\sum X}{N}\right) = 0$$

Transposing and cancelling to solve for b:

$$2b\sum X^2 - 2b(\sum X)\left(\frac{\sum X}{N}\right) = 2\sum XY - 2(\sum X)\left(\frac{\sum Y}{N}\right)$$

Factoring:

$$b\left[\sum X^2 - (\sum X)\left(\frac{\sum X}{N}\right)\right] = \sum XY - (\sum X)\left(\frac{\sum Y}{N}\right)$$

Dividing:

$$b = \frac{\sum XY - \dfrac{(\sum X)(\sum Y)}{N}}{\sum X^2 - \dfrac{(\sum X)^2}{N}}$$

Multiplying by N:

$$b = \frac{N\sum XY - (\sum X)(\sum Y)}{N\sum X^2 - (\sum X)^2}$$

The formulas for a and b such that the sum of the squared deviations about the line is a minimum are

$$a = \overline{Y} - b\overline{X}$$

$$b = \frac{N\sum XY - (\sum X)(\sum Y)}{N\sum X^2 - (\sum X)^2}$$

These expressions provide a means for computing a and b from the original scores such that when these constants are placed into the regression equation ($\tilde{Y} = bX + a$) it will describe precisely the line which best fits the data in the sense of having minimized the squared deviations between the data points and the line (i.e., $\sum(Y_i - \tilde{Y})^2$ will be minimum).

The use of these formulas will be illustrated with the data provided by the five subjects selected previously. Of course, the admissions director mentioned in the original illustration would use as many college students as were available. The more subjects involved in a regression analysis, the more confidence one can have in generalizing its results. However, using just these few subjects will provide the reader with a simple example of the computational routine required. These procedures are presented in Table 5–3. An examination of the formulas reveals that five quantities are needed:

$$N, \sum X, \sum X^2, \sum Y, \text{ and } \sum XY$$

5–3 The Computation of the Regression Equation.

Subject	X	Y	X^2	XY
1	510	1.3	260100	663.0
2	533	.1	284089	53.3
3	603	1.5	363609	904.5
4	670	1.8	448900	1206.0
5	750	3.9	562500	2925.0

$$\sum X = 3066 \quad \sum Y = 8.6 \quad \sum X^2 = 1919198 \quad \sum XY = 5751.8$$

$$(\sum X)^2 = 9400356$$

$$\overline{X} = 613.20 \quad \overline{Y} = 1.72$$

$$N = 5$$

$$b = \frac{N(\sum XY) - (\sum X)(\sum Y)}{N\sum X^2 - (\sum X)^2} = \frac{5(5751.8) - (3066)(8.6)}{5(1919198) - 9400356}$$

$$= \frac{2391.4}{195634} = .012$$

$$a = \overline{Y} - b\overline{X} = 1.72 - (.012)(613.20) = -5.638$$

$$\tilde{Y} = bX + a$$

$$\tilde{Y} = .012X - 5.638$$

The N is the number of *pairs* of scores or the number of subjects, *not* the number of X and Y scores together. The values of b and a are arrived at by substituting into the formulas given above and reducing. The last step is to substitute the resulting constants into the regression equation which results in

$$\tilde{Y} = .012X - 5.638$$

With the regression equation obtained, one may pose the problem the admissions director is constantly faced with. If applicant John Greenley's SAT score is 718, what would one predict his freshman grade average to be? The question is answered easily by substituting $X = 718$ into the regression equation and computing $\tilde{Y}$:

$$\tilde{Y} = .012(718) - 5.638$$
$$\tilde{Y} = 2.978$$

Geometrically this amounts to drawing a vertical line through $X = 718$ parallel to the Y-axis and asking for the Y value at the point of intersection of that vertical line and the regression line.

THE SECOND REGRESSION LINE

All of the discussion has been directed at predicting Y from X. It would appear that if two variables are measured on each person in a group the relationship should be the same regardless of whether one predicts Y from X or X from Y. It is true that the *degree* of relationship is the same regardless of the direction of prediction as will be demonstrated in the next chapter on correlation. However, the regression constants will be different depending upon which variable is the predictor and which is the predicted. This fact is obvious if one considers the SAT-grades example in terms of the y-intercept. When trying to predict grades from SAT scores, the y-intercept of the line was measured in the units of the predicted variable, namely, -5.638 grade points. If the direction of prediction is reversed making SAT scores the predicted dimension and placing it on the ordinate (Y-axis), then the y-intercept for the regression line will be in SAT-score points, not grade points. Obviously, the value of a will be different in these two cases because the measure is different.

The fact that the regression constants are different depending upon which variable is being predicted may be understood further by examining the manner in which a and b were derived. When predicting grades from SAT scores, the criterion for selecting the regression constants is such that $\sum(\text{grade} - \text{predicted grade})^2$ is a minimum. In contrast, when SAT scores are being predicted, the $\sum(\text{SAT} - \text{predicted SAT})^2$ must be a minimum. It happens that making one of these sums a minimum does not guarantee that the other sum will also be minimized by the same line. From another perspective, if one considers a graph (Figure 5–7) with SAT scores on the abscissa and grades on the ordinate, when grades are predicted the squares of the vertical distances between the points and the line are minimized. But, if one uses the same axes and predicts SAT scores, the squares of the horizontal distances between points and regression line would be minimized. This is diagrammed in Figure 5–7. However, making one set of squared distances as small as possible does not simultaneously reduce the other squared distances to a minimum. If the relationship were perfectly linear and all the points fell on the regression line, the two regression lines would coincide. However, since perfect relationships are very rare in the social sciences, there are usually two regression lines.

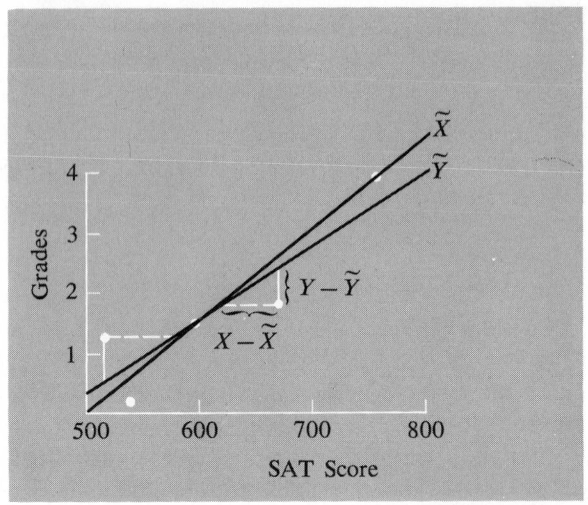

Fig. 5-7. The two regression lines for the sample data, Y on X ($\tilde{Y}$) and X on Y ($\tilde{X}$). The lines connecting a few points to the regression lines indicate the squared distances minimized in determining $\tilde{Y}$ (solid lines) and $\tilde{X}$ (dashed lines).

The formulas which were given above for a and b were for the case in which Y was being predicted from X. This case is sometimes referred to as the **regression of Y on X,** and therefore the regression equation is frequently written

$$\tilde{Y} = b_{yx}X + a_{yx}$$

with the subscript yx meaning the regression of Y on X (Y is predicted). In contrast, for the case in which one is predicting X from knowledge of Y, the regression equation is

$$\tilde{X} = b_{xy}Y + a_{xy}$$

and it is called the **regression of X on Y.** The formulas for the two sets of constants are as follows:

Y on X:

$$b_{yx} = \frac{N(\sum XY) - (\sum X)(\sum Y)}{N\sum X^2 - (\sum X)^2} \qquad a_{yx} = \overline{Y} - b_{yx}\overline{X}$$

X on Y:

$$b_{xy} = \frac{N(\sum XY) - (\sum X)(\sum Y)}{N\sum Y^2 - (\sum Y)^2} \qquad a_{xy} = \overline{X} - b_{xy}\overline{Y}$$

For the example of five subjects used previously in this chapter, the numerical values of these constants for the regression of X on Y would be as follows ($\sum Y^2 = 22.40$):

$$b_{xy} = \frac{N(\sum XY) - (\sum X)(\sum Y)}{N\sum Y^2 - (\sum Y)^2} = \frac{5(5751.8) - (3066)(8.6)}{5(22.40) - (73.96)}$$

$$= \frac{2391.4}{38.04} = 62.87$$

$$a_{xy} = \overline{X} - b_{xy}\overline{Y} = 613.20 - (62.87)(1.72) = 505.06$$

The regression equation would be

$$\tilde{X} = (62.87)Y + 505.06$$

When the two regression lines are plotted on the same graph, Figure 5–7 results. The few lines drawn connecting the points to the regression lines (solid for Y on X, dotted for X on Y) illustrate the distances which are to be squared and minimized in each case.

The two sets of formulas need be of concern only in the case in which prediction is to go in both directions on the basis of the same set of original data. In actual practice, this rarely occurs. Rather, predictions are only made about one of the two variables. Hence, to avoid confusion always label the variable being predicted Y, and the predictor variable X, and use the formulas for the regression of Y on X.

factors in the use of the regression line

The discussion thus far has focused upon describing procedures that attempt to fit a straight line to a set of data points. These procedures may always be carried out regardless of the form of the scatterplot, but ordinarily in the application of regression techniques certain assumptions are made which permit more extensive interpretation of the results of linear regression. Briefly, it is assumed that a linear relationship exists between the two variables in the population and that the sample data reflect this condition to some extent. The following sections of this chapter are concerned with the details of this general assumption and how the interpretation of linear regression analyses may be enriched by making these additional presuppositions.

LINEARITY

The procedures described in the preceding sections are appropriate for data having an underlying linear relationship in the population. A linear relationship exists when the form of the plot of the two variables is a straight line

($Y = bX + a$). If it is not known whether the relationship in the population is linear, a casual examination of the scatterplot of the sample data can sometimes indicate the tenability of this assumption. (Statistical techniques are available that determine more rigorously whether curvilinearity exists in a scatterplot, but they will not be discussed here.) Obviously, if it is doubtful that a linear relationship exists, it is foolish to attempt to fit a straight line to data which would be more appropriately described by some curvilinear trend.

RANGE OF X

One must be careful to restrict predictions to those X values that fall within the range of X values used in the process of determining the regression constants. It is from this original set of data that one examines if the relationship appears to be linear. However, this information on linearity applies only to the range of X values originally used. Therefore, since one's confidence in the assumption of linearity is based only upon the original range of X values, extending the scope of prediction to more extreme X_i exceeds the information on the linearity of regression. Consider an example in which rats were placed under food deprivation for from 0 to 48 hours prior to performing ten trials in a two-choice problem. The solid line in Figure 5–8 represents the hypothetical

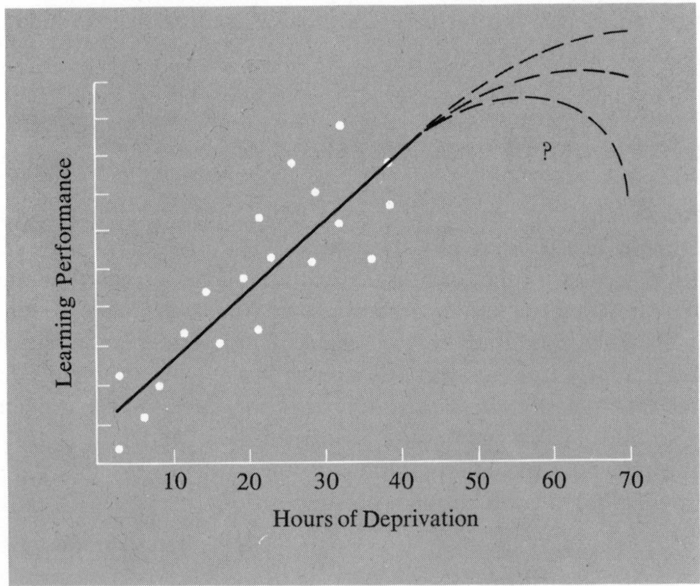

Fig. 5–8. A hypothetical relationship between hours of deprivation and learning performance (solid line) and the ambiguity of the form of the relationship for X values outside of the tested range (dashed lines).

relationship between hours of deprivation and the percent of correct responses. The equation of this hypothetical line is

$$\tilde{Y} = .015X + .02$$

If one wanted to predict performance for 31 hours of deprivation, he would simply substitute $X = 31$ into the equation, obtaining a predicted figure of 48.5% correct responses. If $X = 72$, which is outside of the range of original X values, then the regression equation would predict that 110% of the trials would be correct. Clearly, the relationship between hours of deprivation and learning performance is not linear over such a range of X values. Obviously, performance cannot continue to improve with each extra hour of deprivation because ultimately the animal will die. Therefore, although there may be a linear relationship over parts of the original range of X values, it may not hold true over an extended range of X values. This situation is diagrammed in Figure 5–8. Therefore, it is appropriate to predict only from X values falling within the range of the original values because information on the linearity of the relationship at more extreme values is not available.

STANDARD ERROR OF ESTIMATE

Another set of assumptions is important in the application of the standard error of estimate. One of the purposes in considering regression and the attempt to predict one variable from another was to describe precisely a linear relationship between two variables. Yet, although techniques have now been discussed that will yield the equation for a straight line which best fits the data, the data points only tend to cluster around rather than fall precisely on the line. Thus, although the prediction is that John Greenley would make a 2.6 grade average his freshman year, John's actual performance will probably not be precisely 2.6. It is clear that this predicted value probably will be in error to some extent. However, the degree of inaccuracy may be different for different relationships. What would be useful is to have some sort of numerical index to indicate the extent of the error in prediction. What is required is a measure of the variability of points about the regression line that operates in the same manner as the variance of points about the mean. The greater the variability of the points about the line, the greater the error in prediction.

Although the nature of the distribution of the points in a scatterplot determines the slope of the regression line, it is possible to have scatterplots with regression lines of equal slope but with different amounts of variability of the points about this line. Figure 5–9 displays such a situation.

In Part A the sum of the squared distances, $\sum(Y_i - \tilde{Y})^2$, is quite a bit smaller than for Part B. For any specific prediction it is likely that the predicted Y would be closer to the person's actual Y score in Part A than in Part B, even though both lines are the best fitting lines for their data. The task in this

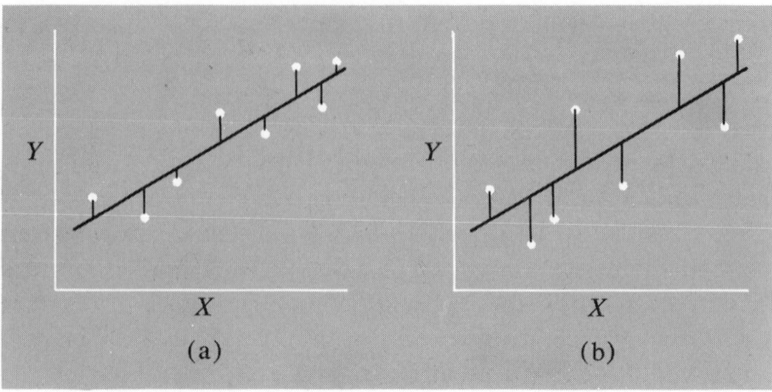

Fig. 5-9. Two regression lines with different amounts of error in prediction. Graph B has larger errors than does Graph A.

section is to develop a quantitative index of the extent of this variability or error in estimating a person's Y score given X.

The statistic needed is the **standard error of estimate,** $s_{y.x}$, read "s y dot x," which is defined to be the square root of the sum of squared deviations of Y_i about the line ($\tilde{Y}$) divided by $(N - 2)$. In symbols,

$$s_{y.x} = \sqrt{\frac{\sum(Y_i - \tilde{Y})^2}{N - 2}}$$

The standard error of estimate is abbreviated $s_{y.x}$, in order to distinguish it from the standard deviation of the Y distribution which is written s_y (s_x for the X distribution), and to indicate that it is appropriate for the regression of Y on X. Consider the logic of this index.

First, since a measure of the variability of points about a value (the line, $\tilde{Y}$) is needed, recall the discussion of variability about the mean in Chapter 3. In that case, an index of variability about a constant value, the mean, was developed by taking the sum of the squared deviations about that mean and dividing them by $N - 1$, to obtain the variance, or its square root, the standard deviation:

$$s_y = \sqrt{\frac{\sum(Y_i - \bar{Y})^2}{N - 1}}$$

The present task is similar: To index the variability of the Y scores, not about their mean, but about the regression line, $\tilde{Y}$. If the sum of these squared deviations, $\sum(Y - \tilde{Y})^2$, is divided by $N - 2$, one has

$$s_{y.x} = \sqrt{\frac{\sum(Y_i - \tilde{Y})^2}{N - 2}}$$

This statistic is very similar to the standard deviation, except that it reflects variation about the regression line ($\tilde{Y}$) rather than about the mean ($\bar{Y}$). Note that while the denominator for the standard deviation was $N - 1$ in order to improve the estimation of σ, the denominator for the standard error of estimate is $N - 2$. This quantity is used to improve $s_{y.x}$ as an estimator of its corresponding population parameter, $\sigma_{y.x}$.

The formula for $s_{y.x}$ given above is a definitional formula. To use it for actual computation would be tedious since a $\tilde{Y}$ would have to be computed for every X. Therefore, an alternative formula is used which will give the identical result but which is easier to compute:

$$s_{y.x} = \sqrt{\left[\frac{1}{N(N-2)}\right]\left[N\sum Y^2 - (\sum Y)^2 - \frac{[N\sum XY - (\sum X)(\sum Y)]^2}{N\sum X^2 - (\sum X)^2}\right]}$$

APPLICATION OF THE STANDARD ERROR OF ESTIMATE

Suppose a student who has taken the SAT test applies to college, and the relationship between SAT and grades would predict a grade average of 1.8. However, it might be of interest not only to predict a specific grade average of 1.8 but to determine an interval of values which is likely to contain the person's actual score. Further, suppose the interval were constructed such that in 95 of every 100 such cases the actual value would fall within the limits of the interval.

In order to determine such an interval, consider the following method as illustrated in Figure 5–10 which diagrams a simple scatterplot with the Y distributions at each value of X also drawn. Each of these six subdistributions has a mean and a standard deviation. If Johnny's X score is 2, and if the distribution of Y_i at $X = 2$ is normal in form, to calculate the limits of the interval one could use the standard normal distribution and the fact that 95% of the cases fall within ± 1.96 standard deviations of the mean. If the mean of the Y_i at $X = 2$ is symbolized by $\bar{Y}_{x=2}$ and the standard deviation of this distribution by $s_{y|x=2}$ (read "the standard deviation of Y given $X = 2$"), then 95% confidence limits for the Y's within the distribution at $X = 2$ would be

$$95\% \text{ limits} = \bar{Y}_{x=2} \pm 1.96(s_{y|x=2})$$

However, if Jane came along with an X score of 4, the mean and standard deviation for the Y distribution at $X = 4$ would have to be computed in order to perform the same service, and so on for all the X values. Such a procedure is tedious, particularly if there are many X values, and thus it would be advantageous if a single measure were available to indicate these means and standard deviations. The $\tilde{Y}$ and the standard error of estimate perform these functions. The regression line, $\tilde{Y}$, provides an estimate of the central tendency of the scores at any given X value. The standard error of estimate, $s_{y.x}$, is a single

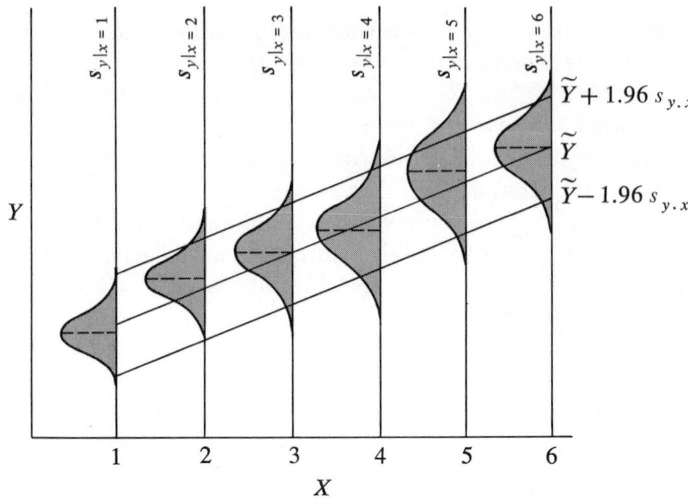

Fig. 5–10. Graph showing the use of the line ($\tilde{Y}$) and the $s_{y.x}$ to construct confidence intervals about the line. The graph also shows the subdistributions of Y_i at each X value.

measure of the variability of the points about $\tilde{Y}$ and could be used to estimate this variability at any single X value. Thus, using these two general measures, $\tilde{Y}$ and $s_{y.x}$, 95% confidence limits are defined by

$$95\% \text{ confidence limits} = \tilde{Y} \pm 1.96 s_{y.x}$$

Of course, not all confidence limits need to be 95% confidence limits. They may have any level of "confidence" associated with them as determined by the coefficient of $s_{y.x}$ in the above expression. If 90% confidence limits are desired, then Table A of Appendix II of the standard normal distribution states that 45% of the area falls between 1.645 standard deviation units and the mean. Thus, 90% confidence limits would be produced by taking

$$\tilde{Y} \pm 1.645 s_{y.x}$$

This entire procedure is contingent upon certain assumptions. Figure 5–10 shows the relationship between the Y distributions at each value of X and the 95% confidence limits which are indicated by two parallel lines, one $1.96 s_{y.x}$ above and the other $1.96 s_{y.x}$ below $\tilde{Y}$. From this sketch it can be seen that some precision is lost for the convenience of using the two general statistics, $\tilde{Y}$ and $s_{y.x}$.

This inaccuracy may not be too severe if three assumptions can be met: (1) linearity, (2) normality of the individual Y distributions at each X value, and (3) homoscedasticity, or the homogeneity of separate Y-distribution variances. One should consider these three assumptions in more detail.

First, the **relationship must be linear.** If it is not linear but curvilinear, then a straight line will not approximate the central tendencies of all the groups. Therefore, one can see in Figure 5–10 that the means of the individual Y distributions do not fall precisely on the line, but this tendency for $\tilde{Y}$ and $\bar{Y}_{x=k}$ not to coincide will be greater if the relationship is not fundamentally linear. Therefore, in order for $\tilde{Y}$ to approximate the central tendency of each subgroup of Y_i the relationship must be linear.

Second, in order to use the proposition that 95% of the cases will fall within ± 1.96 standard deviation units from $\tilde{Y}$, it must be assumed that **each of the Y distributions is normal in form.** If each is not, then this use of $s_{y.x}$ is not appropriate since the necessary conditions only hold for normal distributions.

Third, the standard error of estimate is computed over all the Y subdistributions and is therefore a composite measure of their variability. If, however, the single value $s_{y.x}$ is to be an appropriate index of the variability of each of these separate distributions, then the actual standard deviations $s_{y|x=k}$ should be comparable from one distribution to the other. This comparability of variance is called either "homogeneity of Y-distribution variance" or more commonly, **homoscedasticity.**

The effect of not having homogeneity of variance within each of the Y distributions at each value of X is displayed in Figure 5–11. In this diagram an irregular scatterplot is drawn with its regression line and the lines indicating ± 1.96 standard errors of estimate. The confidence limits for the regression line are not appropriate for most Y distributions at specific values of X because there is not homogeneity of Y-distribution variance across these X values. If the confidence limits were used to indicate the values of Y within which a predicted score would likely fall, they would represent too narrow a range at $X = 3$ but too wide a range at $X = 10$. The use of the standard error of estimate in this manner is appropriate only if the variances of the individual Y distributions are comparable at each value of X. If these variances are homogeneous, a single measure of this dispersion of points about the line (that is, $s_{y.x}$) will suffice to characterize the variability at each value of X. Otherwise, the use of a single measure instead of the specific variance of each individual Y distribution is unwarranted to the extent of the heterogeneity of the variability in Y at each X value.

In summary, to use the standard error of estimate to establish confidence intervals about the regression line one must assume that (1) there is a linear relationship between X and Y so that the regression line is an appropriate description of the relationship, (2) the Y distributions at each X value are all normal so that the percentiles of the standard normal distribution may be appropriately applied, and (3) the variability of these separate Y distributions

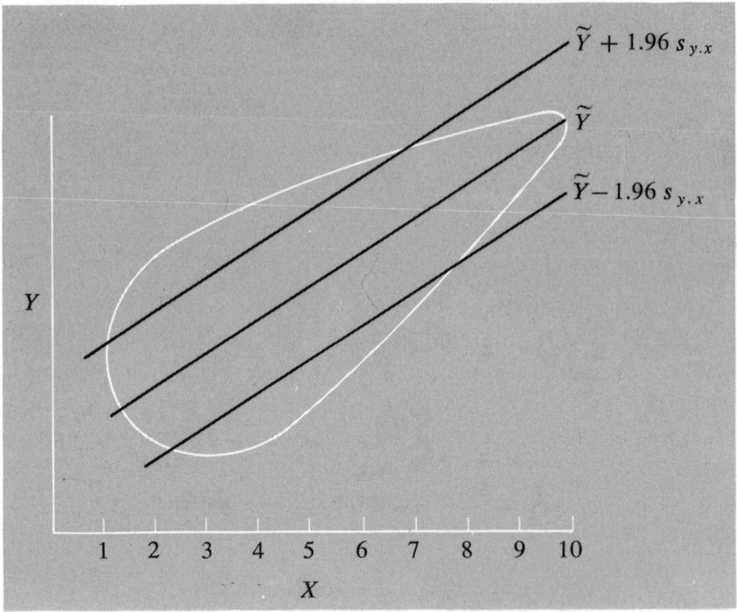

Fig. 5–11. A scatterplot that does not possess homogeneity of subdistribution Y variances (absence of homoscedasticity). Notice that the confidence interval underestimates the range of Y at $X = 3$ but overestimates it at $X = 9$.

is relatively comparable one to another (homoscedasticity) so that the single measure of variability ($s_{y.x}$) will be appropriate for each one.

Are these assumptions ever met? Although they appear to be very restrictive, they can be assumed occasionally, but a large number of scores usually is needed to provide enough cases in each Y distribution to determine if those distributions appear normal and of comparable variability.

FORMULAS

1. Geometry of a Straight Line

$$\text{Slope} = \frac{y_2 - y_1}{x_2 - x_1} \text{ for points } (x_1, y_1) \text{ and } (x_2, y_2) \text{ on the line}$$

y-intercept: Y value at $X = 0$

2. Regression of *Y* on *X*

a. Regression equation

$$\tilde{Y} = b_{yx}X + a_{yx}$$

b. Slope

$$b_{yx} = \frac{N(\sum XY) - (\sum X)(\sum Y)}{N\sum X^2 - (\sum X)^2}$$

c. *y*-intercept

$$a_{yx} = \overline{Y} - b_{yx}\overline{X}$$

d. Standard error of estimate

$$s_{y.x} = \sqrt{\frac{\sum(Y_i - \tilde{Y})^2}{N - 2}}$$

(definitional formula)

$$s_{y.x} = \sqrt{\left[\frac{1}{N(N-2)}\right]\left[N\sum Y^2 - (\sum Y)^2 - \frac{[N(\sum XY) - (\sum X)(\sum Y)]^2}{N\sum X^2 - (\sum X)^2}\right]}$$

(computational formula)

3. Regression of *X* on *Y*

a. Regression equation

$$\tilde{X} = b_{xy}Y + a_{xy}$$

b. Slope

$$b_{xy} = \frac{N(\sum XY) - (\sum Y)(\sum X)}{N\sum Y^2 - (\sum Y)^2}$$

c. *y*-intercept

$$a_{xy} = \overline{X} - b_{xy}\overline{Y}$$

d. Standard error of estimate

$$s_{x.y} = \sqrt{\frac{\sum(X_i - \tilde{X})^2}{N - 2}}$$

(definitional formula)

$$s_{x.y} = \sqrt{\left[\frac{1}{N(N-2)}\right]\left[N\sum X^2 - (\sum X)^2 - \frac{[N(\sum XY) - (\sum Y)(\sum X)]^2}{N\sum Y^2 - (\sum Y)^2}\right]}$$

(computational formula)

EXERCISES

1. Compute the regression constants for the relationships between X and Y, X and W, and Y and W. Also write the regression equation for each of these relationships.

X	Y	W
2	8	10
3	2	7
5	4	1
6	6	5
8	10	2
10	5	3

2. Using the equations from Exercise 1, what would you predict in the following cases?
   (a) $\tilde{Y}$ for $X = 4$
   (b) $\tilde{W}$ for $X = 7$
   (c) $\tilde{W}$ for $Y = 7$
   (d) $\tilde{Y}$ for $X = 15$

3. Construct 95% confidence intervals for your predictions in (a), (b), and (c) of the previous exercise. (Disregard assumptions. See Exercise 8.)

4. The squared deviations $\sum(Y_i - \tilde{Y})^2$ are called squared errors of prediction. Explain the logic of their use for this purpose, and their role in the least squares criterion. Why is the regression line the line of "best fit"?

5. If a salesman receives a base pay of \$200 per month and a 3% commission on his sales, what is the regression equation relating sales and income for this man?

6. Compare the standard error of estimate with a simple standard deviation. In what way are they similar and in what way are they different?

7. Why are there usually two regression lines? Show by using the formula for the slope that if the variances of X and Y are the same, the two regression lines have the same slope. Will the intercepts also be the same under these conditions? Why?

8. In order to use the standard error of estimate to construct confidence limits about the regression line, it is necessary to make three assumptions. Describe these assumptions and explain why these propositions are vital to this application of the $s_{y.x}$.

9. In what way does the regression constant b indicate the "direction" of the relationship?

6

correlation

In the previous chapter on regression, the problem of linear prediction was discussed. It was found that the equation for a straight line relating two variables could be obtained such that the sum of the squared distances between the line and the actual data points was a minimum. Further, the standard error of estimate provided a means of gauging the interval of Y values within which a subject with a given X score was likely to fall. However, the standard error of estimate provides an index of the accuracy of prediction only in terms of the units used to measure the Y variable because its definition is based upon those units: $\sum(Y_i - \tilde{Y})^2$. The $s_{y.x}$ does reflect the extent to which the two variables are related because if $s_{y.x}$ is 10 and $s_{y.w}$ is 5, the relationship between Y and W is stronger than between Y and X (if the Y_i are the same in each case). This comparison of errors of estimation is appropriate if one wants to know whether the verbal or quantitative score of the Scholastic Aptitude Test is a better predictor of the college grades of a certain group of students. But, since the standard error of estimate is always in the units of the predicted variable, it is not possible to compare the strength of linear relationships between two different pairs of variables (e.g., X and Y vs. W and Z). Consequently, it would be useful to have an index of the degree of relationship between two variables that is not expressed in the units of one of the variables and therefore is an index that will permit comparisons to be made between different sets of variables. Such an index of the degree or extent of a linear relationship between two variables is the **correlation coefficient.**

derivation of the correlation coefficient

The approach to developing the formula for the correlation coefficient rests on the fact that the square of the correlation coefficient represents the amount of variability in the Y_i that is associated with differences in the variable X. For example, suppose a reading test were given to a group of children at the termination of first grade. Not every child obtains the same score on this reading test, and the extent to which the scores are dissimilar from child to child is reflected in the variability of the scores (e.g., their variance, s^2). But suppose an intelligence test was also administered and thus the mental age of each child was also available. Now, one might ask what proportion of the variability in reading scores is associated with differences in mental age? If there is a tendency for pupils having high mental ages to also score high in reading, then perhaps a large proportion of the variance in reading scores is associated with differences in the mental ages of the pupils. The square of the correlation coefficient expresses the proportion of variability in the predicted variable (Y_i) that is associated with differences in the X_i and consequently provides an index of the degree of linear relationship between X and Y.

Consider Figure 6–1, which is a scatterplot of a few points and the regression line. The greater the relationship between X and Y, the more variability in Y will be associated with differences in X. For example, if all the points fell precisely on the line, all of the variability in Y would be attributable to X because

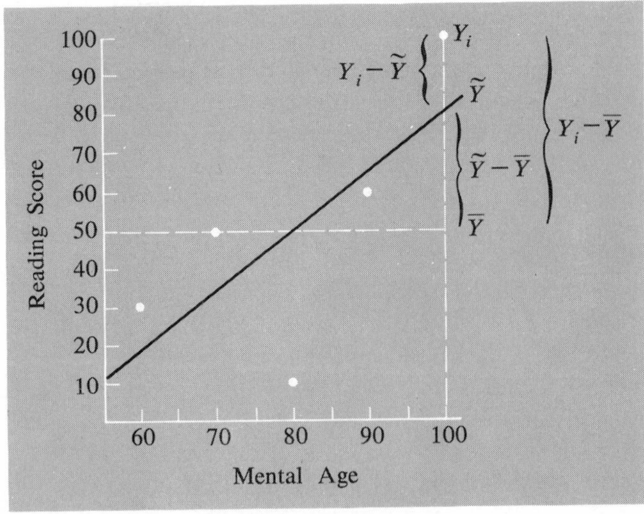

Fig. 6–1. Scatterplot showing three deviations: $(Y_i - \bar{Y})$, $(Y_i - \tilde{Y})$, and $(\tilde{Y} - \bar{Y})$.

Y could be predicted without error from a knowledge of X. No variability in Y would exist that would not be directly predictable from X. Since perfect relationships seldom exist in the social sciences, it will be necessary to examine the nature of the deviations between three points in Figure 6–1 at a given X value: Y_i, the observed point; $\tilde{Y}$, the point on the line predicted on the basis of knowledge of X; and $\bar{Y}$, the mean of the Y_i over all values of X.

Consider the following exercise in attempting to predict Johnny's reading score with no other knowledge at your disposal. In the absence of any additional information, a good estimate of Johnny's reading score would be the mean score for the entire group of children sampled. In the case of the data presented in Figure 6–1, the prediction would be $\bar{Y} = 50$. However, suppose Johnny actually scored 100; then the prediction of 50 would be in error by

$$(Y_i - \bar{Y}) = 100 - 50 = 50$$

Now suppose that one knew that Johnny had a mental age (MA) of 100 and that one also knew the linear relationship between MA and reading score. If one were now asked to predict Johnny's reading score, he would guess the point on the regression line at $X = 100$, namely, $Y = 80$. Again, there would be error in this estimation, in particular

$$(Y_i - \tilde{Y}) = 100 - 80 = 20$$

Notice that although there is still an error, it is less than if $\bar{Y}$ were used to make the prediction. Specifically, the reduction in error is given by

$$(Y_i - \bar{Y}) - (Y_i - \tilde{Y}) = 50 - 20 = 30$$

If the left side of the above expression is simplified, one obtains

$$\begin{aligned}(Y_i - \bar{Y}) - (Y_i - \tilde{Y}) &= Y_i - \bar{Y} - Y_i + \tilde{Y} \\ Y_i - \bar{Y} - Y_i + \tilde{Y} &= (\tilde{Y} - \bar{Y}) \\ (\tilde{Y} - \bar{Y}) &= 80 - 50 = 30\end{aligned}$$

It should be observed that the distance between the point and the mean of the Y_i can be partitioned into two parts:

$$(Y_i - \bar{Y}) = (\tilde{Y} - \bar{Y}) + (Y_i - \tilde{Y})$$

Since $(Y_i - \tilde{Y})$ reflects error still remaining after the prediction with the regression line, $(\tilde{Y} - \bar{Y})$ must represent that segment of $(Y_i - \bar{Y})$ that is associated with X.

However, if one is to speak of variability and proportions of variability, measures of such concepts usually involve squared deviations. It happens that when

$$(Y_i - \bar{Y}) = (\tilde{Y} - \bar{Y}) + (Y_i - \tilde{Y})$$

is squared and summed, all the cross-product terms drop from the expression and the result is

$$\sum(Y_i - \bar{Y})^2 = \sum(\tilde{Y} - \bar{Y})^2 + \sum(Y_i - \tilde{Y})^2$$

This states that the total squared deviations of points about their mean may be partitioned into the sum of two parts. Notice that of the total sum of squared deviations $\sum(Y_i - \bar{Y})^2$, the quantity $\sum(Y_i - \tilde{Y})^2$ represents the squared deviations that still remain after prediction has been made with the regression line. Therefore, $\sum(\tilde{Y} - \bar{Y})^2$ must represent the segment of the total squared deviations in Y_i that indeed are associated with X. Consequently, if $\sum(\tilde{Y} - \bar{Y})^2$ represents the squared deviations in Y associated with X and if $\sum(Y_i - \bar{Y})^2$ represents the total squared deviations in Y, then their ratio

$$\frac{\sum(\tilde{Y} - \bar{Y})^2}{\sum(Y_i - \bar{Y})^2}$$

constitutes the proportion of squared deviations in Y that are associated with differences in X. Often, this ratio is said to express the **proportion of variability** in Y that is associated with differences in X. If the value of the ratio was .55 for the MA-reading example described above, it would mean that 55% of the total variability in reading scores is associated with differences in MA level.

While this ratio indeed provides an index of the degree of relationship by indicating the proportion of variability in Y that is associated with differences in X, it does not reflect the direction of the relationship. Was it positive or negative? That is, were high scores on one variable associated with high scores on the other (positive or direct relationship), or did high scores on one measure relate to low scores on the other (negative or inverse relationship)? Regrettably, since this proportion is a ratio of two positive quantities, it will always be positive. However, consider the fact that although one ordinarily accepts the positive root when one extracts the square root of a number, technically the roots of a number include both a positive and a negative root. Hence, there are really two results in taking the square root of a^2, $+a$ and $-a$, because both $(+a)^2$ and $(-a)^2$ equal a^2. Therefore, one could take the square root of the proportion of variability, accepting the positive root if the relationship between X and Y is positive or the negative root if it is negative.

The **Pearson product moment correlation coefficient,** named after Karl Pearson and symbolized by r, is precisely this quantity:

$$r = \sqrt{\frac{\sum(\tilde{Y} - \bar{Y})^2}{\sum(Y_i - \bar{Y})^2}}$$

Once again the formula which defines a statistic is inconvenient to use in computational work. To use this expression requires that $\tilde{Y}$ be computed for every value of X. However, by substituting the equality ($\tilde{Y} = bX + a$) into the above formula and then substituting the raw-score formulas for both b and a, the above quantity becomes

$$r = \frac{N\sum XY - (\sum X)(\sum Y)}{\sqrt{[N\sum X^2 - (\sum X)^2][N\sum Y^2 - (\sum Y)^2]}}$$

The distinct advantage of this formula, in addition to its ease of computation when large numbers of subjects are involved, is that since the formula for b, the slope of the regression line, was used in its derivation one does not have to be concerned about selecting the positive or negative root to indicate the direction of the relationship. The slope is positive for positive relationships and negative for negative relationships; therefore, since this formula includes the slope, it provides the appropriate sign for r without further labor.

Table 6–1 presents a numerical example of both formulas which yield identical results. The regression line for these data is $\tilde{Y} = .75X + 1.25$.

6–1 Calculation of the Correlation Coefficient.

X	Y	$\bar{Y}$	$\tilde{Y}$	$(Y_i - \bar{Y})^2$	$(Y_i - \tilde{Y})^2$	$(\tilde{Y} - \bar{Y})^2$	X^2	Y^2	XY
9	10	5	8.0	25	4.00	9.00	81	100	90
7	6	5	6.5	1	.25	2.25	49	36	42
5	1	5	5.0	16	16.00	.00	25	1	5
3	5	5	3.5	0	2.25	2.25	9	25	15
1	3	5	2.0	4	1.00	9.00	1	9	3
25	25			46	23.50	22.50	165	171	155

$$r^2 = \frac{\text{Variability Associated with } X}{\text{Total Variability}} = \frac{\sum(\tilde{Y} - \bar{Y})^2}{\sum(Y_i - \bar{Y})^2} = \frac{22.50}{46} = .49$$

$$r = \sqrt{r^2} = \sqrt{.49} = .70$$

Computational Formula

$$r = \frac{N\sum XY - (\sum X)(\sum Y)}{\sqrt{[N\sum X^2 - (\sum X)^2][N\sum Y^2 - (\sum Y)^2]}}$$

$$= \frac{5(155) - (25)(25)}{\sqrt{[5(165) - (25)^2][5(171) - (25)^2]}}$$

$$r = \frac{150}{\sqrt{(200)(230)}} = \frac{150}{\sqrt{46000}} = \frac{150}{214.476} = .70$$

$$r^2 = \text{Proportion of Variance Associated with } X = (.70)^2 = .49$$

$\tilde{Y}$ has been computed for each pair of scores. Columns five through seven yield $\sum(Y_i - \bar{Y})^2$, $\sum(Y_i - \tilde{Y})^2$, and $\sum(\tilde{Y} - \bar{Y})^2$. The square of the correlation coefficient is defined as the proportion of the total variability in Y which is associated with differences in X. In this case $r^2 = .49$. The correlation coefficient, r, is the square root of this value, or .70. In the last three columns of Table 6–1 are the values X^2, Y^2, and XY for use in the computational formula. Again, N is the number of subjects or pairs of scores. These values are substituted into the computational formula, which gives a result of $r = .70$. The square of r is .49, which is the proportion of variance in Y that is associated with differences in X.

properties of the correlation coefficient

THE RANGE OF *r*

The correlation coefficient may assume values from -1 to $+1$. Consider first the case of a perfect linear relationship between X and Y in which the points all fall precisely on a line of non-zero slope (the line is not parallel to the X-axis). In this situation each point Y_i is also a point $\tilde{Y}$, therefore $\sum(\tilde{Y} - \bar{Y})^2$ and $\sum(Y_i - \bar{Y})^2$ are identical, and

$$r = \sqrt{\frac{\sum(\tilde{Y} - \bar{Y})^2}{\sum(Y_i - \bar{Y})^2}} = \sqrt{1} = \pm 1.00$$

Thus, in the case of a perfect relationship the correlation coefficient will equal -1.00 or $+1.00$, depending upon whether the relationship is positive or negative.

Suppose now that there is no relationship between X and Y. The scatterplot may appear to be a rather circular clustering of points (for example, see Figure 6–3C). Here the regression line will be parallel to the X-axis and will be the same line as $\bar{Y}$. Since the two lines, $\tilde{Y}$ and $\bar{Y}$, are identical, then $\sum(\tilde{Y} - \bar{Y})^2$ must be equal to zero, leaving

$$r = \sqrt{\frac{\sum(\tilde{Y} - \bar{Y})^2}{\sum(Y_i - \bar{Y})^2}} = \sqrt{\frac{0}{\sum(Y_i - \bar{Y})^2}} = .00$$

Therefore, when there is no relationship, $r = .00$.

Can r ever be greater than 1.00 or less than -1.00? No, these are the limits of r because it has already been shown that $\sum(\tilde{Y} - \bar{Y})^2$ is always less than or equal to $\sum(Y_i - \bar{Y})^2$ which means that the fraction

$$\frac{\sum(\tilde{Y} - \bar{Y})^2}{\sum(Y_i - \bar{Y})^2}$$

will always be less than or equal to 1.00, and therefore so will r.

Hence, the correlation coefficient ranges in value between -1.00 and $+1.00$. It is ± 1.00 if the points fall precisely on a line of nonzero slope, and it is .00 if there is no relationship at all. If there is no variability in Y_i (they are all the same value), r is not defined. (See Figure 6–3D.)

VARIANCE INTERPRETATION OF r^2

Consider the preceding facts in terms of the proportion of variability of the Y_i that is attributable to X. Suppose there is a grade school composed of children from kindergarten to sixth grade. Consider the heights of these children. Obviously, although this distribution of heights has a mean, most of the scores are not precisely equal to the mean value. They deviate from the mean, and the extent to which they deviate constitutes the total variability in Y_i (in this case, heights). But, careful thought suggests that at least some of this variability in the heights of children is attributable to the fact that the children span a large age range, and there is certainly a relationship between the age of the child and his height. It might be of interest to ask what proportion of the variability in heights is associated with differences in ages. If the figures above were appropriate for this example, $r^2 = .49$ would suggest that 49% of the variability in the heights of the children in the school is attributable to the fact that the children were of different ages. The higher this proportion, the greater the degree of linear relationship between age and height.

Suppose the baby sitter in the example in Chapter 5 had recorded both the hours she worked and the money she earned on sitting jobs over the last year. Obviously, she did not earn the same amount of money each time she sat. That is, there is variability in the per-job return on baby sitting. What proportion of that variability is attributable to the hours worked on each job? If the pairs of points (hours, earnings) were plotted, they would all fall on a straight line with slope equal to the hourly rate. Since the regression line perfectly predicts earnings (Y) from hours worked (X), there is no variability in Y_i which is not predictable from X. Therefore, 100% ($r^2 = 1.00$) of the variability in the Y_i is attributable to X.

Suppose one attempted to relate height and IQ. There is almost no relationship between these variables. The regression line would be horizontal to and $\bar{Y}$ units above the X-axis (i.e., $\tilde{Y} = \bar{Y}$). There is certainly variability in the heights of the subjects in such an observation, but none of this variability is attributable to the fact that the subjects differed in IQ. The fact that 0% of the variability in height is associated with IQ is reflected in the correlation of .00 ($r^2 = .00$, $r = .00$).

THE RELATIONSHIP BETWEEN r AND r^2

It has been said that the square of the correlation coefficient (r^2) may be interpreted as the proportion of variance in Y_i attributable to differences in X.

The correlation coefficient was taken to be the square root of this proportion with the algebraic sign indicating the direction of the relationship. Since r is obviously not the same as r^2, one must exercise caution in interpreting the size of the correlation between two measures. For example, consider the following table:

Correlation: r	Proportion of Variance: r^2
.10	.01
.20	.04
.30	.09
.40	.16
.50	.25
.60	.36
.70	.49
.80	.64
.90	.81
1.00	1.00

Note that a correlation of from .10 to .30 suggests that not very much variance in Y_i is associated with differences in X (1%–9%). In fact, a correlation of .50, which is frequently considered high in psychological and educational research, implies that only 25% of the variance in Y_i is associated with X. That means that 75% of the variability in Y_i is associated with factors other than X (e.g., individual differences, fatigue, etc.). One needs a correlation of .71 before one can say that half of the variability in Y_i is attributable to X. The implication is that in terms of proportion of variance in Y, the **unsquared** correlation coefficient (i.e., r) gives the impression of indicating a higher degree of relationship with X than should be connoted.

THE EFFECT OF ORIGIN AND UNIT UPON *r*

In Chapter 4 it was shown how adding a constant to every score or multiplying every score by a constant affected the value of the mean and variance of that distribution. It was also demonstrated that adding or multiplying (or subtracting and dividing) really amounted to changing the origin and the unit of the measuring scale. An extension of that exercise is to ask what happens to the correlation coefficient if the unit and/or origin of either scale of measurement (X and/or Y) is altered.

The correlation coefficient does not change if every score in either or both distributions is increased or multiplied by a constant.

First consider adding a constant. In the next section it will be shown that (omitting subscripts)

$$r = \frac{\sum(X - \bar{X})(Y - \bar{Y})}{\sqrt{[\sum(X - \bar{X})^2][\sum(Y - \bar{Y})^2]}}$$

If a constant c were added to each X to yield $X + c$ and a constant k were added to each Y to yield $Y + k$,

$$r = \frac{\sum[(X + c) - (\bar{X} + c)][(Y + k) - (\bar{Y} + k)]}{\sqrt{\{\sum[(X + c) - (\bar{X} + c)]^2\}\{\sum[(Y + k) - (\bar{Y} + k)]^2\}}}$$

because adding a constant to every score results in increasing the mean by that constant. But by removing parentheses all the c's and k's subtract out of the expression,

$$r = \frac{\sum(X + \cancel{c} - \bar{X} - \cancel{c})(Y + \cancel{k} - \bar{Y} - \cancel{k})}{\sqrt{[\sum(X + \cancel{c} - \bar{X} - \cancel{c})^2][\sum(Y + \cancel{k} - \bar{Y} - \cancel{k})^2]}}$$

leaving the original formula for r unchanged. Thus, adding or subtracting a constant (c or k may be zero or negative) does not affect the value of r.

Suppose now that every X is multiplied by c and every Y by k (c and k not equal to 0). Recall that if every score is multiplied by a constant the mean of the new distribution equals the constant times the old mean,

$$r = \frac{\sum(cX - c\bar{X})(kY - k\bar{Y})}{\sqrt{[\sum(cX - c\bar{X})^2][\sum(kY - k\bar{Y})^2]}}$$

Remembering that $ab - ac = a(b - c)$ one may reduce this expression to

$$r = \frac{\sum c(X - \bar{X})k(Y - \bar{Y})}{\sqrt{\{\sum[c(X - \bar{X})]^2\}\{\sum[k(Y - \bar{Y})]^2\}}}$$

In the denominator a situation analogous to $(ab)^2 = a^2b^2$ exists. By grouping the constants in front of the summation signs one obtains

$$r = \frac{ck\sum(X - \bar{X})(Y - \bar{Y})}{\sqrt{[c^2\sum(X - \bar{X})^2][k^2\sum(Y - \bar{Y})^2]}}$$

Since $\sqrt{c^2k^2} = ck$,

$$r = \frac{\cancel{c}\cancel{k}\sum(X - \bar{X})(Y - \bar{Y})}{\cancel{c}\cancel{k}\sqrt{[\sum(X - \bar{X})^2][\sum(Y - \bar{Y})^2]}}$$

which leaves the original expression for r unchanged. Therefore, adding or subtracting, multiplying or dividing, or both adding (or subtracting) and multiplying (or dividing) X and/or Y by the same or different nonzero constants does not alter the value of r. More succinctly, r is invariant under transformations of unit and/or origin.

This result has important implications for the use of the correlation coefficient. This fact means that it does not matter if the measurement is in feet or inches, minutes or seconds, units or dozens. The correlation between the variables will be the same. If r indexes the degree of relationship between two variables (e.g., age and height), it must be the case that the degree of association between age and height is the same regardless of whether age is measured in months or years and height is measured in inches or centimeters. It is this property of r which permits using standard scores without altering the size of the correlation. Indeed, the immutability of r to changes in the origin and/or unit of measurement in either one or both of the variables gives this statistic a large range of applications.

THE RELATION BETWEEN CORRELATION AND REGRESSION

slope and correlation Recall the computational formula for the correlation coefficient:

$$r = \frac{N\sum XY - (\sum X)(\sum Y)}{\sqrt{[N\sum X^2 - (\sum X)^2][N\sum Y^2 - (\sum Y)^2]}}$$

By considering the denominator in the same fashion as $\sqrt{ab} = \sqrt{a}\sqrt{b}$ and multiplying the numerator and denominator by $\sqrt{N\sum X^2 - (\sum X)^2}$ one obtains

$$r = \frac{[N\sum XY - (\sum X)(\sum Y)]}{\sqrt{N\sum X^2 - (\sum X)^2}\sqrt{N\sum Y^2 - (\sum Y)^2}} \cdot \frac{\sqrt{N\sum X^2 - (\sum X)^2}}{\sqrt{N\sum X^2 - (\sum X)^2}}$$

which reduces to

$$r = \left(\frac{[N\sum XY - (\sum X)(\sum Y)]}{[N\sum X^2 - (\sum X)^2]}\right)\left(\frac{\sqrt{N\sum X^2 - (\sum X)^2}}{\sqrt{N\sum Y^2 - (\sum Y)^2}}\right)$$

Recalling that

$$b_{yx} = \frac{N\sum XY - (\sum X)(\sum Y)}{N\sum X^2 - (\sum X)^2}$$

and that

$$\frac{s_x}{s_y} = \frac{\sqrt{[N\sum X^2 - (\sum X)^2]/(N-1)}}{\sqrt{[N\sum Y^2 - (\sum Y)^2]/(N-1)}} = \frac{\sqrt{N\sum X^2 - (\sum X)^2}}{\sqrt{N\sum Y^2 - (\sum Y)^2}}$$

one notices that the first fraction in the last expression for r is b_{yx} and that the second is s_x/s_y. Therefore,

$$r = b_{yx}\left(\frac{s_x}{s_y}\right)$$

This expression shows that the correlation coefficient is a joint function of the slope of the regression line and the standard deviations of the two variables. Consequently, the size of r is not simply reflected in the slope of the regression line alone. However, if the scores within the X and Y distributions are converted to standard scores which both have standard deviations of 1, then the formula for the correlation coefficient is

$$r = b_{z_y z_x}$$

In short, when both X and Y distributions are in standard score form, the correlation coefficient is precisely the slope of the regression line. Note, however, that the slope of the line computed with raw scores and the slope computed with standardized scores will not be the same value.

r_{xy} and r_{yx} Ordinarily there will be two regression lines, one for the regression of Y on X and the other for X on Y. However, the correlation coefficient for these two cases is the same. That is, $r_{xy} = r_{yx}$. The truth of this can be readily seen by examining the formula for r:

$$r = \frac{\sum(X - \overline{X})(Y - \overline{Y})}{\sqrt{[\sum(X - \overline{X})^2][\sum(Y - \overline{Y})^2]}}$$

If X and Y are reversed, the formula remains the same.

From an intuitive standpoint this is as it should be. If r is a measure of the degree of relationship between X and Y, the two variables should be related to the same extent regardless of the direction of prediction. Conversely however, the regression lines predict in score units, and if X and Y are not identical scales, then it is reasonable that the regression lines should be different for the two directions of prediction.

$s_{y.x}$ and r The standard error of estimate measures the variability of the data points about the regression line and thus the smaller the $s_{y.x}$ the stronger the linear relationship between X and Y. Further, the stronger the relationship the greater the correlation coefficient. Therefore, it is reasonable to expect that $s_{y.x}$ and r should be related. This association is given by the expression[1]

$$s_{y.x} = s_y\sqrt{1 - r^2}$$

[1] The expression above and the definitional and computational formulas for $s_{y.x}$ given in the previous chapter on regression will yield similar but not identical results. The reason for this discrepancy is that the previous formulas for the sample $s_{y.x}$ have been unbiased estimators of the population standard error. The above formula is not unbiased, but it is presented here because it is used frequently in this form and represents a considerable shortening of computational labor over the previous formulas. Actually, the difference between the two formulas is very small when N is large.

If this expression is transposed so that r^2 is a function of $s_{y.x}$ and s_y, the result is

$$s_{y.x} = s_y\sqrt{1 - r^2}$$

$$\frac{s_{y.x}^2}{s_y^2} = 1 - r^2$$

$$r^2 = 1 - \frac{s_{y.x}^2}{s_y^2}$$

$$r = \sqrt{1 - \frac{s_{y.x}^2}{s_y^2}}$$

This equation states that the size of the relationship as reflected in the correlation coefficient is a function of the relationship between the variability of points about the line (as expressed by $s_{y.x}^2$) and the total variability of the Y scores (s_y^2). More specifically, r will be higher if the fraction

$$\frac{s_{y.x}^2}{s_y^2}$$

is relatively small. In words, the correlation will be high if the variability of the points about the line is small relative to their total variability.

Moreover, since the magnitude of both the $s_{y.x}^2$ and s_y^2 are reflected in a scatterplot, it is possible to judge the relative size of different correlations by observing their graphs.

Consider the graphs in Figure 6–2. Plots A and B have approximately the same variability in Y_i but differ in the extent to which the points cluster about the line. Since the $s_{y.x}$ in A is less than in B, the fraction

$$\frac{s_{y.x}^2}{s_y^2}$$

is smaller and thus the correlation is larger for A than for B. The converse situation is presented in Graphs C and D. The variability of Y_i is greater in D than in C while the $s_{y.x}$ is the same in each. Therefore, the ratio

$$\frac{s_{y.x}^2}{s_y^2}$$

is greater in D than in C, and consequently the correlation is higher in D.

Figure 6–3 provides several examples of different scatterplots with their respective correlation coefficients. Scatterplots A, B, and C reflect the concepts just discussed. Scatterplots D, E, and F represent some interesting special cases. Plot D shows a perfect relationship in the sense of clustering, but one which is maximally imperfect with respect to the variability of Y_i. Here the deviations $\sum(\tilde{Y} - \bar{Y})^2$ and $\sum(Y_i - \bar{Y})^2$ are 0 making $r = \frac{0}{0}$ which is best left as **r is undefined.** This result makes intuitive sense also, because prediction of Y_i is not improved by knowing this relationship since regardless of the X value one

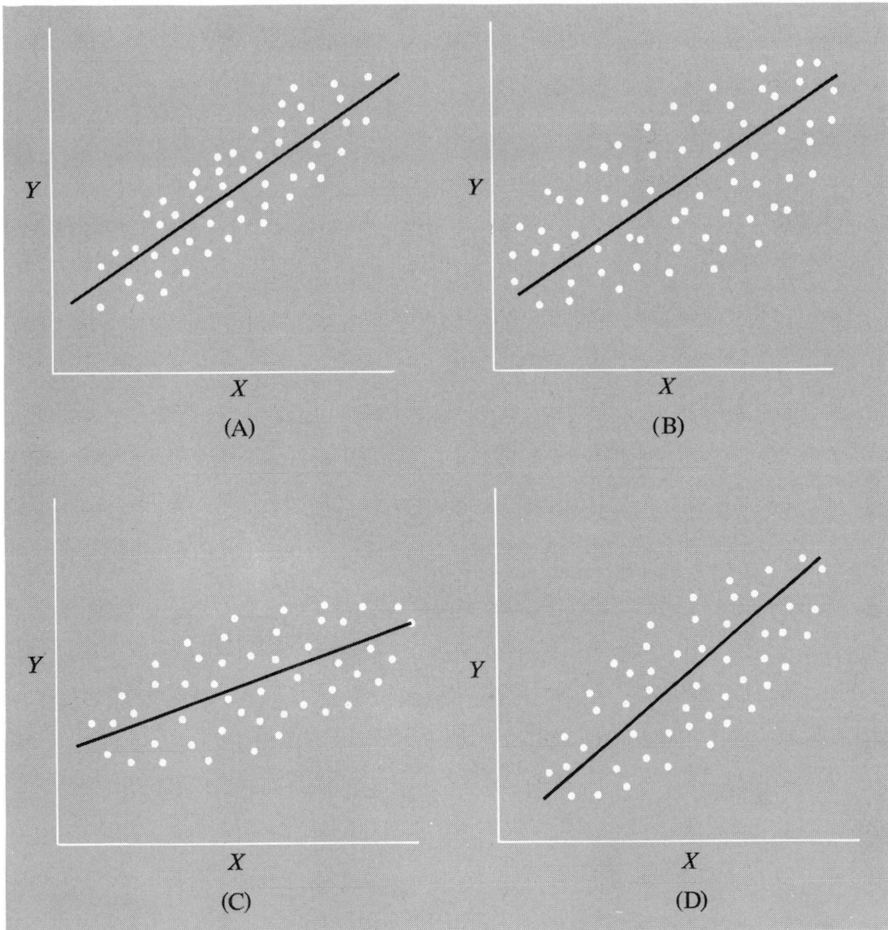

Fig. 6–2. Hypothetical scatterplots. In Graphs A and B the s_y are equivalent but since the $s_{y.x}$ is less in A its correlation is higher. In Graphs C and D, the $s_{y.x}$ are comparable, but since the s_y is greater in D the correlation is higher.

always predicts Y_i to be $\overline{Y}$. Hence, knowledge of the relationship does not assist prediction over using $\overline{Y}$, and the correlation is undefined. However, Plot E shows that if there is perfect clustering of points about a regression line which does not have a slope of 0 (not parallel to the X-axis), then the correlation is 1.00. Plot F depicts the case of a perfect but nonlinear relationship. Depending upon the nature of the curvilinearity, one can obtain r's of various sizes. Thus, it is not valid to conclude that if $r = .00$ there is "no relationship" between X and Y; rather, the conclusion should be that there is no **linear relationship** between X and Y. These facts punctuate the advice to examine the scatterplot before going on with procedures of linear relationship.

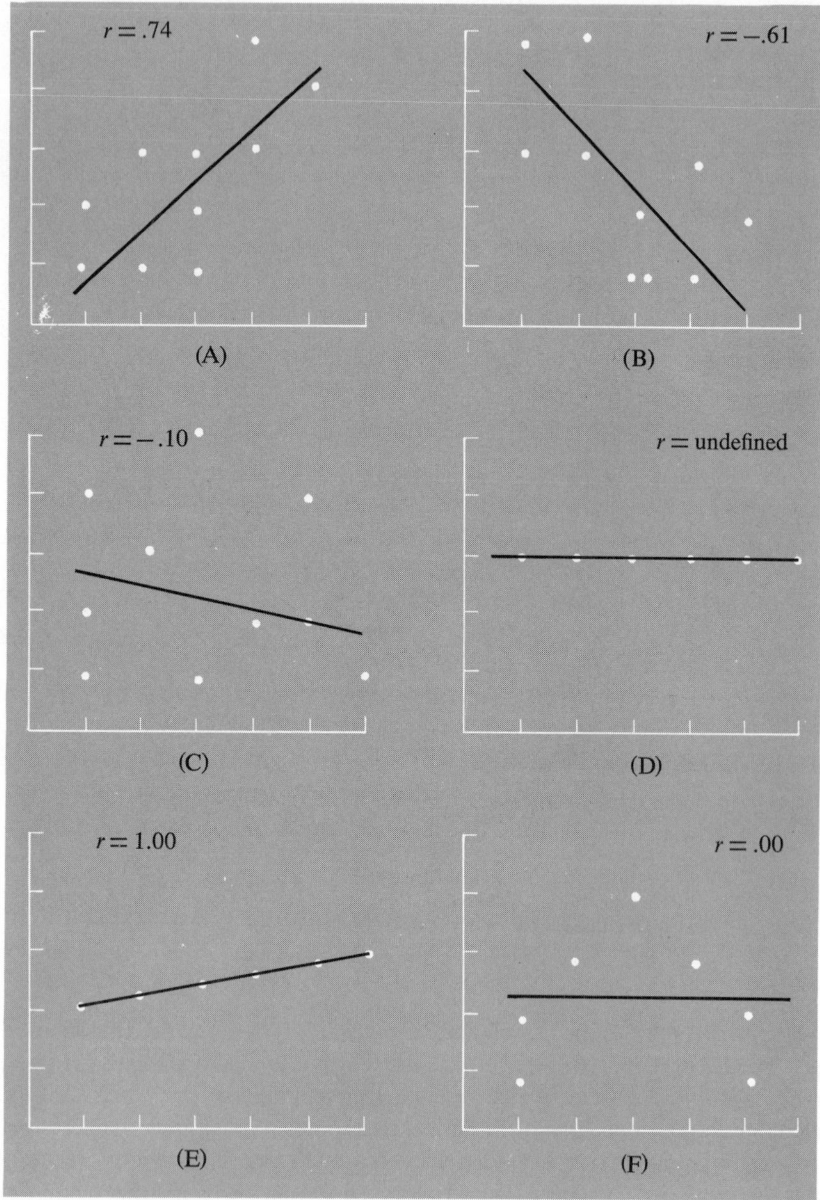

Fig. 6–3. Sample scatterplots with their respective regression lines and correlations.

factors influencing the size of the correlation coefficient

The discussion of correlation up to this point has been concerned with developing a measure of the degree of linear relationship between two variables in a sample. However, in practice one usually wishes to use the sample correlation, r, to estimate the correlation which exists in the larger population whose parameter is symbolized by ρ (pronounced "rho"). The factors mentioned in this section are concerned with the accuracy of r as an estimate of ρ and the factors that determine the size of r.

effect of the range As discussed in a previous section, the size of r is a function of the relative values of $s_{y.x}{}^2$ and $s_y{}^2$ such that r becomes large as $s_y{}^2$ becomes large relative to $s_{y.x}{}^2$. Therefore, if the degree of clustering about the regression line was fairly constant over all segments of the line, then as the range and thus the variance of the Y_i is reduced, the correlation is reduced.

Consider the following example. Suppose a new test of language skills is given to some pupils in grades 1 through 6. Further, the mental age (MA) from a standardized IQ test is also available for each youngster, and the correlation between MA and language skills is computed for the entire sample. A hypothetical plot of this relationship is presented in Figure 6–4. Suppose the cor-

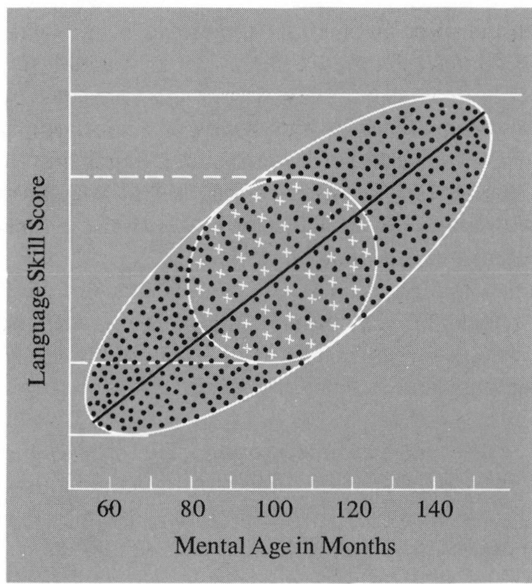

Fig. 6–4. Hypothetical scatterplot showing relatively equal clustering of points about the regression line for a group of pupils and for a subsample of third graders, but a marked reduction in the range of the Y_i for the third graders. The correlation is much larger for the total group than for the subsample.

relation is .76. This result says that for children in grades 1 through 6 the test of language skills is rather closely related to MA. However, now consider the degree of relationship between these two tests just for the third graders. The scores of the third graders are indicated with little X's rather than dots. Notice that for this subsample the variability of the Y_i (amount of vertical dispersion of the scores) is markedly reduced relative to the entire sample. However, the general amount of dispersion about the regression line for the subsample is about equal to that of the entire group of pupils. Since the magnitude of the correlation coefficient is inversely related to the ratio of $s_{y.x}{}^2$ to $s_y{}^2$, the reduction in the variability of the Y_i (i.e., $s_y{}^2$) relative to the dispersion about the line (i.e., $s_{y.x}{}^2$) reduces the size of the correlation coefficient. The correlation for just the third graders might be .28.

Simply put, the size of a correlation is a function of the range (more precisely, the variability) of the Y_i relative to the standard error of estimate. Usually when the sample of scores is restricted, the correlation is less than it would be if the complete range were sampled. The safest course to follow is to limit the interpretation of a correlation to the population from which the sample was drawn. Thus, the correlation of .76 between the test of language skills and MA is appropriate for children in grades 1 through 6, but this figure may not reflect the degree of relationship for children in a portion of that sample (e.g., third graders).

An important application of this fact sometimes occurs when a given test is applied in a new context. Suppose that a test of reading ability is given to children in grades 1 through 6. These scores are correlated with some other criterion of reading competence. A high degree of relationship between the test and the criterion would suggest that the test is a valid indicator of reading ability. Suppose the correlation for the entire sample is .85. Now on the basis of this validity information a reading specialist proposes to use the test on all second graders to single out those students who need special reading instruction. However, when the sample is restricted to second graders, the test may not be nearly as valid as it was for the entire sample. Perhaps, the correlation is only .15 for this subgroup, a figure which would certainly discourage using the test for that particular purpose.

effect of extreme groups The size of r is altered when researchers select extreme groups of subjects in order to compare these groups with respect to certain behaviors. For example, a researcher might select very good and very poor readers in an elementary school in order to evaluate personality factors that may distinguish the groups. In the course of the research an IQ test might be given and the researcher wishes to know the degree of relationship between IQ and reading achievement as measured by a standard reading test. To do so he correlates the two tests, obtaining an $r = .84$. However, since the subjects were either very good or very poor readers, the scores tend to be in two groups as displayed by the dots in Figure 6–5. All the cases which

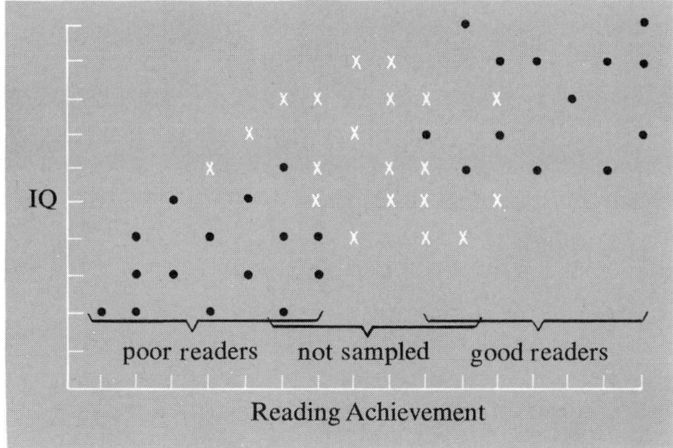

Fig. 6–5. Illustration of a scatterplot for the case in which two extreme groups were selected, poor and good readers (dots). The $r = .84$. The x's indicate students of average reading ability who were not sampled. The r over all subjects is .66. Selection of extreme groups increases r.

would have fallen between these two groups (x's) were eliminated; but if they would have been included in the computation of r, r would equal .66, not .84.

Why should selecting extreme groups on one variable increase the size of r over what would be obtained with more random sampling? This is seen more easily if the following formula for r is considered:

$$r = \frac{\sum(X - \overline{X})(Y - \overline{Y})}{\sqrt{\sum(X - \overline{X})^2 \sum(Y - \overline{Y})^2}}$$

The numerator is composed of the sum of products of the deviation of an X value from its mean and the deviation of a Y value from its mean. Therefore, r becomes large when there are many subjects whose X and Y scores both deviate markedly from their respective means. Consequently, by restricting the sample to extreme groups, one tends to have a disproportionate number of subjects who have scores that deviate considerably from $\overline{X}$ and $\overline{Y}$, respectively. By selecting extreme groups the subjects whose scores would be near the means (which would be located between the two extreme groups) are systematically eliminated, leaving those subjects who have large $(X_i - \overline{X})(Y_i - \overline{Y})$ values to predominate in the group. As a result, the correlation coefficient is likely to be larger than if random sampling had been employed.

combined groups Another caution flag should be waved when the correlation between two variables is computed for subjects who represent a combination of two groups which differ in their mean values on one of the variables. For example, suppose the relationship between mental age and the fear of dying is approximately .10 for a group of first graders but

$-.40$ for sixth graders. However, when the two groups of children are combined into one, the correlation reverses to approximately $+.52$. How is this possible?

Figure 6–6 illustrates what could happen when groups that differ in mean values are combined for the purposes of correlation. The first graders have lower mental ages and are also less concerned with death, and therefore points for them to cluster in the lower left corner of the scatterplot. The correlation between mental age and fear of death within that group is almost zero, $r = .10$. Conversely, the sixth graders have higher mental ages and show considerably more concern about death. Points for them therefore cluster in the upper right corner of the plot. Within this group there is a moderately negative association between mental age and fear of death, $r = -.40$. Now if one considers the scatterplot for these two groups combined it takes on the form of a positive relationship extending from lower left to upper right with two extreme groups to enhance the correlation to $+.52$ which is a highly unrealistic representation of the true state of affairs.[2]

It is quite possible to have any combination of positive and negative correlations between disparate subgroups and the r of their combined group. Figure 6–7 presents some of these possibilities. If the group means are not very different, then combination, while it may change the value of r somewhat, will not do so merely because of the combination itself. If, on the other hand,

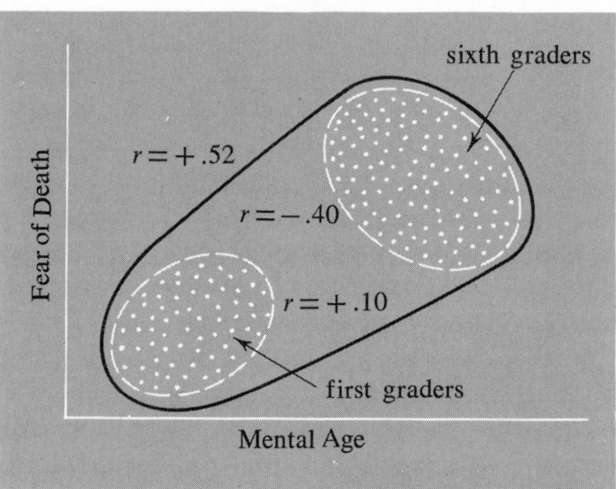

Fig. 6–6. An illustration of how the relationship between mental age and fear of death may be approximately $+.10$ for first graders, $-.40$ for sixth graders, but $+.52$ for these two groups combined.

[2] Although the data on mental age and fear of death are fictitious, they reflect some general trends found in research reported in the following papers: F. C. Jeffers, C. R. Nichols, and C. Eisdorfer, "Attitudes of Older Persons to Death," *Journal of Gerontology*, 1961, XVI, 53–56. A. Mauer, "Adolescent Attitudes toward Death," *Journal of Genetic Psychology*, 1964, CV, 75–90. J. M. Natterson and A. G. Knudson, "Children and Their Mothers: Observations Concerning the Fear of Death in Fatally Ill Children," *Psychosomatic Medicine*, 1960, XXII, 456–465.

the group means are different, the r for the combined sample is not likely to faithfully represent the true situation.

effect of an extreme score Lastly, consider the problem of an extreme case in a sample by examining the scores in Figure 6–8. Most of the scores (dots) cluster in a circular array, but there is one extreme case, x. Without x the correlation is .05, but with it $r = .48$. It is interesting to note, however, that if one of the dots other than x were dropped the correlation would not change a great deal. Thus, only cases which deviate markedly from the general cluster have such a big effect. This is true because the numerator of r contains the expression $\sum(X_i - \overline{X})(Y_i - \overline{Y})$. Therefore, an extreme case can produce a sizeable correlation. Likewise, an extreme case which is deviant from the regression line could also reduce the size of a correlation.

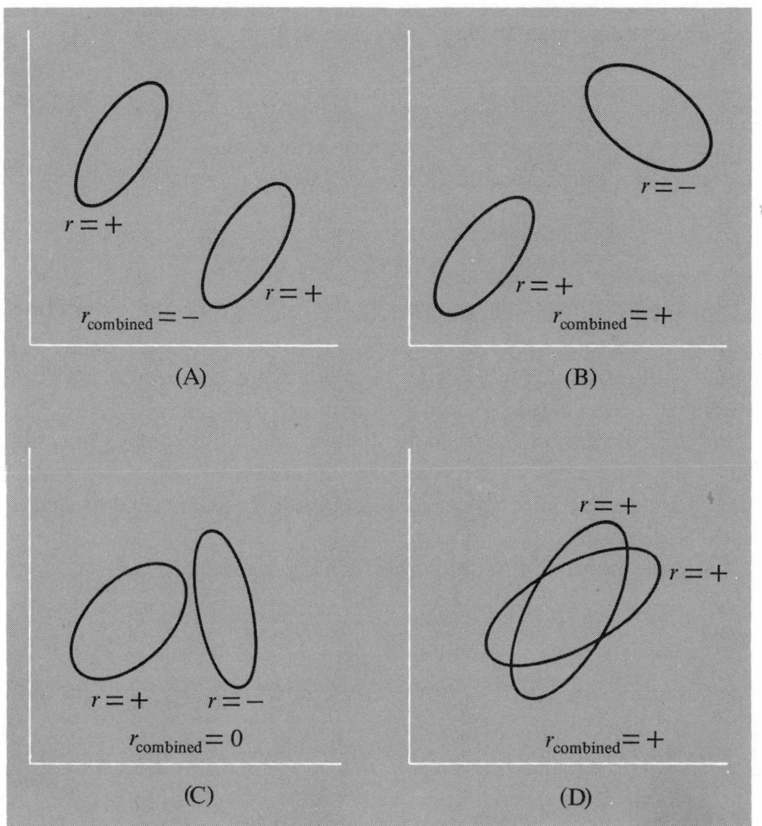

Fig. 6–7. Three examples of what combining two groups of subjects having different means can do to r. Graph D shows that if the two groups have comparable means the r may change somewhat but not merely because of the regrouping.

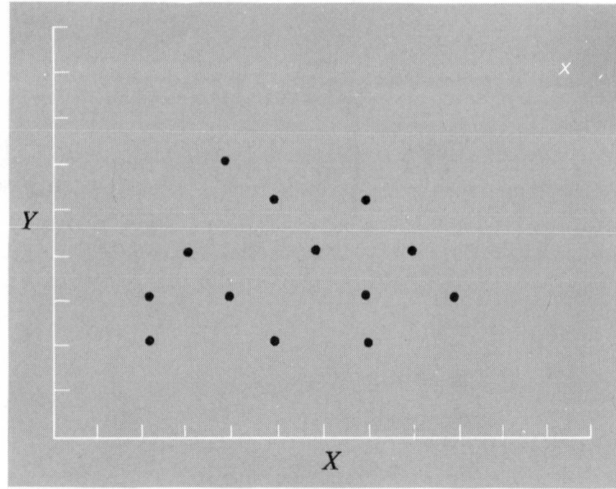

Fig. 6–8. An illustration of the effects of a single extreme case, *x*. Without *x* the correlation is .05, with it $r = .48$.

Ordinarily, if sufficient numbers of cases are sampled in a random manner it is unlikely that such a situation will occur. However, if the sample is small, extreme cases can play a significant role in determining the size of r.

CAUSALITY AND CORRELATION

The correlation coefficient represents the degree of observed association between two variables, not the extent of their causal relationship. Although having a runny nose correlates with having a cold, one would hardly suggest that the runny nose **causes** the cold. We may say that the cold causes the runny nose, but the correlation between runny nose and cold is the same regardless of which way one states it. Because the sun comes up when we wake in the morning does not prompt the megalomaniacal delusion that our getting up causes the sun to rise.

If A correlates with B, three possible causal relationships exist:

A causes B,
B causes A, or
C causes both A and B.

Of course, C may be quite remote with long causal chains interposed before A and B actually occur, but the point is that the possibility that a third variable may produce an observed relationship between A and B implies that one can never infer causality between two variables solely on the basis of their correlation.

This fact has loomed important in certain popular controversies. For example, in the early days of the smoking and cancer issue, it was reported that there was a correlation between the amount of smoking and the likelihood of lung cancer. These data do not compel the conclusion that smoking causes lung cancer. Smoking might do that, but some other factor could cause both the tendency to smoke and the predisposition of the organism toward lung cancer. For example, it may be that relatively nervous people tend to smoke and the more nervous the person, the more he smokes. Further, it could be the case (at least for the purposes of illustration) that nervousness tends to produce a high level of a certain chemical in the person's physiological system that predisposes him toward lung cancer. Thus, it could be the case that nervousness leads both to heavy smoking and a predisposition to lung cancer, and that there is no causal relationship at all between smoking and cancer. Therefore, it must be remembered that a correlation suggests covariation but not necessarily causality.

COMPUTATIONAL PROCEDURES

Although this and previous chapters contain several computational examples, they have been presented as illustrations of isolated techniques. In practice, it is often the case that many of the statistics presented in the last several chapters are computed within the context of a single problem. When this is done, certain computational conveniences are available which facilitate this task. Therefore, Table 6–2 presents an integrated example that displays the calculation of several statistics and also illustrates a short cut for the computational labor. The task is facilitated if three subquantities are computed first:

$$\text{(I)}\ N\sum X^2 - \left(\sum X\right)^2$$
$$\text{(II)}\ N\sum Y^2 - \left(\sum Y\right)^2$$
$$\text{(III)}\ N\sum XY - \left(\sum X\right)\left(\sum Y\right)$$

The table demonstrates how these three subquantities can be used to simplify the computation of the variance, slope, standard error of estimate, and correlation coefficient.

FORMULAS

1. Pearson Product Moment Correlation

$$r = \sqrt{\frac{\sum(\tilde{Y} - \bar{Y})^2}{\sum(Y_i - \bar{Y})^2}} \qquad \text{(definitional formula)}$$

r^2 = proportion of Y variance associated with differences in X.

$$r = \frac{N\sum X_iY_i - (\sum X_i)(\sum Y_i)}{\sqrt{[N\sum X_i^2 - (\sum X_i)^2][N\sum Y_i^2 - (\sum Y_i)^2]}} \qquad \text{(computational formula)}$$

6–2 Complete Computational Example for Several Concepts in Chapters 2 to 6.

Raw Data

SAT	Grades
$\sum X = 3066$	$\sum Y = 8.60$
$(\sum X)^2 = 9400356$	$(\sum Y)^2 = 73.96$
$\sum X^2 = 1919198$	$\sum Y^2 = 22.40$
$N = 5$	$N = 5$

$$\sum XY = 5751.8$$

Intermediate Quantities

$$\text{(I)}\ N\sum X^2 - (\sum X)^2 = 5(1919198) - 9400356 = 195634$$
$$\text{(II)}\ N\sum Y^2 - (\sum Y)^2 = 5(22.40) - 73.96 = 38.04$$
$$\text{(III)}\ N\sum XY - (\sum X)(\sum Y) = 5(5751.8) - (3066)(8.6) = 2391.40$$

Statistical Computations

$$\overline{X} = \frac{\sum X}{N} = \frac{3066}{5} = 613.20$$

$$s_x^2 = \frac{N\sum X^2 - (\sum X)^2}{N(N-1)} = \frac{\text{(I)}}{N(N-1)} = \frac{195634}{5(4)} = 9781.70$$

$$s_x = \sqrt{s_x^2} = \sqrt{9781.70} = 98.90$$

$$\overline{Y} = \frac{\sum Y}{N} = \frac{8.6}{5} = 1.72$$

$$s_y^2 = \frac{N\sum Y^2 - (\sum Y)^2}{N(N-1)} = \frac{\text{(II)}}{N(N-1)} = \frac{38.04}{5(4)} = 1.90$$

$$s_y = \sqrt{s_y^2} = \sqrt{1.90} = 1.38$$

continued

2. Correlation and Regression

$r = b_{yx}\left(\frac{s_x}{s_y}\right)$ (r in terms of slope and variance)

$r = b_{z_y z_x}$ (standard score version of relationship between r and slope)

$r = \sqrt{1 - \frac{s_{y.x}^2}{s_y^2}}$ (r in terms of the variability about the line ($s_{y.x}^2$) relative to the total variability in $Y(s_y^2)$)

6-2 continued

Regression of Y on X

$$b_{yx} = \frac{N(\sum XY) - (\sum X)(\sum Y)}{N\sum X^2 - (\sum X)^2} = \frac{\textbf{(III)}}{\textbf{(I)}} = \frac{2391.4}{195634} = .012$$

$$a_{yx} = \bar{Y} - b\bar{X} = 1.72 - .012(613.20) = -5.638$$

$$\tilde{Y} = b_{yx}X + a_{yx} = .012X - 5.638$$

$$s_{y.x} = \sqrt{\left[\frac{1}{N(N-2)}\right]\left[N\sum Y^2 - (\sum Y)^2 - \frac{[N\sum XY - (\sum X)(\sum Y)]^2}{N\sum X^2 - (\sum X)^2}\right]}$$

$$= \sqrt{\left[\frac{1}{N(N-2)}\right]\left[\textbf{(II)} - \frac{\textbf{(III)}^2}{\textbf{(I)}}\right]}$$

$$= \sqrt{\frac{1}{5(3)}\left[38.04 - \frac{(2391.4)^2}{195634}\right]} = \sqrt{.5873}$$

$$s_{y.x} = .77$$

If $X = 620$, predicted Y:

$$\tilde{Y} = .012(620) - 5.638 = 1.80$$

95% of such cases would fall within the interval:

$$\tilde{Y} \pm 1.96s_{y.x} = 1.80 \pm 1.96(.77) \text{ or } .29 \text{ to } 3.31$$

Correlation

$$r = \frac{N(\sum XY) - (\sum X)(\sum Y)}{\sqrt{[N\sum X^2 - (\sum X)^2][N\sum Y^2 - (\sum Y)^2]}} = \frac{\textbf{(III)}}{\sqrt{\textbf{(I)(II)}}}$$

$$= \frac{2391.40}{\sqrt{(195634)(38.04)}}$$

$$r = .88$$

EXERCISES

1. Below are three scores for each of 9 subjects. Compute the correlation between A and B, A and C, and B and C. Add 5 to each score in Distribution A and then multiply each score by 2. Recompute the correlation between A and B. Explain the effect of changing scales on the correlation.

Subject	A	B	C
1	2	1	8
2	3	3	6
3	3	5	4
4	8	6	2
5	10	7	0
6	5	4	6
7	7	9	3
8	9	5	5
9	6	6	4

2. Compute the following correlation. Then add the score pair (12, 8) and recompute. Why does adding one score change the correlation so much? Can you think of other pairs of scores which would alter the situation in a different direction? Illustrate.

X	Y
2	2
2	3
3	4
4	3
4	6
5	2
5	5

3. If children are divided into two groups containing just the top 50 and bottom 50 children on a First Grade Readiness Test in a school of 500 such children, why might the relationship between IQ and leadership potential as determined by a specially designed test be unreasonably high relative to that obtained on the complete group of 500?

4. What squared deviations are said to compose the "variability" associated with differences in X? Explain the logic of this reasoning.

5. Why are there usually two regression lines but only one correlation for a pair of variables, X and Y?

6. If the point $(\overline{X}, \overline{Y})$ is (15, 25), why does a pair of scores such as (50, 85) seem to influence the regression and correlation between X and Y more than a pair of scores on the order of (10, 22)?

7. Explain why the correlation coefficient is identical to the slope of the regression line if the scores are in standard score form but that this is not the case if raw scores are used.

8. In what way is the ratio of the variability about the regression line relative to the total variability in the Y_i related to the value of r?

9. Discuss and explain whether or not the following combination of values are possible or impossible:
   (a) $N = 2$, $s_{y.x} = 2.5$, $r = .00$
   (b) $N = 25$, $b = .80$, $s_{y.x} = 0$, $r = .65$
   (c) $N = 30$, $b = -.80$, $a = 10$, $r = .70$
   (d) $N = 30$, $r_{xy} = .0$, $r_{xw} = .90$, $r_{yw} = .15$
   (e) $N = 30$, $\overline{X} = 0$, $s_x = 1$, $\overline{Y} = 0$, $s_y = 1$, $b = .60$, $r = .40$
   (f) $r = .50$ for $N = 8$, but r would be $-.30$ if one more score were added

7

introduction to hypothesis testing

In the first six chapters of this book methods have been presented that aid in summarizing and describing groups of measurements. This material is part of **descriptive statistics.** Attention is now turned to another part of statistics: **inferential statistics.**

overview of probability[1]

The purpose of inferential statistics is to assist in making inferences and judgments about what exists on the basis of only partial evidence. This is accomplished by using probability. In a way, most people use probability every day. A college boy observes a girl in one of his classes and concludes that she is "likely" to be his type and so asks her for a date. The weatherman reports there is a 70% chance of rain tomorrow, and the sports reporter states that odds on Fleet Foot in the fourth race at Belmont are 3:2. In each of these examples a statement of probability is made on the basis of only partial evidence. The college girl in the first example may have responded a certain way to class discussion, dressed with a particular flair, and interacted with classmates in a manner that attracted the young man. On the basis of this fragmentary evidence,

[1] The first portion of this chapter is a relatively non-technical discussion of what is meant by a probabilistic statement and the relationship between probability and theoretical relative frequency. This section is primarily designed to provide only enough probability for one to be able to understand the chapters on statistical inference that follow. Chapter 12 is devoted to a more detailed consideration of topics in probability for those who wish to emphasize this aspect of statistics.

he supposes the likelihood that she would be a good date is sufficiently high for him to ask her out. In actuality, she may not be his type at all, but at the time, based upon this limited amount of information, there is a certain probability that she might be. The weatherman's statement that there is a 70% chance of rain tomorrow is based upon weather data existing today and the principles of weather change. The prediction of a 70% chance of rain tomorrow really implies a hypothetical collection of many many days with weather like today. Given this large number of theoretical instances, 70% of the tomorrows would have rain.

In scientific research, probability statements are also used to make inferences and judgments on the basis of only partial information. For example, a social psychologist was interested in the extent to which people could be made to inflict pain on a colleague by the application of social pressure to conform.[2] The social psychologist's experiment was structured so that a male "subject" would join three other men in what was described as an important learning experiment. In this experiment the subject and two other fellows were to teach the third person a simple laboratory task by administering electric shock to the "learner" for his incorrect responses. Actually, though unknown to the subject, the three other people were collaborators of the experimenter. In fact the entire situation, shock, learning, etc., was staged for the subject. Forty subjects were urged by their "colleagues" to turn up the purported shock level as high as possible because it "was essential to the experiment." The "learner" grimaced and squirmed in accordance with the level of shock the subject thought he was administering. Another 40 subjects were not pressured to elevate the presumed shock level. The results showed that those subjects who were not admonished by their colleagues to turn up the shock set their shock controls at an average intensity reading of approximately 3.5 arbitrary units while those subjects who were pressured averaged a shock level of approximately 14 arbitrary units, even though the "learner" screamed and gyrated in response to this much "shock." This experiment showed that for the subjects tested, social pressure seemed to result in the administration of almost three times as much "shock" than if no social pressure was applied.

But, is this result generally true? That is, would the same thing happen if another 80 subjects were recruited and the experiment repeated? The subjects that did participate were sampled from a variety of ages and occupations. Is one to conclude from this experiment that **men in general** behave this way in the face of social pressure? Although the results of the experiment were emphatic, not all "control subjects" administered 3.5 units of "shock" and not all pressured subjects raised the presumed shock to a level of 14. In short, the result of the experiment could have been just a "chance" finding, and if the study were repeated one might obtain a totally different outcome. If this were so, then it would certainly not be fair to infer from this one experiment that on the average

[2] S. Milgram, "Group Pressure and Action against a Person," *Journal of Abnormal and Social Psychology*, 1964, LXIX, 137–143.

men generally will yield to social pressure and inflict pain upon another in the way and to the extent that was reported.

The problem of making inferences of the kind just described could be solved by repeating the experiment and observing whether the same general result occurs. But even if a similar outcome were found in two separate experiments, an incredulous reader might demand a third or a fourth replication. After all, if a coin comes up heads three times in a row, one does not immediately conclude that the coin is loaded or biased. Then, how many replications are necessary before one can be sufficiently confident of the result to warrant the inference that on the average men will yield to social pressure in this kind of a situation? Also, is the difference between 3.5 and 14 big enough to demand the conclusion that, on the average, pressured subjects will turn the shock up higher than non-pressured subjects? How big a difference must there be before one is willing to make the inference that social pressure is a determinant of the extent to which men will inflict pain on others?

In view of these questions, the outcome of a single experiment constitutes only limited and ambiguous evidence about whether the results would be the same or similar for a much larger group of people (or events) than were actually used in the experiment. It would be convenient to have a single numerical index that reflects the uncertainty or ambiguity in deciding upon one prediction or another about what is true for groups larger than the group actually observed. This quantification of uncertainty is conveyed numerically by **probability.** Scientists prefer to use this numerical index of the likelihood of events rather than their personal and subjective feelings of how probable something is. The numerical probability is public knowledge (all scientists can observe and understand it), the probability of one event can be easily compared with the probability of a different event, and certain conventions can be adopted about how high or low the probability must be in order to make one decision or another. Therefore, a knowledge of the concept of probability is essential to understanding the process of inference and decision making in science.

THE CONCEPT OF PROBABILITY

Everyone has some notion of what the concept of probability means as evidenced by our frequent use of the words "likely," "probably," "plausible," etc. At the start of a football game the official flips a coin and everyone assumes that the chances are equal for a head or a tail; that is, the probability of a head is $\frac{1}{2}$ or .50.

If one considers the probability of rolling a five with a fair die, the reasoning is as follows: There are six faces, one of which satisfies the required event (namely obtaining a five). The probability of a five is one in six, $\frac{1}{6}$, or .17. The probability of selecting an ace from an ordinary deck of 52 cards is $\frac{4}{52}$ because there are 52 equally likely possible outcomes, four of which will satisfy the event, drawing an ace.

The determination of a simple probability really implies an **idealized sort of experiment.** In flipping a coin, one actually assumes an experiment in which the coin was tossed over and over again. There are two possible outcomes to a single flip of a coin: a head or a tail. It is assumed that both results are equally likely. On any single throw, either a head or a tail will occur, but over the long range of such flips of a coin, the ratio of heads to all possible outcomes will approach $\frac{1}{2} = .50$. Similarly in drawing a card from a deck, a single draw will result in either an ace or not an ace, but over many many draws the ratio of aces to all other possible outcomes will approach $\frac{4}{52} = \frac{1}{13}$.

In an idealized experiment with a specified number of outcomes, the ratio of the number of outcomes composing an event A relative to the total number of possible outcomes in the experiment approaches the probability of A as the idealized experiment is repeated indefinitely. If the probability of A is symbolized by $P(A)$, the number of outcomes in event A by $\#(A)$, and the total number of outcomes in the idealized experiment by $\#(S)$, then

$$P(A) = \frac{\#(A)}{\#(S)}$$

To illustrate the use of these terms, consider the probability of obtaining a three or higher in a single roll of a die. The idealized experiment is the rolling of a single die. There is a total of six equally likely possible outcomes of such an experiment (e.g., 1, 2, 3, 4, 5, 6), four of which are included in the event A of obtaining a three or higher (e.g., 3, 4, 5, 6). Thus, the number of outcomes composing A is $\#(A) = 4$, and the total number of outcomes in the experiment is $\#(S) = 6$. If the idealized experiment is repeated indefinitely, then the probability of rolling a three or higher is

$$P(A) = \frac{\#(A)}{\#(S)} = \frac{4}{6} = .67$$

There are several points to note about the concept of probability. First, the **probability of an impossible event is 0,** because there would be no outcome that would satisfy the required event (i.e., $\#(A) = 0$). The probability of drawing a joker from a standard deck of 52 cards is

$$P(\text{joker}) = \frac{\#(\text{jokers})}{\#(\text{cards})} = \frac{0}{52} = 0$$

Second, the **probability of drawing any of the possible outcomes is 1.00** because

$$P(\text{any outcome}) = \frac{\#(\text{outcomes})}{\#(\text{outcomes})} = 1.00$$

Therefore, the probability of an event falls someplace between 0 and 1.00.

Third, a **probability statement is always predictive and reflects the ratio of outcomes over the continued repetitions of an idealized experiment.** It is predictive because once it is known that the coin turned up heads, it is no longer probable, it is certain that the coin came up heads. The failure to understand that a probability statement is essentially predictive is illustrated by the golfer who stands sopping wet on the fifth tee cursing the weather man because he predicted showers with a probability of .30. Conceptually, probability is based upon the repeated execution of an idealized experiment and does not reflect what will happen on a single trial of that experiment. For example, the probability of a head in a given coin toss is .50, but everyone knows that the coin decisively will be either heads or tails, not .50 heads. Therefore, when a doctor advises a patient that the probability that some proposed surgery will be successful is .15, the doctor means that in all cases like this 15% of the patients would be cured. But this individual patient will either be cured or not. Therefore, the probability statement applies to a predicted outcome and it reflects the proportion of such circumstances in which a given outcome would occur in the long run. Once the event transpires, it is no longer probable.

Lastly, there is a subtle assumption that in the course of repeating the idealized experiment over and over again that all of the possible causes and combination of causes are appropriately reflected in the collection of results. This is what is meant by the word **chance** or **random.** In flipping a coin over and over again, one makes the assumption for the idealized experiment that all the possible causes that determine the results of coin flips are represented in the experiment an appropriate proportion of the time.

PROBABILITY AND RELATIVE FREQUENCY

By now the reader must have noticed a close association between the determination of probability and the concept of relative frequency introduced in Chapter 2. Recall that theoretical relative frequency is the relative frequency of score values in a distribution that is based upon unlimited sampling. In a sense, it is the distribution of relative frequencies of the results of an idealized experiment based upon an unlimited number of cases. Therefore:

> In an idealized experiment, the probability of an event A equals the theoretical relative frequency of A.

One of the principal implications of such a statement is that a theoretical relative frequency distribution of possible outcomes may be used to determine the probability of different sets of events. For example, suppose Figure 7–1 represents the theoretical relative frequency distribution of IQ of 10-year-old American children. Now consider the probability that a child selected at random from this population would have an IQ greater than 110. According to the conception of probability discussed above in the preceding material, this probability value should be given by the theoretical relative frequency of scores exceeding 110. The approach to determining the probability here rests on equating the **area** (shaded portion) existing between the curve and the abscissa with the concept of **theoretical relative frequency.** For example, the area represented by the shaded portions of the figure constitutes the relative frequencies of all possible outcomes. It has been noted previously (in Chapter 2 and in the preceding material) that the theoretical relative frequency of all events is 1.00. Now, if the shaded portions under the curve in Figure 7–1 represent theoretical relative frequency, then that proportion of it existing between 110 and $+\infty$ (indicated in the figure by cross-hatching) symbolizes the theoretical relative frequency of children having scores greater than 110. Therefore:

> The proportion of the total area under the curve of a theoretical relative frequency distribution that exists between any two points represents the probability of obtaining the events contained within the interval determined by those two points.

For example, consider the probability that a child randomly selected from the population would have an IQ between 85 and 115. This probability is given by

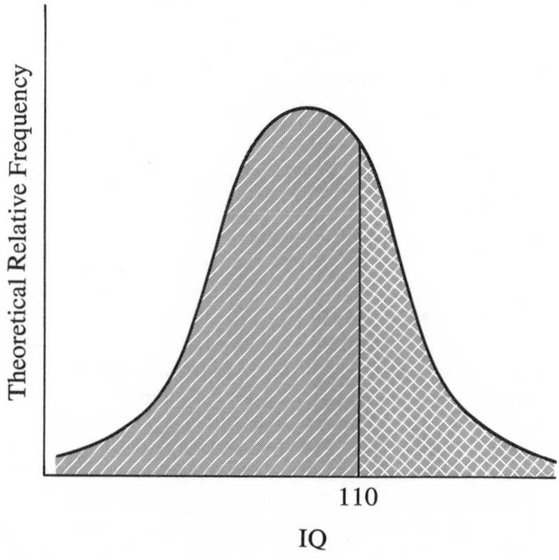

Fig. 7–1. The theoretical relative frequency of the IQ's of 10-year-old American children. The probability of a randomly selected child who has an IQ higher than 110 is indicated by the proportion of the total shaded area represented by the cross-hatched area.

the proportion of the total area that exists between IQ's of 85 and 115 as illustrated in Figure 7–2.

A common example of a theoretical relative frequency distribution is the standard normal distribution (z) described in Chapter 4. The z distribution as presented in Table A of Appendix II is a theoretical relative frequency distribution for the normal distribution based upon unlimited samplings having $\mu = 0$ and $\sigma = 1$. The percentiles listed in Table A correspond not only to the proportion of cases existing between two points but also to the probability of obtaining the score values located between these two points. There are many theoretical relative frequency distributions such as the standard normal whose percentiles are determined and tabled. These distributions will form the basis for making probabilistic statements as outlined in the remainder of this book[3]

EXERCISES

1. Determine the following probabilities:
   (a) Drawing an ace from a deck of 52 playing cards.
   (b) Rolling a two or a one with a die.
   (c) Rolling less than a four with a die.
   (d) Obtaining either a head or a tail in a single flip of a coin.
   (e) Drawing a face card (jack, queen, or king) from a deck of 52 cards.

2. If IQ is distributed normally in the population with a mean of 100 and a standard deviation of 15, what is the probability of randomly selecting a person with an IQ
   (a) of 115 or greater?
   (b) between 90 and 110?
   (c) within two standard deviations on either side of the mean?
   (d) between 95 and 110?
   (e) of either less than 70 or more than 130?

Note: Just as in the examples in Chapter 4, the scores mentioned in Exercise 2 above are conceived to be exactly 115.00, 90.00, 95.00, and 110.00. Although this procedure is most often employed when doing these kinds of problems, a curious result occurs when the question asks for the probability of obtaining a score of exactly 115.00 (as opposed to an interval of scores). The answer is .00, because the amount of area over a single point on a continuous scale is usually considered to be zero. If in fact there are an infinite number of possible scores, the probability of obtaining any single one of them is zero. In practice, however, an IQ score of 115 is considered to represent the interval 114.5 to 115.5, and when this interval is used a nonzero result is obtained. The probability of getting a single score seldom arises in practice, and questions posed in this text can be satisfactorily answered without using real limits.

[3] The equation for a theoretical relative frequency distribution, such as the standard normal and several other distributions to be considered, is known as a **probability** or **density function.** To determine the probability of the occurrence of events located between any two points on the dimension, this function is integrated between these points by the methods of calculus. The values in Table A and other tables in this book represent the results of such a process.

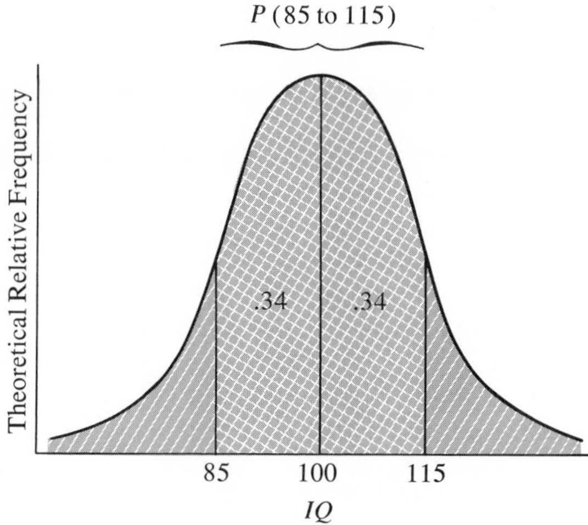

Fig. 7–2. The proportion of the total shaded area that is cross-hatched represents the probability of randomly selecting a child with an IQ between 85 and 115.

sampling and sampling distributions

The task of statistical inference is to make a decision about what exists in a large group of cases (i.e., the population) on the basis of observations made from a small subset of cases (i.e., the sample). Since estimations are to be made from information provided by the sample, the methods used to select this subset of cases are vital to the accuracy of inference. Further, one of the fundamental problems involved in making such decisions is that if another sample were selected, it would likely yield results that are different from those of the first sample. Assuming all experimental conditions were the same for the two samples, this disparity in results from one sample to another is a function of the fact that the same subjects are not involved in each instance. In terms of estimating what is true in the population, this variability of results is "error," and it will be necessary to have a measure of this "sampling error."

METHODS OF SAMPLING

Recall that a **population** is an identifiable group of individuals or events. Characteristics of populations are known as **parameters.** A subset of a population is a **sample,** and quantities computed on a sample are called **statistics.** Often a statistic is used to estimate the value of a parameter. Although unbiasedness has been discussed as one attribute of a good estimator, a statistic used to estimate a parameter is no better than the sample upon which it is computed.

One type of sampling is simple random sampling.

> A **simple random sample** is one in which all elements of the population have an equal probability of being selected.

Suppose you wanted a random sample of students at your university for an opinion poll on the quality and appropriateness of their educational experience. You might obtain a list of all students in the school, go to a **random number table,** and select a sample of 50. A random number table (Table J) is located in Appendix II of this book and consists of rows and columns of random numbers. The numbers are random in the sense that for any single digit position, each of the 10 numbers between 0 and 9 had an equal opportunity to occupy that position. This means that every digit was selected independently of every other digit. Further, not only are all the single digits "random," but all two-, three-, or N-digit numbers are also "random."

It should be observed that if you read down a one-digit column in the table you may feel that these numbers are not very random at all. This is because what most people regard as random is not what "random" in the statistical sense means. For example, if you were to write what you thought was a random sequence of 0's and 1's, you might write 01001001011101, etc. Most people are very hesitant to put more than three of a kind (e.g., 000 or 111) in a row. Yet, in any random selection of four 0 and 1 digits, the probability of 0000 or 1111 is .125 or 125 in every 1000 such sets of four. Look at the first column of numbers in the random number table and observe such a statistically random sequence by letting even numbers be "0" and odd numbers be "1".

To use the table in getting a sample of 50 from a list of 3000 students, assign each student a number between 1 and 3000. Then go to the random number table and mentally block the table off into four-digit columns. Read down the columns until you obtain 50 four-digit numbers that fall between 0001 and 3000 inclusive. The students assigned numbers corresponding to these 50 numbers constitute a randomly selected sample.

In most cases described in this text, **independent random sampling** is required. Although a formal definition of independence is not given until Chapter 12, independence in sampling implies that the selection of any element for inclusion in the sample does not alter the likelihood of drawing any other element of the population into the sample. In almost all cases in which random sampling is required in this text, the implication is that the elements have been independently selected.[4]

[4] Sometimes it is important for an investigator to insure that certain segments of the population are represented in the sample. The political pollsters, for example, attempt to sample the voting public in such a way that each area of the country, each ethnic group, each religious sect, etc. is appropriately represented. Thus, if 10% of the population is Catholic, 10% of the sample would be randomly selected from Catholic voters. Such a sample is called a **proportional stratified random sample.** Since all of the procedures outlined in this text are appropriate for random samples, stratified sampling and its associated statistical procedures will not be considered further.

Since random sampling is the basis for most of the procedures of statistical inference discussed in this text, it would be wise to consider the characteristics of samples that actually are taken in research. For example, suppose one wanted to sample the population of a given town by selecting every two hundredth name in the telephone book. Would this be a random sample of townsfolk, i.e., does each person in the town have an equal opportunity to be selected? This would not be a random sample of townsfolk since people who do not own a phone are systematically excluded by this procedure. Now there are two things one can do to correct the situation. First, a list of all people could be obtained from the city government or census bureau, and the random number table employed. But, this might be a very time-consuming task, and it assumes the availability of the necessary list of all people in the town. The second possibility is to change the definition of the population in accordance with the nature of the sample. Since you cannot get a random sample of "all town people," change the population to "all telephone-owning town people" and discuss the results and conclusions in terms of this group rather than in terms of all residents. The important point is for the researcher to be aware of a possible discrepancy between the population he wants to talk about and the population for which the sample is appropriate.

The tediousness of obtaining a truly random sample is so inhibiting that researchers frequently do not select random samples, but treat their samples statistically as if they were random. For example, a group of rats provided by an animal supplier is not a random selection of rats. Rats are raised in cages set on tiers, some of which are closer to the light than others, and the amount of illumination in the rat's rearing experience can influence some later behavior. Further, when the rats arrive at the laboratory and are assigned to experimental groups, it is sometimes tempting to place the first 10 in one group, the second 10 in the next, etc. But, it happens that the more curious and active rats frequently come over to the side of the shipping box when it is opened. These rats are more accessible and easier to pick up. They are thus selected first and go into the first group if the above procedure is carried out. It is a good idea to use a random number table to determine group assignments, or at least to alternate by assigning one rat to the first group, the next to the second, etc.

Another form of bias in sampling occurs when volunteers are used. College students who volunteer for experiments are probably somewhat different in terms of academic concern, motivation, etc., than those students who do not volunteer. Who volunteers can be an interesting issue in its own right, and it determines what kind of research can and cannot be done. For example, some developmental psychologists are dependent upon mothers to volunteer their infants for observation. It is likely that highly-educated mothers are more receptive to "science's need for subjects" than are more minimally educated mothers. Thus, the sample one obtains is not random because it may contain a preponderance of highly educated families.

How can one safeguard against such bias in one's sample? The best way is simply to be cautious, well read, and aware of what one is doing. In addition, it is advisable to measure the sample you have selected on several dimensions (e.g., age, education, "normality," etc.) appropriate to the research (as long as the measurement of these traits does not influence the subjects in any way) so that readers can judge whether this sample has characteristics similar to the population you want to discuss. The guiding principle is to insure that inferences and generalizations are made to the appropriate population.

SAMPLING DISTRIBUTIONS AND SAMPLING ERROR

It is obvious how certain biases can enter into the sample and make it an inappropriate subset of the population being discussed. However, even when the sample is random and appropriate, it is likely to deviate from the population just because it is a sample of considerably fewer cases than the population possesses.

Suppose the mean score of all second graders in a school system on a reading readiness test was 103 with a standard deviation of 10.5 (e.g., $\mu_x = 103$, $\sigma_x = 10.5$). A random sample of 20 second graders was selected and the mean was 107. The sample mean of 107 is certainly different from the population mean value of 103, yet the sample mean, $\overline{X}$, is an unbiased estimator of the population mean, μ, and the sample was, indeed, randomly selected. What could have produced this difference between sample and population means?

In selecting a random sample the implication is that each subject in the population had an equal **opportunity** to be drawn into the sample, but this does not say that the sample itself will be comparable to the population. One could obtain a sample that happened to have many exceptionally bright children, but nonetheless they might be randomly chosen. Therefore, random samples will differ one from another just because they are samples composed of different individuals.

Suppose instead of one group of 20 subjects 10 random samples of size 20 are picked from the population of all second graders in the school system. The hypothetical mean on the reading test for each of those samples is presented in Table 7–1. Think of these 10 means as being scores in a distribution of means. There would be a mean of such a distribution of means (Mean of the $\overline{X}$'s = 102.9) and a standard deviation (Standard Deviation of the $\overline{X}$'s = 2.81). Such a distribution has a special name and function in statistics.

The distribution of a statistic is called a **sampling distribution.**

Thus, the distribution of the 10 sample means is an empirical sampling distribution. A **theoretical** sampling distribution is a theoretical distribution of a statistic. If samples of size 20 were continually drawn and the mean computed

7–1 Means from 10 samples of size 20.

Sample	Sample Mean ($\bar{X}$)
1	107
2	101
3	100
4	105
5	103
6	99
7	103
8	106
9	100
10	105
	$\sum \bar{X} = 1029$

$$\text{Mean of } \bar{X}\text{'s} = \frac{\sum \bar{X}}{N_{\text{samples}}} = \frac{1029}{10} = 102.9$$

$$\text{Standard Deviation of } \bar{X}\text{'s} = \sqrt{\frac{N_{\text{samples}} \sum \bar{X} - (\sum \bar{X})^2}{N_{\text{samples}}\,(N_{\text{samples}} - 1)}}$$

$$= \sqrt{\frac{10(105955) - (1029)^2}{10(10 - 1)}}$$

$$= 2.81$$

on each one, as the sampling continued the distribution of means would approach the theoretical sampling distribution of the mean for samples of size 20. Actually, sampling distributions are determined by theoretical mathematics and not by repeated sampling as described above, but the meaning of the two approaches is very close.

The sampling distribution represents the third type of distribution to be considered. There is a **population distribution** which is the distribution of scores (whatever they may be) in the population. Usually, this is a theoretical distribution because in actual practice the population is not available. Second, when a sample from the population is selected, this subgroup of scores forms the **sample distribution.** It is from this distribution that various statistics may be computed and used to estimate what exists in the population distribution. The **sampling distribution** is a theoretical distribution of a statistic for samples of size *N* drawn from the population distribution. The sampling distribution is theoretical and conceptually based upon all possible random samples of size *N*. It will be important to maintain the distinction between these three distributions.

standard error of the mean Just as a distribution of scores has certain characteristics (e.g., mean and variance), so, too, does a sampling distribution. Consider the sampling distribution of the mean, the theoretical distribution of means based upon all possible samples of size N from a given population. Such a distribution of means itself will have a mean, which is symbolized by $\mu_{\bar{x}}$ to indicate that it is the theoretical mean of the sample means. It happens that the mean of the sampling distribution of means equals the mean of the population distribution:

$$\mu_{\bar{x}} = \mu_x = \mu$$

The symbol μ without a subscript is customarily used to indicate this value.

In addition to a mean, the sampling distribution of means has a standard deviation which is symbolized by $\sigma_{\bar{x}}$.

> The standard deviation of a sampling distribution of a statistic is called the **standard error** of that statistic.

Consequently, the standard deviation of the sampling distribution of the mean is known as the **standard error of the mean.**

It is exceptionally important for the student to develop a sense for what a standard error reflects. Although the sample mean, $\overline{X}$, is an unbiased estimate of the population mean, μ, the mean computed on a single sample probably will not equal that computed on another sample as illustrated in Table 7–1. There will be variability in sample means. The standard error of the mean, which is the standard deviation of the theoretical sampling distribution of means, is an index that expresses the extent of that variability. Since researchers usually select only one sample, and since the sample mean is used to estimate the population mean, $\sigma_{\bar{x}}$ reflects the amount of variability or error due to sampling in making such an estimate. Consequently, the standard error of the mean is a measure of **sampling error,** the extent to which the value of sample means will vary from one sample of size N to another and thus be inaccurate estimates of μ.

It was stated above that the mean of the sampling distribution of the mean is identical to the mean of the population distribution, $\mu_{\bar{x}} = \mu_x = \mu$. In contrast, the standard deviation of the sampling distribution of the mean is not identical (though it is related) to the standard deviation of the population distribution of raw scores.

> The standard error of the mean, $\sigma_{\bar{x}}$, equals the population standard deviation divided by the square root of the size of the sample upon which the means are based:
>
> $$\sigma_{\bar{x}} = \frac{\sigma_x}{\sqrt{N}}$$

In the preceding example the population standard deviation was 10.5 and the sample size was 20. Therefore, the theoretical standard error of the mean would be

$$\sigma_{\bar{x}} = \frac{\sigma_x}{\sqrt{N}} = \frac{10.5}{\sqrt{20}} = 2.35$$

Thus far, the standard error of the mean has been expressed as a function of the population standard deviation. The population standard deviation may be estimated by the standard deviation of a sample, and thus $\sigma_{\bar{x}}$ may be estimated by $s_{\bar{x}}$:

Since s_x estimates σ_x, an estimate of the standard error of the mean is given by

$$s_{\bar{x}} = \frac{s_x}{\sqrt{N}}$$

which can also be expressed in terms of the raw scores of the sample as

$$s_{\bar{x}} = \frac{s_x}{\sqrt{N}} = \frac{\sqrt{\dfrac{\sum(X_i - \bar{X})^2}{N-1}}}{\sqrt{N}} = \sqrt{\frac{\sum(X_i - \bar{X})^2}{N(N-1)}} = \sqrt{\frac{N\sum X_i^2 - (\sum X_i)^2}{N^2(N-1)}}$$

in which N is the size of the sample of X's.

The preceding formula permits the estimation of the variability of sample means on the basis of the $s_{\bar{x}}$ from one sample. This possibility represents an important saving of labor because many samples do not have to be drawn in order to estimate the degree of variability of sample means (e.g., see Table 7–1).

Examination of the formula for the standard error of the mean, $s_{\bar{x}} = s_x/\sqrt{N}$, reveals a fundamental characteristic of estimating the population mean with a sample mean. Note that the variability of the distribution of sample means decreases as N increases. With large N, the denominator of the expression $s_x/\sqrt{N}$ becomes large, thus reducing the size of the standard error of the mean. Consequently, for large samples one expects $\bar{X}$, the estimate of the population mean μ, to be less variable from sample to sample, and thus a more accurate estimate of μ than if the sample size were smaller. In short, when parameters must be estimated, it is a good idea to have as large a sample as is feasible.

other standard errors The sampling distribution and standard error of the mean have been discussed in detail, but a sampling distribution and standard error exist for any statistic. In each case the logic is the same. Random samples differ in their characteristics, and almost any statistic computed on such samples will also vary somewhat. The theoretical sampling distribution is the distribution of a particular statistic computed on all possible samples of size N, and the standard error of that statistic is the standard deviation of its sampling distribution. Since it is inefficient and costly to collect many samples and repeat an experiment over and over again in order to compute empirically the standard error of a statistic, its value is estimated by using information which can be obtained in one sampling. Thus, it is possible to estimate the sampling error of a statistic by selecting a single sample.

sampling distributions and normality Many of the procedures described in this and remaining chapters rest on the assumption that the sampling distribution of means is normal in form. This is the case if one of two conditions is met.

> Given random sampling, the sampling distribution of the mean approaches a normal distribution if
>
> 1. the population distribution is normal, or
> 2. the size of the sample is large.

If the population distribution is normal, the sampling distribution of the mean will also be normal. However, since one rarely has the population at his disposal, how can one know if the population distribution is normal? One way to make an educated guess is to determine whether a random sample from the population is normally distributed. Another approach is to simply ask what the likelihood is that the population is normally distributed. Some variables are usually not normally distributed because there are a few extreme scores. For example, IQ's of all 21-year olds are probably normally distributed but IQ's of all 21-year old college students are not because low or extremely low scores are not represented as frequently in college groups as extremely high scores. Family income, the latency for a rat to move out of a startbox in a maze, and percent correct on a relatively easy exam are variables that are not usually normally distributed.

Notice that the above variables are bounded on one end of their scales (e.g., $0 income, 0 sec., 100% correct). If the scores tend to fall near the bounded end of the scale, the distribution is likely to be skewed. Fortunately, many of the variables measured in social sciences can be assumed to be normally distributed. When variables are not normal, other statistical techniques may be used (see Chapter 11).

A second way to obtain a normal sampling distribution of the mean is to select a large enough sample. The sampling distribution of the mean will approach a normal distribution as the sample size increases, **even though the population distribution is not normal.** Just how many cases constitute a sufficiently large sample depends upon many factors, one of which is the extent of the departure from normality of the population distribution. If the population distribution does not deviate too much from normality, a sample of size $N = 2$ might produce a sampling distribution of the mean that is quite normal, whereas if the non-normality in the population is severe, N's of 20, 30, or several 100 might be necessary. In short, the sampling distribution of the mean will approach a normal form if the population is normal or if the size of the sample is large.

One of the reasons why normality is necessary for the statistical procedures to be described is the following fact:

> If the population distribution is normal and the observations are independent and randomly selected, the sample mean and variance (and standard deviation) are independent.[5]

Two variables (e.g., $\overline{X}$ and s_x^2 across samples of size N) are independent if they are unrelated in such a way that the value of one does not influence (or relate to) the value of the other (see Chapter 12, page 332). For example, if random samples are drawn from a normal population, then a sample having a mean of 50 is just as likely to have a standard deviation of 12 (or any other particular value) as a sample having a mean of 65. This fact will become important in the succeeding chapters.

It would be good to review slightly. Most of the statistical procedures to be described below are dependent upon several principles. Some of these include: (a) Samples are drawn at random with independent observations. (b) The sampling distribution represents a distribution of a statistic and its standard deviation (standard error) is an expression of the extent to which the statistic will vary from one sample to another (i.e., sampling error). (c) The sampling distribution of the mean is normal if the population is normal or the sample is large. (d) The mean and standard deviation of a random sample from a normal population are independent. Some of these propositions will be important for some techniques while others will be vital for other techniques. Additional assumptions and facts will be introduced as needed.

hypothesis testing

Although the specific techniques of statistical inference vary depending upon the research question being asked, the logic of the general approach is quite similar in these diverse cases. In order to illustrate this logic and the terminology that accompanies it, a relatively simple example will be used. In subsequent chapters, problems closer to those encountered in social sicence will be presented.

[5] Actually, the mean and variance of a sample are independent (unrelated) even if the population distribution is not normal as long as the distribution is symmetrical. A normal distribution is symmetrical, and thus samples from it have independent means and variances. The assumption of normality is made for other reasons as well as this fact.

AN INFORMAL EXAMPLE

Suppose it is known that for the population of rats used for experimentation in a given laboratory the mean number of errorless trials in 200 attempts at a maze is 125, and the standard deviation is 10.5. In symbols, $\mu = 125$ and $\sigma_x = 10.5$. Now suppose that a psychologist has a hunch that injecting a certain drug before each daily maze session might alter performance, but he doesn't know whether it will improve or retard performance. He decides to run a simple experiment. If the results suggest that this drug might have an effect, he will decide to perform a more elaborate study designed to yield more definitive results.[6]

The psychologist proposes to randomly select 20 rats and inject them with the drug before the daily trials. He reasons that if this group behaves in a markedly different manner from non-drugged rats in terms of the number of correct trials, then the drug probably has an effect. The task is to make an inference on the basis of this small group as to whether the drug actually influences learning performance. The problem is how different must the mean of the experimental rats be from the mean of the population of non-drugged rats in order for the psychologist to conclude that the drug has an effect. The non-drugged population standard deviation of 10.5 indicates that not all rats score the mean value of 125. Any single rat might score 110, 138, 98, or 141, for example, without receiving any drug. Consider the situation if a drugged animal were to score 141. True, this is substantially better than the non-drugged population mean of 125, but such a score could also be obtained by a non-drugged rat. In short, how different must the mean of the drugged rats be from the non-drugged population mean in order for the psychologist to decide the drug had an effect?

In order to perform the statistical analysis, it is necessary to assume that the experimental rats are randomly selected from a normally distributed population of rats that has a mean of 125 and standard deviation of 10.5 on this task when no drug is administered. It is to be acknowledged that the tenability of some of these assumptions cannot be evaluated, but the experiment is to be performed as if they were true.

The logic of the general approach is similar to an indirect proof in geometry. Make the hypothesis that the drug has no effect and that the experimental rats represent a random selection from the population of non-drugged rats. One tentatively assumes that this hypothesis (along with the other assumptions stated above) is true; then one gathers data. If the data appear reasonable and

[6] The present example is not intended to illustrate how a scientist would actually pursue the problem suggested by the example. He would be likely to obtain two samples of rats and give one group the drug and not give it to the other. Statistical procedures for comparing the difference between two sample means are described in the next chapter. The example is presented here only because it represents an intermediate step in making the transition between what has been presented before and what is discussed in Chapter 8.

could be expected under these circumstances, perhaps the hypothesis made about the drug having no effect is valid. At least there would be no evidence to the contrary. However, if the data are such that the outcome of the experiment would not be very likely under the hypothesis that the drug has no effect, perhaps this hypothesis is not valid (assuming that the other presuppositions are true).

The key to the above logic is to be able to specify what is a reasonable result under the hypothesis of no drug effect. One method is to ascertain the probability of obtaining whatever mean the experimental rats make if it is proposed that the drug had no effect. Suppose for a moment that only one rat were given the drug instead of 20. Now consider the expression that translates a score (X) into standard score form:

$$z = \frac{X - \mu}{\sigma_x}$$

Under the conditions of this example, the distribution of such z's is the standard normal, a theoretical relative frequency distribution. Since there is an intimate relationship between relative frequency and probability, perhaps this distribution could be used to decide whether any given result is probable or improbable assuming no drug effect. An arbitrary criterion is established. Suppose the psychologist says that if the experimental rat's score is so deviant from the population mean that it should occur in less than 5% of the non-drugged rats, then he will conclude that the drug had an effect. However, since not all rats score the same and some variability is to be expected, if the experimental rat's score is not that extreme, he will conclude that there is not sufficient evidence that the drug has an effect.

When a group of animals rather than a single subject is measured and a mean computed, the question becomes how deviant does the mean of the sample of drugged rats have to be from the population mean of non-drugged rats before one decides the drug has an effect? The formula that translates a single score (X) into a standard normal deviate,

$$z = \frac{X - \mu}{\sigma_x}$$

must be generalized to handle a mean instead of a single score. The above expression indicates the difference between a score and a population mean relative to a measure of the degree of variability of the scores as measured by their standard deviation (σ_x). Means will also vary one from another. The mean of one sample will not be the same as the mean from another sample, and it is likely that no sample mean will precisely equal the population value. Just as the standard deviation of the scores was a measure of the variability or "sampling error" of single scores, the standard error of the mean ($\sigma_{\bar{x}}$) is a measure of the variability or sampling error of means based upon samples of size N.

The rationale for generalizing the preceding formula to the case of means is straightforward. The preceding formula states that a variable minus the population mean of that variable both divided by the standard deviation of the variable is a standard normal deviate if the variable is normally distributed. Now suppose the variable is a mean instead of a score. Then, the formula would state that a sample mean ($\overline{X}$) minus the population mean of such means ($\mu_{\bar{x}} = \mu_x = \mu$) both divided by the standard deviation of such means ($\sigma_{\bar{x}} = \sigma_x/\sqrt{N}$, the standard error of the mean) is a standard normal deviate:

$$z = \frac{\overline{X} - \mu_{\bar{x}}}{\sigma_{\bar{x}}} = \frac{\overline{X} - \mu}{\sigma_x/\sqrt{N}}$$

Since the sampling distribution of the mean is normal in form if the population of scores is normal or if the sample is sufficiently large, the requirement of normality is often met. Consequently, the above formula converts a sample mean into a standard normal deviate, and the percentiles of the standard normal then can be used to assess the likelihood of obtaining a mean of $\overline{X}$ (or one more deviant from μ) in a sample of size N drawn from a population having a mean of μ and standard deviation of σ_x.

More specifically Figure 7–3 is a graph of the standard normal distribution. As related to the example, a z of 0 represents the population mean of 125 correct trials. Since the drug may facilitate or retard learning, a very extreme sample mean may be either larger or smaller than the non-drugged mean of 125 ($z = 0$). Observe the shaded portions of Figure 7–3. The points separating the shaded from the unshaded portions are $z = -1.96$ and $z = +1.96$. If the student will glance at Table A in Appendix II of the standard normal distribution, he will notice that a z of 1.96 cuts the area under the curve so that 47.5% of it

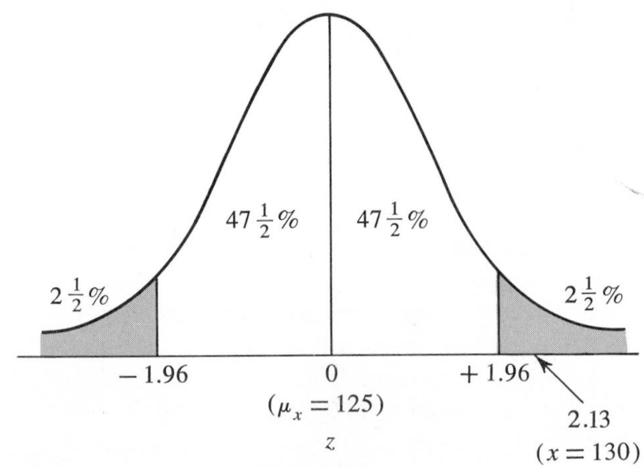

Fig. 7–3. Standard Normal Distribution.

falls between the mean ($z = 0$) and the point ($z = 1.96$), and 2.5% of the area falls between the point and the tail of the graph. Thus, the two shaded segments together represent 5% of the cases. Consequently, when converted to standard normal deviates, means that fall under the shaded portion of the graph in Figure 7–3 will be judged to be so improbable for non-drugged rats (the probability is .05 or less that a sample of non-drugged rats would have a mean in this range) that the psychologist will decide his assumption that the drug has no effect is likely to be wrong. In short, if the mean obtained by the experimental rats results in a z that is less than -1.96 or greater than $+1.96$ (i.e., it falls in the shaded range of values in Figure 7–3), he will decide his data promote the conclusion that the drug had an effect. If the observed mean does not yield such an extreme z value (i.e., it falls between -1.96 and $+1.96$), he will conclude that his data do not support the proposition that the drug has an effect.

Suppose the experiment was now performed and the observed mean of the 20 drugged rats was 130. Converting this mean into a standard normal deviate, one obtains

$$z = \frac{\overline{X} - \mu}{\sigma_x/\sqrt{N}} = \frac{130 - 125}{10.5/\sqrt{20}} = 2.13$$

Looking at Figure 7–3 one would expect to obtain a z score this large in less than 5% of such samples if the drug had no effect. Therefore, although he might be wrong, the psychologist concludes that such a mean is so different from the population mean of non-drugged rats that it is unlikely to have occurred merely because sample means usually differ from the population value. Therefore, he infers that his working hypothesis that the drug had no effect yielded an improbable result, and thus perhaps the assumption is not valid. The drug may have had an effect.

The preceding example illustrates several aspects of the process of hypothesis testing. It will be helpful to consider the same example in more detail and to present the terminology of hypothesis testing.

FORMAL EXAMPLE

statistical assumptions and hypotheses Statistical inference as described above involves making some assumptions and hypotheses about what is true in the population and then asking if the data collected in a sample are concordant with the hypothesis that was tentatively supposed true at the beginning.

It will be helpful to make an arbitrary distinction between assumptions and hypotheses. In the above example, the assumptions were that the experimental rats were randomly sampled and that the non-drugged population has a normal distribution with a mean of 125 and a standard deviation of 10.5. These assumptions are necessary in order to use the statistical techniques described.

Although these propositions are not easily validated and one must proceed as if they were true, within this context these assumptions are not tentative. They are assumed true regardless of whether the drug has an effect or not.

In contrast:

> A **hypothesis** is a statement proposing what is true in some population or populations. Usually it is a proposition about a parameter.

Hypotheses differ from assumptions in that usually two (or more) mutually contradictory hypotheses are offered, one hypothesis is **tentatively** held to be true, and the statistical procedure is designed to facilitate a decision about whether the observed data are in accord with the assumed hypothesis.

> The hypothesis that is tentatively held to be true is called the **null hypothesis** and is customarily symbolized by H_0. The **alternative hypothesis** is represented by H_1.

In the present example, these hypotheses may be stated:

H_0: The observed mean is computed on a sample drawn from a population with $\mu = 125$ (i.e., the drug has no effect).
H_1: The observed mean is computed on a sample drawn from a population with $\mu \neq 125$ (i.e., the drug has some effect).

The statement of these hypotheses appears a little contrived. The logic is that the null hypothesis is tentatively held to be true. Thus, it is assumed that the drug had no effect and that the experimental rats would behave as if they were a group randomly selected from the population of non-drugged rats. If their mean is close enough to the mean of that population, given the variability one would expect as a function of sampling, no doubt will be cast upon this tentative hypothesis. However, if their mean is very deviant from the mean of the non-drugged population relative to the variability expected, perhaps the null hypothesis is not true, and the alternative proposition that the drug actually does have an effect is a more valid characterization of what is really true. Notice that both the set of assumptions and the null hypothesis were held to be true at the beginning. However, the assumptions (e.g., random sampling, normality, etc.) were not made in a tentative fashion. They are assumed to be true regardless of the outcome of the experiment. In contrast, the null hypothesis was **tentatively** held to be true in the manner of an indirect proof in geometry. If the data are not consonant with what would be expected if the null hypothesis were true, then H_0 (not the assumptions) is presumed to be false.

significance level It is crucial to the above logic to decide when the data are or are not consonant with the null hypothesis. In short, how improbable do the data have to be to compel a decision to reject the null hypothesis?

> The **significance level** (or **critical level**), symbolized by α (read "alpha"), is the probability value that forms the boundary between accepting or rejecting the null hypothesis.

The precise value of α is determined somewhat arbitrarily by the researcher (see section on "Determining the Level of Significance" page 163). However, customarily in social science research this value is taken as .05. This means that if the probability is less than .05 that the observed data would be expected to occur if the null hypothesis were true, the null hypothesis will be rejected and the result is said to be "significant at the .05 level" or that "$p < .05$." In the current example, although the non-drugged population mean is 125, some variability of scores and thus of the sample mean is expected. However, extreme departures from $\mu = 125$ relative to the expected variability of means ($\sigma_{\bar{x}} = 10.5/\sqrt{20} = 2.35$) would make the tentative hypothesis of no drug effect unlikely. If the observed mean of the experimental rats was such that one would expect less than 5% of such means based upon 20 non-drugged rats to be as extreme as that actually observed, the null hypothesis of no drug effect will be rejected as being false.

It is important to realize that the probability level of .05 is **arbitrarily** selected **before** the experiment is performed.

decision rules If the significance level is established at .05, for example, how does one decide whether to accept or reject the null hypothesis?

> **Decision rules** are statements that designate the conditions necessary for accepting or rejecting the null hypothesis.

The precise statement of the decision rules depends upon the significance level, the particular computational procedure being used, and the nature of the alternative hypothesis. For the example being considered, the observed mean for the experimental rats ($\overline{X} = 130$) was translated into standard score form ($z = 2.13$). In accordance with the significance level selected, the decision rules are statements that prescribe which observed values of z result in a decision to accept H_0 and which result in a decision to reject H_0.

Recall from the example that a .05 significance level was chosen. Since the mean of the experimental rats was to be converted into standard score form and since the drug could have either a positive or negative effect on learning, two z values must be determined such that $2\frac{1}{2}\%$ of the cases of the standard normal fall below one of the points and $2\frac{1}{2}\%$ lie above the other. Table A in Appendix II lists the areas and z values for the standard normal distribution, and it can be seen that .0250 of the total area falls in the right-hand tail of the distribution beyond a z of 1.96. Since the standard normal is symmetrical, $2\frac{1}{2}\%$ of the distribution also lies in the left-hand tail beyond a $z = -1.96$. Figure 7–3 indicates these values of z, which are called **critical values.** The shaded area under the curve representing 5% of the total area is known as the **critical region** or the **region of rejection.** If the observed z value for the experimental rats falls beyond the critical values, and thus in the shaded region of rejection, it will be regarded as being too extreme to have occurred through sampling error alone under the null hypothesis, and H_0 will be rejected. If the observed value falls between the two points and not in the shaded area, H_0 will not be rejected. A formal statement of these decision rules is as follows:

If z is between -1.96 and $+1.96$ (i.e., $-1.96 < z < 1.96$), accept H_0
If z is less than or equal to -1.96 or if z is greater than or equal to $+1.96$ (i.e., $z \leq -1.96$ or $z \geq 1.96$), reject H_0

computation The statistical procedures take advantage of standardized distributions for which percentiles are available. In the example we have been considering, the standard normal was used but there will be other theoretical distributions employed in different contexts later in the text. The technique involves converting the observed statistic (e.g., the mean) into a standardized form so that this value can be compared with the critical values previously established. Converting to a standardized distribution is necessary so that the percentiles that have been worked out for a few such theoretical distributions can be used for the many different measurements and distributions that researchers encounter.

In order to discriminate observed from critical values of the standardized variable, subscripts are often used. In our example,

$$z_{\text{obs}} = 2.10$$

represents the value corresponding to the observed data while

$$z_{\text{crit}} = \pm 1.96$$

indicates the critical values of z.

interpretation In the example we have been considering, the value of z corresponding to the observed mean of 130 was 2.13, and this falls within the province of the second decision rule which dictates that the null hypothesis is to be rejected. This implies that the obtained mean of 130 ($z = 2.13$) would be expected to occur in less than 5% of such samples of 20 non-drugged rats. Consequently, since it is unlikely that such a value should occur merely as a function of sampling error in picking some rats as opposed to others, the null hypothesis of no drug effect is rejected. Note that the wording is that the null hypothesis is rejected rather than that the alternative hypothesis is accepted. Only one of the two hypotheses, the null hypothesis, was tested.

It was tentatively held to be true and the statistical procedures carried out to determine if the data were concordant with it. Since they were not, H_0 is rejected as probably not being a valid characterization of what exists in the population. Since it was H_0 that was tested, the decision is made in reference to H_0, not H_1.

DECISION ERRORS

Generally, the purpose of statistical inference is to make an educated guess on the basis of a sample of observations as to what is true about a population that is not readily at hand. Since the decision is indeed a guess, it might be wrong.

One kind of error occurs when the decision rules dictate that the null hypothesis should be rejected when, in fact, it is true. That is, the drug **actually** has no effect but the **decision** is that it does. In the present example, the critical region ($\alpha = .05$) represents those values which one would expect samples of non-drugged rats to exhibit 5% of the time or less. Yet, if the drug had no effect but the observed mean for the experimental subjects was sufficiently different from the population mean for non-drugged rats, the decision process would call for the rejection of the null hypothesis and the psychologist will conclude that the drug had an effect. If the null hypothesis is in fact true, these decision procedures would be expected to erroneously reject the null hypothesis 5% of the time.

> A **Type I Error** occurs when the null hypothesis is rejected when it is, in fact, true. Given the validity of the null hypothesis, the probability that it is erroneously rejected by these procedures equals α, the significance level.

There is another type of error that can be made. Suppose the null hypothesis is **actually** wrong, that is, the drug does have an effect; however, the **decision** process may result in accepting the null hypothesis when it should be rejected.

> A **Type II Error** occurs when the null hypothesis is accepted when, in fact, it is false. The probability of this type of error is symbolized by β.

The probability of making a Type II Error cannot be determined unless the population distribution corresponding to H_1 is actually known. Consider Figure 7–4. The distribution labeled H_0 represents the distribution of means (for samples with $N = 20$) of non-drugged rats. The shaded areas in the tails of this distribution constitute the region of rejection. If the null hypothesis is actually true, then this shaded area represents the probability of a Type I Error since means in this region would provoke a decision to reject the null hypothesis. Now shift your attention to the distribution labeled H_1, the distribution of means for drugged rats. Now assume that H_1 is, in fact, true and the drug has

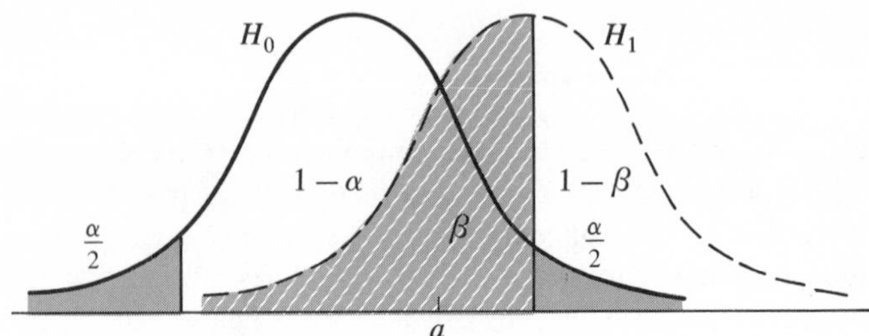

Fig. 7-4. Diagram of the relationship between Type I (α) and Type II (β) errors and power ($1 - \beta$).

an effect. Because of the overlap in the distributions, it is possible that some means would fall close enough to the mean of the non-drugged population so that the psychologist in his decision process would commit a Type II Error by accepting H_0 when it was false. A mean at point a would be such a case. The area labeled β in Figure 7-4 corresponds to means for drugged rats for which the process would erroneously declare that the drug had no effect. It represents the probability of a Type II Error. Because the distribution under H_1 is usually not available, it is usually impossible to estimate the size of β.

There are two other areas to notice in Figure 7-4. The portion of H_0 that is not in the region of rejection represents the probability of correctly accepting $H_0 (p = 1 - \alpha)$. The portion of H_1 that is not part of β represents the probability of correctly rejecting $H_0 (p = 1 - \beta)$. This latter probability is called the **power** of a test. Table 7-2 summarizes these points.

7-2 The 4 Possible Outcomes of a Simple Decision Process and Their Associated Probabilities.

		Actual Situation	
		H_0 is true	**H_0 is false**
Decision	**Reject H_0**	*Type I Error* $p = \alpha$	*Correct Decision* $p = 1 - \beta$ (power)
	Accept H_0	*Correct Decision* $p = 1 - \alpha$	*Type II Error* $p = \beta$

determining the significance level The significance level is the probability of rejecting the null hypothesis when it is, in fact, true (Type I Error). How does one go about setting this level? In a very real sense, the value of α reflects the investigator's feeling of how much error he is willing to tolerate in making a decision to reject H_0. Ordinarily, social scientists accept the ".05 level of significance" as the value of α, but this is merely a convention that has grown up over the years and there is nothing fixed about it. When testing some hypotheses, other levels of significance might be adopted depending upon how critical it is to be wrong in rejecting the null hypothesis. For example, if you were a brain surgeon and were giving a test to determine whether a patient needed a very delicate type of surgery, it might be that you could not afford to risk an operation if the patient really doesn't need one (i.e., if your diagnosis is wrong). Therefore, you might operate only if the probability is less than .01 or .001 that the test result is just a sampling error. However, the more unlikely you make the possibility of incorrectly rejecting the null hypothesis and performing the operation (Type I Error), the more likely a patient with a condition needing an operation will be diagnosed incorrectly as being able to do without it (incorrectly accepting H_0; a Type II Error). In any situation, it is important to remember that the level of significance is arbitrarily established on the basis of the researcher's tolerance for error in his decision-making. However, depending upon the circumstances, the reader may feel differently than the researcher about the size of error he personally feels comfortable in accepting. Therefore, it might be a reasonable procedure to adopt a significance level but to report the actual probability found as a result of testing H_0, regardless of whether one accepts or rejects H_0. In the example, merely compute the value of z and go to the table to find what the probability is of observing a z of that size or larger, given H_0. If there is no over-riding need to make a dichotomous decision, merely stating the significance level corresponding to the actual result and leaving the interpretation of its magnitude up to the reader is probably a good policy.

DIRECTIONAL TESTS

The test of the null hypothesis described in the rats-and-drug example was a **non-directional test.** It was non-directional because the alternative hypothesis (H_1) did not specify the direction of the influence of the drug. Would it help or hinder learning? It only suggested the drug would influence performance, one way or the other. Consequently, the critical region was established so that extreme values in either direction would lead to a decision to reject H_0.

However, suppose this same drug had been found by other scientists to improve the memory of a simple visual discrimination in rats, and the psychologist wonders if its administration will also improve maze learning. Since it is very unlikely that the drug would actually hinder maze learning, he establishes the alternative hypothesis as

> H_1: The observed mean is computed on a sample drawn from a population with $\mu > 125$, (i.e., the drug **facilitates** learning).

This is a **directional** hypothesis since it prescribes that the mean is likely to be higher than 125.

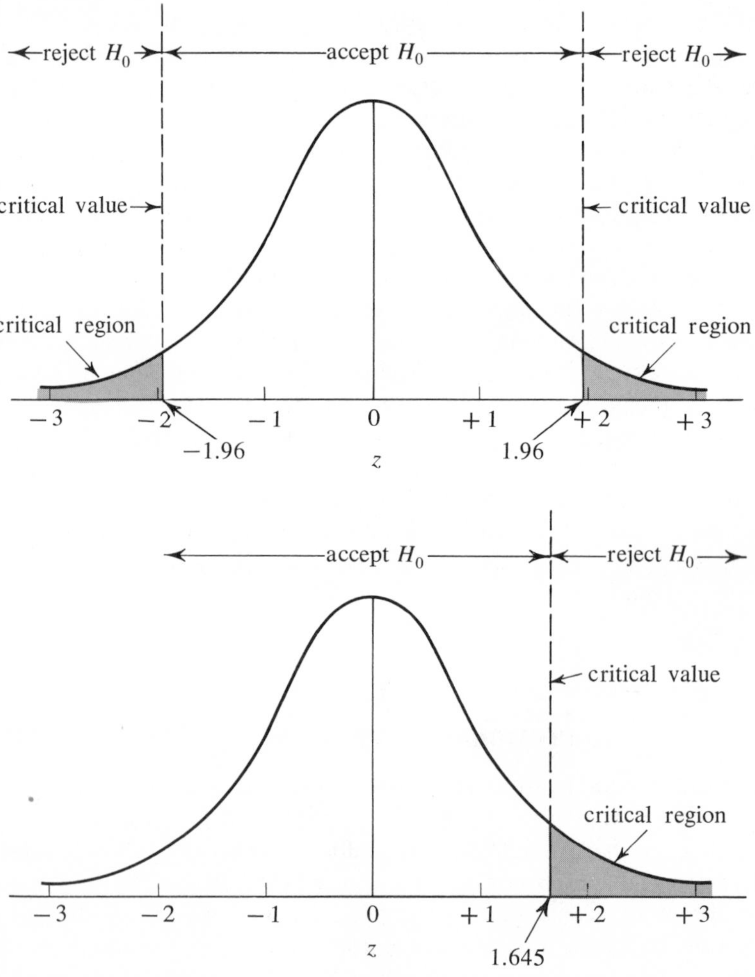

Fig. 7-5. Decision process for a non-directional (two-tailed) test (top) and a directional (one-tailed) test (bottom).

In such an event, it would be unreasonable to divide the critical region into two parts so that extreme means in either direction would lead to rejecting the null hypothesis. Remember the previous research information suggested that the probability is almost zero that drugged rats would exhibit an extremely low mean. Therefore, in order to maintain the significance level at .05, only the extreme 5% of the scores in the right-hand tail of the distribution constitutes the region of rejection. When looking in Table A of the standard normal, one searches for the z value such that .0500 of the area falls between it and the right-hand tail. This value is $z = 1.645$. A comparison of the regions of rejection for these non-directional and directional tests is presented in Figure 7–5.

Since a non-directional test locates the critical region in both tails of the theoretical distribution, it is frequently called a **two-tailed test.** Conversely, since a directional test locates the critical region in only one end of the distribution, it is called a **one-tailed test.**

In determining whether a test is one- or two-tailed, one considers whether there is other evidence or a theory which might predict the result. Then H_1 and the critical values are established in accordance with that prediction. However, this choice of a one- or a two-tailed test **must be made prior to the collection of the data.** That is, the nature of the alternative hypothesis, directional or non-directional, must be established before one knows the experimental result. Otherwise, if one waits until he knows the data and then decides to make a one- instead of a two-tailed test, the theoretical probabilities involved in the significance level (e.g., $\alpha = .05$) are no longer appropriate. Therefore, the statistical hypotheses must be stated before the experiment or observation is performed.

differences between population and sample means with $\sigma_{\bar{X}}$ estimated by $s_{\bar{X}}$

STUDENT'S *t* DISTRIBUTION

The expression used above translating a sample mean into a standard normal deviate is

$$z_{\bar{x}} = \frac{\overline{X} - \mu_{\bar{x}}}{\sigma_{\bar{x}}}$$

In this case $z_{\bar{x}}$ is a standard normal deviate (if the sampling distribution of the mean is normal), $\mu_{\bar{x}}$ is the population mean of the sampling distribution of $\overline{X}$'s determined for all possible samples of size N from the population, and $\sigma_{\bar{x}}$ is the theoretical standard deviation of such $\overline{X}$'s. Up to this point, the formulas presented have always involved a parameter, for example $\sigma_{\bar{x}}$. Regrettably, the value of this parameter is usually not available, so it must be estimated.

The $s_{\bar{x}}$, which is computed on a small sample of cases, is used for this estimation. However, the smaller the sample size the poorer the estimate, and it also happens that the standard normal distribution no longer is appropriate for making the comparisons that are needed. Consequently, when $\sigma_{\bar{x}}$ must be estimated by $s_{\bar{x}}$, particularly when the sample size is small, some theoretical standardized distribution other than the normal must be used. Student's t is such a distribution.

The Student's *t* distribution is a theoretical relative frequency distribution developed by W. S. Gosset who wrote under the name of "Student." When scores are transformed in the following way, the Student's t distribution is appropriate rather than the standard normal:

$$t = \frac{\overline{X} - \mu_{\bar{x}}}{s_{\bar{x}}} = \frac{\overline{X} - \mu}{s_x/\sqrt{N}}$$

The t distribution differs from the standard normal in two major respects. First, while the standard normal requires knowledge of $\sigma_{\bar{x}}$, the t distribution permits this parameter to be estimated by $s_{\bar{x}} = s_x/\sqrt{N}$. Second, there is a different t distribution for each size of sample upon which $s_{\bar{x}}$ is computed. Technically, the appropriate t distribution is determined not by the sample size, N, but by its degrees of freedom, $N - 1$ in this case. Figure 7–6 shows the t distribution for several degrees of freedom. It also depicts the standard normal ($df = \infty$). Notice that the t and z distributions are quite different when the sample size (and thus degrees of freedom) is small, but as the number of degrees of freedom increases the t distribution becomes more and more like the normal.

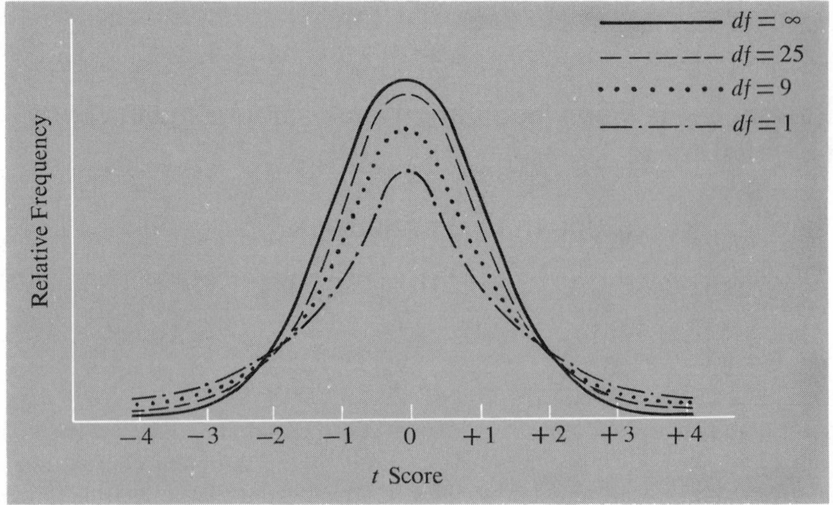

Fig. 7–6. The t distribution for various degrees of freedom. With an infinite number of degrees of freedom, the t and the standard normal (z) distributions are identical.

In fact, when the sample size is allowed to be theoretically infinite, the t and standard normal distributions are identical.[7]

degrees of freedom

The number of degrees of freedom (*df*) for any statistic is the number of components that are free to vary.

The number of degrees of freedom for t is determined by the degrees of freedom for the sampling error $(N - 1)$, which in the case being discussed is simply a standard deviation.

Why does the standard deviation have $N - 1$ degrees of freedom? The main portion of the formula for the sample variance is a sum of squared deviations, $\sum(X_i - \overline{X})^2$. In order to compute such a deviation for any one score in the distribution, the mean, $\overline{X}$, must be known. However, since it is known, one of the deviations can be determined by knowing all the other $N - 1$ deviations. For example, consider the following distribution: 5, 7, 9. The mean is 7. Note what happens if any two of the deviations are computed:

X	$\overline{X}$	$(X - \overline{X})$
5	7	-2
7	7	0
9	7	?

The chart shows that two of the deviations are -2 and 0. Recall now, however, that the sum of the deviations (**not** squared deviations) from the mean is always zero $\{$i.e., $\sum(X - \overline{X}) = 0\}$. Since this is true, the third deviation must be such that when added to the others the sum is zero:

$$\begin{aligned} -2 + 0 + (\text{last deviation}) &= 0 \\ \text{last deviation} &= +2 \end{aligned}$$

It is in this sense that the last deviation to be computed, regardless of which particular score in the distribution is remaining, is not free to vary but is determined. Knowing that the sum of the deviations must add to zero plus the knowledge of the value of the mean and $N - 1$ of the N deviations determine the precise value of the last deviation. Therefore, there are $N - 1$ degrees of freedom associated with the sample variance.

[7] Some texts suggest that if the sample size is 30 or more, the normal and t distributions are similar enough so that the normal distribution (z) may be used even though $s_{\bar{x}}$ has been estimated. While an examination of the tables for z and t in the appendix certainly indicates a great degree of correspondence between the normal and t for samples of 30 or more, it will be the policy of this book to suggest that the t distribution always be used when a parameter is being estimated regardless of sample size. This policy results in greater accuracy in determining probabilities and somewhat less confusion.

The number of degrees of freedom for any statistic is also related to the number of parameters that must be estimated in order to calculate the statistic. For example, $\overline{X}$ is an estimate of the population mean and this estimate must be determined before the standard deviation can be calculated. The number of degrees of freedom for the standard deviation is the number of cases involved (i.e., N) minus the number of parameters being estimated (i.e., 1): $df = N - 1$. The standard error of estimate in the context of regression has $N - 2$ degrees of freedom because the $\tilde{Y}$ in the numerator $\{\sum(Y_i - \tilde{Y})^2\}$ can only be determined if the regression constants a and b are known. The estimation of these two values means that the number of degrees of freedom for $s_{y.x}$ equals $N - 2$.

The present application of the t distribution dictates that t have $N - 1$ degrees of freedom. Other applications of t discussed in the next chapter may have different numbers of df associated with them because different numbers of parameters must be estimated.

APPLICATION OF THE *t* DISTRIBUTION

Suppose the researcher decided to randomly select a sample of 20 rats and give each of them the drug prior to each testing session; but, suppose that the standard deviation of the population of non-drugged rats is not readily available. The population distribution is still regarded as being normal in form with $\mu = 125$. The researcher wishes to test the hypothesis that the observed mean is computed on a sample drawn from a population with $\mu = 125$.

The expression

$$t = \frac{\overline{X} - \mu}{s_x/\sqrt{N}}, \quad df = N - 1$$

changes the unit and origin of the distribution of sample means into standardized t units when $s_x/\sqrt{N}$ is used to estimate $\sigma_{\bar{x}}$. With certain assumptions similar to those invoked to use the standard normal, the t distribution may be employed in the same manner as has been demonstrated with the standard normal distribution. The t distribution is found in Table B of Appendix II and one can determine the probability that a sample with mean $\overline{X}$ and standard deviation s_x could be drawn from a population with $\mu = 125$. Just as for the standard normal, the critical values of t are tabled. The t table presented in Table B is somewhat different from that presented for the standard normal and deserves a brief examination. In general, the table consists of the critical values of t for various significance levels at each of several degrees of freedom. The degrees of freedom are located in the left-most column. To their right one finds various values of t for different significance levels. Since the t (like the z) distribution is symmetrical, a two-tailed test at the .05 level at $N - 1 = 20 - 1 = 19$ degrees of freedom implies that $2\frac{1}{2}\%$ of such t's fall both to the left of -2.093 and to the right of $+2.093$. If a one-tailed test at 19 *df* at the .01 level of significance were appropriate, the entire 1% of the area under the curve falls to the right of 2.539. Thus, the t table gives the critical values of t for various degrees of freedom and levels of significance for both directional (one-tailed) and non-directional tests (two-tailed).

While looking at the t table, one should observe one additional thing about it. First, for any given level of significance the value of t that is required to reject H_0 (critical value of t) becomes smaller as the number of degrees of freedom increases. Consider the third column for a two-tailed test at the .05 level of significance. With only one degree of freedom a $t = 12.706$ is required to reject H_0 whereas a $t = 4.303$ is needed if the $df = 2$. If there are an infinite number of degrees of freedom, $t = 1.96$ is required which is precisely the value of the standard normal distribution for this situation. Thus, as the number of degrees of freedom increases the critical value of t decreases until it approaches the same value that the standard normal would dictate.

Lastly, the smaller the standard error the more likely the null hypothesis will be rejected. This cannot be seen from the t table but it can be appreciated by examining the expression for t:

$$t = \frac{\overline{X} - \mu}{s_x/\sqrt{N}}$$

Since the ratio of two quantities becomes larger as the denominator becomes smaller, it can be seen that the value of t grows larger as the standard error ($s_{\bar{x}} = s_x/\sqrt{N}$) of the mean becomes smaller. Thus, the smaller the standard error the more likely the null hypothesis will be rejected when it is false.

A formal presentation of the solution to this hypothesis testing problem follows:

problem If the mean number of correct trials of the population of non-drugged rats is 125, does the mean of a random sample of 20 rats who are given a drug differ sufficiently from that population to warrant the conclusion that the drug has an effect on learning performance?

hypotheses

H_0: $\overline{X}$ is computed on a sample from a population with $\mu = 125$
H_1: $\overline{X}$ is computed on a sample from a population with $\mu \neq 125$

assumptions It is assumed (1) the rats are randomly and independently sampled, and (2) the population of non-drugged rats is normal with $\mu = 125$.

formula The expression used to convert the observed $\overline{X}$ into the standardized t value is

$$t = \frac{\overline{X} - \mu}{s_x/\sqrt{N}}$$

significance level Assume the .05 level.

critical values Since the alternative hypothesis was non-directional and $\alpha = .05$, t values must be selected so that $2\frac{1}{2}\%$ of the t distribution falls to the left of one and $2\frac{1}{2}\%$ falls to the right of the other critical value. Looking in Table B with $N - 1 = 20 - 1 = 19$ *df*, these critical values are -2.093 and $+2.093$.

decision rules

If t is between -2.093 and $+2.093$, accept H_0
If t is less than or equal to -2.093 or greater than or equal to $+2.093$, reject H_0

computation Suppose the experiment is conducted, the observed mean is 130, and the standard deviation is 9.5. Placing these values into the expression for t one obtains

$$t_{\text{obs}} = \frac{\overline{X} - \mu}{s_x/\sqrt{N}} = \frac{130 - 125}{9.5/\sqrt{20}} = 2.35$$

decision The observed t of 2.35 exceeds the critical values and falls within the province of the second decision rule to reject H_0. It is concluded that given the expected amount of variability in means of samples of size 20 ($s_{\bar{x}} = 9.5/\sqrt{20} = 2.13$), the mean of 130 is too deviant from $\mu = 125$, and thus if the null hypothesis of no drug effect were true, this would be a very unlikely result. Since a mean as extreme as 130 would not likely occur by chance or sampling error alone, the hypothesis of no drug effect is rejected at the $p < .05$ level. The experimenter concludes that the drug may have an effect on learning performance.

SUMMARY OF HYPOTHESIS TESTING

The general procedure for testing a statistical hypothesis is relatively similar in the various situations to be described in this text. Essentially, the researcher is faced with the problem of deciding whether or not the results he will obtain in an experiment represent chance or sampling variability or whether the factors isolated or manipulated actually reflect differences that exist in the populations.

In short, on the basis of sample data, the scientist must make a decision about what exists in a population not available to him. First, certain assumptions about the sampling procedures and the parameters of the populations are made. Second, two (or on occasion more than two) mutually exclusive hypotheses are offered about the population that reflect in statistical terms the researcher's scientific question. One of these hypotheses, the null hypothesis, is tentatively assumed to be true. Third, a significance level is arbitrarily selected; then, as a function of the nature of the alternative hypothesis, the significance level, and the particular theoretical distribution to be used, critical values, and decision rules are established. Fourth, the experiment is conducted and the salient aspects of the data converted into the chosen standardized theoretical distribution. Fifth, the observed transformed statistic is compared with the decision rules, and a decision to accept or reject the null hypothesis is made. If the observed result deviated so much from what would be expected if the null hypothesis were true that it fell in the area of rejection, the tenability of the null hypothesis would be in doubt and it would be rejected. Conversely, if the observed value did not deviate markedly from what would be expected if the null hypothesis were true, the null hypothesis would be accepted, and it is concluded that the observed results deviate from the hypothesized parametric values merely as a function of sampling error.

CONFIDENCE INTERVALS FOR THE MEAN

An important topic in this chapter has been estimating the value of population parameters. Suppose that a psychologist in a school system wanted to know what the average IQ was of the students in a given high school. It is rather expensive to give an IQ test to each student in the school so a random sample of 25 students is tested. Suppose the sample mean is 109 with a standard deviation of 15.

Now if the psychologist were required to estimate with one value the mean IQ in the population of all students in the high school, he would estimate 109. After all, the sample mean is an unbiased estimator of the population mean, and if the sample were indeed random, one would feel somewhat confident that the sample mean of 109 was near the population mean. However, if you were to ask the psychologist if he thought that 109 was exactly the population mean, he would certainly say no. Well, one might pursue, how close do you think 109 is to the population value?

An approach to answering this question is to give a range of values such that one feels reasonably confident that the interval limited by these values contains the population mean. For example, the psychologist might say that he thinks the population mean would likely fall within 6 points of the sample mean, and thus the interval of 103–115 is likely to contain the population mean. It would be helpful to be more precise about this procedure such that one could make a probability statement concerning just how "confident" he was that the suggested interval actually contained the population mean. The procedure for determining such an interval is analogous to that discussed on pages 107–108 with respect to predicting from a regression line.

The interval to be constructed is called a **confidence interval** and the values describing the boundaries of such an interval are the **confidence limits.** The degree of "confidence" in the proposition that the stated interval actually contains the population mean is indicated by a probability value. Of course, one would expect that a very large interval would more likely contain the population value than a very small one (everything else being equal), and thus potentially there are any number of confidence intervals, each having a particular probability associated with it. The most commonly used confidence intervals are the "95% confidence interval" and the "99% confidence interval."

To understand how a 95% confidence interval is determined, consider the data from the above example. The sample mean was 109 and the standard deviation was 15 for a sample of $N = 25$. Now consider the distribution of such sample means—the sampling distribution of the mean. Given the data at hand, the sample mean of 109 is a good estimate of the mean of the sampling distribution of the mean (i.e., the population mean), and $s_x/\sqrt{N} = 15/\sqrt{25} = 3$ is an estimate of the standard deviation of this distribution of means (i.e., the standard error of the mean, $s_{\bar{x}}$). Now recall from the section on "Sampling Distributions and Normality" that under most circumstances the sampling distribution of the mean is normal in form. Lastly, remember from the section on the "Standard Normal Distribution" in Chapter 4 that in a normal distribution 95% of the cases fall within approximately two standard deviations of the mean. To be more exact, Table A indicates that 95% of the cases fall between -1.96 and $+1.96$ standard deviation units of the mean of the standard normal distribution. However, since we are **estimating** the standard error of the mean, the t distribution rather than the standard normal gives a better approximation to the correct number of standard deviation units for the required probability. When one refers to the t table (Table B) with $df = N - 1 = 25 - 1 = 24$ and under two-tailed tests he finds that 95% of the cases should fall within ± 2.064 standard deviation units of the mean. Thus, since the sampling distribution of the mean is normal with estimated mean 109 and standard deviation (i.e., $s_{\bar{x}}$) of 3, then 95% of such sample means should fall within $\pm 2.064 s_{\bar{x}}$ or $2.064(3) = \pm 6.78$ points of the mean. Consequently, one might say that 95% of the means from samples of size 25 would fall between

$$\bar{X} - 2.064 s_{\bar{x}} = 109 - 2.064(3) = 102.22$$

and

$$\bar{X} + 2.064 s_{\bar{x}} = 109 + 2.064(3) = 115.78$$

This interval may also be interpreted to mean that the probability is .95 that the interval of 102.22 to 115.78 contains the population mean. Consider another way to view this interval. Suppose a 95% confidence interval is computed on each sample drawn from this population. If new samples were continually drawn and such intervals calculated, on the average 95% of such intervals would include the population mean value within their limits.

Suppose one wanted to be especially cautious and construct an interval such that 99 times out of 100 it would contain the population mean. Following the same logic as above, one would go to the t table and find the t value for a two-tailed test at .01 with $df = 24$. The value listed is 2.797, and this means that 99% of the cases in a distribution of such sample means are likely to fall within $\pm 2.797 s_{\bar{x}}$ of the mean. Consequently, the 99% confidence limits would be

$$\overline{X} - 2.797 s_{\bar{x}} = 109 - 2.797(3) = 100.609$$

and

$$\overline{X} + 2.797 s_{\bar{x}} = 109 + 2.797(3) = 117.391$$

Note that the probability statement applies to the interval and not to the population mean. The population mean is a fixed value whereas the sample mean and the confidence interval are different from sample to sample. Therefore, the statement that "the probability is p that the population value falls within the interval" is technically bad form because it implies that the value of μ varies and might or might not happen to land in the stated interval. Actually, it is the interval which is variable, and thus a statement with a more correct connotation is that the "probability is p that the interval includes the population value."

FORMULAS

1. Standard Form for a Score

$$z = \frac{X - \mu}{\sigma}$$

2. Standard Form for a Mean

$$z = \frac{\overline{X} - \mu}{\sigma_{\bar{x}}}, \qquad \sigma_{\bar{x}} = \frac{\sigma}{\sqrt{N}}$$

N = Number of cases in the sample for $\overline{X}$

3. Standard Form for a Mean, Parameter Estimated

$$t = \frac{\overline{X} - \mu}{s_{\bar{x}}}, \qquad s_{\bar{x}} = \frac{s_x}{\sqrt{N}}$$

N = Number of cases in the sample for $\overline{X}$

$$df = N - 1$$

EXERCISES

1. Discuss the appropriateness of the following samples for the stated populations.
   (a) Suppose a researcher in education wanted to test the effectiveness of two different teaching methods on college students in his university. He used one method with his 8 A.M. class and the other with his 2 P.M. class.
   (b) A social psychologist is investigating patterns of group dynamics in the context of a jury simulation experiment. He wishes to know the factors involved in the change of attitudes that transpires during jury debate in young adults. His psychology department requires that all students taking "Introduction to Psychology" serve in an experiment. Eighty students select the jury simulation experiment from the twenty possible research projects available to them.
   (c) An advertising man wants to know if housewives like the new style of package that Wonderease Soap Powder comes in. The package has just been displayed on color television, so the advertising man quickly sets up a telephone survey to inquire whether those people who saw the commercial liked the new packaging.

2. A population of 10 scores is listed in this exercise.

$$X_i = 2, 4, 4, 5, 5, 6, 7, 7, 8, 10$$

   Write each score on a piece of paper and place it in a hat. Randomly select 10 samples of size 4 from this population (replace the selected numbers after each drawing of 4), and compute the mean. Create an **empirical** sampling distribution of the mean from these data. Estimate the **theoretical** standard error of the mean first by using the standard deviation of the first sample you select in an appropriate formula and then by computing the standard deviation of the 10 samples you collected. How do you explain the differences in these values? Of what importance is the size of the sample in this process?

3. List the assumptions, hypotheses, formula, significance level (adopt the .05 level), critical values, decision rules, computation, and interpretation of the following tests of hypotheses.
   (a) Determine whether a mean of 84 based upon a sample of 25 is significantly different from a population mean of 81 with a standard deviation of 10.
   (b) What difference would it make if in Example *a* above you did not know the population standard deviation but you did know that the sample $s_x = 10$?
   (c) Suppose that it is known that males in a given area of the world average 62 inches in height. One tribe in the same area and of comparable genetic stock pierces the lips and molds the heads of their young children while the other tribes do not. The natives believe this piercing and molding makes their males grow stronger. A psychological theory also suggests that a moderate amount of stress given in infancy produces skeletally larger adults. The average height of the 36 adult males in this special tribe is 64.5 inches and the standard deviation is 7. Is this information consistent with the theory and tribal beliefs? Why do

these data not constitute proof that the piercing and molding causes this height advantage?[8]

(d) The average IQ of male students at State University that have at least one older brother or sister is 113. A random sample of 121 first-born males was similarly tested and found to have a mean IQ of 117 with a standard deviation of 16. Is it reasonable to conclude that first-born male students have a different IQ than later borns?[9]

4. Determine 90%, 95%, and 99% confidence intervals for the following cases:
   (a) $\overline{X} = 28$, $s_{\bar{x}} = 4$, $N = 30$
   (b) $\overline{X} = 152$, $s_{\bar{x}} = 12$, $N = 16$
   (c) $\sum X = 2400$, $s_x = 20$, $N = 64$
   (d) $\overline{X} = 72$, $\sigma_{\bar{x}} = 5$

[8] Adapted from research reported by T. K. Landauer and J. W. M. Whiting, "Infantile Stimulation and Adult Stature of Human Males," *American Anthropologist*, 1964, LXVI, 1007–1028.

[9] Suggested by research summarized by W. D. Altus, "Birth Order and Its Sequelae," *Science*, 1966, 44–49.

8

elementary techniques of hypothesis testing

The general rationale for hypothesis testing was discussed in Chapter 7. In short, a hypothesis is made about a characteristic of the population. This hypothesis is tentatively held to be true, and then data are collected to determine whether the results are likely to occur within the expected range of sampling error. If the results do not deviate markedly from what would be expected on the basis of sampling variations, there is no reason to doubt the validity of the hypothesis previously supposed to be true. If the results do deviate markedly from what would be expected on this basis, perhaps the hypothesis is not true.

The illustration of this procedure involved knowing the mean number of correct trials of the population of normal rats in a simple learning task. A group of rats were sampled and given a drug before their learning trials. The question was whether the mean of the drugged sample differed "significantly" from the mean of the non-drugged population. If the observed mean differed by an amount that could not be attributed to sampling error, then perhaps the drug had an effect. This was an example of comparing a sample mean with a population mean. However, in most research the population mean is not available, so the experiment would involve two groups of subjects, one that receives the drug and one that does not. The required statistical procedure now becomes one that compares two sample means to determine if these two means are likely to come from populations having the same mean.

the difference between means

Recall the progression of formulas derived in the last chapter. First, the standard normal deviate was presented:

$$z = \frac{X_i - \mu_x}{\sigma_x}$$

Remember that this formula is perfectly general. It states that if the X_i are normally distributed, then each score minus the population mean divided by the population standard deviation of those scores is a standard normal deviate. Now, if the "score" is a mean instead of a raw score, the formula becomes

$$z = \frac{\overline{X} - \mu_{\bar{x}}}{\sigma_{\bar{x}}}$$

Consider letting the basic score be a difference between two means, $\overline{X}_1$ and $\overline{X}_2$. The expression then suggests that normal deviates will be produced if the difference between the sample means $(\overline{X}_1 - \overline{X}_2)$ minus the difference between the population means $(\mu_1 - \mu_2)$ is divided by the standard error of the difference between two means $(\sigma_{\bar{x}_1-\bar{x}_2})$:

$$z = \frac{(\overline{X}_1 - \overline{X}_2) - (\mu_1 - \mu_2)}{\sigma_{\bar{x}_1-\bar{x}_2}}$$

This, then, is an expression that will relate the difference between two means to a theoretical relative frequency distribution, the standard normal, if the distribution of $(\overline{X}_1 - \overline{X}_2)$ is normal.

However, several refinements in such formulas were suggested in the previous chapter. First, the standard error of the difference between means is rarely available, and thus it must be estimated from the sample data. Therefore, $\sigma_{\bar{x}_1-\bar{x}_2}$ must be estimated by $s_{\bar{x}_1-\bar{x}_2}$. However, if parameters are to be estimated, the Student's t distribution rather than the standard normal provides a more accurate estimation of the desired probabilities. Second, in the theory of hypothesis testing, the null hypothesis is tested. When one tests the difference between two means the null hypothesis often is that the two groups of scores come from populations having the same mean value and that the observed difference between the sample means results fortuitously from sampling error. This implies that in the population there is really no difference between μ_1 and μ_2, and thus the expression $(\mu_1 - \mu_2)$ would equal zero. Therefore, the general expression for relating the difference between sample means to its standard error is

$$t = \frac{\overline{X}_1 - \overline{X}_2 - \overbrace{(\mu_1 - \mu_2)}^{0 \text{ by } H_0}}{s_{\bar{x}_1-\bar{x}_2}} = \frac{\overline{X}_1 - \overline{X}_2}{s_{\bar{x}_1-\bar{x}_2}}$$

The final task is to obtain an expression for the standard error of the difference between means. However, this parameter will be estimated differently under various circumstances. Just as the standard error for the mean was a function of the variability of the raw scores ($s_{\bar{x}} = s_x/\sqrt{N}$), the standard error of the difference between means, $s_{\bar{x}_1-\bar{x}_2}$, is a function of the variability within each population. Often the variances of the two groups are fairly comparable, that is, they are **homogeneous.** However, occasionally the variability in one sample is substantially different from the variability in the other group (the variances are **heterogeneous**), and the estimation of $\sigma_{\bar{x}_1-\bar{x}_2}$ requires a slightly different expression. Consequently, the standard error of the difference between means is estimated in a different manner if the variances of the two groups are homogeneous than if they are heterogeneous. Both cases will be considered below.

In addition to the fact that the procedures are different depending upon the variability in the two groups, the statistical techniques are also different if the two groups of scores are measured on different groups of subjects than if they are measured on the same or related subjects. For example, suppose one wanted to know if early visual experience with angular-shaped patterns is better for later visual discrimination between a circle and a triangle than experience with curved patterns. Two groups of rats might be reared, one in an angular and one in a curved environment. Since there are two distinct groups of subjects involved, the groups are called **independent groups.**

In contrast, consider this example. It has been found that if a small electrical current is passed through electrodes in certain brain areas of rats, the rats are stimulated pleasurably. Therefore, rats will perform certain tasks that produce this stimulus. The task in this case is pressing a bar to produce the electrical current. It might be of interest to ask whether stimulation in one area of the brain is as motivating as stimulation in another. If each rat in a single group has one electrode in one brain area (1) and another electrode in a different brain area (2), then the mean number of bar presses that produce the electrical stimulus in one area may be compared with the mean number of responses when the stimulation is given in the other area. But notice here that the two means are derived from two groups of scores both resulting from the behavior of the same group of animals. Each rat contributes a score for Area 1 and also for Area 2. Consequently, these two means are not independent but **correlated.** They are correlated in the following sense. Consider the reasons why scores in a distribution are not all the same. First, there may be differences in the trait being measured and second, there is error. The error is usually considered to embody effects of measurement and individual differences, peculiarities associated with individual subjects. For example, an individual difference considered might be particular sensitivity to electrical stimulation on the part of this specific rat, etc. When the same animals contribute a score to each group, the individual differences are likely to be similar for the two measurements. Therefore, the scores in the two groups are correlated to some extent. Because the scores are correlated the variability of differences between correlated means (the standard error) will be different than for means computed on independent groups of subjects. Consequently, in addition to considering different estimates of standard errors for the case of homogeneous vs. heterogeneous variances, one must also deal with a different standard error if correlated rather than independent groups are involved.

In the next sections, estimates of sampling error will be discussed for several different situations. In all of these cases, an assumption will be made that the population distributions are normal in form. This is called the **assumption of normality.** Recall that in the expressions for a standard normal deviate the "variable" ($X, \overline{X}, \overline{X}_1 - \overline{X}_2$, etc.) must be normally distributed, and the assumption of normality must be made in order to use the percentiles of the standard normal or t distributions. Recall that if the population distribution is normal or the sample size is sufficiently large, then the sampling distribution of the mean is also normal. It is also true that the distribution of the difference between means is normal if the population distributions are normal or if the sample sizes are large.

The assumption of normality of population distributions must be made for all of the procedures described in the next three chapters. Actually, the techniques can be carried out with little loss of accuracy even if some departures from normality are present. However, when the distributions are decidedly not normal and when the samples are small, special procedures must be employed. Such techniques are called **nonparametric tests,** because they do not make such restrictive assumptions. A few of these procedures are discussed in Chapter 11.

In addition to the assumption of normality, it will be assumed that the means are computed on **randomly selected samples** from the population. Further, some assumption will be made about the **variances of the two samples,** and differences in this assumption will result in the use of different formulas with which to estimate the standard error of the difference between means.

Lastly, in every test that is presented, **the null hypothesis is assumed to be true.** This is the very logic of the test. Assume that the null hypothesis is true and ascertain the probability that the observed events could occur given the validity of the null hypothesis. If that probability is reasonable, there is no reason to doubt the truth of the null hypothesis. If that probability is small, perhaps the null hypothesis is not true.

INDEPENDENT GROUPS, HOMOGENEOUS VARIANCES

The formula for estimating the standard error of the difference between means computed on independent groups with homogeneous variances is given by

$$s_{\bar{x}_1-\bar{x}_2} = \sqrt{\left[\frac{(N_1 - 1)s_1^2 + (N_2 - 1)s_2^2}{N_1 + N_2 - 2}\right] \cdot \left[\frac{1}{N_1} + \frac{1}{N_2}\right]}$$

What information does this formula provide? Notice that only the variances of the two groups and the number of cases in each group is required to compute this value. The result is an estimate of the standard deviation of the distribution of differences between pairs of sample means drawn from populations having the same mean (the standard error of the difference between sample means). Consequently, if two groups are sampled and their means computed, $s_{\bar{x}_1-\bar{x}_2}$ provides an estimate of how much variability in the statistic $(\overline{X}_1 - \overline{X}_2)$ should occur merely by randomly drawing pairs of samples from a single population and computing the difference between their means. An example of how this standard error is used is presented below.

research question The question posed previously is whether visual experience with angles as opposed to curves is more important in learning to discriminate between a circle and a triangle.[1] To test this issue, two groups of rats are reared in special cages, one group in a "round" world which has as few angles present as possible but which has curves painted on the side of the cage. The other group is reared in a "square" world that has as few curves as possible but has many angles painted on the sides of the cage. The animals are reared in these special cages from the time their eyes open. They are tested on a circle vs. triangle discrimination by an experiment in which they are taught that water is consistently behind either a circle or a triangle regardless of its position in the test apparatus. The measure of learning is the number of trials on which the rat makes a correct choice (ten trials per day for ten days are given for a total of 100 trials).

statistical hypotheses The null hypothesis is that the observed difference in the mean number of correct responses for the two groups is merely a function of sampling error and that these two groups of subjects are actually derived from a common population. If this were true, the implication would be that the different rearing environments do not affect discrimination learning performance. In terms of population parameters, we have

$$H_0: \mu_1 = \mu_2$$

The alternative hypothesis is that these two samples do not derive from the same population with the attendant implication that the differential rearing environments indeed do produce a difference in learning performance. Symbolically, we have

$$H_1: \mu_1 \neq \mu_2$$

Notice two things. First, the statistical hypotheses are stated in terms of population parameters not statistics. This is because the decision to be made

[1] Based upon but not identical to S. J. Cool, "Some Effects of Early Visual Environments on Adult Discrimination Abilities in the Rat" (Doctoral dissertation, University of Illinois, 1966); R. B. McCall and M. L. Lester, "Differential Enrichment Potential of Visual Experience with Angles vs. Curves" *Journal of Comparative and Physiological Psychology*, 1969, LXIX, 644–648.

really involves what is true about the population(s), rats reared in special environments, not just about the two specific samples observed in this experiment. Second, the alternative hypothesis, H_1, does not specify whether μ_1 is greater or less than μ_2. It just states that the population means are different. This implies that the statistical test should be sensitive to differences in either direction, $\mu_1 > \mu_2$ and $\mu_1 < \mu_2$. In short, a non-directional or two-tailed test is required. A summary of the test of these hypotheses is presented in Table 8–1. These procedures are discussed in the following material.

8–1 Summary of the test of the difference between means for independent groups with homogeneous variances (the round vs. square world example).

Hypotheses

$H_0: \mu_1 = \mu_2$
$H_1: \mu_1 \neq \mu_2$ (non-directional)

Assumptions

1. The two groups are **independent** and sampling is **random.**
2. The two variances are **homogeneous.**
3. The two population distributions and thus $(\overline{X}_1 - \overline{X}_2)$ are **normal,** or the samples are very large.

Decision Rules

Given: .05 significance level, $N_1 + N_2 - 2 = 30\ df$
If $-2.042 < t_{obs} < 2.042$, accept H_0
If $t_{obs} \leq -2.042$ or if $t_{obs} \geq 2.042$, reject H_0

Computation

Square World (*Group* 1)	*Round World* (*Group* 2)
$\overline{X}_1 = 80$	$\overline{X}_2 = 65$
$s_1^2 = 16$	$s_2^2 = 18$
$N_1 = 21$	$N_2 = 11$

$$t_{obs} = \frac{\overline{X}_1 - \overline{X}_2}{\sqrt{\left[\frac{(N_1 - 1)s_1^2 + (N_2 - 1)s_2^2}{N_1 + N_2 - 2}\right] \cdot \left[\frac{1}{N_1} + \frac{1}{N_2}\right]}}$$

$$= \frac{80 - 65}{\sqrt{\left[\frac{(21 - 1)16 + (11 - 1)18}{21 + 11 - 2}\right] \cdot \left[\frac{1}{21} + \frac{1}{11}\right]}}$$

$$t_{obs} = 9.87$$

Interpretation

Reject H_0

formula The formula relating the difference between sample means to its standard error is

$$t = \frac{\overline{X}_1 - \overline{X}_2}{s_{\bar{x}_1 - \bar{x}_2}}$$

in which

$$s_{\bar{x}_1 - \bar{x}_2} = \sqrt{\left[\frac{(N_1 - 1)s_1{}^2 + (N_2 - 1)s_2{}^2}{N_1 + N_2 - 2}\right] \cdot \left[\frac{1}{N_1} + \frac{1}{N_2}\right]}$$

The value of t has $N_1 + N_2 - 2$ degrees of freedom. The standard error of the difference between means must be estimated and this estimation is made on the basis of the variances of the two samples (see preceding formula for $s_{\bar{x}_1 - \bar{x}_2}$). Since the degrees of freedom for each variance is $N - 1$,

$$(N_1 - 1) + (N_2 - 1) = N_1 + N_2 - 2$$

assumptions There are three assumptions for using this formula. First, the two groups of subjects must be **randomly** selected and **independent;** that is, they must be composed of two different sets of subjects that are not matched in their relevant characteristics. Second, the two variances must be **homogeneous.** Later in this chapter a procedure will be discussed that may be used to test this assumption. Third, the two population distributions and thus $(\overline{X}_1 - \overline{X}_2)$ must be **normal** in form. This may be assumed if the population of scores from which these samples are selected is normal or if the number of cases in each sample is very large.

significance level Arbitrarily accept the .05 level of significance.

critical values The critical values will depend upon the degrees of freedom, the nature of the alternative hypothesis, and the level of significance. A glance at Table 8–1 shows that there are 21 and 11 subjects in the groups and thus the degrees of freedom are $(N_1 + N_2 - 2) = (21 + 11 - 2) = 30$. The alternative hypothesis is non-directional and the .05 level has been assumed. From Table B in Appendix II, the critical values are found to be 2.042 and −2.042.

decision rules If the observed (computed) value of t is between −2.042 and +2.042 the null hypothesis of no difference will be accepted. One would conclude that such a difference between means as was observed is well within the range of sampling error. In this event the results would not provide evidence supporting the effectiveness of differential rearing with curves and angles. Conversely, if the observed value of t is larger than or equal to 2.042 or less than or equal to −2.042 the null hypothesis will be rejected. The reasoning would be that the probability that such an observed difference in means merely reflects a sampling difference is too remote and that it is likely that the rearing conditions did affect performance. Symbolically:

$$\text{If } -2.042 < t_{\text{obs}} < 2.042, \text{ accept } H_0$$
$$\text{If } t_{\text{obs}} \leq -2.042 \text{ or if } t_{\text{obs}} \geq 2.042, \text{ reject } H_0$$

computation The computation of the observed t proceeds by listing the relevant known information, the formula for t, the calculation of the components of the formula, and the computation of the result. This work is presented in Table 8–1. The $t_{.05} = 9.87$.

interpretation The observed value of t conforms to the second decision rule, namely to reject H_0. The probability that such a difference between means relative to the variability of such differences could occur merely as a function of sampling error is so small that it is likely that the two means are from samples drawn from two different populations. If the experiment is well conceived, the implication is that the differential rearing conditions produced this difference in observed means.

INDEPENDENT GROUPS, HETEROGENEOUS VARIANCES

In the previous example, the variances of the two subgroups were 16 and 18. Although a method exists to test the significance of the difference between variances that will be discussed later in this chapter, it is clear that these two variances are relatively similar in magnitude. It is possible, however, that the variances of the two groups might be quite different. If this were true, the estimate of the standard error of the difference between means must be adjusted. Special procedures will now be described that appropriately alter either the critical value of t or its degrees of freedom in order to compensate for this heterogeniety of variance.

research question It is known that organisms will respond in a way that results in a stimulus change of some sort. For example, rats, though they are nocturnal animals, will press a bar that results in an increment in the light intensity of the cage. One theory suggests that the amount of change is an important determinant of the extent to which such stimulation will reinforce a response. To test this point two groups of rats are adapted to a cage with a bar in it. After five minutes the rats are allowed to press a bar that increments the intensity of light in the cage for the duration of the bar press. One group of rats experiences a small change in the light intensity while another group has a larger change in light intensity which is contingent upon a bar press.

Is there a difference in the number of bar presses in the ten-minute session produced by the group experiencing a large change in light intensity vs. the group experiencing a small change in the light intensity?[2]

statistical hypotheses The null hypothesis states that the means of the two groups are really drawn from populations that have the same mean. Consequently, the observed difference in the sample means is merely a function of sampling error. The alternative hypothesis is that the two groups are really samples from populations with different means and the disparity between the observed sample means reflects the difference in their population values. Symbolically:

$$H_0: \mu_1 = \mu_2$$
$$H_1: \mu_1 \neq \mu_2$$

Note again that the alternative hypothesis is non-directional. That is, it does not specify whether the larger change will produce more bar pressing than the smaller change or the reverse. It merely suggests that there is a difference, one way or the other. A summary of the test of these hypotheses is presented in Table 8–2.

formula The formula for t remains the same in the general case,

$$t = \frac{\overline{X}_1 - \overline{X}_2}{s_{\bar{x}_1 - \bar{x}_2}}$$

but the standard error of the difference between means is different from that in the previous example:

$$s_{\bar{x}_1 - \bar{x}_2} = \sqrt{\frac{s_1{}^2}{N_1} + \frac{s_2{}^2}{N_2}}$$

assumptions Again, three assumptions are necessary. First, the samples must be **randomly** selected and **independent.** Second, the two population variances are **heterogeneous** rather than homogeneous. Third, the population distributions are **normal** or the sample sizes are very large.

significance level The .05 level of significance shall be selected arbitrarily and a two-tailed (non-directional) test employed because the alternative hypothesis does not specify the direction that a difference might assume.

[2] This example inspired by R. B. McCall, "Stimulus Change and Light-Contingent Bar Pressing," *Journal of Comparative and Physiological Psychology*, 1965, LIX, 258–262. R. B. McCall, "The Initial-Consequent-Change Surface in Light-Contingent Bar Pressing," *Journal of Comparative and Physiological Psychology*, 1966, LXII, 35–42.

8–2 Summary of the test of the difference between means for independent groups with heterogeneous variances (the example of bar pressing for changes in light intensity).

Hypotheses

H_0: $\mu_1 = \mu_2$

H_1: $\mu_1 \neq \mu_2$

Assumptions

1. The two groups are **independent** and sampling is **random.**
2. The two population variances are **heterogeneous.**
3. The two population distributions are **normal** or the samples are very large.

Decision Rules (necessary data displayed below)

$$t_1 = 2.201, \ df = 11, \quad .05 \text{ level}$$

$$t_2 = 2.093, \ df = 19, \quad .05 \text{ level}$$

$$t_{\text{crit}} = \frac{s_{\bar{x}_1}{}^2 t_1 + s_{\bar{x}_2}{}^2 t_2}{s_{\bar{x}_1}{}^2 + s_{\bar{x}_2}{}^2} = \frac{2(2.201) + 3(2.093)}{2 + 3}$$

$$t_{\text{crit}} = \pm 2.136$$

If $-2.136 < t_{\text{obs}} < 2.136$, accept H_0

If $t_{\text{obs}} \leq -2.136$ or $t_{\text{obs}} \geq 2.136$, reject H_0

Computation

Small Change (*Group* 1)	*Large Change* (*Group* 2)
$\bar{X}_1 = 84$	$\bar{X}_2 = 90$
$s_1{}^2 = 24$	$s_2{}^2 = 60$
$N_1 = 12$	$N_2 = 20$
$s_{\bar{x}_1}{}^2 = \frac{s_1{}^2}{N_1} = \frac{24}{12} = 2$	$s_{\bar{x}_2}{}^2 = \frac{s_2{}^2}{N_2} = \frac{60}{20} = 3$

$$t_{\text{obs}} = \frac{\bar{X}_1 - \bar{X}_2}{\sqrt{\frac{s_1{}^2}{N_1} + \frac{s_2{}^2}{N_2}}} = \frac{84 - 90}{\sqrt{\frac{24}{12} + \frac{60}{20}}}$$

$$t_{\text{obs}} = -2.68$$

Interpretation

Reject H_0

critical values and degrees of freedom As has been indicated, because the variances are not very similar (see following data), some correction must be made that will compensate for this bias. The correction may be made by adjusting the critical value of t required to reject H_0. The following procedure is used. Go to the table of critical values of t at the level of significance selected (.05). Using the degrees of freedom associated with the first variance ($N - 1 = 12 - 1 = 11$), determine from the table the critical value corresponding to the .05 level with 11 *df* and call this t_1. Using the degrees of freedom for the second variance, determine t_2 in the same manner. The critical value of t is then

$$t_{\text{crit}} = \frac{s_{\bar{x}_1}{}^2 t_1 + s_{\bar{x}_2}{}^2 t_2}{s_{\bar{x}_1}{}^2 + s_{\bar{x}_2}{}^2}$$

The adjusted critical value for the present example is given in Table 8–2 as $t_{\text{crit}} = 2.136$. The obtained t is then compared with this critical value of t according to the decision rules established (see following).

decision rules The decision rules using the adjusted critical value are as follows:

If $-2.136 < t_{\text{obs}} < 2.136$, accept H_0
If $t_{\text{obs}} \leq -2.136$ or $t_{\text{obs}} \geq 2.136$, reject H_0

computation The data and computation of the observed t are presented in Table 8–2.

interpretation The observed t of -2.68 falls within the second decision rule and thus H_0 is rejected. This implies that the observed difference between the means was too great to have probably occurred by sampling error alone. If the experiment is appropriate, presumably the magnitude of light change does determine the number of responses. Notice that the observed t was negative. This results merely from the arbitrary assignment of the small change group to $\overline{X}_1$. The sign of t makes very little difference in a non-directional test, but in a directional test it becomes very important as will be seen in the next section.

CORRELATED GROUPS

Sometimes the two means to be compared are both measured on the same group of subjects. This means that all of the factors associated with the particular subjects involved influence the score the subject makes under both conditions. This results in some correlation between the scores in the two groups. Under these circumstances, the estimates of the standard error of the difference between means that have been just illustrated are not applicable because they assume that the two groups are independent samples, and if the groups are correlated (e.g., involve the same subjects or closely matched subjects) then the assumption of independence is untenable and other procedures must be used.

research question Suppose it is important as described earlier to ascertain if stimulation of one area of the brain is more reinforcing to a rat than stimulation of another part. An electrode is sunk into both of these areas in each member of a group of 10 rats. After an initial training session, the rats are allowed to press two bars, one of which results in stimulation to one area of the brain and the other of which stimulates the second area. The number of presses on each bar is recorded, and the mean number of presses for stimulation in Area 1 is to be compared with the mean for Area 2. In addition, suppose a set of experiments by other investigators and a current theory strongly suggest that Area 1 should be more effective in producing responses than Area 2. Therefore, the research question asks if Area 1 is a better site for the reinforcing effects of brain stimulation than Area 2.

statistical hypotheses The null hypothesis is the same as it has been in the previous cases. However, because theory and empirical evidence suggest that stimulation of Area 1 may be more reinforcing than stimulation of Area 2, the alternative hypothesis is directional rather than non-directional. That is, based upon other information (theory and data), if there is a difference between the two means the prediction is that the mean for Area 1 will be greater than for Area 2 rather than the reverse. Symbolically:

$$H_0\colon \mu_1 = \mu_2$$
$$H_1\colon \mu_1 > \mu_2$$

A summary of the procedure for testing these hypotheses is presented in Table 8–3.

formula The computational routine for this case differs from the preceding examples, and rests upon the following fact.

> The difference between two means equals the mean difference between pairs of scores.

This states that if the difference between each subject's two scores is computed and the mean of such differences calculated, this mean will equal the mean of the first group of scores minus the mean of the second. Applied to the current situation, if D_i represents the difference between the pair of scores for the ith subject $(X_{1i} - X_{2i})$, then if there were absolutely no difference between the two sample means (i.e., $\overline{X}_1 - \overline{X}_2 = 0$), $\overline{D}$ would also equal zero. Because of

8-3 Summary of the test of the difference between means for correlated groups (the brain stimulation example).

Hypotheses

$H_0: \mu_1 = \mu_2$
$H_1: \mu_1 > \mu_2$ (directional)

Assumptions

1. The data take the form of pairs of scores, and these pairs of observations are **randomly** sampled. Often these two observations are made on the same or closely matched subjects.
2. The population distribution of the D_i is **normal.**

Decision Rules

Given: .01 significance level, $N - 1 = 9$ *df*

If $t_{\text{obs}} < 2.821$, accept H_0
If $t_{\text{obs}} \geq 2.821$, reject H_0

Computation

Subject	*Area* 1	*Area* 2	D_i	D_i^2
1	58	42	16	256
2	45	50	−5	25
3	61	23	38	1444
4	55	50	5	25
5	58	45	13	169
6	90	85	5	25
7	26	30	−4	16
8	35	20	15	225
9	42	50	−8	64
10	48	60	−12	144
			$\sum D_i = 63$	$\sum D_i^2 = 2393$
			$\bar{D} = 6.3$	

$$t_{\text{obs}} = \frac{\sum D_i}{\sqrt{\dfrac{N\sum D_i^2 - (\sum D_i)^2}{N - 1}}}$$

$$t_{\text{obs}} = \frac{63}{\sqrt{\dfrac{10(2393) - (63)^2}{10 - 1}}}$$

$$t_{\text{obs}} = 1.34$$

Interpretation

Accept H_0

sampling error, $\bar{D}$ rarely would be exactly zero even if the two populations did not differ in their means. Therefore, under the null hypothesis that the means of the two samples are both estimates of the same population mean value, the sampling distribution of $\bar{D}$ should also have a mean of zero. Consequently, the statistical question reduces to the probability that $\bar{D}$ should deviate from zero relative to the sampling error of $\bar{D}$:

$$t_{\text{obs}} = \frac{\bar{D} - 0}{s_{\bar{D}}} = \frac{\sum D_i/N}{\sqrt{\dfrac{N\sum D_i^2 - (\sum D_i)^2}{N^2(N-1)}}} = \frac{\sum D_i}{\sqrt{\dfrac{N\sum D_i^2 - (\sum D_i)^2}{N-1}}}$$

The N in the above formula refers to the number of subjects or the number of pairs of scores. Thus, if 12 people are measured both before and after an experimental treatment, $N = 12$.

assumptions The data come in pairs of scores and it is usually presumed that the two types of measures are correlated. Often this results from having the same or closely matched subjects contribute both scores. It is assumed that the pairs are **randomly sampled** and that in the population the D_i are **normally** distributed.

significance level Suppose that the implications of this study are such that it would be exceptionally undesirable to incorrectly reject the null hypothesis. Therefore, the .01 level of significance will be selected.

critical values The test to be performed will involve a directional alternative. This means that the test is one-tailed in that the critical region constitutes only one of the two tails of the t distribution. Since additional information dictates that Area 1 should be better than Area 2, the converse possibility that Area 1 might be poorer in reinforcing bar pressing has become less likely, so unlikely that the probability that this should occur is nearly zero. Under these conditions it is no longer appropriate to expect that a negative value of $\bar{D}$ and thus of t (see preceding formula) might occur, and so the left-hand tail of the theoretical distribution is not included in the critical region. As a result, the critical value appropriate for this test is such that 1% of the area under the curve falls to its right. Looking in the table of t values with $N - 1 = 10 - 1 = 9$ degrees of freedom, one finds the .01 level, one-tailed critical value is 2.821.

Note, however, that if this were a two-tailed test the critical value would be 3.250. One might wonder, if additional information suggests that Area 1 might be better than Area 2, why select a procedure that has a lower critical level than what would be used if a two-tailed alternative were employed? Is this not biasing the result, making it more likely to reject the null hypothesis? If the issue is considered from the standpoint of the meaning of the critical level, this apparent contradiction dissolves. The critical level is an arbitrarily established probability value, the probability that one should erroneously reject the null hypothesis. In terms of a two-tailed test, one could erroneously reject the null hypothesis if Area 1 were greater or less effective in reinforcing behavior, and it is for this reason that the critical region is divided into two parts, one in each tail of the theoretical distribution. However, in the case of the one-tailed test, additional information has suggested that it is very unlikely that the observed value of $\overline{D}$ will fall in one of these regions. Therefore, in order to maintain the probability of erroneously rejecting the null hypothesis at .01 it is necessary to place all of the critical region in the right-hand tail.

decision rules The decision rules are as follows:

$$\text{If } t_{\text{obs}} < 2.821, \text{ accept } H_0$$
$$\text{If } t_{\text{obs}} \geq 2.821, \text{ reject } H_0$$

computation The raw data and computation are illustrated in Table 8–3.

interpretation The observed value of t ($t_{\text{obs}} = 1.34$) is less than the critical value of 2.821, and according to the decision rules one accepts the null hypothesis. This implies that such an observed $\overline{D}$ of 6.3 is within the realm of sampling error for correlated samples of size 10 drawn from populations having the same mean. That is, if the two areas of the brain were identical in their reinforcing potential, with the amount of variability involved it would be quite possible to obtain a sample having a $\overline{D} = 6.3$.

The researcher must conclude that his data provide no evidence that stimulation of Area 1 has more potential reinforcing value than Area 2. This is not to say that the evidence disproves the proposition that Area 1 is better than Area 2. There is a difference between failing to support a proposition and disproving it. Recall that the procedures tested the null hypothesis that there was no difference, and the calculations led to accepting the null hypothesis as being true. However, the alternative hypothesis was **not** tested and rejected. Therefore, the procedures only permit one to say there is no evidence to support the notion that Area 1 is better than Area 2. They do not allow one to say that Area 1 is not better than Area 2 because such a hypothesis was not tested. This is a subtle point, but it is important in governing one's interpretation and thinking with respect to scientific evidence.

homogeneity of variance

The first two tests of the difference between means required knowledge of whether the variances of the two groups were relatively similar (i.e., homogeneous) or different (i.e., heterogeneous). Obviously, the values of the two sample variances will not be precisely identical, but how different must they be before one considers them dissimilar or not homogeneous? This is the same question that has been posed concerning the difference between means: how different do the two means have to be before one rejects the hypothesis that they are computed on random samples from populations having the same mean? The procedure for determining the probability that two variances are computed on samples drawn from populations having the same variance is based upon slightly different reasoning than previously employed.

If the null hypothesis is true and the variances of the two groups are really both estimates of the same population value, then on the average one might expect that the ratio of the two sample variances should be approximately 1.0. However, the value of this ratio would not probably be the same each time a pair of samples is randomly selected. The ratio would vary from sampling to sampling, and a distribution of ratios could be obtained. If pairs of samples were drawn repeatedly from a single population and the ratio of the two variances was computed, in the limit the distribution of such ratios would form a sampling distribution because it would be a distribution of a statistic: s_1^2/s_2^2. Fortunately, the percentiles of this theoretical relative frequency distribution are known in the same manner that the percentiles of the standard normal or t distributions are known.

The theoretical sampling distribution of the ratio of two independent variances is called F.

The F distribution assumes that the two variances are independent, that is, the scores are not correlated (e.g., not based upon the same or matched subjects). Therefore, the use of the F distribution to test the difference between two variances is limited to variances produced by measuring independent groups of subjects.

Recall that the t distribution was different for each number of degrees of freedom. Since the F distribution is the ratio of two independent variances and each variance has a certain number of degrees of freedom associated with it, the F distribution is different for every **pair** of degrees of freedom.

Consequently, the ratio of two variances is distributed as F with $N_1 - 1$ and $N_2 - 1$ degrees of freedom, where $N_1 - 1$ is the degrees of freedom of the variance in the numerator and $N_2 - 1$ is the degrees of freedom of the variance in the denominator.

Table C in Appendix II in the back of this book lists the .05 (roman) and .01 (italic) critical values for F's of various degrees of freedom. To find a critical value, find the column of the table corresponding to the number of degrees of freedom for the variance in the numerator. Then locate the row corresponding to the degrees of freedom for the variance in the denominator of the ratio. Suppose there were 21 and 31 subjects in the groups for the variances in the numerator and denominator of the F ratio, respectively. There would be 20 and 30 degrees of freedom for the F ratio. Locate the intersection of the column labeled 20 and the row labeled 30 degrees of freedom. There are two values at that point. The first (roman) is 1.93 and that is the critical value corresponding to a .05 level test. Below this figure you will find the value 2.55 (italic) which represents the .01 critical value.

The distinction between one-tailed and two-tailed tests does not exist in the same form for the F distribution as it did for the z and t distributions. This is because a convention exists which dictates that:

> In tests of homogeneity of variance the larger of the two variances is always placed in the numerator of the *F* ratio.

Consequently, the obtained value of F is never less than 1.0, and this convention restricts the value of F to only one side of the F distribution. As a result, when testing hypotheses about the homogeneity of variances, the significance levels in the table must be doubled to compensate for the fact that the larger variance is always placed in the numerator. Thus, for this kind of test the critical values listed in the F table for any combination of degrees of freedom represent the .10 and .02 significance levels. In the next chapters, the F distribution will be used within the context of the analysis of variance and then the .05 and .01 levels will be appropriate.

When making directional tests (though this is unusual in this context), the critical values are not altered as above. Rather, the variance **hypothesized** to be larger is placed in the numerator, regardless of its relative size.

EXAMPLE

research question Consider the example given previously about the rats reared in the square vs. the round worlds. In order to select the appropriate formula for testing the difference between the means of those two independent groups of subjects, it must be decided if their variances are homogeneous.

statistical hypotheses The null hypothesis is that the two variances are computed on two random samples drawn from populations having the same variance. In short, $\sigma_1^2 = \sigma_2^2$. The alternative hypothesis is that in the population the variances for animals reared in square and round environments are different. In symbols,

$$H_0\colon \sigma_1^2 = \sigma_2^2$$
$$H_1\colon \sigma_1^2 \neq \sigma_2^2$$

A summary of the procedure for testing these hypotheses is presented in Table 8–4.

8–4 Summary of the test of the differences between two independent variances (the round vs. square world example).

Hypotheses

$H_0: \sigma_1^2 = \sigma_2^2$
$H_1: \sigma_1^2 \neq \sigma_2^2$ (non-directional)

Assumptions

1. The population distributions of the two groups are **normal.**
2. The sample variances are **independent** and sampling is **random.**

Decision Rules

Given: .10 level, $N_1 - 1 = 10$ and $N_2 - 1 = 20$ *df*

If $F_{obs} < 2.35$, accept H_0
If $F_{obs} \geq 2.35$, reject H_0

Computation

Square World	*Round World*
$s_1^2 = 16$	$s_2^2 = 18$
$N_1 = 21$	$N_2 = 11$

$$F_{obs} = \frac{s^2_{larger}}{s^2_{smaller}}, \; df = N_1 - 1, N_2 - 1 \text{ where}$$
$N_1 - 1 = df$ for numerator
$N_2 - 1 = df$ for denominator

$$F_{obs} = \frac{18}{16} = 1.13, \; df = 10, 20$$

Interpretation

Accept H_0

formula The ratio of the larger to the smaller of two independent variances is distributed as F:

$$F = \frac{s^2_{larger}}{s^2_{smaller}}$$

The degrees of freedom are $N_1 - 1$ and $N_2 - 1$, where $N_1 - 1$ refers to the degrees of freedom for the variance in the numerator. In this example there were 11 rats in the round-world group which had a variance of 18 and 21 rats in the square-world group which had a variance of 16. Since the variance for the round-world group was larger, its degrees of freedom ($11 - 1 = 10$) are associated with the numerator and $21 - 1 = 20$ *df* are associated with the denominator of the *F* ratio.

assumptions It is assumed that the samples are **randomly** drawn from **normal** populations and that the samples are **independent.**

significance level Adopt the .10 level.

critical values A "two-tailed test" at the .10 level would ordinarily have 5% of the area in **each tail** compose the critical region. However, because the larger of the two variances will always be placed in the numerator, all the *F* values will be positive. Consequently, the 5% of the area in the right-hand tail actually detects extremely large or small values of *F*. Therefore, the *F* value marking off 5% of the area to its right actually is making a test at the 10% level of significance because of the convention of placing the largest s^2 in the numerator. Therefore, the critical value for 10 and 20 degrees of freedom at the .10 level of significance is 2.35.

decision rules Symbolically:

$$\text{If } F_{\text{obs}} < 2.35, \text{ accept } H_0$$
$$\text{If } F_{\text{obs}} \geq 2.35, \text{ reject } H_0$$

computation The calculations are presented in Table 8–4.

interpretation Since the observed value of *F* (1.13) did not exceed the critical value of 2.35, the first decision rule is realized and the null hypothesis is accepted. This implies that the difference between the two variances is small enough so that such a difference might be expected purely on the basis of sampling error associated with selecting two groups of subjects from populations having the same variance. The two variances are not considered significantly different, and thus the formula that assumes homogeneity of population variances in testing the difference between means is selected.

Notice that in the light-change example illustrating the use of the formulas appropriate for the case in which the variances are **not** considered similar, the ratio of the two variances is

$$F = \tfrac{60}{24} = 2.75, \; df = 19, 11$$

The critical value at the .10 level is approximately 2.66. Since the observed value of *F* exceeds this critical value, the probability that these two variances are both estimates of the same population value is too remote and the null hypothesis of no difference between these variances is rejected. Therefore, the procedures for heterogeneous variances are appropriate for testing the difference between means in this case.

inferences about correlation coefficients

In the previous sections inferences about differences between means and variances were considered. Actually, tests of the significance of differences in population values for two samples may be made with reference to many statistics. In addition to central tendency, one might be interested in inferences about the degree of relationship between two variables. The two sections of this part of the chapter are concerned with whether a significant relationship exists (whether the observed r could come from a population in which the parameter ρ is actually zero) and whether two r's drawn from independent groups of subjects are significantly different from one another.

THE SIGNIFICANCE OF *r*

If a researcher observed a correlation between two variables of .58, he might want to know if an r of this magnitude is merely an imperfect reflection of a population in which that relationship is actually zero, or whether an $r = .58$ faithfully mirrors a population in which a non-zero relationship actually exists. It could be the case that in the population a relationship does not exist between two specified variables. In the course of sampling from such a population in which $\rho = .00$ it might be possible to observe a correlation of .58 or even higher, purely on the basis of sampling error. What is the probability that this could be the case?

research question Some tests of infant development and intelligence contain items that are designed to assess the amount and nature of vocalizations made by the infant. For example, a bell is rung in front of the infant and the presence and extent of the youngster's vocalization in response to this stimulus is measured. Although many items on such infant scales tend to assess motor development and do not seem to relate to later intelligence, it might be reasonable to inquire whether there is a relationship between vocalization in 12-month-old female infants and verbal intelligence at six years of age. Thus, the research question is whether or not there is a relationship between vocalization in 12-month girls and their verbal IQ at six years of age.[3]

statistical hypotheses The data reveal a correlation of .58 between infant vocalization and childhood verbal intelligence for a group of 27 females. However, it is possible that in the population of all females no relationship exists, that is, $\rho = .00$. In such an event, the observed relationship of .58 is merely a

[3] Inspired by J. Cameron, N. Livson, and Nancy Bayley, "Infant Vocalizations and Their Relationship to Mature Intelligence," *Science*, 1967, CLVII, 331–333; T. Moore, "Language and Intelligence: A Longitudinal Study of the First Eight Years," *Human Development*, 1967, X, 88–106.

function of sampling error. Theoretically, it would be possible to continue to select sample after sample of size 27 and compute a correlation on each. The distribution of such sample r's forms the sampling distribution of the correlation coefficient, and its standard deviation is the standard error of r. The null hypothesis states that the observed value of r is typical of such a distribution of sample r's drawn from a population in which this correlation is actually .00. The alternative hypothesis dictates that the observed r is too extreme to be considered a member of such a sampling distribution, and thus it probably reflects a relationship of some non-zero magnitude in the population. Since there is no theory or empirical basis for predicting that such a relationship, if it exists, would be positive or negative, the alternative hypothesis is non-directional. In symbols,

$$H_0: \rho = .00$$
$$H_1: \rho \neq .00$$

A summary of the test of these hypotheses is presented in Table 8–5.

8–5 Summary of the test of the significance of a correlation coefficient (the infant vocalization and IQ example).

Hypotheses

$H_0: \rho = .00$
$H_1: \rho \neq .00$ (non-directional)

Assumptions

1. The population distributions of both X and Y are **normal** in form, and sampling is **random.**

Decision Rules

Given: $\alpha = .05$, a two-tailed test, and $N - 2 = 27 - 2 = 25$ degrees of freedom

If $-2.06 < t_{obs} < 2.06$, accept H_0
If $t_{obs} \leq -2.06$ or $t_{obs} \geq 2.06$, reject H_0

Computation

$$t_{obs} = \frac{r\sqrt{N-2}}{\sqrt{1-r^2}}, \quad df = N - 2 \qquad r = .58 \quad N = 27$$

$$t_{obs} = \frac{.58\sqrt{27-2}}{\sqrt{1-(.58)^2}}, \quad df = 27 - 2 = 25$$

$$t_{obs} = 3.56$$

Interpretation

Reject H_0

statistical formula It can be shown that the difference between a sample value r and its population ρ (if ρ is near zero) divided by an estimate of the standard error of ρ is distributed as t with $N - 2$ degrees of freedom. In symbols,

$$t = \frac{r\sqrt{N-2}}{\sqrt{1-r^2}} \text{ with } N - 2 \text{ degrees of freedom}$$

assumption It is assumed that the sample of X and Y values is randomly selected and that the X and Y population distributions are **normal.**

When both variables, X and Y, are normally distributed, their joint distribution (their scatterplot) is called a **bivariate normal distribution,** and the distribution of the Y_i at any value of X is a normal distribution in the population.

significance level Assume the .05 level of significance.

critical values The critical values of t (Table B) for a two-tailed alternative with critical level of .05 and $N - 2 = 27 - 2 = 25$ degrees of freedom are ± 2.06.

decision rules Given the above information,

If $-2.06 < t_{\text{obs}} < +2.06$, accept H_0
If $t_{\text{obs}} \leq -2.06$ or $t_{\text{obs}} \geq +2.06$, reject H_0

computation The computation of t_{obs} is given in Table 8–5 and $t_{\text{obs}} = 3.56$.

interpretation Since the observed value of t ($t_{\text{obs}} = 3.56$) exceeds the critical value of 2.06, the second decision rule is used and H_0 is rejected. Consequently, the probability that an observed correlation of .58 could be drawn from a population in which the correlation between these two variables is actually zero is too remote to warrant the conclusion that an $r = .58$ could be obtained on the basis of sampling error alone. Therefore, such a hypothesis is rejected with the attendant implication that there is a relationship in the population between vocalization in infant girls and their six-year-old verbal intelligence.

use of tables This general procedure of testing the significance of a correlation coefficient occurs so frequently that tables of critical values of r for a given df and significance level are available. This makes the computation of the above formula unnecessary. Table D in Appendix II in the back of this book gives the value of r needed for significance at specified df and significance levels. In this case with $df = 25$ at the .05 level for a two-tailed test, a correlation of .3809 or higher is needed in order to reject the null hypothesis. Actually, the figure .3809 should be $\pm.3809$ for a two-tailed alternative. Since the observed value of r was .58, this obtained relationship exceeded the critical value of $\pm.3809$.

THE DIFFERENCE BETWEEN TWO CORRELATIONS (INDEPENDENT SAMPLES)

research question The preceding results were obtained from girls. Is there any difference in the degree of this relationship for boys versus girls? It might be the case that the relationship between infant vocalization and six-year-old verbal IQ is stronger or weaker for girls than for boys. To test this a sample of 18 boys was measured at 12 months and six years of age in precisely the same manner as described previously for girls. While the correlation for girls was .58, the correlation for boys was −.09. What is the probability that such a difference in observed correlations could occur merely as a function of sampling error when, in fact, there is no difference between the populations of boys and girls in the degree of this relationship? Note that the two correlations being considered, .58 and −.09, are computed on independent (i.e., different) groups of subjects. The following procedures apply only to this case. Similar but different techniques are required in the event that two correlations computed on the same group of subjects are to be compared.[4]

statistical hypotheses If there is really no difference in the degree of correlation for the two groups (sexes), then the correlation in the population for the boys should equal that parameter for girls ($\rho_1 = \rho_2$). On the other hand, if there is a difference in the magnitude of the relationship for the two groups their population values should not be equal. The alternative in this case is non-directional (two-tailed). If, for some reason, it was anticipated that the boys should demonstrate a lower relationship than the girls, then the alternative hypothesis would state that the ρ_2 for boys is less than the ρ_1 for girls. For the case described above however, the hypotheses are as follows:

$$H_0: \rho_1 = \rho_2$$
$$H_1: \rho_1 \neq \rho_2$$

A summary of the test of these two hypotheses is presented in Table 8–6.

formula The test of these hypotheses is accomplished by first transforming the obtained correlation coefficients according to the following expression:

$$z_r = \tfrac{1}{2}\log_e(1 + r) - \tfrac{1}{2}\log_e(1 - r)$$

Fortunately, this formula has been computed for many values of r and tabled. This r to z transformation is given in Table E in Appendix II in the back of this book. Its use will be described again in the subsequent section on "Computation" and illustrated in Table 8–6.

Once the r to z transformations have been made on each of the two values of r, the difference between the transformed correlation coefficients (z_r) relative

[4] See G. A. Ferguson, *Statistical Analysis in Psychology and Education* (New York: McGraw-Hill, 1966), 188–189.

8-6 Summary of the test of the difference between two correlation coefficients (the vocalization—IQ example).

Hypotheses

$H_0: \rho_1 = \rho_2$
$H_1: \rho_1 \neq \rho_2$ (non-directional)

Assumptions

1. The two sample r's are both computed on **randomly** selected, **independent** samples.
2. The population distributions of X and Y for each correlation are **normal** in form.
3. N_1 and N_2 are both greater than 20.

Decision Rules

Given: $\alpha = .05$ and a two-tailed test

If $-1.96 < z_{obs} < 1.96$, accept H_0

If $z_{obs} \leq -1.96$ or $z_{obs} \geq 1.96$, reject H_0

Computation

Group 1 (Girls): $N_1 = 27$, $r_1 = .58$, $z_{r_1} = .662$
Group 2 (Boys): $N_2 = 18$, $r_2 = -.09$, $z_{r_2} = -.090$

$$z_{obs} = \frac{z_{r_1} - z_{r_2}}{\sqrt{\frac{1}{N_1 - 3} + \frac{1}{N_2 - 3}}}$$

$$z_{obs} = \frac{.662 - (-.090)}{\sqrt{\frac{1}{27 - 3} + \frac{1}{18 - 3}}}$$

$$z_{obs} = 2.28$$

Interpretation

Reject H_0

to the standard error of such differences is given by

$$z = \frac{z_{r_1} - z_{r_2}}{\sqrt{\frac{1}{N_1 - 3} + \frac{1}{N_2 - 3}}}$$

Note that the distribution employed as the theoretical relative frequency distribution is the standard normal (observe that z refers to the standard normal deviate and z_{r_i} refers to the transformed correlations). Because the standard normal is being used and not the t, it is necessary to have an adequate number of cases in the two samples. It is probably best to have N_1 and N_2 each greater than 20.

assumptions There are several assumptions required for performing this test. As always, the sample *r*'s are computed on **randomly** selected samples. Second, it is necessary that the two *r*'s are computed on **independent samples** involving different or unmatched subjects. If this condition were not met, the formula for the sampling error of the difference between correlation coefficients would not be appropriate for reasons similar to those discussed under the testing of the difference in means for independent versus correlated groups. Third, the X and Y distributions for both correlation coefficients must be **normal** in form. Fourth, the two **sample sizes must be greater than 20.**

significance level Assume the .05 level.

critical values A two-tailed test at the .05 level using the standard normal distribution requires an observed z in excess of ± 1.96.

decision rules

$$\text{If } -1.96 < z_{\text{obs}} < +1.96, \text{ accept } H_0$$
$$\text{If } z_{\text{obs}} \leq -1.96 \text{ or } z_{\text{obs}} \geq +1.96, \text{ reject } H_0$$

computation The computation is summarized in Table 8–6. Note that the information given in the problem is stated first. Then the *r*'s are transformed to their corresponding z_r values with the use of Table E. The values are substituted into the formula and a $z_{\text{obs}} = 2.28$ obtained.

interpretation The observed value of z ($z_{\text{obs}} = 2.28$) exceeds the critical values of ± 1.96 and thus conforms to the second decision rule to reject H_0. This implies that the probability that two such correlation coefficients could be drawn from a common population purely on the basis of sampling error is very remote. Therefore, it is likely that these *r*'s represent two populations that have different magnitudes of relationship between infant vocalization and later verbal intelligence. Specifically, it would appear that such a relationship is higher for girls than for boys.

the interpretation of significance

COMPARISON OF H_0: $\rho = .00$ AND H_0: $\rho_1 = \rho_2$

The problem in interpreting just what a "significant difference" might mean can be presented in sharp relief by considering the distinction between testing the null hypothesis that a given correlation is zero (H_0: $\rho = .00$) and the null hypothesis that two correlations are equal (H_0: $\rho_1 = \rho_2$). Suppose the correlation for girls was .58 but the correlation for boys was .35. As illustrated, the $r = .58$ for girls is significant; that is, it is unlikely that such a value was computed on a sample drawn from a population that possesses no correlation at all ($\rho = .00$). More informally, the significant correlation for girls implies that there is a relationship between infant vocalization and verbal IQ for girls. However, if the correlation of $r = .35$ calculated on a sample of 18 boys is tested for the null hypothesis of $\rho = .00$, H_0 is accepted, implying that the relationship is not significant for boys and that there is no evidence of a relationship between vocalization and verbal IQ for boys. Now, when the two correlations (.58 and .35) are compared to determine if they are significantly different from each other (H_0: $\rho_1 = \rho_2$), the test results in accepting the null hypothesis with its attendant interpretation that the relationship is not different for boys and girls. But this combination of results does not seem to make sense. How is it possible that there is a relationship for girls but not for boys while boys and girls do not differ in the amount of this relationship?

This anomaly stems from the fact that tests of hypotheses often are interpreted in terms of a dichotomous decision. Either there is or there is not a relationship or a difference. Although sometimes it is useful to think in these terms, attempting to make a dichotomous decision is a somewhat artificial procedure when the tool employed to make that decision is a probability value that may range from .00 to 1.00 and ordinarily does not fall neatly into two distinct classifications. To illustrate more clearly by citing an extreme example, suppose that with a sample of 32 girls and 32 boys, the correlations were .35 and .34 respectively. With a two-tailed test at the .05 level, the relationship would be judged "significant" for girls but not for boys, yet the two correlations certainly are not significantly different from each other.

In statistical terms, the general situation may be explained by considering the two different sampling distributions that form the basis of these two tests. The sampling distribution of r and that of $r_1 - r_2$ (actually $z_{r_1} - z_{r_2}$) are presented in Figure 8–1. First, when testing the significance of a single correlation coefficient the appropriate sampling distribution is pictured at the top of the graph. The decision rules arbitrarily designate that r's falling beyond a certain point (critical value) are so unlikely to have been sampled from a distribution with $\rho = .00$ that they are deemed to have come from a different population. They may reflect the presence of a non-zero relationship. The critical values and regions have been marked in Figure 8–1 and it is clear that an r of .58 is "significant" in this sense whereas $r = .35$ is not. However, when testing for the difference between two correlations, a different sampling distribution is used, namely the sampling distribution of $r_1 - r_2$ (actually $z_{r_1} - z_{r_2}$), and this graph is presented at the bottom of Figure 8–1. This distribution assumes the null hypothesis that $\rho_1 = \rho_2$. This is quite a different hypothesis from the previous test of the significance of a correlation (H_0: $\rho = .00$). Therefore, it is clear how such a situation could arise. Indeed, it is theoretically possible that both correlations could be individually "nonsignificant" but

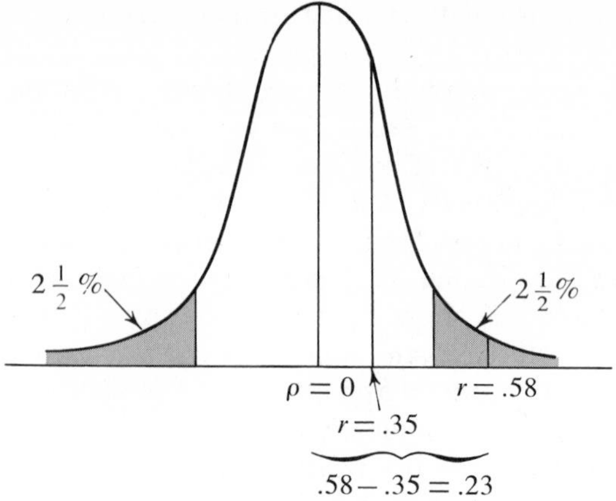

(a) Sampling distribution of r (H_0: $\rho = .00$)

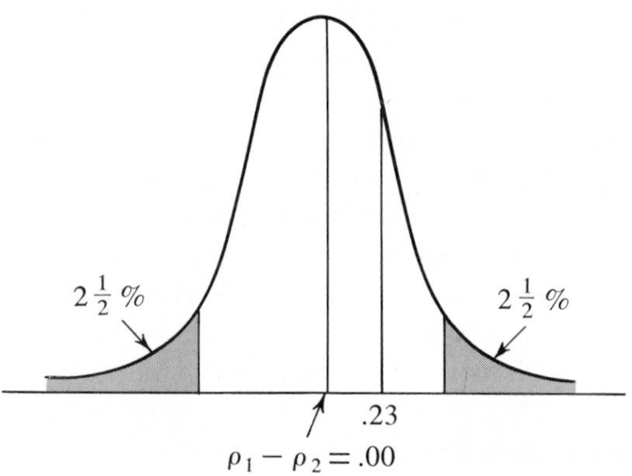

(b) Sampling distribution of $r_1 - r_2$ (H_0: $\rho_1 - \rho_2 = .00$)

Fig. 8–1. The distinction between H_0: $\rho = .00$ and H_0: $\rho_1 - \rho_2 = .00$ illustrated by diagramming the sampling distributions of r and $r_1 - r_2$.

significantly different from each other (e.g., $r_1 = -.35$, $r_2 = +.35$, $N_1 = N_2 = 25$) or each correlation could be significant but there could be no significant difference between them (e.g., $r_1 = .58$, $r_2 = .65$, $N_1 = N_2 = 25$).

How does one interpret such a situation as described? The combination of results is ambiguous. The correlation of .58 for girls is substantial enough to warrant the conclusion that there is probably a relationship between vocalization and IQ for girls. However, the data may be interpreted as being inconclusive for boys (assuming $r = .35$) in that while the correlation is not substantial enough to warrant a firm rejection of the null hypothesis that it reflects a population in which $\rho = .00$, the observed correlation was not so different from the substantial correlation of .58 for girls. Other interpretations are also possible.

PROBABILITY AND "SIGNIFICANCE"

The previous example illustrates how the use of probability to make a dichotomous decision of "significant-nonsignificant" may lead to confusion and ambiguity. There are several problems associated with declaring a statistical difference as either "significant" or "nonsignificant." First, the critical value used to make such a decision is based upon the critical level that is **arbitrarily** selected by the researcher. Thus, whether or not a statistical manipulation is "significant" depends upon the arbitrary selection of the probability of a Type I Error (see Chapter 7). Fortunately (or unfortunately) there is some communality among behavioral scientists as to what level that probability should be. Usually it is placed at .05, and sometimes (though rarely) at .01 or .001. The fact that many of the tables in the appendices of this book list only critical values corresponding to these significance levels attests to this practice.

However, the significant-nonsignificant dichotomy remains artificial. If a correlation of .43 is obtained with 22 subjects, it is deemed significant at the .05 level but a correlation of .42 would not be called significant. Certainly if one concludes that there is a relationship in the event of the correlation of .43 but that there is no relationship in the event of the correlation of .42 he is grossly oversimplifying. This is particularly true in view of the potential influence of a single score on the magnitude of the correlation in a small sample as discussed in a previous chapter. Thus, a single subject could determine whether the relationship is significant or nonsignificant.

In view of these factors, when a dichotomous decision is not required, it is probably best to report the exact probability of the null hypothesis rather than merely whether it was "significant" or "not significant." For example, if a correlation of .40 is obtained on a sample of 20 subjects and a two-tailed test is appropriate, one will observe in Table D that such a value does not reach the required value for significance at the .05 level. However, it does represent a probability that is less than .10 but greater than .05. Therefore, in scientific writing it would be best to state that the probability falls between .10 and .05. In symbols, $.10 < p < .05$. If a correlation were observed to be .58 on a sample of 20 subjects, the probability might be reported as being $p < .01$ regardless of whether the .05 level was originally selected.

PROBABILITY AND *N*

Regretfully, the interpretation of statistical results is more complicated than just described. The critical value often varies with the number of subjects sampled. Suppose a correlation of .35 exists in the population and suppose that such a value was obtained in samples of various sizes. With a two-tailed test at .05, an r of .35 would be statistically significant only if 32 or more subjects were sampled. An examination of Table D shows that the value of r required for significance at .05 decreases as the number of subjects in the sample (i.e., degrees of freedom) increases. Notice that in a sample of 102 cases, a correlation of .195 is significant at the .05 level (two-tailed), but an $r = .75$ is not quite significant if only 7 subjects are involved. In general, the more subjects one samples the more likely it is that he will obtain a significant result if such a condition is actually present in the population.

On the one hand, this is as it should be. The probability value one obtains is intended to be a measure of the uncertainty in the situation. If a coin is tossed four times and it comes up heads on three of those tosses, one does not feel very confident that the coin is biased. The coin might be biased, but how much money would you bet on such a proposition with only that much evidence? Not too much. On the other hand, if the coin is tossed 10,000 times and 7,500 of those tosses result in a head, despite the fact that the same percentage of tosses were heads one would be far more willing to wager that the coin is biased. Therefore, it is not unreasonable that the probability of a given event should be a function of the number of cases involved.

On the other hand, does this mean that scientific results are a function of the tenacity and wealth of the researcher who is capable of including a large number of subjects in his experiments? Not exactly, but it is true that research based upon large samples has more power in the sense that the likelihood of rejecting H_0 when it is in fact false is greater when large rather than small samples are used. Therefore, the use of large samples allows a more sensitive test of the hypotheses.

THE TWO MEANINGS OF "SIGNIFICANCE"

It has become apparent that the appropriate interpretation of scientific results is a complex matter. Of paramount importance is the fact that statistical procedures provide the researcher with a set of tools that can help him interpret the results of his experiments, but that these procedures cannot replace the adequate collection of data under well-controlled conditions.

This proposition implies two important points. First, if the data are sloppily collected and inappropriate to the research question being posed, all the statistical significance in the world will not make the experiment worth while. Statistics do not improve the data or the experiment, they can only facilitate in revealing whatever conclusions lie hidden within that collection of measurements.

The second point is that "statistical significance" does not imply "scientific significance." That is, an experimenter may find emphatic differences between groups, but this information may be totally useless and uninformative. What is important or "scientifically significant" is difficult to define because scientists differ in their opinions on this subject. Further, a given item of data may be useless today but become very important in ten years or more. However, a result that has potential implications for a wide variety of issues (applied or theoretical) or relates to a broad spectrum of topics is an approximate definition of the second meaning of "significant research."

Thus, a great variety of factors are called upon to judge the significance of a scientific result, and such interpretations are made only after much experience with the methods of science and the facts of relevant phenomena.

a comparison of the difference between means and correlation

It will be instructive in order for one to understand more fully the implications of a difference between means and a significant correlation if the two procedures are compared. Fortunately, a very interesting comparison between testing for mean differences vs. correlational procedures exists.[5] The relative role of heredity and environment as factors in development has been a focus of interest for psychologists for some time. More specifically, people have been concerned with whether heredity or environment is responsible for intelligence. One way to approach this issue is to investigate the IQ's of adopted children and their biological and foster mothers. In general, the results have shown a correlation of approximately .35 between a measure of intellectual performance for the biological mothers and one for their children, but a correlation of almost zero between the same measures taken on the foster mothers and the children they reared. By itself, this information would appear to suggest that heredity may be more important than environment in determining intelligence. However, the mean IQ of the children was approximately the same as that of the foster mothers whereas the mean IQ of the biological mothers was much lower. Thus, the children had an average IQ that was much more like their foster mothers than their biological mothers, evidence that seems to implicate environment in the determination of intelligence. How is this pattern of results possible and what does it say about the procedures for testing a difference between means in contrast to a correlation?

Of particular interest for this discussion is the fact that although there was a correlation between the biological mother's intelligence and that of her child, it was also true that the average IQ of the children was higher than that of their biological mothers and more similar to that of their foster mothers. Consider the hypothetical data presented in Figure 8–2. The data presented here have been exaggerated somewhat to illustrate the point more clearly.

Notice first that the scores are plotted according to their value with higher IQ scores at the top, and that they are clustered into scores for biological mothers, children, and foster mothers. The lines connecting pairs of scores

[5] This example suggested by results reported in M. Skodak and H. M. Skeels, "A Final Follow-Up Study of One Hundred Adopted Children," *Journal of Genetic Psychology*, 1949, LXXV, 85–125; M. P. Honzik, "Developmental Studies of Parent-Child Resemblance in Intelligence," *Child Development*, 1957, XXVIII, 215–228.

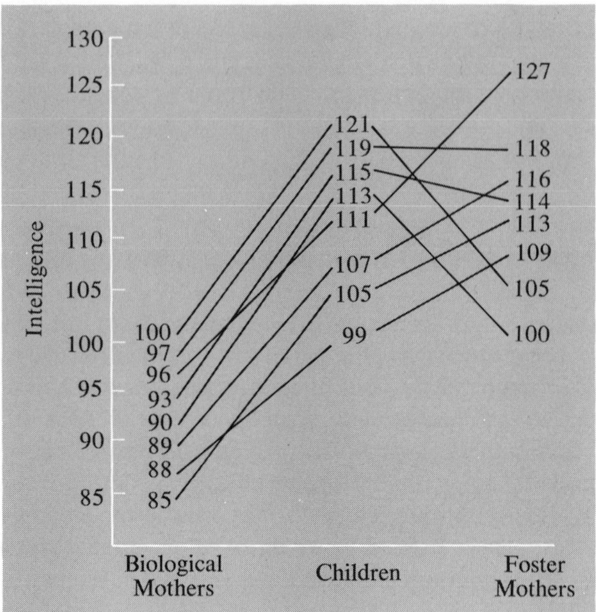

Fig. 8–2. Diagram showing the different meaning of a correlation and the difference between means.

designate which biological mother goes with which child and which child goes with which foster mother. A correlation is high if the lines linking corresponding scores do not cross excessively. Notice that the children tend to line up within their group in much the same order that their biological mothers are assembled, and thus the correlation between biological mother and child in this hypothetical example is fairly high. However, the extensive crossing of lines relating child's IQ and his foster mother's IQ suggests that the relative ordering of children and foster mothers is quite unpredictable and thus the correlation is low. In contrast, the general height (distance from the X axis) of a group on this graph represents the relative score value (e.g., the mean) of the group. It is plain that the children are more like their foster mothers in this respect and less like their biological mothers. Therefore, it is quite possible that two groups of scores may have a correlation but no mean difference, a mean difference but no correlation, no correlation and no mean difference, or a correlation and a mean difference. Further, the correlations may be either positive or negative.

This example attempts to show that correlations and mean differences often present two distinct types of information, both of which are valuable to the interpretation of the general results. Very often, researchers only perform one of these two types of data analyses when, in fact, both could be performed and both could provide different types of information on the processes at work in the experiment or observation. For example, sometimes a test is given before a certain experimental treatment is introduced and then a posttest is given after the experimental treatment. Usually, the researcher looks for a difference in the means of the two groups of scores. Perhaps, an experimental teaching method has been used and the investigator wants to know if the group taught by this method has improved significantly over its performance prior to the experimental program. Suppose that the test of the differences between means is significant, and some improvement was noted. If there is also a correlation between the pretest and posttest, then one can also presume that the program affected each student approximately to the same relative extent: the better students were still at the top of the group on the posttest, and so on. However, if there is no significant correlation, such a result would suggest that although the treatment did raise the mean of the group it seemed to influence some students relatively more than others so that their relative ranking within their group was disrupted. As a consequence, a researcher might wish to further investigate the characteristics of students who tended to improve a disproportionate degree vs. those who did not improve a degree commensurate with the group.

Therefore, the difference between the means of two groups and the correlation between those groups are two independent types of statistics, and they convey different messages about the events and processes being studied.

proportion of variance accounted for

One of the advantages of the correlation coefficient is that r^2 reflects the proportion of the variability in Y that may be attributable to X. Sometimes this fact is stated in terms of the variance in Y **accounted for** by X.

Since the significance of r is influenced by the size of the sample while the proportion of variance accounted for is not, this aspect of the correlation coefficient is quite valuable for one's interpretation of the results of an experiment. For example, frequently in studies involving many subjects it is not uncommon to find statistically significant correlations of .20 or less because of the large N. If $r^2 = (.20)(.20) = .04$, then only 4% of the variance in Y is accounted for by its relationship to X, regardless of the size of the sample.

The same sort of question may be posed about an experiment that involves the relative effectiveness of two different treatments of individuals. For example, if two different teaching methods are used to instruct pupils in reading, a mean reading score for each of the two groups will be obtained and the difference between these means will be tested. However, just as in the case of the correlational example cited above, if enough cases are used, even the slightest of differences may be found to be statistically significant. It would be informative to know how much variability in the scores of the two groups combined is associated with the fact that some pupils were instructed with one teaching method and the others learned by another method.

The proportion of variance accounted for as a function of the differential treatment of two groups of subjects may be estimated by the formula

$$\text{Proportion of Variance} = \frac{t_{obs}^2 - 1}{t_{obs}^2 + N_1 + N_2 - 1}$$

The only values that are needed are the computed value of t (t_{obs}) as determined by the test for the difference between means and the number of subjects in each of the two groups. For example, if the means on a reading test for the two groups ($N_1 = 20$, $N_2 = 25$) were 78 and 62 and $t_{obs} = 2.0$, the proportion of variance in reading score that is attributable to the difference in teaching methods is estimated by[6]

$$\frac{t_{obs}^2 - 1}{t_{obs}^2 + N_1 + N_2 - 1}$$

$$\frac{(2.00)^2 - 1}{(2.00)^2 + 20 + 25 - 1} = .0625$$

Therefore, approximately $6\frac{1}{4}\%$ of the variability in reading score is accounted for by the difference in teaching methods. Note that the above formula may yield a negative result if t is small, in which case it is taken to mean no variance is accounted for by group differences.

FORMULAS

1. Difference between Means

a. Independent groups, homogeneous variances

$$t_{obs} = \frac{\overline{X}_1 - \overline{X}_2}{\sqrt{\left[\frac{(N_1 - 1)s_1^2 + (N_2 - 1)s_2^2}{N_1 + N_2 - 2}\right] \cdot \left[\frac{1}{N_1} + \frac{1}{N_2}\right]}}$$

$$df = N_1 + N_2 - 2$$

[6] Suggested by W. L. Hays, *Statistics for Psychologists* (New York: Holt, Rinehart & Winston, 1963), 327–329.

b. Independent groups, heterogeneous variances

$$t_{\text{obs}} = \frac{\overline{X}_1 - \overline{X}_2}{\sqrt{\dfrac{s_1{}^2}{N_1} + \dfrac{s_2{}^2}{N_2}}}$$

$$df = N_1 + N_2 - 2$$

$$t_{\text{crit}} = \frac{s_{\bar{x}_1}{}^2(t_1) + s_{\bar{x}_2}{}^2(t_2)}{s_{\bar{x}_1}{}^2 + s_{\bar{x}_2}{}^2}$$

c. Correlated groups

$$t_{\text{obs}} = \frac{\sum D_i}{\sqrt{\dfrac{N\sum D_i^2 - (\sum D_i)^2}{N - 1}}}$$

$$df = N - 1$$

2. Test of Homogeneity of Independent Variances

$$F_{\text{obs}} = \frac{s^2_{\text{larger}}}{s^2_{\text{smaller}}}$$

$$df = N_1 - 1,\ N_2 - 1$$

(Double p values listed in Table C for appropriate significance level.)

3. Correlations

a. Test that the correlation is zero

$$t_{\text{obs}} = \frac{r\sqrt{N - 2}}{\sqrt{1 - r^2}}$$

$$df = N - 2$$

(Or look for critical values of r in Table D.)

b. Difference between two independent correlations

$$z = \frac{z_{r_1} - z_{r_2}}{\sqrt{\dfrac{1}{N_1 - 3} + \dfrac{1}{N_2 - 3}}}$$

4. Proportion of Variance

$$\text{Prop. of Var.} = \frac{t_{\text{obs}}{}^2 - 1}{t_{\text{obs}}{}^2 + N_1 + N_2 - 1}$$

EXERCISES

1. Why must it be assumed that the population distribution of the difference between means is normal and under what conditions can such an assumption be met?

2. Why are there two standard errors of the difference between means, one for the case in which the groups have homogeneous variability and the other for the case in which they do not?

3. Why is the test of the difference between means for independent groups not appropriate when the same subjects contribute to both groups of scores?

4. A theory suggests that when people experience cognitive dissonance, conflicting motives or thoughts, they will attempt to reduce this dissonance by altering their perceptions of the circumstances. For example, college students were asked to perform a boring task for a long period of time. Then some were paid \$20 and some were paid \$1 to tell the next student that the task was really interesting and fun. Later, in private, they rated their own actual feelings about the task. The theory predicts that the group which was paid \$20 will not experience as much dissonance when lying about the task because \$20 is a fair wage for that kind of fib. They should rate the task as being quite boring. However, the group which was paid \$1 should experience more dissonance about lying and as a consequence tend to view the task more favorably in order to justify the lie. The ratings (the higher the rating the more interesting the task) for the two groups are below.

   In view of the theory, evaluate these data[7] using the formal organization illustrated in this chapter. Estimate the proportion of variance attributable to the different bribes.

\$20	\$1
3	4
1	8
2	6
4	9
0	3
5	6
4	7
5	10
1	4
3	8

5. Suppose the research question was whether newborn infants spend more time looking at the corners than at the sides of a triangle or vice-versa. An elaborate apparatus permits the determination of precisely where on the stimulus the infant

[7] Inspired by L. C. Festinger and J. M. Carlsmith, "Cognitive Consequences of Forced Compliance," *Journal of Abnormal and Social Psychology*, 1959, LVIII, 203–210.

is fixating his gaze. The length of time that each of eight infants looked at the corners and at the sides of the triangle are presented below. Evaluate these data.[8]

Subject	Corners	Sides
1	10	7
2	23	24
3	16	10
4	19	15
5	23	18
6	12	11
7	18	14
8	16	18

6. Suppose two types of psychotherapy were to be compared for their ability to alleviate anxiety. Two groups of 12 college students were selected from a large group of students in a freshman speech course. The 24 students were picked because through interviews, questionnaires, and physiological measurements they had the highest composite scores for anxiety about giving a speech. Each student then received ten sessions of therapy that followed one of two forms. One type, **behavior therapy,** attempted to teach the subject to relax and mentally associate this state of relaxation with the thought of giving a speech. The other group received **insight therapy** in which the therapist attempted to discern the causes for each person's anxiety and give the person insight into his problem. Later, each student had to give another speech and the same composite score of anxiety was measured. Below are the differences for each subject between his first and second score. High scores indicate a great deal of improvement. Evaluate these data in terms of the effectiveness of the two methods of therapy.[9]

Behavior Therapy	Insight Therapy
25	14
14	12
36	13
21	12
28	15
12	12
19	11
29	11
31	10
22	13
16	12
40	12

[8] Inspired by P. Salapatek and W. Kessen, "Visual Scanning of Triangles by the Human Newborn," *Journal of Experimental Child Psychology*, 1966, III, 155–167.

[9] Inspired by G. L. Paul, *Insight vs. Desensitization in Psychotherapy: An Experiment in Anxiety Reduction* (Stanford: Stanford University Press, 1966).

7. Construct a numerical example in which two groups of 8 scores are significantly different if the same 10 subjects each contributed a score to both groups (i.e., correlated groups) but they are obviously not significantly different if the same numbers were used but they were considered to be from independent groups of subjects.

8. Compute the correlation for the data in Exercise 5 and test to determine if the r is "significant."

9. Suppose that the correlation between the IQ's of 38 sets of identical twins is .87 and the correlation between 27 sets of fraternal twins is .53. Test the obvious theoretical prediction that the correlation is higher for identical than fraternal twins.[10]

10. Below are the data from a study comparing the improvement in reading performance in first grade as a function of two different teachers. Each child was given a pretest at the start of the reading program and a posttest after the training. The scores for these tests and the difference in the two scores for the students in each class follow:

Teacher A

Pupil	Pretest	Posttest	Difference
1	30	36	6
2	14	54	40
3	38	40	2
4	21	65	44
5	35	35	0
6	10	15	5
7	30	29	−1
8	32	70	38

Teacher B

Pupil	Pretest	Posttest	Difference
1	34	49	15
2	21	30	9
3	16	20	4
4	38	63	25
5	27	44	17
6	25	30	5
7	31	50	19
8	15	12	−3
9	17	28	11
10	26	42	16

[10] Inspired by L. Erlenmeyer-Kimling and Lissy F. Jarvik, "Genetics and Intelligence: A Review," *Science*, 1964, CXLII, 1477–1478.

(a) Within each group, test to see if the pupils improved or declined between the pretest and posttest.
(b) Evaluate whether the teachers differed in their teaching effectiveness by testing the difference between the two groups of difference scores.
(c) Correlate the pretest and posttest scores separately for each class. Test to determine if these correlations are significantly different from zero and whether they are different from one another.
(d) How do you interpret and explain the pattern of results obtained above, both in terms of their statistical reasonableness and in terms of what these data show about the two teachers?

9

simple analysis of variance

Techniques that compare the difference between two means were examined in the previous chapter. The null hypothesis for those tests was that the two means were computed on samples drawn from populations having the same means (H_0: $\mu_1 = \mu_2$). However, very often a researcher wishes to compare more than just two means. He asks what the probability is that these several means are all computed on samples drawn from populations having the same means. The statistical procedure that is used to answer this broader question is called the analysis of variance.

Suppose a researcher was interested in the hypothesis that the pupil of the eye enlarges (dilates) when the eye looks at stimuli that are attractive. If such were the case, this response could be a subtle and important indicator of emotion. To test this idea, suppose some male college students are either shown pictures of landscapes, sports action, or female pin-ups. A special camera photographs the eyes of the subjects every half second. Later, these pictures are projected on a large screen and the size of the pupil is measured. Each subject is given a score which corresponds to the amount of change in the size of his pupil while he watches the pictures. Those subjects viewing the pin-up pictures showed an average increase in pupil size of 17 units compared to increases of 9 and 4 units for those watching sports and landscape pictures, respectively.[1]

[1] Adapted from data presented by E. H. Hess, "Attitude and Pupil Size," *Scientific American*, 1965, CCXII, 46–54.

The statistical question is whether these observed differences between group means really reflect population differences provoked by the different pictures or whether these means could have been computed on three randomly sampled groups of subjects from populations having the same mean; hence, the observed differences between them are actually a function of sampling error. The null hypothesis is H_0: $\mu_1 = \mu_2 = \mu_3$.

In the previous chapter, techniques were presented for analyzing the difference between two means. It would be possible to perform such a test between each pair that can be formed from three means (*A*, *B*, *C*): *AB*, *AC*, *BC*. There are several reasons why this procedure is not only undesirable, but inappropriate. First, as the number of means to be compared increases, the number of pairs becomes quite large. For example, although there are only three pairs for three means, there are ten pairs for five means and 28 pairs for eight means. Therefore, the amount of computational labor increases rapidly as the number of means increases.

However, there are more serious reasons for not testing each pair of means. The second argument centers on the accuracy of the probabilistic statement that is to be made after testing a hypothesis. When two means are compared and the .05 level of significance is adopted, over many such comparisons one would expect only 5% of these differences between means to be as great or greater than the critical value under the null hypothesis. That is, if there were 100 pairs of means to be tested and it were assumed that each of the groups came from the same population, one would expect that on the average five of them would show a significant difference by chance or sampling error alone. Further, the significance level of a test of the null hypothesis, for example .05, is meant to imply that an observed *t* that exceeds the critical value would occur in less than five of every 100 **independently** sampled pairs of means drawn from populations having the same mean. If several *t* tests are used to compare the differences between all possible pairs of a set of means, all the pairs are not mutually independent because each group in the set of *k* means is a member of $k - 1$ pairs. Therefore, the significance level appropriate for independent pairs of means is not appropriate when the pairs are not independent. Further, as the number of pairs of means to be tested increases, one begins to expect that some of these tests will turn out to be "significant" by chance alone. If one has a theory or other indication as to which pairs should or should not be significant, this problem is less severe, but most often one does not have such definite predictions.

A last criticism of using several *t* tests in this situation is that frequently the researcher wishes to ask a broader question than whether pairs of means are different. When the psychologist selected landscapes, sports scenes, and pin-ups to show his subjects, he really wanted to know if pupil dilation was a function of this **collection** of these three types of stimuli, not merely whether it was different for members of the various pairs.[2] Thus, the question being asked is frequently broader than the information provided by separate tests between pairs of means.

For these reasons, the analysis of variance provides a more appropriate alternative to answering this type of question than a combination of several t tests between pairs of means.

the logic of the analysis of variance

GENERAL APPROACH

The purpose of the simple analysis of variance is to determine the probability that the means of several groups of scores deviate from one another merely by sampling error. The approach to this purpose taken by the analysis of variance is to partition the variability in the total sample in much the same manner as was done previously in the discussions of correlation and regression. In the previous context, the total variability of Y_i was divided into a portion attributable to X and a portion that was not associated with X. In the case of the analysis of variance the total variability in the scores is partitioned into a portion that reflects differences between the means of the groups and a portion that is not influenced by those differences in means.

The partitioning of variability is performed in such a way that two estimates of the variance of the scores in the population are computed. One of these estimates is based upon the deviation of the group means about the grand mean (mean over all scores in the total analysis). Its size will be influenced both by the variability of individual subjects (since their scores are involved in both the group and grand means) and, in addition, by any differences between group means. Because this variance estimate is based upon the deviation of group means about the grand mean, it is called a **between-groups estimate** of the population variance. In contrast, one could also base an estimate of the variance of the scores in the population on the deviation of scores about their respective group means. It can be shown that such an estimate is not influenced by differences in group means but only by the random variability of individual subjects. Since this estimate is determined by the deviation of scores within each group about their mean, it is known as the **within-groups estimate** of the population variance.

The two variance estimates differ only by virtue of the fact that the between-groups estimate is sensitive to differences between the group means while the

[2] When the researcher designates the specific stimuli in an example of this kind, the stimuli represent a **fixed factor**, whereas when the stimuli are random selections from a population it is called a **random factor**. Since the vast majority of experiments involve fixed factors, the analyses present in this text are appropriate for fixed rather than random factors.

within-groups estimate is not. As these group means become increasingly different from one another, the between-groups variance estimate grows large. However, the null hypothesis being tested is that in the population all the group means are equal (e.g., H_0: $\mu_1 = \mu_2 = \mu_3$). Since the null hypothesis is tentatively held to be true as part of the process of testing its validity, in theory, the between-groups estimate should have no contribution from population differences between means because the means are assumed to be equal to one another under H_0. Thus, under the null hypothesis, the between-groups estimate is influenced only by the same random variation in scores that determines the within-groups estimate.

Therefore, given the null hypothesis, the analysis of variance provides two estimates of the population variance. Presumably, both estimates should be identical to one another except for sampling error. In the previous chapter, the ratio of two independent sample variances (i.e., variance estimates) was said to be distributed as F with degrees of freedom equal to the degrees of freedom for the numerator and the denominator of the ratio, respectively. Therefore, in the present context one can construct the F ratio

$$F = \frac{s^2_{\text{between}}}{s^2_{\text{within}}}$$

and then use the percentiles of the F distribution as found in Table C in Appendix II to determine the probability of obtaining a ratio of this size merely by sampling error. If the ratio is so large that the probability is exceedingly small that s^2_{between} and s^2_{within} estimate the same population variance, then one may assume that the additional influence of differences between group means has inflated the value of s^2_{between}, causing the F ratio to be unusually large. That is, the null hypothesis should be rejected.

The remainder of this section is devoted to expanding and clarifying this rationale.

NOTATION AND TERMINOLOGY

notation It will help to begin by specifying some notation that will serve as a convenient language with which to discuss these concepts. Table 9–1 presents this notation for the general case. Any score, X_{ij} is written with two subscripts. The first or i subscript denotes the subject's number and the second or j subscript indicates the group to which he belongs. Thus, X_{24} would be the second subject in the fourth group. Table 9–1 is arranged to show several subjects in each of the groups. Therefore, the i subscript runs up to n_1 for the first group where n_1 indicates the total number of subjects in the first group. Similarly, n_2 indicates the number of subjects in the second group, and in general n_j denotes the number of subjects in the jth group. There are p groups so the number of subjects in the last group is n_p.

9-1 General notation for the analysis of variance.

Group 1	Group 2	...	Group p	
X_{11}	X_{12}	...	X_{1p}	
X_{21}	X_{22}	...	X_{2p}	
X_{31}	X_{32}	...	X_{3p}	
X_{41}	X_{42}	...	X_{4p}	
$\vdots$	$\vdots$	$\vdots$	$\vdots$	
$X_{n_1 1}$	$X_{n_2 2}$	...	$X_{n_p p}$	
Group Means				**Grand Mean**
$\overline{X}_1 = \frac{\sum_{i=1}^{n_1} X_{i1}}{n_1}$	$\overline{X}_2 = \frac{\sum_{i=1}^{n_2} X_{i2}}{n_2}$	...	$\overline{X}_p = \frac{\sum_{i=1}^{n_p} X_{ip}}{n_p}$	$\overline{X} = \frac{\sum_{j=1}^{p}\sum_{i=1}^{n_j} X_{ij}}{N}$

X_{ij} = score for the ith observation in the jth group

p = number of groups

$$N = n_1 + n_2 + \cdots + n_p = \sum_{j=1}^{p} n_j$$

$$\overline{X}_j = \text{mean for group } j = \frac{\sum_{i=1}^{n_j} X_{ij}}{n_j}$$

$$\overline{X} = \text{grand mean over all groups} = \frac{\sum_{j=1}^{p}\sum_{i=1}^{n_j} X_{ij}}{N}$$

The means of the p groups are designated by $\overline{X}_j$ where the subscript indicates the group number. Thus, $\overline{X}_1$ is the mean of the first group and $\overline{X}_p$ the mean of the last or pth group. In general, $\overline{X}_j$ is the mean of any group (the jth group). If we used the notation previously described, the mean for the jth group would be given by

$$\overline{X}_j = \frac{\sum_{i=1}^{n_j} X_{ij}}{n_j}$$

The grand mean, symbolized by $\overline{X}$ without any subscripts, is the mean of all the scores regardless of group. It can be expressed as

$$\overline{X} = \frac{\sum_{j=1}^{p}\sum_{i=1}^{n_j} X_{ij}}{N}$$

in which N is the total number of subjects or observations,

$$N = \sum_{j=1}^{p} n_j$$

and the double summation signs $\sum_{j=1}^{p} \sum_{i=1}^{n_j} X_{ij}$ direct one to sum the X_{ij} first over all subjects ($i = 1, 2, \ldots n_1$) within the first group ($j = 1$), then over all subjects within the second group ($j = 2$), and so on until and including the last group ($j = p$).

variance terminology The logic of the analysis of variance as briefly sketched above requires two estimates of the population variance, the within-groups and between-groups variance estimates. It will help to refine some terminology and notation about variances at this point. Previously, a sample variance (variance estimate) was defined to be

$$s^2 = \frac{\sum_{i=1}^{n} (X_i - \overline{X})^2}{N - 1}$$

The numerator of this fraction is a sum of squared deviations about the mean, and thus it is known as a **sum of squares** symbolized by ***SS***. The denominator is really the **degrees of freedom** associated with the sum of squares, and is therefore symbolized ***df***. In these terms the variance estimate is really a type of average sum of squares and it is sometimes known as a **mean square** or ***MS***. Consequently, a variance estimate can be symbolized

$$MS = \frac{SS}{df} = \frac{\sum_{i=1}^{n} (X_i - \overline{X})^2}{N - 1} = s^2$$

This merely constitutes a different way of using symbols and terminology from what has been presented before. There is no important conceptual difference. The reason for this translation is that the new terms, MS and SS, are customarily associated with the analysis of variance. Therefore, from now on a variance estimate (e.g., s^2) will be called a mean square or MS.

treatment effect The purpose of the analysis of variance is to estimate the probability that the means of the several groups differ from one another merely by sampling error. The null hypothesis is that in the population the group means are all equal and equal to the grand mean over all the groups. If μ_j represents the population mean for the jth group and μ is the population grand mean, then the null hypothesis is symbolized by

$$H_0\colon \mu_1 = \mu_2 = \cdots = \mu_p = \mu$$

The alternative hypothesis states that in the population the group means are not all equal which is best stated as follows:

$$H_1\text{: Not } H_0$$

Suppose that one called the basis for classifying subjects into the different groups, Factor A, and labeled the different groups $a_1, a_2, \ldots a_p$. In the example being discussed, the "type of picture" is Factor A and the group viewing pin-ups is a_3. In the population, the mean of a_3 is designated as μ_3. Now a **treatment effect** denoted by the Greek letter corresponding to the factor accompanied by a subscript denoting the group (i.e., α_3), is the difference in the population between a group mean and the grand mean.

A treatment effect for group a_j is defined as

$$\alpha_j = \mu_j - \mu$$

To illustrate, suppose in the example cited earlier that **in the population** the means of the landscape, sports, and pin-up groups were not identical to one another, but equal to 6, 10, and 20, respectively. The grand mean is 12. Then ($\alpha_1 = \mu_1 - \mu = 6 - 12 = -6$) represents the treatment effect for rural landscapes, ($\alpha_2 = \mu_2 - \mu = 10 - 12 = -2$) represents the treatment effect for sports, and ($\alpha_3 = \mu_3 - \mu = 20 - 12 = 8$) represents the treatment effect for the pin-ups. Such differences in the population are called treatment effects because very frequently in research the groups of the analysis are distinguished from each other by their different experimental "treatments," such as being shown photos of landscapes, sports, or pin-ups. Also, these differences are known as "effects" because if the subjects are randomly assigned to the groups then presumably these differences between means are the effects of these different treatments. In contrast, note that under the null hypothesis (H_0: $\mu_1 = \mu_2 = \cdots = \mu_p = \mu$) each group mean equals the grand mean, and therefore all treatment effects ($\mu_j - \mu$) would be zero.

PARTITION OF VARIABILITY

derivation of MS As indicated above in the general discussion of rationale, the process underlying the mechanics of the analysis of variance is the partitioning of the total variability of scores into at least two components, one of which is sensitive to differences between group means while the other is not. This partition is quite analogous to that discussed earlier in the context of regression and correlation and illustrated again at the top of Figure 9–1. Recall that the total variability in Y_i was divided into a portion

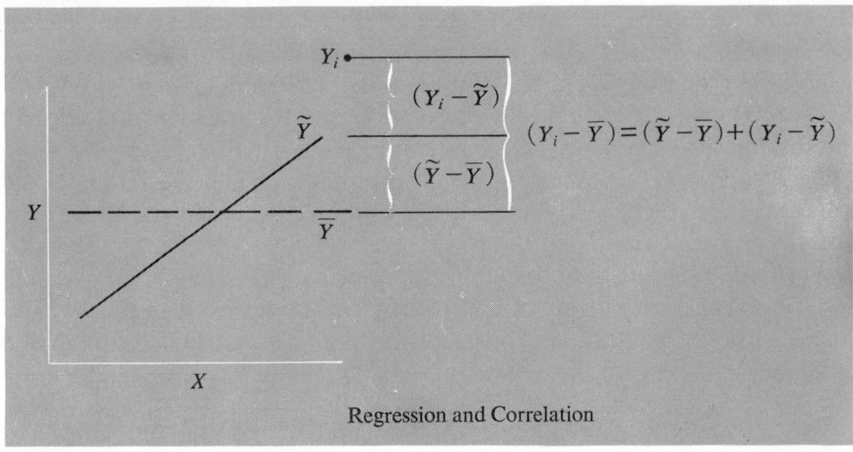

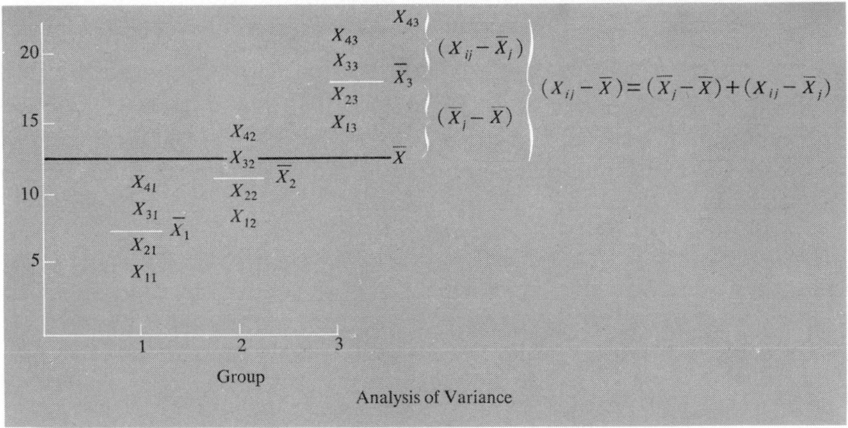

Fig. 9–1. Comparison of the partition of deviations in regression and correlation with those in the analysis of variance.

that was attributable to another variable X and a portion that was not attributable to X (i.e., "error"). For one particular score, the deviations are

$$\begin{array}{ccccc} (Y_i - \bar{Y}) & = & (\tilde{Y} - \bar{Y}) & + & (Y_i - \tilde{Y}) \\ \downarrow & & \downarrow & & \downarrow \\ \text{(Total deviation in } Y_i\text{)} & = & \text{(Deviation due to } X\text{)} & + & \text{(Error)} \end{array}$$

This expression shows that the deviation in Y due to X plus the deviation due to error equals the total deviation in Y.

The bottom half of Figure 9–1 shows how similar the situation is within the context of the analysis of variance. The analysis of variance deals with the relation between groups of scores and some measure made on these subjects, call it X. If the groups represent different amounts of some thing (e.g., age, intelligence, food deprivation, light intensity, etc.), then the situations in regression and the analysis of variance are very similar. The bottom of Figure 9–1 shows the groups along the abscissa and the score values along the ordinate. The scores, X_{ij}, are placed in positions appropriate to their group and score value. The group means and grand mean are indicated. In a manner similar to the case of regression, the total deviations in the scores regardless of group affiliation, $(X_{ij} - \overline{X})$, are partitioned into components associated with the deviation of group means from the grand mean, $(\overline{X}_j - \overline{X})$, plus a portion due to random variability of the scores about their respective group means, $(X_{ij} - \overline{X}_j)$:

$$
\begin{array}{ccccc}
(X_{ij} - \overline{X}) & = & (\overline{X}_j - \overline{X}) & + & (X_{ij} - \overline{X}_j) \\
\downarrow & & \downarrow & & \downarrow \\
\text{(Total deviation} & = & \text{(Deviation between} & + & \text{(Deviation} \\
\text{in } X) & & \text{group mean and} & & \text{within group)} \\
 & & \text{grand mean)} & &
\end{array}
$$

According to this expression, any score may be built up in the following way: Suppose the grand mean of a group of scores is 10, the mean of Group j is 14, and the ith score in Group j deviates from its group mean by -2. In symbols,

$$
\begin{aligned}
\overline{X} &= 10 \\
\overline{X}_j &= 14 \\
(X_{ij} - \overline{X}_j) &= -2
\end{aligned}
$$

Then, according to the previous expression the score may be determined in the following way:

$$
\begin{aligned}
(X_{ij} - \overline{X}) &= (\overline{X}_j - \overline{X}) + (X_{ij} - \overline{X}_j) \\
X_{ij} &= \overline{X} + (\overline{X}_j - \overline{X}) + (X_{ij} - \overline{X}_j) \\
X_{ij} &= 10 + (14 - 10) + (-2) \\
X_{ij} &= 12
\end{aligned}
$$

The above deviations represent contributions that a single score makes to the total variability in a sample of scores. To consider the variability over all samples, these deviations must first be squared (because variability usually implies squared deviations) and then added first within each group and later across all groups. Squaring and summing over the n_j scores in the jth group we have

$$
\sum_{i=1}^{n_j} (X_{ij} - \overline{X})^2 = \sum_{i=1}^{n_j} [(\overline{X}_j - \overline{X}) + (X_{ij} - \overline{X}_j)]^2
$$

The right side of the equation may be treated in the same manner as expansion of the binomial $(a + b)^2 = a^2 + 2ab + b^2$:

$$\sum_{i=1}^{n_j} [(\overline{X}_j - \overline{X})^2 + 2(\overline{X}_j - \overline{X})(X_{ij} - \overline{X}_j) + (X_{ij} - \overline{X}_j)^2]$$

The summation sign may be distributed to all the terms within the brackets.

$$\sum_{i=1}^{n_j} (\overline{X}_j - \overline{X})^2 + \sum_{i=1}^{n_j} 2(\overline{X}_j - \overline{X})(X_{ij} - \overline{X}_j) + \sum_{i=1}^{n_i} (X_{ij} - \overline{X}_j)^2$$

Now consider only the middle term of the above expression,

$$\sum_{i=1}^{n_j} 2(\overline{X}_j - \overline{X})(X_{ij} - \overline{X}_j)$$

Notice that this involves the sum of all the scores about their mean $[\sum(X_{ij} - \overline{X}_j)]$ which is always equal to zero and that the other term $(\overline{X}_j - \overline{X})$ is always a constant with respect to any single group. Consequently, this middle term equals zero and thus vanishes from the total expression leaving

$$\sum_{i=1}^{n_j} (X_{ij} - \overline{X})^2 = \sum_{i=1}^{n_j} (\overline{X}_j - \overline{X})^2 + \sum_{i=1}^{n_j} (X_{ij} - \overline{X}_j)^2$$

A further simplification can be made by observing that the first term on the right side of the equation involves summing the squared deviations of the mean of that group from the grand mean over members of a group. The deviations $(\overline{X}_j - \overline{X})^2$ represent a constant with respect to the summation over individual subjects within a group, and the sum of n constants is n times the constant:

$$\sum_{i=1}^{n_j} (X_{ij} - \overline{X})^2 = n_j(\overline{X}_j - \overline{X})^2 + \sum_{i=1}^{n_j} (X_{ij} - \overline{X}_j)^2$$

The last step is to sum the expression over each group as well as within each group:

$$\underbrace{\sum_{j=1}^{p} \sum_{i=1}^{n_j} (X_{ij} - \overline{X})^2}_{\downarrow} = \underbrace{\sum_{j=1}^{p} n_j(\overline{X}_j - \overline{X})^2}_{\downarrow} + \underbrace{\sum_{j=1}^{p} \sum_{i=1}^{n_j} (X_{ij} - \overline{X}_j)^2}_{\downarrow}$$

(Total squared deviations in X) = (Squared deviations between group means) + (Squared deviations within groups)

Notice that each component of the above expression is a sum of squared deviations (*SS*) and thus is the numerator of a variance estimate or mean square (*MS*). In the terminology of variances introduced earlier in this chapter, these three terms are sums of squares:

$$SS_{\text{total}} = SS_{\text{between}} + SS_{\text{within}}$$

These expressions state that the total sum of squares is composed of the sum of squared deviations of group means from their grand mean (SS_{between}) **plus** the sum of the squared deviations of scores from their respective group means (SS_{within}).

Recall from the general rationale of the analysis of variance that rather than two **sums of squares,** one sensitive to group differences and the other not, two **mean squares** (MS) with these characteristics are required. A variance estimate is a sum of squares divided by its degrees of freedom. Therefore, the degrees of freedom for the sums of squares discussed above must be secured.

For a sample variance, the degrees of freedom (df) equal one less than the number of cases considered for the sum of squares. In the notational scheme described at the beginning of this section, there are N total cases, n_j cases in the jth group, and a total of p groups. The total degrees of freedom in the sample is one less than the total number of cases in the sample or

$$df_{\text{total}} = N - 1$$

The degrees of freedom for SS_{between} should be one less than the number of means in the total sample because SS_{between} is the sum of the squared deviations of each mean about the grand mean. Since there are p means,

$$df_{\text{between}} = p - 1$$

Lastly, the SS_{within} is composed of the sum of the squared deviations of scores about their respective group means. Within a single group the sum of squares

$$\sum_{i=1}^{n_j} (X_{ij} - \overline{X}_j)^2$$

has $n_j - 1$ degrees of freedom. When each of these within-group sum of squares is summed across all the groups to obtain SS_{within}, one also sums the degrees of freedom

$$\sum_{j=1}^{p} (n_j - 1)$$

Distributing the summation sign,

$$\sum_{j=1}^{p} n_j - \sum_{j=1}^{p} (1)$$

replacing the first term by its equivalent, N, and the second term by p because the sum from 1 to p of a constant is p times the constant, one has that the degrees of freedom for SS_{within} are

$$df_{\text{within}} = N - p$$

It happens that the df_{total} equals the sum of the degrees of freedom for SS_{between} plus SS_{within}:

$$df_{\text{total}} = df_{\text{between}} + df_{\text{within}}$$

Therefore, both the sum of squares and the degrees of freedom for the total sample are the sum of a between and a within component.

To obtain a mean square, one simply divides a sum of squares by its degrees of freedom. Therefore, the mean square of the total sample is

$$MS_{\text{total}} = \frac{SS_{\text{total}}}{df_{\text{total}}} = \frac{\sum_{j=1}^{p} \sum_{i=1}^{n_j} (X_{ij} - \overline{X})^2}{N - 1}$$

The mean square sensitive to between-group differences is

$$MS_{\text{between}} = \frac{SS_{\text{between}}}{df_{\text{between}}} = \frac{\sum_{j=1}^{p} n_j(\overline{X}_j - \overline{X})^2}{p - 1}$$

and the mean square not sensitive to group differences (the MS_{within}) is

$$MS_{\text{within}} = \frac{SS_{\text{within}}}{df_{\text{within}}} = \frac{\sum_{j=1}^{p} \sum_{i=1}^{n_j} (X_{ij} - \overline{X}_j)^2}{N - p}$$

One must be careful **not** to suppose that, because

$$SS_{\text{total}} = SS_{\text{between}} + SS_{\text{within}}$$

and

$$df_{\text{total}} = df_{\text{between}} + df_{\text{within}}$$

the total mean square equals the sum of the between and within mean squares. It does not, so one writes

$$MS_{\text{total}} \neq MS_{\text{between}} + MS_{\text{within}}$$

comparison of MS_{between} and MS_{within} In the previous section, formulas for two variance estimates or mean squares were developed. The logic of the analysis of variance rests on the fact that one of these estimates (MS_{between}) can be influenced by population differences between the means of the several groups reflecting treatment effects while the other (MS_{within}) is not so influenced. This section attempts to make this vital discrimination more intuitive.

First, recall the example discussed at the beginning of the chapter. Suppose the amount of pupil dilation registered by the first subject in Group 1 (landscapes) was 10 and that of the first subject in Group 3 (pin-ups) was 16. Why are these two scores different? There are two major possibilities. First, one subject saw landscapes while the other viewed pin-up pictures, and maybe pin-up pictures affect pupil dilation more than landscapes. This contribution to differences between scores stems from possible **treatment effects.** However, in addition to the possibility of treatment effects, one person does not always respond the same as another because of a variety of uncontrolled factors. For example, some subjects just respond more intensely than others, perhaps the test situation is just slightly different in temperature or apparatus position for one subject than another, or a multitude of other possibilities might exist. The entire collection of such potential causes, presumably unrelated to the differences in treatments, is denotatively called **error.** Therefore, differences or variability in scores between different groups may stem from treatment effects and/or error.

In contrast, consider why two scores from subjects in the same group are not identical. First, the two subjects each received the same treatment so that differences in treatment condition cannot be a determinant of variability within a group. However, all of those potential influences subsumed under the concept of error may still be operative. Therefore, in contrast to variability between groups, variability within groups is a function of error but not of treatment effects.

In brief,

SS_{between} reflects treatment effects + error
SS_{within} reflects error

The fact that MS_{between} is sensitive to treatment effects whereas MS_{within} is not may be illustrated with a numerical example. Suppose one consulted a table of random numbers and selected three groups of five numbers each. Since these are random numbers, the three groups are analogous to three samples of size five drawn from a common population (sampling under the null hypothesis). These numbers are displayed in the top half of Table 9–2. The SS_{within} for each group is presented and the within-groups estimate is at the right: $MS_{\text{within}} = 7.33$. The group means are 4, 6, and 5 with a grand mean of 5. The between-groups variance estimate is computed below the listing of the groups and $MS_{\text{between}} = 5.0$.

It is important to remember that, when the groups are randomly sampled from the same population (under the null hypothesis), MS_{between} and MS_{within} are both estimates of the common population variance. Since they are estimates, they will probably not equal each other (in the present case they equal 5.00 and 7.33), but in the long run we would expect them to tend towards being equal.

Now suppose that there are group differences or treatment effects. To implement this condition, 3 units are added to each score in Group 2 and 12 units are added to each score in Group 3. This is equivalent to saying the sports photos are worth 3 extra units of pupillary change and the pin-ups are worth 12 extra units in comparison to rural landscapes.

Consider the two variance estimates presented in the lower half of Table 9–2. Notice that the MS_{within} is precisely the same as it was before the effects were introduced. This is a reflection of the fact that the variance of scores within a group is not influenced by adding a constant to each score in the group. However, the value of MS_{between} was indeed changed as a function of the treatment effects. Now $MS_{\text{between}} = 215.0$. This is because a different constant was added to each of the three groups and thus to the three group means and MS_{between} is sensitive to these differences. It should be clear from this numerical example that the within-groups variance estimator is not influenced by differences in treatment effects whereas the between-groups estimate is influenced by treatment differences.

THE F TEST

The final step in the rationale of the analysis of variance is to compare the two variance estimates under the assumptions of the null hypothesis. The null hypothesis states that in the population the group means are all identical to one another and equal to the grand mean:

$$H_0\colon \mu_1 = \mu_2 = \cdots = \mu_p = \mu$$

Another way of making the same statement is to say that there are no treatment effects:

$$H_0\colon \alpha_1 = \alpha_2 = \cdots = \alpha_p = 0$$

The alternative hypothesis is that these conditions are not so; there are differences between group means or treatment effects:

$$H_1\colon \text{Not } H_0$$

If the null hypothesis is true, MS_{between} and MS_{within} should both estimate the same parameter as they did in the numerical example above before treatment effects were added. Therefore, in the long run the ratio of these two variances or MS's should center around 1.0. The F distribution was discussed in Chapter 8 as a distribution of the ratio of two variances estimating the same parameter. Thus, the percentiles of the F distribution may be used in order to determine the probability of obtaining an F ratio of a specified size purely by sampling error. If the probability is very small that an F of this size is merely a function of sampling error then perhaps the tentative assumption of the null hypothesis of no treatment effects is wrong. This is logical because MS_{between} but not MS_{within} is influenced by treatment effects and a high F ratio means that MS_{between} is large relative to MS_{within}.

independence The use of the F distribution in this fashion is based upon the assumption that the variances in the ratio are independent. When F was used previously, this requirement was assured because the variances were computed on different groups of subjects. In the case of the analysis of variance, the two mean squares are computed on the same subjects. The within-groups estimate is based upon all the scores in the total sample and the between-groups estimate is based upon the group and grand means to which each of

9–2 Numerical illustration of the fact that MS_{between} is influenced by group differences while MS_{within} is not.

Group 1

$$SS_1 = \sum (X_{i1} - \overline{X}_1)^2 \quad \begin{cases} 7 \\ 5 \\ 3 \\ 4 \\ 1 \end{cases}$$

$$SS_1 = 20$$

$$df_1 = 4$$

Group 2

$$SS_2 = \sum (X_{i2} - \overline{X}_2)^2 \quad \begin{cases} 2 \\ 6 \\ 9 \\ 9 \\ 4 \end{cases}$$

$$SS_2 = 38$$

$$df_2 = 4$$

Group 3

$$SS_3 = \sum (X_{i3} - \overline{X}_3)^2 \quad \begin{cases} 9 \\ 3 \\ 5 \\ 6 \\ 2 \end{cases}$$

$$SS_3 = 30$$

$$df_3 = 4$$

$$MS_{\text{within}} = \frac{SS_1 + SS_2 + SS_3}{df_1 + df_2 + df_3}$$

$$MS_{\text{within}} = \frac{20 + 38 + 30}{4 + 4 + 4} = 7.33$$

$$\overline{X}_1 = 4.0 \qquad \overline{X}_2 = 6.0 \qquad \overline{X}_3 = 5.0$$

$$\overline{X} = 5.0$$

$$MS_{\text{between}} = \frac{\sum_{j=1}^{p} n_j(\overline{X}_j - \overline{X})^2}{p - 1}$$

$$MS_{\text{between}} = \frac{5(4 - 5)^2 + 5(6 - 5)^2 + 5(5 - 5)^2}{3 - 1} = 5.0$$

Treatment effect (added to each score) 0	+3	+12	
Group 1 $SS_1 = 20$, $df_1 = 4$ 7, 5, 3, 4, 1	**Group 2** $SS_2 = 38$, $df_2 = 4$ 5, 9, 12, 12, 7	**Group 3** $SS_3 = 30$, $df_3 = 4$ 21, 15, 17, 18, 14	$MS_{\text{within}} = \dfrac{SS_1 + SS_2 + SS_3}{df_1 + df_2 + df_3}$ $MS_{\text{within}} = \dfrac{20 + 38 + 30}{4 + 4 + 4} = 7.33$
$\overline{X}_1 = 4.0$	$\overline{X}_2 = 9.0$	$\overline{X}_3 = 17.0$	$\overline{X} = 10.0$

$$MS_{\text{between}} = \frac{\sum_{j=1}^{p} n_j(\overline{X}_j - \overline{X})^2}{p - 1}$$

$$MS_{\text{between}} = \frac{5(4 - 10)^2 + 5(9 - 10)^2 + 5(17 - 10)^2}{3 - 1} = 215.0$$

these same scores contributes. Therefore, to use the F distribution in order to determine the probability of the null hypothesis, one must demonstrate that the two MS's are independent from one another.

As discussed in Chapter 7 means and variances of samples from populations that are normally distributed are independent. Thus, if the population of scores X_{ij} is normally distributed, $\overline{X}_j$ and s_j^2 are independent.[3] Where several groups of scores are sampled from a normal population, the collection of all the group means ($\overline{X}_j$) is independent of the collection of all the group variances (s_j^2). MS_{between} is based upon the $\overline{X}_j$ while MS_{within} involves the deviation of scores about their mean (e.g., s_j^2). Therefore, MS_{between} and MS_{within} are two independent estimates of the population variance if the population is normally distributed.

the logic of the F test The logic of the F test is now relatively straightforward:

(1) MS_{within} is an estimate of the population variance based upon the deviation of scores about their respective group means. It is not influenced by treatment effects.

(2) MS_{between} is also an estimate of the population variance if the null hypothesis is true. It is based upon the deviations of group means about the grand mean. Since it is influenced by any treatment effects that exist in the population, it is only an estimate of the same population variance if those treatment effects are assumed to be zero, that is, if the null hypothesis is true.

(3) Since the two variance estimates are independent and since the logic of hypothesis testing demands that the null hypothesis be tentatively assumed true, the ratio of these two variance estimates is distributed as F:

$$F = \frac{MS_{\text{between}}}{MS_{\text{within}}}$$

(4) Since under conditions of the null hypothesis the two MS's are estimating the same population value, this ratio should approach a value of 1.0 in the long run. The observed value of F is compared to the sampling distribution of such ratios to determine the probability that such an F value could be obtained merely by sampling error.

(5) If the observed F ratio is very large such that the probability is quite small that an F of this size should be obtained merely by chance, then perhaps the assumption of the null hypothesis (no treatment effects) was not appropriate. If there were treatment effects, MS_{between} would be sensitive to them but MS_{within} would not. Therefore, an improbably large F value might mean that treatment effects, in fact, do exist in the population and the null hypothesis should be rejected.

[3] This is true if the s_j^2 are unbiased estimators.

ASSUMPTIONS UNDERLYING THE ANALYSIS OF VARIANCE

Throughout the course of the previous discussion, several assumptions were made in order to perform the manipulations necessary for the analysis. These assumptions are collected and outlined below. Just why they are necessary and the consequences of violating them will be discussed.

1. homogeneity of within-group variances It is assumed that the populations from which the groups are drawn have equal variances. In symbols,

$$\sigma_1{}^2 = \sigma_2{}^2 = \cdots = \sigma_p{}^2$$

A similar assumption was made in Chapter 8 when one formula for the standard error of the difference between means was based upon homogeneous variance of the two groups while another formula was required if the group variances in the population were not equal (i.e., they were heterogeneous). One reason for this assumption is that it enables MS_{within} to be an appropriate pooling of the variability about each group mean into a single estimate of the population variance. Without homogeneity of variance, one group with a very high variance might contribute disproportionately to this single estimate, and MS_{within} would not be representative of the variability within each group.

There are procedures for testing the homogeneity of variances. In Chapter 8, the F test was employed to test the difference between two sample variances. There are methods that extend such a test to include several variances rather than just two.[4] However, some researchers have argued that these procedures may be influenced by extraneous factors and therefore do not provide an entirely appropriate test of the homogeneity of variance.[5] Further, if a sufficient number of cases are sampled and the number of subjects in each group is the same, moderate violations of this assumption do not alter the result of the analysis of variance very much.

2. independence of groups It is assumed that the groups involved in the analysis are composed of randomly sampled subjects and are independent from one another.

Independence is usually guaranteed by selecting different subjects for the several groups in the analysis and not matching these subjects on any particular basis. However, sometimes it is desirable to have the same subjects contribute scores under each of several different conditions and to have the analysis determine if these correlated groups of scores have different means. There are pro-

[4] B. J. Winer, *Statistical Principles in Experimental Design* (New York: McGraw-Hill, 1962).

[5] W. L. Hays, *Statistics for Psychologists* (New York: Holt, Rinehart & Winston, 1963).

cedures to perform this type of analysis which are called **repeated measures analyses of variance** because subjects are measured under more than one condition.[6] These analyses take into account the fact that if the same subjects contribute measures under more than one condition, the variability in those conditions may be correlated. Thus, an alternative method of estimating the error variance in the population must be used. The difference between independent groups and repeated measures analyses of variance is analogous to the difference between the t test for means from independent vs. correlated groups. The analysis of variance procedures outlined in this text all require independent groups.

3. normality It is assumed that the distribution of each population is normal in form. This condition should be reflected in each of the groups sampled. Each should have a relatively normal distribution.

The assumption of normality is made so that the two variance estimates are independent and so that the F test may be used. It can be shown that the mean and variance of a normal distribution are independent. The MS_{between} is based upon the means of the groups and the MS_{within} is derived from the variability of scores about their respective means (e.g., an s_j^2). If the means are independent from the variability of scores about these group means, then the between-groups and within-groups variance estimates will also be independent.

Violations of the assumption of normality are not terribly damaging if a sufficient number of cases are sampled and the departure from normality is not severe. If the distributions are decidedly not normal, and there are not many cases in each group, a **nonparametric analysis** may be performed. Some nonparametric techniques are presented in Chapter 11.[7]

the null hypothesis As in any hypothesis testing procedure, the null hypothesis is tentatively taken to be true. In symbols,

$$H_0: \mu_1 = \mu_2 = \cdots = \mu_p = \mu$$

or in terms of treatment effects,

$$H_0: \alpha_1 = \alpha_2 = \cdots = \alpha_p = 0$$

In the analysis of variance, MS_{within} and MS_{between} estimate the same population variance only if the null hypothesis is true. The two MS's must estimate the same population parameter in order to use the F ratio which is the ratio of two independent variances estimating a common parameter.

[6] B. J. Winer, *Statistical Principles in Experimental Design* (New York: McGraw-Hill, 1962).

[7] See also S. Siegel, *Nonparametric Statistics* (New York: McGraw-Hill, 1956). J. V. Bradley, *Distribution-Free Statistical Tests* (Englewood Cliffs: Prentice-Hall, 1968).

computational procedures

GENERAL FORMAT

As we discovered in previous chapters, the definitional formulas for statistical quantities are not the most convenient for computational purposes. Table 9–3 gives a general computational scheme for the simple analysis of variance discussed thus far. Part **i** lists the scores in the p groups and several quantities needed for the computations. Under each group is the sum of the scores or total (T_j), the n_j, the mean ($\overline{X}_j$), the sum of squared scores $\left(\sum_{i=1}^{n_j} X_{ij}^2\right)$, and the squared sum of the scores divided by n_j (T_j^2/n_j). (Remember the sum of squared scores ($\sum X^2$) is arrived at by squaring each score and then summing. The squared sum of the scores $(\sum X)^2$ divided by n_j is arrived at by first summing the scores, then squaring the sum and dividing by n_j.) To the right of these group quantities are the totals for the entire sample. Four of the five group quantities are summed: the total sum of scores (T_{total}, sum the T_j), the total number of cases (N, sum the n_j), the total sum of the squared scores

$$\left(\sum_{j=1}^{p}\left(\sum_{i=1}^{n_j} X_{ij}^2\right), \text{sum the } \sum_{i=1}^{n_j} X_{ij}^2\right)$$

and the total of the group squared sum of scores divided by n_j $\left(\sum_{j=1}^{p} T_j^2/n_j, \text{ sum all the } T_j^2/n_j\right)$. These are the basic quantities needed to calculate the sums of squares for the analysis of variance.

Part **ii** lists three intermediate quantities that will facilitate the computation of the *SS*. Quantity (I) consists of the squared total sum of scores divided by $N(T^2{}_{\text{total}}/N$, square T_{total} and divide by N); quantity (II) is simply the total sum of the squared scores as found previously

$$\left[\sum_{j=1}^{p}\left(\sum_{i=1}^{n_j} X_{ij}^2\right)\right]$$

and quantity (III) is the total of the squared sum of scores divided by n_j also calculated previously

$$\left[\sum_{j=1}^{p} \frac{T_j^2}{n_j}\right]$$

Part **iii** of the table lists the formulas for the three sums of squares, the three degrees of freedom, and the two mean squares required for the analysis of variance. Notice that the formulas for the *SS* are expressed in terms of the three intermediate quantities [(I), (II), (III)] previously computed. The degrees of

9–3 General computational procedures.

i.	Group 1	Group 2	. . .	Group p	Total Sample
	X_{11}	X_{12}	. . .	X_{1p}	
	X_{21}	X_{22}	. . .	X_{2p}	
	X_{31}	X_{32}	. . .	X_{3p}	
	$\vdots$	$\vdots$		$\vdots$	
	$X_{n_1 1}$	$X_{n_2 2}$	. . .	$X_{n_p p}$	
Sums	$T_1 = \sum_{i=1}^{n_1} X_{i1}$	$T_2 = \sum_{i=1}^{n_2} X_{i2}$	. . .	$T_p = \sum_{i=1}^{n_p} X_{ip}$	$T_{\text{total}} = \sum_{j=1}^{p} T_j$
n_j	n_1	n_2	. . .	n_p	$N = \sum_{j=1}^{p} n_j$
Means	$\overline{X}_1 = \frac{T_1}{n_1}$	$\overline{X}_2 = \frac{T_2}{n_2}$	. . .	$\overline{X}_p = \frac{T_p}{n_p}$	
Sum of squared scores	$\sum_{i=1}^{n_1} X_{i1}^2$	$\sum_{i=1}^{n_2} X_{i2}^2$	. . .	$\sum_{i=1}^{n_p} X_{ip}^2$	$\sum_{j=1}^{p} \left(\sum_{i=1}^{n_j} X_{ij}^2 \right)$
Squared sum of scores divided by n_j	$\frac{T_1^2}{n_1}$	$\frac{T_2^2}{n_2}$	. . .	$\frac{T_p^2}{n_p}$	$\sum_{j=1}^{p} \left(\frac{T_j^2}{n_j} \right)$

ii.

$$(\text{I}) = \frac{T^2_{\text{total}}}{N} \qquad (\text{II}) = \sum_{j=1}^{p}\left(\sum_{i=1}^{n_j} X_{ij}^2\right) \qquad (\text{III}) = \sum_{j=1}^{p}\left(\frac{T_j^2}{n_j}\right)$$

iii.

$$SS_{\text{between}} = (\text{III}) - (\text{I}) \qquad df_{\text{between}} = p - 1 \qquad MS_{\text{between}} = \frac{SS_{\text{between}}}{df_{\text{between}}}$$

$$SS_{\text{within}} = (\text{II}) - (\text{III}) \qquad df_{\text{within}} = N - p \qquad MS_{\text{within}} = \frac{SS_{\text{within}}}{df_{\text{within}}}$$

$$SS_{\text{total}} = (\text{II}) - (\text{I}) \qquad df_{\text{total}} = N - 1$$

iv.

Summary Table

Source	***df***	***SS***	***MS***	***F***
Between groups	$p - 1$	SS_{between}	MS_{between}	$\frac{MS_{\text{between}}}{MS_{\text{within}}}$
Within groups	$N - p$	SS_{within}	MS_{within}	
Total	$N - 1$	SS_{total}		

freedom are determined by using p (the number of different groups) and N (the total number of subjects in the sample).

Part **iv** of Table 9–3 presents the traditional analysis of variance summary table, a customary display of the information in a simple analysis of variance. The first column is labeled "Source" and this denotes the source of the component of the total variation in the sample. This is followed by the degrees of freedom, sums of squares, mean squares, and F ratio.

NUMERICAL EXAMPLE

research question Some years ago it was discovered that if a person were wired up so that his "brain waves," EEG, heart rate, respiration rate, eye movements, etc. were recorded, it was possible to determine from the pattern of these measures when the person was dreaming.[8] With this method of detecting when a person was dreaming it was then possible to determine whether or not people who were accustomed to dreaming could suddenly do without dreaming. If a person were aroused immediately upon the experimenter's observation of the first signals of the onset of dreaming, the subject could be deprived of 75–80% of his normal dreaming time. Other subjects were aroused during periods in which they were not dreaming so that the number of awakenings of the two groups would be equal. It was found that those subjects who were prevented from dreaming on several consecutive nights spent more time dreaming after the experiment was over than those subjects not deprived of their dreams.

An interesting question about the opportunity to dream is whether deprivation of dreaming would have any effects on personality during the waking day. If normal adults seem to need to dream, perhaps they would become anxious and irritable if the opportunity to dream were curtailed. Consider the following hypothetical experiment.[9] Suppose one group of subjects had their sleep interrupted several times during the evening but never during or immediately before a dream. A second group was aroused an equal number of times, but on two occasions during each evening this wakening was at the onset of a dream. Lastly, a third group was awakened an equal number of times but these subjects were aroused only when they started to dream. The timing of these interruptions could be managed because dreaming often occurs in regular time cycles and the occurrence of a dream could be anticipated. Therefore, three groups of subjects were classified by either no, some, or much dream interruption. These procedures were followed for six consecutive nights. During each day the subjects were interviewed and given some personality tests that were designed to evaluate

[8] For example, see N. Kleitman, "Patterns of Dreaming," *Scientific American*, 1960, CCIII, 82–88.

[9] Based upon, but not identical to W. Dement, "The Effect of Dream Deprivation," *Science*, 1960, CXXXI, 1705–1707.

how anxious and irritable the subjects were. High scores indicated a very upset individual. The score for each subject was the total irritability over the six-day period. The hypothetical results are presented in Tables 9–4 and 9–5. The means for the three groups; no, some, and much interruption, were 4.00, 8.00, and 17.75, respectively. This seems to indicate that the prevention of dreaming produces increased irritability and anxiety in normal adults. But, the observed differences between means could be a function of sampling error when there really is no difference among these three groups in the population. The analysis of variance addresses itself to this question: given the null hypothesis of no differences in the population means, what is the probability that the observed difference between sample means is merely a function of sampling error?

statistical hypotheses The question above boils down to whether there are treatment effects in the population. That is, are the population means for the three groups in fact equal and thus equal to the grand mean, or are they different from one another? Symbolically stated, the null hypothesis is

$$H_0: \mu_1 = \mu_2 = \mu_3 = \mu$$

9–4 Summary of the numerical example of a simple analysis of variance.

Hypotheses

$H_0: \mu_1 = \mu_2 = \mu_3 = \mu$
H_1: Not H_0

Assumptions

1. The population variances for the groups are **homogeneous** (i.e., $\sigma_1{}^2 = \sigma_2{}^2 = \sigma_3{}^2$).
2. The scores in each group are randomly selected and **independent** from the scores in each other group.
3. The population distributions are **normal** in form.

Decision Rules

Given: .05 significance level, $df = 2/12$

If $F_{obs} < 3.88$, accept H_0
If $F_{obs} \geq 3.88$, reject H_0

Computation

See Table 9–5.

$F_{obs} = 24.50$

Interpretation

Reject H_0

9–5 Computational example.

	Group 1 (no interruption)	Group 2 (some interruption)	Group 3 (much interruption)	Total Sample
	7	5	21	
	5	9	15	
	3	12	17	
	4	12	18	
	1	7		
		3		
i. Sums	$T_1 = (7 + 5 + \cdots + 1) = 20$	$T_2 = (5 + 9 + \cdots + 3) = 48$	$T_3 = (21 + 15 + \cdots + 18) = 71$	$T_{\text{total}} = \sum_{j=1}^{p} T_j = 139$
n_j	$n_1 = 5$	$n_2 = 6$	$n_3 = 4$	$N = \sum_{j=1}^{p} n_j = 15$
Means	$\overline{X}_1 = \frac{20}{5} = 4.00$	$\overline{X}_2 = \frac{48}{6} = 8.00$	$\overline{X}_3 = \frac{71}{4} = 17.75$	
Sum of squared scores	$\sum X_{i1}{}^2 = 100$	$\sum X_{i2}{}^2 = 452$	$\sum X_{i3}{}^2 = 1279$	$\sum_{j=1}^{p} \left(\sum_{i=1}^{n_j} X_{ij}{}^2 \right) = 1831$
Squared sum of scores divided by n_j	$\frac{T_1{}^2}{n_1} = \frac{(20)^2}{5} = 80$	$\frac{T_2{}^2}{n_2} = \frac{(48)^2}{6} = 384$	$\frac{T_3{}^2}{n_3} = \frac{(71)^2}{4} = 1260.25$	$\sum_{j=1}^{p} \left(\frac{T_j{}^2}{n_j} \right) = 1724.25$

ii. $(\text{I}) = \dfrac{T^2_{\text{total}}}{N} = \dfrac{(139)^2}{15} = 1288.07$ $\quad (\text{II}) = \sum_{j=1}^{p}\left(\sum_{i=1}^{n_j} X_{ij}^2\right) = 1831$ $\quad (\text{III}) = \sum_{j=1}^{p}\left(\dfrac{T_j^2}{n_j}\right) = 1724.25$

iii.

$$SS_{\text{between}} = (\text{III}) - (\text{I}) = 1724.25 - 1288.07 = 436.18 \qquad df = p - 1 = 3 - 1 = 2$$

$$SS_{\text{within}} = (\text{II}) - (\text{III}) = 1831 - 1724.25 = 106.75 \qquad df = N - p = 15 - 3 = 12$$

$$SS_{\text{total}} = (\text{II}) - (\text{I}) = 1831 - 1288.07 = 542.93 \qquad df = N - 1 = 15 - 1 = 14$$

$$MS_{\text{between}} = \frac{SS_{\text{between}}}{df_{\text{between}}} = \frac{436.18}{2} = 218.09$$

$$MS_{\text{within}} = \frac{SS_{\text{within}}}{df_{\text{within}}} = \frac{106.75}{12} = 8.90$$

iv.

Summary Table

Source	*df*	*SS*	*MS*	*F*
Between groups	2	436.18	218.09	$\dfrac{MS_{\text{between}}}{MS_{\text{within}}} = \dfrac{218.09}{8.90} = 24.50^{**}$
Within groups	12	106.75	8.90	
Total	14	542.93		

Critical values $(df = 2, 12)$ $\quad {}^{*}F_{.05} = 3.88, p < .05$

$\quad {}^{**}F_{.01} = 6.93, p < .01$

The alternative is

$$H_1\text{: Not } H_0$$

A summary of the test of these hypotheses is presented in Table 9–4.

formulas The computational formulas have already been presented in Table 9–3.

assumptions The assumptions underlying this test have been explained previously. They are: (1) **homogeniety of within-group variances**, (2) **independence** of groups and random sampling, and (3) **normality** of the population distributions.

significance level Assume $\alpha = .05$.

critical values The computational work presented in Table 9–5 shows that in this case the numerator of the F ratio has 2 degrees of freedom and the denominator has 12. At $\alpha = .05$ with $df = 2/12$, the critical value for F is 3.88 according to Table C. Notice that although in the test for homogeneity of variance described in Chapter 8, the significance levels in the table were doubled in order to arrive at the correct probabilities (.10, .02), this is not done when using the analysis of variance. The two values given in the table represent the critical values for the .05 and .01 significance levels, respectively.

decision rules The decision rules are:

$$\text{If } F_{\text{obs}} < 3.88, \text{ accept } H_0$$
$$\text{If } F_{\text{obs}} \geq 3.88, \text{ reject } H_0$$

computation The calculations are presented in Table 9–5, following the general procedures set forth in Table 9–4.

interpretation The observed $F = 24.50$. Clearly, this is greater than the required value of 3.88 at $\alpha = .05$. In fact, as presented at the bottom of Table 9–5, the observed value exceeds the critical value for these degrees of freedom when the significance level is .01. Customarily, the .05 level is used as the *minimum* significance level for stating that the data suggest the rejection of the null hypothesis. However, the researcher may indicate when the F exceeds the critical value at a high level of significance. Frequently, the value of F is followed by * or ** (or ***) if it exceeds the critical value for $\alpha = .05$, .01, or .001, respectively. Thus, since 24.50 is larger than the critical value for $\alpha = .01$, this fact is indicated by writing the F value in the summary table as 24.50**. (Actually, $F_{\text{obs}} = 24.50$ exceeds the .001 level, but our table only gives the .01 critical values.)

The obtained F value results in rejection of the null hypothesis. This means the probability that the three means (4, 8, and 17.75) differ merely by sampling error is very small. Therefore, it is likely that the between-groups variance estimate was influenced by treatment effects and the population group means probably do differ from one another. The conclusion is that it is likely that the interruption and prevention of dreaming in adults leads to increased anxiety and irritability.

the relation between the analysis of variance and other statistics

F AND t

If the analysis of variance is simply an extension of the t test to accommodate to more than just two groups, then there should be some relationship between t and F. More specifically, there should be some relationship between the results using the independent-groups, homogeneous-variance t test and the analysis of variance when only two groups are to be compared.

The general nature of the relationship between F and t is

$$F_{1,v} = t_v^2$$

in which the subscripts indicate the degrees of freedom.

This relationship applies both to the observed values of F and t when comparing just two groups and also to the critical values.

Suppose one considers only the first two groups of scores in the experiment on the interruption of dreaming as presented in Table 9–5. One could perform a t test or an analysis of variance to test the difference between these two groups. It happens that because $F_{1,v} = t_v^2$, the two analyses would yield the same general result. Although this fact can be proven algebraically,[10] it will be demonstrated numerically here.

The formula for the independent-groups, homogeneous-variance t test is

$$t_{\text{obs}} = \frac{\overline{X}_1 - \overline{X}_2}{\sqrt{\left[\dfrac{(N_1 - 1)s_1^2 + (N_2 - 1)s_2^2}{N_1 + N_2 - 2}\right] \cdot \left[\dfrac{1}{N_1} + \dfrac{1}{N_2}\right]}}$$

[10] See G. A. Ferguson, *Statistical Analysis in Psychology and Education* (New York: McGraw-Hill, 1966). W. L. Hays, *Statistics for Psychologists* (New York: Holt, Rinehart & Winston, 1963).

Substituting the values for the means, N_j, and variances for these two groups, one obtains

$$t_{\text{obs}} = \frac{4 - 8}{\sqrt{\left[\frac{(5-1)5 + (6-1)13.6}{5+6-2}\right]\left[\frac{1}{5} + \frac{1}{6}\right]}} = \frac{4}{\sqrt{3.58}}$$

If an analysis of variance were performed on these two groups the intermediate quantities would be

$$(\text{I}) = 420.36 \qquad (\text{II}) = 552.00 \qquad (\text{III}) = 464.00$$

The sums of squares, degrees of freedom, and mean squares between- and within-groups are

$$\begin{aligned} SS_{\text{between}} &= 43.64 & df_{\text{between}} &= 1 & MS_{\text{between}} &= 43.64 \\ SS_{\text{within}} &= 88.00 & df_{\text{within}} &= 9 & MS_{\text{within}} &= 9.78 \end{aligned}$$

The resulting F_{obs} is

$$F_{\text{obs}} = \frac{43.64}{9.78} = 4.46$$

Now, if

$$F = t^2$$

then does

$$4.46 \stackrel{?}{=} \left(\frac{4}{\sqrt{3.58}}\right)^2$$

It does within rounding error. This then constitutes an example of the fact that for the case of two groups, the observed values of F computed by the analysis of variance and t computed by the appropriate t test are equivalent. In this sense, the t test is a special case (when $p = 2$) of the analysis of variance. Alternatively, the analysis of variance is a direct extension of the t test to more than two groups.

The critical values of F and t are also related in the same manner. The square of the critical value for t at a specified significance level and with degrees of freedom v will equal the corresponding F for degrees of freedom equal to 1 and v. For example, at $\alpha = .05$ (two-tailed) and with 17 *df*, the critical value of t is

$$t_{\text{crit}} = 2.11$$

At the same significance level with degrees of freedom equal to 1 and 17, the required F is

$$F_{\text{crit}} = 4.45$$

If

$$F_{1,v} = t_v^{\,2}$$

then the following should hold:

$$4.45 \stackrel{?}{=} (2.11)^2$$

It does.

Therefore, F and t are directly related and the analysis of variance is an extension of the t test between means to more than two groups.

PROPORTION OF VARIANCE ATTRIBUTABLE TO TREATMENTS

The analysis of variance as customarily used does not indicate the proportion of the total variability in the scores that is attributable to the differences between group means. If the observed F is "significant" this result indicates that the differences between group means are probably not simply a function of sampling error, but such a result does not indicate the proportion of the total variability in the scores that is attributable to these treatment effects. It can be seen from the table of critical values that the size of F required for significance becomes smaller and smaller as the number of degrees of freedom increases. Because tests of H_0 are more powerful when N is large, even a very small difference in treatment means may be sufficient to result in a "significant difference" if the sample size is very large. However, the importance of such an effect in terms of the proportion of the total variability that is accounted for by these treatment effects might be quite trivial.

The proportion of variance accounted for by differences between population means may be estimated from a simple analysis of variance by the following formula.[11]

$$\text{Proportion of variance} = \frac{SS_{\text{between}} - (p - 1)\, MS_{\text{within}}}{SS_{\text{total}} + MS_{\text{within}}}$$

In the example on the effects of the prevention of people's having a normal amount of dreaming on their state of anxiety and irritability, the following values were obtained:

$$\begin{aligned} SS_{\text{between}} &= 436.18 \\ SS_{\text{total}} &= 542.93 \\ MS_{\text{within}} &= 8.90 \\ p - 1 &= 2 \end{aligned}$$

[11] Hays (*op. cit.*) reports that this estimate depends upon the assumption that there are equal numbers of cases in each group or that the n_j are proportional to the number of such cases of each type that exist in the population. Further, this estimate may be negative in which case it is assumed to be .00.

Substituting into the preceding proportion-of-variance expression,

$$\text{Proportion of variance} = \frac{436.18 - (2)8.90}{542.93 + 8.90} = \frac{418.38}{551.83} = .76$$

one finds that 76% of the variance in scores may be attributable to the treatment effect.

This is a rather high value for research in the social sciences. Very frequently, significant differences between groups may be obtained but the proportion of variance accounted for is on the order of 10% or 20%. This means that although the variable being investigated probably makes a difference (treatment effects do exist), the magnitude of its contribution to the total variability is quite small. Thus, the estimation of the proportion of variance accounted for by a given treatment effect is a valuable aid to interpreting the scientific importance of that variable.

EXERCISES

1. The following sets of numbers were obtained from a random number table.

Group 1	Group 2	Group 3
1	6	1
4	2	2
4	1	2
9	3	4
3	0	3
		7
		9

   (a) Compute the analysis of variance.
   (b) Add three to each score in Group 2 and six to each score in Group 3. This process is analogous to the existence of what in the population? Now, compute the analysis of variance again and explain any differences between this result and that found in Part (a).
   (c) Return to the original numbers as given above and add 20 to the last score in each group. Recompute the analysis of variance and explain any differences you observe.

2. Suppose the "error" component of your score is 3, the grand mean is 10, and the treatment effect associated with your group is −5. What is your score?

3. Explain how the partition of variability in the analysis of variance is analogous to the partition of variability in regression and correlation.

4. An experiment was designed to test the possibility that the expectancy a teacher has about her children somehow becomes translated into actions that help to produce the expected characteristics (i.e., it is a self-fulfilling expectancy).[12] Children in the first grade of an elementary school were all given an intelligence test, but the teachers in the school thought it was a test for "late bloomers," children who would show sudden spurts of intellectual growth. The experimenters then selected three small groups of children **at random** and wrote to the teachers that the test showed the members in Group 1 probably would not demonstrate any particularly large growth spurts in the next year, the members of Group 2 would show a moderate amount, and those in the third group would show a great deal of advancement in the next year. Remember, the children were actually picked at random for these groups. A year later, the children were tested again. The difference in IQ is given below. Test the hypothesis that there were no differences among the groups in IQ change. If teacher expectancy had an effect, determine the proportion of variance accounted for by the manipulation of expectancies.

Group 1	Group 2	Group 3
3	10	14
2	4	25
6	1	10
0	14	19
1	5	15
5	3	9
	9	18

[12] Based upon but not identical to a study by R. Rosenthal and Lenore F. Jacobson, "Teacher Expectations for the Disadvantaged." *Scientific American*, 1968, CCXVIII, 19–23.

10

two-factor analysis of variance

The simple analysis of variance as described in Chapter 9 tests the likelihood that several sample means are actually diverse reflections of the same population mean and differ only because of sampling. It was assumed that these groups represented some type of one-dimensional classification: different amounts of food deprivation, different teaching programs, different makes of cars, etc. The point is that the several groups could be classified as being different levels or types of a *single* category of events, treatments, stimuli, etc.

In actual practice, scientists more frequently view the groups involved in their experiments as belonging to more than one classification, and it is the purpose of this chapter to consider the extension of simple analysis of variance to the case in which the groups fall into a two-way classification scheme. For example, suppose one were interested in the question of whether vicarious reward or punishment would influence the extent to which children will imitate a model. Consider the following experiment.[1] Forty boys and forty girls are randomly selected from a given school. Each child sees a movie in which an adult hits, pounds, pushes, and otherwise assaults a large plastic doll with a weighted base (called a Bobo doll). Half of the children of each sex see a film in which the adult aggressor is rewarded by another adult with praise and congratulations for her vicious attack while half of the children see the aggressor punished with verbal reprimands for his violent behavior. After seeing the movie, all children are brought into a room with several age-appropriate toys including the Bobo doll. In a ten-minute play session, the number of imitated aggressive responses to the Bobo doll are counted. There are four groups in this experiment: (1) boys who

[1] Based upon A. Bandura, D. Ross, and S. A. Ross, "Imitation of Film-Mediated Aggressive Models," *Journal of Abnormal and Social Psychology*, 1963, LXVI, 3–11.

see the aggressor rewarded, (2) boys who see the aggressor punished, (3) girls who see the aggressor rewarded, and (4) girls who see the aggressor punished. These four groups do not represent different levels of a single dimension, but rather each group belongs both to a classification based upon the sex of its subjects and to a classification based upon seeing the aggressor rewarded or punished.

If a single classification scheme is called a **factor** and each division within it a **level** (though these divisions need not necessarily represent different **amounts** of that factor—e.g., the sex factor with levels male and female), then the above example represents a **two-factor** experiment or **design** with two levels of each factor. Designating a factor by a capital letter and each level by a subscripted lower case letter of the same character, the example described above can be expressed in a tabular fashion as follows:

		Factor B (Vicarious Reinforcement) b_1 **(reward)**	b_2 **(punishment)**
Factor A (Sex)	a_1 (males)	males who see aggressor rewarded	males who see aggressor punished
	a_2 (females)	females who see aggressor rewarded	females who see aggressor punished

Suppose the average number of imitative aggressive responses for each of the four groups was as follows:

		Factor B (Vicarious Reinforcement) b_1 **(reward)**	b_2 **(punishment)**	
Factor A (Sex)	a_1 (males)	25	5	15
	a_2 (females)	19	3	11
		22	4	13

In addition to representing the group means, the "marginal" numbers represent the mean number of imitative responses for males (15) and females (11) "collapsed" over (i.e., disregarding the different) reinforcement conditions, and the mean number for subjects watching a rewarded aggressor (22) and a punished aggressor (4) "collapsed" over sex of subject. The grand mean number of responses for all subjects is 13.

Three types of questions could be asked about data collected in accordance with this classification scheme. First, is there a significant difference between the levels of Factor *A*? In this case, do boys imitate aggressive behavior more than do girls? Specifically, does the difference between the means of 15 and 11 represent a difference that exists in the population or is this observed result merely a function of sampling error? Second, is there a significant difference between the levels of Factor *B*? In this case, does the vicarious experience of seeing the aggressor rewarded or punished influence the extent to which children will imitate? Is the difference between the means of 22 and 4 within the realm of sampling error? Third, is there an **interaction** between the influence of sex and the tendency to be influenced by vicarious reinforcement such that the effect of rewarding or punishing the aggressor is different for boys than for girls? Alternatively, such a result may be interpreted to mean that the difference in the tendency to imitate aggressive behavior between boys and girls is different depending upon whether the aggressor is rewarded or punished.

The possible differences between levels of Factor *A* or levels of Factor *B* collapsed over the other factor are called **main effects,** while a potential joint result of both these factors is known as an **interaction.** The meaning of these terms can be appreciated best by examining graphs of possible results of the two-factor example just described. In Figure 10–1, Graph A depicts the case in which all the means are approximately the same and there are no main effects and no interaction. Graph B describes one main effect: males imitate more than females. Notice that the reward and punishment conditions did not appear to influence the amount of imitation. Graph C illustrates a main effect for vicarious reinforcement with no effects for sex and no interaction. In short, children of both sexes imitated more if the aggressor was rewarded than if he was punished and the amount of imitation was the same for both sexes.

In Graph D, there appears to be an effect both for reinforcement and for sex of the child. In general, males imitated more than females and the reward condition generated more imitation than the punishment condition. There is no interaction in Graph D because the difference between males and females is about the same within each of the reinforcement conditions. Another way to say this is that the lines for each sex are approximately parallel indicating that the reinforcement conditions had a comparable effect on both sexes.

Graphs E and F depict interactions between sex and vicarious reinforcement. *The nature of an interaction is such that the effect for one variable is not the same under all conditions of the other variable.* In Graph E, whether the model was

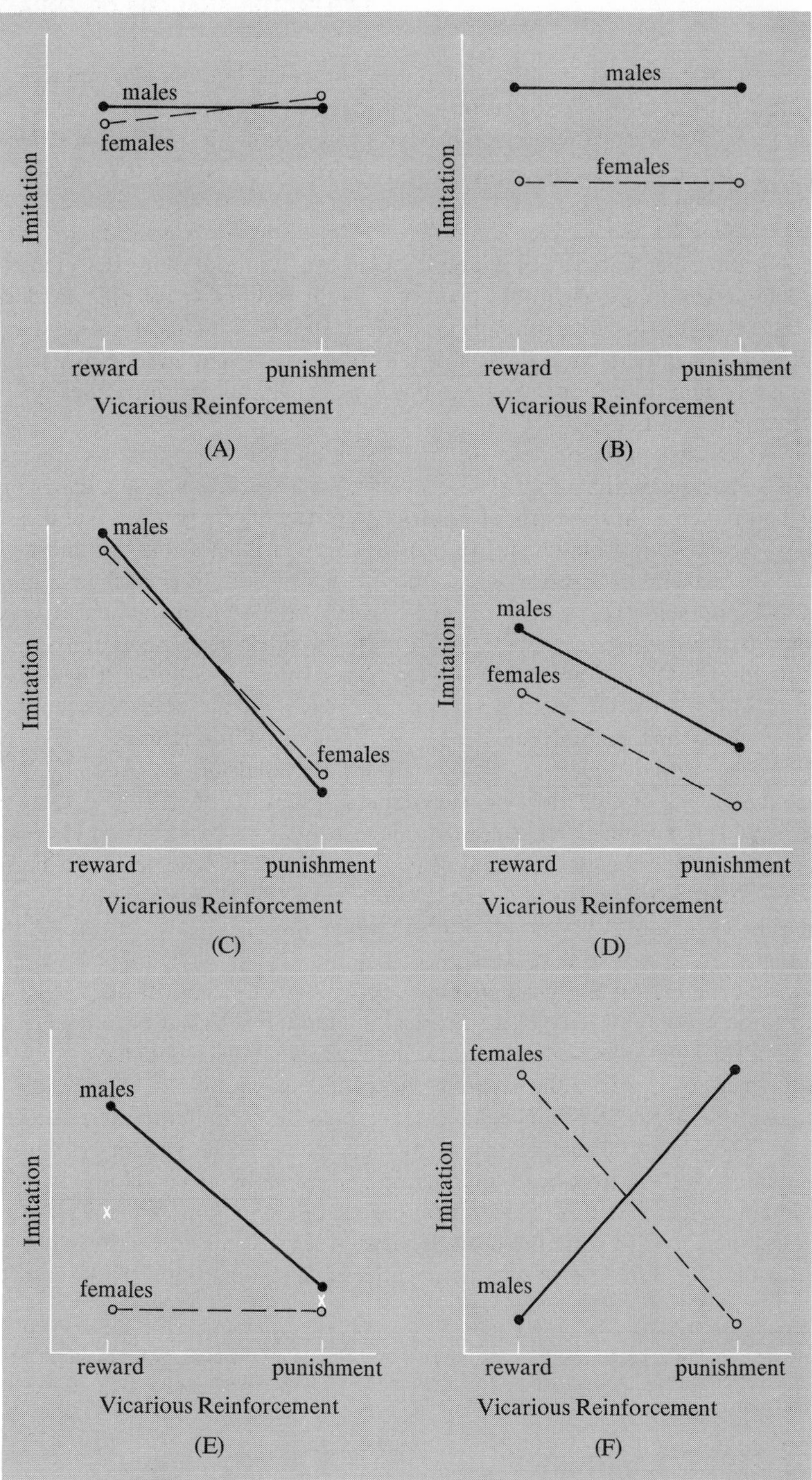

Fig. 10–1. Examples of some possible main effects and interactions.

rewarded or punished made a difference for males but not for females. In Graph F, the influence for vicarious reinforcement had opposite effects for the two sexes. A rewarded aggressor produced more imitation in females than a punished aggressor, but the reverse was true for males. Notice that there is no main effect for vicarious reinforcement nor for sex.

In summary, a **main effect** is a difference in means for a given factor disregarding the other factor. For example, males may imitate more than females. An **interaction** occurs when the effect for a factor is different for different levels of the other factor. For example, the effect of vicarious reinforcement may depend on or **interact** with the sex of the child. Males may imitate a rewarded aggressor more than a punished one but females will not imitate either type of aggressor very much.

From another point of view, an interaction may be thought of as occurring when a specific combination of levels of factors generates a result that would not be predicted on the basis of knowledge of the effects of each factor separately. An analogy from chemistry provides a vivid illustration.[2] Suppose you had two beakers, each filled with a liquid. Specifically, one beaker contains hydrochloric acid (HCl), and if a nickel were dropped into the acid it would soon dissolve leaving a copper coin. Suppose the other beaker contains sodium hydroxide (NaOH). If ground beef were placed into this solution it would disappear in a short while. Both beakers contain highly toxic substances that have severe effects on common substances. If the two solutions were mixed, one might suspect that the effects would be even more deleterious. Actually, however, the mixing of HCl and NaOH produces salty water ($NaCl + H_2O$ or salt and water) after a time, and, except for the taste, may be drunk safely. Here is an instance in which the combination of two variables each of which has a known deteriorating property is not a simple addition of effects which make the combination even more damaging. Rather, when the chemicals are mixed they **interact** in such a way that their effect is quite unlike what might have been predicted merely on the basis of knowing what each chemical does by itself. Thus, one way to conceive of a statistical interaction is that it occurs when the result of the joint influence of two variables is not what one would have predicted on the basis of knowing the separate effects of each variable.

In many analysis of variance designs, any possible combination of results can occur. There may be one or two significant main effects with or without an interaction or there may be an interaction and no main effects. However, when an interaction is found to be significant, generally one ignores the significance or insignificance of the main effects. That is, if there is an interaction, that fact means that the influence of one factor differed depending upon the level of the

[2] The author is indebted to R. M. Liebert for calling this example to his attention. Of course, someone could predict the result of mixing HCl and NaOH on the basis of his familiarity with these chemicals. From a superficial standpoint, however, the example is analogous to statistical interaction.

other factor. Since a main effect represents a difference in means for one variable collapsed over the different conditions of the other factor, the occurrence of an interaction indicates that collapsing over the other factor is not meaningful since the effects for Factor A are not the same within each level of Factor B. For example, consider Graph E in Figure 10–1. The small x's indicate the means for the reward and punishment conditions collapsed over the sex of the subject. It might be the case that the difference between these two means (the x's) is significant, and one would conclude that a rewarded aggressor produces more imitation than a punished aggressor. However, if the interaction depicted in that graph is also significant, it says that vicarious reinforcement makes a difference only for males and not for females, thus qualifying the general interpretation of the main effect for reinforcement. Consequently, if an interaction is significant, generally any main effects that are also significant are disregarded.[3]

THE LOGIC OF TWO-FACTOR ANALYSIS OF VARIANCE[4]

The logic of two-factor analysis of variance is a direct extension of the rationale underlying simple analysis of variance. To review, in simple analysis of variance the total sum of squares was partitioned into two components, each of which provided an estimate of the variability in the population **if** the null hypothesis that the population mean of each group is the same value is taken to be true. However, one of these variance estimates was based upon the deviations of the group means about the grand mean (between-groups estimate) while the other was derived on the basis of the deviations of the scores about their respective group means (within-groups estimate). If the null hypothesis is true, these are both estimates of the same population value. However, since the between-groups estimate involves the group means, its size will depend upon the extent that the group means differ from one another. Consequently, if the between-groups estimate is very large relative to the within-groups estimate (which is not influenced by differences between group means), then one might conclude that the tentative presumption that these groups were all samples from the same population (i.e., the null hypothesis) may not be true. The ratio of the

[3] This general "rule" does have an exception in the event that an interaction exists but all levels of one group are significantly higher than the corresponding levels of the other group. The analysis would yield a main effect and an interaction. For example, suppose in Graph E of Figure 10-1 the line for males was substantially higher than for females under each of the reinforcement conditions. If the males evidenced more imitation than females under reward and under punishment conditions in addition to having the pattern difference displayed in Graph E, then the main effect for sex as well as the interaction would be meaningful. Determining if a main effect should be interpreted when an interaction is also present is a subtle issue and beyond the scope of this text.

[4] This discussion will be restricted to fixed factors, independent groups, and equal cell sizes as discussed later.

between- to within-groups estimate is distributed as F, and by determining the percentile of the observed ratio in this theoretical relative frequency distribution one can assign a probability to the possibility of obtaining such a ratio by sampling error alone. If the probability is sufficiently small, the null hypothesis of no difference between the population means is rejected.

In two-factor analysis of variance, the total sum of squares is usually partitioned into four components. Just as for simple analysis of variance, the variance estimates are called **mean squares** (MS). In the case of a double classification, the four mean squares all estimate the same population variance **if** it can be assumed (among other things) that the population means are all equal (i.e., the null hypothesis is true).[5] However, three of the four estimates are sensitive to certain aspects of the data, while the fourth estimate is not. Consider these several sources of variability and their variance estimates.

One estimate of the variability in the population (symbolized by MS_A) is based upon the deviations of the means for the levels of Factor A (collapsed over Factor B) about the grand mean. This estimate is analogous to the between-groups estimate in a simple analysis of variance involving only the groups of Factor A. As such, its size is sensitive to differences between the means of the levels of Factor A. However, under the null hypothesis differences between these means are merely a reflection of sampling error.

A second estimate of the variability in the population (symbolized by MS_B) is based upon the deviations of the means for the levels of Factor B (collapsed over Factor A) about the grand mean. As such, it is analogous to MS_A except that the means for the levels of Factor B are used. This estimate is sensitive to differences between the means for Factor B.

A third estimate of the variability in the population (symbolized by MS_{AB}) is based upon the deviations of each group mean from what would be predicted on the basis of the knowledge of the two main effects. This mean square is sensitive to the possible interaction between Factors A and B.

Finally, the fourth estimate of the population variability is derived in the same manner as the within-groups estimate in simple analysis of variance (MS_{within}). It is based upon the deviations of each score from its respective group mean. As such, it is not sensitive to differences between groups or between levels of factors. Therefore, the within-groups estimate may be used as a standard against which the size of the other estimates may be evaluated.

The ratio of the mean square for Factor A divided by the mean square within-groups provides a test of the null hypothesis that the means of the levels of A differ from one another merely as a function of sampling error. Under the null hypothesis, the size of this ratio should not be very large since both variances presumably estimate the same value under H_0. However, since MS_A is sensitive to differences between the means for Factor A, the ratio will be large to the extent that those means deviate from one another. If they are

[5] Technically, there are several null hypotheses as discussed in the following material.

very different, the ratio will be so large that the probability that these deviations derive merely from sampling error is exceedingly remote, and the null hypothesis may be rejected. The conclusion would be that the means for the levels of Factor A are "significantly different" from one another.

Similarly, the ratio of the mean square for Factor B divided by MS_{within} reflects the extent to which the means for the levels of Factor B differ from one another. The general rationale for testing the null hypothesis that such differences are merely a function of sampling error is similar to that just described for Factor A.

Analogously, the ratio of MS_{AB} divided by MS_{within} tests the proposition that an interaction between Factors A and B exists in the population.

In short, the logic of double classification analysis of variance is a direct extension of that employed for simple analysis of variance. The total sum of squares is partitioned into components that are each sensitive to different aspects of the classification scheme. Under the null hypothesis, all the groups in the design are randomly selected and have the same population mean. If this is true, the sample means of the groups and the means for the levels of the two factors should deviate only by sampling error. Since MS_A, MS_B, and MS_{AB} are sensitive to different characteristics of the design while MS_{within} is not influenced by these characteristics, the ratio of each of the three mean squares to MS_{within} provides an F ratio that tests the null hypothesis that selected means differ only to an extent expected by sampling error.

derivation of formulas

NOTATION AND TERMINOLOGY

The raw score notation follows the general plan described for the simple one-factor analysis of variance except that an additional subscript is necessary. This notation is summarized in Table 10–1. A single score is indicated by X_{ijk} which represents the ith individual in the jth level of Factor A and the kth level of Factor B. There are a total of p levels of Factor A and q levels of Factor B. It will be assumed that there are an equal number of subjects in each of the jk groups and this number is n.[6] To obtain the mean of any group (for example the jkth group), one simply sums the individual scores within it and divides by n:

$$\overline{X}_{jk} = \frac{\sum_{i=1}^{n} X_{ijk}}{n}$$

[6] The two-factor techniques described in this text demand that there are an equal number of subjects per cell and that n is greater than 1. Special procedures do exist for the case in which the groups do not have equal numbers of subjects and/or $n = 1$. See, for example, B. J. Winer, *Statistical Principles in Experimental Design* (New York: McGraw-Hill, 1962).

10–1 Summary of Raw Score Notation for the Two-Factor Analysis of Variance.

		Factor B			
		b_1	b_2	$\cdots$	b_q
Factor A	a_1	X_{111} X_{211} X_{311} $\vdots$ X_{n11}	X_{112} X_{212} X_{312} $\vdots$ X_{n12}	$\cdots$ $\cdots$ $\cdots$ $\cdots$	X_{11q} X_{21q} X_{31q} $\vdots$ X_{n1q}
		$\overline{X}_{11} = \frac{\sum_{i=1}^{n} X_{i11}}{n}$	$\overline{X}_{12} = \frac{\sum_{i=1}^{n} X_{i12}}{n}$	$\cdots$	$\overline{X}_{1q} = \frac{\sum_{i=1}^{n} X_{i1q}}{n}$
	a_2	X_{121} X_{221} X_{321} $\vdots$ X_{n21}	X_{122} X_{222} X_{322} $\vdots$ X_{n22}	$\cdots$ $\cdots$ $\cdots$ $\cdots$	X_{12q} X_{22q} X_{32q} $\vdots$ X_{n2q}
		$\overline{X}_{21} = \frac{\sum_{i=1}^{n} X_{i21}}{n}$	$\overline{X}_{22} = \frac{\sum_{i=1}^{n} X_{i22}}{n}$	$\cdots$	$\overline{X}_{2q} = \frac{\sum_{i=1}^{n} X_{i2q}}{n}$
		$\vdots$	$\vdots$	$\cdots$	$\vdots$
	a_p	X_{1p1} X_{2p1} X_{3p1} $\vdots$ X_{np1}	X_{1p2} X_{2p2} X_{3p2} $\vdots$ X_{np2}	$\cdots$ $\cdots$ $\cdots$ $\cdots$	X_{1pq} X_{2pq} X_{3pq} $\vdots$ X_{npq}
		$\overline{X}_{p1} = \frac{\sum_{i=1}^{n} X_{ip1}}{n}$	$\overline{X}_{p2} = \frac{\sum_{i=1}^{n} X_{ip2}}{n}$	$\cdots$	$\overline{X}_{pq} = \frac{\sum_{i=1}^{n} X_{ipq}}{n}$

n = the number of subjects in each group

a_j = the jth level of Factor A

p = the number of levels of Factor A

b_k = the kth level of Factor B

q = the number of levels of Factor B

X_{ijk} = the ith score in the jkth group

$$\frac{\sum_{i=1}^{n} X_{ijk}}{n} = \overline{X}_{jk} = \text{the mean of the } jk\text{th group}$$

Table 10–2 summarizes the notation for the several means involved in such a two-factor classification. Any cell mean (i.e., the *jk*th) is given by $\overline{X}_{jk}$. If the mean is for a single level of Factor *A* (i.e., the *j*th) in which all the subjects in the level (regardless of the classification on Factor *B*) are included, the symbol

$$\overline{X}_{j.}$$

is used in which the dot (.) indicates the factor which has been summed over (in this case Factor *B*). The mean of the *k*th level of Factor *B* is represented by

$$\overline{X}_{.k}$$

and the grand mean computed for all subjects across all levels of Factors *A* and *B* is given by

$$\overline{X}_{..}$$

THE PARTITION OF VARIABILITY

Recall from the previous chapter on simple analysis of variance that a treatment effect was defined to be the difference, in the population, between a group mean and the grand mean. Such a treatment effect was estimated by the difference between a sample group mean and the grand mean over all groups in the sample:

$$\text{estimated treatment effect } a_j = \overline{X}_j - \overline{X}$$

Suppose the means for the example described above are those presented in Table 10–3. In the two-factor classification, there are several sources of treatment effects. For example, for Factor *A* (sex) the treatment effect for males would be estimated by the difference between the mean for Level 1 of Factor *A* ($\overline{X}_{1.}$) and the grand mean ($\overline{X}_{..}$):

$$\begin{aligned} \text{effect for } a_1 &= (\overline{X}_{1.} - \overline{X}_{..}) \\ a_1 &= 15 - 13 \\ a_1 &= +2 \end{aligned}$$

Similarly, the treatment effect for Level 2 of Factor *A* (females) is estimated by[7]

$$\begin{aligned} \text{effect for } a_2 &= (\overline{X}_{2.} - \overline{X}_{..}) \\ a_2 &= 11 - 13 \\ a_2 &= -2 \end{aligned}$$

[7] Recall that a treatment effect is estimated by the difference between a sample group mean and the grand mean. As such, negative treatment effects merely imply that one would expect a particular group to have less of the behavior in question relative to the grand mean. For example, the estimated treatment effect of -2 for females implies that on the average females displayed two fewer imitative responses than the average for the entire sample. It does not mean simply that females show -2 imitative responses.

10–2 Summary of Notation for Means for the Two-Factor Analysis of Variance.

		Factor B				
		b_1	b_2	$\dots$	b_q	**Means for the levels of Factor A**
Factor A	a_1	$\overline{X}_{11}$	$\overline{X}_{12}$	$\dots$	$\overline{X}_{1q}$	$\overline{X}_{1.} = \dfrac{\sum_{k=1}^{q}\sum_{i=1}^{n} X_{i1k}}{nq}$
	a_2	$\overline{X}_{21}$	$\overline{X}_{22}$	$\dots$	$\overline{X}_{2q}$	$\overline{X}_{2.} = \dfrac{\sum_{k=1}^{q}\sum_{i=1}^{n} X_{i2k}}{nq}$
	$\vdots$	$\vdots$	$\vdots$		$\vdots$	$\vdots$
	a_p	$\overline{X}_{p1}$	$\overline{X}_{p2}$		$\overline{X}_{pq}$	$\overline{X}_{p.} = \dfrac{\sum_{k=1}^{q}\sum_{i=1}^{n} X_{ipk}}{nq}$
Means for the levels of Factor B		$\overline{X}_{.1} = \dfrac{\sum_{j=1}^{p}\sum_{i=1}^{n} X_{ij1}}{pn}$	$\overline{X}_{.2} = \dfrac{\sum_{j=1}^{p}\sum_{i=1}^{n} X_{ij2}}{pn}$	$\dots$	$\overline{X}_{.q} = \dfrac{\sum_{j=1}^{p}\sum_{i=1}^{n} X_{ijq}}{pn}$	**Grand Mean** $\overline{X}_{..} = \dfrac{\sum_{k=1}^{q}\sum_{j=1}^{p}\sum_{i=1}^{n} X_{ijk}}{npq}$

n = the number of subjects in each group
a_j = the jth level of Factor A
p = the number of levels of Factor A
b_k = the kth level of Factor B
q = the number of levels of Factor B
$\overline{X}_{j.}$ = the mean for level j of Factor A
$\overline{X}_{.k}$ = the mean for level k of Factor B
$\overline{X}_{..}$ = the grand mean

10–3 Means for the Example Described in the Text.

		Factor *B* (Vicarious Reinforcement) b_1 (reward)	b_2 (punishment)	
Factor *A* (Sex)	a_1 (males)	25	5	15
	a_2 (females)	19	3	11
		22	4	13

In general,

$$\text{effect for } a_j = (\overline{X}_{j.} - \overline{X}_{..})$$

Similarly, the treatment effects for levels of Factor *B* (vicarious reinforcement) are estimated by

$$\text{effect for } b_1 = (\overline{X}_{.1} - \overline{X}_{..})$$
$$b_1 = 22 - 13$$
$$b_1 = +9$$

$$\text{effect for } b_2 = (\overline{X}_{.2} - \overline{X}_{..})$$
$$b_2 = 4 - 13$$
$$b_2 = -9$$

In general,

$$\text{effect for } b_k = (\overline{X}_{.k} - \overline{X}_{..})$$

An interaction between Factors *A* and *B* occurs when the observed values differ from what would be predicted on the basis of the two factors alone. To illustrate, disregard any differences between individual subjects for a moment, and suppose one were to predict the means in each cell of the above design solely on the basis of the estimated treatment effects for Factor *A* (sex) and Factor *B* (vicarious reinforcement).

Table 10–4 presents the predictions of the means of each cell in the design on the basis of the two factors alone. The grand mean (13) is taken as a base in each case. Since a treatment effect is represented by the difference between the group mean and the grand mean, the treatment effects can be added to the grand mean to estimate the mean value for each cell. Thus, in the upper left-hand cell for males who viewed a rewarded aggressor, the grand mean (13) plus the estimated treatment effect for being male (+2) plus the estimated treatment

10–4 Estimation of Means from the Two Factors Alone.

		Factor B (Vicarious Reinforcement) b_1 (reward)	b_2 (punishment)	Estimated Treatment Effect
Factor A (Sex)	a_1 (males)	$13 + 2 + 9 = 24$	$13 + 2 - 9 = 6$	$+2$
	a_2 (females)	$13 - 2 + 9 = 20$	$13 - 2 - 9 = 2$	-2
	Estimated Treatment Effects	$+9$	-9	Grand Mean 13

effect for seeing a rewarded aggressor (+9) are added to obtain the estimated cell mean of 24. Similar procedures have been followed for the other cells.

Table 10–5 shows that these estimates of the cell means based upon the factors of sex and vicarious reinforcement alone were not totally accurate. Each cell of the following table gives the estimated value minus the actual mean.

The estimated cell mean of 24 for males seeing a rewarded aggressor missed the actual value (25) by −1 unit. Similar deviations were observed for the other cells. These deviations represent the difference between what the treatment effects for the factors of sex and vicarious reinforcement alone would predict and what the observed value is. These differences represent an **interaction** between Factor A (sex) and Factor B (vicarious reinforcement), effects that are unique to the specific combinations of sex and reinforcement.

10–5 Observed Sample Means Minus Estimated Values.

		Factor B (Vicarious Reinforcement) b_1 (reward)	b_2 (punishment)
Factor A (Sex)	a_1 (males)	$24 - 25 = -1$	$6 - 5 = 1$
	a_2 (females)	$20 - 19 = 1$	$2 - 3 = -1$

In short, the treatment effect for interaction is estimated by taking the actual cell mean ($\overline{X}_{jk}$) and subtracting the grand mean ($\overline{X}_{..}$) and the treatment effects for the two main effects [($\overline{X}_{j.} - \overline{X}_{..}$) and ($\overline{X}_{.k} - \overline{X}_{..}$)]. The main effects are subtracted from the cell mean along with the grand mean because the interaction represents the difference between the actual mean and what would have been predicted on the basis of the two main effects. In symbols, a treatment effect for interaction is estimated by

$$\begin{aligned} \text{effect for } ab_{jk} &= \overline{X}_{jk} - [\overline{X}_{..} + (\overline{X}_{j.} - \overline{X}_{..}) + (\overline{X}_{.k} - \overline{X}_{..})] \\ &= \overline{X}_{jk} - [\overline{X}_{..} + \overline{X}_{j.} - \overline{X}_{..} + \overline{X}_{.k} - \overline{X}_{..}] \\ ab_{jk} &= \overline{X}_{jk} - \overline{X}_{j.} - \overline{X}_{.k} + \overline{X}_{..} \end{aligned}$$

A cell mean can be thought of as being composed of the grand mean plus the treatment effects for Factor A, Factor B, and their interaction:

$$\text{Cell mean} = \overline{X}_{..} + (\overline{X}_{j.} - \overline{X}_{..}) + (\overline{X}_{.k} - \overline{X}_{..}) + (\overline{X}_{jk} - \overline{X}_{j.} - \overline{X}_{.k} + \overline{X}_{..})$$

The next step is to recall that each subject does not usually score the same as each other subject in his group. Once the mean of the cell is known, each subject within the cell (X_{ijk}) deviates from the cell mean by

$$X_{ijk} - \overline{X}_{jk}$$

Therefore, any particular score (X_{ijk}) may be conceived to be the sum of the grand mean, the treatment effects for Factors A and B, and the interaction of A and B, plus the deviation of the score from the cell mean (within groups):

$$\begin{aligned} \underbrace{X_{ijk}}_{\text{a score}} &= \underbrace{\overline{X}_{..}}_{\text{grand mean}} + \underbrace{(\overline{X}_{j.} - \overline{X}_{..})}_{\text{effect for } A} + \underbrace{(\overline{X}_{.k} - \overline{X}_{..})}_{\text{effect for } B} + \underbrace{(\overline{X}_{jk} - \overline{X}_{j.} - \overline{X}_{.k} + \overline{X}_{..})}_{\text{effect for the interaction of } A \text{ and } B} \\ &\quad + \underbrace{(X_{ijk} - \overline{X}_{jk})}_{\text{within groups}} \end{aligned}$$

SUMS OF SQUARES, DEGREES OF FREEDOM, MEAN SQUARES, *F*'s

sums of squares In order to pursue the partitioning of the total variability, one must have an expression for total variability. This is represented by the sum of squared deviations of the scores about the grand mean, in this case $\sum_{i=1}^{n} \sum_{j=1}^{p} \sum_{k=1}^{q} (X_{ijk} - \overline{X}_{..})^2$. One can obtain an expression for the total sum of squared deviations in terms of treatment effects by transposing the grand mean from the right to the left side of the previous expression:

$$\begin{aligned} (X_{ijk} - \overline{X}_{..}) = (\overline{X}_{j.} - \overline{X}_{..}) + (\overline{X}_{.k} - \overline{X}_{..}) + (\overline{X}_{jk} - \overline{X}_{j.} - \overline{X}_{.k} + \overline{X}_{..}) \\ + (X_{ijk} - \overline{X}_{jk}) \end{aligned}$$

If this equation is squared and summed over all scores, all of the cross-product terms can be shown to be zero, just as in the case for the simple analysis of variance described on page 223. The result is

$$\sum_{i=1}^{n}\sum_{j=1}^{p}\sum_{k=1}^{q}(X_{ijk}-\overline{X}_{..})^2 = nq\sum_{j=1}^{p}(\overline{X}_{j.}-\overline{X}_{..})^2 + np\sum_{k=1}^{q}(\overline{X}_{.k}-\overline{X}_{..})^2$$
$$+\, n\sum_{j=1}^{p}\sum_{k=1}^{q}(\overline{X}_{jk}-\overline{X}_{j.}-\overline{X}_{.k}+\overline{X}_{..})^2 + \sum_{i=1}^{n}\sum_{j=1}^{p}\sum_{k=1}^{q}(X_{ijk}-\overline{X}_{jk})^2$$

Each of these sums of squared deviations is a **sum of squares** (*SS*). The sum of squared deviations of individual scores from the grand mean represents the total sum of squares:

$$SS_{\text{total}} = \sum_{i=1}^{n}\sum_{j=1}^{p}\sum_{k=1}^{q}(X_{ijk}-\overline{X}_{..})^2$$

The sum of squared deviations of the means for the levels of Factor *A* about the grand mean is the sum of squares for Factor *A* (the coefficient of *nq* represents the result of summing constants):

$$SS_A = nq\sum_{j=1}^{p}(\overline{X}_{j.}-\overline{X}_{..})^2$$

The sum of squared deviations of the means of the levels of Factor *B* about the grand mean is the sum of squares for Factor *B*:

$$SS_B = np\sum_{k=1}^{q}(\overline{X}_{.k}-\overline{X}_{..})^2$$

The sum of squared deviations of the cell means minus the grand mean and treatment effects for Factor *A* and *B* is the sum of squares for interaction:

$$SS_{AB} = n\sum_{j=1}^{p}\sum_{k=1}^{q}(\overline{X}_{jk}-\overline{X}_{j.}-\overline{X}_{.k}+\overline{X}_{..})^2$$

Finally, the sum of squared deviations of the individual scores about their own group mean represents the sum of squares for within groups:

$$SS_{\text{within}} = \sum_{i=1}^{n}\sum_{j=1}^{p}\sum_{k=1}^{q}(X_{ijk}-\overline{X}_{jk})^2$$

Just as was the case previously, the total sum of squares equals the sum of the component sums of squares:

$$SS_{\text{total}} = SS_A + SS_B + SS_{AB} + SS_{\text{within}}$$

This is what is meant by partitioning. The total sum of squares is divided into separate components which sum to SS_{total} and which represent different sources of variability (Factor *A*, Factor *B*, interaction, within groups).

degrees of freedom As before, the variance estimates (mean squares, MS) are obtained by dividing each of these sums of squares by its appropriate degrees of freedom. The total sum of squares involves the squared deviation of each score from the grand mean. Thus, the number of degrees of freedom for SS_{total} will be one less than the total number of observations in the entire design. If there are n subjects per group and pq groups, the total number of subjects is npq, which may be abbreviated by N. Therefore,

$$df_{\text{total}} = npq - 1 = N - 1$$

The sum of squares for Factor A involves the squared deviation of each of the Factor A means from the grand mean. There are p such means, so the degrees of freedom for the Factor A variance estimate are

$$df_A = p - 1$$

Similarly, Factor B has q levels, so the degrees of freedom are

$$df_B = q - 1$$

The degrees of freedom for interaction are slightly less intuitive. This sum of squares involves the cell means, but the grand mean and all marginal means (means for all levels of the main factors) are also involved. Therefore, the task is to determine how many cell means in the table are free to vary given the grand mean and all marginal means. Consider, for example, a 3 × 2 table:

?	?		10
			20
10	15	20	15

A little thought indicates that once the values for any two cells are established, for example the ones with question marks, then the means of the remaining cells can be determined. The open cells must have a value that would make the average within that row (or column) equal to the marginal average which is given. Therefore, in the above example, there are two degrees of freedom for interaction. The number of cells free to vary is always the product of (the number of rows minus one) times (the number of columns minus one) because one vacant cell in any row (or column) can be determined. Consequently, the degrees of freedom for interaction are

$$df_{AB} = (p - 1)(q - 1)$$

The sum of squares within groups is composed of the squared deviations of the scores about their own mean. Within any one group, $n - 1$ of those scores are free to vary. Since there are pq groups in the design, the degrees of freedom for SS_{within} are

$$df_{\text{within}} = pq(n - 1)$$
$$= pqn - pq$$
$$df_{\text{within}} = N - pq$$

Notice that in a manner similar to that used for the sums of squares, the degrees of freedom for the total equal the sum of the degrees of freedom for the component sources of variability:

$$df_{\text{total}} = df_A + df_B + df_{AB} + df_{\text{within}}$$

mean squares The mean squares for the several sources of variability are given by the sums of squares divided by their respective degrees of freedom:

$$MS_A = \frac{SS_A}{df_A}$$

$$MS_B = \frac{SS_B}{df_B}$$

$$MS_{AB} = \frac{SS_{AB}}{df_{AB}}$$

$$MS_{\text{within}} = \frac{SS_{\text{within}}}{df_{\text{within}}}$$

F ratios Once the mean squares have been determined, F ratios may be constructed to test the significance of the several possible treatment effects. The following F ratios may be formed:

$$F_A = \frac{MS_A}{MS_{\text{within}}}$$

$$F_B = \frac{MS_B}{MS_{\text{within}}}$$

$$F_{AB} = \frac{MS_{AB}}{MS_{\text{within}}}$$

In each case, under the null hypothesis the numerator and denominator are both estimates of the same population value. However, the numerators (in contrast to MS_{within}) are sensitive to differences in particular sets of means. To the extent that these means differ from one another, the numerator of the F ratio will become large relative to its denominator. If the resulting ratio is so large that the probability is very small that an observed value of its size could be reasonably expected under the null hypothesis, then H_0 is rejected and one concludes that the differences between the means of the effect being considered are so great that they are not likely to be merely a result of sampling differences.[8]

NUMERICAL ILLUSTRATION OF TREATMENT EFFECTS

It will be helpful to observe in a numerical example how the presence of treatment effects is reflected in the results of an analysis of variance.

Table 10–6 presents a 2 × 2 analysis of variance using randomly selected numbers between 0 and 10 as the scores. Since the numbers are presumably randomly selected, it can be assumed that the null hypotheses are true and that in the population the group means are all equal. With certain additional assumptions, the population variance could be estimated by variances computed on these data in a variety of ways. It should not matter if variability is appropriately computed by taking scores about their cell means, means for the levels of one factor or another about the grand mean, etc. They should all estimate the same population variance. While these different estimates will probably not equal one another, if H_0 is true they should deviate from each other only by sampling error.

The sum of squares for Factor A reflects the extent to which the means for levels of A deviate from the grand mean. The $SS_A = 12.8$. Similarly, the sum of squares for Factor B reflects the deviations of the means for the levels of B about the grand mean. The $SS_B = 7.20$. The interaction sum of squares represents the degree to which the cell means deviate from the grand mean plus the treatment effects for the respective levels of A and B. In this case, $SS_{AB} = 3.20$. Finally, the sum of squares within groups is computed by taking the squared deviation of each score about its own group mean. The $SS_{\text{within}} = 75.6$. The lower portion of Table 10–6 presents the traditional summary of the analysis of variance. The mean squares (MS) are calculated by dividing the SS by its degrees of freedom (df), and the F's are obtained by dividing the MS for A, B, or AB by the MS_{within}. Since according to the F table given in Table C the critical value for F with 1 and 16 degrees of freedom is 4.49 at $p < .05$, none of the effects in this example is significant.

Now consider the analysis presented in Table 10–7. The same numbers are used except that 10 has been added to each score in both the b_2 groups. This is analogous to introducing a treatment effect for Factor B. Observe how the several sums of squares respond to this specific manipulation. First, as one might expect, the sum of squares for Factor B increases considerably as a function of this change (and so does the total sum of squares). However, notice that the sums of squares for A, AB, and within groups do not change. This example illustrates how a selective introduction of a specific main effect is reflected only in the appropriate sum of squares.

[8] A discussion of the assumptions required for this analysis appears in a later section.

10–6 Two-Factor Analysis of Variance with No Effects.

		Factor B b_1	b_2	
Factor A	a_1	5 4 3 4 2 $\overline{X}_{11} = 3.6$	8 9 4 2 5 $\overline{X}_{12} = 5.6$	$\overline{X}_{1.} = 4.6$
	a_2	6 7 5 8 4 $\overline{X}_{21} = 6.0$	6 9 5 9 3 $\overline{X}_{22} = 6.4$	$\overline{X}_{2.} = 6.2$
		$\overline{X}_{.1} = 4.8$	$\overline{X}_{.2} = 6.0$	$\overline{X}_{..} = 5.4$

$$SS_A = nq \sum_{j=1}^{p} (\overline{X}_{j.} - \overline{X}_{..})^2$$
$$= (5)(2)[(4.6 - 5.4)^2 + (6.2 - 5.4)^2]$$
$$SS_A = 12.80$$

$$SS_B = np \sum_{k=1}^{q} (\overline{X}_{.k} - \overline{X}_{..})^2$$
$$= (5)(2)[(4.8 - 5.4)^2 + (6.0 - 5.4)^2]$$
$$SS_B = 7.20$$

Interaction

$$SS_{AB} = n \sum_{j=1}^{p} \sum_{k=1}^{q} (\overline{X}_{jk} - \overline{X}_{j.} - \overline{X}_{.k} + \overline{X}_{..})^2$$
$$= 5[(3.6 - 4.6 - 4.8 + 5.4)^2 + (5.6 - 4.6 - 6.0 + 5.4)^2 + (6.0 - 6.2 - 4.8 + 5.4)^2 + (6.4 - 6.2 - 6.0 + 5.4)^2]$$
$$SS_{AB} = 3.20$$

Within Groups

$$SS_{\text{within}} = \sum_{i=1}^{n} \sum_{j=1}^{p} \sum_{k=1}^{q} (X_{ijk} - \overline{X}_{jk})^2$$
$$SS_{\text{within}} = 75.60$$

Source	*df*	*SS*	$MS = \frac{SS}{df}$	$F = \frac{MS}{MS_{\text{within}}}$
A	$p - 1 = 1$	12.80	12.80	2.71
B	$q - 1 = 1$	7.20	7.20	1.52
AB	$(p - 1)(q - 1) = 1$	3.20	3.20	.68
Within	$N - pq = 16$	75.60	4.72	
Total	$N - 1 = 19$	98.80		

10–7 Sample Two-Factor Diagram with a Treatment Effect Added to b_2

		Factor B		
		b_1	$b_2\ (+10)$	
Factor A	a_1	5 4 3 4 2 $\overline{X}_{11} = 3.6$	18 19 14 12 15 $\overline{X}_{12} = 15.6$	$X_{1.} = 9.6$
	a_2	6 7 5 8 4 $\overline{X}_{21} = 6.0$	16 19 15 19 13 $\overline{X}_{22} = 16.4$	$\overline{X}_{2.} = 11.2$
		$\overline{X}_{.1} = 4.8$	$\overline{X}_{.2} = 16.0$	$\overline{X}_{..} = 10.4$

$$SS_A = nq \sum_{j=1}^{p} (\overline{X}_{j.} - \overline{X}_{..})^2$$
$$= (5)(2)[(9.6 - 10.4)^2 + (11.2 - 10.4)^2]$$
$$SS_A = 12.80$$

$$SS_B = np \sum_{k=1}^{q} (\overline{X}_{.k} - \overline{X}_{..})^2$$
$$= (5)(2)[(4.8 - 10.4)^2 + (16.0 - 10.4)^2]$$
$$SS_B = 627.20$$

Interaction

$$SS_{AB} = n \sum_{j=1}^{p} \sum_{k=1}^{q} (\overline{X}_{jk} - \overline{X}_{j.} - \overline{X}_{.k} + \overline{X}_{..})^2$$
$$= 5[(3.6 - 9.6 - 4.8 + 10.4)^2 + (15.6 - 9.6 - 16.0 + 10.4)^2 + (6.0 - 11.2 - 4.8 + 10.4)^2 + (16.4 - 11.2 - 16.0 + 10.4)^2]$$
$$SS_{AB} = 3.20$$

Within Groups

$$SS_{\text{within}} = \sum_{i=1}^{n} \sum_{j=1}^{p} \sum_{k=1}^{q} (X_{ijk} - \overline{X}_{jk})^2$$
$$SS_{\text{within}} = 75.60$$

Source	df	SS	$MS = \frac{SS}{df}$	$F = \frac{MS}{MS_{\text{within}}}$
A	$p - 1 = 1$	12.80	12.80	2.71
B	$q - 1 = 1$	627.20	627.20	132.89
AB	$(p - 1)(q - 1) = 1$	3.20	3.20	.68
Within	$N - pq = 16$	75.60	4.72	
Total	$N - 1 = 19$	718.80		

Now turn to the analysis presented in Table 10–8. Here, the same numbers as in Table 10–6 are used again, but 10 has been added only to the scores in the upper right-hand cell, ab_{12}. Since this difference is not added to the entire b_2 level (as was just done in Table 10–7) but only to b_2 within the a_1 level, the result should be an interaction between Factors A and B since the pattern of results for the levels of B depends upon or interacts with the level of A. As anticipated, the analysis shows an increase in the sum of squares for interaction, SS_{AB}, but observe that the sums of squares for A and B also increase. Only the SS_{within} remains uninfluenced by this change. The inflation of SS_A and SS_B in response to the increment of a single cell results from the fact that such a manipulation does indeed change the means of the respective levels of A and B. The SS_{within} is not altered because adding a constant to any group of scores does not change the variability of those particular scores about their mean.

These comparisons illustrate how the analysis of variance is sensitive to different types of treatment effects. It shows how the SS_A and SS_B reflect differences in the marginal means, how SS_{AB} is changed when one but not another cell within a single level of one factor is altered, and how SS_{within} remains uninfluenced by changes in cell or level means. Consequently, if the null hypothesis is true and the groups are all random samples having the same population mean, these sums of squares all estimate the same value. However, to the extent that treatment effects exist for A, B, and/or AB, their respective mean squares will be inflated, but the mean square within groups will not be altered because it is not sensitive to differences between cell or level means. Consequently, it is appropriate to construct three F ratios, $\frac{MS_A}{MS_{\text{within}}}$, $\frac{MS_B}{MS_{\text{within}}}$, and $\frac{MS_{AB}}{MS_{\text{within}}}$, which will test the existence of treatment effects in the population.

The above examples also demonstrate that when an interaction exists, additional treatment effects for Factor A or Factor B may not be too meaningful. Recall that in Table 10–8 only cell ab_{12} was deliberately incremented, yet the sum of squares for Factors A and B as well as for the AB interaction were increased. Thus, the existence of interactions of some forms may also produce significant main effects even when only one cell is markedly different from the others. When a significant interaction is obtained, the data should be graphed in order to interpret the results.

ASSUMPTIONS UNDERLYING TWO-FACTOR ANALYSIS OF VARIANCE

Two-factor analyses of variance make some of the same assumptions that are required in a single-factor analysis and for the same reasons.

First, the groups of the design must be **independent** from one another, and the observations **randomly sampled.** This assumption is necessary so that the variability within each group is not correlated with the variability within another group. While all the analysis-of-variance procedures described in this text as-

10-8 Sample Two-Factor Design with a Treatment Effect Added to Cell ab_{12}

		Factor B: b_1	b_2	
Factor A	a_1	5, 4, 3, 4, 2	(+10) 18, 19, 14, 12, 15	$\bar{X}_{1.} = 9.6$
		$\bar{X}_{11} = 3.6$	$\bar{X}_{12} = 15.6$	
	a_2	6, 7, 5, 8, 4	6, 9, 5, 9, 3	$\bar{X}_{2.} = 6.2$
		$\bar{X}_{21} = 6.0$	$\bar{X}_{22} = 6.4$	
		$\bar{X}_{.1} = 4.8$	$\bar{X}_{.2} = 11.0$	$\bar{X}_{..} = 7.9$

$$SS_A = nq \sum_{j=1}^{p} (\bar{X}_{j.} - \bar{X}_{..})^2$$
$$= (5)(2)[(9.6 - 7.9)^2 + (6.2 - 7.9)^2]$$
$$SS_A = 57.80$$

$$SS_B = np \sum_{k=1}^{q} (\bar{X}_{.k} - \bar{X}_{..})^2$$
$$= (5)(2)[(4.8 - 7.9)^2 + (11.0 - 7.9)^2]$$
$$SS_B = 192.20$$

Interaction

$$SS_{AB} = n \sum_{j=1}^{p} \sum_{k=1}^{q} (\bar{X}_{jk} - \bar{X}_{j.} - \bar{X}_{.k} + \bar{X}_{..})^2$$
$$= 5[(3.6 - 9.6 - 4.8 + 7.9)^2 + (15.6 - 9.6 - 11.0 + 7.9)^2 + (6.0 - 6.2 - 4.8 + 7.9)^2 + (6.4 - 6.2 - 11.0 + 7.9)^2]$$
$$SS_{AB} = 168.20$$

Within Groups

$$SS_{\text{within}} = \sum_{i=1}^{n} \sum_{j=1}^{p} \sum_{k=1}^{q} (X_{ijk} - \bar{X}_{jk})^2$$
$$SS_{\text{within}} = 75.60$$

Source	df	SS	$MS = \frac{SS}{df}$	$F = \frac{MS}{MS_{\text{within}}}$
A	$p - 1 = 1$	57.80	57.80	12.24
B	$q - 1 = 1$	192.20	192.20	40.72
AB	$(p - 1)(q - 1) = 1$	168.20	168.20	35.63
Within	$N - pq = 16$	75.60	4.72	
Total	$N - 1 = 19$	493.80		

sume independent groups, techniques do exist for handling situations in which the groups are not independent, such as a before-after experiment in which the same subjects are measured before and then after a special treatment is administered.[9]

A second assumption is that the population distributions of each group in the design are **normal** in form and have equal variances (i.e., **homogeneity of variance**). The assumption of normality is made so that the variance estimates in the F ratio are independent, and homogeneity of variance is needed so that MS_{within} represents an appropriate pooling of the variability within each group of the design.

Third, the procedures assume that the factors involved in the design are **fixed.** There are two types of factors, **random** and **fixed.** A random factor is one for which the levels are randomly selected. For example, suppose a researcher were interested in the effects of a new teaching program vs. an old teaching program at schools in a particular school system. If the school system is very large, perhaps not all the schools will be analyzed. Consequently, three of them are randomly drawn from a hat and thus compose the three levels of the Factor A (schools) in the analysis. In this case, Factor A (schools) would be a random factor. However, if the researcher designated which particular schools were to be entered into the analysis, perhaps because of their size, socioeconomic makeup, geographical location, etc., then these schools would not be randomly selected from the population of schools but chosen from some "fixed" subgroups of schools which form the levels of Factor A (schools). Factor A (schools) would then be a **fixed** factor. It is possible to have a two-factor analysis variance in which one factor is fixed and the other is random. This is called a **mixed model.** The procedures outlined in this text are only applicable to the **fixed model** (both factors are fixed), since this is the most common of the three designs. Techniques for analyzing the random and mixed models can be found elsewhere.[10]

Finally, the techniques outlined here have assumed that there are an **equal number of cases** in each group and that there is **more than one observation per cell.** Again, procedures do exist for the case in which the cells are unequal with respect to n.[11]

computation

COMPUTATIONAL FORMULAS

Just as with previous techniques, the definitional formulas are not the most convenient ones to use for computational purposes. A more satisfactory set of

[9] See "repeated measures designs," B. J. Winer, *Statistical Principles in Experimental Design* (New York: McGraw-Hill, 1962).

[10] *Ibid.*

[11] *Ibid.*

computational procedures is outlined in Table 10–9. Recall that n = the number of subjects in each group, N is the total number of subjects in the design, p = the number of levels of Factor A, q = the number of levels of Factor B, and X_{ijk} = the score for the ith subject in the jth level of A and kth level of B.

Part **i** of Table 10–9 displays the raw data. The T's represent various totals (sums) and the system of subscripts is identical to that previously described for cell and level means. Thus, T_{jk} is the total for the jkth cell, $T_{j.}$ is the total for the jth level of A summed over all levels of B, $T_{.k}$ is the sum for the kth level of B summed over all levels of A, and $T_{..}$ is the grand total accumulated over all observations in all conditions. A matrix of these sums is presented in Part **ii** of Table 10–9.

Part **iii** presents five quantities that facilitate the computation of the analysis of variance. Quantity (I) is the grand total squared, then divided by the total N in the design. Quantity (II) is simply the sum of all squared scores. Quantity (III) is the sum of the squared total for each level of Factor A divided by nq, and Quantity (IV) is the sum of the squared totals for each level of Factor B divided by np. Quantity (V) is the sum of the squares of all cell totals divided by n.

Part **iv** presents the formulas for obtaining all the necessary quantities for the analysis of variance summary table. Notice that the sums of squares are computed quite easily by adding and subtracting the intermediate quantities displayed in Part **iii.** The sum of the degrees of freedom and the sum of the SS should equal df_{total} and SS_{total}, respectively.

Although the computational work for this relatively simple and small two-factor analysis of variance is not particularly overburdening, the computational labor becomes tedious if the number of subjects is rather large. Also, there are three- and four-factor (or more) analyses of variance which demand considerably more labor in their calculations. Fortunately, if the analysis is very large or several such analyses are to be performed, the researcher may use a computer to perform the calculations. In fact, programs exist to execute almost all of the statistical computations presented in this volume. The computational routines described in this text are appropriate for use with the more common hand calculators because they are more frequently available to students. However, if small programmed calculators or large computers are available, their use will certainly facilitate the computational procedures. A caution is in order, however. These machines only do the computation, they do not select the appropriate statistical test, evaluate the tenability of the assumptions, determine whether a one- or two-tailed test is appropriate, or interpret the results. There is a danger in using a statistical test without having studied it thoroughly, and sometimes people yield to the temptation to use a computer because it's so easy without having sufficient knowledge to use its output correctly. Computer programs should be used only after the student is thoroughly familiar with a given statistical tool, and one way to become familiar with it is to perform the calculations of several analyses by hand.

10–9 Computational Formulas for Two-Factor Analysis of Variance.

i. Raw Data

	Factor B b_1	b_2	$\cdots$	b_q	**Row Sums**
a_1	X_{111} X_{211} X_{311} $\vdots$ X_{n11} $T_{11} = \sum_{i=1}^{n} X_{i11}$	X_{112} X_{212} X_{312} $\vdots$ X_{n12} $T_{12} = \sum_{i=1}^{n} X_{i12}$	$\cdots$	X_{11q} X_{21q} X_{31q} $\vdots$ X_{n1q} $T_{1q} = \sum_{i=1}^{n} X_{i1q}$	$T_{1.} = \sum_{i=1}^{n} \sum_{k=1}^{q} X_{i1k}$
Factor A a_2	X_{121} X_{221} X_{321} $\vdots$ X_{n21} $T_{21} = \sum_{i=1}^{n} X_{i21}$	X_{122} X_{222} X_{322} $\vdots$ X_{n22} $T_{22} = \sum_{i=1}^{n} X_{i22}$	$\cdots$	X_{12q} X_{22q} X_{32q} $\vdots$ X_{n2q} $T_{2q} = \sum_{i=1}^{n} X_{i2q}$	$T_{2.} = \sum_{i=1}^{n} \sum_{k=1}^{q} X_{i2k}$
$\vdots$	$\vdots$	$\vdots$	$\cdots$	$\vdots$	$\vdots$
a_p	X_{1p1} X_{2p1} X_{3p1} $\vdots$ X_{np1} $T_{p1} = \sum_{i=1}^{n} X_{ip1}$	X_{1p2} X_{2p2} X_{3p2} $\vdots$ X_{np2} $T_{p2} = \sum_{i=1}^{n} X_{ip2}$	$\cdots$	X_{1pq} X_{2pq} X_{3pq} $\vdots$ X_{npq} $T_{pq} = \sum_{i=1}^{n} X_{ipq}$	$T_{p.} = \sum_{i=1}^{n} \sum_{k=1}^{q} X_{ipk}$
Column Sums	$T_{.1} = \sum_{i=1}^{n} \sum_{j=1}^{p} X_{ij1}$	$T_{.2} = \sum_{i=1}^{n} \sum_{j=1}^{p} X_{ij2}$	$\cdots$	$T_{.q} = \sum_{i=1}^{n} \sum_{j=1}^{p} X_{ijq}$	$T_{..} = \sum_{i=1}^{n} \sum_{j=1}^{p} \sum_{k=1}^{q} X_{ijk}$

ii. Table of Sums

		Factor B: b_1	b_2	$\dots$	b_q	Row Sums
Factor A	a_1	T_{11}	T_{12}	$\dots$	T_{1q}	$T_{1.}$
	a_2	T_{21}	T_{22}	$\dots$	T_{2q}	$T_{2.}$
	$\vdots$	$\vdots$	$\vdots$	$\vdots$	$\vdots$	$\vdots$
	a_p	T_{p1}	T_{p2}	$\dots$	T_{pq}	$T_{p.}$
Column Sums		$T_{.1}$	$T_{.2}$	$\dots$	$T_{.q}$	$T_{..}$

iii. Intermediate Quantities

$$(\mathrm{I}) = \frac{T_{..}^{\,2}}{N} \qquad (\mathrm{II}) = \sum_{i=1}^{n}\sum_{j=1}^{p}\sum_{k=1}^{q} X_{ijk}^{\,2} \qquad (\mathrm{III}) = \frac{\sum_{j=1}^{p} T_{j.}^{\,2}}{nq} \qquad (\mathrm{IV}) = \frac{\sum_{k=1}^{q} T_{.k}^{\,2}}{np} \qquad (\mathrm{V}) = \frac{\sum_{j=1}^{p}\sum_{k=1}^{q} T_{jk}^{\,2}}{n}$$

iv. Summary Table

Source	*df*	*SS*	*MS*	*F*
A	$p-1$	(III) − (I)	$\frac{SS_A}{df_A}$	$\frac{MS_A}{MS_{\text{within}}}$
B	$q-1$	(IV) − (I)	$\frac{SS_B}{df_B}$	$\frac{MS_B}{MS_{\text{within}}}$
AB	$(p-1)(q-1)$	(V) + (I) − (III) − (IV)	$\frac{SS_{AB}}{df_{AB}}$	$\frac{MS_{AB}}{MS_{\text{within}}}$
Within	$N-pq$	(II) − (V)	$\frac{SS_{\text{within}}}{df_{\text{within}}}$	
Total	$N-1$	(II) − (I)		

10–10 Computational Example of a Two-Factor Analysis of Variance.

i. Raw Data

Factor A (rearing)		Factor B (breed) b_1 (basenjis)	b_2 (shetland)	b_3 (terriers)	b_4 (beagles)
	a_1 (indulged)	1	7	6	9
		4	10	9	7
		3	10	7	10
		1	9	8	10
		2	6	5	8
		2	8	10	9
	a_2 (disciplined)	5	9	1	2
		1	9	0	6
		4	8	3	3
		1	10	1	4
		2	5	2	5
		3	8	4	3

ii. Table of Sums

	b_1	b_2	b_3	b_4	
a_1	$T_{11} = (1 + \cdots + 2) = 13$	$T_{12} = (7 + \cdots + 8) = 50$	$T_{13} = (6 + \cdots + 10) = 45$	$T_{14} = (9 + \cdots + 9) = 53$	$T_{1.} = 161$
a_2	$T_{21} = (5 + \cdots + 3) = 16$	$T_{22} = (9 + \cdots + 8) = 49$	$T_{23} = (1 + \cdots + 4) = 11$	$T_{24} = (2 + \cdots + 3) = 23$	$T_{2.} = 99$
	$T_{.1} = 29$	$T_{.2} = 99$	$T_{.3} = 56$	$T_{.4} = 76$	$T_{..} = 260$

iii. Intermediate Quantities

$$(\text{I}) = \frac{T_{..}^2}{N} = \frac{(260)^2}{48} = 1408.3333$$

$$(\text{II}) = \sum_{i=1}^{n} \sum_{j=1}^{p} \sum_{k=1}^{q} X_{ijk}^2 = (1^2 + 4^2 + 3^2 + \cdots + 5^2 + 3^2) = 1896.0000$$

$$(\text{III}) = \frac{\sum_{j=1}^{p} T_{j.}^2}{nq} = \frac{(161^2 + 99^2)}{(6)(4)} = 1488.4167$$

$$(\text{IV}) = \frac{\sum_{k=1}^{q} T_{.k}^2}{np} = \frac{(29^2 + \cdots + 76^2)}{(6)(2)} = 1629.5000$$

$$(\text{V}) = \frac{\sum_{j=1}^{p} \sum_{k=1}^{q} T_{jk}^2}{n} = \frac{(13^2 + 16^2 + \cdots + 53^2 + 23^2)}{6} = 1801.6667$$

iv. Sums of Squares and Degrees of Freedom

$$SS_A = (\text{III}) - (\text{I}) = 1488.4167 - 1408.3333 = 80.0834$$
$$df_A = p - 1 = 2 - 1 = 1$$

$$SS_B = (\text{IV}) - (\text{I}) = 1629.5000 - 1408.3333 = 221.1667$$
$$df_B = q - 1 = 4 - 1 = 3$$

$$SS_{AB} = (\text{V}) + (\text{I}) - (\text{III}) - (\text{IV}) = 1801.6667 + 1408.3333 - 1488.4167 - 1629.5000 = 92.0833$$
$$df_{AB} = (p - 1)(q - 1) = (1)(3) = 3$$

$$SS_{\text{within}} = (\text{II}) - (\text{V}) = 1896.0000 - 1801.6667 = 94.3333$$
$$df_{\text{within}} = N - pq = 48 - (2)(4) = 40$$

$$SS_{\text{total}} = (\text{II}) - (\text{I}) = 1896.0000 - 1408.3333 = 487.6667$$
$$df_{\text{total}} = N - 1 = 48 - 1 = 47$$

v. Summary Table

Source	*df*	*SS*	*MS*	*F*
A (Rearing)	1	80.0834	80.0834	33.96[a]
B (Breed)	3	221.1667	73.7222	31.26[a]
AB (Rearing × Breed)	3	92.0833	30.6944	13.02[a]
Within	40	94.3333	2.3583	
Total	47	487.6667		

[a] $p < .01$

FORMAL EXAMPLE

The issue of nature-nurture (the relative contributions of heredity and environment to the behavior of organisms) has been a popular topic for many years. Not too long ago, people believed that most development was predetermined by the genes and that development was merely the unfolding of the plan of the genes. Now, the most common position is called interactionism. This theory states that the roles of heredity and environment are conceived to work in concert. One cannot talk about the role of heredity without specifying the environment and vice versa. In short, heredity and environment interact to produce the behavior we observe.

One illustration of the notion of interactionism is that the same environmental experience affects different species in dissimilar ways. For example, suppose twelve dogs from each of four different breeds (basenji, shetland sheepdog, wire-haired fox terrier, beagle) were either indulged or disciplined between the third and eighth week of their lives.[12] The indulged animals were encouraged in play, aggression, and climbing on their supine handler. In contrast, the disciplined dogs were restrained on their handler's lap, taught to sit, stay, come on command, etc. The indulged-disciplined treatment was inspired by reports that overindulged children often cannot inhibit their impulses in structured situations. Consequently, the test of the effects of these treatments was to take each animal into a room with his handler and a bowl of meat. The dog was hungry but the handler prevented him from eating for three minutes by hitting the animal on the rump with a rolled newspaper and shouting "no." After this period of restraint, the handler left the room and the length of time it took the dog to begin to eat the meat (latency) was recorded. Presumably, if the observations on children translate to dogs, the indulged animals should go to the food more quickly (record shorter latencies) than the disciplined dogs.

A simplified set of hypothetical data is presented in Part **i** of Table 10–10. Factor A (rearing condition) has two levels, **indulged and disciplined.** Factor B is breed and has four levels. Note that the "levels" of Factor B do not constitute a continuum but rather separate categories. Consider some possible results. It may be that the disciplined dogs will refrain from eating the food while the indulged will feast quickly. In this case, one would expect that the analysis of variance would yield a significant effect for Factor A. Another result might be that regardless of rearing condition, some breeds generally go to the food more rapidly than others, in which case there would be a significant effect for Factor B. Lastly, the effect of indulged or disciplined rearing may take different forms for the several breeds. For one breed the rearing treatment might make a difference whereas for another it might not or it might even have an opposite effect. In this event, the analysis would yield a significant interaction between

[12] Inspired by but not identical to D. G. Freedman, "Constitutional and Environmental Interactions in Rearing of Four Breeds of Dogs," *Science*, 1958, CXXVII, 585–586.

rearing and breed. If an interaction of this form were significant, then any main effects for rearing and breed would be disregarded. Part **ii** of Table 10–10 gives the totals for each cell of the design and the marginal totals. Part **iii** presents the computation of the intermediate quantities, Part **iv** displays the calculation of the sums of squares and degrees of freedom, and the summary of the analysis is given in Part **v**.

In the present example, the critical values of F for 3 and 40 degrees of freedom are 2.84 and 4.31 for tests at the .05 and .01 levels, respectively. The observed F for interaction is 13.02, a value that exceeds the critical level at $p < .01$. The F's for the main effects are calculated for completeness of presentation. A formal summary of this analysis is presented in Table 10–11.

10–11 Summary of the Numerical Example of a Two-Factor Analysis of Variance.

Hypotheses

Factor A

H_0: $\alpha_1 = \alpha_2 = 0$
H_1: Not H_0

Factor B

H_0: $\beta_1 = \beta_2 = \beta_3 = \beta_4 = 0$
H_1: Not H_0

AB Interaction

H_0: $\alpha\beta_{11} = \alpha\beta_{12} = \ldots = \alpha\beta_{24} = 0$
H_1: Not H_0

Assumptions

1. The groups are **independent** from one another and the observations are **randomly sampled.**
2. The population distributions of each group are **normal** and have equal variances (**homogeneity of variance**).
3. The factors are **fixed,** and there are n observations ($n > 1$) per group. (**equal n's**)

Decision Rules (.05 level)

	Factor A ($df = 1/40$)	**Factor B ($df = 3/40$)**	**AB Interaction ($df = 3/40$)**
Accept H_0 if:	$F_{obs} < 4.08$	$F_{obs} < 2.84$	$F_{obs} < 2.84$
Reject H_0 if:	$F_{obs} \geq 4.08$	$F_{obs} \geq 2.84$	$F_{obs} \geq 2.84$

Computation (See Table 10–10.)

$F_{obs} = 33.96$	$F_{obs} = 31.26$	$F_{obs} = 13.02$

Interpretation

Since the F for interaction exceeds the critical level the null hypothesis is rejected. It is concluded that the effects of indulgent and disciplined rearing are not the same for each breed of dog.

A plot of the data, presented in Figure 10–2, will help to interpret the significant interaction. Note that the graph is not a polygon but a **bar graph** consisting of bars for the indulged and disciplined groups within each breed. The vertical height of the bars represents the mean length of latency to eat the meat in the test situation. A tall bar indicates a long hesitation. The bar graph is used in this context rather than connected points because the abscissa (breed) represents discrete categories and not points along a continuum.

An interaction implies that differences between levels of one factor are not the same within each level of the other factor. In terms of the example, the difference between indulged and disciplined dogs is not the same within each breed of animal. This can be seen most clearly in the graph (Figure 10–2). Notice that the basenjis ate the food quickly, regardless of whether they were indulged or disciplined. The shetlands also showed little difference between rearing conditions but seemed to begin eating late in the period. In contrast, the rearing conditions did seem to affect the terriers and beagles since it appeared that the indulged dogs of these two breeds took longer to go to the food than their disciplined companions.

The significant interaction means that the indulged-disciplined manipulation affected some breeds differently from others. More generally, an environmental experience may affect some strains but not others. It is tempting to conclude more specifically that the rearing variable affected terriers and beagles but not basenjis or shetlands. Technically, the significant interaction does not apply to particular pairs of comparisons within the total design but rather indicates that

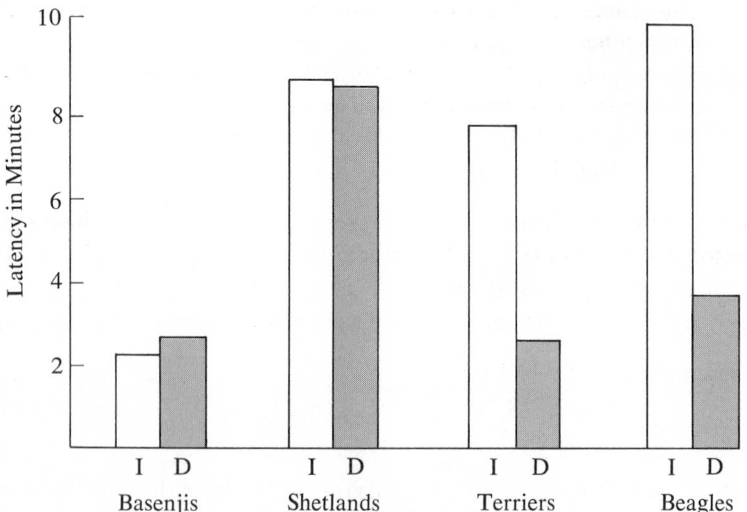

Fig. 10–2. Results for the Rearing (indulged, disciplined) × Breed experiment in which a significant interaction occurred.

the rearing treatment was different within breeds, all four breeds considered at once. If the researcher had reason to be particularly concerned with some specific comparisons within a breed prior to the time of the experiment, he might test the difference between means with a t test or other procedure for making **a priori comparisons** (i.e., before the fact) within the total design. However, most frequently a theory or other justification for examining specific pairs of means within a total design does not present itself prior to the experiment. Rather, it is often only after the results are available that the researcher decides he would like to compare specific pairs. For example, suppose the scientist performing the above study did not have any specific reasons before the experiment for testing the difference between indulged and disciplined animals within any one particular breed. However, after the data were collected, he noticed that there was a significant interaction and the graph suggested that the rearing variable affected the terriers and beagles but not the others. He might wonder if there would be significant differences between the two means for each of the breeds. If he now performs a simple t test between these pairs of means, the resulting probability levels will not be appropriate. They are not correct because the researcher would probably not have tested them if the interaction was not significant or if he had not noticed in the graph that there appeared to be a difference for some breeds and not others. Consequently, in the group of such **a posteriori comparisons** (i.e., after the fact) that this researcher makes there would be a high number of significant differences even if the null hypotheses of no difference were actually true because he only makes such tests when the data suggest that there will be a significant difference in a pair. It is in this sense that **a posteriori** tests "capitalize on chance" and some correction must be made in order to accommodate to this. The theory behind choosing which correction to use in such after-the-fact comparisons is beyond the scope of this text, but the interested reader is referred to Winer's more advanced book on the analysis of variance.[13]

ESTIMATING THE PROPORTION OF VARIANCE

As with the simple analysis of variance, it is informative to know the proportion of variance in the dependent variable that is associated with each factor in the design. The fact that a significant F ratio was obtained implies that something systematic or nonrandom is probably influencing the result, but it provides no information concerning how much of the total variability in the measure is associated with this nonrandom influence. Specifically, not all dogs in the example described waited the same length of time before going for the meat. There was variability in their latencies. What proportion of this total variability is associated with (or could be predicted from) the fact that some animals were treated with indulgence or discipline (i.e., Factor A)? What proportion is

[13] Winer, *op. cit.*

associated with the different breeds of dogs involved (Factor B)? Finally, suppose one knew both the rearing treatment and the breed of dog, what additional proportion of the variance can be accounted for by the combination of both these factors (AB interaction)?

These proportions of variance may be estimated with the following formulas.[14]

$$\text{For Factor } A\text{:} \quad \frac{SS_A - (p-1)MS_{\text{within}}}{MS_{\text{within}} + SS_{\text{total}}}$$

$$\text{For Factor } B\text{:} \quad \frac{SS_B - (q-1)MS_{\text{within}}}{MS_{\text{within}} + SS_{\text{total}}}$$

$$\text{For } AB \text{ Interaction:} \quad \frac{SS_{AB} - (p-1)(q-1)MS_{\text{within}}}{MS_{\text{within}} + SS_{\text{total}}}$$

Substituting the values found in the illustrative example, one obtains:

$$\text{For Factor } A\text{:} \quad \frac{80.0834 - (2-1)(2.3583)}{2.3583 + 487.6667} = .16$$

$$\text{For Factor } B\text{:} \quad \frac{221.1667 - (4-1)(2.3583)}{2.3583 + 487.6667} = .44$$

$$\text{For } AB \text{ Interaction:} \quad \frac{92.0833 - (2-1)(4-1)(2.3583)}{2.3583 + 487.6667} = .17$$

These results indicate that 16% of the total variability in latency is associated with the rearing treatment, 44% is accounted for by the breed, and an additional 17% is accounted for by the unique combination of rearing treatment and breed.

INTERPRETATION

The preceding example revealed a "significant" effect for the interaction between rearing treatment and breed of dog. Judging from the graph of this interaction, one might conclude that the difference in rearing treatment affects some breeds but not others. The fact that a "significant difference" was found indicates that the observed differences in group means are sufficiently large that it is likely that they did not occur simply because of sampling error. However, whether a given effect is "statistically significant" depends in part on the number of cases in the design. Even the smallest difference in means could be found to be statistically significant if a large enough sample were collected. Therefore, the importance attached to a "significant" difference depends to some extent upon the size of the sample.

[14] For a more detailed discussion of these procedures, see Hays, *op. cit.*, 406–407.

From the above discussion one can appreciate that a "significant" result implies that something nonrandom is probably occurring but it does not describe the extent of that influence on the observed behavior. Calculating the proportion of the total variability in the data associated with each factor provides some information on this second question. In the example, it would seem that rearing environment, breed, and the combination of rearing and breed are associated with a relatively large segment of the total variability in the data. It is the proportion of variability that helps to indicate the "importance" of the influence of the variables being studied. If rearing, breed, and their interaction collectively only accounted for 10% of the variance in latencies even though the effects were statistically significant, the scientist might decide to search for variables that are associated with the other 90% of the variability. Of course, it must be remembered that the extent of an effect is a function of what was studied. Breed of dog might account for much less variance if only terriers and beagles were used or if the other factor in the design was a more potent governor of this behavior than was the rearing treatment.

But even if the variables investigated demonstrate statistical significance and are associated with sizable portions of the total variability in the data, the statistical procedures themselves do not guarantee that these factors *caused* the observed differences. The analysis only reports that the difference observed probably was not random and was associated with a sizable portion of the total variability. The design and execution of the experiment, not the statistics, comment upon the possible causal effects of the variables studied. Quite sizable and significant effects might have been produced not by breed or rearing, but by the behavior of the experimenter when he prevented the dog from eating during the first three minutes of the test situation. Though it was not the case, suppose for the sake of the discussion that the experimenter tested all the shetlands first and really punished the dogs severely for going near the food. As a result, the dogs of both rearing groups tended to avoid the food, some for the entire ten-minute test situation. Feeling that the punishment was too severe, the experimenter could have tested the basenjis next and unconsciously reduced the level of punishment. However, since all the basenjis ate very quickly and since the experimenter sensed that none of the hypothesized rearing differences seemed to be appearing, it is possible that the experimenter might have subsequently punished the remaining disciplined dogs harder than the indulged animals and produced the rearing differences reported. Although this example is somewhat contrived to punctuate the point, experimenter bias has been found to influence the outcomes of experiments,[15] and it is entirely possible that the effects suggested by the example could be produced by this kind of "extraneous" variable if appropriate experimental procedures are not followed.

[15] See, for example, R. Rosenthal, *Experimenter Effects in Behavioral Research* (New York: Appleton-Century-Crofts, 1966).

The point to remember is that the statistical procedures can not discriminate between what effects are caused by the variables investigated or by other influences not under the experimenter's direct control. Causal inferences can be made only when the design of the experiment is such that if a difference is found there exists no possible cause for this difference other than the variables manipulated directly by the researcher. In short, statistics is a set of methods that serve to describe and quantify data in such a way that inferences may be made by an orderly process; the art of experimental design, not statistics, speaks to discerning the causes of the observed effects.

EXERCISES

1. Distinguish in your own words between a main effect and an interaction. Give three examples of an interaction in terms of common events.

2. If the different sums of squares add to SS_{total} and the different degrees of freedom sum to df_{total}, do the different mean squares sum to a MS_{total}, and why?

3. The following is a rather random set of data:

		Factor B: b_1	b_2
Factor A	a_1	4	2
		7	9
		5	1
		2	4
	a_2	4	5
		8	6
		1	1
		4	10

Compute the analysis of variance on these data. Now add 10 to each score in the a_2 level and recompute. Explain the differences and similarities in results between the first and second computation. Now take the original data and add 10 to each score in cell ab_{11} and recompute. Compare all three analyses and explain the similarities and differences.

4. If the interaction in an analysis of variance design is significant, why might the main effects be ignored? Illustrate.

5. An important social topic is the effects of marijuana. Twenty-four college men are selected, 12 of whom are regular users of marijuana, ordinary cigarettes, and

alcohol and 12 who are regular users of cigarettes and alcohol but who have never used marijuana before.[16] It is assumed that there are no other differences between these two groups of subjects (an assumption that may not be true). Within each group, user and non-user, six subjects smoked two marijuana cigarettes in the laboratory while six subjects smoked placebo cigarettes that taste and smell like marijuana but have no effect. A short time after smoking, all subjects took a set of perceptual-motor tests of skills required for driving. The researcher wanted to know if marijuana had more of an effect on driving skills than a placebo, if users responded differently from non-users, and if there was an interaction. The scores the subjects received are as follows:

Regular users receiving marijuana
42, 35, 48, 26, 55, 47

Regular users receiving placebo
35, 52, 43, 45, 49, 38

Naïve users receiving marijuana
60, 45, 55, 39, 47, 42

Naïve users receiving placebo
47, 42, 51, 37, 49, 48

Evaluate these data with the analysis of variance. Draw up a formal summary of the analysis, display all computation, compute the proportion of variance for each significant source of variability in the design, graph any results, and interpret the experiment.

6. Suppose the same researchers were interested in comparing the "high" achieved by subjects who are regular users vs. those who are naïve to marijuana relative to subjects who are given placebos. Twenty-eight subjects participated, 14 men who were regular users and 14 men who were not (naïve). Half of each group smoked two marijuana cigarettes in the laboratory and half smoked two placebos. An elaborate system of questions and tasks were given a short time after the smoking took place, and the resultant score reflected the degree of "high" as reported by the subject and as evaluated by the clinical impressions of the attending physician. The greater the score, the greater the "high." Following the procedures of the previous question, evaluate and interpret the following data:

Regular user receiving marijuana
29, 33, 19, 23, 27, 21, 25

Regular user receiving placebo
17, 21, 19, 22, 18, 14, 23

Naïve user receiving marijuana
14, 10, 17, 9, 11, 13, 15

Naïve user receiving placebo
15, 12, 10, 16, 11, 12, 9

[16] Data and results are hypothetical but represent an extrapolation of a study cautiously reported by A. T. Weil, N. E. Zinberg, and J. M. Nelson, "Clinical and Psychological Effects of Marihuana in Man," *Science*, 1968, CLXII, 1234–1242.

11

nonparametric techniques

parametric versus nonparametric tests

A variety of techniques have been presented in the preceding chapters that test certain statistical hypotheses. In order to use these tests appropriately, several assumptions must hold about the population distributions. For example, the t test of the difference between two independent means requires that sampling is random and that the two population distributions are normal and have the same variance. Since one almost never has precise knowledge about the population, only guesses about the tenability of some of these assumptions can be made. Furthermore, there are times when certain of the assumptions simply cannot be met. For example, if a very easy examination is given to a class there may be many scores of 100% and only a few scores as low as 80%. This distribution would be markedly skewed to the left and decidedly not normal. Therefore, there is a need for statistical techniques that may be used when some of the assumptions required by the previously described procedures cannot be met. Since the assumptions usually are statements about the parameters of population distributions (e.g., equal variances) and these parameters must be estimated from the data, techniques that make such assumptions are called **parametric** tests. Methods that make fewer (or at least different) assumptions about the populations involved are known as **nonparametric** or **distribution-free** tests.

Although nonparametric tests are frequently used because certain assumptions cannot be made about the populations involved, a researcher may select a nonparametric technique to analyze his data for other reasons as well. Sometimes the variables in question are measured with ordinal or even nominal scales (see Chapter 2). Parametric tests are not usually appropriate in such cases. For example, suppose an educator wants to correlate the scores from a new test of reading achievement with a teacher's rank ordering of her pupils on reading proficiency. The teacher's rankings represent an ordinal scale. Thus, a nonparametric index of the degree of relationship would be more appropriate than the Pearson *r*. In another context, one may want to know if boys or girls are more likely to approve or disapprove of a certain moral standard. In this case, both variables (sex and approve-disapprove) are nominal in character, and parametric tests for such data are simply not available. Thus, when measurement is nominal or ordinal in character, a nonparametric test may be the only choice.

If nonparametric techniques do not require the assumptions that parametric techniques do, then why are they not always used? There are several reasons why parametric procedures are more common and traditionally preferred to nonparametric procedures when everything else is equal. One major reason is that parametric methods usually have a greater **power efficiency** than do nonparametric methods. Power-efficiency is a technical concept that refers to the probability that the test will reject the null hypothesis when that hypothesis is, in fact, false (correctly reject H_0).[1] If the difference between the central tendency of two groups is being considered, a *t* test is more likely to detect a population difference than is an appropriate nonparametric test for the given *N*'s.

Another reason why parametric methods are often preferred is that they provide information that nonparametric methods do not. For example, in the two-factor analysis of variance, a test for an interaction may be made. It is more difficult to assess this type of effect with nonparametric methods.

A final consideration is more subtle. Frequently, parametric and nonparametric tests do not address themselves to precisely the same question and are sensitive to different aspects of the data. For example, if one wants to know whether the mean of one group differs from the mean of another in the population, a parametric test makes a rather direct assessment of this question, given the assumptions. A nonparametric test designed to make a similar evaluation may actually ask whether one distribution is different from another *in any way*, and distributions may differ not only in central tendency but also in variability, skewness, etc. Thus, although parametric and nonparametric tests are often intimately related, situations can occur in which a "significant" difference will be obtained with one technique and not with another because sometimes parametric and nonparametric tests evaluate slightly different aspects of the data.

In short, parametric tests possess the advantage of having relatively more power-efficiency (everything else equal) and sometimes providing relatively

[1] For a more detailed discussion of power-efficiency, see S. Siegel, *Nonparametric Statistics* (New York: McGraw-Hill, 1956) 20.

more information about a phenomenon (e.g., interactions in the analysis of variance). However, several assumptions about the population must be made in order to obtain these benefits. When the assumptions about population distributions cannot be made or when the data are nominal or ordinal, a nonparametric method may be more appropriate.

The techniques presented in this chapter are samples of some of the most common nonparametric methods. Many others exist and the interested reader is referred to books by Bradley and by Siegel[2] for more complete coverage of this area.

tests on independent samples

PEARSON CHI-SQUARE TESTS

Occasionally, the social scientist collects independent and random samples of observations and wishes to compare them in terms of the similarity with which these observations are distributed among several discrete and mutually exclusive categories. Suppose that two groups of subjects are randomly selected. The two groups may be boys and girls, students and nonstudents, athletes and nonathletes, etc. Now, suppose the social scientist has a set of several discrete categories into which any particular subject may be classified. For example, subjects may be judged to have "warm," "neutral," or "cold" personalities or to have several levels of agreement or disagreement with a given statement or political figure. No matter what the classification system, the categories must be exhaustive and mutually exclusive so that each subject will belong to one and and only one category.

The statistical question that is to be asked is whether the groups differ in the relative distribution of observations among the different categories. The null hypothesis is that in the population the two groups do not differ in their relative frequency distributions of people among the categories. The alternative hypothesis is that the groups do differ. Notice that H_1 does not specify how they differ, but only that the two relative distributions are not the same in some way.

Sometimes these hypotheses are interpreted in terms of a possible dependence or contingency between the two bases of classification. For example, if groups of college men and women were asked whether they approved, disapproved, or were neutral with respect to the "new morality" as described in a short statement which each subject read, the null hypothesis might be viewed as suggesting that opinion about the new morality is independent of the sex of subject. The alternative hypothesis is that there is a dependence, that is, the relative distribu-

[2] J. V. Bradley, *Distribution-Free Statistical Tests* (Englewood Cliffs: Prentice-Hall, 1968). S. Siegel, *Nonparametric Statistics* (New York: McGraw-Hill, 1956).

tion of approving, disapproving, and neutral responses is contingent upon the sex of the respondents.

Several assumptions must be made. First, it must be assumed that **the two samples are independent** from one another. This usually implies that different and unrelated sets of subjects are selected. Second, the subjects within each group must be **randomly** and **independently** sampled. Third, each observation must qualify for **one and only one category** in the classification scheme. Fourth, the **sample size must be relatively large.** The latter assumption will be discussed further.

The data can be cast into an $r \times c$ table in which r refers to the number of rows and c indicates the number of columns. For the preceding example concerning the "new morality," one would have

	Men	Women	
Approve	58	35	93
Neutral	11	25	36
Disapprove	10	23	33
	79	83	162

Suppose the numbers in the cells represent the frequencies of responses in each category. It can be seen that 79 men and 83 women were sampled and a total of 93 people approved the new morality as defined by the written statement.

If there were really no difference in the relative frequencies of the two distributions, then the same proportion of the sample for each sex should have responded within each category. Since one does not know what proportion of college students in the population, men and women combined, approve, disapprove, or are neutral relative to the statement, these proportions must be estimated from the observed data. For example, $\frac{93}{162} = 57.41\%$ of the college students selected approved of the statement. Since there were 79 men, 57.41% of 79 or 45.35 should have approved the statement if there were no differences in the distribution of response for the two sexes. The 45.35 men is an **expected frequency** for the cell "men-approve." The same process may be used to obtain the expected frequency of each cell in the table. The computation of expected frequencies is most often stated in the following terms:

> To compute the **expected frequency** for any cell, multiply the total for the row in which the cell falls by the total for the column in which the cell falls, and divide this product by the total number of cases in the table.

In terms of the "men-approve" cell, the expected frequency is given by

$$\frac{(93)(79)}{162} = 45.35$$

Since $\frac{93}{162}$ is the proportion of the total sample approving and 79 is the number of males in the sample, this method is identical to the logic described previously.

If the expected frequencies are computed in this manner for each cell, the observed frequencies (symbolized by O) and the expected frequencies (symbolized by E) for the sample data would be as follows:

	Men	**Women**
Approve	$O = 58$ $E = 45.35$	$O = 35$ $E = 47.65$
Neutral	$O = 11$ $E = 17.56$	$O = 25$ $E = 18.44$
Disapprove	$O = 10$ $E = 16.09$	$O = 23$ $E = 16.91$

If the calculation of the expected frequencies is correct, the row and column sums of the expected frequencies will equal the sums of the observed frequencies.

We now have a set of expected frequencies given that the null hypothesis of the equivalence of population distributions within the categories for the two groups is true and given the observed marginal values. Given the observed and expected frequencies, the task is to determine some index of the extent to which the observed frequencies are determined on the basis of the equivalence of the distributions of the groups (H_0). An index of the difference between observed and expected frequencies must reflect the extent to which the distributions of the observed frequencies differ for the groups sampled. The following expression represents such an index and its sampling distribution approximates a theoretical distribution called **chi square** (χ^2):

$$\chi_{\text{obs}}^2 = \sum_{j=1}^{r} \sum_{k=1}^{c} \frac{(O_{jk} - E_{jk})^2}{E_{jk}}$$

in which O_{jk} = the observed number of frequencies in the cell corresponding to the intersection of the jth row and kth column,

E_{jk} = the expected number of frequencies in the cell corresponding to the intersection of the jth row and kth column,

r = the number of rows, and

c = the number of columns

The formula simply directs one to take the difference between the observed and expected frequencies for each cell, square it, divide by the expected frequency, and sum over all cells. The resulting value is distributed as chi square with degrees of freedom

$$df = (r - 1)(c - 1)$$

where r is the number of rows and c the number of columns in the table of frequencies.

The percentiles of the chi square distribution for each number of degrees of freedom are known, and Table F in Appendix II lists values of chi square for selected percentiles (significance levels) at several *df*. In the present case, the table of data has three rows and two columns, thus there are $(r - 1)(c - 1) = (3 - 1)(2 - 1) = 2$ degrees of freedom. The critical value for a test at the .05 level of significance is 5.99. If the observed value of chi square, symbolized by $\chi_{\text{obs}}{}^2$, exceeds the critical value, the null hypothesis, H_0, is rejected. If not, H_0 is accepted.

For the data presented, the calculation of χ^2 proceeds as follows:

$$\chi_{\text{obs}}{}^2 = \frac{(58 - 45.35)^2}{45.35} + \frac{(35 - 47.65)^2}{47.65} + \frac{(11 - 17.56)^2}{17.56} + \frac{(25 - 18.44)^2}{18.44} + \frac{(10 - 16.09)^2}{16.09} + \frac{(23 - 16.91)^2}{16.91}$$

$$\chi_{\text{obs}}{}^2 = 16.17$$

Since the observed value of 16.17 exceeds the critical value of 5.99 and, in fact, is beyond the critical value for a test at the .001 level, the null hypothesis is rejected. It can be assumed that the data indicate that the distribution of approval-disapproval of the stated version of the new morality is different for the two sexes. Apparently, college men are more likely to endorse such a statement than are college women.

A more formal summary of this example is presented in Table 11–1.

When the assumptions were listed for performing such a test, it was noted that a large sample is required. The approximation to the theoretical chi square distribution is not very good for small samples and thus the probabilities are somewhat inaccurate. Obviously, the question becomes how large must the sample be for the approximation to be sufficiently close. Unfortunately, the closeness of the approximation is a function of many factors, and a single rule of thumb is not totally adequate. However, if a conservative guideline were needed, it would probably be best not to have any expected frequency less than 5. If the table is only 2×2 in size, then no expected frequency should be less than 10. Notice that the requirement is based upon the **expected** frequencies, not the observed frequencies (but the E_{jk} are indirectly a function of sample size).

11–1 Formal Summary of $r \times c$ Chi Square Test Example.

Hypotheses

H_0: Given the observed marginals, the distributions of frequencies in the population are not different for the two groups (sexes).
H_1: Given the observed marginals, these distributions are different for the two groups (sexes).

Assumptions

1. The two groups are **independent.**
2. The subjects for each group are **randomly** and **independently** selected.
3. Each observation must qualify for **one and only one category.**
4. The sample size must be fairly large such that **no expected frequency is less than 5, for r or c greater than 2, or less than 10 if $r = c = 2$.**

Decision Rules

Given: .05, and a $3 \times 2[df = (r - 1)(c - 1) = 2]$ table

If ${\chi_{obs}}^2 < 5.99$, accept H_0
If ${\chi_{obs}}^2 \geq 5.99$, reject H_0

Computation (See text.)

$${\chi_{obs}}^2 = \sum_{j=1}^{r} \sum_{k=1}^{c} \frac{(O_{jk} - E_{jk})^2}{E_{jk}}$$

$${\chi_{obs}}^2 = 16.17$$

Interpretation

Reject H_0

SPECIAL APPLICATIONS OF CHI SQUARE

four-fold tables The above procedures are stated generally in terms of an $r \times c$ table. Although the example is for a 3×2 table, theoretically the size of the table may be quite large as long as there are sufficient numbers of cases so that the expected frequencies in each cell are at least 5.

Actually, one of the most frequent applications of the chi square procedures is for a 2×2 table, also called a **four-fold contingency table.** The application of the technique is the same as described above except that the computation is simplified by the following:

	Category I	Category II	
Group I	a	b	$a + b$
Group II	c	d	$c + d$
	$a + c$	$b + d$	N

$$\chi_{\text{obs}}^2 = \frac{N(|ad - bc| - N/2)^2}{(a + b)(c + d)(a + c)(b + d)}$$

The notation $|ad - bc|$ means the absolute value of $(ad - bc)$. If the data are cast into the four-fold table as presented, then the computation of χ^2 follows the formula given. This formula contains a correction called *Yates correction for continuity* that is intended to make the approximation to the theoretical chi square distribution more precise.[3]

When the data are cast in this form, the statistical question is really whether the proportion of one group evidencing a given behavior is different from the proportion of another group. In terms of the preceding table, does the proportion $a/(a + b)$ reflect a population value that is different from that estimated by the proportion of $c/(c + d)$?

example It has been casually observed by some psychiatrists that there appears to be an association between the occurrence of schizophrenic breaks in pregnant women and the sex of their offspring. If this is true and the biochemical process mediating the phenomenon were discovered, then one would be on the track of a potential biochemical correlate of mental illness. Some type of drug treatment for schizophrenia might grow out of such knowledge.

Subjects were randomly selected from women who either had a schizophrenic break during the first month after conception or had a break within one month

[3] Although this "correction" is commonly used, under some circumstances its use actually results in a poorer approximation. For a discussion of this issue see: F. Adler, "Yates' Correction and the Statisticians," *Journal of the American Statistical Association*, 1951, XLVI, 490–501; W. G. Cochran, "The Test of Goodness of Fit," *Annals of Mathematical Statistics*, 1952, XXIII, 315–345. The formula for χ^2 without the correction is

$$\chi^2 = \frac{N(ad - bc)^2}{(a + b)(c + d)(a + c)(b + d)}$$

after delivering their infant.[4] The sex of their offspring was noted. Thus, each person included was independently sampled and fell into one and only one of the four categories:

	Offspring		
	Male	**Female**	
Schizophrenic Break Within One Month of:			
Conception	5	24	29
Delivery	28	8	36
	33	32	65

The observed frequencies given in the table indicate that for the 29 women who experienced a break within the first month after conception, 24 offspring were female. For the 36 women who broke within the first month after delivery, 28 offspring were male. A calculation of the expected frequencies for this table indicates that none is less than 10, and thus the assumption of sample size is met.

The null hypothesis being tested is that there is no dependency between the time of the schizophrenic break and the sex of the offspring. Another way to say this is that the proportion of males and females born to women evidencing a break within a month after conception is the same as the proportion of males and females born to women evidencing a break within a month after delivery. The alternative hypothesis is that there is a dependency (or contingency) between the time of a schizophrenic break and the sex of the offspring.

The decision rules at the .05 level for

$$df = (r - 1)(c - 1) = (2 - 1)(2 - 1) = 1$$

are that H_0 will be accepted if $\chi_{obs}{}^2$ is less than 3.84 but H_0 will be rejected if the observed value is equal to or greater than 3.84.

The computation of $\chi_{obs}{}^2$ proceeds according to the formula given for four-fold tables:

$$\chi^2 = \frac{N(|ad - bc| - N/2)^2}{(a + b)(c + d)(a + c)(b + d)}$$

$$= \frac{65(|5(8) - 24(28)| - 65/2)^2}{(29)(36)(33)(32)}$$

$$\chi^2 = 21.19$$

[4] Inspired by M. A. Taylor, "Sex Ratios of Newborns: Associated with Prepartum and Postpartum Schizophrenia," *Science*, 1969, CLXIV, 723–724 and Erratum, *Science*, 1969, CLXV, 380. But see also F. T. Melges, "Postpartum Psychiatric Reactions: Time of Onset and Sex Ratio of Newborns," *Science*, CLXVI, 1026–1027.

Since the observed value of 21.19 is greater than the critical value of 3.84 (also greater than the critical value at the .001 level), the null hypothesis is rejected. There is good evidence that the time of a schizophrenic break and the sex of the offspring are related according to this data.

goodness of fit Another application of the Pearson chi square techniques occurs when independently sampled observations fall into one of several pre-established categories, all of which are part of a single classification scheme. For example, suppose that for voter polls, it is known that yearly income is a determinant of voter trends. Consequently, when a sample is selected for predicting voter behavior, special care is taken to insure that it reflects the appropriate proportion of voters in the last election who had various levels of income. Suppose the income categories of concern to the pollster are pre-established. Then, any randomly selected voter will fall into one and only one of these income categories. In a sense, this type of design is an $r \times 1$ table since there is only one classification scheme having r categories.

Suppose that the pollster asks each new interviewer whom he hires to collect a sample of 400 voters. Sometimes, new recruits stray from the established sampling methods and tend to obtain biased samples. A young college student may be deliberately persistent in getting low-income voters in the sample out of concern for their voice in national affairs. An upper-middle class housewife might not want to visit slum neighborhoods and consequently obtain a sample that is disproportionately populated with high-income voters. Therefore, the pollster assesses his new recruits by comparing the distribution of income levels in the sample they obtain with the distribution for all voters in the last national election.

From the standpoint of the Pearson chi square analysis, the current example is simply a one-classification procedure in which the expected frequencies are determined by some previous information or expectancy. The research question is somewhat different also. In the previous cases, there have been two or more distributions of observations with the question being whether the relative frequencies in those distributions were the same from group to group. Now one group is being sampled and the question is whether the distribution of their responses conforms to some pre-established criterion.

The same assumptions are required for this analysis as for the previous cases. Observations must be **independently and randomly sampled,** the **response must fall into one and only one category,** and the **sample must be fairly large** (i.e., the expected frequencies must be greater than 10 if only two categories are used, and more than 5 if there are more than two categories). Another precaution is that the **classification scheme must be pre-established.** That is, the definition of each category must be clearly stated *before* the data are collected.

Suppose one new interviewer sampled 400 voters and the distribution of incomes was that listed in Table 11–2. The pollster wishes to know if the new interviewer's sample differs significantly from the income distribution recorded during the last national election. The null hypothesis for such a test would be that the sample represents a random selection from a population that does not differ in the distribution of income of voters from the last election. The alternative is that the population from which the interviewer sampled does not have the same income distribution as the last election.

The formula for calculating χ_{obs}^2 remains the same as before, but it now has $df = j - 1$ where j is the number of categories in the single classification scheme. Since the pollster is far more interested in being overly critical of his new interviewers than in allowing a biased worker to escape uninstructed, he sets the significance level at .20. Consequently, the critical value is obtained from Table F with $df = 5$ (table has six categories) and is 7.29. The decision rules follow:

$$\text{If } \chi_{obs}^2 < 7.29, \text{ accept } H_0$$
$$\text{If } \chi_{obs}^2 \geq 7.29, \text{ reject } H_0$$

The hypothetical data are presented below in Table 11–2.

11–2 Hypothetical Data for a Test of Goodness of Fit.

Annual Income	Current Sample	Percent Voting in Last Election	Expected Frequency Based upon Last Election
Greater than $20,000	28	.08	32
$15,000–$20,000	65	.18	72
$10,000–$15,000	80	.23	92
$7,000–$10,000	132	.31	124
$4,000–$7,000	77	.17	68
Less than $4,000	18	.03	12
Total	400	1.00	400

In the interviewer's sample, 28 people had incomes over $20,000. The percentage of people voting in the last election having that high an income was 8%. In a sample of 400, one would expect .08(400) = 32 people to have an income at this level if the null hypothesis is taken to be valid. The computation of χ_{obs}^2 proceeds as follows:

$$\chi_{obs}^2 = \sum_j \frac{(O_j - E_j)^2}{E_j}$$

$$= \frac{(28 - 32)^2}{32} + \frac{(65 - 72)^2}{72} + \frac{(80 - 92)^2}{92}$$

$$+ \frac{(132 - 124)^2}{124} + \frac{(77 - 68)^2}{68} + \frac{(18 - 12)^2}{12}$$

$$\chi_{obs}^2 = 7.45$$

Since the observed value of 7.45 exceeds the critical value of 7.29, the pollster decides that such a result is too extreme to be simply a function of sampling differences and he judges that the new interviewer has biased the sample.

discussion There is some concern among statisticians about the appropriate use of the Pearson chi square procedures outlined in this section. Some scholars feel that the assumptions are quite restrictive and that the approximation to the theoretical chi square distribution is rather poor. Other statisticians do not feel as strongly about this point. Because these procedures are very common, the student should be acquainted with them. However, before straying very far from the assumptions, the sophisticated student might consult Bradley[5] for a list of cautions and references on the use of these procedures.

MANN-WHITNEY *U* TEST FOR THE DIFFERENCE BETWEEN TWO POPULATIONS

If two samples are randomly and independently selected and if there is an underlying continuous distribution and at least ordinal scale measurement, then the Mann-Whitney U test may be used to evaluate the difference between the two population distributions. The U test is one of the most popular alternatives to the parametric t test.

The assumptions stated above are quite minimal. **Random** and **independent sampling** with **independent groups** is required. It is also assumed that there is an underlying **continuous scale of measurement** (see Chapter 2). Lastly, the **measurement scale must be at least ordinal** in character.

The null hypothesis is that the populations from which the two samples are drawn are identical. The alternative hypothesis is that these two populations are not identical. Note that this is not equivalent to testing the difference between two population means because two distributions could be quite different in form but have identical means. Therefore, it is theoretically possible to obtain a statistically significant result with the U test when in fact the means are identical. From a practical standpoint, the general shapes of the distributions of two

[5] Bradley, *op. cit.*, 248.

groups within a single experiment are not often markedly different. When the form of the distributions are similar then the U test does compare the central tendencies of the groups. Thus, if the sample distributions are similar, the results of the U test are often interpreted in terms of differences in central tendency; if the distributions are not similar, the results must be viewed in terms of the difference between the distributions in general.

The rationale for the test is based upon the premise that if two distributions of equal size are identical and if the observations from each group are lined up in rank order (i.e., smallest first), then the scores from the two groups should be well mixed in that ordered sequence. If they are well mixed, then the number of scores in Group A that precede each of the scores in Group B should equal (approximately) the number of scores in B that precede each of the scores in A. If the scores in Group A tend to be smaller than those in B, then more of the A scores will precede B scores when the scores are rank ordered.

The statistic based upon an extension of this type of rationale is the U. Suppose that the sets of scores for Groups A and B are as follows:

$$A = \{5, 9, 17, 3\}$$
$$B = \{1, 8, 28, 20, 18\}$$

Now arrange the scores in order beginning with the smallest score but retain the group identity of each observation. Then assign each score a rank beginning with rank "1" for the smallest score:

Score	1	3	5	8	9	17	18	20	28
Group	*B*	*A*	*A*	*B*	*A*	*A*	*B*	*B*	*B*
Rank	1	2	3	4	5	6	7	8	9

Although the computation of U can be accomplished by using a summing technique, a more convenient method requires that the total (T_j) of the ranks for one group be obtained. For the example just presented,

$$T_A = 2 + 3 + 5 + 6 = 16$$

The statistic U is then given by

$$U_{\text{obs}} = n_A n_B + \frac{n_A(n_A + 1)}{2} - T_A$$

in which n_A and n_B are the numbers of cases in Groups A and B, respectively. For the present example

$$U_{\text{obs}} = 4(5) + \frac{4(4 + 1)}{2} - 16$$
$$U_{\text{obs}} = 14$$

n ≤ 20 If n for each group is 20 or less, Table G in Appendix II gives the critical values for U. A separate table is presented for different significance levels. In each case, the rows and columns represent different numbers of cases for the two groups (it makes no difference which group is used for the rows and which for the columns). At the intersection of the appropriate row and column, two values of U are given, one smaller than the other. These two values indicate the **region of acceptance,** such that if the observed U falls between these two values, H_0 is **accepted.** If the observed value is less than or equal to the lower value in the table or greater than or equal to the larger value in the table, H_0 is rejected.

n ≥ 20 If n for either group is greater than 20, then Table G cannot be used. It happens that with such a large sample, the observed value of U approaches a normal distribution with

$$\text{mean} = \frac{n_A n_B}{2}$$

and

$$\text{standard deviation} = \sqrt{\frac{(n_A)(n_B)(n_A + n_B + 1)}{12}}$$

Consequently, if the size of a group is greater than 20 and the difference in sample sizes of the two groups is not too great, the significance of U_{obs} may be determined by calculating

$$z = \frac{U_{\text{obs}} - n_A n_B/2}{\sqrt{\frac{(n_A)(n_B)(n_A + n_B + 1)}{12}}}$$

which approaches the standard normal distribution. In this event, critical values may be obtained by consulting Table A.

ties Occasionally, the values of scores are tied.[6] For example, consider the set of scores {13, 15, 15, 18}. The score of 13 receives rank 1. The two scores of 15 are given the average of the next two ranks. These two ranks are ranks 2 and 3 and their average is 2.5. Consequently, the two

[9] The method of handling tied observations suggested in this chapter is a common and convenient one, but it has certain technical liabilities. Most rank-order statistics assume an underlying continuous distribution. If this is true, ties in scores result from imprecision of measurement. If more precise methods were available no ties would exist. Consequently, in this instance the occurrence of ties is not a true reflection of what really exists. The issue of just how to handle ties is not firmly resolved, and Bradley (*op. cit.*) presents a good though sophisticated discussion of the alternatives. One approach advocated by Siegel (*op. cit.*) is to use the average-rank technique presented in the text and correct for ties with special formulas. However, Siegel points out, the corrections do not change the result very much even when a large proportion of the scores are tied. Bradley notes that under some conditions the average-rank approach actually biases the outcome in one direction or another rather than yielding a

scores of 15 each receive a rank of 2.5. Notice, that the score of 18 is then assigned a rank of 4. It is not given a rank of 3 because this rank was used in the previous averaging. If three or more scores are tied, each score receives the average rank that these scores would have received if they were distinct. Similarly, the next score(s) begin with the next unused rank. An example of ranking with several ties follows:

Score	13	13	16	19	19	22	22	22	28	28	30
Rank	1.5	1.5	3	4.5	4.5	7	7	7	9.5	9.5	11

small sample illustration Freudian theory is based in part upon the premise that man is born with certain innate drives and needs, one of which centers around his mouth, an oral need. Another important concept is that the energy system of an organism is closed, so that if a need is blocked from satisfaction the need does not dissipate but will express itself in other ways. For example, a person might be frustrated in his oral needs as a young child and because of this dammed up need he performs a great deal of oral activity as an adult (e.g., he smokes). It would be reasonable under this theory to suppose that if during the early months of life oral needs (e.g., the need for sucking) were not exercised, and thus frustrated, there should be more oral activity later in order to make up for this frustration. Conversely, from a learning standpoint, if an infant were not allowed to suck, one might not expect him to learn to suck on other objects later in life.

For example, an experiment is run in which four infants are fed from special cups as soon as possible after birth.[7] Another six infants are fed on bottles

---

result that is itself a type of average or medium approximation. The simplest alternative to this problem appears to be to treat the tie scores as if they were not tie scores, selecting the ranks in the manner *least* favorable to rejecting the null hypothesis. Then, rerank the observations, this time treating the ties in a manner *most* favorable to rejecting the null hypothesis. As a result, one obtains two test statistics, one most and one least favorable toward rejecting the null hypothesis. If both statistics fall into the region of rejection, the null hypothesis may be unambiguously rejected. If both fall outside the rejection region, the null hypothesis may be accepted without ambiguity. However, if one value does and the other does not fall within the rejection region, no clear decision can be made. In short, most of the methods discussed in this chapter technically assume that no ties exist. Since ties are common in social science, some procedures must be followed to handle them, and the choice of which method to follow rests on technical considerations largely beyond the scope of this text. However, the careful student will note that the method of handling ties is an issue, and he will be sensitive to the possible qualifications their presence may make upon the accuracy of his conclusions.

[7] Inspired by, but not identical to R. R. Sears and G. W. Wise, "Relation of Cup Feeding in Infancy to Thumbsucking and the Oral Drive." *American Journal of Orthopsychiatry*, 1950, XX, 123–138.

throughout the course of infancy much as the average American child is. After eight months of these experiences, samples of the infants' behavior are made to determine how much of the time the infants suck their thumbs. These measures were expressed in terms of the proportion of time spent sucking during the observations.

The assumptions are that the **subjects are randomly and independently sampled** and that **the scale of measurement** (percent thumb sucking) **is continuous and of an ordinal nature.**

The null hypothesis is that the population distribution for cup-fed babies is the same as for bottle-fed babies. The alternative hypothesis is that these distributions are different in some way. The .05 level will be adopted.

The data are presented in the following table in which *C* indicates cup feeding and *B* bottle feeding. The scores are percentages.

Group	*C*	*C*	*C*	*B*	*B*	*C*	*B*	*B*	*B*	*B*
Score	3	5	6	9	10	12	13	13	16	24
Rank	1	2	3	4	5	6	7.5	7.5	9	10

U_{obs} is computed as follows with the cup-fed group called Group A:

$$\begin{aligned} U_{\text{obs}} &= n_A n_B + \frac{n_A(n_A + 1)}{2} - T_A \\ &= 4(6) + \frac{4(5)}{2} - 12 \\ U_{\text{obs}} &= 22 \end{aligned}$$

Looking at Table G for a two-tailed test at the .05 level, one finds the critical values of U for $n = 4,6$ are 2 and 22. The observed value of U is 22 and since this equals the critical value for U, H_0 is rejected. The distributions are probably different, and it would appear that cup-fed infants suck their thumbs less, though they presumably experience more frustration of their oral needs because of the reduced opportunity to suck.

large sample illustration The same issue that motivated the above experiment, inspired a similar experiment with dogs.[8] Dogs were randomly and independently sampled and arbitrarily assigned to one of two rearing conditions. As pups, the dogs were bottlefed with nipples having either

[8] Inspired by, but not identical to D. M. Levy, "Experiments on the Sucking Reflex and Social Behavior in Dogs," *American Journal of Orthopsychiatry*, 1934, IV, 203–224.

very large holes allowing the milk to flow freely or small holes which demanded more sucking in order for a dog to obtain a sufficient meal. After being weaned the dogs were tested for the amount of non-nutritive sucking they did in a structured situation. The logic of the experiment suggests that if there is an innate drive to suck, not sucking during rearing should frustrate this drive and lead to more oral behavior later. Thus, the dogs being fed through big holes should have a more frustrated need to suck because they did not suck as much during infancy. In contrast, the small-holes group had to suck a great deal, and all this oral activity presumably reduced the need for sucking behavior later. If a learning orientation is assumed, just the opposite predictions might be made. A great deal of sucking should produce a strong habit of sucking.

Twenty-five dogs were assigned to the little-hole group and 24 to the big-hole group. The subjects were randomly and independently selected and the amount of time spent in oral activity is on a continuous scale having ordinal properties. The null hypothesis is that the populations from which these two samples are drawn are identical. The alternative is that the population distributions are not identical in every respect.

Since the sample sizes are large (greater than 20), the standard normal approximation will be used. For a two-tailed alternative at the .05 level, the observed z must be less than or equal to -1.96 or greater than or equal to 1.96 in order to reject H_0.

The data and computation are presented in Table 11–3 and a formal summary of the procedure is presented in Table 11–4. The data are arranged in increasing order of score value within each group. Then, disregarding group affiliation, the scores are rank ordered, and the total of the ranks for the two groups is determined. The value of U_{obs} is computed in Table 11–3.

The formula approximating the standard normal is given in Table 11–3 and the corresponding values entered. The resulting observed z is 2.07 which complies with the second decision rule and the null hypothesis is rejected. The interpretation is that the groups probably do differ in the population and an examination of the data indicate that according to the Freudian orientation, dogs reared without much sucking opportunity (big-hole group) showed more oral behavior than the animals given much sucking opportunity (small-hole group) early in life.

KRUSKAL-WALLIS TEST FOR *k* INDEPENDENT SAMPLES

The Mann-Whitney U test for two samples may be generalized to several independent samples. As such, the test for several groups would be analogous to the simple parametric analysis of variance but without making several of its assumptions. The most common approach to this kind of analysis is known as the Kruskal-Wallis test.

11–3 Data and Computation for Large-Sample Mann-Whitney *U* Test.

Little Holes Score	Little Holes Rank	Big Holes Score	Big Holes Rank
8	2	3	1
10	3	22	9
11	4.5	27	10
11	4.5	29	11.5
12	6	30	13
18	7	36	14
21	8	51	23
29	11.5	51	23
45	15	51	23
46	16	59	26
49	18	65	27
49	18	74	30
49	18	76	31.5
50	20.5	76	31.5
50	20.5	81	33.5
57	25	83	35
71	28	96	40.5
73	29	98	42
81	33.5	122	44
89	36	135	45
90	37	142	46
93	38	159	47
94	39	183	48
96	40.5	190	49
109	43	$n_B = 24$	$T_B = 703.5$
$n_A = 25$	$T_A = 521.5$		

$$U_{\text{obs}} = n_A n_B + \frac{n_A(n_A + 1)}{2} - T_A$$

$$= 25(24) + \frac{25(25 + 1)}{2} - 521.5$$

$$U_{\text{obs}} = 403.5$$

11–4 Formal Summary of Large-Sample Illustration of Mann-Whitney *U* Test.

Hypotheses

H_0: The population distributions from which the samples are drawn are identical.

H_1: These populations are not identical.

Assumptions

1. The observations are **randomly** and **independently** sampled, and the two groups are **independent** from one another.
2. The measurement scale is **continuous** and has at least **ordinal** properties.

Decision Rules

Since the sample is large ($n > 20$), the standard normal approximation will be used. For a two-tailed test at .05, the decision rules are

If $-1.96 < z_{obs} < 1.96$, accept H_0

If $z_{obs} \leq -1.96$ or $z_{obs} \geq 1.96$, reject H_0

Computation

The value of U_{obs} is calculated in Table 11–3. The standard normal approximation is given by

$$z_{obs} = \frac{U_{obs} - n_A n_B/2}{\sqrt{\dfrac{(n_A)(n_B)(n_A + n_B + 1)}{12}}}$$

$$= \frac{403.5 - 24(25)/2}{\sqrt{\dfrac{(24)(25)(24 + 25 + 1)}{12}}}$$

$$z_{obs} = 2.07$$

Interpretation

Since $z_{obs} = 2.07$ exceeds the critical value, H_0 is rejected.

Suppose three **independent groups** of subjects are **randomly selected.** Suppose also, that the groups each receive different treatments, that the dependent variable has a **continuous distribution,** and that it is measured with at least an **ordinal scale.** Last, assume that there are **at least five observations per group.**[9]

The null hypothesis is that the three samples have identical population distributions, while the alternative hypothesis is that their population distributions are different. If the distributions have the same form, this difference implies that the scores are higher or lower in some of the groups than in others.

[9] For procedures to handle the case in which there are less than five observations in a group, see Siegel, *op. cit.*, 185–188.

The method of handling the data is quite comparable to the Mann-Whitney test. Consider the following sample data.

Groups					
1		**2**		**3**	
Score	**Rank**	**Score**	**Rank**	**Score**	**Rank**
21	1	35	5	28	2
29	3	39	7	31	4
38	6	45	8	52	9
54	10	58	11	79	16
60	12.5	60	12.5	80	17
71	15	63	14	83	18
$n_1 = 6$	$T_1 = 47.5$	89	19	$n_3 = 6$	$T_3 = 66$
		$n_2 = 7$	$T_2 = 76.5$		

The scores are arranged into groups in ascending order of score value. Then, without regard to group affiliation, all the observations are ranked, with the smallest score value being assigned a rank of 1. If any scores are ties, each tie score receives the average of the ranks available for those scores. The ranks for each group are totaled within each group, and this total is signified by T_j for the jth group.

The general rationale is that if the groups are distributed in the same way and with the same central tendency, then the averages of the ranks for the several groups should be approximately equal. To the extent that the scores in one group are higher than those in the others, the several averages will be unequal. Obviously, the averages are not likely to be precisely equal, but under the null hypothesis will differ because of sampling error. When the differences in average ranks become so great that it is implausible to attribute them to mere sampling error, the tentative assumption of the null hypothesis is rejected and the existence of treatment effects in the population is suspected.

This logic is translated into a formula for the statistic H which reflects the extent to which the sum of the ranks for the several groups differ from one another. The formula for H is

$$H_{\text{obs}} = \left[\frac{12}{N(N+1)}\right]\left[\sum_{j=1}^{k} \frac{T_j^2}{n_j}\right] - 3(N+1)$$

in which

k = the number of groups in the analysis
n_j = the number of observations in the jth group
$N = \sum n_j$, the total number of observations in the analysis
T_j = the total of the ranks in the jth group.

The formula directs one to sum the ranks in each group and square this total.

Divide each squared total by the number of observations in that particular group, and sum across all groups to obtain

$$\sum_{j=1}^{k} \frac{T_j^2}{n_j}$$

Enter this and N into the above expression for H.

The sampling distribution of the statistic H has approximately the same form as chi square with $k - 1$ degrees of freedom (k = the number of groups). This approximation is close only when there are at least five observations per group and the accuracy of the approximation improves as N increases.

In the present case, there are three groups so the degrees of freedom for H are $k - 1 = 3 - 1 = 2$. The critical value of chi square with $df = 2$ is 5.99 as obtained from Table F. Thus, if H_{obs} is greater than or equal to 5.99, the null hypothesis of equivalence of population distributions will be rejected.

The computation for the data provided is straightforward.

$$H_{\text{obs}} = \left[\frac{12}{N(N+1)}\right]\left[\sum_{j=1}^{k} \frac{T_j^2}{n_j}\right] - 3(N+1)$$

$$= \left[\frac{12}{19(19+1)}\right]\left[\frac{(47.5)^2}{6} + \frac{(76.5)^2}{7} + \frac{(66)^2}{6}\right] - 3(19+1)$$

$$H_{\text{obs}} = 1.20$$

Since the value of H_{obs} does not exceed the critical level, the observed differences between the samples are within the realm of sampling error and the null hypothesis of no population differences is accepted.

example In Chapter 10, a study was mentioned that involved showing a movie to young children and noting whether or not they would imitate the aggressive actions of an adult more if the adult was seen to be rewarded for such behavior[10] The parallels to violence and aggression on television are obvious. Suppose there were three different groups of children in the experiment. All children saw a movie of an adult striking and otherwise assaulting a large doll, Bobo. After this behavior, the film ending depicted one of three consequences to the aggressor. Either she was rewarded with praise, punished with reprimands, or nothing at all happened to her. Each of the three groups of children saw a different ending. The question was whether this vicarious experience with reinforcement would determine the percentage of imitative aggressive behaviors in a ten-minute test situation in which each child was placed in a room with Bobo and other toys.

The assumptions for a Kruskal-Wallis test can be met. The subjects were randomly selected and assigned to independent groups. The dependent variable

[10] After A. Bandura, D. Ross, and S. A. Ross, "Imitation of Film-Mediated Aggressive Models," *Journal of Abnormal and Social Psychology*, 1963, LXVI, 3–11.

is the percent of responses the child makes which are imitations of the aggressor, and this variable is theoretically continuous and ordinal in nature.

The hypothesis to be tested is that the population distributions for the three conditions in the experiment are identical. The alternative hypothesis is that these distributions are not the same in some way.

Since there are three groups, the degrees of freedom for this test are $k - 1 = 3 - 1 = 2$. The test statistic H is distributed as chi square, and Table F shows the critical value for such a test to be 5.99. Thus, if the value of H_{obs} is greater than or equal to 5.99 the null hypothesis will be rejected. Otherwise, it will be accepted.

The data and the computation of H_{obs} are presented in Table 11–5. H_{obs} is found to be 13.91 which exceeds the critical value at .05 (and at .01 as well), and H_0 is rejected. The analysis suggests that the populations from which these three groups are drawn do differ in some way, and an examination of the data implies that a child is more likely to imitate as a function of the extent to which positive consequences derive from the aggressor's behavior. A formal summary of this analysis is presented in Table 11–6.

11–5 Data and Computation for the Kruskal-Wallis Test Example.

Punished		Nothing		Rewarded	
Score (%)	Rank	Score (%)	Rank	Score (%)	Rank
0	1	2	3	8	13.5
1	2	3	5	12	16.5
3	5	4	7.5	13	18
3	5	6	10.5	16	20.5
4	7.5	7	12	19	22
5	9	10	15	21	23
6	10.5	12	16.5	22	24
8	13.5	14	19	23	25
		16	20.5		
$n_1 = 8$	$T_1 = 53.5$	$n_2 = 9$	$T_2 = 109$	$n_3 = 8$	$T_3 = 162.5$

$$H = \left[\frac{12}{N(N+1)}\right]\left[\sum_{j=1}^{k} \frac{T_j^2}{n_j}\right] - 3(N+1)$$

$$= \left[\frac{12}{25(25+1)}\right]\left[\frac{(53.5)^2}{8} + \frac{(109)^2}{9} + \frac{(162.5)^2}{8}\right] - 3(25+1)$$

$$H = 13.91$$

$$df = k - 1 = 3 - 1 = 2$$

11–6 Formal Summary of Kruskal-Wallis Test Example.

Assumptions

1. Subjects are **randomly and independently sampled** and divided into ***k*** **independent groups** with all $n_j \geq 5$.
2. The underlying dimension is **continuous** and the measurement scale is at least **ordinal.**

Hypotheses

H_0: The population distributions from which the groups are sampled are identical.
H_1: These distributions are different in some way.

Decision Rules

Given: the .05 level of significance and that H is distributed as chi square (Table F) with $k - 1 = 3 = 2\,df$

If $H_{\text{obs}} < 5.99$, accept H_0
If $H_{\text{obs}} \geq 5.99$, reject H_0

Computation (See Table 11–4.)

$$H_{\text{obs}} = \left[\frac{12}{N(N+1)}\right]\left[\sum_{j=1}^{k} \frac{T_j^2}{n_j}\right] - 3(N+1)$$

$$H_{\text{obs}} = 13.91$$

Interpretation

Since $H_{\text{obs}} = 13.91$ exceeds the critical value of 5.99, H_0 is rejected.

correlated samples

WILCOXON TEST FOR TWO CORRELATED SAMPLES

All of the tests described in this chapter thus far have been for independent samples, groups of observations on separate or unmatched subjects. Just as special procedures were required for the t test when the sets of observations were made on the same or matched subjects, so too a different nonparametric analysis must be made when the samples are not independent. One of the most common distribution-free tests for this situation is the Wilcoxon test for correlated or matched samples.

If the same subjects are measured under two conditions or if matched pairs of subjects provide a score under each of two conditions and if the measurement is ordinal both within pairs and between pair differences, then the Wilcoxon test may be used to test the null hypothesis that the population distributions corresponding to the two types of observations are identical.

Suppose that a special program is designed to provide children with broadening sociocultural experiences. It is also of interest to observe whether this program improves children's language skills. Seven children are enrolled in the program and each is administered a test of linguistic development at the beginning and at the end of the program. The researcher wishes to know if there was any change in linguistic behavior even though no direct attempt was made to teach language.

There are a few assumptions which the Wilcoxon test makes but they are less restrictive than those required for the appropriate t test. First, the subjects must be **randomly** selected. Second, the scale of measurement must at least be **ordinal** in nature. Also, each subject will have a pair of scores and these two values will probably differ. One could obtain a distribution of these differences, and the test assumes that these differences also fall on an ordinal scale (i.e., the differences may be ordered in magnitude).

The null hypothesis is that the population distributions under the two conditions are identical. The alternative hypothesis is that they are not identical. Usually, particularly if the distributions are symmetrical, this is taken to mean that the central tendency of one distribution is higher than that of the other.

The procedure requires that the matched pairs of scores be subtracted in order to obtain their difference and that the algebraic sign of the difference be retained. Following this, the absolute values of the differences are assigned ranks starting with a rank of 1 for the smallest difference. Recall that the signs of the differences were retained but that the rankings were made without regard to sign. The ranks may now be attributed to positive and negative differences between the two groups. If there is no difference between the groups, then one would expect that the sum of the ranks associated with positive differences between the groups would be about equal to the sum of the ranks associated with negative differences between the groups. Since under this circumstance, the total of all ranks would be divided relatively evenly between positive and negative differences and thus the smaller of these two sums would take on its largest value under the null hypothesis of no difference. If there is a difference between groups, then either the positive or negative sum of ranks will be quite a bit smaller than the other. As the difference between groups increases, the smaller of the two sums gets smaller and smaller. The sampling distribution of this smaller sum is known and when the observed total becomes sufficiently small as to be unlikely to have arisen solely because of sampling error, the null hypothesis of no difference is rejected.

Suppose the data presented in Table 11–7 are for the seven children in the hypothetical example of a sociocultural enrichment program:

11–7 Hypothetical Data for Wilcoxon Test Example.

Subject	Pretest	Posttest	Difference d_i	Absolute Difference $\lvert d_i \rvert$	Rank Difference	Signed Rank Difference
A	74	76	−2	2	3	−3
B	81	80	1	1	1.5	1.5
C	85	89	−4	4	6	−6
D	79	88	−9	9	7	−7
E	92	95	−3	3	4.5	−4.5
F	83	80	3	3	4.5	4.5
G	87	86	1	1	1.5	1.5

$$T_+ = 7.5$$
$$T_- = 20.5$$
$$W_{obs} = 7.5$$

The seven subjects and their scores on the pretest and posttest are listed, and the difference between these scores, d_i, is computed. Then the absolute values of these differences are taken and ranked, assigning the rank of 1 to the lowest absolute difference. If a difference is zero, then it is dropped from the analysis and the total N (the number of **paired** observations) is reduced by the number of such zero differences. If some of the absolute differences are of equal value, these ties are assigned the average of the ranks that they would have received if they had been distinct.

After the absolute differences have been ranked, the last column of the above table merely repeats the rank that each matched pair received but the algebraic sign of the difference in score values is attached to the rank. Now, two quantities are computed, T_+ which is the total of the ranks having positive signs associated with them in the last column of the table and T_- which is the sum of those ranks having negative signs. The statistic of interest is W_{obs} which is simply the smaller of T_+ and T_-. If the two groups are similar to one another, these two totals will be about equal. As the difference between groups increases so does the difference between T_+ and T_-, and W_{obs} (the smaller of the two) takes on a smaller and smaller value. When W_{obs} becomes sufficiently small relative to its sampling distribution, H_0 is rejected.

For N (the number of **paired** observations sampled less the number of pairs having zero differences in scores) between 6 and 25, the critical values for the sampling distribution of W as a function of N for several levels of significance and for one- and two-tailed tests are presented in Table H. If W_{obs} **is less than or equal to** the tabled critical value, H_0 is rejected and a difference in the population is presumed. In the present illustration, $N = 7$, and if the test is taken to be non-directional at the .05 level, the critical value is 2. Since W_{obs} is greater than this critical value, H_0 is accepted and the observed differences between the pretest and posttest are attributed to sampling error.

For N greater than 25, an approximation to the standard normal may be used (actually the approximation is sufficiently good so that it may be used with $N \geq 10$). The conversion to a standard normal deviate is given by the following:

$$z_{obs} = \frac{W_{obs} - N(N+1)/4}{\sqrt{\dfrac{N(N+1)(2N+1)}{24}}}$$

For the sake of illustration, when the values obtained in the illustration are substituted into this expression one has

$$z_{obs} = \frac{7.5 - 7(7+1)/4}{\sqrt{\dfrac{7(7+1)[2(7)+1]}{24}}}$$

$$z_{obs} = -1.10$$

For a two-tailed test, the critical values at the .05 level would be -1.96 and 1.96. If the observed value of z falls between -1.96 and 1.96, H_0 is accepted. Since -1.10 does occur in this interval, a conclusion of no population difference is drawn. If the test were one-tailed, the critical region would be entirely in the **left-hand** tail of the standard normal, with $z = -1.64$ as the critical value.

example One fundamental principle in the sensorimotor development of organisms is the apparent close relationship between visual and auditory perceptual processes on the one hand and the opportunity for the organism to physically interact with his environment on the other. Some theorists have suggested that in order for visual and auditory stimuli to really have an effect on the organism, they must be associated with the feedback of physical interaction with the stimulus environment. One application of this theory was made in the following experiment.[11] Eight pairs of kittens, the members of

[11] Inspired by R. Held and A. Hein, "Movement-Produced Stimulation in the Development of Visually-Guided Behaviors," *Journal of Comparative and Physiological Psychology*, 1963, LVI, 872–876.

each pair coming from the same litter, were reared in darkness until they were 10 weeks of age. They then received visual stimulation for only a short period each day under very special conditions. The two kittens of each pair were placed into a vertically oriented cylindrical apparatus with stripes painted on the side. One member of each pair was allowed to move about the apparatus at will. However, he wore a harness which was attached by means of a system of pulleys and gears to a "gondola-like" carriage that held the other kitten. A post in the center of the apparatus prevented one member of the pair from seeing the other, and the circumstances were arranged so that the visual experience of the two kittens was quite similar. If the theory is correct, the freely active kitten should show faster development on visual-motor tasks than the kitten carried passively through the environment in the gondola. A series of tasks that measure visual-motor development were used and each subject received a score indicating his proficiency on such a test battery.

It is assumed that the pairs of kittens are randomly selected. The test battery yields a score such that the measurement within pairs and between differences in pairs is at least ordinal in character.

The null hypothesis is that the population distributions for active and passive kittens are identical. The alternative hypothesis is that these distributions are not the same in some way. The data, computation, and formal summary for this example appear in Table 11–8. Notice that for pair *D*, the difference between the two kittens is zero and this fact eliminates the pair from the analysis. Consequently, the N is reduced from 8 to 7. The negative ranks have the smaller total ($T- = 2$), and Table H reveals that the critical value for W is 2 for a two-tailed test at $\alpha = .05$. Since the observed and critical values are equal, the null hypothesis is rejected. This study supports the theory that feedback from physical interaction with the stimulus environment is a catalytic element in the enrichment potential of the sensory environment.

rank-order correlation

SPEARMAN RANK-ORDER CORRELATION COEFFICIENT

The Pearson product moment correlation coefficient introduced in Chapter 6 may be applied to ordinal as well as interval or ratio data. Often, if the data are markedly skewed, measurements made with an interval or ratio scale are transformed to ranks before the correlation is computed. When the Pearson product moment correlation is applied to rank orderings, it is called Spearman's rank-order correlation, and it is symbolized by r_S.

11–8 Summary for the Wilcoxon Test Example.

Hypotheses

H_0: The population distributions for the two matched groups of observations are identical.
H_1: These two distributions are not identical.

Assumptions

1. The pairs of subjects are **randomly selected** (or the same subjects are measured under two different conditions).
2. **Ordinal measurement** is available both within pairs and between the N differences between members' scores.

Decision Rules

Given: the .05 level, $N = 7$ (see below), and a two-tailed alternative

If $W_{\text{obs}} > 2$, accept H_0
If $W_{\text{obs}} \leq 2$, reject H_0

Computation

Pair	Active Kitten	Passive Kitten	d_i	$\lvert d_i \rvert$	Rank i	Signed Rank d_i
A	4	2	2	2	5	5
B	3	0	3	3	7	7
C	1	0	1	1	2	2
D	2	2	0	0	eliminated	
E	5	3	2	2	5	5
F	1	2	−1	1	2	−2
G	3	1	2	2	5	5
H	5	4	1	1	2	2

N = number of pairs minus the number of zero differences

$N = 7$

$T_+ = 26$
$T_- = 2$
$W_{\text{obs}} = 2$

Interpretation

Since the observed W equals the critical value, the null hypothesis is rejected and the observed difference in the pairs is taken not to be due merely to sampling error.

Suppose that a group of 15 nursery children were being observed by two judges who were asked to rank the children on their social aggressiveness. Thus, each judge would rank order the 15 children, assigning a rank of 1 to the child presumed to have the least aggressive behavior and a rank of 15 to the child presumed to have the most aggressive tendencies. The question is to what extent do the two judges agree in their ranking. The assumptions for computing such an index are that the subjects are **randomly** sampled and the measurement is at least **ordinal.**

Suppose the data are

Pupil	Judge I	Judge II	d_i	d_i^2
A	1	3	−2	4
B	4	4	0	0
C	5	8	−3	9
D	10	5	5	25
E	8	2	6	36
F	14	15	−1	1
G	7	9	−2	4
H	2	6	−4	16
I	12	14	−2	4
J	9	7	2	4
K	15	13	2	4
L	3	1	2	4
M	13	12	1	1
N	11	10	1	1
O	6	11	−5	25
		$N = 15$	$\sum d_i = 0$	$\sum d_i^2 = 138$

In the present case, the raw data were themselves rank orderings of the subjects by two different judges. If the data were numbers of aggressive acts, for example, these measurements would have to be rank ordered before proceeding. Notice, however, that in contrast to some of the previous rank-order statistical tests, observations are **ranked only within, not across, a condition.** That is, for an index of relationship, each subject has two scores, one measuring one attribute (or made under one condition) and the other measuring another attribute. The observations are ranked for each attribute separately. Ties may be handled as before by assigning the average of the ranks that the tied observations would otherwise have received.

The method proceeds by computing the difference (d_i) between the ranks for each subject and then squaring each of these differences. The sum of the squared differences in ranks $\left(\sum_{i=1}^{N} d_i^2\right)$ and the number of **pairs of observations** (N) are entered into the following formula for r_S:

$$r_S = 1 - \left[\frac{6\left(\sum_{i=1}^{N} d_i^2\right)}{N^3 - N}\right]$$

For the data presented above:

$$r_S = 1 - \left[\frac{6(138)}{15^3 - 15}\right]$$

$$r_S = .75$$

The formula given above for the Spearman rank-order correlation is a simplification of the formula for the Pearson product-moment correlation as applied to ranked data. It can be shown that when the Pearson formula is applied to data that have been ranked, the expression can be reduced to the formula given above for r_S. This means that if the Pearson formula were applied to the data above, a correlation of .75 would result. However, suppose a set of data measured on an interval or ratio scale were available and a Pearson correlation computed. Now, if these same data were subsequently transformed to ranks and the Spearman formula used, the Pearson and Spearman correlations would not be identical. In short, when applied to the same ranked data r and r_S will yield identical coefficients; but an r computed on interval or ratio data and an r_S computed on the rankings for that same data will not be identical (but probably will be quite close).

TESTING THE SIGNIFICANCE OF r_S

As with Pearson r, it is desirable to be able to test the hypothesis that the observed value of r_S is really computed on a sample drawn from a population in which the correlation is actually zero and that the observed value is merely a function of sampling error.

Using the data presented in the previous section, the null hypothesis would be that the observed Spearman correlation of .75 is based upon a sample from a population in which the correlation is actually zero (that is, $H_0: \rho_S = 0$). The alternative hypothesis is that a nonzero correlation actually does exist in the population ($H_1: \rho_S \neq 0$). The assumptions are that the subjects were **randomly** selected and that the measurement was at least **ordinal.**

Table I[12] lists critical values for the Spearman correlation for samples of size $N = 5$ to $N = 30$ for several levels of significance and for directional and

[12] The values in this table are exact for $N \leq 10$, but approximate for other values of N. Note also that the entries in the table may be regarded as + (positive) or − (negative).

nondirectional tests. If the observed correlation equals or exceeds the value in the table for specified N, α, and type of test (one- or two-tailed), the null hypothesis is rejected. For the present case, $N = 15$, $\alpha = .05$, and the alternative is directional since one would predict that the judges would tend to agree. Thus, the critical value of r_S is .447. Since the observed correlation of .75 is greater than the critical value, H_0 is rejected and it is concluded that the two judges do evidence some degree of concordance in their evaluations of the children.

For $N > 30$, the following expression translates r_S into an approximation to Student's t distribution with $N - 2$ degrees of freedom:

$$t = \frac{r_S\sqrt{N-2}}{\sqrt{1-r_S{}^2}}$$

example The following example illustrates the computation of r_S and a test to determine if the population correlation is zero.

Suppose a new test designed to diagnose reading skill has become available. Mrs. Smith, a reading consultant for a public school system, would like to use the test to screen children in the schools in order to select those that need remedial work. Since there are several hundred pupils, a single test must be used for this purpose. However, in order to evaluate whether the new test will serve this function, Mrs. Smith randomly selects 20 pupils and performs a comprehensive workup on each child based upon scores on several specialized tests, reading samples, and clinical techniques. As a result of this extensive evaluation, she ranks each of the 20 children in terms of general reading skills, a rank of 1 going to the least capable student. After this workup, she administers the new diagnostic test. She wants to know the degree of relationship between the test and her thorough evaluation and to test whether this correlation is significantly different from zero.

The assumptions are that the subjects were randomly sampled and that the rankings and test scores both constitute ordinal scales. The null hypothesis for testing r_S is that the observed value deviates from a population correlation of zero only because of sampling error (H_0: $\rho_S = 0$). The directional alternative is that a positive relationship exists between the two forms of evaluation (H_1: $\rho_S > 0$).

The decision rules are based upon the critical values which are obtained from Table I. From the table with $N = 20$ and a one-tailed test at the .05 level, the required value of r_S is .381. Thus, the decision rules are that if the observed value of r_S is less than .381, accept H_0; otherwise reject H_0.

The data are presented in Table 11–9. Notice that the scores on the reading test must first be converted to ranks, while the teacher's evaluations are already in this form. The value of d_i represents the difference **in ranks** for the two measures. The $N = 20$ and the $\sum_{i=1}^{n} d_i{}^2 = 628$.

11–9 Data for the Spearman Rank-Order Correlation Example.

Pupil	Reading Test Score	Rank of Test Score	Teacher Ranking	d_i	d_i^2
A	38	1	11	−10	100
B	67	7	13	−6	36
C	72	10	5	5	25
D	43	2	10	−8	64
E	91	18	15	3	9
F	54	5	12	−7	49
G	63	6	9	−3	9
H	78	12	6	6	36
I	69	9	4	5	25
J	74	11	8	3	9
K	85	14	14	0	0
L	98	20	19	1	1
M	46	3	7	−4	16
N	52	4	3	1	1
O	68	8	1	7	49
P	80	13	16	−3	9
Q	93	19	17	2	4
R	87	16	20	−4	16
S	86	15	2	13	169
T	89	17	18	−1	1

$$N = 20, \sum_{i=1}^{N} d_i^2 = 628$$

Table 11–10 presents a formal summary of the procedure for testing the significance of this r_S. The value of the correlation is found to be .528 with a critical value of .381. Since the observed value exceeds the critical value in the right tail, H_0 is rejected. It is concluded that the observed correlation probably does reflect a nonzero relationship in the population.

11–10 Summary of Spearman Rank-Order Correlation Coefficient Example.

Assumptions

1. The sample is **randomly** selected.
2. The measurement is at least **ordinal** in character.

Hypotheses

$$H_0: \rho_S = 0$$
$$H_0: \rho_S > 0$$

Decision Rules

Given: a one-tailed alternative, the .05 level, and $N = 20$

If $r_S < .381$, accept H_0.
If $r_S \geq .381$, reject H_0.

Computation

Given: from Table 11–9 that $N = 20$ and $\sum_{i=1}^{N} d_i^2 = 628$

$$r_S = 1 - \left[\frac{6 \sum_{i=1}^{N} d_i^2}{N^3 - N}\right]$$
$$= 1 - \left[\frac{6(628)}{20^3 - 20}\right]$$
$$r_S = .528$$

Interpretation

Since the observed value of r_S corresponds with the second decision rule, H_0 is rejected and it is concluded that a nonzero correlation probably exists in the population.

discussion Because the approximations to theoretical sampling distributions for samples of intermediate size are somewhat less accurate than might be desired, some statisticians and researchers prefer another method of assessing rank correlation. This statistic is called Kendall's *tau,* and the procedures for testing its significance are more precise than for the Spearman coefficient. The Kendall procedure reflects a slightly different rationale, and thus the two coefficients are not precisely equivalent. Procedures for the use of "tau" are outlined in Siegel (*op. cit.*) and Bradley (*op. cit.*).

when to use nonparametric tests

At the beginning of this chapter, nonparametric tests were said to have advantages over parametric tests if the data were measured with a nominal or ordinal scale or if the assumptions of normality and/or equal variances could not be met. When the data are measured in a nominal or ordinal scale, nonparametric techniques are almost always required. However, if an interval or ratio scale is available, parametric tests may still be appropriate even if the assumptions of normality and homogeneity of variance are not tenable. Without going into detail, the parametric t test is not influenced a great deal by violations of either of these two assumptions, particularly if the sample size is rather large. Therefore, if the skewness or heterogeneity is not too severe and the sample size is large, a t test may still be appropriate. Furthermore, recall that for several nonparametric tests, it must be assumed that the two distributions have relatively equivalent shapes in order to interpret the results of the analysis in terms of the difference between the central tendencies of the groups. Some statisticians feel that this assumption is just as restrictive, if not more so, than the assumptions of normality and homogeneity of variance required for the parametric t test. This opinion, plus the fact that the t test can tolerate moderate violations of its assumptions, prompt some scholars to favor the parametric over the nonparametric test in all but the most extreme situations.

Consequently, if the data are measured in a nominal or ordinal scale, use the nonparametric test appropriate to the research question. However, if interval or ratio data are available, the choice is not so clear. If the departure from normality or homogeneity of variance is not too great and the sample size is substantial, the t test is still probably an appropriate technique; otherwise, use a nonparametric test.

FORMULAS

1. Chi Square

a. For $r \times c$ tables:

$$\chi_{\text{obs}}{}^2 = \sum_{j=1}^{r} \sum_{k=1}^{c} \frac{(O_{jk} - E_{jk})^2}{E_{jk}}$$

in which

O_{jk} = the observed frequency of the jkth cell
E_{jk} = the expected frequency of the jkth cell
r = the number of rows
c = the number of columns

Refer to the Chi Square Distribution with

$$df = (r - 1)(c - 1)$$

b. For 2 × 2 tables:

a	*b*
c	*d*

$$\chi^2 = \frac{N(|ad - bc| - N/2)^2}{(a + b)(c + d)(a + c)(b + d)}$$

Refer to the Chi Square Distribution with

$$df = 1$$

2. Mann-Whitney *U* Test for Two Independent Samples

a. For $n \leq 20$:

$$U_{\text{obs}} = n_A n_B + \frac{n_A(n_A + 1)}{2} - T_A$$

in which

n_A = the number of observations in Group A
n_B = the number of observations in Group B
T_A = the total of the ranks for Group A

Refer to the U Distribution with n_A and n_B.

b. For $n \geq 20$:

$$z = \frac{U_{\text{obs}} - n_A n_B/2}{\sqrt{\dfrac{(n_A)(n_B)(n_A + n_B + 1)}{12}}}$$

in which U_{obs}, n_A, and n_B are defined above.
Refer to the Standard Normal Distribution (z).

3. Kruskal-Wallis Test for *k* Independent Samples

$$H_{\text{obs}} = \left[\frac{12}{N(N + 1)}\right]\left[\sum_{j=1}^{k} \frac{T_j^2}{n_j}\right] - 3(N + 1)$$

in which

k = the number of groups in the analysis
n_j = the number of observations in the jth group
$N = \sum n_j$ the total number of observations in the analysis
T_j = the total of the ranks in the jth group

Refer H_{obs} to the Chi Square Distribution with

$$df = k - 1$$

4. Wilcoxon Test for Two Correlated Samples

a. For $N \leq 25$:

W_{obs} = the smaller of the sum of the ranks associated with positive differences in pairs of scores (T_+) and the sum of the ranks associated with negative differences (T_-).

Refer to the W Distribution.

b. For $N > 25$:

$$z_{\text{obs}} = \frac{W_{\text{obs}} - N(N+1)/4}{\sqrt{\dfrac{N(N+1)(2N+1)}{24}}}$$

in which W_{obs} is defined as above and

N = the number of pairs of observations

Refer to Standard Normal Distribution (z).

5. Spearman Rank-Order Correlation Coefficient

$$r_S = 1 - \left[\frac{6\left(\sum_{i=1}^{N} d_i^2\right)}{N^3 - N}\right]$$

in which

N = the number of pairs of observations
d_i = the difference in ranks for the ith pair of scores

a. For $N \leq 30$:

Refer to table of critical values for r_S.

b. For $N > 30$:

$$t = \frac{r_S\sqrt{N-2}}{\sqrt{1 - r_S^2}}$$

Refer to Student's t Distribution with

$$df = N - 2$$

EXERCISES

1. Under what conditions might a researcher prefer to use a nonparametric rather than a parametric statistical technique?

2. To what does **power-efficiency** refer? For a given N, are parametric tests or comparable nonparametric tests more powerful?

3. Suppose men and women were randomly sampled and asked whether they approved or disapproved of the President's foreign policy. Of the 59 women sampled, 39 approved and 20 disapproved whereas only 30 of 62 men approved. Test the hypothesis that there is no difference between men and women with respect to the percent that approve of the President's policies.

4. A man draws 60 balls from an urn and replaces each one after examining its color. The man drew 15 red, 29 green, and 16 blue balls. Test the hypothesis that the urn really contains an equal number of each color.

5. A sample of children were observed from 3 to 12 years of age and their IQ was tested periodically. It was found that 45 children showed increases in the general trend of their IQ's over this age period while 37 displayed essentially declining trends. The mothers of these children were seen in their homes during this period and the home visitor rated each mother on the extent to which she expected intellectual success and encouraged her child in its pursuit. The data follow:

		Amount of Maternal Aspiration		
		Low	Medium	High
IQ Trend over Age	Increased	7	15	27
	Decreased	30	9	11

Test the hypothesis that there is no difference in the distribution of maternal aspiration for intellectual success for the children that evidenced IQ increases than for those showing declines.

6.

A	B	C
28	34	51
33	31	72
14	20	21
6	18	13
9	15	53
14	22	44
21	30	48
24	54	61

Above is a set of data. Perform the following nonparametric statistical tests on these data:

(a) Assume that Groups *A*, *B*, and *C* are independent random samples. Test the hypothesis that there is no difference between the population distributions for Groups *A* and *B*. For Groups *A* and *C*. For Groups *B* and *C*.

(b) Assuming that the three groups are independent, test the hypothesis that in the population these three groups do not differ.

(c) Conceptually, what is the difference between the questions in parts (a) and (b)? Is there an advantage to one over the other, and if so, what?

(d) Suppose that the first score in each group is a measure on a single subject before, during, and after a certain treatment. Test the hypothesis that the measurements in *A* are from a population distribution comparable to that from which the scores in *B* were drawn. Compare *A* and *C* for the same question. *B* and *C*.

(e) Compare the result you obtained for Group *A* vs. Group *B* when you tested it in Part (a) with the result when you tested it in Part (d). How do you explain any differences in the results of these two tests?

(f) Making the same assumptions as in Part (d), perform a Pearson product-moment correlation on Groups *A* and *C*, and then rank the data separately within each group. Perform both a Pearson and a Spearman correlation procedure on these rankings. Compare the results you obtained in these three cases and state the general conclusion that you have illustrated.

(g) Test the Spearman correlation computed in Part (f) above for the hypothesis that the correlation in the population is zero. Compute the Spearman correlation for the data in *A* and *B* and test this correlation in the same manner. Do the same for the data in *B* and *C*.

7. Consider the following practical situation. Suppose that a father comes home from work after a hard day and sits down with his wife and five-year-old child for dinner. The wife asks the husband, "How was your day, dear?" The retort is, "It was . . . ," in which ". . ." is a set of expletives not in the best social and child-rearing traditions. The mother may censor her husband in front of the child by saying, "Jim, you really shouldn't swear like that in front of Junior," or she could continue the conversation without commenting on the profanity. The question is, under which of these maternal response conditions is the child more likely to remember the profanity? Suppose it were possible to perform such a study in which some fathers were verbally censored while others were not.[13] Later, the child was asked what his father had said in response to the question of, "How

		Child's Memory of Profanity		
		None	**Some**	**All**
Mother's Response to Profanity	**Censors Father**	4	22	24
	No Response	14	19	16

[13] Inspired by but not identical to R. M. Liebert, and L. E. Fernandez, "Effects of Vicarious Consequences on Imitative Performance," *Child Development*, in press.

was your day?" The responses are scored as either not remembering anything, remembering a portion of the father's response, or remembering all of it. The numbers of children responding at each level are presented on the preceding page. Test the hypothesis that the mother's response to the father's profanity does not influence the ability of the child to remember the event.

8. It happens that boys have more reading problems than do girls in the United States. One explanation of this fact is that the reading materials used in many schools in the United States are not very masculine in their content. It may be that boys would do better in reading if the material were about rockets, athletics, science, etc., rather than about home and family. To test this notion, a school system divided its first grades into two types. In half the classes, both sexes used the traditional (presumably feminine) materials. In the other classes males used masculine materials and the females were taught with the traditional materials. Of 450 boys in the non-sex-appropriate group, 42 were said to have reading problems but in the group where the material was sex-appropriate, 31 of 475 boys developed reading problems. Test the hypothesis that the sex-role appropriateness of reading material does not influence the acquisition of reading skills for boys.

9. A dress designer wishes to evaluate women's preferences for certain types of clothes. The designer has five general styles of dresses and all of his creations are essentially variations on these five motifs. The designer sets up a style show and typical examples of the five styles are modeled. Afterwards, all five styles are shown simultaneously and the women in the audience cast a written ballot indicating their favorite dress. The number of votes for the five dresses were 25, 36, 19, 31, 29, respectively. Test the hypothesis that women show no differential preference among the five styles.

10. One hypothesis about thumbsucking in infants and children is that the behavior is a learned habit. An interesting question is how children come to learn it. It happens that all normal infants have a "rooting reflex" in which stroking the side of the mouth with a finger (for example) elicits a widening of the mouth, a turning of the head to the side of the tactile stimulus, and a propensity to suck the finger. This reflex is useful in helping the infant find his mother's breast. However, when an infant sleeps, it is customary to place the child on his stomach and his arms lie on each side of his head. The thumb may easily contact the side of the mouth, and the infant "roots" and sucks his thumb. Perhaps he learns the habit in this context. If infants could be prevented from rooting and sucking their thumbs when they go to sleep and wake up, presumably they would not develop as strong a habit for this behavior.[14] Suppose nylon mittens were put on the hands of nine infants just before they went to sleep and removed when they got up, thus preventing thumbsucking. Eleven other infants were reared without the gloves. In an observation period of several hours when the infants were nine months of age, the amount of time the infant sucked his thumb was recorded. The data follow. With the appropriate nonparametric technique, test the hypothesis that the wearing of mittens does not alter the amount of thumbsucking in the observation.

[14] Inspired by but not identical to Lorna S. Benjamin, "The Beginning of Thumbsucking," *Child Development*, 1967, XXXVIII, 1079–1088.

Mittens	Control
4	7
10	15
6	7
14	8
1	8
0	16
5	11
13	11
9	35
	19
	21

11. Given the following data, calculate the means and medians for the two groups and use the appropriate parametric t test to compare the two groups. Then compute a Mann-Whitney U test on the same data. Compare the results of the two tests. Explain any differences and attempt to draw some conclusions about when nonparametric tests might be more appropriate than parametric tests. In what way is the difference between the mean and the median similar to the difference between a parametric and a nonparametric test in this example?

A	*B*
10	16
11	17
12	18
13	19
14	20
15	21
62	24

12. The concept of reminiscence in learning refers to the improvement in performance of a learned task after a period of "rest" following an initial practice period. The effect often appears in tasks requiring motor learning. For example, a pursuit rotor is a machine on which a spot of light moves in a circular pattern and the subject attempts to keep the point of a pencil-like stylus on the moving dot. The apparatus is such that it can monitor the length of time the point of the stylus is actually on the spot of light. Each of several randomly selected subjects is allowed 25 seconds of practice on the pursuit rotor and then given a rest of either .5, 1, or 3 minutes. This is followed by a test period on the rotor. The number of seconds in contact with the spot during the test is given below for the three groups.[15]

[15] Inspired by but not identical to A. L. Iron, "Reminiscence in Pursuit-Rotor Learning as a Function of Length of Rest and Amount of Pre-Test Practice," *Journal of Experimental Psychology*, 1949, XXXIX, 492–499.

Using the appropriate nonparametric technique, test the hypothesis that the amount of rest does not alter postrest performance.

Rest in Minutes		
.5	1.0	3.0
21	32	42
32	55	58
26	62	63
49	24	71
51	53	56
41	35	13
19	59	65
27		54
		68

13. Twelve culturally deprived children are given an intensive preschool enrichment program in an attempt to raise their IQ's. They are tested first after one month of training and then at the end of the first year. The IQ's of the children for these two testings follow. By using the appropriate nonparametric technique, test the hypothesis that the program had no effect on the IQ's of the youngsters.

Child	One Month	One Year
A	89	103
B	95	97
C	82	100
D	101	98
E	91	96
F	85	88
G	96	97
H	93	105
I	86	99
J	99	110
K	90	107
L	84	86

14. For the data in Exercise 13, using r_S, determine the degree of relationship between the first testing and the second for the 12 children. Test the hypothesis that in the population the relationship is zero. On psychological and educational grounds, how do you interpret the result observed in Exercise 13 in view of this additional information?

12

further topics in probability

set theory

SETS AND RELATIONS AMONG SETS

A discussion of probability is greatly facilitated if it can be couched in the terms of set theory. Therefore, some very elementary definitions and operations of set theory will be presented first.

A **set** is a well-defined collection of things.

The ordinary concept of a set, such as a set of drinking glasses or a set of carving knives, is quite analogous to the mathematical notion of a set. The critical implication in the definition is that there is some rule or quality that the objects in the set possess which determines, unequivocally, whether or not they are contained in the specified set. For example, husbands are a set. Every human male, if he is married, is a member of the set of husbands. If he is not married, if he is a "she", if he is a giraffe, etc., then he is not a member of the set, husbands. Thus, a set is a collection of objects which are distinguishable from all other objects on the basis of some particular characteristic.

An **element** of a set is any one of its members.

It is customary to arbitrarily label a set by some capital letter, such as, A, B, C, etc., and to denote an element of a set with a small letter, such as, a, b, c, etc.

There are two special sets that should be mentioned, the universal and the empty set.

> The **universal set** includes all objects to be considered in any one discussion. It is symbolized by S.
>
> The **empty** or **null set,** contains no elements. It is symbolized by $\emptyset$.

A very important concept for the study of probability is that of subset.

> If every element in set A is also an element of set B, then A is a **subset** of B.

Since the phrase "is a subset of" is rather long and cumbersome, it is customary to write it with the symbol $\subseteq$.

One of the primary applications of the set and subset to statistics are their analogy to the concepts of population and sample. A sample is a subset of the population. In Figure 12–1 one might consider the entire space, S (the universal set), as the population composed of all male college students. Perhaps the sample is only composed of male college students attending State University and is symbolized by A. Further, the researcher randomly selects only a few male college students at State, symbolized by B. Thus, $A \subseteq S$, $B \subseteq S$, and $B \subseteq A$.

> If S is the entire space and A is a subset of S, then the symbol A', read "not A," denotes the set of all elements in S which are **not** in A. A' is called the **complement** of A.[1]

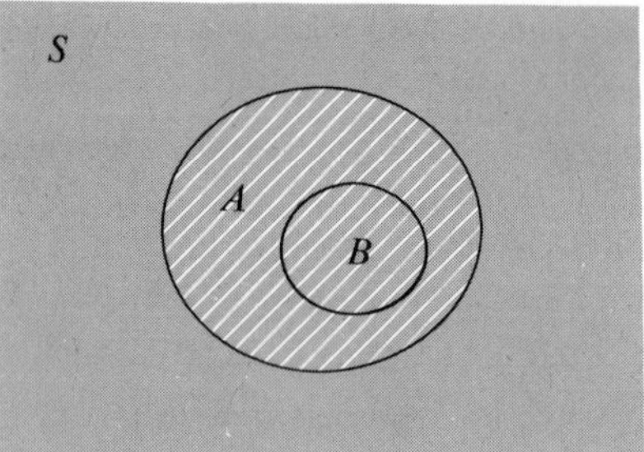

Fig. 12–1. Set-subset relationship. S is the set of all male college students, A is male college students at State, and B is a small sample of the males at State.

[1] Other symbols used for the complement of A include $\bar{A}$, $\tilde{A}$, and $\sim A$.

If S includes all the integers from 1 to 10, and A includes 1, 4, 5, 8, and 9, then A' includes 2, 3, 6, 7, and 10. The complement relationship is displayed in Figure 12–2. The shaded portion is A'.

> If every element in A is also an element of B and if every element in B is also an element of A, then A **equals** B (i.e., if $A \subseteq B$ and $B \subseteq A$, then $A = B$).

If $A = \{1, 2, 5, 9\}$ and $B = \{5, 1, 9, 2\}$, then $A = B$. Note that the order of the elements in A and B is irrelevant.

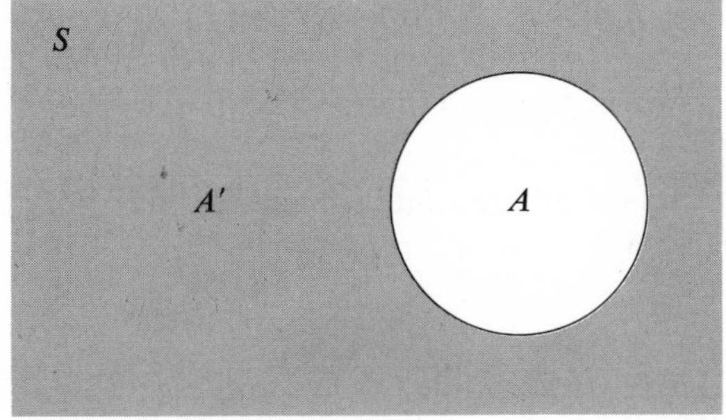

Fig. 12–2. Complementation. S is the universal set, A is a subset of S, and A' (not A) is the complement of A since it contains all the elements in S which are not in A.

OPERATIONS

> Given two sets, A and B, the **union** of A and B is the set of all elements which (1) are in A, **or** (2) are in B, **or** (3) are in both A and B.

The word "union" is symbolized by $\cup$ so that A union B (the union of A and B) is written $A \cup B$.

Figure 12–3 illustrates the concept of union in which the shaded area represents the union of A and B, symbolized $A \cup B$. The crucial word to remember about the concept of union is "or." The criterion for including any element in the union of A and B is whether that element is contained in A **or** B **or** both A and B. For example, if A includes $\{1, 2, 3, 4, 5\}$ and B includes $\{3, 4, 5, 6, 7, 8\}$, then $A \cup B = \{1, 2, 3, 4, 5, 6, 7, 8\}$. Notice that numbers contained in both A

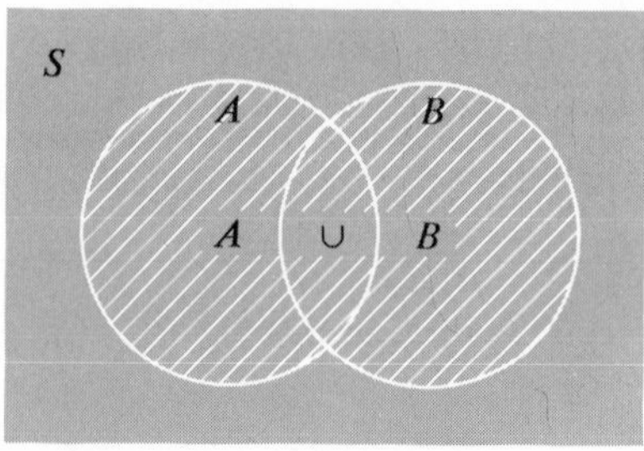

Fig. 12–3. Union. A union B ($A \cup B$) is represented by the shaded area. $A \cup B$ contains all elements in A, in B, or in both A and B.

and B are not represented twice in $A \cup B$. That is, $A \cup B$ is **not** equal to $\{1, 2, 3, 4, 5, 3, 4, 5, 6, 7, 8\}$.

> Given two sets, A and B, the **intersection** of A and B contains all elements which are in both A **and** B, but not A or B alone. The symbol for "intersection" is $\cap$, and A intersection B is written $A \cap B$.

Figure 12–4 illustrates the intersection of A and B in which $A \cap B$ is the shaded portion of the diagram.

Thus, if

$$A = \{1, 2, 3, 4, 5\} \text{ and}$$
$$B = \{3, 4, 5, 6, 7, 8\}$$

then

$$A \cap B = \{3, 4, 5\}$$

Here the emphasis is on the word "and" because in order for an element to be a member of the intersection of A and B ($A \cap B$), it must be contained in both A **and** B. The intersection represents the common portion of two sets, or the elements shared by two sets.

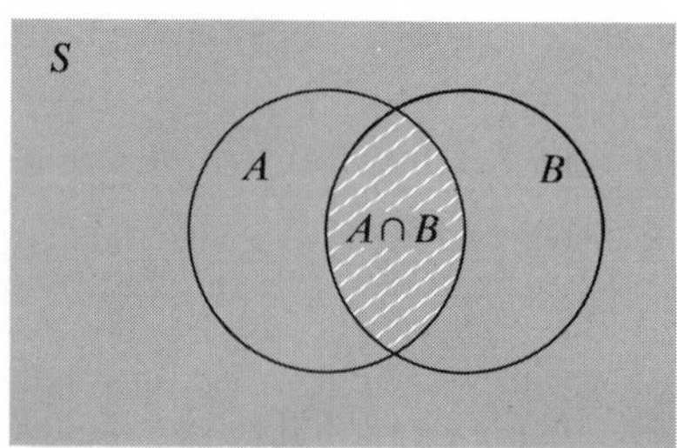

Fig. 12–4. Intersection. $A \cap B$, is represented by the shaded area which includes all elements which are members of set A and set B simultaneously.

It is useful to be more explicit about the distinction between union (∪) and intersection (∩). An element belongs to the **union** of A and B, if it qualifies under **any one** of the following criteria:

(1) If it is a member of A
(2) If it is a member of B
(3) If it is a member of both A and B

However, in order to determine if an element qualifies for inclusion in the **intersection** of A and B, (3) is the only criterion. An element must be a member of both A and B. The difference between the important words in the definitions also highlights the distinction between union and intersection. $A \cup B$ contains elements which are in A **or** B **or** in both A and B; whereas $A \cap B$ contains only those elements which are in both A **and** B simultaneously.

There is a special case of intersection which defines a particular relationship between two sets that should be pointed out. Suppose $A \cap B$ contains no elements, that is, $A \cap B = \emptyset$. Such a condition says that A and B share no common elements, no element in A is also in B and no element in B is also in A. If $A \cap B = \emptyset$, then A and B are called **disjoint sets,** because there is no common element to "join" them together. Figure 12–5 illustrates a pair of disjoint sets. Another example of disjoint sets is A and A'. Recall that A' contains all elements not in A and is called the complement of A. It is clear that for any set A, A and A' are disjoint.

A summary of the terms and concepts discussed in this section is presented in Table 12–1.

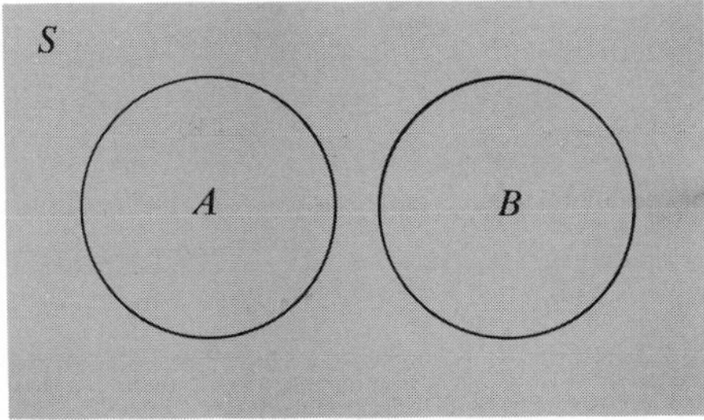

Fig. 12–5. Two disjoint sets. $A \cap B = \emptyset$, that is, A and B share no common elements.

simple classical probability

In probability, the collection of all the elements of the idealized experiment is called the **sample space,** symbolized by S. The elements of this set are known as **elementary events** or **outcomes.** An **event** is any subset of elements in S. Therefore, an "event" may be an elementary event, a subset set of elementary events, or all

12-1 Terminology of Set Theory.

Set Theory

1. **Set:** A well-defined collection of things.
2. **Element:** A member of a set.
3. **Universal Set, S:** The set of all objects under discussion.
4. **Empty Set, $\emptyset$:** The set containing no elements.
5. **Subset:** If every element in A is also in B, A is a subset of B (i.e., $A \subseteq B$).
6. **Complement:** Set A' is the complement of set A if it contains every element in S which is not also in A.
7. **Equality:** Set A equals set B if every element in A is also in B and every element in B is also in A (i.e., if $A \subseteq B$ and $B \subseteq A$, $A = B$).
8. **Union:** The union of sets A and B, $A \cup B$, is the set of all elements which are (1) in A, (2) in B, or (3) in both A and B.
9. **Intersection:** The intersection of A and B, $A \cap B$, is the set of all elements which are in both A and B simultaneously.
10. **Disjoint Sets:** Two sets are disjoint if they share no common elements (i.e., $A \cap B = \emptyset$).

elementary events (i.e., S). Thus, in the idealized experiment of rolling a single die, the sample space consists of the set of six elementary events (or outcomes): 1, 2, 3, 4, 5, and 6. An event in this idealized experiment may be a roll of three or less $\{1, 2, 3\}$, a roll of a deuce $\{2\}$, or a roll of an even number $\{2, 4, 6\}$. **Simple classical probability** involves making probabilistic statements on a sample space whose elementary events are all equally likely to occur. This is why discussions of probability frequently employ the flipping of coins, drawing of cards, rolling of dice, etc., because all these experiments have equally likely elementary events.

As indicated in Chapter 7, in the classical case, the probability of an event A is defined to be the number of outcomes in A divided by the number of outcomes in the sample space, S. If $P(A)$ indicates the "probability of A" and "$\#(A)$" indicates the "number of outcomes in A," then the classical definition of probability is given by

$$P(A) = \frac{\#(A)}{\#(S)}$$

In the tossing of a coin the sample space consists of the two equally likely outcomes, heads and tails, and the probability of a head is

$$P\text{ (Head)} = \frac{\#\text{ (Head)}}{\#\text{ (Possible Outcomes)}} = \frac{1}{2}$$

In the idealized experiment of throwing a die, the sample space consists of the equally likely alternatives $\{1, 2, 3, 4, 5, 6\}$, and the probability of throwing a two is $\frac{1}{6}$. The probability of a five is also $\frac{1}{6}$. The probability of a four or less is $\frac{4}{6}$.

The determination of probability in the classical case consists of three steps. First, determine if the sample space contains equally likely events. Second, count the elementary events that compose the event A in question. Third, count the total number of elementary events in the sample space, S. Then the probability of A is the number of elementary events in A divided by the number of elementary events in S. In terms of set theory, the probability of an event A is the ratio of the number of elements in the subset A to the number of elements in S.

There are two simple axioms implied by the classical definition of probability. These were mentioned earlier and are now translated into the terminology of set and probability theory.

The first axiom is that

$$P(\emptyset) = .00$$

which states that the probability of an impossible event is .00.

If there are no possible ways of achieving an event A, the number of outcomes in A is zero, and the equation for probability becomes $P(\emptyset) = \dfrac{0}{\#(S)}$ which is always 0.

The second axiom is that

$$P(S) = 1.00$$

which states that the probability that some event in the sample space occurs is 1.00.

Consider the probability of getting either a head or a tail in a single toss of a coin. Since there are no other alternatives besides a head or a tail, the probability of getting one of them is 1.00. Mathematically, the probability of the sample space is

$$P(S) = \frac{\#(S)}{\#(S)} = 1.00$$

These two axioms together imply that the probability of any event will fall between 0 and 1.00, inclusive. Further, the second axiom implies that the sum of the probabilities of all possible elementary events in the sample space equals 1.00. The $P(\text{Head}) = .5$ and the $P(\text{Tail}) = .5$, and their sum is 1.00.

SOME IMPORTANT DEFINITIONS

mutually exclusive events

Two events, A and B, of the same idealized experiment are considered to be **mutually exclusive** if they share no elementary events, that is, A and B are disjoint sets ($A \cap B = \emptyset$).

This implies that if one event has occurred, the other has not. Consider the event A of drawing a king on a single draw from a special deck only composed of all the jacks, queens, and kings of a regular deck. Abbreviate the cards by giving them two initials, the first for the denomination and the second for the suit (e.g., the King of Spades by KS, etc.). Since event A is drawing a king, set A contains four elements (all the kings):

$$A = \{KS, KC, KH, KD\}$$

Now let event B be drawing a queen in a single draw. Set B also contains four elements:

$$B = \{QS, QC, QH, QD\}$$

Note first that there is no element in A which is also in B. Therefore, A and B are disjoint sets and consequently $A \cap B = \emptyset$. Note also that if on a single draw A occurs, B has not occurred; if you draw a king you do not also draw a queen on that draw.

In contrast, consider now the events of drawing a king (A) and drawing a red card (B) from this special deck:

$$A = \{KH, KD, KS, KC\}$$
$$B = \{KH, KD, QH, QD, JH, JD\}$$

These events are not mutually exclusive because they have two common elements, $\{KH, KD\}$, therefore $\#(A \cap B) = 2$ not 0, and A and B are not disjoint. Further, it is not necessarily true that if A occurs B does not occur, because if the king of hearts or diamonds is drawn, then both event A and event B have simultaneously occurred.

Therefore, two events are mutually exclusive if their sets are disjoint and the occurrence of one event precludes the occurrence of the other.

independent events[2]

Two events are said to be **independent** if the occurrence of one event does not alter the probability that the other event will occur.

[2] The definition given here is linked to the independence of trials of an idealized experiment. A more precise definition of independence is given on p. 332.

Suppose one takes the 12 picture cards from a deck of cards (jacks, queens, kings) and shuffles them. Consider the event A of drawing a king. Since there are four kings in the deck there are four ways of obtaining the event A (i.e., $\#(A) = 4$), and there are 12 cards in all (i.e., $\#(S) = 12$). Therefore, the probability of A is

$$P(A) = \frac{\#(A)}{\#(S)} = \frac{4}{12} = \frac{1}{3}$$

Now suppose the card actually drawn, whatever it was, is returned to the deck, the cards are reshuffled, and one considers the probability of event B of drawing a king on the second draw from the deck. Again, there are four ways of drawing a king and 12 total possibilities, therefore the probability of B is

$$P(B) = \frac{\#(A)}{\#(S)} = \frac{4}{12} = \frac{1}{3}$$

Now the probability of drawing a king on the second draw is not changed as a function of the occurrence of the first event. In fact, from the standpoint of event B, it does not matter whether the initial draw (the draw of the first event) is a king or not, because in any case the card is replaced in the deck. The deck is shuffled, and one redraws with the probability of $\frac{4}{12}$ of selecting a king on the second draw. Since the probability of event B is unaltered by the occurrence of event A, A and B are said to be independent events.

dependent events

Two events are said to be **dependent** if the occurrence of one event alters the probability of the other.

In the previous example for independent events cards were drawn from the sample deck and replaced. Consider now the situation in which the first card drawn is not returned to the deck. That is, suppose one draws **without** replacement. The probability of drawing a king on the first try is still $\frac{4}{12}$ or $\frac{1}{3}$. But suppose that whatever is picked on that first draw, king or not, it is set aside and not returned to the deck. Now what is the probability of selecting a king on the second draw? Well, it depends upon what is picked on the first draw. For example, if event A occurs and a king is selected on the first draw and it is not replaced into the deck, then for the second choice there is a total of 11 cards left, three of which are kings. Therefore, in this case the probability of event B, selecting a king on the second draw, is $\frac{3}{11}$. But, suppose a jack rather than a king were selected on the first try and it is not replaced. Now there is a total of 11 cards to pick on the second draw, but four not three of them are kings. Therefore the probability of event B in this case is $\frac{4}{11}$. Clearly, when drawing without replacement the probability of B depends upon whether event A has or has not occurred. Therefore, A and B are said to be dependent events.

conditional probability

Conditional probability is the probability that an event will occur given that some other event has already occurred. The probability that event B shall occur given the fact that event A has already occurred is written

$$P(B \mid A)$$

which is read "the probability of B given A."

Thus, in the previous illustration of dependent events, the conditional probability of B given A (the probability of a king given that a king had been drawn without replacement) was

$$P(B \mid A) = \tfrac{3}{11}$$

Recall that A' means all events in the sample space except A. Suppose A' indicates drawing a card other than a king on the first selection. Therefore, the conditional probability of B given A' (the probability of a king given that a non-king was drawn) is

$$P(B \mid A') = \tfrac{4}{11}$$

Another example of conditional probability is the probability of selecting a red ball on the second draw when drawing is done without replacement from an urn containing three red and six green balls. This probability is "conditional" upon what is drawn on the first try since the ball is not replaced. If a red ball is drawn the first time, the probability is $\frac{2}{8} = \frac{1}{4}$ that one obtains a red ball on the second draw since two of the eight balls left after the first draw are red. Alternatively, if a green ball had been selected first, the probability of drawing a red ball on the next selection is $\frac{3}{8}$. In symbols, if drawing a red ball on the first try is event A (A' is drawing a green one) and drawing a red ball the second try is event B, then

$$P(B \mid A) = \tfrac{2}{8}$$
$$P(B \mid A') = \tfrac{3}{8}$$

Although it is necessary to have some knowledge about independence and dependence to lead into the discussion of conditional probabilities, it is now possible to use the notion of conditional probability to define independence. If A and B are independent, the probability of B is uninfluenced by whether or not A has occurred, and the probability of B is the same whether A is given or not. Therefore, we define independence as follows.

Two events A and B are defined to be **independent** if

$$P(B \mid A) = P(B)$$

In the case of drawing with replacement, the probability of event B, drawing a king on the second try, was $\frac{4}{12} = \frac{1}{3}$. The probability of drawing a king on the second try given that a king had turned up on the first try was also $\frac{4}{12} = \frac{1}{3}$, since the first king was returned to the deck before reshuffling. Therefore, A and B are independent because in drawing with replacement

$$P(B) = \tfrac{1}{3}$$
$$P(B \mid A) = \tfrac{1}{3}$$

and therefore

$$P(B \mid A) = P(B)$$

An interesting application (or lack of application) of the concept of independence is known as the **gambler's fallacy.** The gambler's fallacy is the failure to appreciate the independence of some events that occur in a sequence, and it is epitomized when a gambler who has lost 10 straight times at dice feels that he has a better than average chance of winning the next game because of his long string of misfortune. Another example is the wife who feels that after five boys in a row, surely the probability of having a girl as a sixth child is greater than .50. Actually the theoretical probabilities of these events do not change as these people suppose. The probability of having a girl (or a boy) is approximately .50 for any given birth, and the sex of the child for any given birth is probably independent of the sex of the child on the preceding birth. Therefore, the probability of having a girl is approximately .50 whether it is one's first child or whether the child will have 10 brothers (or sisters) upon its arrival. So, too, for the gambler, just because he has had a bad losing streak, it is no more likely that he will win the next game than if he had a fantastic winning streak in progress.

Games of chance are very likely to be independent in actuality as well as theoretically. On the other hand, if a basketball team loses 10 games in a row and they come up against their rival school which is of approximately equal ability, the probabilities of winning the game may be more than .50 if the team is highly spirited and wishes to beat its rival and salvage an otherwise poor season. Of course, it could be less than .50 if the 10 losses have so demoralized the team that it can hardly face the humiliation of playing another game. Thus, although the independence of events is an important characteristic in assessing probabilities, in practice, it is sometimes difficult to determine if events are independent or not.

independence and mutually exclusive events compared

Although the ideas of independent and mutually exclusive events appear to be very similar, they should not be confused. The difference between them is that mutually exclusive refers to the sharing or not sharing of elements of sets whereas independence is defined in terms of the probabilities of two events. Therefore,

Mutually Exclusive Events: $A \cap B = \emptyset$
Independent Events: $P(B \mid A) = P(B)$

probability of complex events

PROBABILITY OF A ∩ B

The probability that two events, A and B, both occur is

$$P(A \cap B) = P(A)P(B \mid A)$$

This means that the probability that both A and B occur is the probability of A times the probability of B given that A has occurred.

In the special case when A and B are independent events, $P(B \mid A) = P(B)$ (which is the definition of independent events). Therefore, substituting $P(B)$ for $P(B \mid A)$ in the above expression, we have the following:

The probability that two **independent** events A and B both occur is

$$P(A \cap B) = P(A)P(B)$$

Consider the logic of these propositions. Suppose one had the small deck of cards used previously that only contains the four kings, queens, and jacks. Consider the event of drawing two consecutive kings without replacement. This event is really composed of two events: A, the event of drawing a king on the first selection, and B, the event of drawing a king on the second selection. In terms of the events A and B, the complex event of drawing two consecutive kings amounts to the intersection of A and B ($A \cap B$). This is because the elements that will satisfy the two conditions must be members of both set A (the collection of events in which a king is drawn on the first try) and also set B (the collection of events in which a king is drawn on the second try). In terms of the diagram in Figure 12–4 earlier in the chapter, drawing two consecutive kings is represented by the shaded portion which contains elements falling both in A and also in B. Hence, the task is to ascertain the probability of $A \cap B$.

Considering the laws of classical probability, the result should be given by

$$P(A \cap B) = \frac{\#(A \cap B)}{\#(S)}$$

How many elementary events are in $A \cap B$ and how many are in S? First, consider drawing two kings. There are four ways of drawing the first one. Hence $\#(A) = 4$. The next requirement is the number of ways of drawing a king given that one has already been selected on the first draw. In symbols one wants $\#(B \mid A)$, which is 3, because if one king has been selected, three remain. Now then, how many ways are there to pick two consecutive kings? Table 12–2 lists all the possible ways. From this table it is clear that for every king that could be drawn on the first try, there are three that could be drawn on the second

12–2 The Number of Ways of Getting Two Consecutive Kings, $(A \cap B)$.		
First Draw	**Second Draw**	**Number of Ways**
King of Spades	{King of Clubs King of Hearts King of Diamonds	3
King of Clubs	{King of Spades King of Hearts King of Diamonds	3
King of Hearts	{King of Spades King of Clubs King of Diamonds	3
King of Diamonds	{King of Spades King of Clubs King of Hearts	3
[First Draw (A)] × [Second Draw $(B \mid A)$] = [Total $(A \cap B)$] 4 × 3 = 12		

try. Therefore, the total number of ways two kings can be drawn without replacement is

$$\#(A \cap B) = [\#(A)] \times [\#(B \mid A)] = (4)(3) = 12$$

The solution is similar for the number of events in the sample space, S. There are 12 cards that could be selected on the first draw and 11 cards remaining for selection on the second draw. Therefore, one might partition the total sample space up into S_A, the total number of selections possible on the first draw, and $S_{B|A}$, the total number of possibilities on the second draw given that the first has occurred. Therefore, the total number of ways of selecting two cards is

$$\#(S) = [\#(S_A)] \times [\#(S_{A|B})] = (12)(11) = 132$$

We now have expressions for the number of ways to select two consecutive kings, $\#(A \cap B)$, and the number of ways to select two consecutive cards, $\#(S)$; thus, the probability of getting two kings without replacement is

$$P(A \cap B) = \frac{\#(A \cap B)}{\#(S)} = \underbrace{\frac{[\#(A)]}{[\#(S_A)]}} \times \underbrace{\frac{[\#(B \mid A)]}{[\#(S_{AB})]}} = \frac{4}{12} \times \frac{3}{11} = \frac{12}{132}$$

$$P(A \cap B) = [P(A)] \times [P(B \mid A)] = \frac{4}{12} \times \frac{3}{11} = \frac{12}{132}$$

Observe that the first part of the above expression is $P(A)$ and the second part is the conditional probability of B given A, $P(B \mid A)$, and that the probability of the intersection of two events equals the probability of A times the conditional probability of B given A. In the case being illustrated, the probability of drawing two consecutive kings is $\frac{4}{12} \times \frac{3}{11} = \frac{12}{132} = .09$. This means that if you were to repeatedly draw two consecutive cards from the special deck, on the average you might expect that 9 of every 100 such pairs would be a pair of kings.

example Suppose you have a budding romance going with a sharp girl you discovered in your statistics class. You ask her to take a walk in the country with you after her afternoon laboratory. She says she would like that but sometimes the lab runs late and there would not be time. The likelihood that she will be able to go is only about .50. Further, the weather man says there is a 40% chance of rain today, which means the probability of no rain is .60. Though you are both hardy souls, let's assume you will not go if it rains. What is the probability you take your date for a walk in the country?

Define event A to be "your date gets out of lab on time," and event B to be "it does not rain." Thus, the complex event of your girl having the time **and** there being no rain is $A \cap B$, the probability of which is given by

$$P(A \cap B) = P(A)P(B \mid A)$$

Since the probability of rain is not changed by whether or not your girl gets out of the lab on time, A and B are independent, and $P(B \mid A) = P(B)$. Therefore, the required probability is given by

$$P(A \cap B) = P(A)P(B)$$

Since $P(A) = .50$ and $P(B) = .60$,

$$P(A \cap B) = P(A)P(B) = (.50)(.60) = .30$$

In other words, on the average you would make it to the country on only 30 of every 100 such occasions.

discussion Please note that one needs to remember only that

$$P(A \cap B) = P(A)P(B \mid A)$$

This formula includes the case in which A and B are independent when $P(B \mid A) = P(B)$. Thus, there is no need to try to retain two formulas when one will do.

Second, the real problem in using this expression for the probability of the intersection of two events is translating the verbal statement of the problem into events A and B, and then determining if the intersection of A and B is required. Most often, the intersection of A and B is needed if the problem states (or could be restated to say) that both A **and** B must occur to satisfy the complex condition. The key word is "and":

(1) You must draw a king on the first try **and** on the second.
(2) Your date must finish lab early **and** it must not rain.

The word "and" signifies that the joint occurrence of A and B is required, and thus $A \cap B$ is an appropriate description of the problem.

expression for conditional probability The previous discussion provides an expression for the conditional probability of B given A:

$$P(A \cap B) = P(A)P(B \mid A)$$

Dividing by $P(A)$ and transposing, we have

$$P(B \mid A) = \frac{P(A \cap B)}{P(A)}$$

Therefore, the conditional probability of B given A equals the probability that A and B occur divided by the probability of A. In symbols:

$$P(B \mid A) = \frac{P(A \cap B)}{P(A)}$$

If the probability that your team wins a two-game basketball tournament is .15 [$P(A \cap B) = .15$] and the probability of winning your first game is .50 [$P(A) = .50$], then before the tournament begins you can speculate that the probability that you win the tournament given that you win the first game is

$$P(B \mid A) = \frac{P(A \cap B)}{P(A)} = \frac{.15}{.50} = .30$$

PROBABILITY OF $A \cup B$

The probability of the occurrence of either one of two events, A or B, that is, $A \cup B$, is

$$P(A \cup B) = P(A) + P(B) - P(A \cap B)$$

This states that the probability that either A or B occurs equals the probability of A plus the probability of B minus the probability of $A \cap B$. However, the probability of $A \cap B$ is zero if A and B are mutually exclusive. (This is because in that case $A \cap B = \emptyset$ and $P(\emptyset) = .00$.) Therefore, if A and B are mutually exclusive events, the preceding formula is simplified:

If A and B are **mutually exclusive,** the probability that either A or B occurs is

$$P(A \cup B) = P(A) + P(B)$$

This states that if A and B are mutually exclusive the probability that either A or B occurs is the sum of the probabilities of A and B. Let us examine the logic of this proposition with an example.

We will return to the special deck of 12 cards. What is the probability of selecting either a king or a red card? If A is the event of selecting a king and B the event of selecting a red card, then $A \cup B$ is the event of selecting either a king or a red card. The shaded area in Figure 12–3 earlier in the chapter corresponds to this union of A and B. Thus, the problem is to determine

$$P(A \cup B) = \frac{\#(A \cup B)}{\#(S)}$$

The question now becomes one of ascertaining the number of elementary events in $A \cup B$. If the cards are abbreviated as before (e.g., *Q*ueen of *D*iamonds = QD), then

$$\begin{aligned}\#(A) &= (KH, KD, KS, KC) = 4\\ \#(B) &= (KH, KD, QH, QD, JH, JD) = 6\end{aligned}$$

In order for an element to qualify for A $\cup$ B it must be either in A or in B. But, the total number of elements in $A \cup B$ is not merely the sum of $\#(A)$ and $\#(B)$ because then the king of hearts (KH) and the king of diamonds (KD) would be counted twice since they are in both A and B (i.e., A and B are not mutually exclusive). But any elements in both A and B compose the intersection of $A \cap B$, and therefore in order to count these common elements once not twice one subtracts the $\#(A \cap B)$ from the sum of $\#(A)$ and $\#(B)$, obtaining

$$\begin{aligned}\#(AUB) &= \#(A) + \#(B) - \#(A \cap B)\\ &= \quad 4 \quad + \quad 6 \quad - \quad 2 \quad = 8\end{aligned}$$

Thus there are eight possible cards which are either in A or in B:

$$\#(A \cup B) = (KS, KC, KH, KD, QH, QD, JH, JD) = 8$$

The $\#(S)$ for the case of drawing one card from a deck of 12 is 12. Therefore, the probability of $A \cup B$ should be given by

$$\begin{aligned}P(A \cup B) &= \frac{\#(A \cup B)}{\#(S)} = \frac{\#(A) + \#(B) - \#(A \cap B)}{\#(S)}\\ &= \frac{4 + 6 - 2}{12} = \frac{8}{12} = .67\end{aligned}$$

However, this expression may be simplified to

$$\begin{aligned}P(A \cup B) &= \underbrace{\frac{\#(A)}{\#(S)}} + \underbrace{\frac{\#(B)}{\#(S)}} - \underbrace{\frac{\#(A \cap B)}{\#(S)}} = \frac{4}{12} + \frac{6}{12} - \frac{2}{12} = .67\\ P(A \cup B) &= P(A) + P(B) - P(A \cap B) = \frac{4}{12} + \frac{6}{12} - \frac{2}{12} = .67\end{aligned}$$

which shows that the probability of the union of A and B equals the probability of A plus the probability of B minus the probability of $A \cap B$.

example Suppose a student applied to two graduate schools, A and B. He assessed the chances of getting into each as $P(A) = .10$ and $P(B) = .25$. What is the probability of getting into either school A or school B? Since either A or B satisfies the required outcome, the probability is given by

$$P(A \cup B) = P(A) + P(B) - P(A \cap B) = .10 + .25 - (.10)(.25) = .325$$

example What is the probability of getting an odd number or a six in a single roll of a die? If A is the event of getting an odd number and B the event of getting a six, then the required probability is

$$P(A \cup B) = P(A) + P(B) - P(A \cap B) = \tfrac{3}{6} + \tfrac{1}{6} - 0 = \tfrac{4}{6}$$

Note that A and B are mutually exclusive and therefore the $P(A \cap B) = 0$.

discussion Once again, only the first formula needs to be remembered since for the case in which A and B are mutually exclusive one merely sets one of the terms equal to zero rather than changing the nature of the formula.

Although these probabilistic laws have been stated only in terms of two events, the formulas can be generalized to cases involving more than two events. For example, if A, B, and C are **independent,** then

$$P(A \cap B \cap C) = P(A)P(B)P(C)$$

If A, B, and C are all **mutually exclusive,** then

$$P(A \cup B \cup C) = P(A) + P(B) + P(C)$$

The word "or" in a verbal statement of a problem tends to imply that the union of two or more events is required, just as the presence of the word "and" signals the intersection of two or more events.

Thus, the above discussion on the probability of the union of two events dealt with

(1) either a king **or** a red card,
(2) getting accepted at either school A **or** B, and
(3) rolling an odd number **or** a six.

example Consider a last example which involves a combination of union and intersection. What is the probability of selecting either an ace or a king on the first draw and a red card or a face card (J, Q, K) on the second draw from an ordinary deck of 52 cards if selection is performed with replacement? Let

A = an ace on the first draw
B = a king on the first draw
C = a red card on the second draw
D = a face card on the second draw

Reducing the statement of the problem to symbols, the required complex event is (A **or** B) **and** (C **or** D), and thus the probability is

$$P[(A \cup B) \cap (C \cup D)]$$

First observe that the two events $(A \cup B)$ and $(C \cup D)$ are independent since the selection is performed with replacement. Further, A and B are mutually exclusive whereas C and D are not. Therefore, expanding the above expression,

$$P[(A \cup B) \cap (C \cup D)] = [P(A) + P(B)] \times [P(C) + P(D) - P(C \cap D)]$$

Now,

$$\begin{aligned} P(A) &= \tfrac{4}{52} = \tfrac{1}{13} \\ P(B) &= \tfrac{4}{52} = \tfrac{1}{13} \\ P(C) &= \tfrac{26}{52} = \tfrac{1}{2} \\ P(D) &= \tfrac{12}{52} = \tfrac{3}{13}, \text{ and} \\ P(C \cap D) &= P(C)P(D) = (\tfrac{1}{2})(\tfrac{3}{13}) = \tfrac{3}{26} \end{aligned}$$

Hence, the result is

$$[\tfrac{1}{13} + \tfrac{1}{13}][\tfrac{1}{2} + \tfrac{3}{13} - \tfrac{3}{26}] = (\tfrac{2}{13})(\tfrac{8}{13}) = \tfrac{16}{169} = .095$$

methods of counting

Since the classical definition of probability rests on the principle of taking the ratio of the number of elementary events in A divided by the number of elementary events in S, it is necessary to be able to assess the number of outcomes in a complex event in some manner other than enumerating each of them. Determining how many different basketball teams can be put on the court if you have ten players each of whom can play any position is very tedious if one has to write out all 252 five-man teams. Therefore, some counting methods are required to facilitate this task.

PERMUTATIONS

A **permutation** of a set of objects or events is an ordered sequence. The number of ordered sequences of r objects which can be selected from n objects is symbolized by

$${}_nP_r$$

which is read "the permutations of n things taken r at a time."

If one has four objects, A, B, C, and D, then $ABCD$, $ACBD$, $ADBC$, $ADCB$ are some of the 24 possible permutations of the four objects taken four at a time. If these four objects were taken two at a time, then AB, BA, AC, CA, AD, DA,

BC, CB, etc., are some of the 12 permutations of four objects taken two at a time. Note that the definition states "ordered sequences." That means that AB and BA are two different permutations, i.e., order makes a difference.

The number of permutations of n things taken r at a time, ${}_nP_r$, equals

$${}_nP_r = \frac{n!}{(n-r)!}$$

This expression involves the symbol $n!$, read "n factorial" which is defined as

$$n! = n(n-1)(n-2)(n-3)\ldots(1)$$

Thus, $5! = (5)(4)(3)(2)(1) = 120$. Further $0! = 1$.

If in the expression for the number of permutations, $r = n$, the number of permutations of n things (taken n at a time) equals

$${}_nP_n = \frac{n!}{(n-n)!} = \frac{n!}{0!} = n!$$

Let us examine the logic behind these expressions.

Suppose one has five objects, A, B, C, D, and E. Consider first the number of permutations of these five objects taken five at a time, i.e., ${}_nP_n = {}_5P_5$. Think of the task as having to fill five positions. There are five possible objects with which to fill the first position. For every one of those five selections, the second position may be filled with any one of the four remaining objects, since an ordered sequence does not permit selecting with replacement. This means that there are $(5)(4) = 20$ ways of filling the first two positions. Note that one multiplies because *for every one* of the first five possibilities, there exists four ways to fill the second. The third position may be filled with any one of the three remaining objects, there are two ways to fill the fourth, and only one object (or way) remains for the last position. Therefore, the total number of ordered sequences or permutations of five things is

$$(5)(4)(3)(2)(1) = 5! = 120$$

There are 5! ways of ordering five objects. In general, there are $n!$ permutations of n things (taken n at a time),

$${}_nP_n = n!$$

Now consider the number of permutations of five things taken only three at a time, i.e., ${}_nP_r = {}_5P_3$. There are five ways to fill the first position, four ways to fill the second position, and three ways to fill the third position and that is all. Thus one multiplies

$${}_nP_r = n(n-1)(n-2)\ldots(n-r+1) = (5)(4)(3) = 60$$

However, mathematically the same result is arrived at by dividing $n!$ by $(n - r)!$:

$$_nP_r = \frac{n!}{(n-r)!} = \frac{(5)(4)(3)\cancel{(2)}\cancel{(1)}}{\cancel{(2)}\cancel{(1)}} = (5)(4)(3) = 60$$

Thus, the expression for the number of permutations of n things taken r at a time is

$$_nP_r = n(n-1)(n-2)\ldots(n-r+1) = \frac{n!}{(n-r)!}$$

This formula is consistent with the previously discussed case of $n!$ permutations of n things taken n at a time ($r = n$):

$$_nP_r = {}_nP_n = \frac{n!}{(n-n)!} = \frac{n!}{(0)!} = \frac{n!}{1} = n!$$

(Note: Remember $0! = 1$.)

example What is the probability of picking first, second, and third in a race involving seven horses? There is only one way to pick the three horses and assign them to the proper places (event A) but there are $_7P_3$ ways of ordering three of seven horses (S). The required probability is

$$P(A) = \frac{\#(A)}{\#(S)} = \frac{1}{_7P_3} = \frac{1}{\frac{7!}{(7-3)!}} = \frac{1}{\frac{(7)(6)(5)\cancel{(4)}\cancel{(3)}\cancel{(2)}\cancel{(1)}}{\cancel{(4)}\cancel{(3)}\cancel{(2)}\cancel{(1)}}} = \frac{1}{(7)(6)(5)} = \frac{1}{210}$$

$$P(A) = .0048$$

Therefore, if there was a crowd of 10,000 people, none of whom had any information on the horses and all of whom guessed randomly, on the average 48 people would pick the first three horses to finish in order.

COMBINATIONS[3]

A **combination** is any set of objects or events regardless of their internal order. The number of groups of r objects that can be selected from n objects is symbolized by $_nC_r$ and given by

$$_nC_r = \frac{n!}{(n-r)!r!}$$

When the number of combinations of n things taken n at a time is desired, only one combination exists. Note also that while AB and BA are two different *permutations* of A and B, they are the *same combination;* permutations are

[3] This text uses the symbol $_nC_r$ for the number of combinations of n things taken r at a time, while some other books use $\binom{n}{r}$.

ordered sequences while combinations are subsets and are not considered with regard to the order of their elements. Consider the logic of determining ${}_nC_r$.

Recall that the number of permutations of n objects taken r at a time is

$$_nP_r = \frac{n!}{(n - r)!}$$

Thus, if $n = 5$ and $r = 3$,

$$_5P_3 = \frac{5!}{2!} = 60$$

The number of combinations, however, is much less than 60, because many of the permutations are just reorderings of a single combination. Table 12–3 presents the 60 permutations of five things taken three at a time, but they are arranged into groups corresponding to the ten combinations. It can be seen that there are six permutations for every combination of five things taken three at a time. In general, if objects are to be taken r at a time there will be $r!$ permutations for every combination. Thus, since there are three elements in each group, there are $3! = (3)(2)(1) = 6$ permutations for each combination as indicated by the groupings of six in Table 12–3. Just as one divides the number of inches by 12 in order to obtain length in feet, one divides the number of permutations by $r!$ in order to obtain the number of combinations since there are $r!$ permutations for every combination. Therefore, the expression for combinations is

$$_nC_r = \frac{_nP_r}{r!} = \frac{\dfrac{n!}{(n - r)!}}{r!} = \frac{n!}{(n - r)!r!}$$

12–3 The Sixty Permutations and Ten Combinations (Underlined) of Five Things Taken Three at a Time.

ABC	*ABD*	*ABE*	*ACD*	*ACE*
ACB	*ADB*	*AEB*	*ADC*	*AEC*
BCA	*BAD*	*BAE*	*CAD*	*CAE*
BAC	*BDA*	*BEA*	*CDA*	*CEA*
CAB	*DAB*	*EAB*	*DAC*	*EAC*
CBA	*DBA*	*EBA*	*DCA*	*ECA*
ADE	*BCD*	*BCE*	*BDE*	*CDE*
AED	*BDC*	*BEC*	*BED*	*CED*
DAE	*CBD*	*CBE*	*DBE*	*DCE*
DEA	*CDB*	*CEB*	*DEB*	*DEC*
EAD	*DBC*	*EBC*	*EBD*	*ECD*
EDA	*DCB*	*ECB*	*EDB*	*EDC*

example A football coach has seven guards on his team. If it does not make any difference who plays the right or the left position, how many different pairs of guards can he field? Since order is unimportant, this amounts to asking how many combinations of seven things taken two at a time are there?

$$_7C_2 = \frac{7!}{5!2!} = \frac{(7)(6)(5)(4)(3)(2)(1)}{(5)(4)(3)(2)(1)(2)(1)} = 21$$

example What is the probability of being dealt a poker hand (five cards) containing all spades? If A is the event of being dealt all spades, one must get any of the many combinations of 13 cards in that suit taken five at a time. The sample space S includes the number of five-card hands in a deck of 52 cards. The required probability is

$$P(A) = \frac{_{13}C_5}{_{52}C_5} = \frac{\frac{13!}{8!5!}}{\frac{52!}{47!5!}} = \frac{(13)(12)(11)(10)(9)}{(52)(51)(50)(49)(48)}$$

$$P(A) = .0005$$

EXERCISES

1. Determine which of the following events are mutually exclusive:
   (a) flipping a head, flipping a tail with one toss of a fair coin.
   (b) rolling a three or greater, rolling an even number with a die.
   (c) drawing a red card, drawing an ace.
2. Determine which of the following events are independent:
   (a) flipping a head on the first toss and a tail on the second toss of a coin.
   (b) selecting an ace and then selecting a king when drawing is done with replacement. When drawing is done without replacement.
   (c) having a boy as a first child and having a girl as a second.
3. What is the relationship between conditional probability and independence?
4. Determine the following probabilities:
   (a) In a deck of 12 cards (4 jacks, 4 queens, 4 kings), what is the probability of drawing a jack or a queen? A red card or a jack?
   (b) What is the probability of obtaining either (1) at least three, or, (2) less than two in a single roll of a die? At least three or an even number in a single roll of a die?
   (c) What is the probability of rolling two successive 6's with a die?
   (d) If an urn contains three red and four green balls, what is the probability of selecting a green ball given that a red ball has been drawn on the first selection

and not replaced? And replaced? If drawing is without replacement, what is the probability of selecting two successive green balls? a red and then a green ball?

5. Determine the following permutations:
   (a) ${}_5P_5$ (b) ${}_4P_2$ (c) ${}_6P_4$

6. If a room has 8 chairs, how many different seating arrangements are there if 10 people come in?

7. Determine the following combinations:
   (a) ${}_4C_4$ (b) ${}_5C_2$ and ${}_5C_3$ (c) ${}_7C_3$

8. How many different relay teams of four men could a coach put together if he had seven swimmers to choose from? If the order of swimming made a difference, then how many could he put together?

9. What is the probability of being dealt a five-card hand with all clubs? Of one suit?

10. What is the probability of naming the three top horses (regardless of specific position) in a field of 8? What is the probability of correctly designating first, second, and third positions from the field of 8? Given that you have picked the top three horses, what is the probability of correctly assigning them to the first three positions?

advanced probability problems

basketball teams If a basketball coach has six guards, five forwards, and two centers, how many different teams could be composed? (A basketball team has two guards, two forwards, and a center.) The coach must pick two of six guards (${}_6C_2$), two of five forwards (${}_5C_2$), **and** one of two centers (${}_2C_1$):

$$({}_6C_2)({}_5C_2)({}_2C_1) = \frac{6!}{4!2!} \times \frac{5!}{3!2!} \times \frac{2!}{1!1!} = 300 \text{ teams}$$

poker hands What is the probability of getting the royal flush (ten, jack, queen, king, ace of spades) in poker? Since order is irrelevant, there are ${}_{52}C_5 = 2{,}598{,}960$ hands in poker. There is only one combination which will provide the 10, J, Q, K, A of spades, or ${}_5C_5 = 1$, therefore,

$$P(A) = \frac{{}_5C_5}{{}_{52}C_5} = \frac{1}{2{,}598{,}960} = .00000038$$

What is the probability of getting the royal flush, 10, J, Q, K, A in any suit? If ${}_5C_5 = 1$ is the number of ways of obtaining this flush in spades, then if the required event can be obtained with any one of the four suits, the number of ways must be $({}_5C_5)({}_4C_1)$ and the probability is

$$P(A) = \frac{({}_5C_5)({}_4C_1)}{{}_{52}C_5} = \frac{(1)(4)}{2{,}598{,}960} = \frac{4}{2{,}598{,}960} = .0000015$$

What is the probability of getting four of a kind in poker? There are three requirements for this to happen. One needs to get all four cards at a given face value $({}_4C_4)$ **and** the four of a kind could be at any of the 13 face values $({}_{13}C_1)$ **and** the fifth card of the hand could be any one of the 48 that were not already drawn $({}_{48}C_1)$. Thus

$$P\text{ (four of a kind)} = \frac{({}_4C_4)({}_{13}C_1)({}_{48}C_1)}{{}_{52}C_5} = \frac{624}{2{,}598{,}960} = .00024$$

no duplication If an elevator starts with four people in it in a building with six floors, what is the probability that no two people leave the elevator at the same stop? If each individual is to get off on a separate floor, then some combination of four of the six floors must be selected, ${}_6C_4$. If duplication *were* allowed, then each of the four people has six floors to choose from for a total of $(6)(6)(6)(6) = (6)^4$ possible arrangements of people and floors. Therefore, the probability is

$$P(A) = \frac{{}_6C_4}{(6)^4} = \frac{15}{1296} = .012$$

birthday problem The same type of problem as described above has become rather famous in a different form.[4] What is the probability that in a group of 23 people there will be at least two people with the same birthday disregarding the year of birth? This can be worked best by subtracting the probability of no duplication from 1.00. First assume that birthdays are randomly distributed during the year and that the year has 365 days, two assumptions which while not quite true do permit an approximate solution. Now, 23 people must each have a different birthday which event can occur in ${}_{365}C_{23}$ ways. If duplication *is* allowed, each person has the possibility of having a birthday on any of the 365 days, which for a group of 23 people results in $(365)(365)\ldots = (365)^{23}$ different possible distributions of birthdays and people. The resulting probability of no duplication is

$$P(A) = \frac{{}_{365}C_{23}}{(365)^{23}} = .50 \text{ (approximately)}$$

Therefore, the probability of finding some sort of duplication of birthdays in a group of 23 people is (1.00 − .50) or about 50–50, a fairly astounding result. The probability of a duplication of birthdays in a group of 10 people is approxi-

[4] See W. Feller, *An Introduction to Probability Theory and Its Application* (New York: Wiley, 1962).

mately .12 and in a group of 30 it is .71. Therefore, it is an even bet that in a group of 23 or more, there is at least some duplication of birthdays. Since most people attach a much lower probability to these events than is appropriate, this problem illustrates how poorly we subjectively estimate the probabilities of complex events.

binomial probability In six tosses of a coin, what is the probability of obtaining exactly two heads? It is important to notice that the question does not specify the order in which the heads and tails must appear. It only requires that exactly two of the six tosses be heads. Therefore, the solution to this problem may be achieved by first ascertaining the probability of any single sequence of two heads and four tails and then determining how many such sequences are possible.

One potential sequence is (H, H, T, T, T, T). The probability of a head on any single flip is $\frac{1}{2}$ and the probability of a tail is also $\frac{1}{2}$. The probability of getting two heads in succession is $(\frac{1}{2})(\frac{1}{2})$, of two heads followed by a tail is $(\frac{1}{2})(\frac{1}{2})(\frac{1}{2})$, and of (H, H, T, T, T, T) is $(\frac{1}{2})(\frac{1}{2})(\frac{1}{2})(\frac{1}{2})(\frac{1}{2})(\frac{1}{2}) = \frac{1}{64}$.

Further, the probability of the sequence (T, T, T, H, H, T) is also

$$(\tfrac{1}{2})(\tfrac{1}{2})(\tfrac{1}{2})(\tfrac{1}{2})(\tfrac{1}{2})(\tfrac{1}{2}) = \tfrac{1}{64}$$

and the probability of any particular sequence of two heads and four tails is $\frac{1}{64}$.

How many such sequences of two heads and four tails are there? It happens that the number of sequences of two heads in six tosses is the same as the number of combinations of six things taken two at a time:

$${}_6C_2 = \frac{6!}{2!(6-2)!} = 15$$

Therefore, since the event of two heads in six flips can occur in 15 different ways each with a probability of $\frac{1}{64}$, the required answer is given by the sum of these 15 probabilities (since they are mutually exclusive) or

$$\tfrac{1}{64} + \tfrac{1}{64} + \cdots + \tfrac{1}{64} = 15(\tfrac{1}{64}) = \tfrac{15}{64}$$

This problem is an example of **binomial probability,** and the process of finding its solution may be formalized into a general expression.

> In a sequence of n independent trials that have only two outcomes (arbitrarily call them "success" and "failure") with the probability p of a success and probability q of a failure (note that $q = 1 - p$) the probability of r successes in n trials is
>
> $${}_nC_r p^r q^{n-r}$$
>
> or
>
> $$\frac{n!}{r!(n-r)!} p^r q^{n-r}$$

To illustrate further, suppose an urn contained one red and three green balls. If the ball is returned to the urn after each drawing, what is the probability of selecting three reds in five tries? A "success" is defined as the selection of a red ball. Since on any one trial there is only one of four red balls in the urn, the probability of a success is one-fourth ($p = \frac{1}{4}$). Since $q = 1 - p$ and since three of the four balls available on any one trial are "failures", $q = \frac{3}{4}$. The required event is to obtain three red balls ($r = 3$) in five draws ($n = 5$). Therefore, the desired probability is

$$\frac{n!}{r!(n-r)!} p^r q^{n-r}$$

$$\frac{5!}{3!(5-3)!} \left(\frac{1}{4}\right)^3 \left(\frac{3}{4}\right)^{5-3} = \frac{90}{1024} = .088$$

FORMULAS

1. Classical probability:

a. $P(A) = \dfrac{\#(A)}{\#(S)}$

b. $P(\emptyset) = \dfrac{\#(\emptyset)}{\#(S)} = \dfrac{0}{\#(S)} = 0$

c. $P(S) = \dfrac{\#(S)}{\#(S)} = 1.00$

2. Probability of an intersection:

a. $P(A \cap B) = P(A)P(B \mid A)$

b. If A and B are independent (i.e., $P(B \mid A) = P(B)$), then $P(A \cap B) = P(A)P(B)$.

3. Conditional probability:

$$P(B \mid A) = \frac{P(A \cap B)}{P(A)}$$

4. Probability of a union:

a. $P(A \cup B) = P(A) + P(B) - P(A \cap B)$

b. If A and B are mutually exclusive (i.e., $A \cap B = \emptyset$), then $P(A \cup B) = P(A) + P(B)$.

5. Permutations:

a. ${}_nP_r = \dfrac{n!}{(n-r)!}$

b. ${}_nP_n = n!$

6. Combinations:

$$_nC_r = \frac{n!}{(n-r)!r!}$$

7. Binomial probability, the probability of *r* successes in *n* trials:

$$P(r, n, p) = \frac{n!}{(n-r)!r!} p^r q^{n-r}$$

in which p = the probability of a success,
q = the probability of a failure, and
$p + q = 1$

EXERCISES

1. If drawing is done without replacement, what is the probability of getting an ace and *then* a king in two successive draws from a deck of 52 cards? Of just getting an ace and a king in two draws?
2. If there is room for a captain and two co-pilots on a space mission and four captains and eight co-pilots are available, how many different crews could be sent?
3. What is the probability of getting a five-card poker hand with two aces and three kings in it? With a straight flush in it (five consecutive cards of the same suit, e.g., 3, 4, 5, 6, and 7 of diamonds)?
4. If five people enter a room with seven chairs and each person mentally picks out a chair to sit in, what is the probability that no two people select the same seat?
5. In an urn containing four yellow and seven blue balls, what is the probability of drawing a yellow and a blue ball if drawing is without replacement? Of drawing three yellow and a blue?
6. What is the probability of obtaining four heads in seven flips of a coin? At least five heads? At most, six heads?

appendix I

appendix I

review of basic mathematics

Almost invariably a class of students in statistics contains students whose mathematical background varies from a knowledge of high school algebra to a knowledge of differential equations. This broad range of ability makes it difficult to begin a course in statistics unless some common level of mathematical experience can be assumed. The following section contains a review of several basic mathematical concepts and operations including symbols, fractions, factorials, exponents, factoring, and square roots. Since this is meant to be a review, some students will not need to spend much time on this section while others would profit from a fairly serious study of this material.[1] It would be best for students to check themselves by working the exercises at the end of the section.

SYMBOLS

The study of mathematics is greatly facilitated by the use of symbols. However, some students feel that their basic problem with mathematical material is precisely the symbolism. Actually, this problem probably occurs because the students do not take time to learn what the symbols mean. It will be helpful if the reader does not proceed until he can readily interpret all the symbols presented to that point.

Most symbols will be introduced as they arise in the text. However, in addition to the signs of equality ($=$) and inequality ($\neq$) and those signs for the four basic mathematical operations ($+$, $-$, $\times$ and $\div$), the student should be intimately familiar with signs denoting inequalities. The symbol

$$>$$

means "is greater than." The expression

$$5 > 3$$

is read "5 is greater than 3" and

$$a > b$$

[1] Those students needing a more thorough review of the concepts presented in this section and additional material relevant to this text are referred to Helen Walker, *Mathematics Essential for Statistics* (New York: Holt, Rinehart and Winston, 1951).

F. Ayers, Jr., *Schaum's Outline of Theory and Problems of First Year College Mathematics* (New York: Schaum, 1958).

is read "a is greater than b." Conversely, the symbol

$$<$$

means "is less than." The expression

$$3 < 5$$

is read "3 is less than 5" and

$$b < a$$

is read "b is less than a." Some students remember the difference between these two symbols by recalling that the wide or open end of the symbol (as opposed to the vertex) is always next to the larger quantity.

Sometimes an expression of the following type will be encountered:

$$-1.96 < t < 1.96$$

This statement means that t is greater than -1.96 but less than 1.96. More simply, t lies between -1.96 and 1.96. If one wants to state the opposite fact, namely that t falls outside this interval of -1.96 to 1.96, one customarily writes

$$t < -1.96 \text{ or } t > 1.96$$

Occasionally, it is desirable to write that some quantity is "greater than or equal to" some other quantity. This fact can be written with the symbol

$$\geq$$

To show that z assumes values of 2.56 or greater, write

$$z \geq 2.56$$

Similarly, the symbol

$$\leq$$

means "less than or equal to," and if z were less than or equal to zero one could write

$$z \leq 0$$

FRACTIONS

addition and subtraction In order for one to add fractional quantities, the denominators of the two fractions must be equal. Thus, to add $\frac{1}{2}$ and $\frac{1}{3}$ it is necessary to change both fractions to sixths by multiplying the first by $\frac{3}{3}$ and the second by $\frac{2}{2}$:

$$\tfrac{1}{2} + \tfrac{1}{3} = ?$$

$$\tfrac{1}{2}\left(\tfrac{3}{3}\right) + \tfrac{1}{3}\left(\tfrac{2}{2}\right) = \tfrac{3}{6} + \tfrac{2}{6} = \tfrac{5}{6}$$

More generally, to add $\frac{a}{b} + \frac{c}{d}$,

$$\frac{a}{b} + \frac{c}{d} = \frac{a}{b}\left(\frac{d}{d}\right) + \frac{c}{d}\left(\frac{b}{b}\right) = \frac{ad}{bd} + \frac{cb}{bd} = \frac{ad + cb}{bd}$$

multiplication The product of two fractions equals the product of the two numerators divided by the product of the two denominators. To multiply $\frac{1}{2}$ times $\frac{3}{5}$, one proceeds as follows:

$$\frac{1}{2} \cdot \frac{3}{5} = \frac{(1)(3)}{(2)(5)} = \frac{3}{10}$$

In general, multiply $\frac{a}{b}$ times $\frac{c}{d}$, as follows:

$$\frac{a}{b} \cdot \frac{c}{d} = \frac{ac}{bd}$$

Frequently, if large numbers are involved or if long strings of fractions are to be multiplied, some of the terms in the numerator may be cancelled by terms in the denominator. This amounts to dividing the numerator and denominator by the same number. The following example shows how cancellation can simplify the multiplication of fractions.

$$\frac{1}{\cancel{2}} \cdot \frac{\cancel{3}}{\cancel{8}_{\cancel{2}}} \cdot \frac{\cancel{4}}{\cancel{9}_{\cancel{3}}} \cdot \frac{\overset{\overset{3}{\cancel{9}}}{\cancel{18}}}{19} = \frac{3}{2(19)} = \frac{3}{38}$$

division To divide one fraction by another, invert the divisor and multiply. Divide $\frac{1}{2}$ by $\frac{1}{3}$:

$$\tfrac{1}{2} \div \tfrac{1}{3} = \tfrac{1}{2} \cdot \tfrac{3}{1} = \tfrac{3}{2} = 1.5$$

In general,

$$\frac{a}{b} \div \frac{c}{d} = \frac{a}{b} \cdot \frac{d}{c} = \frac{ad}{bc}$$

Remember also that

$$\frac{0}{n} = 0$$

and that

$$\frac{n}{0} = \text{undefined}$$

FACTORIALS

In some probability problems (Chapter 12) it is necessary to multiply a positive integer by each of the integers having a value less than that integer ending with 1. This string of multiplications of integers is called a *factorial* and the sign "!" following the largest integer in the string is used to indicate this operation. For example, 3!, read "three factorial," would equal

$$3! = 3 \cdot 2 \cdot 1 = 6$$

In general, $n!$ means

$$n! = n(n-1)(n-2)(n-3)\cdots(1)$$

Note also by convention that

$$0! = 1$$

EXPONENTS

An exponent is a number written as a superscript to a base number which signifies that the base number should be multiplied by itself as many times as indicated by the exponent. Therefore,

$$2^3 = 2 \cdot 2 \cdot 2 = 8$$

and more generally

$$n^r = \underbrace{n \cdot n \cdot n \cdots n}_{r \text{ times}}$$

Note also that

$$n^1 = n$$

and

$$n^0 = 1$$

addition and subtraction Generally, numbers with exponents cannot be added or subtracted without first multiplying as directed by the exponent. This is true even if the numbers have the same base. For example, $2^2 + 2^3$ is handled by performing the indicated multiplication and then adding:

$$2^2 + 2^3 = 2 \cdot 2 + 2 \cdot 2 \cdot 2 = 4 + 8 = 12$$

multiplication The product of two exponential quantities with the *same base number* is that base number raised to the sum of the two exponents. For example,

$$(2^2)(2^3) = 2^{2+3} = 2^5$$

because

$$(2^2)(2^3) = (2 \cdot 2)(2 \cdot 2 \cdot 2) = 2^5$$

More generally,

$$(n^r)(n^s) = n^{r+s}$$

If the exponents *do not have the same base number* (e.g., $2^4 \times 3^4$), this procedure does not apply and the multiplication should be carried out first.

division The quotient of two exponential quantities with the same base number is that base raised to the difference between the exponent of the numerator and that of the denominator. For example,

$$\frac{2^3}{2^2} = 2^{3-2} = 2^1 = 2$$

More generally,

$$\frac{n^r}{n^s} = n^{r-s}$$

It is helpful to remember in this context that in the expression n^r/n^s, if s is larger than r, then the result has a negative exponent. Negative exponents mean that a reciprocal $\left(\frac{1}{\text{number}}\right)$ is taken before the multiplication is carried out. For example,

$$\frac{2^4}{2^7} = 2^{4-7} = 2^{-3} = \frac{1}{2^3} = \frac{1}{2 \cdot 2 \cdot 2} = \frac{1}{8}$$

fractions A fraction raised to a power equals the ratio of the numerator raised to that power divided by the denominator raised to that power. For example,

$$\left(\frac{3}{5}\right)^2 = \frac{3^2}{5^2} = \frac{9}{25}$$

More generally,

$$\left(\frac{r}{s}\right)^n = \frac{r^n}{s^n}$$

binomial exponentiation Many of the algebraic manipulations presented in this text require the student to understand the squaring of a binomial. For the quantity $(a + b)^2$,

$$(a + b)^2 = a^2 + 2ab + b^2$$

This result is obtained by taking the square of the first term in the binomial (e.g., a^2), plus 2 times the product of the two terms in the binomial ($2ab$), plus the square of the second term (b^2). A more common problem is to expand $(a - b)^2$. This is accomplished in the same way but with attention to the signs:

$$(a - b)^2 = a^2 + 2a(-b) + (-b)^2 = a^2 - 2ab + b^2$$

Again, the result equals the square of the first term, plus 2 times the product of the two terms [e.g., $2(a)(-b) = -2ab$], plus the square of the last term [$(-b)^2 = b^2$]. The student must remember that these procedures apply to any binomial regardless of the specific terms. This text will use the symbol X and $\overline{X}$ to refer to quantities which will be defined later, and quite frequently it will be necessary to expand $(X - \overline{X})^2$. The result is generated just as in the examples above:

$$(X - \overline{X})^2 = X^2 - 2X\overline{X} + \overline{X}^2$$

FACTORING AND SIMPLIFICATION

Factoring an algebraic expression implies the following type of manipulation:

$$ax + ay = a(x + y)$$

Factoring is often used to simplify algebraic expressions. Consider the following example:

$$\frac{-a(b - c) - (c - ab)}{a - 1}$$

Carrying out the appropriate multiplications in the numerator, one obtains

$$\frac{-ab - a(-c) - (c - ab)}{a - 1}$$

and simplifying the signs of certain expressions, one obtains

$$\frac{-ab + ac - c + ab}{a - 1}$$

By subtracting,

$$\frac{ac - c}{a - 1}$$

factoring,

$$\frac{c(a - 1)}{a - 1}$$

and dividing, one finds the expression reduces to

$$c$$

Sometimes in the course of simplifying an expression it helps to divide each term in the numerator by the denominator:

$$\frac{a - b}{c} = \frac{a}{c} - \frac{b}{c}$$

However, the student must discriminate. The above manipulation is correct but the following manipulations are *incorrect*.

$$\frac{c}{a - b} \neq \frac{c}{a} - \frac{c}{b}$$

$$\frac{a - b}{c - d} \neq \frac{a}{c} - \frac{b}{d}$$

ROOTS

double roots It must be remembered that technically the square root of a^2 is $\pm a$ since both $(a)^2$ and $(-a)^2$ equal a^2. Ordinarily, just the positive root is accepted as the answer, but there will be occasions in which it is necessary to remember that two roots do exist.

(5) Test of the difference between two correlated means. *Hypotheses.* $H_0{:}\mu_1 = \mu_2$. $H_1{:}\mu_1 \neq \mu_2$. *Assumptions.* The data are in the form of pairs of scores which were randomly sampled and the population of the D_i is normally distributed. *Decision rules.* Given .05 level, $df = N - 1 = 7$, two-tailed test. If $-2.365 < t_{\text{obs}} < 2.365$, accept H_0. If $t_{\text{obs}} \leq -2.365$ or $t_{\text{obs}} \geq 2.365$, reject H_0. *Computation.*

$$t_{\text{obs}} = \frac{\sum D}{\sqrt{(N\sum D^2 - (\sum D)^2)/(N-1)}} = \frac{18}{\sqrt{(8(100) - (18)^2)/7}} = 2.46$$

Interpretation. Reject H_0, the observed difference between means is too large to be due to sampling error. The infants looked at the corners more than at the sides. **(6)** Test for homogeneity of variance. *Hypotheses.* $H_0{:}\sigma_1^2 = \sigma_2^2$. $H_1{:}\sigma_1^2 \neq \sigma_2^2$. *Assumptions.* The population distributions of the two groups are normal, the sample variances are independent, and random sampling was used. *Decision rules.* Given .10 level, $df = N_1 - 1 = 11$ and $N_2 - 1 = 11$. If $F_{\text{obs}} > 2.82$, accept H_0. If $F_{\text{obs}} \geq 2.82$, reject H_0. *Computation.* $F_{\text{obs}} = s^2_{\text{largest}}/s^2_{\text{smallest}} = 75.90/1.84 = 41.25$. Reject H_0, and use independent groups, heterogeneous variance t test between means. Test of difference between means (independent groups, heterogeneous variances). *Hypotheses:* $H_0{:}\mu_1 = \mu_2$. $H_1{:}\mu_1 \neq \mu_2$. *Assumptions.* The two groups are independent and they are drawn from normal populations with heterogeneous variances. *Decision rules.* Given .05 level, $df = N_1 - 1 = 11$ and $N_2 - 1 = 11$, two-tailed test.

$$t_{\text{crit}} = \frac{s_{\bar{x}_1}^{\,2} t_1 + s_{\bar{x}_2}^{\,2} t_2}{s_{\bar{x}_1}^{\,2} + s_{\bar{x}_2}^{\,2}} = \frac{6.33(2.201) + .15(2.201)}{6.33 + .15}$$

$t_{\text{crit}} = 2.20$. If $-2.20 < t_{\text{obs}} < 2.20$, accept H_0. If $t_{\text{obs}} \leq -2.20$ or $t_{\text{obs}} \geq 2.20$, reject H_0. *Computation.*

$$t_{\text{obs}} = \frac{\bar{X}_1 - \bar{X}_2}{\sqrt{s_1^2/N_1 + s_2^2/N_2}} = \frac{24.42 - 12.25}{\sqrt{75.90/12 + 1.84/12}} = 4.77$$

Interpretation. Reject H_0, the difference in observed means is too great to be simply a function of sampling error. There is a difference between the two therapeutic approaches. **(7)** Verify that the following set of numbers satisfies the conditions of this problem.

A	*B*
2	1
4	3
6	5
8	7
10	9
12	11
14	13
16	15

(8) *Hypotheses.* $H_0{:}\rho = 0$. $H_1{:}\rho \neq 0$. *Assumptions.* The population distributions of the two variables are normal and sampling is random. *Decision rules.* Given .05, $df = N - 2 = 6$, two-tailed test. If $-.7067 < r_{\text{obs}} < .7067$, accept H_0. If $r_{\text{obs}} \leq -.7067$ or $r_{\text{obs}} \geq .7067$, reject H_0. Values obtained from Table D. *Computation.* $r_{\text{obs}} = .85$. *Interpretation.* Reject H_0, the observed correlation is too large to be simply a function of sampling error. **(9)** *Hypotheses.* $H_0{:}\rho_1 = \rho_2$. $H_1{:}\rho_1 > \rho_2$. *Assumptions.* The r's are computed on randomly and independently selected samples, the population distributions of X and Y for each correlation are normal, and N_1 and N_2 are both greater than 20. *Decision rules.* Given .05, one-tailed test. If $z_{\text{obs}} < 1.645$, accept H_0. If $z_{\text{obs}} \geq 1.645$, reject H_0. *Computation.*

$$z_{\text{obs}} = \frac{z_{r_1} - z_{r_2}}{\sqrt{1/(N_1 - 3) + 1/(N_2 - 3)}} = \frac{1.333 - .590}{\sqrt{1/(38 - 3) + 1/(27 - 3)}} = 2.80$$

Interpretation. Reject H_0, the difference between the correlations is too large to be a simple function of sampling error. The correlation between the IQs of identical twins is higher than between the IQs of fraternal twins. **(10a)** t test for correlated groups. Teacher A. $H_0{:}\mu_1 = \mu_2$. $H_1{:}\mu_1 \neq \mu_2$. Given .05 level, $df = N - 1 = 7$, two-tailed test. If $-2.365 < t_{\text{obs}} < 2.365$, accept H_0. If $t_{\text{obs}} \leq 2.365$ or $t_{\text{obs}} \geq 2.365$, reject H_0. $t_{\text{obs}} = 2.37$. Reject H_0, the children improved. Teacher B. $H_0{:}\mu_1 = \mu_2$. $H_1{:}\mu_1 \neq \mu_2$. Given .05 level, $df = N - 1 = 9$, two-tailed test. If $-2.262 < t_{\text{obs}} < 2.262$, accept H_0. If $t_{\text{obs}} \leq -2.262$ or $t_{\text{obs}} \geq 2.262$, reject H_0. $t_{\text{obs}} = 4.51$. Reject H_0, the children improved. **(10b)** F test for homogeneity of variance. $H_0{:}\sigma_1{}^2 = \sigma_2{}^2$. $H_1{:}\sigma_1{}^2 \neq \sigma_2{}^2$. Given .10 level, $df = 7, 9$. If $F_{\text{obs}} < 3.29$, accept H_0. If $F_{\text{obs}} \geq 3.29$, reject H_0. $F_{\text{obs}} = 5.85$. Reject H_0, the variances are heterogeneous. t test for independent groups, heterogeneous variances. $H_0{:}\mu_1 = \mu_2$. $H_1{:}\mu_1 \neq \mu_2$. $t_{\text{crit}} = 2.35$. If $-2.35 < t_{\text{obs}} < 2.35$, accept H_0. If $t_{\text{obs}} \leq -2.35$ or $t_{\text{obs}} \geq 2.35$, reject H_0. $t_{\text{obs}} = .66$. Accept H_0, the observed difference between teachers is within the realm of sampling error. **(10c)** Teacher A. $H_0{:}\rho_1 = 0$. $H_1{:}\rho_1 \neq 0$. Given .05 level, $df = 6$, two-tailed test. If $-.7067 < r_{\text{obs}} < .7067$, accept H_0. If $r_{\text{obs}} \leq -.7067$ or $r_{\text{obs}} \geq .7067$, reject H_0. $r_{\text{obs}} = .13$. Accept H_0, the observed correlation could have occurred by sampling error. Teacher B. $H_0{:}\rho_2 = 0$. $H_1{:}\rho_2 \neq 0$. Given .05 level, $df = 8$, two-tailed test. If $-.6319 < r_{\text{obs}} < .6319$, accept H_0. If $r_{\text{obs}} \leq -.6319$ or $r_{\text{obs}} \geq .6319$, reject H_0. $r_{\text{obs}} = .96$. Reject H_0, the probability that $r_{\text{obs}} = .96$ could come from a population with $\rho = .00$ is too small. A correlation exists between pretest and posttest scores. Test for the difference between two r's. $H_0{:}\rho_1 = \rho_2$. $H_1{:}\rho_1 \neq \rho_2$. Given .05 level, two-tailed test. If $-1.96 < z_{\text{obs}} < 1.96$, accept H_0. If $z_{\text{obs}} \leq -1.96$ or $z_{\text{obs}} \geq 1.96$, reject H_0. $z_{\text{obs}} = -3.10$. Reject H_0, the difference between the two correlations is too large to be a function of sampling error. **(10d)** The data and analyses indicate that children in both classes improved over the period between pretest and posttest, and pupils in the two classes did not differ in the amount of this improvement. These data by themselves do not indicate that these pupils improved more than they would have under another teaching method or even without any special program of instruction. The fact that there was a correlation between pretest and posttest scores for Teacher B but not for Teacher A suggests that the classroom practices of Teacher A influence some students more than others while the teaching of B seems to promote the same relative improvement in all her pupils.

chapter 9

(1a) *Hypotheses.* $H_0{:}\mu_1 = \mu_2 = \mu_3 = \mu$. H_1: Not H_0. *Assumptions.* Homogeneity and normality of population group variances, random sampling, and independent groups. *Decision rules.* If $F_{obs} < 3.74$, accept H_0. If $F_{obs} \geq 3.74$, reject H_0. *Computation.* **pg. 244.**

$T_1 = 21$	$T_2 = 12$	$T_3 = 28$	$T_{total} = 61$
$n = 5$	$n_2 = 5$	$n_3 = 7$	$N = 17$
$\overline{X}_1 = 4.2$	$\overline{X}_2 = 2.4$	$\overline{X}_3 = 4.0$	
$\sum X_{i1}^2 = 123$	$\sum X_{i2}^2 = 50$	$\sum X_{i3}^2 = 164$	$\sum\sum X_{ij}^2 = 337$
$\dfrac{T_1^2}{n_1} = 88.2$	$\dfrac{T_2^2}{n_2} = 28.8$	$\dfrac{T_3^2}{n_3} = 112.0$	$\dfrac{\sum T_j^2}{n_j} = 229$

(I) = 218.8824 (II) = 337.0000 (III) = 229.0000

$SS_{between} = 10.1176$	$df_{between} = 2$	$MS_{between} = 5.0588$
$SS_{within} = 108.0000$	$df_{within} = 14$	$MS_{within} = 7.7143$
$SS_{total} = 118.1176$	$df_{total} = 16$	

Source	*df*	*SS*	*MS*	*F*
Between Groups	2	10.1176	5.0588	.66
Within Groups	14	108.0000	7.7143	
Total	16	118.1176		

Interpretation. Accept H_0, the observed means are similar enough so that their small differences could be attributable to sampling error. **(1b)** Adding different constants to the groups is analogous to introducing a treatment difference. Reanalyzing, MS_{within} remains the same ($MS_{within} = 7.7143$) while $MS_{between}$ reflects the introduction of mean differences ($MS_{between} = 57.4706$). $F_{obs} = 7.45$ which is greater than the critical value of 3.74 and leads to rejecting H_0. **(1c)** Adding 20 to the last score in each group will increase within-group variability ($MS_{within} = 81.9184$) but will influence between-group variability very little ($MS_{between} = 4.4538$). $F_{obs} = .05$, accept H_0.
(2) $X_{ij} = \overline{X} + (\overline{X}_j - \overline{X}) + (X_{ij} - \overline{X}_j) = 8$.
(3) See page 220 of text.

(4)

Source	*df*	*SS*	*MS*	*F*
Between Groups	2	582.5738	291.2869	14.74**
Within Groups	17	335.9762	19.7633	
Total	19	918.5500		

chapter 10

pg. 280. **(1)** See pages 248–251 of text.
(2) No, for the same reason that 2 + 3 = 5 and 1 + 4 = 5 but $\frac{2}{1} + \frac{3}{4} \neq \frac{5}{5}$. Can you apply this numerical fact to explaining why?
(3a) *Hypotheses.* Factor A. $H_0: \alpha_1 = \alpha_2 = 0$. H_1: Not H_0. Factor B. $H_0: \beta_1 = \beta_2 = 0$. H_1: Not H_0. AB Interaction. $H_0: \alpha\beta_{11} = \alpha\beta_{12} = \alpha\beta_{21} = \alpha\beta_{22} = 0$. H_1: Not H_0. *Assumptions.* The groups are independent and randomly sampled with $n > 1$ from populations having normal distributions and homogeneous variances. The factors are fixed. *Decision rules.* For all tests $df = 1, 12$, and $\alpha = .05$. If $F_{\text{obs}} < 4.75$, accept H_0. If $F_{\text{obs}} \geq 4.75$, reject H_0. *Computation.* (I) = 333.0625, (II) = 455.0000, (III) = 334.6250, (IV) = 333.6250, (V) = 338.2500.

Source	*df*	*SS*	*MS*	*F*
A	1	1.5625	1.5625	.16
B	1	.5625	.5625	.06
AB	1	3.0625	3.0625	.31
Within	12	116.7500	9.7292	
Total	15	121.9375		

Interpretation. Accept H_0 for all tests.
(3b) *Computation.* (I) = 1463.0625, (II) = 2035.0000, (III) = 1914.6250, (IV) = 1463.6250, (V) = 1918.2500.

Source	*df*	*SS*	*MS*	*F*
A	1	451.5625	451.5625	46.41**
B	1	.5625	.5625	.06
AB	1	3.0625	3.0625	.31
Within	12	116.7500	9.7292	
Total	15	571.9375		

By increasing the scores in a single level of Factor A, only the total sum of squares and SS_A are increased. **(3c)** *Computation.* (I) = 798.0625, (II) = 1215.0000, (III) = 874.6250, (IV) = 883.6250, (V) = 1098.2500.

Source	*df*	*SS*	*MS*	*F*
A	1	76.5625	76.5625	7.87*
B	1	85.5625	85.5625	8.79*
AB	1	138.0625	138.0625	14.19**
Within	12	116.7500	9.7292	
Total	15	416.9375		

By increasing the scores in a single cell, the total sum of squares increases with most of the increment given to SS_{AB}, but SS_A and SS_B also become larger. SS_{within} does not change because adding a constant to each score does not alter the variability of scores about their mean. The fact that SS_A and SS_B are increased as well as SS_{AB} is one reason why sometimes when a significant interaction exists, the presence of main effects are difficult to interpret. Discuss this issue with respect to the current problem. **(4)** See page 251 in text and previous problem. **(5)** *Computation.* (I) = 48330.3750, (II) = 49643.0000, (III) = 48422.4167, (IV) = 48331.4167, (V) = 48445.5000.

Source	*df*	*SS*	*MS*	*F*
User	1	92.0417	92.0417	1.54
Drug	1	1.0417	1.0417	<1
User × Drug	1	22.0417	22.0417	<1
Within	20	1197.5000	59.8750	
Total	23	1312.6251		

Interpretation. None of the observed F's even approached the critical value ($\alpha = .05$) of 4.35 indicating that there is no evidence that marijuana altered perceptual performance and that naive users were affected differently than regular users.
(6) *Computation.* (I) = 8400.8928, (II) = 9491.0000, (III) = 9071.2142, (IV) = 8479.7857, (V) = 9204.4286.

Source	*df*	*SS*	*MS*	*F*
User	1	670.3214	670.3214	56.14**
Drug	1	78.8929	78.8929	6.61*
User × Drug	1	54.3215	54.3215	4.55*
Within	24	286.5714	11.9405	
Total	27	1090.1072		

Proportion of variance. 60% for User, 6% for Drug, and 4% for User × Drug.

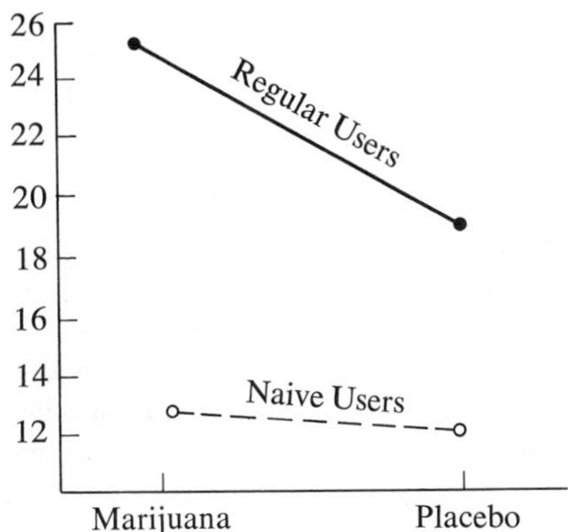

Interpretation. All F's exceeded the critical value of 4.26 and thus the three H_0 are rejected. From the graph and the fact that 60% of the variance was accounted for by differences between regular marijuana users and those naive to it, it is clear that users report better "highs" than non-users, even for the placebos (it would appear). Although the effect for marijuana verses placebo was significant, it seems that such a result is produced mainly by the regular users since the interaction is also significant. Thus, it would appear that regular users discriminate the difference between marijuana and a placebo better than non-users.

chapter 11

pg. 318. **(1)** A nonparametric test might be used if nominal or ordinal data are involved or if some of the assumptions of the parametric test (e.g., homogeneity of variance, normality) cannot be met. **(2)** Power-efficiency is the probability that the statistical test will correctly reject the null hypothesis. For a given N, parametric tests are more powerful than analogous nonparametric tests. **(3)** *Hypotheses.* Chi Square 2×2 Table. H_0: Given the observed marginals, the distributions of frequencies in the population are not different for the two sexes. H_1: These distributions are different. *Assumptions.* The groups are independent with subjects randomly and independently sampled. Each subject must qualify for one and only one category and $n > 10$. *Decision rules.* Given .05 level, $df = 1$. If $\chi_{\text{obs}}^2 < 3.84$, accept H_0. If $\chi_{\text{obs}}^2 \geq 3.84$, reject H_0. *Computation.* $\chi_{\text{obs}}^2 = 3.18$. *Interpretation.* Accept H_0. **(4)** Chi Square goodness of fit test. $\chi_{\text{obs}}^2 = 6.10$ which exceeds the critical value of $\chi_{\text{crit}}^2 = 5.99$ with $df = 2$. H_0 that there are an equal number of balls of each color is rejected. **(5)** Chi Square 2×3 Table. $\chi_{\text{obs}}^2 = 22.50$ which exceeds the critical value of 5.99 ($df = 2$). Reject H_0. Children who showed increases in IQ over age were more likely to have had mothers who held high aspirations for their children than if an IQ decrease was observed. **(6a)** Mann-Whitney U Test. *Hypotheses.* H_0: The population distributions are identical. H_1: The population distributions are not identical. *Assumptions.* The observations are randomly and independently sampled, the groups are independent, and the measurement scale is continuous with ordinal properties. *Decision rules.* Given .05 level, $n_A = 8$, $n_B = 8$. If $13 < U_{\text{obs}} < 51$, accept H_0. If $U_{\text{obs}} \leq 13$ or $U_{\text{obs}} \geq 51$, reject H_0. *Computation.* $U_{\text{obs}} = 47$. *Interpretation.* Accept H_0. For Groups A and C. *Computation.* $U_{\text{obs}} = 54.5$, reject H_0. For Groups B and C. *Computation.* $U_{\text{obs}} = 47$, accept H_0. **(6b)** Kruskal-Wallis Test for 3 Independent Samples. *Hypotheses.* H_0: The three population distributions are identical. H_1: The population distributions are not identical. *Assumptions.* Subjects are randomly and independently sampled, the groups are independent with $n_j > 5$, the measurement scale is continuous with ordinal properties. *Decision rules.* Given .05 level, $df = 2$ (Chi Square, Table F). If $H_{\text{obs}} < 5.99$, accept H_0. If $H_{\text{obs}} \geq 5.99$, reject H_0. *Computation.* $H_{\text{obs}} = 7.03$. *Interpretation.* Reject H_0. **(6c)** Exercise 6b asks whether three groups differ in the population, whereas Exercise 6a asks whether a specific pair of groups differ. They are different questions and different statistical tests must be used. The three tests on pairs are not an appropriate substitute for the test on all three groups considered simultaneously. Why? **(6d)** Wilcoxon Test. Groups A and B. *Hypotheses.* H_0: The population distributions are identical. H_1: The distributions are different. *Assumptions.* The subjects are randomly selected and ordinal measurement is available both within and between pairs of scores. *Decision rules.* Given .05 level, $N = 8$, and two-tailed test. If $W_{\text{obs}} > 3$, accept H_0. If $W_{\text{obs}} \leq 3$, reject H_0. *Computation.*

$W_{obs} = 1$. *Interpretation.* Reject H_0. For Groups A and C. $W_{obs} = 0$, reject H_0. For Groups B and C, $W_{obs} = 2$, reject H_0. **(6e)** The difference between A and B is not significant when the scores are conceived to be from independent groups but (6a) is significant when the scores are conceived to be pairs of scores from the same 8 subjects. This is possible because in (a) the groups are compared relative to the variability within groups whereas in (d) the difference between scores is compared relative to the variability of such differences. **(6f)** Pearson correlation on raw data from Groups A and C equals .76. After ranking within each group, the r and r_S both equal .71. The correlations on the ranked data are equivalent because the Spearman formula is the Pearson coefficient applied to ranked data. The correlations on the raw and ranked data differ because the data are different. **(6g)** For Groups A and C. *Hypotheses.* H_0: $\rho_S = 0$. H_1: $\rho_S \neq 0$. *Assumptions.* The sample is randomly selected and has ordinal measurement. *Decision rules.* Given .05 and two-tailed test with $N = 8$. If $-.715 < r_S < .715$, accept H_0. If $r_S \leq -.715$ or $r_S \geq .715$, reject H_0. *Computation.* $r_S = .708$. *Interpretation.* Accept H_0, but observe that the probability that such an r_S could be obtained by sampling error alone is $p < .06$. For Groups A and B. $r_S = .875$, reject H_0. For Groups B and C. $r_S = .548$, accept H_0. (7) Chi Square 2 × 3 Table. $\chi_{obs}^2 = 7.36$. $df = 2$, $\chi_{crit}^2 = 5.99$, reject H_0. If father is censored the child is more likely to remember the profane response of father. **(8)** Chi Square 2 × 2 Table. $\chi_{obs}^2 = 2.13$. $\chi_{crit}^2 = 3.84$ for .05 level with $df = 1$ and two-tailed test. Accept H_0. **(9)** Chi Square test of goodness of fit. $\chi_{obs}^2 = 5.86$. $\chi_{crit}^2 = 9.49$, $df = 4$, .05 level, two-tailed. Accept H_0. **(10)** Mann-Whitney U Test. $U_{obs} = 79$, $U_{crit} = 23$ and 76 for $n = 9, 11$, .05 level, two-tailed test. Reject H_0. **(11)** For Group A, $\overline{X} = 19.57$, $M_d = 13$; for Group B, $\overline{X} = 19.29$, $M_d = 19$. t test for the difference between independent groups, heterogeneous variances. $t_{obs} = .04$, not significant. Mann-Whitney U test. $U_{obs} = 42$. $U_{crit} = 8, 41$. Reject H_0. The means of the groups are very similar but the medians are somewhat different. Because of the distributions (e.g., $X = 62$) the median is more appropriate. The $X = 62$ elevates the mean of Group A and makes its variance quite large. The t test is not significant. When the data are ranked, the 62 does not exert such an influence and the U test is significant. The median and U test both predominantly use the ordinal characteristics of the scale. **(12)** Kruskal-Wallis Test for three independent samples. $H_{obs} = 7.78$. $H_{crit} = 5.99$. Reject H_0. **(13)** Wilcoxon Test. $W_{obs} = 4.5$. $W_{crit} = 17$ for $N = 12$, .05 level, one-tailed. Reject H_0. **(14)** $r_S = .27$. Critical value of $r_S = .504$ for $N = 12$, at .05 level, one-tailed. Accept H_0. This result suggests that although the children generally improved during the year, this improvement was not particularly uniform among all children.

chapter 12

(1) Only a is mutually exclusive. **(2)** a, b (if drawing is with replacement), and c are independent. **(3)** Events A and B are independent if and only if $P(B \mid A) = P(B)$ in which $P(B \mid A)$ is the conditional probability of B given A. **(4a)** 2/3, 2/3; **(4b)** 5/6, 5/6; **(4c)** 1/36; **(4d)** 2/3, 4/7, 2/7, 2/7. **(5a)** 120; **(5b)** 12; **(5c)** 360. **(6)** 1,814,400. **(7a)** 1; **(7b)** 10, 10; **(7c)** 35. **(8)** 35,840. **(9)** 1/56, 1/336, 1/6. pg. 344

pg. 349. **(1)** $\frac{4}{52} \times \frac{4}{51} = \frac{16}{2652}, \frac{32}{2652}$. **(2)** 112. **(3)** 24/2,598,960 = .000009, 41184/2,598,960 = .0158. **(4)** 21/16807 = .00125. **(5)** 56/110 = .51, 672/7920 = .0848. **(6)** 35/128, 29/128, 127/128.

appendix I

(1a) $\frac{5}{7}$; **(1b)** $\frac{9}{10}$; **(1c)** $\frac{98}{99}$; **(1d)** $\frac{3}{2}$; **(1e)** $\frac{1}{6}$; **(1f)** $\frac{7}{9}$; **(1g)** $\frac{59}{180}$. **(2a)** $\frac{2}{9}$; **(2b)** $\frac{2}{7}$; **(2c)** 1; **(2d)** $\frac{8}{9}$; **(2e)** $\frac{6}{5}$; **(2f)** $\frac{16}{5}$. **(3a)** 24; **(3b)** 20; **(3c)** 480. **(4a)** 27; **(4b)** 18; **(4c)** 24; **(4d)** 7; **(4e)** $2^7 = 128$; **(4f)** 144; **(4g)** 1; **(4h)** 4; **(4i)** $\frac{25}{9}$; **(4j)** $\frac{27}{125}$; **(4k)** $\frac{25}{54}$. **(5a)** $a^2 + 2ab + b^2$; **(5b)** $a^2 - 2ab + b^2$; **(5c)** $X^2 - 2X\overline{X} + \overline{X}^2$; **(5d)** $(cd)^2 - 2abcd + (ab)^2$ or $c^2d^2 - 2abcd + a^2b^2$; **(5e)** c; **(5f)** $\frac{ca - b}{c}$ or $a - \frac{b}{c}$; **(5g)** $\frac{(d + c)}{(d - c)}$; **(6a)** 38; **(6b)** 359; **(6c)** 69.3; **(6d)** .75; **(6e)** 31.5; **(6f)** 10.9; **(6g)** 108.1.

glossary of symbols

glossary of symbols

Symbol	Meaning
a	Regression constant representing the y-intercept. It is also written with paired subscripts (a_{yx}, a_{xy}) which denote whether the regression is Y on X or X on Y.
α	Unsubscripted alpha is the significance level in hypothesis testing, which is also the probability of a Type I error.
α_j	Subscripted alpha is the treatment effect in the population for the jth level of Factor A.
a_j	Single subscripted a_j is the estimated treatment effect for the jth level of Factor A.
$\alpha\beta_{jk}$	Treatment effect in the population for the jkth cell in two-factor analysis of variance.
b	Regression constant indicating the slope of the regression line. It is also written with paired subscripts (b_{yx}, b_{xy}) which indicate whether the regression is Y on X or X on Y, and with multiple subscripts ($b_{z_y z_x}$) indicating the value is for standardized variables z_y and z_x.
β	Unsubscripted beta represents the power of a statistical test.
β_k	Subscripted beta is a treatment effect in the population for the kth level of Factor B.
c	Often used to denote any non-zero constant.
°C	Degrees centigrade.
$_nC_r$	The number of combinations (order irrelevant) of n things taken r at a time.
χ^2	Chi squared, a test statistic used in several nonparametric tests. It is often subscripted to indicate if the value is an observed (χ^2_{obs}), or a critical one (χ^2_{crit}).
Cum. f	Cumulative frequency.
Cum. Rel. f	Cumulative relative frequency.
D_i	The difference between pairs of scores (e.g., in the t test for the difference between means for correlated groups).

Symbol	Meaning
d_i	The difference between ranks of paired scores (e.g., in Spearman's rank-order correlation).
df	Degrees of freedom.
E_{jk}	The expected frequency for the jkth cell.
e	The base of Napierian logarithms, $e = 2.7183\ldots$.
F	A test statistic, usually the ratio of two independent variances. It is sometimes subscripted to indicate if the value is an observed (F_{obs}) or a critical one (F_{crit}).
f	Frequency.
°F	Degrees Fahrenheit.
H	Test statistic for the Kruskal-Wallis test.
H_0	The null hypothesis.
H_1	The alternative hypothesis.
i	The size of a class interval.
k	Often used to denote any non-zero constant.
L	The lower limit of the interval containing the median.
$\log_e$	The logarithm to the base e; also the natural or Napierian logarithm. Sometimes written ln in other contexts.
$\log_{10}$	The logarithm to the base 10. Most frequently written without subscript.
μ	The population mean. It is also written with subscripts, for example, $\mu_{\bar{x}}$, indicating the population mean of the distribution of sample means.
M_d	The Median.
M_o	The mode.
MS	Mean square or variance estimate in the analysis of variance. It is often written with subscripts indicating the mean square for a particular source of variability (e.g., MS_{between}, MS_{AB}, etc.).
N	The total number of subjects, observations, or paired observations (check the precise definition for each application).

Symbol	Meaning
n	The number of subjects or observations within a specific subgroup of a larger sample.
n_b	The number of scores falling below the lower limit of the interval containing the median.
n_w	The number of scores within the interval containing the median.
O_{jk}	The observed frequency for the *jk*th cell.
$P(A)$	The probability of event *A*.
$P(B \mid A)$	The conditional probability of the event *B*, given that event *A* has already occurred.
p	The probability that the observed data could be obtained if the null hypothesis were true.
$P_{.n}$	The *n*th percentile point.
${}_nP_r$	The number of permutations (order considered) of *n* things taken *r* at a time.
π	A constant equal to 3.1416 . . . .
r	The sample Pearson product-moment correlation coefficient.
r^2	The estimated proportion of variance in *Y* attributable to *X* (the square of the correlation coefficient).
ρ	The population correlation coefficient.
r_s	The sample Spearman rank-order correlation coefficient.
ρ_s	The population Spearman rank-order correlation.
Rel. *f*	Relative frequency.
S	The universal set or sample space.
s	The sample standard deviation. It is also written with subscripts indicating the variable or statistic for which the standard deviation applies (e.g., s_x, the standard deviation of the *S*'s; $s_{\bar{x}}$, the standard error of the mean; $s_{\bar{x}_1-\bar{x}_2}$, the standard error of the difference between two means).
s^2	The sample variance. It is also written with subscripts (see *s*).
σ	The population standard deviation. It is also written with subscripts (see *s*).
σ^2	The population variance. It is also written with subscripts (see *s*).
$s_{y.x}$	The sample standard error of estimate in regression.
$\sigma_{y.x}$	The population standard error of estimate.
$s_{y\mid x=2}$	The sample standard deviation of the *Y*'s at $X = 2$.
$\sigma_{y\mid x=2}$	The population standard deviation of the *Y*'s at $X = 2$.
SS	Sum of squares. It is often written with subscripts indicating the mean square for a particular source of variability (e.g., SS_{between}, SS_{AB}, etc.).
$\sum X_i$	The sum of the X_i for $i = 1$ to N. It is also written without limits on the summation sign and subscripts, $\sum X$.
T	A total, sometimes written with subscripts indicating which scores are summed.
t	Student's *t* test statistic. It is also written with subscripts indicating the value is an observed (t_{obs}) or a critical one (t_{crit}), or indicating the value of *t* at $p = .05$ ($t_{.05}$), etc.
U	The test statistic for the Mann-Whitney U test. It is also written with subscripts indicating the value is an observed (U_{obs}) or a critical one (U_{crit}).
X_i	The *i*th score of a variable. Other letters (e.g., Y_i, W_i, etc.) are also used to denote variables.
$\bar{X}$	The sample mean. Any variable with a bar over it signifies the mean of that variable (e.g., $\bar{Y}$). It is also written with subscripts indicating the levels and factors involved (e.g. $\bar{X}_{j.}$, $\bar{X}_{.k}$, $\bar{X}_{..}$, etc.).
$\tilde{Y}$	The value of *Y* predicted on the basis of the regression line. One may also find $\tilde{X}$, when the regression is for *X* on *Y*.
W	The test statistic for the Wilcoxon test. It is also written with subscripts indicating if the value is an observed (W_{obs}) or a critical one (W_{crit}).
z	A standard normal deviate. It is also written with subscripts indicating if the value is an observed (z_{obs}) or a critical one (z_{crit}).

Symbol	Meaning
z_r	A transformed value of the correlation coefficient, r.
A'	The prime after a capital letter A (for example) indicates the set complement to A (i.e., all elements not in A).
$\subseteq$	The sign $\subseteq$ in $A \subseteq B$ indicates that A is a subset of B.
$\cup$	The sign $\cup$ in $A \cup B$ indicates union, the set of elements that are in either A, in B, or in both A and B.
$\cap$	The sign $\cap$ in $A \cap B$ indicates intersection, the set of elements that are in A and in B.
$=$	"is equal to"
$\neq$	"is not equal to"
$<$	"is less than"
$\leq$	"is less than or equal to"
$>$	"is greater than"
$\geq$	"is greater than or equal to"
$\pm$	"plus or minus"
$\sqrt{\ }$	"square root of"
$\lvert\ \rvert$	"the absolute value of"
∞	Infinity
$\emptyset$	The null or empty set.
*, **, ***	The stated observed value of the test statistic is significant at the .05(*), the .01(**), or the .001(***) level.

index

index

Abscissa, 29
Absolute zero point. *See* Scales of measurement
Analysis of variance (simple), 214–44
assumptions, 231–32
between-groups variance estimate, 216–32
comparison of between and within mean square, 225–27
computational procedures, 233–41
derivation of formulas, 220–25
F test, 227–30
formal numerical example, 236–41
general logic, 216–32
notation, 217–20
partition of variability, 220–27
proportion of variance, 243–44
relation to *t* test, 241–43
versus multiple *t* tests, 215–16
within-groups variance estimate, 216–32
Analysis of variance (two-factor), 246–80
a posteriori comparisons, 277
a priori comparisons, 277
assumptions, 266–68
computational procedures, 268–73
derivation of formulas, 253–63
extension of simple analysis of variance, 246–47
fixed model, 268
formal computational example, 272–77
general logic, 251–53
interactions, 248–51
main effects, 248–51
notation, 253–55
partition of variability, 255–59
proportion of variance, 277–78
treatment effects (numerical illustration), 263–67
unequal cell size, 268
Asymptotic curve, 77
Average, 5. *See also* Mean
Axes, 29

Bar graph, 276
Bimodal distribution, 45
Binomial exponentiation, review of basic math, 357
Binomial probability, 347–48
formula, 349
Bivariate normal distribution, 197

Central tendency, 32, 38–47. *See also* Mean; Median; Mode
comparison of mean, median, and mode, 45–47
measures of, 38–47
Chance, 142
Chi square distribution, table, 373
Chi square tests, 284–93
caution in use, 293
formulas, 315–16
four-fold contingency table, 288–91
goodness of fit, 291–93
Class interval. *See* Frequency distribution
Combinations, 342–44, 349
Complement (set theory), 324, 328
Conditional probability, 332–33, 337, 348
Confidence intervals:
for the mean, 171–73
for the regression line, 107–10
Constant (versus a variable), 11
Continuity, Yates correction for, 289
Continuous variable, 11
Correlation, 113–33
causality, 132–33
relation to regression, 114–18, 122–26
Correlation coefficient:
comparison of test for the difference between means and correlation, 205–207
comparison of a test for the significance of *r* versus the difference between two *r*s, 200–202
computation, 117, 133–35
derivation, 114–18
factors influencing size, 127–32
changes in unit and origin, 120–22
combining groups, 129–31
extreme groups, 128–29

Correlation coefficient (con't.)
extreme score, 131–32
range, 127–28
formulas, 116–17, 133
properties, 118–26
range of values, 118–19
relationship to standard error of estimate and variability in *Y* distribution, 123–26
slope, 122–23
standard error of estimate, 123–26
tests of significance:
difference between two independent correlations, 198–200
significance of *r*, 195–97
summary of formulas, 209
table of critical values for the Pearson product moment correlation, 371
table of critical values for the Spearman rank-order correlation, 379
two regression lines, 123
variance interpretation, 119–20
Critical level, in hypothesis testing, 158–59
Critical region, in hypothesis testing, 160
Critical values, in hypothesis testing, 160
Cumulative frequency distribution. *See* Frequency distributions
Curvilinear relationship, 88

Data, definition, 1
Decision errors in hypothesis testing, 161–63
significance levels, 161–63
Type I and II, 161
Decision rules in hypothesis testing, 159–60
Degrees of freedom, definition, 167–68
Density function, 144
Dependent events, 331. *See also* Independent events
Descriptive statistics, 1, 138
Directional test of hypothesis, 163–65
Discrete variable, 11
Disjoint sets, 327–28
Distribution-free tests. *See* Nonparametric techniques

Element (in set theory), 323, 328
Elementary event, 327–28
Empty set, 324, 328
Error:
linear prediction, 97. *See also* Standard error of estimate
simple analysis of variance, 226
Estimation, 47–49
Event, in probability, 327–28
Expectation ("expected value"), 49
Expected frequency, in Chi square tests, 285–87
Exponents, review of basic math, 356

F distribution, 191–92, 217, 227–30
relationship to *t*, 241–43
table, 367
Factor, in analysis of variance, 247–48
fixed, 216, 268
random, 216, 268
Factorial, review of basic math, 355
Factoring, review of basic math, 358
Fixed model, in analysis of variance, 268
Formula:
computational, 54
definitional, 54
Fractions, review of basic math, 354
Frequency distributions, 19–36
class interval, 22, 26–27
construction, summary illustration, 28–29
cumulative frequency, 24
cumulative relative frequency, 24
grouped data, 23, 25–29
how differ one from another, 32–36
lowest interval, 27
midpoint of an interval, 28
number of class intervals, 25–26
relative frequency, 21
theoretical relative, 78
Frequency histogram, 29, 31–32
Frequency polygon, 29–32

Galton, Francis, 95
Gambler's fallacy, 333
Gosset, W. S., 166
Graphs, 29–36
cumulative frequency histogram and polygon, 31–32
frequency histogram, 29
frequency polygon, 29–31
relative frequency histogram and polygon, 31

Histogram, 29–32
Homogeneity of variance:
in analysis of variance, 231, 268
in testing difference between means, 178–86
Homoscedasticity, 109
Hypotheses, in hypothesis testing, 157–58
Hypothesis testing, introduction, 138–73
directional and non-directional tests, 163–65
example, 154–65
standard normal distribution, 155–57
Hypothesis testing, techniques, 176–208
correlation coefficients, 195–200
differences between means, 177–90
homogeneity of variance, 190–94
significance, 200–205

Idealized experiment. *See* Probability
Impossible event, in probability, 329
Independence, 153, 332–33
Independent events, 330–31
compared with mutually exclusive events, 333
probability of the intersection of two independent events, 334–37
Inferential statistics, 2, 138
Interaction, in analysis of variance, 248–51, 257–59
Interpolation in tables, review of basic math, 361
Interquartile range, 62
Intersection, 326–28, 348
compared with union, 327
probability, 334–37
Interval scale, 9

Kendall's *tau*, 314–15
Kruskal-Wallis test, 298–304, 316–17
Kurtosis, 33

Least-squares criterion in regression, 95–99
Leptokurtic distribution, 33–35
Linear relationship, 86–88
Linearity, and linear regression, 103–104

Main effect, in analysis of variance, 248–51
Mann-Whitney *U* test, 293–98, 316
Mann-Whitney *U* distribution, table, 374
Marginal numbers, 248
Mean, as a measure of central tendency, 38–39, 49, 58
comparison with median and mode, 45–47
deviations about, 39
relationship to variance, 153
role in the variance, 52
squared deviations about, 40–42
Means, tests for differences, 177–90, 208–209
assumptions, 179
comparison of test of difference between means and correlation, 205–207
correlated groups, 186–90
independent groups, heterogeneous variances, 183–86
independent groups, homogeneous variances, 179–83
independent versus correlated groups, 178–79
proportion of variance accounted for, 207–208
Mean square, in analysis of variance, 219
Measurement, definition, 1. *See also* Scales of measurement
Median, 5, 41–47, 59
comparison with mean and mode, 45–47
Mode, 45–47, 59
bimodal, 45–46
comparison with mean and median, 45–47
Mutually exclusive events, 330, 333
probability of union of two, 337–40

Nominal scale, 11
Non-directional test of hypothesis, 163–65
Non-linear relationships, 88
Nonparametric techniques, 179, 232, 282–317
Chi square tests, 284–93
formulas, 315–17
Kruskal-Wallis test, 298–304
Mann-Whitney *U* test, 293–98
Spearman rank-order correlation coefficient and test, 308–15
tied observations, 295–96
versus parametric, 282–84
Wilcoxon text, 304–308

Normal distribution, 77–84
  formula, 77
  relationship between mean and variance in, 153
Normal distribution, standard normal, 78–84
  applications, 80–84
  deviates, 79
  standard scores, 83–84
  table, 364
Normality:
  assumption in simple analysis of variance, 232
  assumption in two-factor analysis of variance, 268
  determination, 152
Null hypothesis, 158
Null set, 324

One-tailed tests of hypotheses, 163–65
Ordinal scale, 10
Ordinate, 29
Origin. *See* Scales of measurement
Outcome, in probability, 327–28

Parameter, 48–49, 145
Pearson, Karl, 116
Pearson product moment correlation coefficient, 116. *See also* Correlation coefficient
Percentiles, 61–65
  computation, 62–65
  rank versus point, 61
Permutations, 340–42, 348
Platykurtic distribution, 35
Polygon. *See* Graphs
Population, 47–48, 145
Power (power-efficiency), 162, 283
Prediction. *See* Regression
Probability, 138–44, 323–49
  area under a curve, 143
  binomial, 347–48
  birthday problem, 346
  chance, 142
  combinations, 342–44
  conditional, 332–33
  dependent events, 331
  distribution, 78
  formulas, 348–49
  idealized experiment, 141
  independent events, 330–31
  independent and mutually exclusive events compared, 333
  intersection of two events, 334–37
  mutually exclusive events, 330
  overview, 138–44
  permutations, 340–42
  problems, advanced, 345–48
  randomness, 142
  relative frequency, 142–44
  simple classical, 141, 327–29
  standard normal distribution, 144
  uncertainty, 3
  union of two events, 337–40
Proportion of variance
  correlation, 119–20
  difference between means, 207–208
  simple analysis of variance, 243–44
  two-factor analysis of variance, 277–78
Proportional stratified random sample, 146

Quartile, upper and lower, 61–62

r to z_r, table of transformations, 372
Random numbers, 146
  table, 380
Randomness, 142
Random sample
  independence, 146
  problems in obtaining, 147–48
  proportional stratified, 146
  simple, 146
Range, 51, 59
Rank-order correlation coefficient and test, 308–15
Ratio scale, 9
Real limits, 12–13, 27–28, 51
Reciprocals, table, 382
Region of rejection, 160
Regression, 86–110
  computational procedures, 110–11, 133–35
  constants, 88–101, 110–11
  equation for a straight line, 87–94, 110–11
  error in prediction, 97
  factors in application, 103–10
  least squares criterion, 95–99
  linearity, 94, 103–104
  non-linear, 88
  prediction, 100–101
  second regression line, 101–103
  standard error of estimate, 105–10
Regression toward the mean, 95

Relationship. *See* Correlation, regression
  degree of, 101
  direct, 90
  inverse, 90
  linear, 125–26
  negative, 90
  positive, 90
Relative frequency distribution, 21, 78
Relative standing, measures of, 61–84
Repeated-measures analyses of variance, 232
Rounding numbers, 13–14

Sample, 47–48, 145
Sample space, 327–28
Sampling distribution, 148–53. *See also* Standard error theoretical versus empirical, 148
Sampling, methods of, 145–48
Sampling error, standard error as a measure of, 150
Scales of measurement, 7–11, 66–72
  change of unit, origin, 67–72
    effects on the mean, 67–69
    effects on the variance and standard deviation, 69–72
  properties, 7–8
    absolute zero, 8
    equal interval, 8
    magnitude, 8
  types, 9–11
    interval, 9
    nominal, 11
    ordinal, 10
    ratio, 9
Scatterplot, 94
Set theory, 323–28
  complementation, 324
  disjoint sets, 327
  element, 323
  empty or null set, 324
  equivalence, 325
  intersection, 326–27
  set, 323, 328
  subset, 324
  terminology, 328
  union, 325–27
  universal set, 324
Significance:
  interpretation of, 200–205, 278–80
  N, 203–204
  probability, 203
Significance level, 158–59, 163, 240
Simplification, review of basic math, 358
Skewness, 35, 46
Slope, 88–91, 110–11
  correlation, 122–23
  direction of relationship, 90–91
Spearman rank-order correlation coefficient, 308–15, 317
Square roots, table, 382
Square roots (extracting), review of basic math, 359
Squares, table, 382
Standard deviation, 53–59
  properties as measure of variability, 55–58
Standard distributions, 78–84
Standard error, 150–52
Standard error of estimate, 105–11
  application, 107–10
  assumptions for use, 108–10
  correlation coefficient, 123–26
Standard error of the mean, 150–53
  normality, 152–53
  N, 151
Standard normal distribution and deviates. *See* Normal distribution
Standard scores, 73–77
  change in the unit and origin, 73–74
  mean and variance of distribution, 74–77, 84
  relation to normal distribution, 77-80
  standard deviation units, 75
  use in comparing performance on several measures, 75–76
Stated limits, 27
Statistics:
  descriptive, 1, 138
  inferential, 2, 138
  study of, 1–6
  versus parameters, 48, 145
Straight line, equation, 92
Straight line relationship. *See* Regression
Student's *t* distribution. *See t* distribution
Subset, 324, 328
Sum of squares, in analysis of variance, 219
Summation sign, 14–17
Symbols, review of basic math, 353

t distribution, 165–70
  application, 168–70
  F, 241–43
  table, 366

extracting the square root The square root of a number is frequently desired in statistical manipulations and it is quite helpful if the student can perform this operation without tables. The following is a description of how to proceed. Suppose the square root of 184.3 is desired. First, using the decimal point as a starting place, separate the digits into pairs working away from the decimal point in both directions:

```
1    84.30    00
```

Next, consider only the first group of digits, the "1" in this case. Pose the question, "What number when multiplied by itself will be less than or equal to 1?" The answer is "1." Write this "division" as follows:

```
      1
    ____________________
 1 | 1    84.30    00
```

Continue the square-root operation as follows:

```
      1
    ____________________
 1 | 1    84.30    00
   | 1
   |__________
     0    84
```

Notice that the next *pair* of digits (8 and 4), not just the next single digit, was brought down. Now, double whatever number is in the answer at this point (e.g., 1) and place it to the left of the "84" (the preceding zero has been dropped):

```
      1    ?
    ____________________
 1 | 1    84.30    00
   | 1
   |__________
 2?     | 84
        |_____
```

Notice that the 1 was doubled to 2 but another digit is required and that place is reserved with a question mark in two places, one in the answer and one in the current divisor. The question mark represents some digit such that the digit times the current divisor (2?) is close to but less than or equal to 84. The "?" equals 3 because $3 \times 23 = 69$ which is less than 84. Just as in long division, the required number must be the largest such integer. In this case 4 is too large because $4 \times 24 = 96$ which is greater than 84, so 3 is the largest appropriate integer. After the familiar multiplication and subtraction, this procedure is repeated:

```
      1    3.?
    ____________________
   | 1    84.30    00
 1 | 1
   |__________
     23 | 84
        | 69
        |_____
    26? | 1530
        |_____
```

The current divisor of 26? is obtained by doubling the current answer (13) and affixing an unknown digit (?). Again the question is what does "?" equal to make $? \times 26? \leq$

1530? The answer is 5 because $5 \times 265 = 1325$ which is less than but close to 1530. The number 6 would be too large because $6 \times 266 = 1596 > 1530$.

```
          1     3.5     ?
     1 |  1    84.30   00
       |  1
        ------------
        23  |  84
            |  69
             ----------
         265 | 1530
             | 1325
              ----------
        270? | 205 00
```

Notice that in order to obtain the next divisor the current answer is doubled but the decimal point is ignored. Thus, the current divisor is 270? not 27.0?. Again, note that a *pair* of zeros not just one was brought down into the remainder. The appropriate value for "?" is now 7:

```
          1     3.5     7
       |  1    84.30   00
       |  1
        ------------
        23  |  84
            |  69
             ----------
         265 | 1530
             | 1325
              ----------
        2707 |  20500
             |  18949
              ----------
                 1551
```

In long division to round the answer appropriately one frequently asks if two times the remainder is more than the divisor. If it is, one rounds the answer up, otherwise the answer remains as it is. Thus, one might be tempted to say, "Since twice the current remainder of 1551 is 3102 which is greater than 2707, round the answer to 13.58." This procedure does not always work in extracting square roots because the current divisor will not be the divisor in the next step. The best policy is to carry the extraction one step beyond the desired accuracy. If the answer is required only to tenths, 13.6 is the result.

table of squares and square roots Appendix II, Table K in the back of this book lists the squares and square roots of each integer from 1 to 1000. The square of 28 is obtained simply by finding 28 in the first column headed N and looking to the next column labeled N^2 in that row to find the answer of 784. The square root of 28 is found in the third column which lists 5.2915 as the $\sqrt{N}$.

The precise number of interest may not be listed in Appendix II. For example, suppose one wanted to know the square root of 6.25. The table will actually provide the precise answer if one conceives of 6.25 as $\frac{625}{100}$. Since

$$\sqrt{\frac{625}{100}} = \frac{\sqrt{625}}{\sqrt{100}} = \frac{\sqrt{625}}{10}$$

one needs only to find the square root of 625 and divide it by 10. The table lists the square root of 625 to be 25, and dividing that by 10 yields the square root of 6.25 as 2.5.

To obtain the square root of 75300, think of 75300 as 100 × 753 and thus its square root as

$$\sqrt{(100)(753)} = \sqrt{100}\,\sqrt{753} = 10\sqrt{753}$$

The root listed for 753 is 27.4408 and 10 times this gives the desired answer of 274.408.

These illustrations show that if a number can be factored into two or more numbers which are available in the table, the same general procedure as described may be used.

INTERPOLATION

Interpolation is a procedure for using tables, such as that for square roots, and obtaining an approximation for numbers that are not listed in the table. For example, consider the square root of 13.67. Such a number is not listed in Appendix II and suppose a method other than factoring must be used. If the root is computed by the long method described previously, the answer is 3.6973. An approximation to this value can be obtained by interpolating within the square root table as illustrated in the following manner:

Number	*Square Root*	*Difference*		*Partition of Difference*	
31	3.6056		$\frac{2}{3}$		→ 3.6056
		.1361		.0907	→ + .0907
13.67					→ 3.6963
14	3.7417		$\frac{1}{3}$	.0454	
				.1361	

The square root of 13 is 3.6056 and the square root of 14 is 3.7417 (as shown from the table in Appendix II). Since the square root of 13.67 is desired, the result should fall somewhere between the root for 13 and the root for 14. In fact, the basic logic of interpolation is that the answer should fall between these two roots in the same ratio that 13.67 falls between 13 and 14. The table shows 13 and 14 and their corresponding square roots as reproduced here. The number in question, 13.67, falls two-thirds of the way between 13 and 14. Thus, the difference in the roots for 13 and 14, namely .1361 is partitioned into two parts, two-thirds (.0907) and one-third (.0454). Since 13.67 falls two-thirds of the way between 13 and 14, then two-thirds of the difference between the roots of 13 and 14 should be added to the root of 13 in order to approximate the square root of 13.67. This result is 3.6963. Notice that it is not identical to the correct answer of 3.6973, but for some purposes this approximation will be sufficiently accurate.

The application of the general procedure of interpolation is not limited to finding square roots. As the reader will note, there are many tables in the back of this book and frequently interpolation may be required to obtain a value which is not listed there.

EXERCISES

1. Perform the indicated operations.
   a. $\frac{2}{7} + \frac{3}{7}$
   b. $\frac{3}{5} + \frac{3}{10}$
   c. $\frac{4}{9} + \frac{6}{11}$
   d. $\frac{7}{2} + \frac{3}{7}$
   e. $\frac{1}{2} - \frac{1}{3}$
   f. $\frac{5}{6} - \frac{1}{18}$
   g. $\frac{7}{9} - \frac{9}{20}$
2. Perform the indicated operations.
   a. $\frac{2}{3} \cdot \frac{1}{3}$
   b. $\frac{3}{7} \cdot \frac{2}{3}$
   c. $\frac{27}{54} \cdot \frac{2}{3} \cdot \frac{15}{18} \cdot \frac{3}{5} \cdot 6$
   d. $\frac{2}{3} \div \frac{3}{4}$
   e. $\frac{4}{5} \div \frac{2}{3}$
   f. $\frac{8}{11} \div \frac{5}{22}$
3. Simplify the following.
   a. $4!$
   b. $\dfrac{5!}{3!}$
   c. $\dfrac{3!6!}{9}$
4. Simplify the following.
   a. 3^3
   b. $3^2 + 3^2$
   c. $4^2 + 2^3$
   d. $2^4 - 3^2$
   e. $2^3 \cdot 2^4$
   f. $3^2 \cdot 4^2$
   g. $3^3 \div 3^3$
   h. $4^3 \div 4^2$
   i. $5^2 \div 3^2$
   j. $(\frac{3}{5})^3$
   k. $(\frac{2}{3})^3 \div (\frac{4}{5})^2$
5. Expand and simplify the following expressions.
   a. $(a + b)^2$
   b. $(a - b)^2$
   c. $(X - \overline{X})^2$
   d. $(cd - ab)^2$
   e. $\dfrac{(b - c)(-a) + (ab - c)}{a - 1}$
   f. $\dfrac{ca - b}{c}$
   g. $\dfrac{dab + cba}{ab(d - c)}$
6. First, determine the square root without using tables and then use the tables to determine the square root of each of the following.
   a. 1444
   b. 128,881
   c. 4800
   d. .57
   e. 992.5
   f. 118.2
   g. 11695

appendix II

tables

Table A. Areas under the Standard Normal Curve

z	0 z	0 z
0.00	.0000	.5000
0.01	.0040	.4960
0.02	.0080	.4920
0.03	.0120	.4880
0.04	.0160	.4840
0.05	.0199	.4801
0.06	.0239	.4761
0.07	.0279	.4721
0.08	.0319	.4681
0.09	.0359	.4641
0.10	.0398	.4602
0.11	.0438	.4562
0.12	.0478	.4522
0.13	.0517	.4483
0.14	.0557	.4443
0.15	.0596	.4404
0.16	.0636	.4364
0.17	.0675	.4325
0.18	.0714	.4286
0.19	.0753	.4247
0.20	.0793	.4207
0.21	.0832	.4168
0.22	.0871	.4129
0.23	.0910	.4090
0.24	.0948	.4052
0.25	.0987	.4013
0.26	.1026	.3974
0.27	.1064	.3936
0.28	.1103	.3897
0.29	.1141	.3859
0.30	.1179	.3821
0.31	.1217	.3783
0.32	.1255	.3745
0.33	.1293	.3707
0.34	.1331	.3669
0.35	.1368	.3632
0.36	.1406	.3594
0.37	.1443	.3557
0.38	.1480	.3520
0.39	.1517	.3483
0.40	.1554	.3446
0.41	.1591	.3409
0.42	.1628	.3372
0.43	.1664	.3336
0.44	.1700	.3300
0.45	.1736	.3264
0.46	.1772	.3228
0.47	.1808	.3192
0.48	.1844	.3156
0.49	.1879	.3121
0.50	.1915	.3085
0.51	.1950	.3050
0.52	.1985	.3015
0.53	.2019	.2981
0.54	.2054	.2946
0.55	.2088	.2912
0.56	.2123	.2877
0.57	.2157	.2843
0.58	.2190	.2810
0.59	.2224	.2776
0.60	.2257	.2743
0.61	.2291	.2709
0.62	.2324	.2676
0.63	.2357	.2643
0.64	.2389	.2611
0.65	.2422	.2578
0.66	.2454	.2546
0.67	.2486	.2514
0.68	.2517	.2483
0.69	.2549	.2451
0.70	.2580	.2420
0.71	.2611	.2389
0.72	.2642	.2358
0.73	.2673	.2327
0.74	.2704	.2296
0.75	.2734	.2266
0.76	.2764	.2236
0.77	.2794	.2206
0.78	.2823	.2177
0.79	.2852	.2148
0.80	.2881	.2119
0.81	.2910	.2090
0.82	.2939	.2061
0.83	.2967	.2033
0.84	.2995	.2005
0.85	.3023	.1977
0.86	.3051	.1949
0.87	.3078	.1922
0.88	.3106	.1894
0.89	.3133	.1867
0.90	.3159	.1841
0.91	.3186	.1814
0.92	.3212	.1788
0.93	.3238	.1762
0.94	.3264	.1736
0.95	.3289	.1711
0.96	.3315	.1685
0.97	.3340	.1660
0.98	.3365	.1635
0.99	.3389	.1611
1.00	.3413	.1587
1.01	.3438	.1562
1.02	.3461	.1539
1.03	.3485	.1515
1.04	.3508	.1492
1.05	.3531	.1469
1.06	.3554	.1446
1.07	.3577	.1423
1.08	.3599	.1401
1.09	.3621	.1379
1.10	.3643	.1357
1.11	.3665	.1335
1.12	.3686	.1314
1.13	.3708	.1292
1.14	.3729	.1271
1.15	.3749	.1251
1.16	.3770	.1230
1.17	.3790	.1210
1.18	.3810	.1190
1.19	.3830	.1170
1.20	.3849	.1151
1.21	.3869	.1131
1.22	.3888	.1112
1.23	.3907	.1093
1.24	.3925	.1075
1.25	.3944	.1056
1.26	.3962	.1038
1.27	.3980	.1020
1.28	.3997	.1003
1.29	.4015	.0985
1.30	.4032	.0968
1.31	.4049	.0951
1.32	.4066	.0934
1.33	.4082	.0918
1.34	.4099	.0901
1.35	.4115	.0885
1.36	.4131	.0869
1.37	.4147	.0853
1.38	.4162	.0838
1.39	.4177	.0823
1.40	.4192	.0808
1.41	.4207	.0793
1.42	.4222	.0778
1.43	.4236	.0764
1.44	.4251	.0749
1.45	.4265	.0735
1.46	.4279	.0721
1.47	.4292	.0708
1.48	.4306	.0694
1.49	.4319	.0681
1.50	.4332	.0668
1.51	.4345	.0655
1.52	.4357	.0643
1.53	.4370	.0630
1.54	.4382	.0618
1.55	.4394	.0606
1.56	.4406	.0594
1.57	.4418	.0582
1.58	.4429	.0571
1.59	.4441	.0559
1.60	.4452	.0548
1.61	.4463	.0537
1.62	.4474	.0526
1.63	.4484	.0516
1.64	.4495	.0505

Source: Runyon and Haber, *Fundamentals of Behavioral Statistics*, 1967, Addison-Wesley, Reading, Mass.

Table A (continued)

z	0 z	0 z	z	0 z	0 z	z	0 z	0 z
1.65	.4505	.0495	2.22	.4868	.0132	2.79	.4974	.0026
1.66	.4515	.0485	2.23	.4871	.0129	2.80	.4974	.0026
1.67	.4525	.0475	2.24	.4875	.0125	2.81	.4975	.0025
1.68	.4535	.0465	2.25	.4878	.0122	2.82	.4976	.0024
1.69	.4545	.0455	2.26	.4881	.0119	2.83	.4977	.0023
1.70	.4554	.0446	2.27	.4884	.0116	2.84	.4977	.0023
1.71	.4564	.0436	2.28	.4887	.0113	2.85	.4978	.0022
1.72	.4573	.0427	2.29	.4890	.0110	2.86	.4979	.0021
1.73	.4582	.0418	2.30	.4893	.0107	2.87	.4979	.0021
1.74	.4591	.0409	2.31	.4896	.0104	2.88	.4980	.0020
1.75	.4599	.0401	2.32	.4898	.0102	2.89	.4981	.0019
1.76	.4608	.0392	2.33	.4901	.0099	2.90	.4981	.0019
1.77	.4616	.0384	2.34	.4904	.0096	2.91	.4982	.0018
1.78	.4625	.0375	2.35	.4906	.0094	2.92	.4982	.0018
1.79	.4633	.0367	2.36	.4909	.0091	2.93	.4983	.0017
1.80	.4641	.0359	2.37	.4911	.0089	2.94	.4984	.0016
1.81	.4649	.0351	2.38	.4913	.0087	2.95	.4984	.0016
1.82	.4656	.0344	2.39	.4916	.0084	2.96	.4985	.0015
1.83	.4664	.0336	2.40	.4918	.0082	2.97	.4985	.0015
1.84	.4671	.0329	2.41	.4920	.0080	2.98	.4986	.0014
1.85	.4678	.0322	2.42	.4922	.0078	2.99	.4986	.0014
1.86	.4686	.0314	2.43	.4925	.0075	3.00	.4987	.0013
1.87	.4693	.0307	2.44	.4927	.0073	3.01	.4987	.0013
1.88	.4699	.0301	2.45	.4929	.0071	3.02	.4987	.0013
1.89	.4706	.0294	2.46	.4931	.0069	3.03	.4988	.0012
1.90	.4713	.0287	2.47	.4932	.0068	3.04	.4988	.0012
1.91	.4719	.0281	2.48	.4934	.0066	3.05	.4989	.0011
1.92	.4726	.0274	2.49	.4936	.0064	3.06	.4989	.0011
1.93	.4732	.0268	2.50	.4938	.0062	3.07	.4989	.0011
1.94	.4738	.0262	2.51	.4940	.0060	3.08	.4990	.0010
1.95	.4744	.0256	2.52	.4941	.0059	3.09	.4990	.0010
1.96	.4750	.0250	2.53	.4943	.0057	3.10	.4990	.0010
1.97	.4756	.0244	2.54	.4945	.0055	3.11	.4991	.0009
1.98	.4761	.0239	2.55	.4946	.0054	3.12	.4991	.0009
1.99	.4767	.0233	2.56	.4948	.0052	3.13	.4991	.0009
2.00	.4772	.0228	2.57	.4949	.0051	3.14	.4992	.0008
2.01	.4778	.0222	2.58	.4951	.0049	3.15	.4992	.0008
2.02	.4783	.0217	2.59	.4952	.0048	3.16	.4992	.0008
2.03	.4788	.0212	2.60	.4953	.0047	3.17	.4992	.0008
2.04	.4793	.0207	2.61	.4955	.0045	3.18	.4993	.0007
2.05	.4798	.0202	2.62	.4956	.0044	3.19	.4993	.0007
2.06	.4803	.0197	2.63	.4957	.0043	3.20	.4993	.0007
2.07	.4808	.0192	2.64	.4959	.0041	3.21	.4993	.0007
2.08	.4812	.0188	2.65	.4960	.0040	3.22	.4994	.0006
2.09	.4817	.0183	2.66	.4961	.0039	3.23	.4994	.0006
2.10	.4821	.0179	2.67	.4962	.0038	3.24	.4994	.0006
2.11	.4826	.0174	2.68	.4963	.0037	3.25	.4994	.0006
2.12	.4830	.0170	2.69	.4964	.0036	3.30	.4995	.0005
2.13	.4834	.0166	2.70	.4965	.0035	3.35	.4996	.0004
2.14	.4838	.0162	2.71	.4966	.0034	3.40	.4997	.0003
2.15	.4842	.0158	2.72	.4967	.0033	3.45	.4997	.0003
2.16	.4846	.0154	2.73	.4968	.0032	3.50	.4998	.0002
2.17	.4850	.0150	2.74	.4969	.0031	3.60	.4998	.0002
2.18	.4854	.0146	2.75	.4970	.0030	3.70	.4999	.0001
2.19	.4857	.0143	2.76	.4971	.0029	3.80	.4999	.0001
2.20	.4861	.0139	2.77	.4972	.0028	3.90	.49995	.00005
2.21	.4864	.0136	2.78	.4973	.0027	4.00	.49997	.00003

Table B. Critical Values of t

	Level of significance for one-tailed test					
	.10	.05	.025	.01	.005	.0005
	Level of significance for two-tailed test					
df	.20	.10	.05	.02	.01	.001
1	3.078	6.314	12.706	31.821	63.657	636.619
2	1.886	2.920	4.303	6.965	9.925	31.598
3	1.638	2.353	3.182	4.541	5.841	12.941
4	1.533	2.132	2.776	3.747	4.604	8.610
5	1.476	2.015	2.571	3.365	4.032	6.859
6	1.440	1.943	2.447	3.143	3.707	5.959
7	1.415	1.895	2.365	2.998	3.499	5.405
8	1.397	1.860	2.306	2.896	3.355	5.041
9	1.383	1.833	2.262	2.821	3.250	4.781
10	1.372	1.812	2.228	2.764	3.169	4.587
11	1.363	1.796	2.201	2.718	3.106	4.437
12	1.356	1.782	2.179	2.681	3.055	4.318
13	1.350	1.771	2.160	2.650	3.012	4.221
14	1.345	1.761	2.145	2.624	2.977	4.140
15	1.341	1.753	2.131	2.602	2.947	4.073
16	1.337	1.746	2.120	2.583	2.921	4.015
17	1.333	1.740	2.110	2.567	2.898	3.965
18	1.330	1.734	2.101	2.552	2.878	3.922
19	1.328	1.729	2.093	2.539	2.861	3.883
20	1.325	1.725	2.086	2.528	2.845	3.850
21	1.323	1.721	2.080	2.518	2.831	3.819
22	1.321	1.717	2.074	2.508	2.819	3.792
23	1.319	1.714	2.069	2.500	2.807	3.767
24	1.318	1.711	2.064	2.492	2.797	3.745
25	1.316	1.708	2.060	2.485	2.787	3.725
26	1.315	1.706	2.056	2.479	2.779	3.707
27	1.314	1.703	2.052	2.473	2.771	3.690
28	1.313	1.701	2.048	2.467	2.763	3.674
29	1.311	1.699	2.045	2.462	2.756	3.659
30	1.310	1.697	2.042	2.457	2.750	3.646
40	1.303	1.684	2.021	2.423	2.704	3.551
60	1.296	1.671	2.000	2.390	2.660	3.460
120	1.289	1.658	1.980	2.358	2.617	3.373
∞	1.282	1.645	1.960	2.326	2.576	3.291

Source: Table B is taken from Table III of Fisher and Yates, *Statistical Tables for Biological, Agricultural and Medical Research,* published by Oliver and Boyd,, Ltd., Edinburgh, and by permission of the authors and publishers.

The value listed in the table is the critical value of t for the number of degrees of freedom listed in the left column for a one- or two-tailed test at the significance level indicated at the top of each column. If the observed t is *greater than or equal to* the tabled value, reject H_0.

Table **C.** Critical Values of F (.05 level in roman type, .01 level in bold face)

Degrees of freedom for lesser mean square [denominator]	Degrees of freedom for greater mean square [numerator]																								
	1	2	3	4	5	6	7	8	9	10	11	12	14	16	20	24	30	40	50	75	100	200	500	∞	
1	161 **4,052**	200 **4,999**	216 **5,403**	225 **5,625**	230 **5,764**	234 **5,859**	237 **5,928**	239 **5,981**	241 **6,022**	242 **6,056**	243 **6,082**	244 **6,106**	245 **6,142**	246 **6,169**	248 **6,208**	249 **6,234**	250 **6,261**	251 **6,286**	252 **6,302**	253 **6,323**	253 **6,334**	254 **6,352**	254 **6,361**	254 **6,366**	1
2	18.51 **98.49**	19.00 **99.00**	19.16 **99.17**	19.25 **99.25**	19.30 **99.30**	19.33 **99.33**	19.36 **99.36**	19.37 **99.37**	19.38 **99.39**	19.39 **99.40**	19.40 **99.41**	19.41 **99.42**	19.42 **99.43**	19.43 **99.44**	19.44 **99.45**	19.45 **99.46**	19.46 **99.47**	19.47 **99.48**	19.47 **99.48**	19.48 **99.49**	19.49 **99.49**	19.49 **99.49**	19.50 **99.50**	19.50 **99.50**	2
3	10.13 **34.12**	9.55 **30.82**	9.28 **29.46**	9.12 **28.71**	9.01 **28.24**	8.94 **27.91**	8.88 **27.67**	8.84 **27.49**	8.81 **27.34**	8.78 **27.23**	8.76 **27.13**	8.74 **27.05**	8.71 **26.92**	8.69 **26.83**	8.66 **26.69**	8.64 **26.60**	8.62 **26.50**	8.60 **26.41**	8.58 **26.35**	8.57 **26.27**	8.56 **26.23**	8.54 **26.18**	8.54 **26.14**	8.53 **26.12**	3
4	7.71 **21.20**	6.94 **18.00**	6.59 **16.69**	6.39 **15.98**	6.26 **15.52**	6.16 **15.21**	6.09 **14.98**	6.04 **14.80**	6.00 **14.66**	5.96 **14.54**	5.93 **14.45**	5.91 **14.37**	5.87 **14.24**	5.84 **14.15**	5.80 **14.02**	5.77 **13.93**	5.74 **13.83**	5.71 **13.74**	5.70 **13.69**	5.68 **13.61**	5.66 **13.57**	5.65 **13.52**	5.64 **13.48**	5.63 **13.46**	4
5	6.61 **16.26**	5.79 **13.27**	5.41 **12.06**	5.19 **11.39**	5.05 **10.97**	4.95 **10.67**	4.88 **10.45**	4.82 **10.29**	4.78 **10.15**	4.74 **10.05**	4.70 **9.96**	4.68 **9.89**	4.64 **9.77**	4.60 **9.68**	4.56 **9.55**	4.53 **9.47**	4.50 **9.38**	4.46 **9.29**	4.44 **9.24**	4.42 **9.17**	4.40 **9.13**	4.38 **9.07**	4.37 **9.04**	4.36 **9.02**	5
6	5.99 **13.74**	5.14 **10.92**	4.76 **9.78**	4.53 **9.15**	4.39 **8.75**	4.28 **8.47**	4.21 **8.26**	4.15 **8.10**	4.10 **7.98**	4.06 **7.87**	4.03 **7.79**	4.00 **7.72**	3.96 **7.60**	3.92 **7.52**	3.87 **7.39**	3.84 **7.31**	3.81 **7.23**	3.77 **7.14**	3.75 **7.09**	3.72 **7.02**	3.71 **6.99**	3.69 **6.94**	3.68 **6.90**	3.67 **6.88**	6
7	5.59 **12.25**	4.74 **9.55**	4.35 **8.45**	4.12 **7.85**	3.97 **7.46**	3.87 **7.19**	3.79 **7.00**	3.73 **6.84**	3.68 **6.71**	3.63 **6.62**	3.60 **6.54**	3.57 **6.47**	3.52 **6.35**	3.49 **6.27**	3.44 **6.15**	3.41 **6.07**	3.38 **5.98**	3.34 **5.90**	3.32 **5.85**	3.29 **5.78**	3.28 **5.75**	3.25 **5.70**	3.24 **5.67**	3.23 **5.65**	7
8	5.32 **11.26**	4.46 **8.65**	4.07 **7.59**	3.84 **7.01**	3.69 **6.63**	3.58 **6.37**	3.50 **6.19**	3.44 **6.03**	3.39 **5.91**	3.34 **5.82**	3.31 **5.74**	3.28 **5.67**	3.23 **5.56**	3.20 **5.48**	3.15 **5.36**	3.12 **5.28**	3.08 **5.20**	3.05 **5.11**	3.03 **5.06**	3.00 **5.00**	2.98 **4.96**	2.96 **4.91**	2.94 **4.88**	2.93 **4.86**	8
9	5.12 **10.56**	4.26 **8.02**	3.86 **6.99**	3.63 **6.42**	3.48 **6.06**	3.37 **5.80**	3.29 **5.62**	3.23 **5.47**	3.18 **5.35**	3.13 **5.26**	3.10 **5.18**	3.07 **5.11**	3.02 **5.00**	2.98 **4.92**	2.93 **4.80**	2.90 **4.73**	2.86 **4.64**	2.82 **4.56**	2.80 **4.51**	2.77 **4.45**	2.76 **4.41**	2.73 **4.36**	2.72 **4.33**	2.71 **4.31**	9
10	4.96 **10.04**	4.10 **7.56**	3.71 **6.55**	3.48 **5.99**	3.33 **5.64**	3.22 **5.39**	3.14 **5.21**	3.07 **5.06**	3.02 **4.95**	2.97 **4.85**	2.94 **4.78**	2.91 **4.71**	2.86 **4.60**	2.82 **4.52**	2.77 **4.41**	2.74 **4.33**	2.70 **4.25**	2.67 **4.17**	2.64 **4.12**	2.61 **4.05**	2.59 **4.01**	2.56 **3.96**	2.55 **3.93**	2.54 **3.91**	10
11	4.84 **9.65**	3.98 **7.20**	3.59 **6.22**	3.36 **5.67**	3.20 **5.32**	3.09 **5.07**	3.01 **4.88**	2.95 **4.74**	2.90 **4.63**	2.86 **4.54**	2.82 **4.46**	2.79 **4.40**	2.74 **4.29**	2.70 **4.21**	2.65 **4.10**	2.61 **4.02**	2.57 **3.94**	2.53 **3.86**	2.50 **3.80**	2.47 **3.74**	2.45 **3.70**	2.42 **3.66**	2.41 **3.62**	2.40 **3.60**	11
12	4.75 **9.33**	3.88 **6.93**	3.49 **5.95**	3.26 **5.41**	3.11 **5.06**	3.00 **4.82**	2.92 **4.65**	2.85 **4.50**	2.80 **4.39**	2.76 **4.30**	2.72 **4.22**	2.69 **4.16**	2.64 **4.05**	2.60 **3.98**	2.54 **3.86**	2.50 **3.78**	2.46 **3.70**	2.42 **3.61**	2.40 **3.56**	2.36 **3.49**	2.35 **3.46**	2.32 **3.41**	2.31 **3.38**	2.30 **3.36**	12
13	4.67 **9.07**	3.80 **6.70**	3.41 **5.74**	3.18 **5.20**	3.02 **4.86**	2.92 **4.62**	2.84 **4.44**	2.77 **4.30**	2.72 **4.19**	2.67 **4.10**	2.63 **4.02**	2.60 **3.96**	2.55 **3.85**	2.51 **3.78**	2.46 **3.67**	2.42 **3.59**	2.38 **3.51**	2.34 **3.42**	2.32 **3.37**	2.28 **3.30**	2.26 **3.27**	2.24 **3.21**	2.22 **3.18**	2.21 **3.16**	13

Source: Reproduced by permission from *Statistical Methods*, 5th edition by George B. Snedecor, copyright 1956 by the Iowa State University Press.

The values in the table are the critical values of F for the degrees of freedom listed over the columns (the degrees of freedom for the greater mean square or numerator of the F ratio) and the degrees of freedom listed for the rows (the degrees of freedom for the lesser mean square for the denominator of the F ratio). The critical value for the .05 level of significance is presented first (roman type) followed by the critical value at the .01 level (bold face). If the observed value is *greater than or equal to* the tabled value, reject H_0.

Table C (continued)

Degrees of freedom for lesser mean square [denominator]	Degrees of freedom for greater mean square [numerator]																								
	1	2	3	4	5	6	7	8	9	10	11	12	14	16	20	24	30	40	50	75	100	200	500	∞	
14	4.60 **8.86**	3.74 **6.51**	3.34 **5.56**	3.11 **5.03**	2.96 **4.69**	2.85 **4.46**	2.77 **4.28**	2.70 **4.14**	2.65 **4.03**	2.60 **3.94**	2.56 **3.86**	2.53 **3.80**	2.48 **3.70**	2.44 **3.62**	2.39 **3.51**	2.35 **3.43**	2.31 **3.34**	2.27 **3.26**	2.24 **3.21**	2.21 **3.14**	2.19 **3.11**	2.16 **3.06**	2.14 **3.02**	2.13 **3.00**	14
15	4.54 **8.68**	3.68 **6.36**	3.29 **5.42**	3.06 **4.89**	2.90 **4.56**	2.79 **4.32**	2.70 **4.14**	2.64 **4.00**	2.59 **3.89**	2.55 **3.80**	2.51 **3.73**	2.48 **3.67**	2.43 **3.56**	2.39 **3.48**	2.33 **3.36**	2.29 **3.29**	2.25 **3.20**	2.21 **3.12**	2.18 **3.07**	2.15 **3.00**	2.12 **2.97**	2.10 **2.92**	2.08 **2.89**	2.07 **2.87**	15
16	4.49 **8.53**	3.63 **6.23**	3.24 **5.29**	3.01 **4.77**	2.85 **4.44**	2.74 **4.20**	2.66 **4.03**	2.59 **3.89**	2.54 **3.78**	2.49 **3.69**	2.45 **3.61**	2.42 **3.55**	2.37 **3.45**	2.33 **3.37**	2.28 **3.25**	2.24 **3.18**	2.20 **3.10**	2.16 **3.01**	2.13 **2.96**	2.09 **2.98**	2.07 **2.86**	2.04 **2.80**	2.02 **2.77**	2.01 **2.75**	16
17	4.45 **8.40**	3.59 **6.11**	3.20 **5.18**	2.96 **4.67**	2.81 **4.34**	2.70 **4.10**	2.62 **3.93**	2.55 **3.79**	2.50 **3.68**	2.45 **3.59**	2.41 **3.52**	2.38 **3.45**	2.33 **3.35**	2.29 **3.27**	2.23 **3.16**	2.19 **3.08**	2.15 **3.00**	2.11 **2.92**	2.08 **2.86**	2.04 **2.79**	2.02 **2.76**	1.99 **2.70**	1.97 **2.67**	1.96 **2.65**	17
18	4.41 **8.28**	3.55 **6.01**	3.16 **5.09**	2.93 **4.58**	2.77 **4.25**	3.66 **4.01**	2.58 **3.85**	2.51 **3.71**	2.46 **3.60**	2.41 **3.51**	2.37 **3.44**	2.34 **3.37**	2.29 **3.27**	2.25 **3.19**	2.19 **3.07**	2.15 **3.00**	2.11 **2.91**	2.07 **2.83**	2.04 **2.78**	2.00 **2.71**	1.98 **2.68**	1.95 **2.62**	1.93 **2.59**	1.92 **2.57**	18
19	4.38 **8.18**	3.52 **5.93**	3.13 **5.01**	2.90 **4.50**	2.74 **4.17**	2.63 **3.94**	2.55 **3.77**	2.48 **3.63**	2.43 **3.52**	2.38 **3.43**	2.34 **3.36**	2.31 **3.30**	2.26 **3.19**	2.21 **3.12**	2.15 **3.00**	2.11 **2.92**	2.07 **2.84**	2.02 **2.76**	2.00 **2.70**	1.96 **2.63**	1.94 **2.60**	1.91 **2.54**	1.90 **2.51**	1.88 **2.49**	19
20	4.35 **8.10**	3.49 **5.85**	3.10 **4.94**	2.87 **4.43**	2.71 **4.10**	2.60 **3.87**	2.52 **3.71**	2.45 **3.56**	2.40 **3.45**	2.35 **3.37**	2.31 **3.30**	2.28 **3.23**	2.23 **3.13**	2.18 **3.05**	2.12 **2.94**	2.08 **2.86**	2.04 **2.77**	1.99 **2.69**	1.96 **2.63**	1.92 **2.56**	1.90 **2.53**	1.87 **2.47**	1.85 **2.44**	1.84 **2.42**	20
21	4.32 **8.02**	3.47 **5.78**	3.07 **4.87**	2.84 **4.37**	2.68 **4.04**	2.57 **3.81**	2.49 **3.65**	2.42 **3.51**	2.37 **3.40**	2.32 **3.31**	2.28 **3.24**	2.25 **3.17**	2.20 **3.07**	2.15 **2.99**	2.09 **2.88**	2.05 **2.80**	2.00 **2.72**	1.96 **2.63**	1.93 **2.58**	1.89 **2.51**	1.87 **2.47**	1.84 **2.42**	1.82 **2.38**	1.81 **2.36**	21
22	4.30 **7.94**	3.44 **5.72**	3.05 **4.82**	2.82 **4.31**	2.66 **3.99**	2.55 **3.76**	2.47 **3.59**	2.40 **3.45**	2.35 **3.35**	2.30 **3.26**	2.26 **3.18**	2.23 **3.12**	2.18 **3.02**	2.13 **2.94**	2.07 **2.83**	2.03 **2.75**	1.98 **2.67**	1.93 **2.58**	1.91 **2.53**	1.87 **2.46**	1.84 **2.42**	1.81 **2.37**	1.80 **2.33**	1.78 **2.31**	22
23	4.28 **7.88**	3.42 **5.66**	3.03 **4.76**	2.80 **4.26**	2.64 **3.94**	2.53 **3.71**	2.45 **3.54**	2.38 **3.41**	2.32 **3.30**	2.28 **3.21**	2.24 **3.14**	2.20 **3.07**	2.14 **2.97**	2.10 **2.89**	2.04 **2.78**	2.00 **2.70**	1.96 **2.62**	1.91 **2.53**	1.88 **2.48**	1.84 **2.41**	1.82 **2.37**	1.79 **2.32**	1.77 **2.28**	1.76 **2.26**	23
24	4.26 **7.82**	3.40 **5.61**	3.01 **4.72**	2.78 **4.22**	2.62 **3.90**	2.51 **3.67**	2.43 **3.50**	2.36 **3.36**	2.30 **3.25**	2.26 **3.17**	2.22 **3.09**	2.18 **3.03**	2.13 **2.93**	2.09 **2.85**	2.02 **2.74**	1.98 **2.66**	1.94 **2.58**	1.89 **2.49**	1.86 **2.44**	1.82 **2.36**	1.80 **2.33**	1.76 **2.27**	1.74 **2.23**	1.73 **2.21**	24
25	4.24 **7.77**	3.38 **5.57**	2.99 **4.68**	2.76 **4.18**	2.60 **3.86**	2.49 **3.63**	2.41 **3.46**	2.34 **3.32**	2.28 **3.21**	2.24 **3.13**	2.20 **3.05**	2.16 **2.99**	2.11 **2.89**	2.06 **2.81**	2.00 **2.70**	1.96 **2.62**	1.92 **2.54**	1.87 **2.45**	1.84 **2.40**	1.80 **2.32**	1.77 **2.29**	1.74 **2.23**	1.72 **2.19**	1.71 **2.17**	25
26	4.22 **7.72**	3.37 **5.53**	2.98 **4.64**	2.74 **4.14**	2.59 **3.82**	2.47 **3.59**	2.39 **3.42**	2.32 **3.29**	2.27 **3.17**	2.22 **3.09**	2.18 **3.02**	2.15 **2.96**	2.10 **2.86**	2.05 **2.77**	1.99 **2.66**	1.95 **2.58**	1.90 **2.50**	1.85 **2.41**	1.82 **2.36**	1.78 **2.28**	1.76 **2.25**	1.72 **2.19**	1.70 **2.15**	1.69 **2.13**	26

The function, $F = e$ with exponent $2z$, is computed in part from Fisher's table VI (7). Additional entries are by interpolation, mostly graphical.

Table C (continued)

Degrees of freedom for lesser mean square [denominator]	Degrees of freedom for greater mean square [numerator]																								
	1	2	3	4	5	6	7	8	9	10	11	12	14	16	20	24	30	40	50	75	100	200	500	∞	
27	4.21 **7.68**	3.35 **5.49**	2.96 **4.60**	2.73 **4.11**	2.57 **3.79**	2.46 **3.56**	2.37 **3.39**	2.30 **3.26**	2.25 **3.14**	2.20 **3.06**	2.16 **2.98**	2.13 **2.93**	2.08 **2.83**	2.03 **2.74**	1.97 **2.63**	1.93 **2.55**	1.88 **2.47**	1.84 **2.38**	1.80 **2.33**	1.76 **2.25**	1.74 **2.21**	1.71 **2.16**	1.68 **2.12**	1.67 **2.10**	27
28	4.20 **7.64**	3.34 **5.45**	2.95 **4.57**	2.71 **4.07**	2.56 **3.76**	2.44 **3.53**	2.36 **3.36**	2.29 **3.23**	2.24 **3.11**	2.19 **3.03**	2.15 **2.95**	2.12 **2.90**	2.06 **2.80**	2.02 **2.71**	1.96 **2.60**	1.91 **2.52**	1.87 **2.44**	1.81 **2.35**	1.78 **2.30**	1.75 **2.22**	1.72 **2.18**	1.69 **2.13**	1.67 **2.09**	1.65 **2.06**	28
29	4.18 **7.60**	3.33 **5.42**	2.93 **4.54**	2.70 **4.04**	2.54 **3.73**	2.43 **3.50**	2.35 **3.33**	2.28 **3.20**	2.22 **3.08**	2.18 **3.00**	2.14 **2.92**	2.10 **2.87**	2.05 **2.77**	2.00 **2.68**	1.94 **2.57**	1.90 **2.49**	1.85 **2.41**	1.80 **2.32**	1.77 **2.27**	1.73 **2.19**	1.71 **2.15**	1.68 **2.10**	1.65 **2.06**	1.64 **2.03**	29
30	4.17 **7.56**	3.32 **5.39**	2.92 **4.51**	2.69 **4.02**	2.53 **3.70**	2.42 **3.47**	2.34 **3.30**	2.27 **3.17**	2.21 **3.06**	2.16 **2.98**	2.12 **2.90**	2.09 **2.84**	2.04 **2.74**	1.99 **2.66**	1.93 **2.55**	1.89 **2.47**	1.84 **2.38**	1.79 **2.29**	1.76 **2.24**	1.72 **2.16**	1.69 **2.13**	1.66 **2.07**	1.64 **2.03**	1.62 **2.01**	30
32	4.15 **7.50**	3.30 **5.34**	2.90 **4.46**	2.67 **3.97**	2.51 **3.66**	2.40 **3.42**	2.32 **3.25**	2.25 **3.12**	2.19 **3.01**	2.14 **2.94**	2.10 **2.86**	2.07 **2.80**	2.02 **2.70**	1.97 **2.62**	1.91 **2.51**	1.86 **2.42**	1.82 **2.34**	1.76 **2.25**	1.74 **2.20**	1.69 **2.12**	1.67 **2.08**	1.64 **2.02**	1.61 **1.98**	1.59 **1.96**	32
34	4.13 **7.44**	3.28 **5.29**	2.88 **4.42**	2.65 **3.93**	2.49 **3.61**	2.38 **3.38**	2.30 **3.21**	2.23 **3.08**	2.17 **2.97**	2.12 **2.89**	2.08 **2.82**	2.05 **2.76**	2.00 **2.66**	1.95 **2.58**	1.89 **2.47**	1.84 **2.38**	1.80 **2.30**	1.74 **2.21**	1.71 **2.15**	1.67 **2.08**	1.64 **2.04**	1.61 **1.98**	1.59 **1.94**	1.57 **1.91**	34
36	4.11 **7.39**	3.26 **5.25**	2.86 **4.38**	2.63 **3.89**	2.48 **3.58**	2.36 **3.35**	2.28 **3.18**	2.21 **3.04**	2.15 **2.94**	2.10 **2.86**	2.06 **2.78**	2.03 **2.72**	1.98 **2.62**	1.93 **2.54**	1.87 **2.43**	1.82 **2.35**	1.78 **2.26**	1.72 **2.17**	1.69 **2.12**	1.65 **2.04**	1.62 **2.00**	1.59 **1.94**	1.56 **1.90**	1.55 **1.87**	36
38	4.10 **7.35**	3.25 **5.21**	2.85 **4.34**	2.62 **3.86**	2.46 **3.54**	2.35 **3.32**	2.26 **3.15**	2.19 **3.02**	2.14 **2.91**	2.09 **2.82**	2.05 **2.75**	2.02 **2.69**	1.96 **2.59**	1.92 **2.51**	1.85 **2.40**	1.80 **2.32**	1.76 **2.22**	1.71 **2.14**	1.67 **2.08**	1.63 **2.00**	1.60 **1.97**	1.57 **1.90**	1.54 **1.86**	1.53 **1.84**	38
40	4.08 **7.31**	3.23 **5.18**	2.84 **4.31**	2.61 **3.83**	2.45 **3.51**	2.34 **3.29**	2.25 **3.12**	2.18 **2.99**	2.12 **2.88**	2.07 **2.80**	2.04 **2.73**	2.00 **2.66**	1.95 **2.56**	1.90 **2.49**	1.84 **2.37**	1.79 **2.29**	1.74 **2.20**	1.69 **2.11**	1.66 **2.05**	1.61 **1.97**	1.59 **1.94**	1.55 **1.88**	1.53 **1.84**	1.51 **1.81**	40
42	4.07 **7.27**	3.22 **5.15**	2.83 **4.29**	2.59 **3.80**	2.44 **3.49**	2.32 **3.26**	2.24 **3.10**	2.17 **2.96**	2.11 **2.86**	2.06 **2.77**	2.02 **2.70**	1.99 **2.64**	1.94 **2.54**	1.89 **2.46**	1.82 **2.35**	1.78 **2.26**	1.73 **2.17**	1.68 **2.08**	1.64 **2.02**	1.60 **1.94**	1.57 **1.91**	1.54 **1.85**	1.51 **1.80**	1.49 **1.78**	42
44	4.06 **7.24**	3.21 **5.12**	2.82 **4.26**	2.58 **3.78**	2.43 **3.46**	2.31 **3.24**	2.23 **3.07**	2.16 **2.94**	2.10 **2.84**	2.05 **2.75**	2.01 **2.68**	1.98 **2.62**	1.92 **2.52**	1.88 **2.44**	1.81 **2.32**	1.76 **2.24**	1.72 **2.15**	1.66 **2.06**	1.63 **2.00**	1.58 **1.92**	1.56 **1.88**	1.52 **1.82**	1.50 **1.78**	1.48 **1.75**	44
46	4.05 **7.21**	3.20 **5.10**	2.81 **4.24**	2.57 **3.76**	2.42 **3.44**	2.30 **3.22**	2.22 **3.05**	2.14 **2.92**	2.09 **2.82**	2.04 **2.73**	2.00 **2.66**	1.97 **2.60**	1.91 **2.50**	1.87 **2.42**	1.80 **2.30**	1.75 **2.22**	1.71 **2.13**	1.65 **2.04**	1.62 **1.98**	1.57 **1.90**	1.54 **1.86**	1.51 **1.80**	1.48 **1.76**	1.46 **1.72**	46
48	4.04 **7.19**	3.19 **5.08**	2.80 **4.22**	2.56 **3.74**	2.41 **3.42**	2.30 **3.20**	2.21 **3.04**	2.14 **2.90**	2.08 **2.80**	2.03 **2.71**	1.99 **2.64**	1.96 **2.58**	1.90 **2.48**	1.86 **2.40**	1.79 **2.28**	1.74 **2.20**	1.70 **2.11**	1.64 **2.02**	1.61 **1.96**	1.56 **1.88**	1.53 **1.84**	1.50 **1.78**	1.47 **1.73**	1.45 **1.70**	48

Table C (continued)

Degrees of freedom for lesser mean square [denominator]	Degrees of freedom for greater mean square [numerator]																								
	1	2	3	4	5	6	7	8	9	10	11	12	14	16	20	24	30	40	50	75	100	200	500	∞	
50	4.03 **7.17**	3.18 **5.06**	2.79 **4.20**	2.56 **3.72**	2.40 **3.41**	2.29 **3.18**	2.20 **3.02**	2.13 **2.88**	2.07 **2.78**	2.02 **2.70**	1.98 **2.62**	1.95 **2.56**	1.90 **2.46**	1.85 **2.39**	1.78 **2.26**	1.74 **2.18**	1.69 **2.10**	1.63 **2.00**	1.60 **1.94**	1.55 **1.86**	1.52 **1.82**	1.48 **1.76**	1.46 **1.71**	1.44 **1.68**	50
55	4.02 **7.12**	3.17 **5.01**	2.78 **4.16**	2.54 **3.68**	2.38 **3.37**	2.27 **3.15**	2.18 **2.98**	2.11 **2.85**	2.05 **2.75**	2.00 **2.66**	1.97 **2.59**	1.93 **2.53**	1.88 **2.43**	1.83 **2.35**	1.76 **2.23**	1.72 **2.15**	1.67 **2.06**	1.61 **1.96**	1.58 **1.90**	1.52 **1.82**	1.50 **1.78**	1.46 **1.71**	1.43 **1.66**	1.41 **1.64**	55
60	4.00 **7.08**	3.15 **4.98**	2.76 **4.13**	2.52 **3.65**	2.37 **3.34**	2.25 **3.12**	2.17 **2.95**	2.10 **2.82**	2.04 **2.72**	1.99 **2.63**	1.95 **2.56**	1.92 **2.50**	1.86 **2.40**	1.81 **2.32**	1.75 **2.20**	1.70 **2.12**	1.65 **2.03**	1.59 **1.93**	1.56 **1.87**	1.50 **1.79**	1.48 **1.74**	1.44 **1.68**	1.41 **1.63**	1.39 **1.60**	60
65	3.99 **7.04**	3.14 **4.95**	2.75 **4.10**	2.51 **3.62**	2.36 **3.31**	2.24 **3.09**	2.15 **2.93**	2.08 **2.79**	2.02 **2.70**	1.98 **2.61**	1.94 **2.54**	1.90 **2.47**	1.85 **2.37**	1.80 **2.30**	1.73 **2.18**	1.68 **2.09**	1.63 **2.00**	1.57 **1.90**	1.54 **1.84**	1.49 **1.76**	1.46 **1.71**	1.42 **1.64**	1.39 **1.60**	1.37 **1.56**	65
70	3.98 **7.01**	3.13 **4.92**	2.74 **4.08**	2.50 **3.60**	2.35 **3.29**	2.23 **3.07**	2.14 **2.91**	2.07 **2.77**	2.01 **2.67**	1.97 **2.59**	1.93 **2.51**	1.89 **2.45**	1.84 **2.35**	1.79 **2.28**	1.72 **2.15**	1.67 **2.07**	1.62 **1.98**	1.56 **1.88**	1.53 **1.82**	1.47 **1.74**	1.45 **1.69**	1.40 **1.62**	1.37 **1.56**	1.35 **1.53**	70
80	3.96 **6.96**	3.11 **4.88**	2.72 **4.04**	2.48 **3.56**	2.33 **3.25**	2.21 **3.04**	2.12 **2.87**	2.05 **2.74**	1.99 **2.64**	1.95 **2.55**	1.91 **2.48**	1.88 **2.41**	1.82 **2.32**	1.77 **2.24**	1.70 **2.11**	1.65 **2.03**	1.60 **1.94**	1.54 **1.84**	1.51 **1.78**	1.45 **1.70**	1.42 **1.65**	1.38 **1.57**	1.35 **1.52**	1.32 **1.49**	80
100	3.94 **6.90**	3.09 **4.82**	2.70 **3.98**	2.46 **3.51**	2.30 **3.20**	2.19 **2.99**	2.10 **2.82**	2.03 **2.69**	1.97 **2.59**	1.92 **2.51**	1.88 **2.43**	1.85 **2.36**	1.79 **2.26**	1.75 **2.19**	1.68 **2.06**	1.63 **1.98**	1.57 **1.89**	1.51 **1.79**	1.48 **1.73**	1.42 **1.64**	1.39 **1.59**	1.34 **1.51**	1.30 **1.46**	1.28 **1.43**	100
125	3.92 **6.84**	3.07 **4.78**	2.68 **3.94**	2.44 **3.47**	2.29 **3.17**	2.17 **2.95**	2.08 **2.79**	2.01 **2.65**	1.95 **2.56**	1.90 **2.47**	1.86 **2.40**	1.83 **2.33**	1.77 **2.23**	1.72 **2.15**	1.65 **2.03**	1.60 **1.94**	1.55 **1.85**	1.49 **1.75**	1.45 **1.68**	1.39 **1.59**	1.36 **1.54**	1.31 **1.46**	1.27 **1.40**	1.25 **1.37**	125
150	3.91 **6.81**	3.06 **4.75**	2.67 **3.91**	2.43 **3.44**	2.27 **3.14**	2.16 **2.92**	2.07 **2.76**	2.00 **2.62**	1.94 **2.53**	1.89 **2.44**	1.85 **2.37**	1.82 **2.30**	1.76 **2.20**	1.71 **2.12**	1.64 **2.00**	1.59 **1.91**	1.54 **1.83**	1.47 **1.72**	1.44 **1.66**	1.37 **1.56**	1.34 **1.51**	1.29 **1.43**	1.25 **1.37**	1.22 **1.33**	150
200	3.89 **6.76**	3.04 **4.71**	2.65 **3.88**	2.41 **3.41**	2.26 **3.11**	2.14 **2.90**	2.05 **2.73**	1.98 **2.60**	1.92 **2.50**	1.87 **2.41**	1.83 **2.34**	1.80 **2.28**	1.74 **2.17**	1.69 **2.09**	1.62 **1.97**	1.57 **1.88**	1.52 **1.79**	1.45 **1.69**	1.42 **1.62**	1.35 **1.53**	1.32 **1.48**	1.26 **1.39**	1.22 **1.33**	1.19 **1.28**	200
400	3.86 **6.70**	3.02 **4.66**	2.62 **3.83**	2.39 **3.36**	2.23 **3.06**	2.12 **2.85**	2.03 **2.69**	1.96 **2.55**	1.90 **2.46**	1.85 **2.37**	1.81 **2.29**	1.78 **2.23**	1.72 **2.12**	1.67 **2.04**	1.60 **1.92**	1.54 **1.84**	1.49 **1.74**	1.42 **1.64**	1.38 **1.57**	1.32 **1.47**	1.28 **1.42**	1.22 **1.32**	1.16 **1.24**	1.13 **1.19**	400
1000	3.85 **6.66**	3.00 **4.62**	2.61 **3.80**	2.38 **3.34**	2.22 **3.04**	2.10 **2.82**	2.02 **2.66**	1.95 **2.53**	1.89 **2.43**	1.84 **2.34**	1.80 **2.26**	1.76 **2.20**	1.70 **2.09**	1.65 **2.01**	1.58 **1.89**	1.53 **1.81**	1.47 **1.71**	1.41 **1.61**	1.36 **1.54**	1.30 **1.44**	1.26 **1.38**	1.19 **1.28**	1.13 **1.19**	1.08 **1.11**	1000
∞	3.84 **6.64**	2.99 **4.60**	2.60 **3.78**	2.37 **3.32**	2.21 **3.02**	2.09 **2.80**	2.01 **2.64**	1.94 **2.51**	1.88 **2.41**	1.83 **2.32**	1.79 **2.24**	1.75 **2.18**	1.69 **2.07**	1.64 **1.99**	1.57 **1.87**	1.52 **1.79**	1.46 **1.69**	1.40 **1.59**	1.35 **1.52**	1.28 **1.41**	1.24 **1.36**	1.17 **1.25**	1.11 **1.15**	1.00 **1.00**	∞

Table D. Critical Values of the Pearson Product Moment Correlation Coefficient

	Level of significance for one-tailed test				
	.05	.025	.01	.005	.0005
	Level of significance for two-tailed test				
$df = N-2$	.10	.05	.02	.01	.001
1	.9877	.9969	.9995	.9999	1.0000
2	.9000	.9500	.9800	.9900	.9990
3	.8054	.8783	.9343	.9587	.9912
4	.7293	.8114	.8822	.9172	.9741
5	.6694	.7545	.8329	.8745	.9507
6	.6215	.7067	.7887	.8343	.9249
7	.5822	.6664	.7498	.7977	.8982
8	.5494	.6319	.7155	.7646	.8721
9	.5214	.6021	.6851	.7348	.8471
10	.4973	.5760	.6581	.7079	.8233
11	.4762	.5529	.6339	.6835	.8010
12	.4575	.5324	.6120	.6614	.7800
13	.4409	.5139	.5923	.6411	.7603
14	.4259	.4973	.5742	.6226	.7420
15	.4124	.4821	.5577	.6055	.7246
16	.4000	.4683	.5425	.5897	.7084
17	.3887	.4555	.5285	.5751	.6932
18	.3783	.4438	.5155	.5614	.6787
19	.3687	.4329	.5034	.5487	.6652
20	.3598	.4227	.4921	.5368	.6524
25	.3233	.3809	.4451	.4869	.5974
30	.2960	.3494	.4093	.4487	.5541
35	.2746	.3246	.3810	.4182	.5189
40	.2573	.3044	.3578	.3932	.4896
45	.2428	.2875	.3384	.3721	.4648
50	.2306	.2732	.3218	.3541	.4433
60	.2108	.2500	.2948	.3248	.4078
70	.1954	.2319	.2737	.3017	.3799
80	.1829	.2172	.2565	.2830	.3568
90	.1726	.2050	.2422	.2673	.3375
100	.1638	.1946	.2301	.2540	.3211

Source: Table D is taken from Table VII of Fisher and Yates, *Statistical Tables for Biological, Agricultural, and Medical Research,* published by Oliver and Boyd, Ltd., Edinburgh, and by permission of the authors and publishers.

If the observed value of r is *greater than or equal to* the tabled value for the appropriate level of significance (columns) and degrees of freedom (rows), then reject H_0. The degrees of freedom are the number of pairs of scores minus two, or $N - 2$.

Table **E.** Transformation of r to z_r

r	z_r	r	z_r	r	z_r	r	z_r	r	z_r
.000	.000	.200	.203	.400	.424	.600	.693	.800	1.099
.005	.005	.205	.208	.405	.430	.605	.701	.805	1.113
.010	.010	.210	.213	.410	.436	.610	.709	.810	1.127
.015	.015	.215	.218	.415	.442	.615	.717	.815	1.142
.020	.020	.220	.224	.420	.448	.620	.725	.820	1.157
.025	.025	.225	.229	.425	.454	.625	.733	.825	1.172
.030	.030	.230	.234	.430	.460	.630	.741	.830	1.188
.035	.035	.235	.239	.435	.466	.635	.750	.835	1.204
.040	.040	.240	.245	.440	.472	.640	.758	.840	1.221
.045	.045	.245	.250	.445	.478	.645	.767	.845	1.238
.050	.050	.250	.255	.450	.485	.650	.775	.850	1.256
.055	.055	.255	.261	.455	.491	.655	.784	.855	1.274
.060	.060	.260	.266	.460	.497	.660	.793	.860	1.293
.065	.065	.265	.271	.465	.504	.665	.802	.865	1.313
.070	.070	.270	.277	.470	.510	.670	.811	.870	1.333
.075	.075	.275	.282	.475	.517	.675	.820	.875	1.354
.080	.080	.280	.288	.480	.523	.680	.829	.880	1.376
.085	.085	.285	.293	.485	.530	.685	.838	.885	1.398
.090	.090	.290	.299	.490	.536	.690	.848	.890	1.422
.095	.095	.295	.304	.495	.543	.695	.858	.895	1.447
.100	.100	.300	.310	.500	.549	.700	.867	.900	1.472
.105	.105	.305	.315	.505	.556	.705	.877	.905	1.499
.110	.110	.310	.321	.510	.563	.710	.887	.910	1.528
.115	.116	.315	.326	.515	.570	.715	.897	.915	1.557
.120	.121	.320	.332	.520	.576	.720	.908	.920	1.589
.125	.126	.325	.337	.525	.583	.725	.918	.925	1.623
.130	.131	.330	.343	.530	.590	.730	.929	.930	1.658
.135	.136	.335	.348	.535	.597	.735	.940	.935	1.697
.140	.141	.340	.354	.540	.604	.740	.950	.940	1.738
.145	.146	.345	.360	.545	.611	.745	.962	.945	1.783
.150	.151	.350	.365	.550	.618	.750	.973	.950	1.832
.155	.156	.355	.371	.555	.626	.755	.984	.955	1.886
.160	.161	.360	.377	.560	.633	.760	.996	.960	1.946
.165	.167	.365	.383	.565	.640	.765	1.008	.965	2.014
.170	.172	.370	.388	.570	.648	.770	1.020	.970	2.092
.175	.177	.375	.394	.575	.655	.775	1.033	.975	2.185
.180	.182	.380	.400	.580	.662	.780	1.045	.980	2.298
.185	.187	.385	.406	.585	.670	.785	1.058	.985	2.443
.190	.192	.390	.412	.590	.678	.790	1.071	.990	2.647
.195	.198	.395	.418	.595	.685	.795	1.085	.995	2.994

Source: From Edwards, A. L., *Statistical Methods for the Behavorial Sciences,* 1965, Holt, Rinehart and Winston, New York.

Table F. Critical Values of Chi Square

	Level of significance for one-tailed test					
	.10	.05	.025	.01	.005	.0005
	Level of significance for two-tailed test					
df	.20	.10	.05	.02	.01	.001
1	1.64	2.71	3.84	5.41	6.64	10.83
2	3.22	4.60	5.99	7.82	9.21	13.82
3	4.64	6.25	7.82	9.84	11.34	16.27
4	5.99	7.78	9.49	11.67	13.28	18.46
5	7.29	9.24	11.07	13.39	15.09	20.52
6	8.56	10.64	12.59	15.03	16.81	22.46
7	9.80	12.02	14.07	16.62	18.48	24.32
8	11.03	13.36	15.51	18.17	20.09	26.12
9	12.24	14.68	16.92	19.68	21.67	27.88
10	13.44	15.99	18.31	21.16	23.21	29.59
11	14.63	17.28	19.68	22.62	24.72	31.26
12	15.81	18.55	21.03	24.05	26.22	32.91
13	16.98	19.81	22.36	25.47	27.69	34.53
14	18.15	21.06	23.68	26.87	29.14	36.12
15	19.31	22.31	25.00	28.26	30.58	37.70
16	20.46	23.54	26.30	29.63	32.00	39.29
17	21.62	24.77	27.59	31.00	33.41	40.75
18	22.76	25.99	28.87	32.35	34.80	42.31
19	23.90	27.20	30.14	33.69	36.19	43.82
20	25.04	28.41	31.41	35.02	37.57	45.32
21	26.17	29.62	32.67	36.34	38.93	46.80
22	27.30	30.81	33.92	37.66	40.29	48.27
23	28.43	32.01	35.17	38.97	41.64	49.73
24	29.55	33.20	36.42	40.27	42.98	51.18
25	30.68	34.38	37.65	41.57	44.31	52.62
26	31.80	35.56	38.88	42.86	45.64	54.05
27	32.91	36.74	40.11	44.14	46.96	55.48
28	34.03	37.92	41.34	45.42	48.28	56.89
29	35.14	39.09	42.69	46.69	49.59	58.30
30	36.25	40.26	43.77	47.96	50.89	59.70
32	38.47	42.59	46.19	50.49	53.49	62.49
34	40.68	44.90	48.60	53.00	56.06	65.25
36	42.88	47.21	51.00	55.49	58.62	67.99
38	45.08	49.51	53.38	57.97	61.16	70.70
40	47.27	51.81	55.76	60.44	63.69	73.40
44	51.64	56.37	60.48	65.34	68.71	78.75
48	55.99	60.91	65.17	70.20	73.68	84.04
52	60.33	65.42	69.83	75.02	78.62	89.27
56	64.66	69.92	74.47	79.82	83.51	94.46
60	68.97	74.40	79.08	84.58	88.38	99.61

Source: Table F is taken from Table IV of Fisher and Yates, *Statistical Tables for Biological, Agricultural and Medical Research,* published by Oliver and Boyd, Ltd., Edinburgh, and by permission of the authors and publishers.

The table lists the critical values of chi square for the degrees of freedom shown at the left for tests corresponding to those significance levels heading each column. If the observed value of χ^2_{obs} is *greater than or equal to* the tabled value, reject H_0.

Table G. Critical Values of the Mann–Whitney *U* for a One–Tailed Test at .005 or a Two–Tailed Test at .01

n_2 \ n_1	1	2	3	4	5	6	7	8	9	10	11	12	13	14	15	16	17	18	19	20
1	--	--	--	--	--	--	--	--	--	--	--	--	--	--	--	--	--	--	--	--
2	--	--	--	--	--	--	--	--	--	--	--	--	--	--	--	--	--	--	0 38	0 40
3	--	--	--	--	--	--	--	--	0 27	0 30	0 33	1 35	1 38	1 41	2 43	2 46	2 49	2 52	3 54	3 57
4	--	--	--	--	--	0 24	0 28	1 31	1 35	2 38	2 42	3 45	3 49	4 52	5 55	5 59	6 62	6 66	7 69	8 72
5	--	--	--	--	0 25	1 29	1 34	2 38	3 42	4 46	5 50	6 54	7 58	7 63	8 67	9 71	10 75	11 79	12 83	13 87
6	--	--	--	0 24	1 29	2 34	3 39	4 44	5 49	6 54	7 59	9 63	10 68	11 73	12 78	13 83	15 87	16 92	17 97	18 102
7	--	--	--	0 28	1 34	3 39	4 45	6 50	7 56	9 61	10 67	12 72	13 78	15 83	16 89	18 94	19 100	21 105	22 111	24 116
8	--	--	--	1 31	2 38	4 44	6 50	7 57	9 63	11 69	13 75	15 81	17 87	18 94	20 100	22 106	24 112	26 118	28 124	30 130
9	--	--	0 27	1 35	3 42	5 49	7 56	9 63	11 70	13 77	16 83	18 90	20 97	22 104	24 111	27 117	29 124	31 131	33 138	36 144
10	--	--	0 30	2 38	4 46	6 54	9 61	11 69	13 77	16 84	18 92	21 99	24 106	26 114	29 121	31 129	34 136	37 143	39 151	42 158
11	--	--	0 33	2 42	5 50	7 59	10 67	13 75	16 83	18 92	21 100	24 108	27 116	30 124	33 132	36 140	39 148	42 156	45 164	48 172
12	--	--	1 35	3 45	6 54	9 63	12 72	15 81	18 90	21 99	24 108	27 117	31 125	34 134	37 143	41 151	44 160	47 169	51 177	54 186
13	--	--	1 38	3 49	7 58	10 68	13 78	17 87	20 97	24 106	27 116	31 125	34 125	38 144	42 153	45 163	49 172	53 181	56 191	60 200
14	--	--	1 41	4 52	7 63	11 73	15 83	18 94	22 104	26 114	30 124	34 134	38 144	42 154	46 164	50 174	54 184	58 194	63 203	67 213
15	--	--	2 43	5 55	8 67	12 78	16 89	20 100	24 111	29 121	33 132	37 143	42 153	46 164	51 174	55 185	60 195	64 206	69 216	73 227
16	--	--	2 46	5 59	9 71	13 83	18 94	22 106	27 117	31 129	36 140	41 151	45 163	50 174	55 185	60 196	65 207	70 218	74 230	79 241
17	--	--	2 49	6 62	10 75	15 87	19 100	24 112	29 124	34 148	39 148	44 160	49 172	54 184	60 195	65 207	70 219	75 231	81 242	86 254
18	--	--	2 52	6 66	11 79	16 92	21 105	26 118	31 131	37 143	42 156	47 169	53 181	58 194	64 206	70 218	75 231	81 243	87 255	92 268
19	--	0 38	3 54	7 69	12 83	17 97	22 111	28 124	33 138	39 151	45 164	51 177	56 191	63 203	69 216	74 230	81 242	87 255	93 268	99 281
20	--	0 40	3 57	8 72	13 87	18 102	24 116	30 130	36 144	42 158	48 172	54 186	60 200	67 213	73 227	79 241	86 254	92 268	99 281	105 295

(Dashes in the body of the table indicate that no decision is possible at the stated level of significance.)

Source: From Mann, H. B., and Whitney, D. R., "On a test of whether one of two random variables is a stochastically larger than the other," *Annals of Mathematical Statistics,* 1947, **18,** 50-60, and Auble, D., "Extended tables for the Mann-Whitney statistic," *Bulletin of the*

Table G. Critical Values of the Mann–Whitney U for a One–Tailed Test at .01 or a Two–Tailed Test at .02

n_2 \ n_1	1	2	3	4	5	6	7	8	9	10	11	12	13	14	15	16	17	18	19	20
1	--	--	--	--	--	--	--	--	--	--	--	--	--	--	--	--	--	--	--	--
2	--	--	--	--	--	--	--	--	--	--	--	--	0 26	0 28	0 30	0 32	0 34	0 36	1 37	1 39
3	--	--	--	--	--	--	0 21	0 24	1 26	1 29	1 32	2 34	2 37	2 40	3 42	3 45	4 47	4 50	4 52	5 55
4	--	--	--	--	0 20	1 23	1 27	2 30	3 33	3 37	4 40	5 43	5 47	6 50	7 53	7 57	8 60	9 63	9 67	10 70
5	--	--	--	0 20	1 24	2 28	3 32	4 36	5 40	6 44	7 48	8 52	9 56	10 60	11 64	12 68	13 72	14 76	15 80	16 84
6	--	--	--	1 23	2 28	3 33	4 38	6 42	7 47	8 52	9 57	11 61	12 66	13 71	15 75	16 80	18 84	19 89	20 94	22 98
7	--	--	0 21	1 27	3 32	4 38	6 43	7 49	9 54	11 59	12 65	14 70	16 75	17 81	19 86	21 91	23 96	24 102	26 107	28 112
8	--	--	0 24	2 30	4 36	6 42	7 49	9 55	11 61	13 67	15 73	17 79	20 84	22 90	24 96	26 102	28 108	30 114	32 120	34 126
9	--	--	1 26	3 33	5 40	7 47	9 54	11 61	14 67	16 74	18 81	21 87	23 94	26 100	28 107	31 113	33 120	36 126	38 133	40 140
10	--	--	1 29	3 37	6 44	8 52	11 59	13 67	16 74	19 81	22 88	24 96	27 103	30 110	33 117	36 124	38 132	41 139	44 146	47 153
11	--	--	1 32	4 40	7 48	9 57	12 65	15 73	18 81	22 88	25 96	28 104	31 112	34 120	37 128	41 135	44 143	47 151	50 159	53 167
12	--	--	2 34	5 43	8 52	11 61	14 70	17 79	21 87	24 96	28 104	31 113	35 121	38 130	42 138	46 146	49 155	53 163	56 172	60 180
13	--	0 26	2 37	5 47	9 56	12 66	16 75	20 84	23 94	27 103	31 112	35 121	39 130	43 139	47 148	51 157	55 166	59 175	63 184	67 193
14	--	0 28	2 40	6 50	10 60	13 71	17 81	22 90	26 100	30 110	34 120	38 130	43 139	47 149	51 159	56 168	60 178	65 187	69 197	73 207
15	--	0 30	3 42	7 53	11 64	15 75	19 86	24 96	28 107	33 117	37 128	42 138	47 148	51 159	56 169	61 179	66 189	70 200	75 210	80 220
16	--	0 32	3 45	7 57	12 68	16 80	21 91	26 102	31 113	36 124	41 135	46 146	51 157	56 168	61 179	66 190	71 201	76 212	82 222	87 233
17	--	0 34	4 47	8 60	13 72	18 84	23 96	28 108	33 120	38 132	44 143	49 155	55 166	60 178	66 189	71 201	77 212	82 224	88 234	93 247
18	--	0 36	4 50	9 63	14 76	19 89	24 102	30 114	36 126	41 139	47 151	53 163	59 175	65 187	70 200	76 212	82 224	88 236	94 248	100 260
19	--	1 37	4 53	9 67	15 80	20 94	26 107	32 120	38 133	44 146	50 159	56 172	63 184	69 197	75 210	82 222	88 235	94 248	101 260	107 273
20	--	1 39	5 55	10 70	16 84	22 98	28 112	34 126	40 140	47 153	53 167	60 180	67 193	73 207	80 220	87 233	93 247	100 260	107 273	114 286

(Dashes in the body of the table indicate that no decision is possible at the stated level of significance.)

Institute of Educational Research at Indiana University, 1953, **1**, No. 2, as used in Runyon and Haber, *Fundamentals of Behavorial Statistics,* 1967, Addison-Wesley, Reading, Mass.

If the observed value of U falls between the two values presented in the table for n_1 and n_2, *accept* H_0. Otherwise, reject H_0.

Table G. Critical Values of the Mann–Whitney *U* for a One–Tailed Test at .025 and a Two–Tailed Test at .05

n_2 \ n_1	1	2	3	4	5	6	7	8	9	10	11	12	13	14	15	16	17	18	19	20
1	--	--	--	--	--	--	--	--	--	--	--	--	--	--	--	--	--	--	--	--
2	--	--	--	--	--	--	--	0 16	0 18	0 20	0 22	1 23	1 25	1 27	1 29	1 31	2 32	2 34	2 36	2 38
3	--	--	--	--	0 15	1 17	1 20	2 22	2 25	3 27	3 30	4 32	4 35	5 37	5 40	6 42	6 45	7 47	7 50	8 52
4	--	--	--	0 16	1 19	2 22	3 25	4 28	4 32	5 35	6 38	7 41	8 44	9 47	10 50	11 53	11 57	12 60	13 63	13 67
5	--	--	0 15	1 19	2 23	3 27	5 30	6 34	7 38	8 42	9 46	11 49	12 53	13 57	14 61	15 65	17 68	18 72	19 76	20 80
6	--	--	1 17	2 22	3 27	5 31	6 36	8 40	10 44	11 49	13 53	14 58	16 62	17 67	19 71	21 75	22 80	24 84	25 89	27 93
7	--	--	1 20	3 25	5 30	6 36	8 41	10 46	12 51	14 56	16 61	18 66	20 71	22 76	24 81	26 86	28 91	30 96	32 101	34 106
8	--	0 16	2 22	4 28	6 34	8 40	10 46	13 51	15 57	17 63	19 69	22 74	24 80	26 86	29 91	31 97	34 102	36 108	38 111	41 119
9	--	0 18	2 25	4 32	7 38	10 44	12 51	15 57	17 64	20 70	23 76	26 82	28 89	31 95	34 101	37 107	39 114	42 120	45 126	48 132
10	--	0 20	3 27	5 35	8 42	11 49	14 56	17 63	20 70	23 77	26 84	29 91	33 97	36 104	39 111	42 118	45 125	48 132	52 138	55 145
11	--	0 22	3 30	6 38	9 46	13 53	16 61	19 69	23 76	26 84	30 91	33 99	37 106	40 114	44 121	47 129	51 136	55 143	58 151	62 158
12	--	1 23	4 32	7 41	11 49	14 58	18 66	22 74	26 82	29 91	33 99	37 107	41 115	45 123	49 131	53 139	57 147	61 155	65 163	69 171
13	--	1 25	4 35	8 44	12 53	16 62	20 71	24 80	28 89	33 97	37 106	41 115	45 124	50 132	54 141	59 149	63 158	67 167	72 175	76 184
14	--	1 27	5 37	9 47	13 51	17 67	22 76	26 86	31 95	36 104	40 114	45 123	50 132	55 141	59 151	64 160	67 171	74 178	78 188	83 197
15	--	1 29	5 40	10 50	14 61	19 71	24 81	29 91	34 101	39 111	44 121	49 131	54 141	59 151	64 161	70 170	75 180	80 190	85 200	90 210
16	--	1 31	6 42	11 53	15 65	21 75	26 86	31 97	37 107	42 118	47 129	53 139	59 149	64 160	70 170	75 181	81 191	86 202	92 212	98 222
17	--	2 32	6 45	11 57	17 68	22 80	28 91	34 102	39 114	45 125	51 136	57 147	63 158	67 171	75 180	81 191	87 202	93 213	99 224	105 235
18	--	2 34	7 47	12 60	18 72	24 84	30 96	36 108	42 120	48 132	55 143	61 155	67 167	74 178	80 190	86 202	93 213	99 225	106 236	112 248
19	--	2 36	7 50	13 63	19 76	25 89	32 101	38 114	45 126	52 138	58 151	65 163	72 175	78 188	85 200	92 212	99 224	106 236	113 248	119 261
20	--	2 38	8 52	13 67	20 80	27 93	34 106	41 119	48 132	55 145	62 158	69 171	76 184	83 197	90 210	98 222	105 235	112 248	119 261	127 273

(Dashes in the body of the table indicate that no decision is possible at the stated level of significance.)

Table G. Critical Values of the Mann–Whitney *U* for a One–Tailed Test at .05 or a Two–Tailed Test at .10

n_2 \ n_1	1	2	3	4	5	6	7	8	9	10	11	12	13	14	15	16	17	18	19	20
1	--	--	--	--	--	--	--	--	--	--	--	--	--	--	--	--	--	--	0 19	0 20
2	--	--	--	--	0 10	0 12	0 14	1 15	1 17	1 19	1 21	2 22	2 24	2 26	3 27	3 29	3 31	4 32	4 34	4 36
3	--	--	0 9	0 12	1 14	2 16	2 19	3 21	3 24	4 26	5 28	5 31	6 33	7 35	7 38	8 40	9 42	9 45	10 47	11 49
4	--	--	0 12	1 15	2 18	3 21	4 24	5 27	6 30	7 33	8 36	9 39	10 42	11 45	12 48	14 50	15 53	16 56	17 59	18 62
5	--	0 10	1 14	2 18	4 21	5 25	6 29	8 32	9 36	11 39	12 43	13 47	15 50	16 54	18 57	19 61	20 65	22 68	23 72	25 75
6	--	0 12	2 16	3 21	5 25	7 29	8 34	10 38	12 42	14 46	16 50	17 55	19 59	21 63	23 67	25 71	26 76	28 80	30 84	32 88
7	--	0 14	2 19	4 24	6 29	8 34	11 38	13 43	15 48	17 53	19 58	21 63	24 67	26 72	28 77	30 82	33 86	35 91	37 96	39 101
8	--	1 15	3 21	5 27	8 32	10 38	13 43	15 49	18 54	20 60	23 65	26 70	28 76	31 81	33 87	36 92	39 97	41 103	44 108	47 113
9	--	1 17	3 24	6 30	9 36	12 42	15 48	18 54	21 60	24 66	27 72	30 78	33 84	36 90	39 96	42 102	45 108	48 114	51 120	54 126
10	--	1 19	4 26	7 33	11 39	14 46	17 53	20 60	24 66	27 73	31 79	34 86	37 93	41 99	44 106	48 112	51 119	55 125	58 132	62 138
11	--	1 21	5 28	8 36	12 43	16 50	19 58	23 65	27 72	31 79	34 87	38 94	42 101	46 108	50 115	54 122	57 130	61 137	65 144	69 151
12	--	2 22	5 31	9 39	13 47	17 55	21 63	26 70	30 78	34 86	38 94	42 102	47 109	51 117	55 125	60 132	64 140	68 148	72 156	77 163
13	--	2 24	6 33	10 42	15 50	19 59	24 67	28 76	33 84	37 93	42 101	47 109	51 118	56 126	61 134	65 143	70 151	75 159	80 167	84 176
14	--	2 26	7 35	11 45	16 54	21 63	26 72	31 81	36 90	41 99	46 108	51 117	56 126	61 135	66 144	71 153	77 161	82 170	87 179	92 188
15	--	3 27	7 38	12 48	18 57	23 67	28 77	33 87	39 96	44 106	50 115	55 125	61 134	66 144	72 153	77 163	83 172	88 182	94 191	100 200
16	--	3 29	8 40	14 50	19 61	25 71	30 82	36 92	42 102	48 112	54 122	60 132	65 143	71 153	77 163	83 173	89 183	95 193	101 203	107 213
17	--	3 31	9 42	15 53	20 65	26 76	33 86	39 97	45 108	51 119	57 130	64 140	70 151	77 161	83 172	89 183	96 193	102 204	109 214	115 225
18	--	4 32	9 45	16 56	22 68	28 80	35 91	41 103	48 114	55 123	61 137	68 148	75 159	82 170	88 182	95 193	102 204	109 215	116 226	123 237
19	0 19	4 34	10 47	17 59	23 72	30 84	37 96	44 108	51 120	58 132	65 144	72 156	80 167	87 179	94 191	101 203	109 214	116 226	123 238	130 250
20	0 20	4 36	11 49	18 62	25 75	32 88	39 101	47 113	54 126	62 138	69 151	77 163	84 176	92 188	100 200	107 213	115 225	123 237	130 250	138 262

(Dashes in the body of the table indicate that no decision is possible at the stated level of significance.)

Table H. Critical Values of W for the Wilcoxon Test

	Level of significance for one-tailed test					Level of significance for one-tailed test			
	.05	.025	.01	.005		.05	.025	.01	.005
	Level of significance for two-tailed test					Level of significance for two-tailed test			
N	.10	.05	.02	.01	N	.10	.05	.02	.01
5	0	--	--	--	28	130	116	101	91
6	2	0	--	--	29	140	126	110	100
7	3	2	0	--	30	151	137	120	109
8	5	3	1	0	31	163	147	130	118
9	8	5	3	1	32	175	159	140	128
10	10	8	5	3	33	187	170	151	138
11	13	10	7	5	34	200	182	162	148
12	17	13	9	7	35	213	195	173	159
13	21	17	12	9	36	227	208	185	171
14	25	21	15	12	37	241	221	198	182
15	30	25	19	15	38	256	235	211	194
16	35	29	23	19	39	271	249	224	207
17	41	34	27	23	40	286	264	238	220
18	47	40	32	27	41	302	279	252	233
19	53	46	37	32	42	319	294	266	247
20	60	52	43	37	43	336	310	281	261
21	67	58	49	42	44	353	327	296	276
22	75	65	55	48	45	371	343	312	291
23	83	73	62	54	46	389	361	328	307
24	91	81	69	61	47	407	378	345	322
25	100	89	76	68	48	426	396	362	339
26	110	98	84	75	49	446	415	379	355
27	119	107	92	83	50	466	434	397	373

Source: From F. Wilcoxon, S. Katte, and R. A. Wilcox, *Critical Values and Probability Levels for the Wilcoxon Rank Sum Test and the Wilcoxon Signed Rank Test,* New York, American Cyanamid Co., 1963, and F. Wilcoxon and R. A. Wilcox, *Some Rapid Approximate Statistical Procedures,* New York, Lederle Laboratories, 1964 as used in Runyon and Haber, *Fundamentals of Behavioral Statistics,* 1967, Addison-Wesley, Reading, Mass.

For a given N (the number of pairs of scores), if the observed value is *less than or equal to* the value in the table for the appropriate level of significance, then reject H_0.

Table I. Critical Values for the Spearman Rank-Order Correlation Coefficient

	Significance level for a one-tailed test at			
	.05	.025	.005	.001
	Significance level for a two-tailed test at			
N	.10	.05	.01	.002
5	.900	1.000		
6	.829	.886	1.000	
7	.715	.786	.929	1.000
8	.620	.715	.881	.953
9	.600	.700	.834	.917
10	.564	.649	.794	.879
11	.537	.619	.764	.855
12	.504	.588	.735	.826
13	.484	.561	.704	.797
14	.464	.539	.680	.772
15	.447	.522	.658	.750
16	.430	.503	.636	.730
17	.415	.488	.618	.711
18	.402	.474	.600	.693
19	.392	.460	.585	.676
20	.381	.447	.570	.661
21	.371	.437	.556	.647
22	.361	.426	.544	.633
23	.353	.417	.532	.620
24	.345	.407	.521	.608
25	.337	.399	.511	.597
26	.331	.391	.501	.587
27	.325	.383	.493	.577
28	.319	.376	.484	.567
29	.312	.369	.475	.558
30	.307	.363	.467	.549

Source: Glasser, G. J., and R. F. Winter, "Critical Values of the Coefficient of Rank Correlation for Testing the Hypothesis of Independence," *Biometrika,* 48, 444 (1961).

If the observed value of r_S is *greater than or equal to* the tabled value for the appropriate level of significance, reject H_0. Note that the left-hand column is the number of pairs of scores, not the number of degrees of freedom.

Table J. Random Numbers

22 17 68 65 84	68 95 23 92 35	87 02 22 57 51	61 09 43 95 06	58 24 82 03 47
19 36 27 59 46	13 79 93 37 55	39 77 32 77 09	85 52 05 30 62	47 83 51 62 74
16 77 23 02 77	09 61 87 25 21	28 06 24 25 93	16 71 13 59 78	23 05 47 47 25
78 43 76 71 61	20 44 90 32 64	97 67 63 99 61	46 38 03 93 22	69 81 21 99 21
03 28 28 26 08	73 37 32 04 05	69 30 16 09 05	88 69 58 28 99	35 07 44 75 47
93 22 53 64 39	07 10 63 76 35	87 03 04 79 88	08 13 13 85 51	55 34 57 72 69
78 76 58 54 74	92 38 70 96 92	52 06 79 79 45	82 63 18 27 44	69 66 92 19 09
23 68 35 26 00	99 53 93 61 28	52 70 05 48 34	56 65 05 61 86	90 92 10 70 80
15 39 25 70 99	93 86 52 77 65	15 33 59 05 28	22 87 26 07 47	86 96 98 29 06
58 71 96 30 24	18 46 23 34 27	85 13 99 24 44	49 18 09 79 49	74 16 32 23 02
57 35 27 33 72	24 53 63 94 09	41 10 76 47 91	44 04 95 49 66	39 60 04 59 81
48 50 86 54 48	22 06 34 72 52	82 21 15 65 20	33 29 94 71 11	15 91 29 12 03
61 96 48 95 03	07 16 39 33 66	98 56 10 56 79	77 21 30 27 12	90 49 22 23 62
36 93 89 41 26	29 70 83 63 51	99 74 20 52 36	87 09 41 15 09	98 60 16 03 03
18 87 00 42 31	57 90 12 02 07	23 47 37 17 31	54 08 01 88 63	39 41 88 92 10
88 56 53 27 59	33 35 72 67 47	77 34 55 45 70	08 18 27 38 90	16 95 86 70 75
09 72 95 84 29	49 41 31 06 70	42 38 06 45 18	64 84 73 31 65	52 53 37 97 15
12 96 88 17 31	65 19 69 02 83	60 75 86 90 68	24 64 19 35 51	56 61 87 39 12
85 94 57 24 16	92 09 84 38 76	22 00 27 69 85	29 81 94 78 70	21 94 47 90 12
38 64 43 59 98	98 77 87 68 07	91 51 67 62 44	40 98 05 93 78	23 32 65 41 18
53 44 09 42 72	00 41 86 79 79	68 47 22 00 20	35 55 31 51 51	00 83 63 22 55
40 76 66 26 84	57 99 99 90 37	36 63 32 08 58	37 40 13 68 97	87 64 81 07 83
02 17 79 18 05	12 59 52 57 02	22 07 90 47 03	28 14 11 30 79	20 69 22 40 98
95 17 82 06 53	31 51 10 96 46	92 06 88 07 77	56 11 50 81 69	40 23 72 51 39
35 76 22 42 92	96 11 83 44 80	34 68 35 48 77	33 42 40 90 60	73 96 53 97 86
26 29 13 56 41	85 47 04 66 08	34 72 57 59 13	82 43 80 46 15	38 26 61 70 04
77 80 20 75 82	72 82 32 99 90	63 95 73 76 63	89 73 44 99 05	48 67 26 43 18
46 40 66 44 52	91 36 74 43 53	30 82 13 54 00	78 45 63 98 35	55 03 36 67 68
37 56 08 18 09	77 53 84 46 47	31 91 18 95 58	24 16 74 11 53	44 10 13 85 57
61 65 61 68 66	37 27 47 39 19	84 83 70 07 48	53 21 40 06 71	95 06 79 88 54
93 43 69 64 07	34 18 04 52 35	56 27 09 24 86	61 85 53 83 45	19 90 70 99 00
21 96 60 12 99	11 20 99 45 18	48 13 93 55 34	18 37 79 49 90	65 97 38 20 46
95 20 47 97 97	27 37 83 28 71	00 06 41 41 74	45 89 09 39 84	51 67 11 52 49
97 86 21 78 73	10 65 81 92 59	58 76 17 14 97	04 76 62 16 17	17 95 70 45 80
69 92 06 34 13	59 71 74 17 32	27 55 10 24 19	23 71 82 13 74	63 52 52 01 41
04 31 17 21 56	33 73 99 19 87	26 72 39 27 67	53 77 57 68 93	60 61 97 22 61
61 06 98 03 91	87 14 77 43 96	43 00 65 98 50	45 60 33 01 07	98 99 46 50 47
85 93 85 86 88	72 87 08 62 40	16 06 10 89 20	23 21 34 74 97	76 38 03 29 63
21 74 32 47 45	73 96 07 94 52	09 65 90 77 47	25 76 16 19 33	53 05 70 53 30
15 69 53 82 80	79 96 23 53 10	65 39 07 16 29	45 33 02 43 70	02 87 40 41 45
02 89 08 04 49	20 21 14 68 86	87 63 93 95 17	11 29 01 95 80	35 14 97 35 33
87 18 15 89 79	85 43 01 72 73	08 61 74 51 69	89 74 39 82 15	94 51 33 41 67
98 83 71 94 22	59 97 50 99 52	08 52 85 08 40	87 80 61 65 31	91 51 80 32 44
10 08 58 21 66	72 68 49 29 31	89 85 84 46 06	59 73 19 85 23	65 09 29 75 63
47 90 56 10 08	88 02 84 27 83	42 29 72 23 19	66 56 45 65 79	20 71 53 20 25
22 85 61 68 90	49 64 92 85 44	16 40 12 89 88	50 14 49 81 06	01 82 77 45 12
67 80 43 79 33	12 83 11 41 16	25 58 19 68 70	77 02 54 00 52	53 43 37 15 26
27 62 50 96 72	79 44 61 40 15	14 53 40 65 39	27 31 58 50 28	11 39 03 34 25
33 78 80 87 15	38 30 06 38 21	14 47 47 07 26	54 96 87 53 32	40 36 40 96 76
13 13 92 66 99	47 24 49 57 74	32 25 43 62 17	10 97 11 69 84	99 63 22 32 98

Source: Table J is taken from Table XXXIII of Fisher and Yates, *Statistical Tables for Biological, Agricultural and Medical Research,* published by Oliver and Boyd, Ltd., Edinburgh, and by permission of the authors and publishers.

Table J (continued)

10 27 53 96 23	71 50 54 36 23	54 31 04 82 98	04 14 12 15 09	26 78 25 47 47
28 41 50 61 88	64 85 27 20 18	83 36 36 05 56	39 71 65 09 62	94 76 62 11 89
34 21 42 57 02	59 19 18 97 48	80 30 03 30 98	05 24 67 70 07	84 97 50 87 46
61 81 77 23 23	82 82 11 54 08	53 28 70 58 96	44 07 39 55 43	42 34 43 39 28
61 15 18 13 54	16 86 20 26 88	90 74 80 55 09	14 53 90 51 17	52 01 63 01 59
91 76 21 64 64	44 91 13 32 97	75 31 62 66 54	84 80 32 75 77	56 08 25 70 29
00 97 79 08 06	37 30 28 59 85	53 56 68 53 40	01 74 39 59 73	30 19 99 85 48
36 46 18 34 94	75 20 80 27 77	78 91 69 16 00	08 43 18 73 68	67 69 61 34 25
88 98 99 60 50	65 95 79 42 94	93 62 40 89 96	43 56 47 71 66	46 76 29 67 02
04 37 59 87 21	05 02 03 24 17	47 97 81 56 51	92 34 86 01 82	55 51 33 12 91
63 62 06 34 41	94 21 78 55 09	72 76 45 16 94	29 95 81 83 83	79 88 01 97 30
78 47 23 53 90	34 41 92 45 71	09 23 70 70 07	12 38 92 79 43	14 85 11 47 23
87 68 62 15 43	53 14 36 59 25	54 47 33 70 15	59 24 48 40 35	50 03 42 99 36
47 60 92 10 77	88 59 53 11 52	66 25 69 07 04	48 68 64 71 06	61 65 70 22 12
56 88 87 59 41	65 28 04 67 53	95 79 88 37 31	50 41 06 94 76	81 83 17 16 33
02 57 45 86 67	73 43 07 34 48	44 26 87 93 29	77 09 61 67 84	06 69 44 77 75
31 54 14 13 17	48 62 11 90 60	68 12 93 64 28	46 24 79 16 76	14 60 25 51 01
28 50 16 43 36	28 97 85 58 99	67 22 52 76 23	24 70 36 54 54	59 28 61 71 96
63 29 62 66 50	02 63 45 52 38	67 63 47 54 75	83 24 78 43 20	92 63 13 47 48
45 65 58 26 51	76 96 59 38 72	86 57 45 71 46	44 67 76 14 55	44 88 01 62 12
39 65 36 63 70	77 45 85 50 51	74 13 39 35 22	30 53 36 02 95	49 34 88 73 61
73 71 98 16 04	29 18 94 51 23	76 51 94 84 86	79 93 96 38 63	08 58 25 58 94
72 20 56 20 11	72 65 71 08 86	79 57 95 13 91	97 48 72 66 48	09 71 17 24 89
75 17 26 99 76	89 37 20 70 01	77 31 61 95 46	26 97 05 73 51	53 33 18 72 87
37 48 60 82 29	81 30 15 39 14	48 38 75 93 29	06 87 37 78 48	45 56 00 84 47
68 08 02 80 72	83 71 46 30 49	89 17 95 88 29	02 39 56 03 46	97 74 06 56 17
14 23 98 61 67	70 52 85 01 50	01 84 02 78 43	10 62 98 19 41	18 83 99 47 99
49 08 96 21 44	25 27 99 41 28	07 41 08 34 66	19 42 74 39 91	41 96 53 78 72
78 37 06 08 43	63 61 62 42 29	39 68 95 10 96	09 24 23 00 62	56 12 80 73 16
37 21 34 17 68	68 96 83 23 56	32 84 60 15 31	44 73 67 34 77	91 15 79 74 58
14 29 09 34 04	87 83 07 55 07	76 58 30 83 64	87 29 25 58 84	86 50 60 00 25
58 43 28 06 36	49 52 83 51 14	47 56 91 29 34	05 87 31 06 95	12 45 57 09 09
10 43 67 29 70	80 62 80 03 42	10 80 21 38 84	90 56 35 03 09	43 12 74 49 14
44 38 88 39 54	86 97 37 44 22	00 95 01 31 76	17 16 29 56 63	38 78 94 49 81
90 69 59 19 51	85 39 52 85 13	07 28 37 07 61	11 16 36 27 03	78 86 72 04 95
41 47 10 25 62	97 05 31 03 61	20 26 36 31 62	68 69 86 95 44	84 95 48 46 45
91 94 14 63 19	75 89 11 47 11	31 56 34 19 09	79 57 92 36 59	14 93 87 81 40
80 06 54 18 66	09 18 94 06 19	98 40 07 17 81	22 45 44 84 11	24 62 20 42 31
67 72 77 63 48	84 08 31 55 58	24 33 45 77 58	80 45 67 93 82	75 70 16 08 24
59 40 24 13 27	79 26 88 86 30	01 31 60 10 39	53 58 47 70 93	85 81 56 39 38
05 90 35 89 95	01 61 16 96 94	50 78 13 69 36	37 68 53 37 31	71 26 35 03 71
44 43 80 69 98	46 68 05 14 82	90 78 50 05 62	77 79 13 57 44	59 60 10 39 66
61 81 31 96 82	00 57 25 60 59	46 72 60 18 77	55 66 12 62 11	08 99 55 64 57
42 88 07 10 05	24 98 65 63 21	47 21 61 88 32	27 80 30 21 60	10 92 35 36 12
77 94 30 05 39	28 10 99 00 27	12 73 73 99 12	49 99 57 94 82	96 88 57 17 91
78 83 19 76 16	94 11 68 84 26	23 54 20 86 85	23 86 66 99 07	36 37 34 92 09
87 76 59 61 81	43 63 64 61 61	65 76 36 95 90	18 48 27 45 68	27 23 65 30 72
91 43 05 96 47	55 78 99 95 24	37 55 85 78 78	01 48 41 19 10	35 19 54 07 73
84 97 77 72 73	09 62 06 65 72	87 12 49 03 60	41 15 20 76 27	50 47 02 29 16
87 41 60 76 83	44 88 96 07 80	83 05 83 38 96	73 70 66 81 90	30 56 10 48 59

Table **K.** Table of Squares, Square Roots, and Reciprocals

N	N^2	$\sqrt{N}$	$1/N$	N	N^2	$\sqrt{N}$	$1/N$
1	1	1.0000	1.000000	41	1681	6.4031	.024390
2	4	1.4142	.500000	42	1764	6.4807	.023810
3	9	1.7321	.333333	43	1849	6.5574	.023256
4	16	2.0000	.250000	44	1936	6.6332	.022727
5	25	2.2361	.200000	45	2025	6.7082	.022222
6	36	2.4495	.166667	46	2116	6.7823	.021739
7	49	2.6458	.142857	47	2209	6.8557	.021277
8	64	2.8284	.125000	48	2304	6.9282	.020833
9	81	3.0000	.111111	49	2401	7.0000	.020408
10	100	3.1623	.100000	50	2500	7.0711	.020000
11	121	3.3166	.090909	51	2601	7.1414	.019608
12	144	3.4641	.083333	52	2704	7.2111	.019231
13	169	3.6056	.076923	53	2809	7.2801	.018868
14	196	3.7417	.071429	54	2916	7.3485	.018519
15	225	3.8730	.066667	55	3025	7.4162	.018182
16	256	4.0000	.062500	56	3136	7.4833	.017857
17	289	4.1231	.058824	57	3249	7.5498	.017544
18	324	4.2426	.055556	58	3364	7.6158	.017241
19	361	4.3589	.052632	59	3481	7.6811	.016949
20	400	4.4721	.050000	60	3600	7.7460	.016667
21	441	4.5826	.047619	61	3721	7.8102	.016393
22	484	4.6904	.045455	62	3844	7.8740	.016129
23	529	4.7958	.043478	63	3969	7.9373	.015873
24	576	4.8990	.041667	64	4096	8.0000	.015625
25	625	5.0000	.040000	65	4225	8.0623	.015385
26	676	5.0990	.038462	66	4356	8.1240	.015152
27	729	5.1962	.037037	67	4489	8.1854	.014925
28	784	5.2915	.035714	68	4624	8.2462	.014706
29	841	5.3852	.034483	69	4761	8.3066	.014493
30	900	5.4772	.033333	70	4900	8.3666	.014286
31	961	5.5678	.032258	71	5041	8.4261	.014085
32	1024	5.6569	.031250	72	5184	8.4853	.013889
33	1089	5.7446	.030303	73	5329	8.5440	.013699
34	1156	5.8310	.029412	74	5476	8.6023	.013514
35	1225	5.9161	.028571	75	5625	8.6603	.013333
36	1296	6.0000	.027778	76	5776	8.7178	.013158
37	1369	6.0828	.027027	77	5929	8.7750	.012987
38	1444	6.1644	.026316	78	6084	8.8318	.012821
39	1521	6.2450	.025641	79	6241	8.8882	.012658
40	1600	6.3246	.025000	80	6400	8.9443	.012500

Source: J. W. Dunlap and A. K. Kurtz, *Handbook of Statistical Monographs, Tables and Formulas.* New York: World Book Company, 1932, as used in A. L. Edwards, *Statistical Methods for the Behavioral Sciences,* 1954, Holt, Rinehart and Winston, New York.

Table K (continued)

N	N^2	$\sqrt{N}$	$1/N$	N	N^2	$\sqrt{N}$	$1/N$
81	6561	9.0000	.012346	121	14641	11.0000	.00826446
82	6724	9.0554	.012195	122	14884	11.0454	.00819672
83	6889	9.1104	.012048	123	15129	11.0905	.00813008
84	7056	9.1652	.011905	124	15376	11.1355	.00806452
85	7225	9.2195	.011765	125	15625	11.1803	.00800000
86	7396	9.2736	.011628	126	15876	11.2250	.00793651
87	7569	9.3274	.011494	127	16129	11.2694	.00787402
88	7744	9.3808	.011364	128	16384	11.3137	.00781250
89	7921	9.4340	.011236	129	16641	11.3578	.00775194
90	8100	9.4868	.011111	130	16900	11.4018	.00769231
91	8281	9.5394	.010989	131	17161	11.4455	.00763359
92	8464	9.5917	.010870	132	17424	11.4891	.00757576
93	8649	9.6437	.010753	133	17689	11.5326	.00751880
94	8836	9.6954	.010638	134	17956	11.5758	.00746269
95	9025	9.7468	.010526	135	18225	11.6190	.00740741
96	9216	9.7980	.010417	136	18496	11.6619	.00735294
97	9409	9.8489	.010309	137	18769	11.7047	.00729927
98	9604	9.8995	.010204	138	19044	11.7473	.00724638
99	9801	9.9499	.010101	139	19321	11.7898	.00719424
100	10000	10.0000	.010000	140	19600	11.8322	.00714286
101	10201	10.0499	.00990099	141	19881	11.8743	.00709220
102	10404	10.0995	.00980392	142	20164	11.9164	.00704225
103	10609	10.1489	.00970874	143	20449	11.9583	.00699301
104	10816	10.1980	.00961538	144	20736	12.0000	.00694444
105	11025	10.2470	.00952381	145	21025	12.0416	.00689655
106	11236	10.2956	.00943396	146	21316	12.0830	.00684932
107	11449	10.3441	.00934579	147	21609	12.1244	.00680272
108	11664	10.3923	.00925926	148	21904	12.1655	.00675676
109	11881	10.4403	.00917431	149	22201	12.2066	.00671141
110	12100	10.4881	.00909091	150	22500	12.2474	.00666667
111	12321	10.5357	.00900901	151	22801	12.2882	.00662252
112	12544	10.5830	.00892857	152	23104	12.3288	.00657895
113	12769	10.6301	.00884956	153	23409	12.3693	.00653595
114	12996	10.6771	.00877193	154	23716	12.4097	.00649351
115	13225	10.7238	.00869565	155	24025	12.4499	.00645161
116	13456	10.7703	.00862069	156	24336	12.4900	.00641026
117	13689	10.8167	.00854701	157	24649	12.5300	.00636943
118	13924	10.8628	.00847458	158	24964	12.5698	.00632911
119	14161	10.9087	.00840336	159	25281	12.6095	.00628931
120	14400	10.9545	.00833333	160	25600	12.6491	.00625000

Table K (continued)

N	N^2	$\sqrt{N}$	$1/N$	N	N^2	$\sqrt{N}$	$1/N$
161	25921	12.6886	.00621118	201	40401	14.1774	.00497512
162	26244	12.7279	.00617284	202	40804	14.2127	.00495050
163	26569	12.7671	.00613497	203	41209	14.2478	.00492611
164	26896	12.8062	.00609756	204	41616	14.2829	.00490196
165	27225	12.8452	.00606061	205	42025	14.3178	.00487805
166	27556	12.8841	.00602410	206	42436	14.3527	.00485437
167	27889	12.9228	.00598802	207	42849	14.3875	.00483092
168	28224	12.9615	.00595238	208	43264	14.4222	.00480769
169	28561	13.0000	.00591716	209	43681	14.4568	.00478469
170	28900	13.0384	.00588235	210	44100	14.4914	.00476190
171	29241	13.0767	.00584795	211	44521	14.5258	.00473934
172	29584	13.1149	.00581395	212	44944	14.5602	.00471698
173	29929	13.1529	.00578035	213	45369	14.5945	.00469484
174	30276	13.1909	.00574713	214	45796	14.6287	.00467290
175	30625	13.2288	.00571429	215	46225	14.6629	.00465116
176	30976	13.2665	.00568182	216	46656	14.6969	.00462963
177	31329	13.3041	.00564972	217	47089	14.7309	.00460829
178	31684	13.3417	.00561798	218	47524	14.7648	.00458716
179	32041	13.3791	.00558659	219	47961	14.7986	.00456621
180	32400	13.4164	.00555556	220	48400	14.8324	.00454545
181	32761	13.4536	.00552486	221	48841	14.8661	.00452489
182	33124	13.4907	.00549451	222	49284	14.8997	.00450450
183	33489	13.5277	.00546448	223	49729	14.9332	.00448430
184	33856	13.5647	.00543478	224	50176	14.9666	.00446429
185	34225	13.6015	.00540541	225	50625	15.0000	.00444444
186	34596	13.6382	.00537634	226	51076	15.0333	.00442478
187	34969	13.6748	.00534759	227	51529	15.0665	.00440529
188	35344	13.7113	.00531915	228	51984	15.0997	.00438596
189	35721	13.7477	.00529101	229	52441	15.1327	.00436681
190	36100	13.7840	.00526316	230	52900	15.1658	.00434783
191	36481	13.8203	.00523560	231	53361	15.1987	.00432900
192	36864	13.8564	.00520833	232	53824	15.2315	.00431034
193	37249	13.8924	.00518135	233	54289	15.2643	.00429185
194	37636	13.9284	.00515464	234	54756	15.2971	.00427350
195	38025	13.9642	.00512821	235	55225	15.3297	.00425532
196	38416	14.0000	.00510204	236	55696	15.3623	.00423729
197	38809	14.0357	.00507614	237	56169	15.3948	.00421941
198	39204	14.0712	.00505051	238	56644	15.4272	.00420168
199	39601	14.1067	.00502513	239	57121	15.4596	.00418410
200	40000	14.1421	.00500000	240	57600	15.4919	.00416667

Table K (continued)

N	N^2	$\sqrt{N}$	$1/N$	N	N^2	$\sqrt{N}$	$1/N$
241	58081	15.5242	.00414938	281	78961	16.7631	.00355872
242	58564	15.5563	.00413223	282	79524	16.7929	.00354610
243	59049	15.5885	.00411523	283	80089	16.8226	.00353357
244	59536	15.6205	.00409836	284	80656	16.8523	.00352113
245	60025	15.6525	.00408163	285	81225	16.8819	.00350877
246	60516	15.6844	.00406504	286	81796	16.9115	.00349650
247	61009	15.7162	.00404858	287	82369	16.9411	.00348432
248	61504	15.7480	.00403226	288	82944	16.9706	.00347222
249	62001	15.7797	.00401606	289	83521	17.0000	.00346021
250	62500	15.8114	.00400000	290	84100	17 0294	.00344828
251	63001	15.8430	.00398406	291	84681	17.0587	.00343643
252	63504	15.8745	.00396825	292	85264	17.0880	.00342466
253	64009	15.9060	.00395257	293	85849	17.1172	.00341297
254	64516	15.9374	.00393701	294	86436	17.1464	.00340136
255	65025	15.9687	.00392157	295	87025	17.1756	.00338983
256	65536	16.0000	.00390625	296	87616	17.2047	.00337838
257	66049	16.0312	.00389105	297	88209	17.2337	.00336700
258	66564	16.0624	.00387597	298	88804	17.2627	.00335570
259	67081	16.0935	.00386100	299	89401	17.2916	.00334448
260	67600	16.1245	.00384615	300	90000	17.3205	.00333333
261	68121	16.1555	.00383142	301	90601	17.3494	.00332226
262	68644	16.1864	.00381679	302	91204	17.3781	.00331126
263	69169	16.2173	.00380228	303	91809	17.4069	.00330033
264	69696	16.2481	.00378788	304	92416	17.4356	.00328947
265	70225	16.2788	.00377358	305	93025	17.4642	.00327869
266	70756	16.3095	.00375940	306	93636	17.4929	.00326797
267	71289	16.3401	.00374532	307	94249	17.5214	.00325733
268	71824	16.3707	.00373134	308	94864	17.5499	.00324675
269	72361	16.4012	.00371747	309	95481	17.5784	.00323625
270	72900	16.4317	.00370370	310	96100	17.6068	.00322581
271	73441	16.4621	.00369004	311	96721	17.6352	.00321543
272	73984	16.4924	.00367647	312	97344	17.6635	.00320513
273	74529	16.5227	.00366300	313	97969	17.6918	.00319489
274	75076	16.5529	.00364964	314	98596	17.7200	.00318471
275	75625	16.5831	.00363636	315	99225	17.7482	.00317460
276	76176	16.6132	.00362319	316	99856	17.7764	.00316456
277	76729	16.6433	.00361011	317	100489	17.8045	.00315457
278	77284	16.6733	.00359712	318	101124	17.8326	.00314465
279	77841	16.7033	.00358423	319	101761	17.8606	.00313480
280	78400	16.7332	.00357143	320	102400	17.8885	.00312500

Table K (continued)

N	N^2	$\sqrt{N}$	$1/N$	N	N^2	$\sqrt{N}$	$1/N$
321	103041	17.9165	.00311526	361	130321	19.0000	.00277008
322	103684	17.9444	.00310559	362	131044	19.0263	.00276243
323	104329	17.9722	.00309598	363	131769	19.0526	.00275482
324	104976	18.0000	.00308642	364	132496	19.0788	.00274725
325	105625	18.0278	.00307692	365	133225	19.1050	.00273973
326	106276	18.0555	.00306748	366	133956	19.1311	.00273224
327	106929	18.0831	.00305810	367	134689	19.1572	.00272480
328	107584	18.1108	.00304878	368	135424	19.1833	.00271739
329	108241	18.1384	.00303951	369	136161	19.2094	.00271003
330	108900	18.1659	.00303030	370	136900	19.2354	.00270270
331	109561	18.1934	.00302115	371	137641	19.2614	.00269542
332	110224	18.2209	.00301205	372	138384	19.2873	.00268817
333	110889	18.2483	.00300300	373	139129	19.3132	.00268097
334	111556	18.2757	.00299401	374	139876	19.3391	.00267380
335	112225	18.3030	.00298507	375	140625	19.3649	.00266667
336	112896	18.3303	.00297619	376	141376	19.3907	.00265957
337	113569	18.3576	.00296736	377	142129	19.4165	.00265252
338	114244	18.3848	.00295858	378	142884	19.4422	.00264550
339	114921	18.4120	.00294985	379	143641	19.4679	.00263852
340	115600	18.4391	.00294118	380	144400	19.4936	.00263158
341	116281	18.4662	.00293255	381	145161	19.5192	.00262467
342	116964	18.4932	.00292398	382	145924	19.5448	.00261780
343	117649	18.5203	.00291545	383	146689	19.5704	.00261097
344	118336	18.5472	.00290698	384	147456	19.5959	.00260417
345	119025	18.5742	.00289855	385	148225	19.6214	.00259740
346	119716	18.6011	.00289017	386	148996	19.6469	.00259067
347	120409	18.6279	.00288184	387	149769	19.6723	.00258398
348	121104	18.6548	.00287356	388	150544	19.6977	.00257732
349	121801	18.6815	.00286533	389	151321	19.7231	.00257069
350	122500	18.7083	.00285714	390	152100	19.7484	.00256410
351	123201	18.7350	.00284900	391	152881	19.7737	.00255754
352	123904	18.7617	.00284091	392	153664	19.7990	.00255102
353	124609	18.7883	.00283286	393	154449	19.8242	.00254453
354	125316	18.8149	.00282486	394	155236	19.8494	.00253807
355	126025	18.8414	.00281690	395	156025	19.8746	.00253165
356	126736	18.8680	.00280899	396	156816	19.8997	.00252525
357	127449	18.8944	.00280112	397	157609	19.9249	.00251889
358	128164	18.9209	.00279330	398	158404	19.9499	.00251256
359	128881	18.9473	.00278552	399	159201	19.9750	.00250627
360	129600	18.9737	.00277778	400	160000	20.0000	.00250000

Table K (continued)

N	N^2	$\sqrt{N}$	$1/N$	N	N^2	$\sqrt{N}$	$1/N$
401	160801	20.0250	.00249377	441	194481	21.0000	.00226757
402	161604	20.0499	.00248756	442	195364	21.0238	.00226244
403	162409	20.0749	.00248139	443	196249	21.0476	.00225734
404	163216	20.0998	.00247525	444	197136	21.0713	.00225225
405	164025	20.1246	.00246914	445	198025	21.0950	.00224719
406	164836	20.1494	.00246305	446	198916	21.1187	.00224215
407	165649	20.1742	.00245700	447	199809	21.1424	.00223714
408	166464	20.1990	.00245098	448	200704	21.1660	.00223214
409	167281	20.2237	.00244499	449	201601	21.1896	.00222717
410	168100	20.2485	.00243902	450	202500	21.2132	.00222222
411	168921	20.2731	.00243309	451	203401	21.2368	.00221729
412	169744	20.2978	.00242718	452	204304	21.2603	.00221239
413	170569	20.3224	.00242131	453	205209	21.2838	.00220751
414	171396	20.3470	.00241546	454	206116	21.3073	.00220264
415	172225	20.3715	.00240964	455	207025	21.3307	.00219780
416	173056	20.3961	.00240385	456	207936	21.3542	.00219298
417	173889	20.4206	.00239808	457	208849	21.3776	.00218818
418	174724	20.4450	.00239234	458	209764	21.4009	.00218341
419	175561	20.4695	.00238663	459	210681	21.4243	.00217865
420	176400	20.4939	.00238095	460	211600	21.4476	.00217391
421	177241	20.5183	.00237530	461	212521	21.4709	.00216920
422	178084	20.5426	.00236967	462	213444	21.4942	.00216450
423	178929	20.5670	.00236407	463	214369	21.5174	.00215983
424	179776	20.5913	.00235849	464	215296	21.5407	.00215517
425	180625	20.6155	.00235294	465	216225	21.5639	.00215054
426	181476	20.6398	.00234742	466	217156	21.5870	.00214592
427	182329	20.6640	.00234192	467	218089	21.6102	.00214133
428	183184	20.6882	.00233645	468	219024	21.6333	.00213675
429	184041	20.7123	.00233100	469	219961	21.6564	.00213220
430	184900	20.7364	.00232558	470	220900	21.6795	.00212766
431	185761	20.7605	.00232019	471	221841	21.7025	.00212314
432	186624	20.7846	.00231481	472	222784	21.7256	.00211864
433	187489	20.8087	.00230947	473	223729	21.7486	.00211416
434	188356	20.8327	.00230415	474	224676	21.7715	.00210970
435	189225	20.8567	.00229885	475	225625	21.7945	.00210526
436	190096	20.8806	.00229358	476	226576	21.8174	.00210084
437	190969	20.9045	.00228833	477	227529	21.8403	.00209644
438	191844	20.9284	.00228311	478	228484	21.8632	.00209205
439	192721	20.9523	.00227790	479	229441	21.8861	.00208768
440	193600	20.9762	.00227273	480	230400	21.9089	.00208333

Table K (continued)

N	N^2	$\sqrt{N}$	$1/N$	N	N^2	$\sqrt{N}$	$1/N$
481	231361	21.9317	.00207900	521	271441	22.8254	.00191939
482	232324	21.9545	.00207469	522	272484	22.8473	.00191571
483	233289	21.9773	.00207039	523	273529	22.8692	.00191205
484	234256	22.0000	.00206612	524	274576	22.8910	.00190840
485	235225	22.0227	.00206186	525	275625	22.9129	.00190476
486	236196	22.0454	.00205761	526	276676	22.9347	.00190114
487	237169	22.0681	.00205339	527	277729	22.9565	.00189753
488	238144	22.0907	.00204918	528	278784	22.9783	.00189394
489	239121	22.1133	.00204499	529	279841	23.0000	.00189036
490	240100	22.1359	.00204082	530	280900	23.0217	.00188679
491	241081	22.1585	.00203666	531	281961	23.0434	.00188324
492	242064	22.1811	.00203252	532	283024	23.0651	.00187970
493	243049	22.2036	.00202840	533	284089	23.0868	.00187617
494	244036	22.2261	.00202429	534	285156	23.1084	.00187266
495	245025	22.2486	.00202020	535	286225	23.1301	.00186916
496	246016	22.2711	.00201613	536	287296	23.1517	.00186567
497	247009	22.2935	.00201207	537	288369	23.1733	.00186220
498	248004	22.3159	.00200803	538	289444	23.1948	.00185874
499	249001	22.3383	.00200401	539	290521	23.2164	.00185529
500	250000	22.3607	.00200000	540	291600	23.2379	.00185185
501	251001	22.3830	.00199601	541	292681	23.2594	.00184843
502	252004	22.4054	.00199203	542	293764	23.2809	.00184502
503	253009	22.4277	.00198807	543	294849	23.3024	.00184162
504	254016	22.4499	.00198413	544	295936	23.3238	.00183824
505	255025	22.4722	.00198020	545	297025	23.3452	.00183486
506	256036	22.4944	.00197628	546	298116	23.3666	.00183150
507	257049	22.5167	.00197239	547	299209	23.3880	.00182815
508	258064	22.5389	.00196850	548	300304	23.4094	.00182482
509	259081	22.5610	.00196464	549	301401	23.4307	.00182149
510	260100	22.5832	.00196078	550	302500	23.4521	.00181818
511	261121	22.6053	.00195695	551	303601	23.4734	.00181488
512	262144	22.6274	.00195312	552	304704	23.4947	.00181159
513	263169	22.6495	.00194932	553	305809	23.5160	.00180832
514	264196	22.6716	.00194553	554	306916	23.5372	.00180505
515	265225	22.6936	.00194175	555	308025	23.5584	.00180180
516	266256	22.7156	.00193798	556	309136	23.5797	.00179856
517	267289	22.7376	.00193424	557	310249	23.6008	.00179533
518	268324	22.7596	.00193050	558	311364	23.6220	.00179211
519	269361	22.7816	.00192678	559	312481	23.6432	.00178891
520	270400	22.8035	.00192308	560	313600	23.6643	.00178571

Table K (continued)

N	N^2	$\sqrt{N}$	$1/N$	N	N^2	$\sqrt{N}$	$1/N$
561	314721	23.6854	.00178253	601	361201	24.5153	.00166389
562	315844	23.7065	.00177936	602	362404	24.5357	.00166113
563	316969	23.7276	.00177620	603	363609	24.5561	.00165837
564	318096	23.7487	.00177305	604	364816	24.5764	.00165563
565	319225	23.7697	.00176991	605	366025	24.5967	.00165289
566	320356	23.7908	.00176678	606	367236	24.6171	.00165017
567	321489	23.8118	.00176367	607	368449	24.6374	.00164745
568	322624	23.8328	.00176056	608	369664	24.6577	.00164474
569	323761	23.8537	.00175747	609	370881	24.6779	.00164204
570	324900	23.8747	.00175439	610	372100	24.6982	.00163934
571	326041	23.8956	.00175131	611	373321	24.7184	.00163666
572	327184	23.9165	.00174825	612	374544	24.7386	.00163399
573	328329	23.9374	.00174520	613	375769	24.7588	.00163132
574	329476	23.9583	.00174216	614	376996	24.7790	.00162866
575	330625	23.9792	.00173913	615	378225	24.7992	.00162602
576	331776	24.0000	.00173611	616	379456	24.8193	.00162338
577	332929	24.0208	.00173310	617	380689	24.8395	.00162075
578	334084	24.0416	.00173010	618	381924	24.8596	.00161812
579	335241	24.0624	.00172712	619	383161	24.8797	.00161551
580	336400	24.0832	.00172414	620	384400	24.8998	.00161290
581	337561	24.1039	.00172117	621	385641	24.9199	.00161031
582	338724	24.1247	.00171821	622	386884	24.9399	.00160772
583	339889	24.1454	.00171527	623	388129	24.9600	.00160514
584	341056	24.1661	.00171233	624	389376	24.9800	.00160256
585	342225	24.1868	.00170940	625	390625	25.0000	.00160000
586	343396	24.2074	.00170648	626	391876	25.0200	.00159744
587	344569	24.2281	.00170358	627	393129	25.0400	.00159490
588	345744	24.2487	.00170068	628	394384	25.0599	.00159236
589	346921	24.2693	.00169779	629	395641	25.0799	.00158983
590	348100	24.2899	.00169492	630	396900	25.0998	.00158730
591	349281	24.3105	.00169205	631	398161	25.1197	.00158479
592	350464	24.3311	.00168919	632	399424	25.1396	.00158228
593	351649	24.3516	.00168634	633	400689	25.1595	.00157978
594	352836	24.3721	.00168350	634	401956	25.1794	.00157729
595	354025	24.3926	.00168067	635	403225	25.1992	.00157480
596	355216	24.4131	.00167785	636	404496	25.2190	.00157233
597	356409	24.4336	.00167504	637	405769	25.2389	.00156986
598	357604	24.4540	.00167224	638	407044	25.2587	.00156740
599	358801	24.4745	.00166945	639	408321	25.2784	.00156495
600	360000	24.4949	.00166667	640	409600	25.2982	.00156250

Table K (continued)

N	N^2	$\sqrt{N}$	$1/N$	N	N^2	$\sqrt{N}$	$1/N$
641	410881	25.3180	.00156006	681	463761	26.0960	.00146843
642	412164	25.3377	.00155763	682	465124	26.1151	.00146628
643	413449	25.3574	.00155521	683	466489	26.1343	.00146413
644	414736	25.3772	.00155280	684	467856	26.1534	.00146199
645	416025	25.3969	.00155039	685	469225	26.1725	.00145985
646	417316	25.4165	.00154799	686	470596	26.1916	.00145773
647	418609	25.4362	.00154560	687	471969	26.2107	.00145560
648	419904	25.4558	.00154321	688	473344	26.2298	.00145349
649	421201	25.4755	.00154083	689	474721	26.2488	.00145138
650	422500	25.4951	.00153846	690	476100	26.2679	.00144928
651	423801	25.5147	.00153610	691	477481	26.2869	.00144718
652	425104	25.5343	.00153374	692	478864	26.3059	.00144509
653	426409	25.5539	.00153139	693	480249	26.3249	.00144300
654	427716	25.5734	.00152905	694	481636	26.3439	.00144092
655	429025	25.5930	.00152672	695	483025	26.3629	.00143885
656	430336	25.6125	.00152439	696	484416	26.3818	.00143678
657	431649	25.6320	.00152207	697	485809	26.4008	.00143472
658	432964	25.6515	.00151976	698	487204	26.4197	.00143266
659	434281	25.6710	.00151745	699	488601	26.4386	.00143062
660	435600	25.6905	.00151515	700	490000	26.4575	.00142857
661	436921	25.7099	.00151286	701	491401	26.4764	.00142653
662	438244	25.7294	.00151057	702	492804	26.4953	.00142450
663	439569	25.7488	.00150830	703	494209	26.5141	.00142248
664	440896	25.7682	.00150602	704	495616	26.5330	.00142045
665	442225	25.7876	.00150376	705	497025	26.5518	.00141844
666	443556	25.8070	.00150150	706	498436	26.5707	.00141643
667	444889	25.8263	.00149925	707	499849	26.5895	.00141443
668	446224	25.8457	.00149701	708	501264	26.6083	.00141243
669	447561	25.8650	.00149477	709	502681	26.6271	.00141044
670	448900	25.8844	.00149254	710	504100	26.6458	.00140845
671	450241	25.9037	.00149031	711	505521	26.6646	.00140647
672	451584	25.9230	.00148810	712	506944	26.6833	.00140449
673	452929	25.9422	.00148588	713	508369	26.7021	.00140252
674	454276	25.9615	.00148368	714	509796	26.7208	.00140056
675	455625	25.9808	.00148148	715	511225	26.7395	.00139860
676	456976	26.0000	.00147929	716	512656	26.7582	.00139665
677	458329	26.0192	.00147710	717	514089	26.7769	.00139470
678	459684	26.0384	.00147493	718	515524	26.7955	.00139276
679	461041	26.0576	.00147275	719	516961	26.8142	.00139082
680	462400	26.0768	.00147059	720	518400	26.8328	.00138889

Table K (continued)

N	N^2	$\sqrt{N}$	$1/N$	N	N^2	$\sqrt{N}$	$1/N$
721	519841	26.8514	.00138696	761	579121	27.5862	.00131406
722	521284	26.8701	.00138504	762	580644	27.6043	.00131234
723	522729	26.8887	.00138313	763	582169	27.6225	.00131062
724	524176	26.9072	.00138122	764	583696	27.6405	.00130890
725	525625	26.9258	.00137931	765	585225	27.6586	.00130719
726	527076	26.9444	.00137741	766	586756	27.6767	.00130548
727	528529	26.9629	.00137552	767	588289	27.6948	.00130378
728	529984	26.9815	.00137363	768	589824	27.7128	.00130208
729	531441	27.0000	.00137174	769	591361	27.7308	.00130039
730	532900	27.0185	.00136986	770	592900	27.7489	.00129870
731	534361	27.0370	.00136799	771	594441	27.7669	.00129702
732	535824	27.0555	.00136612	772	595984	27.7849	.00129534
733	537289	27.0740	.00136426	773	597529	27.8029	.00129366
734	538756	27.0924	.00136240	774	599076	27.8209	.00129199
735	540225	27.1109	.00136054	775	600625	27.8388	.00129032
736	541696	27.1293	.00135870	776	602176	27.8568	.00128866
737	543169	27.1477	.00135685	777	603729	27.8747	.00128700
738	544644	27.1662	.00135501	778	605284	27.8927	.00128535
739	546121	27.1846	.00135318	779	606841	27.9106	.00128370
740	547600	27.2029	.00135135	780	608400	27.9285	.00128205
741	549081	27.2213	.00134953	781	609961	27.9464	.00128041
742	550564	27.2397	.00134771	782	611524	27.9643	.00127877
743	552049	27.2580	.00134590	783	613089	27.9821	.00127714
744	553536	27.2764	.00134409	784	614656	28.0000	.00127551
745	555025	27.2947	.00134228	785	616225	28.0179	.00127389
746	556516	27.3130	.00134048	786	617796	28.0357	.00127226
747	558009	27.3313	.00133869	787	619369	28.0535	.00127065
748	559504	27.3496	.00133690	788	620944	28.0713	.00126904
749	561001	27.3679	.00133511	789	622521	28.0891	.00126743
750	562500	27.3861	.00133333	790	624100	28.1069	.00126582
751	564001	27.4044	.00133156	791	625681	28.1247	.00126422
752	565504	27.4226	.00132979	792	627264	28.1425	.00126263
753	567009	27.4408	.00132802	793	628849	28.1603	.00126103
754	568516	27.4591	.00132626	794	630436	28.1780	.00125945
755	570025	27.4773	.00132450	795	632025	28.1957	.00125786
756	571536	27.4955	.00132275	796	633616	28.2135	.00125628
757	573049	27.5136	.00132100	797	635209	28.2312	.00125471
758	574564	27.5318	.00131926	798	636804	28.2489	.00125313
759	576081	27.5500	.00131752	799	638401	28.2666	.00125156
760	577600	27.5681	.00131579	800	640000	28.2843	.00125000

Table K (continued)

N	N^2	$\sqrt{N}$	$1/N$	N	N^2	$\sqrt{N}$	$1/N$
801	641601	28.3019	.00124844	841	707281	29.0000	.00118906
802	643204	28.3196	.00124688	842	708964	29.0172	.00118765
803	644809	28.3373	.00124533	843	710649	29.0345	.00118624
804	646416	28.3549	.00124378	844	712336	29.0517	.00118483
805	648025	28.3725	.00124224	845	714025	29.0689	.00118343
806	649636	28.3901	.00124069	846	715716	29.0861	.00118203
807	651249	28.4077	.00123916	847	717409	29.1033	.00118064
808	652864	28.4253	.00123762	848	719104	29.1204	.00117925
809	654481	28.4429	.00123609	849	720801	29.1376	.00117786
810	656100	28.4605	.00123457	850	722500	29.1548	.00117647
811	657721	28.4781	.00123305	851	724201	29.1719	.00117509
812	659344	28.4956	.00123153	852	725904	29.1890	.00117371
813	660969	28.5132	.00123001	853	727609	29.2062	.00117233
814	662596	28.5307	.00122850	854	729316	29.2233	.00117096
815	664225	28.5482	.00122699	855	731025	29.2404	.00116959
816	665856	28.5657	.00122549	856	732736	29.2575	.00116822
817	667489	28.5832	.00122399	857	734449	29.2746	.00116686
818	669124	28.6007	.00122249	858	736164	29.2916	.00116550
819	670761	28.6182	.00122100	859	737881	29.3087	.00116414
820	672400	28.6356	.00121951	860	739600	29.3258	.00116279
821	674041	28.6531	.00121803	861	741321	29.3428	.00116144
822	675684	28.6705	.00121655	862	743044	29.3598	.00116009
823	677329	28.6880	.00121507	863	744769	29.3769	.00115875
824	678976	28.7054	.00121359	864	746496	29.3939	.00115741
825	680625	28.7228	.00121212	865	748225	29.4109	.00115607
826	682276	28.7402	.00121065	866	749956	29.4279	.00115473
827	683929	28.7576	.00120919	867	751689	29.4449	.00115340
828	685584	28.7750	.00120773	868	753424	29.4618	.00115207
829	687241	28.7924	.00120627	869	755161	29.4788	.00115075
830	688900	28.8097	.00120482	870	756900	29.4958	.00114943
831	690561	28.8271	.00120337	871	758641	29.5127	.00114811
832	692224	28.8444	.00120192	872	760384	29.5296	.00114679
833	693889	28.8617	.00120048	873	762129	29.5466	.00114548
834	695556	28.8791	.00119904	874	763876	29.5635	.00114416
835	697225	28.8964	.00119760	875	765625	29.5804	.00114286
836	698896	28.9137	.00119617	876	767376	29.5973	.00114155
837	700569	28.9310	.00119474	877	769129	29.6142	.00114025
838	702244	28.9482	.00119332	878	770884	29.6311	.00113895
839	703921	28.9655	.00119190	879	772641	29.6479	.00113766
840	705600	28.9828	.00119048	880	774400	29.6648	.00113636

Table K (continued)

N	N^2	$\sqrt{N}$	$1/N$	N	N^2	$\sqrt{N}$	$1/N$
881	776161	29.6816	.00113507	921	848241	30.3480	.00108578
882	777924	29.6985	.00113379	922	850084	30.3645	.00108460
883	779689	29.7153	.00113250	923	851929	30.3809	.00108342
884	781456	29.7321	.00113122	924	853776	30.3974	.00108225
885	783225	29.7489	.00112994	925	855625	30.4138	.00108108
886	784996	29.7658	.00112867	926	857476	30.4302	.00107991
887	786769	29.7825	.00112740	927	859329	30.4467	.00107875
888	788544	29.7993	.00112613	928	861184	30.4631	.00107759
889	790321	29.8161	.00112486	929	863041	30.4795	.00107643
890	792100	29.8329	.00112360	930	864900	30.4959	.00107527
891	793881	29.8496	.00112233	931	866761	30.5123	.00107411
892	795664	29.8664	.00112108	932	868624	30.5287	.00107296
893	797449	29.8831	.00111982	933	870489	30.5450	.00107181
894	799236	29.8998	.00111857	934	872356	30.5614	.00107066
895	801025	29.9166	.00111732	935	874225	30.5778	.00106952
896	802816	29.9333	.00111607	936	876096	30.5941	.00106838
897	804609	29.9500	.00111483	937	877969	30.6105	.00106724
898	806404	29.9666	.00111359	938	879844	30.6268	.00106610
899	808201	29.9833	.00111235	939	881721	30.6431	.00106496
900	810000	30.0000	.00111111	940	883600	30.6594	.00106383
901	811801	30.0167	.00110988	941	885481	30.6757	.00106270
902	813604	30.0333	.00110865	942	887364	30.6920	.00106157
903	815409	30.0500	.00110742	943	889249	30.7083	.00106045
904	817216	30.0666	.00110619	944	891136	30.7246	.00105932
905	819025	30.0832	.00110497	945	893025	30.7409	.00105820
906	820836	30.0998	.00110375	946	894916	30.7571	.00105708
907	822649	30.1164	.00110254	947	896809	30.7734	.00105597
908	824464	30.1330	.00110132	948	898704	30.7896	.00105485
909	826281	30.1496	.00110011	949	900601	30.8058	.00105374
910	828100	30.1662	.00109890	950	902500	30.8221	.00105263
911	829921	30.1828	.00109769	951	904401	30.8383	.00105152
912	831744	30.1993	.00109649	952	906304	30.8545	.00105042
913	833569	30.2159	.00109529	953	908209	30.8707	.00104932
914	835396	30.2324	.00109409	954	910116	30.8869	.00104822
915	837225	30.2490	.00109290	955	912025	30.9031	.00104712
916	839056	30.2655	.00109170	956	913936	30.9192	.00104603
917	840889	30.2820	.00109051	957	915849	30.9354	.00104493
918	842724	30.2985	.00108932	958	917764	30.9516	.00104384
919	844561	30.3150	.00108814	959	919681	30.9677	.00104275
920	846400	30.3315	.00108696	960	921600	30.9839	.00104167

Table K (continued)

N	N^2	$\sqrt{N}$	$1/N$	N	N^2	$\sqrt{N}$	$1/N$
961	923521	31.0000	.00104058	981	962361	31.3209	.00101937
962	925444	31.0161	.00103950	982	964324	31.3369	.00101833
963	927369	31.0322	.00103842	983	966289	31.3528	.00101729
964	929296	31.0483	.00103734	984	968256	31.3688	.00101626
965	931225	31.0644	.00103627	985	970225	31.3847	.00101523
966	933156	31.0805	.00103520	986	972196	31.4006	.00101420
967	935089	31.0966	.00103413	987	974169	31.4166	.00101317
968	937024	31.1127	.00103306	988	976144	31.4325	.00101215
969	938961	31.1288	.00103199	989	978121	31.4484	.00101112
970	940900	31.1448	.00103093	990	980100	31.4643	.00101010
971	942841	31.1609	.00102987	991	982081	31.4802	.00100908
972	944784	31.1769	.00102881	992	984064	31.4960	.00100806
973	946729	31.1929	.00102775	993	986049	31.5119	.00100705
974	948676	31.2090	.00102669	994	988036	31.5278	.00100604
975	950625	31.2250	.00102564	995	990025	31.5436	.00100503
976	952576	31.2410	.00102459	996	992016	31.5595	.00100402
977	954529	31.2570	.00102354	997	994009	31.5753	.00100301
978	956484	31.2730	.00102249	998	996004	31.5911	.00100200
979	958441	31.2890	.00102145	999	998001	31.6070	.00100100
980	960400	31.3050	.00102041	1000	1000000	31.6228	.00100000

answers to the exercises

answers to the exercises

chapter 2

pg. 17. **(1a)** ordinal; **(1b)** ratio; **(1c)** nominal; **(1d)** the difference centers on the fact that the centigrade scale is interval while the Kelvin is ratio. **(2)** Student No. 8 has a rank of 2 and Student No. 7 a rank of 3. Their ranks as well as their scores (10 and 9, respectively) differ by one point. In contrast, Student No. 9 also differs from Student No. 8 by a rank of one, but he has 8 more score points. Thus, when scores are transformed to ranks, the equal interval property will be lost. **(3a)** continuous; **(3b)** discrete; **(3c)** continuous; **(3d)** discrete. **(4a)** .5–1.5; **(4b)** 17.5–18.5; **(4c)** 76.5–77.5; **(4d)** 1.05–1.15; **(4e)** 24.25–24.35; **(4f)** 1002.35–1002.45; **(4g)** 3.835–3.845; **(4h)** 12.605–12.615; **(4i)** 129.795–129.805. **(5a)** 4.6; **(5b)** 3.5; **(5c)** 2.1; **(5d)** 6.8; **(5e)** 8.0. **(6a)** 19; **(6b)** 12; **(6c)** 8; **(6d)** 21; **(6e)** 40; **(6f)** 69; **(6g)** 103; **(6h)** 361. **(7a)** 57; **(7b)** 207; **(7c)** 120; **(7d)** 15; **(7e)** 22. **(8a)** $k + 1$; **(8b)** 1; **(8c)** $1 + \dfrac{\sum Z}{Nk(\sum Z + 1)}$.

pg. 36. **(1)**

Class Interval	Real Limits	Interval Size	Midpoint	f	Rel. f	Cum. f	Cum. Rel. f
88–95	87.5–95.5	8	91.5	4	.08	50	1.00
80–87	79.5–87.5	8	83.5	3	.06	46	.92
72–79	71.5–79.5	8	75.5	5	.10	43	.86
64–71	63.5–71.5	8	67.5	7	.14	38	.76
56–63	55.5–63.5	8	59.5	7	.14	31	.62
48–55	47.5–55.5	8	51.5	8	.16	24	.48
40–47	39.5–47.5	8	43.5	6	.12	16	.32
32–39	31.5–39.5	8	35.5	5	.10	10	.20
24–31	23.5–31.5	8	27.5	3	.06	5	.10
16–23	15.5–23.5	8	19.5	1	.02	2	.04
8–15	7.5–15.5	8	11.5	1	.02	1	.02
				$N = 50$			

Eleven intervals of size 8 were selected but 9 to 12 intervals might have been picked as long as they covered the range of scores and the lower stated limit of the first interval was evenly divisible by the interval size. See Table 2–7 in text, page 28. **(2)** See examples of graphs in text, paying close attention to the points mentioned in the text.

(3)

Class Interval	Real Limits	Interval Size	Midpoint	f	Rel. f	Cum. f	Cum. Rel. f
50–51	49.5–51.5	2	50.5	1	.02	60	1.00
48–49	47.5–49.5	2	48.5	0	.00	59	.98
46–47	45.5–47.5	2	46.5	2	.03	59	.98
44–45	43.5–45.5	2	44.5	4	.07	57	.95
42–43	41.5–43.5	2	42.5	5	.08	53	.88
40–41	39.5–41.5	2	40.5	8	.13	48	.80
38–39	37.5–39.5	2	38.5	12	.20	40	.67
36–37	35.5–37.5	2	36.5	10	.17	28	.47
34–35	33.5–35.5	2	34.5	9	.15	18	.30
32–33	31.5–33.5	2	32.5	4	.07	9	.15
30–31	29.5–31.5	2	30.5	4	.07	5	.08
28–29	27.5–29.5	2	28.5	1	.02	1	.02
				$N = 60$			

As in Problem 1, fewer or more than 12 intervals might have been used. See text for examples of graphs.

(4)

Class Interval	Real Limits	Interval Size	Midpoint	f	Rel. f	Cum. f	Cum. Rel. f
2.8–3.1	2.75–3.15	.4	2.95	2	.07	28	1.00
2.4–2.7	2.35–2.75	.4	2.55	3	.11	26	.93
2.0–2.3	1.95–2.35	.4	2.15	9	.32	23	.82
1.6–1.9	1.55–1.95	.4	1.75	4	.14	14	.50
1.2–1.5	1.15–1.55	.4	1.35	6	.21	10	.36
.8–1.1	.75–1.15	.4	.95	3	.11	4	.14
.4– .7	.35– .75	.4	.55	1	.04	1	.04
				$N = 28$			

chapter 3

(1) means = 5.29, 6.40, 4.55, 7.22; medians = 6.00, 7.50, 5.00, 5.67; modes = 7, 9, 2 and 6, 6. **(2a)** mean or median because distribution is not highly skewed; **(2b)** median because distribution is skewed to the left; **(2c)** mean and median are acceptable since distribution is rather symmetrical but the modes should also be mentioned since dis- **pg. 50.**

tribution is bimodal; **(2d)** median because of the extreme score. **(3)** If a distribution is highly skewed, the median is often selected as the measure of central tendency. Why? **(4a)** 6; **(4b)** 5.5; **(4c)** 2.75; **(4d)** 2.875; **(4e)** 10.75.

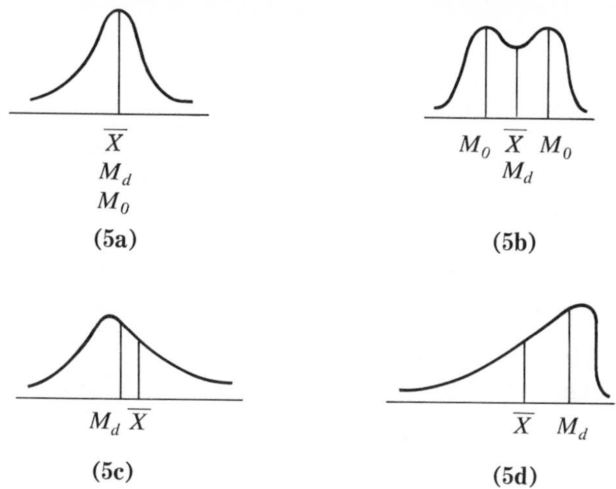

(5a) (5b) (5c) (5d)

(6) The sum of the deviations about the median (6) is -5, making the sum of the deviations about the median less than the deviations about the mean. Remember, it is the sum of the *squared* deviations (not unsquared) about the mean which is smaller than about any other value (the median included). **(7)** $41 > 37.4287$, yes. **(8)** A sample is a subgroup of a population, but that population may in turn be a subgroup (i.e., a sample) of a larger group or population. Can you illustrate with an example? **(9)** Much effort will be made to determine estimates (statistics) of population values that we do not know (parameters). **(10)** Both are unbiased estimates of μ. Can you explain why?

pg. 60. **(1)** see text p. 51. **(2)** The range is based upon only the two most extreme scores, not all the scores, and the range is a statistic that itself is quite variable from one sample to another. **(3a)** $\overline{X} = 7.5$, $s^2 = .67$, $s = .82$; **(3b)** $\overline{X} = 7.00$, $s^2 = 8.67$, $s = 2.95$; **(3c)** $\overline{X} = 7.00$, $s^2 = 11.43$, $s = 3.38$. **(4)** The denominator $N - 1$ is used so that s^2 is an unbiased estimator of σ^2. What does unbiased mean? **(5)** Yes; No, not without correcting for the difference in the unit of measurement. **(6)** See text p. 55 for a discussion of this issue.

chapter 4

pg. 66. **(1a)** 59.5; **(1b)** 78; **(1c)** 50; **(1d)** 85; **(1e)** 71.83; **(1f)** 72.17; **(1g)** 78.25; **(1h)** 73. **(2a)** $P_{.1125}$; **(2b)** $P_{.445}$; **(2c)** $P_{.7625}$; **(2d)** $P_{.65}$; **(2e)** $P_{.175}$; **(2f)** $P_{.3125}$; **(2g)** $P_{.85}$; **(2h)** $P_{.075}$.

(1a) 60, 64, 8; **(1b)** 38, 64, 8; **(1c)** 500, 6400, 80; **(1d)** 10, 2.56, 1.60; **(1e)** -43.75, 1, 1. **(2a)** 2, .25, 50; **(2b)** 40, 36, 6; **(2c)** 45, 225, 15. **pg. 73.**

(1) Percentiles only reflect ordinal position (i.e., the proportion of the group falling below a given score) and do not indicate how far the other scores were from a given percentile value. Standard scores take into account the variability of the distribution. **(2)** See page 75 of text. **(3)** $\overline{X} = 8.00$, $s = 2.37$; $z_i = -1.27, -.42, -.42, 0, .42, 1.69$; $\bar{z} = 0$, $s_z = 1.00$; yes, because a distribution of standard scores has a mean of 0 and a standard deviation of 1. **(4)** Relative frequency or the proportion of cases falling between two specified values on the abscissa. **(5)** .50; .50; .1587; .8413. **(6a)** .6826; **(6b)** .1359; **(6c)** .0668; **(6d)** .0500; **(6e)** .0100. **(7a)** $\pm 3\sigma$; **(7b)** 29, 47. **(8a)** .7486; **(8b)** .1587; **(8c)** .5793. **(9a)** 63.24; **(9b)** 44.60 approximately; **(9c)** 31.39. **(10a)** .6231; **(10b)** .1574; **(10c)** .0036. **pg. 84.**

chapter 5

(1a) $b_{yx} = .21$, $a_{yx} = 4.69$; **(1b)** $b_{wx} = -.81$, $a_{wx} = 9.26$; **(1c)** $b_{wy} = -.0082$, $a_{wy} = 4.7178$. **(2a)** 5.48; **(2b)** 3.59; **(2c)** 4.66; **(2d)** $X = 15$ not within the range of original X values. **(3a)** $s_{y.x} = 3.11$, $-.62$ to 11.58; **(3b)** $s_{w.x} = 2.63$, -1.56 to 8.74; **(3c)** $s_{w.y} = 3.79$, -2.75 to 12.07. **(4)** See page 95 of text. **(5)** $\tilde{Y} = .03X + 200$ in which $\tilde{Y}$ = predicted income and X = dollar value of sales. **(6)** Both are measures of variability, but one reflects variability about a mean and the other variability about a regression line. **(7)** See page 101 of text. **pg. 112.**

$$b_{y.x} = \frac{N(\sum XY) - (\sum X)(\sum Y)}{N\sum X^2 - (\sum X)^2} \qquad b_{x.y} = \frac{N(\sum XY) - (\sum Y)(\sum X)}{N\sum Y^2 - (\sum Y)^2}$$

$$s_x^{\,2} = \frac{N\sum X^2 - (\sum X)^2}{N(N-1)} \qquad s_y^{\,2} = \frac{N\sum Y^2 - (\sum Y)^2}{N(N-1)}$$

Since N is the same value in all the above formulas, $N(N-1)$ is the same for $s_x^{\,2}$ and $s_y^{\,2}$. If $s_x^{\,2} = s_y^{\,2}$, then $N\sum X^2 - (\sum X)^2 = N\sum Y^2 - (\sum Y)^2$. The numerators of b_{yx} and b_{xy} are always equal and if $s_x^{\,2} = s_y^{\,2}$, then their denominators are also equal. Therefore, if $s_x^{\,2} = s_y^{\,2}$, then $b_{yx} = b_{xy}$ and the two regression lines have the same slopes. The intercepts will not usually be equal in this case:

$$a_{yx} = \overline{Y} - b_{yx}\overline{X}$$
$$a_{xy} = \overline{X} - b_{xy}\overline{Y}$$

Even if $b_{yx} = b_{xy}$, $\overline{Y}$ would have to equal $\overline{X}$ for $a_{yx} = a_{xy}$. **(8)** See page 109 of text. **(9)** If b is positive, the relationship is positive; if b is negative, the relationship is negative.

chapter 6

(1) $r_{AB} = .70$, $r_{AC} = -.77$, $r_{BC} = -.82$; $r_{2(A+5)\ B} = .70$; Changing the unit and/or origin of a scale (even for only one of the two scales) does not alter the correlation be- **pg. 135.**

tween the two variables. **(2)** $r_{xy} = .32$, $r_{x'y'} = .77$. The correlation changes because the score pair (12, 8) deviates markedly from $(\overline{X}, \overline{Y})$. In a small sample such an extreme score can alter the correlation coefficient to a considerable degree. Adding the points (12, −8) or (−12, 8) would shift r in the opposite direction. **(3)** See page 128 of text. **(4)** $\sum(\tilde{Y}_i - \overline{Y})^2$, the total sum of squares of points about their mean can be partitioned into the following components:

$$\sum(\tilde{Y}_i - \overline{Y})^2 = \sum(\tilde{Y}_i - \overline{Y})^2 + \sum(Y_i - \tilde{Y}_i)^2.$$

The $\sum(Y_i - \tilde{Y}_i)^2$ represent the squared deviations of the points about the regression line, that is, the error remaining after predicting Y from X. The $\sum(\tilde{Y}_i - \overline{Y})^2$ is that portion of the total which is not error, that is, the variability in Y_i associated with X. **(5)** The two regression lines result from the fact that minimizing the squared deviations between points and the line for Y_i does not minimize these deviations for the X_i. However, the *degree* of linear relationship as reflected in r is the same regardless of the direction of prediction. **(6)** Extreme points influence the regression constants and r more than points near $(\overline{X}, \overline{Y})$ because their deviations from $(\overline{X}, \overline{Y})$, being large, contribute disproportionately to the numerators of b and r when they are squared. **(7)** Since $r = b_{yx}(s_x/s_y)$, when scores are standardized, $s_x = s_y = 1$, making $s_x/s_y = 1$. The result is $r = b_{z_y z_x}$. **(8)** Since $r^2 = 1 - s_{y.x}{}^2/s_y{}^2$, the correlation becomes larger as $s_{y.x}{}^2/s_y{}^2$ becomes smaller. **(9a)** Impossible, with an N of 2, both points would fall precisely on the regression line and $s_{y.x}$ would be 0 not 2.5; **(9b)** Impossible, if $s_{y.x} = 0$, r must be ± 1.00; **(9c)** Impossible, if b is negative, r must be negative; **(9d)** Possible; **(9e)** Impossible, the means and standard deviations indicate that X and Y are in standard score form and thus r must equal b; **(9f)** Possible.

chapter 7

pg. 144. **(1a)** 4/52; **(1b)** 1/3; **(1c)** 1/2; **(1d)** 1.00; **(1e)** 3/13. **(2a)** $P = .1587$; **(2b)** $P = .5028$; **(2c)** $P = .9544$; **(2d)** $P = .6221$; **(2e)** $P = .0456$.

pg. 174. **(1a)** An 8 A.M. class appeals to only some students. One might wonder if the sample of students in an 8 A.M. class was typical of college students and whether it would be composed of a different type of student than a 2 P.M. class; **(1b)** Although all students must participate in an experiment, they can select which they want to do. Are those who volunteer for a jury experiment, as opposed to some other type, typical of all college students? **(1c)** Are those people who own color TV sets typical of shoppers in general? **(2)** The values differ because they estimate a common parameter ($\sigma_{\overline{x}}$) on the basis of a different set of scores. The larger the N the less error (variability) is in the estimate. **(3a)** *Assumptions.* The members of the sample are randomly and independently selected and the population involved is normal with $\mu = 81$ and $\sigma = 10$. *Hypotheses.* H_0: $\overline{X}$ is computed on a sample from a population with $\mu = 81$. H_1: $\overline{X}$ is computed on a sample from a population with $\mu \neq 81$. *Formula.*

$$z = \frac{\overline{X} - \mu}{\sigma_{\overline{x}}} = \frac{\overline{X} - \mu}{\sigma_x/\sqrt{N}}$$

Significance level. Assume $\alpha = .05$. *Critical values.* -1.96 and $+1.96$ for a two-tailed test. *Decision rules.* If z_{obs} is between -1.96 and $+1.96$, accept H_0; If z_{obs} is less than or equal to -1.96 or more than or equal to $+1.96$, reject H_0. *Computation.* $z_{obs} = 1.50$. *Interpretation.* Accept H_0, the observed mean deviates from the population mean by an amount that is within the range of sampling error. **(3b)** One would then use the formula for t with $df = 24$ rather than the z distribution. The critical values of t would be ± 2.064 for a two-tailed test at $\alpha = .05$, and the decision rules would be: If t_{obs} is between -2.064 and $+2.064$, accept H_0. If t_{obs} is less than or equal to -2.064 or more than or equal to $+2.064$, reject H_0. Because s_x is also 10, the observed t would be calculated by

$$t_{obs} = \frac{\overline{X} - \mu}{s_x/\sqrt{N}} = \frac{84 - 81}{10/\sqrt{25}} = 1.50$$

This would result in the same decision (i.e., accept H_0) and interpretation as in Problem **3a. (3c)** *Assumptions.* The members of the sample are randomly and independently selected and the population of non-pierced males is normal with a mean of 62 inches. *Hypotheses.* H_0: $\overline{X}$ is computed on a sample from a population with $\mu = 62$. H_1: $\overline{X}$ is computed on a sample from a population with $\mu > 62$. (Notice that this is a directional alternative. Why?) *Formula.*

$$t = \frac{\overline{X} - \mu}{s_{\overline{x}}} = \frac{\overline{X} - \mu}{s_x/\sqrt{N}}$$

Significance level. Assume $\alpha = .05$. *Critical value.* From Table B with $df = N - 1 = 35$, one-tailed, $\alpha = .05$: $+1.691$ (approximately; obtained by interpolation). *Decision rules.* If t_{obs} is less than 1.691, accept H_0. If t_{obs} is greater than or equal to 1.691, reject H_0. *Computation.*

$$t_{obs} = \frac{\overline{X} - \mu}{s_x/\sqrt{N}} = \frac{64.5 - 62}{7/\sqrt{36}} = 2.14$$

Interpretation. Reject H_0, the observed mean of 64.5 is greater than would be expected to occur from errors of sampling from a population with $\mu = 62$. This result does not constitute proof that the piercing and molding causes increased height since factors that cause or are related to determining which cultures pierce and mold might also produce skeletally tall males (e.g., diet, genetic stock, amount of sunshine, etc.). **(3d)** *Assumptions.* The sample of first borns is randomly and independently selected and the mean of the later-born population is 113. *Hypotheses.* H_0:$\overline{X}$ is computed on a sample from a population with $\mu = 113$. H_1:$\overline{X}$ is computed on a sample from a population with $\mu \neq 113$. *Formula.*

$$t = \frac{\overline{X} - \mu}{s_{\overline{x}}} = \frac{\overline{X} - \mu}{s_x/\sqrt{N}}$$

Significance level. Assume $\alpha = .05$. *Critical values.* Given a two-tailed test, $df = N - 1 = 120$, $\alpha = .05$: $t_{crit} = \pm 1.98$. *Decision rules.* If t_{obs} is between -1.98 and $+1.98$, accept H_0. If t_{obs} is less than or equal to -1.98 or more than or equal to $+1.98$,

reject H_0. *Computation.*

$$t_{obs} = \frac{\overline{X} - \mu}{s_x/\sqrt{N}} = \frac{117 - 113}{16/\sqrt{121}} = 2.76$$

Interpretation. Reject H_0, the observed mean is too deviant from $\mu = 113$ to be simply a function of sampling error. **(4a)** 19.82 to 36.18, 16.976 to 39.024; **(4b)** 126.428 to 177.572, 116.636 to 187.364; **(4c)** 32.5 to 42.5 approximately (no interpolation in Table B used), 30.85 to 44.15 approximately; **(4d)** 62.2 to 81.8, 59.12 to 84.88.

chapter 8

pg. 210. **(1)** The assumption of normality is made so that the standard normal or the t distribution may be used to determine the required probability. This assumption can be made if the population distribution(s) are normal or if the sample size is sufficiently large. **(2)** In order to make such a statistical test, an estimate of the standard error of the difference between means is required and this estimate is based upon the two sample variances. One estimate may be made if those variances can be assumed to be equal while another estimate (and correction) must be used if they are not. **(3)** When the same subjects produce both groups of scores, the individual differences that characterize those subjects influence the scores in both groups causing them to be correlated to some extent. This correlation affects the accuracy of the estimate of the standard error of the difference between means based upon independent groups, so another procedure must be used. **(4)** Test for homogeneity of variance. *Hypotheses.* $H_0{:}\sigma_1{}^2 = \sigma_2{}^2$. $H_1{:}\sigma_1{}^2 \neq \sigma_2{}^2$. *Assumptions.* The population distributions of the two groups are normal, the sample variances are independent, and random sampling was used. *Decision rules.* Given .10 level, $df = N_1 - 1 = 9$ and $N_2 - 1 = 9$. If $F_{obs} < 3.18$, accept H_0. If $F_{obs} \geq 3.18$, reject H_0. *Computation.* $F = s^2_{largest}/s^2_{smallest} = 5.39/3.07 = 1.76$. *Interpretation.* Accept H_0, the difference between the variances is within the range expected by sampling error. Use a t test for homogeneous variances to compare means. Test for the difference between means. *Hypotheses.* $H_0{:}\mu_1 = \mu_2$. $H_1{:}\mu_1 < \mu_2$. *Assumptions.* The two groups are independent, selected by random sampling, with normal populations having homogeneous variances. *Decision rules.* Given .05 level and $df = N_1 + N_2 - 2 = 18$, one-tailed test. If $-1.734 < t_{obs}$, accept H_0. If $t_{obs} \leq -1.734$, reject H_0. *Computation.*

$$t_{obs} = (\overline{X}_1 - \overline{X}_2)\Big/\sqrt{\left[\frac{(N_1 - 1)s_1{}^2 + (N_2 - 1)s_2{}^2}{N_1 + N_2 - 2}\right]\cdot\left[\frac{1}{N_1} + \frac{1}{N_2}\right]}$$

$$t_{obs} = (2.8 - 6.5)\Big/\sqrt{\left[\frac{(10 - 1)3.07 + (10 - 1)5.39}{10 + 10 - 2}\right]\cdot\left[\frac{1}{10} + \frac{1}{10}\right]} = -4.02$$

Interpretation. Reject H_0, the observed difference in means is too great to be a simple result of sampling error. The dissonance theory is supported. *Proportion of variance.*

$$\text{Prop. of Var.} = \frac{t^2 - 1}{t^2 + N_1 + N_2 - 1} = \frac{(4.02)^2 - 1}{(4.02)^2 + 10 + 10 - 1} = 43\%$$